BROKEN
NATION

2013

To
David

love
Mum & Jack
xx

Christmas 2013

BROKEN NATION

Australians in the Great War

JOAN BEAUMONT

ALLEN&UNWIN
SYDNEY • MELBOURNE • AUCKLAND • LONDON

First published in 2013

Allen & Unwin
83 Alexander Street
Crows Nest NSW 2065
Australia
Phone: (61 2) 8425 0100
Email: info@allenandunwin.com
Web: www.allenandunwin.com

Cataloguing-in-Publication details are available
from the National Library of Australia
www.trove.nla.gov.au

ISBN 978 1 74175 138 3

Internal design by Lisa White
Maps by Keith Mitchell
Index by Trevor Matthews
Set in 12/17 pt Minion by Midland Typesetters, Australia
Printed and bound in Australia by Griffin Press

10 9 8 7 6 5 4 3 2 1

For my father, a child in World War I, who, as a man,
believed that no one should be forced to kill

CONTENTS

LIST OF ILLUSTRATIONS

LIST OF ILLUSTRATIONS

Chapter 5, pages 400–1

The 4th Light Horse Regiment in the Jordan Valley
The charge at Beersheba?
The 1st Light Horse Brigade before the attack on Jericho

Chapter 5, pages 484–5

Hughes and Australian soldiers, 1918
The Australian Flying Corps No. 4 Squadron at Pas-de-Calais
The AIF 2nd Division memorial at Mont St Quentin

Chapter 6, pages 520–1

Crowds in Martin Place, Sydney, awaiting the armistice
An Australian sapper comes home
VAD nurses during the 'Spanish' influenza pandemic
Nurses and patients at the Anzac Hostel, Brighton, Victoria

LIST OF TABLES AND FIGURES

Tables

Figures

LIST OF MAPS

PREFACE

The centenary of World War I and the landing at Gallipoli will no doubt fill bookstores across Australia with numerous accounts of the nation's role in this conflict. These will swell the already voluminous literature on Australian military history that has been published over the last two decades to meet and fuel a growing popular interest in the memory of war. So why this book?

It has been written to provide what is still lacking in the literature: a comprehensive history of Australians at war in the period 1914–19 that integrates battles, the home front, diplomacy and memory. Not surprisingly, perhaps, Australian military history has been dominated by the history of battles and military units. Battle, after all, is the essence of war, and the Anzac 'legend'—which is the most enduring legacy of World War I for Australians today—is a story about soldiers and their behaviour in battle. But World War I involved more than fighting and killing. Sometimes called the first 'total' war, it was a conflict in which civilians mattered. Theirs, after all, was the majority experience. Even though a remarkable number of Australians enlisted and served overseas—nearly 417,000 and 330,000 respectively from a population of fewer than five million—most Australians stayed at home. Among men aged 18 to 60, nearly 70 per cent did not enlist. In essence, then, the story of Australians at war is about more than the Australian Imperial Force (AIF) at war.

Moreover, it was the Australian population on the home front—a term that was coined during World War I in recognition of its importance—who underpinned the national war effort. They did not fight, but they accepted casualties on a scale that would be unthinkable today. Many thousands of them mobilised their resources—labour, money, emotional energy, and organisational and practical skills—to assist the war effort. Many more endured economic dislocation and a reduced standard of living. Most critically, whatever the terrible cost, the majority of Australians supported the war, believing that the cause for which their men were fighting was just. Some national populations in World War I ultimately lost the will to fight—notably, those of Russia in 1917 and, to some degree, Germany in late 1918. But despite the fact that Australians were profoundly divided on the questions of military conscription and the equity of the sacrifices being demanded of them, the will to continue the war survived. It was not universal—by mid-1918, the industrial labour movement was demanding an end to the war by a negotiated peace—but it was widespread enough for there not to be a general collapse of morale on the home front. In addition, although there was a rising level of violence in political life and the working class was radicalised by the experience of the war, Australians did not opt for revolution.

The home front therefore needs to be seen as an essential part of the national experience of war. It should be imagined as being in a dialogue with the battlefront. Often civilians and soldiers are assumed to have been in separate spheres—as, in many ways, they were. Physically, Australian civilians were remote from the conflict. They did not experience the occupation, bombing, starvation or homelessness that were the lot of many European peoples. Nor, as civilians, could they truly comprehend the horrors of battle in modern industrial warfare: the almost intolerable noise of artillery; the terror of arbitrary obliteration; the obscene injuries inflicted by shrapnel, machine guns, flame throwers, bayonets and gas; the misery of life in the trenches in winter and the foulness of gangrene and trench foot.

Yet Australians at home were not emotionally quarantined from World War I. The men of the AIF wrote home, often graphically, about wounds and death—even about the incompetence of those commanding them. Much of their fear, discomfort, despair and cynicism about the war escaped the pen of the censor. Even when soldiers did keep silent, trying to reassure their already anxious families, the enormous casualty lists brought catastrophe into numerous homes and communities. The bodies of the wounded, who returned to Australia from mid-1915 onwards, also testified to the mutilation, disfigurement and violence of the war.

Hence every dimension of Australian life in 1914–18 was affected by the knowledge of what was happening in Gallipoli, France, Belgium and the Middle East. Nowhere was this clearer than in the ebb and flow of voluntary recruitment and the two referenda about conscription in 1916 and 1917. These stirred raw passion, hysteria and rancour not just because of the gravity of the issues at stake but because they were played out against the backdrop of mass grief and the greatest battles of attrition in which the British imperial armies fought, the Somme and Third Ypres.

In turn, events on the battlefront were shaped—positively and negatively— by what happened at home. Like all armies in a democratic age, the men of the AIF looked to the home front for affirmation of their efforts. Evidence that they had been remembered—even if this took the now anachronistic form of 'comforts' prepared by an industry of voluntary patriotic workers— was essential. The commander of the AIF for much of the war, General Sir William Birdwood, at least thought this, telling Australians in 1920 that the high morale of Australian solders was 'maintained very largely, because here in their homeland, you good people never let them forget that you were always with them, rejoicing with them in their days of triumph and sympathising with them in their hardship'.[1]

In contrast, the decline of voluntary recruitment and the rejection of conscription conveyed ambiguous messages about home-front support. Even though many soldiers themselves opposed conscription—much to the chagrin of Prime Minister W.M. (Billy) Hughes—they bore the consequences of the widening gap between reinforcements and casualties in the latter years of the war. By 1918, the five Australian divisions were seriously under strength, and their battalions—so central to the AIF's esprit de corps—were being forcibly disbanded in the face of near-mutiny by the troops affected. Had the war continued into 1919, the Australian narrative might not have ended in triumphalism, but rather in retrenchment and decline—and perhaps even rebellion. There might even have been an Australian version of the 'stab in the back' theory that so infected German political life after the war.

A further reason for positioning the home front centrally in an Australian history of World War I is that it was here that much of the intangible damage of the war occurred. Of course, it was the men of the AIF—the more than 60,000 dead and 153,000 wounded—who bore the physical injuries of the war, the most significant pain in a grisly hierarchy of suffering. But their families and the Australian political system and social fabric were also left injured and maimed. After the early consensus of 1914–15 evaporated, Australians were increasingly polarised around the question of how the military and economic cost of the war should be borne. The resulting disputes—over conscription, cost of living increases and the obligations of citizenship—left Australia divided along faultlines that lasted at least a generation: the volunteer against the 'shirker'; the conscriptionist against the anti-conscriptionist; and—though sectarianism was not created by the war—the Catholic against the Protestant. The insults, calumny and accusations that each had traded with the other in the hysteria of the war years were not forgotten, and they continued to poison public life for many years. Although it is difficult to quantify, post-war Australian society seemed less tolerant of difference, more fearful of radicalism and more xenophobic. Most notably, the split of the Australian Labor Party under the pressures of war cut short its emergence as a reforming party of national government and ushered in a long period of dominance of federal politics by the non-Labor parties. In much of the recent memory 'boom', this negative legacy of the war has been elided.

However, if this book aims to reinstate the home front in the history of Australians at war, it does not dispute the centrality of fighting to any account of World War I. On the contrary, it tries to provide a comprehensive account of the battles in which Australians fought—in Gallipoli, France, Belgium and the Middle East—in a form that is accessible to the general reader. The current memory 'boom', fuelled as it is by national pride, a surge of interest in family genealogy and a fascination with mass trauma and victimhood, has established its own elite set of battles. Gallipoli is clearly pre-eminent for Australians and universally known. Villers-Bretonneux, Pozières, the Somme and Fromelles also seem to be recognised beyond the circles of military and battlefield tour enthusiasts. But if the experience of teaching in a major tertiary institution is any guide, this is often where knowledge of World War I battles ends.

However, Australian defence forces fought in many more battles and theatres of war than those. When in 1938 the national memorial was being completed at Villers-Bretonneux, the list of battles approved for inscription were the Somme, Pozières, Bapaume, Bullecourt, Messines, Menin Road, Polygon Wood, Broodseinde, Poelcapelle, Passchendaele, Avre, Ancre, Villers-Bretonneux, Lys, Hazebrouck, Hamel, Amiens, Albert, Chuignes, Mont St Quentin, Epehy, Hindenburg Line, St Quentin Canal and Beaurevoir Line.[2]

It was inevitable that some of these battles would be forgotten. All historical writing and memory—be it at the level of the individual or the collective (the family, the community or the nation)—is selective. What we remember is shaped as much by the priorities and values of the present as by the realities of the past. Hence another aim of this book is to explore how it is that certain memories of battle in World War I have survived to dominate national memory today. 'National memory', it must be said, is a concept that needs to be used with caution. As Jay Winter reminds us:

> States do not remember; individuals do, in association with other people. If the term 'collective memory' has any meaning at all, it is the process through which different collectives, from groups of two to groups in their thousands, engage in acts of remembrance together.[3]

The focus of this book is therefore on the *processes*—the commemorative rituals, the installation of memorials, the organisation of 'pilgrimages' and the production of cultural media—by which particular episodes of World War I have survived to dominate memory today. What these processes—which involve a dynamic and symbiotic interaction between what might be called 'agents of memory' at various levels of Australian society—reveal is that the hierarchy of 'sites of memory' in 2013 is not that of 1919. When the five divisions of the AIF came to choose the locations for their dedicated memorials, they chose Pozières (1st Division), Mont St Quentin (2nd Division), Sailly-le-Sec (3rd Division), Bellenglise (4th Division) and Polygon Wood (5th Division). These battles do not map easily onto today's commemorative priorities. Where, for example, is Fromelles, a battle now at the heart of Australian national memory? Who today knows where Bellenglise can be found?

The men of the AIF, it seems, chose to be remembered not for their defeats but for their victories. Gallipoli, perhaps, was the exception—although even this was remembered as a 'triumph' in the sense that it was the dramatic storming of the cliffs by the initial landing forces on 25 April 1915 and their survival against the odds that became legendary. In contrast, the dominant mode of understanding in the memory of war today is catastrophe and trauma. As the French historians Stéphane Audoin-Rouzeau and Annette Becker have observed, in 1998 the commemorations of the end of World War I depicted combatants as 'mere non-consenting victims [, and] mutineers and rebels [as] the only true heroes'.[4]

Yet if we owe anything to the generation that fought and died in World War I—and the rhetoric of the centenary anniversaries will almost certainly suggest that we do—it is to try to remember the war as they saw it. In particular, we must acknowledge—if not condone—the values for which they were prepared to fight. The dominant narrative of World War I in the Western world has become one of futility: of a war in which the losses were never matched by the gains; in which lives were wasted by incompetent and profligate military commanders; and in which military victory failed to bring any lasting peace to Europe. There is good reason for this, but it should not be forgotten that Australians had clearly identified war aims in World War I. These included the maintenance of British global imperial power, the protection of the White Australia Policy, the guaranteeing of Australian security in the Pacific, the defence of democracy against German tyranny and aggression, and the protection of the rights of small nations such as Belgium. Some of the values that inform these aims we still embrace; others we struggle to understand. No one born after the decline of British global power, for example, can begin to comprehend the ideological fervour and passionate sense of loyalty to empire that sustained many Australians through four terrible years of war.

The final aim of this book, therefore, is to examine how these war aims and values were pursued and contested, both in the home-front debates about the war and in the sphere of imperial and international relations. When Australians went to war in August 1914, it was not only because they shared Britain's war aims but because London controlled Australia's diplomatic relations with the rest of the world. The growing sense of national consciousness that World War I spawned did little to challenge imperial loyalty as the hegemonic value, but it did start a process of change in the status of Australia and other Dominions within and outside the empire. Like other Dominion leaders, in 1917–18 Hughes came to demand a greater voice in imperial decision-making and a recognition on the part of decision-makers in London that Australia's and Britain's interests were not always one and the same.

Hughes had his successes, and in 1919 Australia would for the first time be granted independent representation at a major international conference, the Paris Peace Conference. But on many counts the diplomatic gains of the war were small—and scarcely commensurate with the cost of the war in blood and money. On the one hand, Australia retained control of the strategically important German colonies to its north, albeit under a mandate of the new League of Nations. Hughes also succeeded, as he saw it, in protecting the restrictive immigration policy of White Australia by blocking the Japanese attempt to gain international affirmation of the principle of racial equality. But when it came to other core Australian interests, such as reparations for the country's war debt, Hughes confronted the reality of the severe limits to Australia's influence and power. The Treaty of Versailles, a deeply flawed compromise between power politics and the liberal internationalism of US President Woodrow Wilson, was therefore a bitter disappointment to him and his colleagues.

World War I, in fact, had transformed the world order that Australia had gone to war to defend. By 1918, the dynastic monarchies of Germany, Russia and Austria-Hungary had collapsed, the Ottoman Empire had disintegrated and Bolshevism had triumphed in Russia. Germany's attempt to dominate Europe had, it seemed, been checked, but the price paid for victory was the erosion of the British global dominance whose preservation was a core war aim for many Australians. The United States, though entering the war only in 1917, had emerged to challenge the centuries-long dominance of Europe. Japan, the nation whose expansionist intentions were of serious concern to

Australians, had also capitalised on the war to enhance its strategic position in the Asia-Pacific region. All of this was not as obvious in 1919 as it was in 1942, when British imperial power in the Asia-Pacific collapsed humiliatingly at Singapore, but enough of it was evident for Hughes to view the peace settlement as a defeat for Australia and a victory for the United States.

In the realm of diplomacy, therefore, the Australian experience of World War I was again one of loss. How intriguing, then, that the war that caused such damage should have spawned what is now the foundational narrative of Australian nationalism. Beginning almost as soon as the AIF landed at Gallipoli in 1915, the Anzac 'legend' would gain a firm hold on the cultural imagination of the Australian media and public. It was a version of events that overstated the performance and uniqueness of the Australian 'digger', but which—possibly because of its hyperbole—was rapidly incorporated into the commemorative rituals of Anzac Day from the time of its first celebration in 1916. In essence, the legend claimed that Australian men—drawn from a society whose lifestyle and social structures predisposed them to be exceptional fighters—had made a decisive contribution to Allied victory and had performed exceptional feats in war. Not only had they proved themselves worthy of the Anglo-Saxon race and their forebears who had conquered the Australian bush; most importantly, the AIF—whose voluntary tradition was singular—had manifested qualities and solidarity in battle that stood as a model for future generations.

It was as if the sheer scale of Australia's loss during World War I demanded a narrative of hyperbole that invested its profound trauma with meaning. Certainly Australians invested more energy in building war memorials during and after the war than any other nation: some 1500 to 2000 were constructed—probably the highest rate for any country that fought the war. In many cases, these memorials also perpetuated the divisions of the war by listing not just the dead but the men who had volunteered to serve in the Australian Imperial Force and survived.[5]

In the decades that followed World War I, the Anzac 'legend' would become the dominant narrative of the war, in the sense that it would come to be seen as natural and incontestable even by those who were not part of the elites or institutions that created and promulgated it. It would survive and evolve across the century, performing the 'mythic' function of a story about the past that serves as a 'charter' for the present, justifying later institutions and maintaining their existence. With effortless ease, it would incorporate the service of the men and women who followed their fathers' example and served in World War II. It would survive—only just—the bitterness of the Vietnam War, the next divisive debate about conscription and the radical and feminist movements of the 1960s. Then, when the decline of the Anzac 'legend' and its rituals seemed almost terminal, it would be reinvented in the new nationalism of the late twentieth century. Now focused on the core attributes of endurance, courage, sacrifice and mateship, 'Anzac' is invoked not just by politicians, but by sportsmen, policemen and others who champion the values of the collective and team over the individual, to stand for 'what it means to be Australian'. How and why this happened—and why a narrative that met the needs of Australians in World War I should continue to have such cultural dominance and emotional power in a radically different Australia a century later—is yet to be explained. But that is the subject of another book.[6]

Charles Bean

This book contains many references to C.E.W. (Charles) Bean. It is impossible to write a history of Australians during World War I without quoting this influential historian. Born in England, where he studied classics and law, Bean came to Australia in 1904. Employed as a teacher and then a journalist, in 1909 he went to the west of New South Wales to write a series of articles on the wool industry for the *Sydney Morning Herald*. Here in the Australian bush he formed lasting views about the importance of its lifestyle in shaping Australian cultural values and concepts of masculinity.

Though he spent the years 1910–12 in England, Bean returned to Australia in 1913. When war broke out in August 1914, he won the vote of the Australian Journalists Association to be Australia's first official war correspondent. He defeated Keith Murdoch, father of Rupert, who would also go on to play a significant role in the Australian history of World War I.

Bean travelled to Egypt with the 1st Australian Imperial Force (AIF) in 1914 and accompanied the force to Gallipoli. For the remainder of the war he was often at the front line, observing the action and forming a deep attachment to the Australian troops. Quite early in the war, he decided that the only memorials that would be worthy of the AIF were a history of their role in World War I and a war museum in Australia. Hence, while writing journalism for immediate publication at home, Bean also kept a diary and filled 283 notebooks with observations of the battles in which the AIF was taking part. Appointed the official historian of the war, he also led a mission to Gallipoli in early 1919 before returning to Australia and beginning work on the official history series.

Over the next two decades, he would write six volumes of this monumental work (the six that dealt with the infantry divisions) and edit eight more. Bean would also write a condensed history of the war, *Anzac to Amiens*. When completed in 1942, the official history project amounted to nearly four million words—in the days before computers!

Many decades later, the official histories remain an indispensable resource for the historian of Australia's experience of war. This is not just because of their readability and data but because Bean's eyewitness accounts of the war at the tactical level were never replicated. Anyone seeking to understand the way in which battle played out for the Australian soldier, as opposed to his commanders, cannot avoid reading Bean.

Bean is also of central importance because of the role he played in creating the Anzac 'legend' or 'myth'. While living with Australian soldiers in 1915–18, he developed a profound respect not only for their seemingly natural fighting ability but for the distinctive qualities that, as Bean saw it, underpinned this prowess: their independence of spirit, their ability to think independently, their resourcefulness, their egalitarian ethos and, above all, their mateship. These characteristics, which Bean attributed to the relatively classless nature of Australian society and the influence of the bush, were celebrated in the official histories and other writings that he published after the war. In these, Bean also gave voice to the view that resonates strongly in Australian political culture even today: that 'it was on the 25th of April, 1915, that the consciousness of Australian nationhood was born'.[7]

Bean was not alone in promulgating a narrative of the war that celebrated the brilliance and distinctiveness of the AIF. It was a version of the past that many others—including the press, politicians and the commander of the Australian Corps in 1918, General Sir John Monash—embraced and developed during and after World War I. But it was Bean who articulated the almost mythic representation of the AIF most consistently and eloquently, and who worked tirelessly to enshrine the memory of the AIF in the Australian War Memorial in Canberra, opened during the next world war, in 1941. Unique in its being a memorial, a museum and a research centre in one, the War Memorial remains the custodian of a national memory of war into the twenty-first century.[8] Hence, as both a historian and agent of memory, Bean stands as a colossus whom no historian of Australia in World War I can ignore.

A note on statistics

There will always be variations between sets of statistics of battle casualties, particularly in a war as vast and complex as World War I. End dates, for example, are always problematic. At what date do we stop attributing deaths by wounds to a specific battle or to the war itself? Should deaths from the influenza pandemic of 1918–19 be counted as war deaths? And what of the many young men who died prematurely in the 1920s of the injuries they had sustained in 1914–18?

This book uses, where possible, the statistics of the Australian War Memorial, *The Official History of Australia in the War of 1914–18* or the national census of 1911. Where other sources are used, these are cited in an endnote. Preference is also given to statistics that give an order of magnitude, since a precise number is often contested.

Key data for any history of World War I are the monthly enlistments for the Australian Imperial Force (AIF), which remained an exclusively volunteer force from 1914 to 1918. These are the figures over which recruitment officials agonised during the war and that, for the historian, provide some measure of the shifting moods of the Australian population. Enlistment data are provided in Appendix 2: 'AIF enlistments by month, 1915–18'. Numerical data can be found in Ernest Scott's volume of the official history, *Australia During the War*,[9] now digitised on the Australian War Memorial website at <www.awm.gov.au/histories/first_world_war>.

ACKNOWLEDGEMENTS

The original inspiration for this book came from Ian Bowring, then a commissioning editor at Allen & Unwin. His tolerance of my ever-receding delivery dates, as I tried to reconcile my academic leadership role with my personal research agenda at Deakin University and, from 2008, at the Australian National University, was essential to the book finally coming to life.

There are many people to whom I owe thanks. First, my academic colleagues at the Strategic and Defence Studies Centre, Australian National University, David Horner, Brendan Taylor and Hugh White: they provided me with a visiting fellowship in 2007 and, from 2012, with the congenial academic home within which the final 'big push' to complete the book was made. Sally Walker, formerly Vice Chancellor of Deakin University, allowed me to take up the ANU fellowship while I held a senior management role at Deakin. Glenda Lynch, my ever patient research assistant, undertook countless hours of painstaking and exemplary archival work. Keith Mitchell was meticulous in his production of the maps, adapting, with the ready agreement of John Coates, the original maps in the definitive *An Atlas of Australia's War*, vol. VII, *The Australian Centenary History of Defence* (Melbourne: Oxford University Press, 2001).

At various stages my manuscript was read and commented upon by colleagues and friends: Jean Bou, Ken Cooper, David Horner, Neville Meaney and Robin Prior. I cannot thank them too much for their willingness to do

ACKNOWLEDGEMENTS

this. Finally, the staff at Allen & Unwin, Foong Ling Kong, Angela Handley, Sue Jarvis and Liz Keenan, provided ongoing and meticulous editorial and production support.

The Australian War Memorial granted me permission to cite liberally *The Official History of Australia in the War of 1914–1918*. Memorial staff also provided expert and timely advice on copyright matters relating to its rich private record collection. Craig Tibbits and Kelda McManus are particularly to be thanked. So, too, are the family of C.E.W. Bean and the descendants of soldiers of the 1st Australian Imperial Force, who agreed to my quoting the private diaries, letters and memoirs which add such colour and authenticity to the narratives of battle.

Sarah Lethbridge of the Noel Butlin Archives Centre, Australian National University, was also a much valued source of support on all matters relating to this unique national archive of labour history.

And then there are my daughters: Diana Beaumont, Caroline Burrows and Julia Rhyder. They have been unfailingly loyal, interested and supportive, keeping faith in 'The Book', even as it seemed more a matter of their mother's imagination than a reality.

ABBREVIATIONS AND ACRONYMS

AANS	Australian Army Nursing Service
AIF	Australian Imperial Force
AFC	Australian Flying Corps
ALP	Australian Labor Party
AN&MEF	Australian Naval & Military Expeditionary Force
ANU	Australian National University
AWM	Australian War Memorial
Bde	Brigade
EEF	Egyptian Expeditionary Force
FPWC	Federal Parliamentary War Committee
IWC	Imperial War Cabinet
IWW	Industrial Workers of the World
LH	Light Horse
MEF	Mediterranean Expeditionary Force
NAA	National Archives of Australia
NLA	National Library of Australia
RSL	Returned and Services League
RSSILA	Returned Sailor's and Soldier's Imperial League of Australia
SMH	*Sydney Morning Herald*
US	United States
USL	Universal Service League
VAD	Voluntary Aid Detachment

PROLOGUE
Joe Russell's War

Clarence Joe Russell, known to his family as Joe, volunteered to serve in the Australian Imperial Force (AIF) on 4 December 1916. This was not an obvious time to enlist. Across Australia, only 2617 men volunteered that month. Many more—nearly 21,000—had enlisted two months earlier, in September and October 1916. Thinking that the national referendum on conscription for overseas service would result in a 'yes' vote, they had decided to save face by volunteering rather than waiting to be conscripted. But Joe Russell had not.

Joe was probably thought by many of his peers in Adelaide, South Australia, to be a 'shirker'. He was 31 years of age, 5 feet 9¾ inches (1.8 metres) tall, a grocer and unmarried: he was very much an 'eligible'. But he hesitated, so family memory would have it, until his girlfriend shamed him by handing him a white feather, a symbol of cowardice that had become popular in wartime Britain.

We do not know what emotions Joe felt when, on 10 February 1917, he boarded a ship for France, where the five infantry divisions of the AIF were deployed. Unlike the many thousands of men who rushed to enlist in the first months of the war, he knew he risked injury or death. In the Battle of the Somme in 1916 alone, the armies of the British Empire had suffered 432,000 casualties. Many men had already returned to Australia with terrible injuries received at Fromelles, the Somme or in the failed Gallipoli campaign of April to December 1915. But Joe went to France nonetheless.

He arrived in the United Kingdom on 2 May 1917 and joined the 50th Battalion (4th Division) in France on 25 August. There, one of the most infamous battles of the war—the Third Battle of Ypres—was in train. It had begun on 31 July 1917 with grand hopes on the part of the Commander-in-Chief of the British Expeditionary Force, General (Sir) Douglas Haig, of breaking through to the English Channel and shattering the stalemate that had existed on the Western Front since 1914. But by the time Joe arrived, the land around Ypres was a morass of mud and shell holes full of fetid water. The rain had started early in the campaign. The water table in that region of Belgium was high, and the irrigation systems used to reclaim the land had been destroyed by incessant artillery bombardments. Struggling to make their way across a surreal landscape on duckboards or slippery paths, men and horses sank into the mud. By the time the campaign ended on 10 November, perhaps 310,000 British and Commonwealth forces, and 200,000 German soldiers, had been killed, or were wounded or missing. Some 38,000 of the Commonwealth casualties were Australian.

Joe was wounded on 26 September 1917. He was probably part of the attack on Polygon Wood—or, to be more accurate, the pockmarked hill with skeletal trunks of shattered trees that was all that remained of the wood. On that day, when in fact the weather was better, the battle began with a creeping barrage, an artillery attack that protected advancing infantry by delivering a curtain of shells landing just ahead of them. In the words of C.E.W. Bean, the accredited Australian journalist on the Western Front:

> the shell-bursts raised a wall of dust and smoke which appeared almost to be solid. So dense was the cloud that individual bursts, except the white puffs of shrapnel above its near edge, could not be distinguished. Roaring, deafening, it rolled ahead of the troops 'like a Gippsland bushfire'.[10]

Somewhere in the midst of all this, just one month and a day after he had arrived in France, Joe was wounded in his left leg. He was evacuated to the

7th Canadian General Hospital at Étaples, but on the way (again according to family memory) he and the stretcher-bearers carrying him were buried by shellfire. He was dug out of the suffocating dirt of France, only to be buried alive again before reaching the casualty clearing station.

Perhaps on this long journey, Joe's leg wound became infected. The high-explosive shells used on the Western Front showered the battlefield with jagged fragments that embedded soil and pieces of clothing in the men's flesh. These were the days before antibiotic drugs, and it was difficult to keep wounds clean. Gangrene, with its 'unutterably foul smell', set in. By the time Joe reached Guilford, England, in October 1917, his leg had to be amputated. He was fortunate in that he survived the operation—6 per cent of soldiers who had their limbs amputated on the Western Front did not.[11]

Joe was repatriated to Australia, arriving home in April or May 1918. In his total overseas service of about a year, he had been in battle, it seems, for only a few hours. He probably killed very few Germans. Perhaps all he had done for his country was to lose his leg. The girl who had given him the white feather did not marry Joe. With a pension of £3 per fortnight and his British War Medal and Victory Medal, he moved in with his two sisters, Edith Russell and Lydia Errington, and his five-year-old niece, Edna. Lydia had been widowed, not by the war but by the 'Spanish' influenza pandemic that killed at least 50 million people around the world in 1918–19. Many people thought this haemorrhagic fever was attributable to the war. Perhaps it had originated with rats feeding on the corpses in the trenches of France and Belgium; certainly it had been spread around the world by the movement of troops whose immune systems may have been weakened by the stresses of active service. So even though Lydia's husband, Ernest Errington, had remained in Australia, serving in Adelaide's 4th Military District Headquarters Band, she received a 'Dead Man's Penny', that bronze plaque issued by the government to the families of men who died in the war, with the inscription 'He died for freedom and honour'.[12]

Joe, Edna and the grieving Lydia were dependent on Joe's work as a cobbler and the income from Edith's small grocery store in Grote Street, central

Adelaide. Joe slept in the front bedroom, where for years after the war he would have nightmares, reliving those moments when he was smothered by the dirt of France. He would struggle in his sleep to get out of bed, forgetting his missing leg and falling to the floor. Edna, the only child in this traumatised family, would rush to his bedroom to help him.

Eventually Joe married and had one son. But he remained Edna's surrogate father. Complete with wooden leg, he walked her down the aisle when in 1934 she married a young teacher and Methodist lay preacher, Cliff Magor, in the Flinders Street Baptist Church. It is a long aisle, sloping quite steeply downwards to the altar, so it must have been difficult for Joe. He died, aged 53, in April 1938.

This is only one of some 330,000 stories of Australian men and women who served overseas in the war that soon became known as 'The Great War'. Thousands of Australian families endured the aftermath of this massive conflict, and handed their stories down from one generation to the next. Joe Russell's story starts this history only because he was my great-uncle. Lydia was my grandmother; Ernest my grandfather; Edna my mother. As a child, I heard the story of Joe's white feather and lost leg many times. As a child, I took little notice of it—except for the macabre details of his nightmares and his falling out of bed. Only now do I recognise that Joe is one of the reasons why I have written this book. His war service was reluctant, short and ineffectual, yet in its own way it was courageous. Had not he, and millions of other men, been willing to fight—whatever their reservations and fears—the armies of 1914–18 could not have fought World War I for more than four terrible years.

1

1914
Going to war

No democracy of the twenty-first century could fight World War I. Between August 1914 and November 1918, at least nine million military personnel and civilians died. Some 61,520 of them were from Australia. A further 153,500 Australians were wounded or gassed and more than 3600 taken prisoner. In all, over 330,000 men and women served overseas. This was at a time when the Australian population was less than five million.[1]

How can we comprehend the willingness of Australians to tolerate such losses when today the death of a single soldier in combat triggers a spasm of media attention and political anxiety? How can we even imagine casualties on such a scale? To put them into some kind of perspective: World War I accounts for nearly 60 per cent of all Australian deaths in international conflicts since a contingent of colonials left for an imperial adventure in the Sudan in 1885. World War II, in contrast, caused around 39,760 deaths, even though it was a far more destructive conflict globally and Australia faced the threat of invasion for the first time since white settlement. Fewer men were killed and wounded in the ten years of the Vietnam War than on 19 July 1916, the day the Australian Imperial Force (AIF) fought at Fromelles in France. What made the men of the AIF persevere in the face of such terrible losses? What did they think they were fighting for? And what gave meaning to the deaths of these fathers, husbands, brothers and sons for the families who grieved at home?

We can probably never fully understand, living as we do in an individualistic, materialistic and secular society where the death of the young is treated as almost intolerable. But if we are to try, we need to begin not with Gallipoli and 25 April 1915, which dominate Australians' memory of the war today, but with Europe and 4 August 1914. World War I was, after all, a European war—one that, thanks to imperialism's global stretch, sucked into its maw millions of people around the world. It was also the belief of many Australians that what happened in Europe directly affected their lives and interests that made them willing to support the war through four years of bitter loss and dispute at home.

The outbreak of war

Historians of World War I often talk of the 'last summer' of Europe. They invoke haunting Impressionist images of young men and women in long skirts and broad-brimmed hats picnicking, unaware of imminent disaster. But in Australia it was winter when the first signs of war appeared in mid-1914. As the official historian of the Australian home front, Ernest Scott, put it:

> The almond trees, heralds of the coming spring while winter still blanched the grass with morning frosts, were white with blossom. At Mildura and Renmark miles of orange groves glowed yellow . . . The peach trees and the apple orchards were beginning to bud. Nearly seventy-eight million sheep and eleven million head of cattle were nibbling the herbage . . . In the wheat belt there was the largest area under crop that Australia had ever known.

Although it was winter, it was terribly dry. The country was preoccupied with drought, and also with a federal election. Unable to control the House of Representatives, the Liberal Prime Minister Joseph Cook, in office only since June 1913, had forced a double dissolution in the hope of securing working majorities in both houses of parliament.[2]

Australian politicians were therefore campaigning far from the seat of the federal government in Melbourne when late in June came news of an act of violence in Eastern Europe that would ultimately lead to war. On 28 June, the heir to the Hapsburg monarchy of Austria-Hungary, Archduke Franz Ferdinand, and his wife were assassinated in Sarajevo while visiting Bosnia, a territory annexed by Austria-Hungary only in 1908. The murders were not of global significance, and the quality press in Australia gave them serious coverage for only a few days. The violence was understood to be a symptom of wider problems in the tottering multinational empire of Austria-Hungary—in particular, the centrifugal forces of nationalism and self-determination in the Balkans. Russia, another great authoritarian monarchy of Europe, was known to be supporting the political aspirations of the Slavic peoples beyond its own borders. It seemed that all that held Austria-Hungary together was its monarch, Franz Joseph, who had been on the throne since 1848.

However, Franz Joseph was 84 years of age and the murdered archduke was the heir to his throne. Franz Joseph's only son had died in a scandalous incident with his mistress in 1889, while his favourite brother, who had been installed as emperor of Mexico in one of the more bizarre imperial episodes of the nineteenth century, had been executed by Mexican republicans in 1867. The troubles of European royalty then—as now—made for good reading, and an Adelaide newspaper, *The Register*, commented on 30 June:

> Verily the old monarch [Franz Joseph] has had to drink deeply of the cup of humiliation and woe, and his pale face and bent body, recently enfeebled by illness, presented a pathetic spectacle as, on being informed of the latest remorseless stroke of his evil Destiny, he murmured with deep feeling 'I am spared nothing!'

Soon, however, the Australian press moved back to covering the federal election and another remote crisis with which many recent immigrants to Australia identified more strongly: the issue of self-government, or Home Rule, for Ireland.

By late July, however, it was clear that events in Europe were spinning out of control. The Austro-Hungarian government accused Bosnia's neighbour, Serbia, of complicity in the assassination of the archduke, and on 23 July it issued an ultimatum demanding that the Serbian government take action in relation to internal policing and suppression of propaganda against Austria-Hungary. The Serbian government appeared to acquiesce in these demands, even though they compromised its sovereignty, but the Austro-Hungarian government, with the support of its ally Germany, proceeded to mobilise seven army corps against Serbia.

This started a sequence of tit-for-tat mobilisations that rapidly escalated the crisis beyond the Balkans. Feeling obliged to support the cause of pan-Slavism in Eastern Europe, the Russian government responded to Austria's mobilisation against Serbia by taking measures to mobilise its own massive army. Austria-Hungary, in turn, declared war on Serbia on 28 July. Russia then started partial mobilisation and two days later, when it seemed Germany would support Austria, upgraded this to full mobilisation. Since war with Russia now seemed imminent, Austria ordered a general mobilisation of its own forces. Germany, in turn, ordered its army to mobilise, sending an ultimatum to Russia demanding that it cease all military action within twelve hours. When Moscow failed to respond, Germany declared war on Russia on 1 August. In response, France, an ally of Russia, ordered a general mobilisation, a decision that triggered Germany's declaration of war on France two days later. The following day, Germany attacked France through Belgium, a country whose neutrality had been guaranteed by the Treaty of London of 1839. Britain, which was not only a guarantor of Belgian neutrality but aligned with France, then declared war on Germany on 4 August. Within thirteen days of the Austro-Hungarian ultimatum to Serbia, all of the five so-called Great Powers of Europe—Austria-Hungary, France, Germany, Great Britain and Russia—were at war. There had not been a war on this scale since 1815.

Historians have debated ever since why this catastrophic escalation of tensions occurred so rapidly in July and August 1914. There had been numerous diplomatic crises between the European powers in the preceding decades, but these had been managed without resorting to general war. Assassinations were quite common as a means of making a political point. Why, then, did the killing of Archduke Ferdinand in the remote town of Sarajevo become the 'shot heard around the world'? Why did the European states find themselves locked into a seemingly uncontrollable sequence of mobilisation and counter-mobilisation that escalated the July crisis into a general European war? Who, if anyone, was to blame?

A traditional explanation is the rigidity of the military alliance system in Europe. In the late nineteenth century the major European powers had progressively grouped themselves into opposing diplomatic and military camps: the Triple Alliance of 1882, consisting of Germany, Austria-Hungary and Italy, on the one hand; and the Franco-Russian Alliance of 1892, on the other. Britain had aligned itself with France in 1904 through the Entente Cordiale with the aim of containing Germany. It was this system of mutual obligation that triggered the successive mobilisations of the European powers in July and August 1914.

However, military alliances of themselves do not cause wars. Rather, in 1914 the alliances reflected new and powerful structural changes in the European system that, grinding like tectonic plates, were producing the tensions that erupted into war in 1914. The legitimacy of the authoritarian dynastic monarchies that ruled Austria-Hungary, Germany and Russia was being challenged by the ideologies of nationalism, liberalism, socialism and self-determination. Beyond Europe, most of the powers were competing in Africa and Asia for the strategic and economic spoils of empire. Finally, industrialisation was generating major changes in the balance of power that had provided stability since the end of the Napoleonic wars in 1815, particularly the industrialisation of Germany.

Formed as a federal nation state only in 1871 after a series of short and successful wars launched by Prussia, Germany was Europe's fastest growing industrial power. Its gross national product multiplied six times between 1870 and 1913. Its coal production increased more than seven times over the same period; steel production grew fifteenfold. The German population also increased by nearly 60 per cent between 1871 and 1910.[3] The problem that this posed for Europe was that, left unchecked, Germany might dominate the Continent. The French, with a smaller population, slower economic growth and an obsession to reverse their defeat in the Franco-Prussian War of 1870–71, could not tolerate this.

Nor could the British: over the centuries, their traditional foreign policy goal had been to maintain the balance of power on the Continent, intervening only when—as in the case of the French Revolutionary and Napoleonic wars from 1792 to 1815—one European power was threatening to become hegemonic. Now Germany seemed to be doing this, while also mounting an even more troubling challenge to the naval supremacy on which Britain's global power depended. Britain's 'two-power' standard, whereby it aimed to maintain a fleet large enough to contain the two next greatest naval powers at any given time, was slipping from its grasp as Germany launched a naval race from 1906 on, building dreadnought class ships to match the most modern technology of the Royal Navy.

All these structural changes were potentially explosive because of the militarisation of Europe. In the years before 1914, defence budgets grew dramatically as diplomatic tensions rose and jingoistic lobby groups and militaristic popular presses agitated for increased defence spending. Much of this military expenditure funded the new technologies of war that would cause such carnage in World War I. But the actual size of European armies and navies also increased alarmingly in the late nineteenth century. With the exception of Britain, all major powers maintained armies of several million men (including reserves).

Even at the time, it seemed that Europe had gone insane. The 'two armed camps' appeared to be drifting uncontrollably towards war in some Social Darwinist struggle for survival. 'The situation in Europe is desperate', wrote *The Register* on 1 August, 'because of the ascendancy of militarism in Vienna, St. Petersburg and Berlin. Well-equipped armies, aggregating millions of officers and men, are like dogs straining at the leash.' Slipping into more Australian imagery the next day, it declared:

When a mischievous boy stamps his foot on an ants' nest a scene is produced similar to that observable on the Continent today. Austria has stamped her foot, and the surface of Europe swarms with soldiers, mobilizing in millions, hurrying hither and thither like myriads of angry and excited ants.[4]

Such were the risks inherent in the huge arsenals of Europe that the outbreak of war has sometimes been explained as an accident: as the British wartime Prime Minister David Lloyd George put it in his war memoirs, Europe 'slithered over the brink into the boiling cauldron of war'. But arms races of themselves do not cause wars. At the height of the Cold War, the Soviet and Western blocs possessed nuclear weapons that could have caused mutual obliteration many times over, but these were never used. Ultimately, it is individual politicians who make the decisions—or, more often, the misjudgements—that lead to war. In July and August 1914 a small coterie of advisers around Franz Joseph of Austria decided to take punitive action against Serbia, even though it was possible that Russia would not back down. Russian Tsar Nicholas II, under pressure from his military advisers, decided to support Serbia and order general mobilisation. The British government, after an agonising prevarication that probably inflamed the crisis, decided on the advice of the Foreign Secretary Sir Edward Grey and the First Lord of the Admiralty Winston Churchill to support France and Belgium, believing that it had to act 'to prevent the whole of the West of Europe opposite us from falling under the domination of a single power'. Most importantly, Kaiser Wilhelm II and his military leaders gave unqualified support to Austria when it wished to attack Serbia, even though Germany was not bound to do so by the terms of the Triple Alliance and its decision risked war against Russia. Whether the Germans actually aspired to dominate Europe and to make a 'grab for world power' has been the subject of passionate debate from 1919 to today. More probably, Germany's decision-making processes were chaotic and Kaiser Wilhelm, rather than being rational, resolute and calculating, simply failed to provide the direction and coordination of Germany's foreign and defence policy that would have stopped it from stumbling into war.[5]

Germany's decision to go to war was critically important because of the peculiarities of its pre-war strategic planning. Once France and Russia were allies, Germany was faced with a nightmare scenario of simultaneous wars in the east and the west. This could only be managed, the German military leadership concluded in the years before 1914, by defeating France quickly. In the event of a general European war, therefore, they planned to first strike through Belgium, neutralising France before turning to meet the Russians in the east. This was in itself a gamble, but it was compounded by the fact that the violation of Belgian neutrality might bring Britain into the war. Indeed, it was Germany's disregard for Britain's treaty with Belgium—that 'scrap of paper', as Chancellor Theobald von Bethmann-Hollweg famously put it—that finally tipped the balance in favour of war among the wavering decision-makers in London.

Australia's 'decision' for war

World War I, then—though it later came to be popularly seen as futile—was about core issues concerning the balance of power in Europe. But why did this matter to Australians? Why did they follow the Gadarene-swine rush of European nations into war? The answer lies partly in the fact that Australia was not an independent international actor in 1914. Even though at Federation the Commonwealth government had gained control over what the constitution called 'external affairs', this ambiguous power was not interpreted by politicians to mean the right to manage Australia's diplomatic relations with the rest of the world. Rather, these were assumed to remain the prerogative of London, which conducted foreign policy on behalf of the whole British Empire. Hence, in August 1914 when Britain declared war it did so in the expectation that Australia and other Dominions would follow.[6]

The Australian government might have protested. London failed to consult it during the crisis of July 1914, even though it had given assurances to Australia and the other Dominions (Canada, New Zealand and South Africa) at the Imperial Conference of 1911 that it would keep them informed on the formulation of imperial foreign policy. But the Cook government accepted the British decision without question, believing that the issues for which Britain was going to war—the defence of the rights of small nations, such as Belgium, and the need to contain Germany's power—were also core interests of Australia.

As many Australians saw it, the wider strategic arguments for supporting Britain were compelling. Ever since European settlement in 1788, they had struggled to feel secure in the vast land mass they had occupied. With their small population and the Asian masses to their north, they could not hope to defend the continent's long coastline. Only Britain's global power could contain the ambitions of other European empires and the rising power of Japan in the Asia-Pacific region, and only the Royal Navy could keep open the sea lanes of communication on which Australia's international trade depended. Hence, all of Australian defence planning in the decades preceding World War I had been positioned within a framework of imperial defence.

This did not mean that Australian governments had completely abdicated any role in defence planning prior to 1914. On the contrary, in the years after Federation, the ragbag of colonial forces that the Commonwealth inherited had been integrated into a small national army, consisting mainly of artillery and administrative staff. In addition, in 1911 Australia had introduced a system of compulsory military training of young men for home defence and, in the face of some opposition from the Admiralty, taken the momentous step of creating its own navy. Its centrepiece was a modern battle cruiser, HMAS *Australia*, which arrived to great public enthusiasm in October 1913.[7]

This planning reflected a growing awareness on the part of Australians that their strategic interests were not always identical to Britain's or the Empire's. In particular, Britain could not be guaranteed to share the depth of Australian concerns about Japan, which had expanded into Korea and, to the astonishment of Australians and Europeans, annihilated the Russian fleet in the Battle of Tsushima in 1905. Instead, in 1902 Britain had actually signed an alliance with Japan. Suffering from what we would now call 'strategic overstretch', it thought this was the best way to guarantee British interests in the Pacific. But for Australians, already fearful of invasion by the Asian 'hordes', this was anything but reassuring. As a cartoon in *Truth* put it on 8 August 1914:

> The scene is changed!
> The brown man is brother!
> Alas, for dear Australia White!
> The Japs are pals of Mother![8]

Yet whatever their reservations about the Anglo-Japanese alliance, the vast majority of Australians saw no option but to continue to rely upon, and do all they could to strengthen, the system of imperial defence. Any further erosion of British power globally would simply increase Australia's exposure, not just to Japan, but to German imperial ambitions in the Asia-Pacific.

This strategic logic was underpinned by a profound cultural and emotional identification with the United Kingdom. Over half a million Australians, of a total population of 4.3 million in 1911, had been born in England, Wales, Scotland or Ireland. Many more were of Anglo-Celtic descent. For most of these men and women, there was no contradiction in being 'Australian' and 'British' at the same time. Rather, Britain was the source of all that was best in culture, architecture, education, and political and legal institutions. Australians also gloried in the 'crimson thread of kinship', as the politician Henry Parkes had called it, that bound them to the British race, ensuring the purity of White Australia, a core value of the young Australian Federation. Loyalty to Britain, then, was much more than strategic pragmatism: as Lloyd Robson put it in 1982, it 'had all the depth and comprehensiveness of a religion'.[9]

In fact, as the war years would show, the depth of this identification with Britain varied according to class, denomination and ethnicity. Imperial loyalty was not universal, but rather the dominant value of those who held political, cultural and economic power in Australia. However, it pervaded public life and education. Classrooms across the nation displayed world maps studded with reassuring splashes of imperial red. Empire Day (24 May, the anniversary of Queen Victoria's birthday) was the occasion for celebrating the glories of the British Empire, while books such as W.H. Fitchett's *Deeds That Won the Empire* (1897) socialised young Australians into tales of imperial heroism. The values that the empire supposedly affirmed—discipline, duty and service in the collective good—were also inculcated through movements such as the Boy Scouts (itself a progeny of an imperial war) and the system of universal military training.

Australia's offer of support

Hence the question facing the Australian government in August 1914 was not whether Australians should be at war, but what kind of contribution they should make to the imperial war effort. Cook's small Cabinet met to discuss this question on 3 August at the urging of the governor-general, Sir Ronald Craufurd Munro Ferguson, a Scottish peer and former British politician who took his vice-regal responsibilities as the channel of communication between Australia and London extremely seriously. Given the primitive communications (there was no domestic air travel and all telegraphic communications had to be coded), only five of ten Cabinet ministers were present at this important meeting. Cook was in the chair. A migrant from the United Kingdom with 'an atavistic attachment to the British Empire', he believed that war 'would unite the nation and prepare individuals and classes to eschew vain things and sacrifice their interests for the good of the whole'. (He was also a teetotaller and a Methodist lay preacher.) His attorney-general, William Irvine, born in Ireland, similarly had no doubts that 'When England is at war we are at war. There is no half way home . . . we are not only bound to abide by [the British government's] decision, but to give them every assistance that lies in our power.'[10]

Predictably, then, after receiving advice from senior army and navy leaders, the Cabinet decided to place the vessels of the Royal Australian Navy (RAN) under the immediate control of the Royal Navy. This was consistent with all pre-war defence planning, which assumed an integrated Anglo-Australian naval strategy within the Asia-Pacific region. The head of the RAN was a British officer, and its personnel had been trained to be wholly interchangeable with those of the Royal Navy. However, the Cabinet went further. It also agreed to offer London an expeditionary force of some 20,000 men that could be deployed as the British authorities wished while Australia covered the costs of its maintenance. Imperial loyalties aside, it seems that the Cabinet was influenced by the fact that the Canadian government had already offered London an even larger force: initially 20,000 men, but soon increased to 33,000. New Zealand, too, had promised an expeditionary force on 31 July. As Scott says, the Cabinet wanted to prove that Australia was 'not less eager, though a little late'.[11]

The target of 20,000 men was ambitious. Australia had only a very small permanent army and the *Defence Act* of 1903 prohibited its use overseas—a restriction imposed precisely out of fear that Australia might be obligated to provide troops for the empire in time of war. Hence, all members of the new expeditionary force would have to be volunteers. Admittedly, some 20,000 men had volunteered to serve in the Boer War a decade or so earlier, but if the rates of evasion of the compulsory military training scheme were any indication, young Australian men had a limited appetite for the soldier's life.[12]

However, the Cabinet had no doubt that its decision to create what later became known as the Australian Imperial Force (AIF) would have bipartisan support. During the ongoing election campaign, political leaders of both parties had competed to prove themselves the more patriotic. Cook, while addressing an election meeting at Horsham, in the wheat district of Victoria, had declared on 31 July that if war broke out in Europe, 'I want to make quite clear that all our resources in Australia are in the Empire and for the Empire, and for the preservation and security of the Empire.' When he predicted that Armageddon was coming and that Australians might have to go and fight on the other side of the world, his audience cheered and applauded—even though many of them were of German origin. The leader of the Australian Labor Party (ALP), Andrew Fisher, went one better. Although he was not as enamoured of the British connection as Cook and Irvine, and elements of his party advocated the resolution of international disputes by arbitration, Fisher, like socialists around the world, chose national over international solidarity. At a meeting at Colac, Victoria, also on 31 July, he coined the phrase that would echo down the years as symbolic of Australia's unreserved commitment to war: 'Should the worst happen after everything has been done that honour will permit, Australians will stand beside our own to help and defend her to our last man and last shilling.' It was a view echoed on the other side of the continent, where the leader of the Liberal opposition in Perth declared that Western Australians would be loyal to the empire to the 'last shilling and last man'.[13]

Such was the bipartisanship about going to war that William Morris (Billy) Hughes, a senior member of the federal Labor opposition, proposed that the federal election should be suspended during the international crisis; it could be 'declared off', like a football game, in favour of a political truce. Continuity of government, he argued, could be ensured if the proclamation dissolving parliament were revoked or if the current parliamentarians were returned unopposed. In effect, he was arguing for a government of national unity, but the proposal was unworkable. It did not appeal to Fisher, and was quickly forgotten.[14]

Support for the war was also strident in the mainstream press. The Melbourne *Age* agreed on 3 August that Australia should follow Canada and New Zealand and 'maintain inviolate the fabric of the [British] Empire'. Britain had been driven to abandon its policy of splendid isolation in Europe 'in order to preserve a balance of power . . . that was menaced by the portentous development of the Teutonic hegemony'. The Adelaide *Register*, meanwhile, declared on 4 August that 'the Dominions regard the mother country's quarrels as their own'. Lapsing into an execrable piece of imperial poetry, it intoned:

> To all the loyal hearts who long
> To keep our British Empire whole!
> To all our noble sons, the strong
> New England of the Southern Pole!
> To England under Indian skies,
> To those dark millions of her realm—
> Hands all around!
> God the traitor's hope confound!
> To this great name of England, drink, my friends,
> And all her glorious Empire round and round!

The *Sydney Morning Herald* joined the chorus, claiming on 3 August to speak for the whole of Australia when it said that Australians would support Britain 'to the utmost limit of their resources'. 'We know that our security and our independence depend on the victory of the British arms. We know that if we were to stand aside we could not be certain of our national existence for a year or for a day.' On 6 August it trumpeted: 'It is our baptism of fire. Australia knows something of the flames of war, but its realities have never been brought so close as they will be in the near future.' In Western Australia, too, there were assurances in the press that: 'No shadow of doubt rests upon the loyalty of the Australian people [to the Motherland].'[15]

The leaders of Australia's churches also spoke strongly in favour of imperial loyalty. In the 1911 census, 98 per cent of Australians claimed to be Christian. The majority of these were Protestants with historical connections to Britain. Not everyone regularly attended church or mass, but those who did heard from the pulpit that while war might be a scourge, it was a calamity visited upon the human race to chastise it for its lack of righteousness. Christians must view it as an opportunity for spiritual renewal. T.E. Ruth, the charismatic pastor of Collins Street Baptist Church in Melbourne and a recent immigrant to Australia, declaimed:

> Clear and certain as the shining of the sun in the Australian sky, the call came to our nation to honour its word, to risk its sovereignty, its soldiery, its ships, its men, and its money, to its last man and its last penny, to the last shred of its power, to the remotest outposts of its influence, rather than repudiate its solemn pledge to maintain the independence of smaller nations and fulfil its destiny in the higher civilisation of the race. We are fighting not for territory but for truth, not for the aggrandisement of the British Empire, but for the defence of British integrity, not for the development of our own military prowess, but for the overthrow of the most presumptuous and arrogant militarism that has ever menaced the peace of the world, and the progress of its peoples.

In the Victorian town of Bright, the Anglican minister also declared that: 'We are British first, and Australian second . . . Let us then offer the best of our manhood and let us speak with our pocket in helping the Empire in its time of need.' At St John's Church, Fremantle, the state of the empire was compared with that of Jerusalem when Jesus lamented over it. Even the Catholic church hierarchy, who claimed to speak for the 22 per cent of the population who identified themselves as Catholic, supported the imperial cause. There was little of the bitter sectarianism that would poison Australian public life later in the war.[16]

There were, however, some voices of dissent—mostly on the left of politics. *Labor Call*, the official organ of the Political Labor Council of Victoria, judged the war to be a calamity, 'only slaughter and carnage'. It predicted it would end with 'revolution and the dethronement of monarchs'. The *Australian Worker*, the official organ of the Australian Workers' Union, edited by the articulate Henry Boote, also saw the war as 'a phase of capitalist society' for which there was no extenuating reason: no great principle lay behind it and no vital issue that would justify loss of life: 'It is false to say that war strengthens and uplifts a nation. That is one of those monstrous fallacies invented to excuse men in the evil they do . . . God help Australia! God help England! God help Germany! God help us!' *The Bulletin*, the long-standing nationalist weekly, meanwhile concluded on 20 August that:

> If ever there was a 'capitalist' or 'trade war' this is surely one'. [The war] is essentially a business one. It will unquestionably ruin many capitalists of all nationalities. All wars do. But, on the other hand, it will make fortunes for other capitalists—as every war does.[17]

There was also opposition to the war on the part of a few radical women. The feminist and suffragette Vida Goldstein publicly called upon women 'of all nations' to 'show their common bond of motherhood':

> [It is] a fearful reflection on 2000 years of Christianity that men have rushed into war before using every combined effort to prevent this appalling conflict . . . The time has come for women to show that they,

as givers of life, refuse to give their sons as material for slaughter, and
that they recognise that human life must be the first consideration of
nations.[18]

However, such voices, which would become louder and more insistent as the
war progressed, were scarcely heard in August 1914.

Why did they volunteer?

What did individual Australians think—the men who were to volunteer
for the AIF and the women who were to send them? It is hard to know. In
1914 there were no public opinion polls, no talkback radio, no exit polls at
the polling booths for the federal election held on 5 September. Journalists
did not thrust microphones into voters' faces demanding their impromptu
emotional reactions to war and tragedy.

Traditionally, it is claimed that Australians welcomed the war, naïvely
confident that that it would be over by Christmas. Ernest Scott, writing in
1936, claimed that 'a passionate thrill of patriotic feeling' touched 'the hearts
of every class in the country'. In his 1982 study of the AIF, Lloyd Robson
maintained that 'Australians had made up their minds and were ready and
indeed terrifyingly willing to go to war'.[19]

Much has been made of the fact that, as the crisis in Europe worsened
in late July and early August, large crowds gathered in streets and public
spaces. In Melbourne, for example, a crowd of mostly men gathered outside
the *Argus* office waiting for the posting of cables about developments in
Europe. In the country towns of north-eastern Victoria, too, there were
apparently spontaneous parades in the streets and large crowds in the
pubs, while school and church bells rang for up to an hour to announce
the outbreak of war.

But crowds of themselves tell us little. We do not know how large they
were, nor why these Australians came out onto the streets. Perhaps it *was* war
fever, the euphoric 'spirit of 1914' that was manifest in the capitals of Europe.
In Germany, for example, excited crowds assembled throughout the country.

Among them, in Berlin, was the young Adolf Hitler, who 'fell down on [his] knees and thanked heaven from an overflowing heart for granting [him] the good fortune of being permitted to live at this time'. In London, too, about 12,000 people massed outside Buckingham Palace while crowds in Trafalgar Square greeted the declaration of war with 'a great roar of defiance'. Years later, Lloyd George would claim that the 'warlike crowds that thronged Whitehall and poured into Downing Street' forced the government's hand when it was deliberating whether to go to war.[20]

Yet perhaps it was simple curiosity that brought people onto the streets in Australia, or the desire to be the first to get the news, or the need to connect with others at a time when the future seemed so insecure. In Perth the crowds were quiet rather than jingoistic. The war was greeted not with cheers but with a day of prayer organised by the Western Australian Council of Churches. People gathering at the Congregational Church in St Georges Terrace happened to be opposite one of the major newspaper offices. Many stayed there until after midnight, waiting for further news from Europe.[21]

A more reliable indicator of public enthusiasm for war was the rush of volunteers for the AIF. On the day recruiting offices opened, 10 August, 2000 men volunteered in Sydney alone. Within two weeks, this had increased to 10,000, while 7000 men had enlisted in Victoria. New South Wales and Victoria contained about two-thirds of the Australian population, but across the nation recruiting depots were busy. Men who were rejected for medical or other reasons moved from state to state in search of a depot that would accept them. Other men volunteered in cohorts. Most famously, the elite Melbourne school Scotch College formed a group of 71 'Old Scotchies'. A dux of the school and editor of the school magazine, James Drummond Burns, was to publish in May 1915 one of the most quoted expressions of imperial loyalty:

> The bugles of England were blowing o'er the sea,
> As they had called a thousand years, calling now to me;
> They wake me from dreaming in the dawning of the day,
> The bugles of England—and how could I stay?[22]

It took only a month for the government's initial target of 20,000 volunteers to be reached. In fact, the interest in recruitment was so strong (by the end of the year there were over 52,000 volunteers) that Australia was soon able to offer Britain a further infantry brigade and two brigades of mounted troops. This was despite stringent fitness requirements for recruits at this time. Men had to be at least eighteen years of age (the upper age limit fluctuated to as high as 45) and 5 feet 6 inches (1.67 metres) tall, and possess good eyesight and good teeth (supposedly so they could eat hard army biscuits).[23]

Again, we know little about what motivated men to enlist. As Richard White has said, we can assume that 'Australians did not necessarily join the war for the same reasons Australia did'. The letters and diaries that the volunteers wrote home tell us little of their reasons for joining up. Men usually began writing home after they had joined the AIF. Often they said little about their subjective state: thoughts and emotions became locked in stylistic conventions when written down. Moreover, their letters home were written with an eye to avoiding censorship and minimising the anxiety of parents and girlfriends. Even diaries kept during service abroad could be self-censored, written in the expectation that someday another person would read them. Hence fear, doubt, anger and regret could be repressed, though this was not always the case.[24]

As for later memoirs of war experiences, another possible entrée into the mental world of Australian soldiers, these were commonly written by the better educated soldiers. Inevitably, too, they were retrospective. Memories were mediated through later life experiences and external cultural influences. As White has said, 'the experience of war itself has important effects on the men's explanations as to why they were there, and different explanations are required for different purposes at different points in a soldier's career'.[25]

The same is true of oral recollections, which, rehearsed time and again at reunions, often come to reflect a wider collective and cultural memory. Alistair Thomson found when interviewing World War I veterans in the 1980s that their memories of war had 'changed over time and in relation to the public, national narratives':

Through participation in collective remembrance, ex-servicemen enjoyed recognition and affirmation of a particular, positive Anzac identity, and they articulated their memories of the war using the public narratives of the [Anzac] legend. This memory composure was essential for individual peace of mind but, in the process, memories that were not recognised by the legend were displaced and marginalised.[26]

We can therefore only surmise that Australian men volunteered for the AIF for many different reasons, some perhaps difficult to articulate. Some men, it seems, were driven by pragmatism. Drought and the disruption of the Australian economy in the first months of the war created considerable unemployment. The pay in the AIF was good. For privates, it was six shillings a day—a rate intended (when rations and accommodation were taken into account) to be comparable to the wage of an Australian worker. A New Zealand soldier, in contrast, received 5 shillings, while a British infantryman at the start of the war was paid only 1 shilling a day (later raised to 3 shillings). Hence an early volunteer, Robert Antill, wrote to his family from military camp in November 1914:

> One thing its not bad money here 5/- a day and clothes and food thats nearly good as Cabinet Making and not half as hard. You may thint it funny mee turning up such a good job but it was like this Philpott had only about 3 days work left for us and things are so bad out here for there is a drought on . . . so I thorrt I would join the army.

Other 'push factors' driving men to enlist may have been difficulties in personal relationships, the monotony of life in Australian cities or the loneliness of working in the bush. To quote White again: 'Perhaps the greatest tragedy of the war was not the deaths of those who had everything to live for but the lives of those for whom a single chance to do something different was worth dying for.'[27]

The 'pull factors' included the chance to travel and to see family in Britain. In all, some 18 per cent of recruits in the AIF were men who had been born in the United Kingdom. British-born Australians were marginally over-represented in the AIF, especially in the early days of recruitment. John Simpson Kirkpatrick, who was to become an enduring Australian icon as 'the man with the donkey' at Gallipoli, was one such Briton, looking for the chance to return to England even before the war began. There were probably many more like him: men who had not made a go of it in Australia but could justify their return home by becoming soldiers of the empire.[28]

Some men seem also to have enlisted as an adventure. They wanted to be part of the stoush, to have 'a dig at the Germans'. Alternatively, they had served in earlier wars and the militia, liked soldiering and wanted to be back in action. Neville Howse, the man who won Australia's first Victoria Cross during the Boer War and would later head the AIF's medical services, was one of these. He left his home within a few hours of being called to duty, even though he was 51 years of age and the father of four children aged one to eight. 'What are you thinking of at your age!' his wife asked, with good reason.[29]

Perhaps Howse and others thought the war would be short, but many people sensed that that it would be long and costly. Cook warned on 31 August that the conflict would be 'of considerable duration'. In the House of Representatives on 14 October, he repeated that: 'The war will be a tremendously long one, taxing all our resources and those of the whole of the Empire and of the Allies. There can be only one ending, I believe, but that will only be through tremendous suffering and self-sacrifice on the part of our Empire.' *The Register* meanwhile cited the work of the Polish strategist Ivan Bloch, who in 1898 predicted the trenches, attrition and stalemate of modern industrial war. It warned on 3 August:

> The building up of organizations of war, with all their expensive appliances for wholesale human slaughter, [has been] conducted and engineered in dead and deliberate earnest for campaigns which will be among the most sanguinary and ruinous in the world's history.[30]

However, young men are inclined to think they are indestructible. In the twenty-first century, they drive cars recklessly and do BASE jumping and underwater cave diving. In 1914 they went to war. At this time, too, death was much more a part of life. Richard White has estimated that 15 per cent of deaths between 1901 and 1910 were of Australians between 20 and 39 years of age, the age bracket that provided most AIF recruits. The mortality rate in the AIF was ultimately around 20 per cent, so the odds of surviving were not dramatically different if a man stayed at home.[31]

What of patriotism and imperial loyalty, the values so dominant in Australian public discourse? These almost certainly mattered, at least for young educated men. Members of social and political elites tend to find little dissonance between their personal values and the prevailing ideology. For them, private and public discourse become seamlessly integrated. Hence, Malcolm Stirling, a young man studying law at the University of Melbourne, could write to his mother on 28 April 1915:

> I'm afraid you will not be pleased with this letter, but I can't help it. I have made up my mind to go to the war and am writing to get your consent and Dad's . . . The War, instead of getting better is getting blacker every day: and I think it is the duty of every responsible person to do his share . . . This isn't a sudden whim. It is a growing desire that has now become so strong that I *must* go.

In this same letter Stirling went on to reflect on the professional advantages of serving in the war. However, duty was the language he invoked—possibly unconsciously—to justify his decision to himself and to his parents.[32]

Whatever the motives of men who volunteered in 1914, we can be confident that the mix changed as the war continued. By mid-1915, when Stirling enlisted, it was impossible to view the war as an adventure. The massive casualties on Gallipoli and the Western Front left no doubt that there was a significant risk of death or injury for anyone who served. The men who volunteered then therefore were not naïve or pragmatic. Rather they were part of what has been called 'the mystery of "second acceptance"'. They knew the consequences of enlisting but did so—compelled, it seems, by a sense of obligation, a conviction that the war was just, a fear that the Allies might lose the war and, as the pressure for recruitment intensified, by the burden of peer opinion and the humiliation of being stigmatised, as Joe Russell was, as a 'shirker'.[33]

The first months of war

As individual Australians pondered their choices and obligations, the war was taking a very different course from that anticipated by the military leaders who launched it. On 2 August, the Germans invaded Luxembourg, capturing the railway lines that were essential for their armies' strategic mobility. Two days later they launched an attack with 52 divisions through Belgium and Luxembourg, using significant forces in Lorraine as a pivot for their great wheeling movement to the north. Their advance through Belgium met more resistance than expected, although the main Belgian forces under King Albert withdrew into a fortified 'national redoubt' around Antwerp, on the coast. It was not until 16 August that the vital Belgian fortress of Liège fell to the Germans, opening the way for their armies on the right to advance into France along the corridor of the River Meuse.

In these opening battles there was little coordination between the Belgians and their allies. Even though the French had anticipated a German thrust through Belgium, they proceeded to implement their own pre-war strategic plan, based on a philosophy of the all-out offensive (*attaque à outrance*). Leaving only one army in the area of the Belgian frontier, the French attacked the German forces further south, in the Ardennes and on the River Sambre, a tributary of the Meuse. However, this 'battle of the frontiers', from 20 to 24 August, soon proved 'a comprehensive Allied débâcle'. The French armies lost a staggering 75,000 men (27,000 of them on one day alone, 22 August). German losses were much lighter. To the north, meanwhile, the small British Expeditionary Force had crossed the Channel and met the German forces for the first time at Mons in Belgium on 23 August. It, too, was soon forced to retreat because of the greater strength of the German First Army and the withdrawal of the French Fifth Army on its right. By the end of August, both British and French armies were being forced back on the defensive.[34]

However, the French forces had not been completely destroyed, and their retreat was so rapid that they avoided being encircled. The Germans also faced increasing problems of supply and communication. Their armies had little in the way of motorised transport, and much of what they had soon broke down. All their supplies and equipment therefore had to be carried beyond the railheads by men and horses. Soon the 84,000 horses of the First Army, which needed two million pounds of fodder a day, were dying for lack of feed. Soldiers, too, became exhausted fighting and carrying heavy packs in the summer heat.

As these implacable logistical realities made it difficult to reinforce the German right wing, the German Chief of the General Staff, Helmuth von Moltke, decided on a strategy of double envelopment of the French armies. On 26 August, he ordered an attack in Lorraine with the aim of driving the French forces apart. But then, when it seemed that victory was almost secure, he detached two corps from the right flank of his forces in France and sent them to reinforce the armies confronting the offensive that the Russians had launched in East Prussia. It was a decision that was much criticised later, but von Moltke's commanders in France were optimistic, and it seemed that East Prussia was in danger of being invaded.

Hence, although the German right wing had almost reached Paris by early September, it lacked the strength to encircle the capital as originally planned. Instead it turned east to the north of Paris—only to find that when it then tried to cross the Marne in an effort to take the city, the balance of power had shifted. The French counter-attacked on 4 September and a gap of some 40 kilometres opened between the German First and Second Armies. With the First Army in danger of being outflanked, and communications between the armies collapsing, the Germans decided to retreat, even though they had not been defeated in the field. With this critical Battle of the Marne, from 5 to 12 September, the German advance into France was halted.[35]

At the same time, the Eastern Front was erupting not only in East Prussia but also further south in Galicia (a province of Austria, now in Poland). The Russians, with their massive but inadequately equipped army, tried to deliver simultaneous blows against both Germany and Austria-Hungary. But each offensive was weaker than if they had concentrated their forces, and they failed disastrously in the north. Between 24 and 31 August, the German commanders Paul von Hindenburg and Erich Ludendorff—men who were later to dominate their nation's war strategy—achieved one of the most devastating victories of the war, at Tannenberg. Some 50,000 Russians were killed or wounded and a further 92,000 soldiers and 500 guns captured. German casualties were between 10,000 and 15,000. Yet despite this defeat, the Russians were able to replace their losses. The continued fighting in September around the Mansurian Lakes and the German–Russian border showed that Tannenberg, though a major victory for the Germans, had not been decisive.

Further south, the Austrians invaded Serbia on 12 August, even though it would have been more rational to concentrate their forces against the Russian threat emerging in Galicia. They met well-led and well-entrenched Serbian forces and lost some 24,000 casualties compared with 17,000 Serbs. In Galicia, they soon experienced an even greater debacle. Advancing 'in blazing heat across featureless plains with little effective cavalry reconnaissance . . . [and] blundering into superior Russian forces whose artillery took a terrible toll', the Hapsburg forces lost some 100,000 dead, 220,000 wounded and 100,000 prisoners of war, as well as substantial oil supplies and rich arable land in Bukovina and Galicia. They never really recovered. Already fragile because of the army's multinational character (it included Czech and Slav units whose reliability was questionable), the Austro-Hungarian forces increasingly needed German power to prop them up.[36]

Capturing German New Guinea

As the crisis in Europe unfolded, the Australian and New Zealand governments went into battle much closer to home. The German Pacific naval squadron, based at Tsingtao (Qingdao) in China, was in a position to threaten the lines of communication between Australia and Britain, disrupting imperial trade and intercepting the transporting of Dominion troops to Europe. However, its operations relied on a chain of communication stations in German colonies that stretched from Samoa to the Caroline Islands.

On 6 August, the British government asked the Australian and New Zealand governments to mount expeditions to capture the wireless stations in Samoa, New Guinea, Nauru and Yap, in the Pelew Islands (Palau). Well aware of the strategic and potential commercial importance of these German colonies, the Australians quickly cobbled together an expeditionary force of some 1000 infantry, 500 naval reservists, and signals and medical personnel. In command was a militia officer, Colonel William Holmes, while Neville Howse (the doctor who had rushed from home in a matter of hours) was the principal medical officer. The navy, whose role in World War I is often overlooked, provided support in the form of the *Australia*, the new light cruiser *Sydney*, the cruiser *Encounter* (on loan from the Royal Navy), three destroyers, *Warrego*, *Parramatta* and *Yarra*, and Australia's only two submarines, *AE1* and *AE2*.

The Australian Naval and Military Expeditionary Force (AN&MEF), as it was called, was seen off in Sydney by crowds still excited about the prospect of war:

> Along Oxford Street the girls from the ribbon store brought out rolls of red, white and blue ribbon, which was cut up and fixed on bayonet points, in hats, on sleeves—anywhere where it would show up. Flags were in evidence all along the line [of the march], practically every other man having a flag or patriotic emblem of some kind waving from his rifle. Not a few friends and relatives marched side by side in the ranks all the way from the barracks to Fort Macquarie.[37]

After two weeks' training on Palm Island, off Townsville, the force sailed for Rabaul. A young doctor, Brian Pockley, wrote to his parents on the night of 10 September:

> We make a night attack at 3 am tonight. Probably there will be no opposition at all as on a previous occasion when the two destroyers and the Sydney entered Simpsonhaven and steamed peacefully out again after a landing party had destroyed their post office . . . Personally I think it will be a very pleasant little picnic.[38]

Rabaul was defended by some 300 German and 'native' troops, who had prepared trenches along the main road leading to the wireless station at Bitapaka. They were soon overwhelmed by the Australian force. With the German governor agreeing to capitulate, the British flag was raised, and the local population was advised in pidgin that: 'No more 'um Kaiser. God Save 'um King.'[39] Six Australians were killed in the operation, one of whom was Pockley, shot while attending a wounded man.

From Rabaul, the Australian forces moved on to occupy other German territories south of the equator. One of the two submarines, the *AE1*, and its crew of 35, disappeared—perhaps while carrying out diving practice, or after striking a rock. A poem penned in memory of the submariners tried to capture the horror of their claustrophobic end:

> Pent in their iron cell they sank beneath the waves
> Untouched by shot or shell they drifted to their graves
> Until their painful breath at last began to fail
> Upon their way to death; let pity draw the veil.
> They could not strike one blow, but out of sound and sight
> Of comrade or of foe they passed to endless night
> Deep down on the ocean's floor, far from the wind and sun
> They rest forever more.[40]

Although the crew of the *AE1* were eulogised as being 'no less for Empire lost', the Rabaul campaign was rather anti-climactic. It may have extended 'in a few more places on the map of the world those red colored spots of which we Britishers are all so proud', as Holmes put it, but his men had been 'spoiling for a fight': 'like young foxhounds, [they] would be all the better as soldiers if they were blooded'. When offered the chance to volunteer for the AIF, most men of the AN&MEF took it. The Australian administration remained on the islands, however, staking Australia's claim to retain control of these former German colonies after the war.[41]

Significantly, these colonies did *not* include the strategic territories that the Germans held further north in Micronesia: the Marshall, Pelew, Caroline and Mariana islands. Although the Australian government was planning to occupy these islands after it had taken New Guinea, it was pre-empted by the Japanese, who entered the war on the side of the Allied Powers on 23 August—and then occupied the German colonies north of the equator in late September and early October. Neither Australia nor the British Foreign Office welcomed this move, fearing—with good cause—that the Japanese would use the war in Europe to extend their influence in China and the Pacific. But the Admiralty needed the Japanese navy: to police the North Pacific, to assist in controlling the German cruisers *Scharnhorst* and *Gneisenau*, then roaming these seas, and to supplement Allied naval strength in Europe. In addition, no one in London wished to cause gratuitous offense to their Japanese ally. So the Australian government had no choice but to accept the *fait accompli* of the Japanese occupation, trusting in the caveat that the British imposed on the Japanese to the effect that the occupation of the German colonies to the north of the equator was without prejudice to any post-war arrangements. As it happened, when this principle came to be tested in the peace settlement of 1919, Australia had no more interest than the Japanese in respecting it![42]

The creation of the Australian Imperial Force

Meanwhile, in Australia, the newly formed AIF was preparing to leave for Europe. The man appointed to command the force was Major-General William Throsby Bridges. Generals tend not to become heroes in Australia, where soldiers or 'diggers' dominate popular mythology, but Bridges was something of an exception—if only because he died of wounds in May 1915 at Gallipoli. Like many leaders of the time, he was a man of the British Empire. Born in Scotland, he had served in both the Sudan Contingent, raised to rescue General Gordon at Khartoum, and in the Boer War of 1899–1902. Beginning his Australian career as an artillery officer in the New South Wales defence force in the 1880s, he had held a succession of positions in Australian intelligence and defence planning in the decades after Federation. He had founded the Royal Military College, Duntroon, and in 1914 was inspector-general, the most senior appointment in the Australian Army.

It was Bridges who gave the Australian Imperial Force its name. It was an astute choice, affirming imperial loyalty but staking Australia's claim to have an army with a distinctive national character. Significantly, Bridges also insisted that Australian units should not be subsumed into the British order of battle, as the War Office in London proposed, but rather that they should remain discrete formations. As C.E.W. Bean later wrote:

> Had [the Australian force] fought through the war in the form favoured by the [British] Army Council, there would have been no Anzac Corps. Australia would have had to its credit no 'Landing', no Lone Pine, neither Pozières nor Broodseinde, no Villers-Bretonneux, not Mont St. Quentin, neither Romani nor Damascus, no battle of the Hindenburg Line ... The Australian nation would not have existed in the same sense as to-day.[43]

The AIF had several characteristics that would shape its character and wartime experience. Most notably, thanks to the already mentioned restrictions of the *Defence Act*, it was a volunteer army. Its performance would be seen as a test, not of professional competence but of the national character. For many Australians watching how their men coped in combat, it was the citizen in arms, not a regular soldier, who was being affirmed in battle.[44]

The AIF was also recruited on a regional basis, with infantry and light horse units linked, wherever possible, to the various states and regions. This fuelled local identification and pride in a way that benefited morale and future recruitment. The 'Pals' or 'Chums' battalions in Britain were likewise formed on the premise that men who knew each other would have a stronger esprit de corps. However, the negative side of regional recruitment was that battle losses would fall particularly heavily on the communities from which these units were drawn.[45]

Finally, the AIF was not well trained—at least initially. More than a third of the infantry and a quarter of the Light Horse in the first contingent had no previous connection with military life. Only a minority had served in the militia or fought in earlier imperial wars. Bean, who more than any other individual would create the legendary narrative of Anzacs that emerged from the war, thought the lack of training for the AIF was never 'the main difficulty':

> The bush [he would claim in his official history] still sets the standard of personal efficiency even in the Australian cities. The bushman is the hero of the Australian boy; the arts of the bush life are his ambition; his most cherished holidays are those spent with country relatives or in camping out. He learns something of half the arts of a soldier by the time he is ten years old—to sleep comfortably in any shelter, to cook meat or bake flour, to catch a horse, to find his way across country by day or night, to ride, or, at the worst, to 'stick on'. The Australian of the bush is frequently called upon to fight bush-fires; and fighting bush-fires, more than any other human experience, resembles the fighting of a pitched battle.[46]

However, this was a deeply romanticised view. Even in 1914, Australia was one of the most urbanised societies in the world. War in Gallipoli and on the Western Front would show that Australians needed training and battlefield experience before they became an effective fighting force. Skill in fighting bushfires helped little in confronting artillery and machine guns. Rather, as Jeffrey Grey puts it, the 1st Division of the AIF was 'probably the worst-trained formation ever sent from Australia's shores'.[47]

The first sailings of the AIF

Bridges wanted the AIF to sail for Europe within a month of the first recruitment. Logistically, this was a huge undertaking. Camps sprang up to house the volunteers: at Randwick racecourse in Sydney; Broadmeadows outside Melbourne; Morphettville in Adelaide; and Enoggera in Queensland. Some 60,000 pairs of boots were found within four weeks. Assuming that the AIF would arrive in the European winter, the Department of Defence Contracts Branch bought as much khaki cloth, blankets, woollen underwear, socks and shirts as it could find. It also commandeered the output of all the woollen factories in the country. The AIF uniform that emerged was drab: a functional pea-soup shade, with the buttons and rising-sun badge oxidised to prevent their glinting in the sun and making the soldier a target. With loose sleeves buttoned at the wrist, baggy breeches and leather leggings, it was hardly the dress of heroes.

In battle, the AIF would rely heavily on the logistical support of the British Army, but there was some local capacity to support the war effort. Prior to 1914, the Department of Defence had accumulated large quantities of army stores for use in the event of war. A small arms factory had been established at Lithgow, in New South Wales, as had a facility for manufacturing explosives at Maribyrnong, Melbourne, and a harness factory at Clifton Hill. (Cavalry were expected to play a major role in the coming war, and most military transport was then horse-drawn.) For all this, there was chaos as newly appointed commanding officers battled to get supplies for their units.

Still, by 21 September the first units of the AIF were ready to sail for Europe on transports converted from passenger liners and cargo ships. Their departure was delayed by the presence of German warships in the Indian Ocean threatening the route that the transports would take. It was not until 1 November, when the Admiralty had found the necessary escorts, that the convoy (of 26 Australian and ten New Zealand transports) sailed from its assembly point in King George Sound, off Albany in Western Australia. Among the vessels protecting it were two Australian cruisers (*Melbourne* and *Sydney*), the British *Minotaur*, and—ironically, given contemporary fears— the Japanese armoured cruiser *Ibuki*.

As the convoy was crossing the Indian Ocean, HMAS *Sydney* was diverted to intercept the German cruiser *Emden*, which was known to be attacking the Cocos Islands and the cable and wireless station that formed part of the British imperial communications system. Outranking the *Emden* in speed, range of guns and weight, the *Sydney* soon crippled the German ship on 8 November, at the cost of only twelve Australian casualties. The captain of the *Sydney* boarded the *Emden*, to be confronted with a scene of devastation:

My God, what a sight! . . . Everybody on board was demented by shock, and fumes, and the roar of shells bursting among them. She was a shambles. Blood, guts, flesh and uniforms were scattered all about. One of our shells had landed behind a gun shield, and had blown the whole gun crew into one pulp. You couldn't even tell how many men there had been.[48]

In Australia and Britain, however, the news of the sinking was cause for exultation. The British magazine *Punch* carried images of the *Emden* as a fox in the jaws of an Australian lion, while other foreign papers congratulated Australia for having taken the initiative and created its own navy. Jingoism aside, there were sound strategic reasons to welcome the sinking of the *Emden*. Together with a British victory over the German navy on 8 December 1914 near the Falkland Islands, in which the *Scharnhorst* and *Gneisenau* were sunk, it had the effect of neutralising the German naval threat in the Pacific. The first convoy made its way safely to Suez and Egypt, where the Australian and New Zealand troops disembarked for training, and over the next two years, Australian and New Zealand troop convoys could sail from Australia without escort.

The improved security in the Indian Ocean meant that only one other convoy would depart from Albany, in December 1914, but such is the power of the trope of 'the first'—the first convoy, the 'baptism of fire' and so on—that Albany would acquire considerable commemorative significance in later decades. Fifty-four years later, it would become the site of a dramatic statue of an Australian Light Horseman defending a New Zealander near his wounded horse, a replica of a statue originally installed in Port Said but destroyed by Egyptian nationalists in 1956. Later still, in 1985, when the memory of World War I had become inclusive enough to honour a former enemy, the channel from King George Sound to the open sea was renamed the Ataturk Channel. A statue to Atatürk, who as Mustafa Kemal thwarted the Anzac attacks on the Gallipoli peninsula in 1915, was also installed, overlooking the place from which the AIF sailed. The association of Albany with the war against the Turks is not immediately self-evident, except for the fact that the men who

Crowds farewelling the 12th Battalion of the Australian Imperial Force as it marched through the streets of Hobart, Tasmania, on 14 October 1914 prior to embarking for service overseas. (AWM H11609)

THE STRUGGLE FOR SUPREMACY.

The left-wing response to World War I was shaped by the conviction that there was an even more important struggle, for supremacy between capitalism—here represented by the bloated plutocrat—and labour. (*Australian Worker*, 15 October 1914; Noel Butlin Archives Centre, ANU)

Charles (C.E.W.) Bean, war correspondent and official historian, in Egypt in January 1915. Beneath him is Mena Camp. (AWM G01658)

The Australian soldier as the bushman stereotype: the 12th Regiment training at Holsworthy Camp near Liverpool, New South Wales. (AWM A03315)

sailed in this first convoy served in Gallipoli, but this gesture was a quid pro quo for the Turkish government's agreement on the 75th anniversary of the Gallipoli campaign to rename the beach on which the AIF came ashore in 1915 'Anzac Cove'. The installation of a memorial to Atatürk at the head of Anzac Parade, Canberra, was also a gesture of reciprocity on this anniversary. Perhaps not surprisingly, then, when the centenary of the Gallipoli campaign came to be planned in 2011 and 2012, one of the commemorative events on which there was early agreement was a re-enactment of the departure of the first AIF convoy from Albany.

The home front

The Australian population, meanwhile, was making the difficult adjustment to war. World War I has often been called the first 'total war': total in the sense that it demanded the mobilisation of the 'home front'—a term coined in this conflict—as much as the battle front. Victory in an industrialised war depended not just on the performance of armies but on the willingness of civilians to tolerate mass casualties, to accept lower standards of living, to support the armies in the field through patriotic voluntary work, and to produce munitions and supplies for the armies in the field.

Given Australia's geographical distance from the battlefields, the impact of the war was not as profound as on many European societies. Australia was not occupied as were Belgium, northern France and parts of Eastern Europe. Nor was it flooded with refugees or millions of soldiers undergoing training or taking leave from the front. Nor were Australian civilians targeted by that new and indiscriminate weapon of war, the bomber. Nonetheless, the impact of World War I on Australian society was to be profound. The casualty rate would prove to be one of the highest per capita of the war, there would be serious disruption of the Australian economy and erosion of living conditions, and the political consensus of August 1914 would quickly dissolve, leading to bitter and lasting internal divisions.

In 1914, Australia had one of the highest standards of living in the world but its economy was highly exposed to international trade fluctuations. With a small domestic market, it formed part of a wider imperial economy in which the Dominions and colonies provided primary products to the metropolitan power, which in turn provided manufactured goods, equipment and investment capital. Australia's manufactures accounted in 1913 for only 13.4 per cent of gross domestic product, while wool, wheat and minerals were the key exports. In time, the demands of the war for raw materials would deliver benefits to these and other sectors of the economy. Australia would become a major supplier of frozen meat to Britain and its allies, and of wool for the millions of uniforms required for the Allied defence forces. Import substitution would also give a boost to local manufacturing industries such as textiles, leather goods and chemicals.[49]

However, the immediate impact of the war was to create a crisis of adaptation. There was an immediate and, it would prove, lasting shortage of the shipping on which most internal and all international trade depended. With the outbreak of war, enemy ships made a run for home or neutral ports, while British ship owners stopped sailings until the risk of shipping being sunk by the enemy was neutralised. In addition, on 7 August an embargo was imposed on all trade with enemy countries, and controls were placed on trade with other countries through which the enemy might source commodities indirectly. Belgium and the north of France also became battle zones. In 1913–14, about 25 per cent of Australian wool exports had gone to Germany and a further 40 per cent to France and Belgium. Much of the wool production, which represented one-third of exports in value terms, was therefore in danger of not being sold, while the pastoral industry faced immediate cash-flow and credit problems. Other smaller industries dependent on trade with Germany and Central Europe, such as opals and pearling, quickly stagnated.[50]

Another significant sector of the Australian economy, base metals (lead, tin, copper and zinc), was largely controlled by several German companies in 1914. After becoming attorney-general in September 1914, Hughes became determined—almost to the point of obsession—to exclude any German influence from the Australian economy, not only during but after the war.

He moved quickly to transfer control of the metal industries to Anglo-Australian interests. The Broken Hill Proprietary Company Ltd (BHP), in the process of building a relatively small steel plant at Newcastle when war broke out, grew during the war to become a major domestic steel producer as it replaced British imports. However, in the short term, the base-metals mines of Broken Hill and Tasmania laid off many men. So too did the coal mines of New South Wales. Job opportunities also declined in the rural industries, which were already suffering the effects of drought. By the end of 1914, the national unemployment rate had risen from 5.7 per cent to 11 per cent. In Queensland it was worse, soaring from 4.3 per cent to 17.7 per cent of the unionised workforce.[51]

By late 1914, there were also signs of alarming increases in the prices of essential commodities. Initially these were caused by drought and a panic reaction to anticipated shortages. But as the war continued, inflationary pressures in the economy grew. The cost of financing the war was to prove huge, and it would require a complex mix of fiscal responses, including taxation, war loans raised from the Australian public, loans from the British government and funds raised on the London money market. With the Commonwealth government's taxation powers in 1914 limited largely to customs, excise and a land tax, it would move in 1915–16 to levy income tax (formerly only at the state level) and entertainment taxes. It also printed extra money to assist its financial operations. The value of Australian notes in circulation increased from £9.57 million in June 1914 to £56.95 million in June 1920. The reserve of bullion, available because Australia was one of the world's largest producers of gold, was used to back the increased note issue, but it fuelled the rise in the price level. Within a year of the outbreak of war, the price of some staple goods had doubled. In Melbourne, bread was 50 per cent more expensive in May 1915 than it had been in June 1914; flour cost 86.9 per cent more and butter was 62.5 per cent dearer. Nearly all other food and household necessities had also increased in price. Wages, meanwhile, failed to rise commensurately, and to maintain purchasing power.[52]

Rising prices, unemployment and inflation are political dynamite at the best of times, but even more explosive in wartime. A democratic society can be mobilised to fight a war on a mass scale only if there is manifest equality of personal and economic sacrifices. Any hint that some citizens are profiting from the suffering of others corrodes the political consensus. Rising prices became a politically sensitive issue almost as soon as the men of the AIF set sail for the battlefield. 'Profiteering'—the word entered the language at this time—became an obsession of the radical left, while the 'fat man' or plutocrat, making excessive profits from the war by selling weapons and commodities at inflated prices, soon emerged as a cartoon stereotype. As early as August 1914, the *Australian Worker* was criticising Melbourne companies that donated £500 to a patriotic fund but dealt harshly with their employees. A few weeks later, it observed that monetary sacrifice from capitalists seemed too easy: 'Having thus vicariously displayed their patriotism they return to the business of profit sharing while the other fellow goes fighting.'[53]

In response to growing public concern, various state governments agreed soon after the war began to control the price of food. On 31 August 1914, the federal government also set up a royal commission to consider economic controls that might be needed to ensure the supply of food and other essentials if the war continued 'for a year or more'. But state legislation was administered unevenly or emasculated by the conservative state upper houses, while the commission had no power to fix prices. The issue of prices was to remain highly contentious into 1915 and beyond.[54]

The Australian political system that had to manage these changes was fluid and relatively unstable. The federal bureaucracy was less than fifteen years old, the balance between state and Commonwealth power was strongly in favour of the states, and the federal political party system was in its infancy. In the first years after Federation there had been a series of short-lived coalitions between political groupings, none of which could govern in its own right. A major faultline within conservative and liberal politics was the dispute between free traders and protectionists. As the power of the ALP grew, however, the non-Labor forces in 1909 fused to form what became the Liberal Party, and protectionism triumphed as an enduring national policy. However, it was a 'New Protectionism', under which industries only received the benefits of tariff protection if they reciprocated by paying fair and reasonable wages to their employees.[55]

The ALP, which formed a majority government federally for the first time from 1910 to 1913, had emerged from the trade union movement in response to the economic depression of the 1890s and a series of bitter strikes and lockouts. Trade union membership in 1914 was high, at over half a million workers, representing not only those in manufacturing industries but unskilled workers in mines, on the wharves and ships, and rural workers—for example, shearers. This powerful industrial movement dominated the ALP at the local branch level and ensured its early electoral success. Whereas the first British Labour government was not elected until 1924, in 1914 Labor was in power in three of the six Australian states—New South Wales, Tasmania and Western Australia. At the federal level, it formed minority or majority governments three times before winning the September 1914 election.[56]

Despite—or possibly because of—its electoral success, the ALP was experiencing growing tensions between its political leadership and its industrial base. The party had come into existence with a vision of using political power to improve the conditions of Australian workers, eradicating inequality, privilege and social injustice. However, although it embarked on a reform agenda when in office—including creating the Commonwealth Bank in 1911—electoral success necessitated compromises and brought with it the obligation to champion the interests of all Australians, regardless of class. It also became clear to the political arm of the labour movement that, if it were to maintain power for more than a short period, it must extend its electoral base beyond the unions, the industrial suburbs and the mining towns. However, Labor policy was approved at annual conferences dominated by the industrial movement. Parliamentarians, who were bound by a pledge to implement these policies, increasingly chafed at the constraints this seemed to impose on their flexibility and their capacity for manoeuvre and leadership in office. Their critics on the left, in turn, construed their willingness to compromise as evidence of corruption by the spoils of office.[57]

At the heart of these disputes were ideological debates about the nature of the labour movement. Should it be pragmatic, willing to use political power to improve worker conditions by piecemeal reform, 'civilising' rather than destroying capitalism? Or was it socialist—even Marxist—seeking to introduce state control of the means of production and destroy an irredeemably iniquitous capitalist system? Should the working classes rely on the Commonwealth Arbitration Court created by the first Labor government in 1905 to control employment conditions and industrial conflict? Or should they pursue change though the 'direct' action of the strike? The more militant approach, heavily influenced by syndicalist and anarchist theorists in Europe and the United States, began to penetrate the trade union movement in the years before 1914. In particular, the Industrial Workers of the World (IWW), an international workers' syndicalist movement, had gained a significant presence.

Union militancy was fuelled by bitter experiences in major industrial disputes in the decade before the war: the Victorian railways (1903), the Broken Hill mines (1908), the New South Wales coal mines (1909–10), the Queensland sugar mills (1911) and the Brisbane general strike (1912). In almost all of these disputes, the unions were defeated—partly owing to the willingness of state governments to back the employers and pass punitive legislation against the strikers. Sobered by these defeats and the high levels of unemployment, the unions would be quiescent in the first year of the war, but the fractures between the industrial and political wings of the labour movement had the potential to split wide open as the demands and costs of the war intensified.

The new wartime government

It fell to Andrew Fisher, who led the ALP to victory in the election of 5 September, to manage these tensions. In many ways he had the credentials to be an effective wartime leader. He was an able, principled politician who had served two previous terms as prime minister (1908–09 and 1910–13). With a deep commitment to a non-doctrinaire socialism, he had not only overseen a period of reform but also taken the lead in issues of national defence. In 1909 his government had initiated the scheme of compulsory military service and he was one of the architects of the RAN, resisting the pressure from London for Australia to continue to subsidise vessels in the Royal Navy rather than create its own fleet unit. Fisher also had some experience in international negotiation, having attended the Imperial Conference in London in 1911, where he argued for greater consultation on foreign policy.

However, for all these qualifications, Fisher would find that 'war was not his metier', as Neville Meaney has put it. Although he had unhesitatingly supported Australia's commitment to the war, personally he thought that war was a scourge. Like many of his Labor colleagues, he believed that international arbitration was a preferable way to resolve conflicts between nations. As a Scottish immigrant, Fisher also lacked the almost instinctually passionate attachment to the British Empire of Cook, Irvine and, for that matter, his own Labor colleague, Hughes. As mentioned, Fisher had no time for Hughes' rather maverick proposal to suspend the federal election in August, since this would involve Labor surrendering all hope of continuing with its program of social and political reform, to which Fisher remained committed.[58]

One of the first acts of Fisher's new government was to introduce a raft of legislation related to management of the war: the *Crimes Act*, the *Trading with the Enemy Act* and the *War Precautions Act*. The last was to prove exceptionally important, since it gave the executive branch of government the power to govern by decree through regulations 'for securing the public safety and defence of the Commonwealth'. It would play a critical role in wartime politics and is worth citing in detail. Under the *War Precautions Act* it was an offence to publish or attempt to elicit any information that might be useful to the enemy. This was uncontroversial, but the Act also prohibited any person from encouraging, by any means, disloyalty or hostility to the British Empire and its cause. It was also an offence under the Act to spread false information likely to cause disaffection or alarm, or to disseminate information likely to interfere with the success of Australia's military forces, or their recruiting, training, discipline or administration. Government officials were also empowered to search any premises where there might be publications containing injurious matter, and to destroy such material if found. Beyond that, Australians were prohibited from printing or distributing material that had been forbidden by the censor, and were even prevented from revealing or implying in publications that material had been altered, added or removed by the censor.

There is always a tension in time of war between the rights of citizens and the needs of national security, and there was some concern, even on Cook's part, when the *War Precautions Act* was pushed through parliament by Hughes in late September 1914, that it gave too much discretion to the agencies of the government. Some parliamentarians feared that it would allow the government to proclaim 'something like martial law', and the member for the South Australian seat of Angus, which included the majority German district of the Barossa Valley, questioned the clause that allowed the government to deem naturalised Australians aliens. Yet the Act was passed. There was a pervasive sense among federal parliamentarians that the war would be the greatest 'not of the century, but . . . of the world's history', as one member of the Senate put it. Extraordinary measures seemed necessary to protect the interests of Australia. Other countries had either dissolved their parliaments soon after the outbreak of war or ceded significant emergency powers to their executive branches. Moreover, the powers sought, Hughes argued, were inherent in all governments—a view which Irvine supported, arguing that 'In time of war Governments do . . . many things not authorised by law.'[59]

Hughes also gave assurances to parliament that the government would use the new powers as sparingly as possible. However, when he replaced Fisher as prime minister in October 1915, Hughes would exploit the provisions of the *War Precautions Act*, not just for waging the war but for domestic political advantage. As the war continued, the regulations accompanying the Act were enlarged and amended by Hughes and his solicitor-general, Robert Garran, until there were more than a hundred of them. With remarkable detail, these regulations controlled the lives and political activities of Australians, reflecting the increasingly authoritarian nature of the Australian state at war.

The 'enemy within the gates'

One of the first groups to feel the impact of the government's emergency powers was Australians of German and Austro-Hungarian or other enemy descent. The 1911 census identified nearly 33,000 residents who had been born in Germany, and more than 2700 born in Austria-Hungary. There were also 74,508 Lutherans, a denominational affiliation that suggested German descent. Within the various Australian states there were identifiable 'German' areas: the Barossa Valley and Mount Barker in South Australia; around Wagga Wagga in New South Wales; the Mallee district in Victoria; and the Darling Downs in Queensland.[60]

It was reasonable to assume that at least some of these people might pose a security risk, given their conflicting loyalties, and in the first weeks of war the Australian government moved to control their movements and identify any suspicious behaviour. On 10 August 1914, all Germans were required to report to the nearest police station to register their personal details. They also had to sign parole declarations promising that they would not take any action prejudicial to the British Empire during the war. Austrian-Australians followed a week later when war was declared between Britain and Austria. Information collated by the police was forwarded to intelligence departments within military headquarters, which soon became 'a considerable secret service operation . . . [covering] practically all of Australia'.[61]

Aware of their vulnerability, German-Australian communities rushed to affirm their commitment to the British cause, sending declarations to state governors and the governor-general. Some wrote to the press appealing for understanding of their predicament:

Just consider our position for one moment . . . My wife is an Australian, My children and grandchildren are Australians. I have been 30 years here. I have spent the greater and most valuable part of my life in Australia. I dearly love it, and would not live in any other land. I have close relations in Germany; 18 sons of cousins are under arms now. I have an uncle in Russia. Two of his sons are under arms against their cousins, six of my relations are serving under French colours, and five are in the English Army. Here is a whole family, and not the only one, fighting against each other.[62]

It was not a time for tolerance or reason, however. In the hothouse atmosphere of August–September 1914, letters poured in to the newspapers questioning the loyalty of Australians of enemy descent. On 20 August, for example, the Melbourne *Argus* carried a letter claiming that 'On all sides I have heard Germans denounce England . . . Every German, whether naturalised or not, should be interned and put out of harm's way.' The following day another self-appointed custodian of national security argued, 'We are too soft and easy and lenient with the German resident . . . The country is full of Germans who fatten our trade, and openly "barrack" for Germany. . . . Very stern measures are imperative with a people so devoid of honour.' In the minority were those who spoke up for German-Australians:

Where is our much vaunted British fair play? By all means let the authorities take every necessary precaution to safeguard the national interest but to brand as suspect all naturalised aliens of German extraction and to deprive them of their livelihood, is dastardly in the extreme.[63]

Military headquarters also began to receive reports from the public about imminent threats of attack. An airship was 'spotted' over New South Wales, while raiders were thought to be lurking in Bass Strait. Flashlights were observed in the Dandenongs. Was it an enemy agent, transmitting messages in Morse code to vessels offshore? In fact, the lights were probably a picture-show man flashing his electric lamps at intervals along a road in an effort to attract local residents to his entertainment, or a rabbit trapper making the nightly rounds of his traps with a hurricane lamp. The 'airship' was actually a meteorite, and the German 'submarines', spotted from a seaside town, were whales.[64]

Some of this hysteria was fuelled by hyperactive imagination; some by personal malice and debt-settling. One anonymous sleuth, 'All for Empire', for example, wrote: 'Mr. A —— of B —— Street does not work, but is plentifully supplied with money, which he spends freely. His wife pretends to go out washing, but she has not been out for four weeks; this does not keep him!' However, the anti-German sentiment was also inflamed, especially in later years of the war, by the propaganda used to mobilise Australians for the war effort. Like so much of Australian political discourse of the time, this invoked racial stereotypes. Whereas before the war German-Australians had been welcome immigrants, thought to share a similar 'Aryan' background to the British, now the country from which they originated was demonised as the home of 'Huns'. Germany was a nation of '20th-century Vandals filled with an unholy lust for world dominion', *The Argus* of 11 September 1914 claimed. In cartoons and political discourse, the descendants of Goethe, Schiller and Beethoven were morphed into rapists, militarists decked in *Pickelhauben* and boots, and monsters committing war crimes. Every week *The Bulletin* carried cartoons, particularly by the artist Norman Lindsay, that portrayed the Germans as ape-like giants, disrobing women, crucifying victims and looming over the peoples they had occupied, their hands dripping with blood. These images might have been difficult to reconcile with one's bespectacled German neighbour, but they created the emotional distance that converted many Australians into 'good haters'.[65]

This visceral propaganda was fuelled by a stream of atrocity stories that started to emanate from Belgium in the first weeks of the war. As the German armies advanced on their path of conquest, refugees flooded into France, bringing tales of atrocities against civilians: Belgian women and children used as human shields; civilians shot, mutilated, bayoneted or hanged; priests and nuns shot; even children having their hands cut off. In federal parliament, on 14 October 1914, the Liberal senator Thomas Bakhap declared:

> We read how our enemies, in the wildest paroxysms of bestial fury, pursue shrieking maids and matrons in Belgium . . . A great many people believe that in this day of The Hague Convention war is conducted somewhat on ball-room lines, but war is a very pitiless and terrible business . . . [war] is hell.[66]

Some of these stories were later found to be exaggerated, but there was considerable substance to them. As the German armies met unexpectedly fierce resistance in Belgium, they developed a paranoid fear of civilians acting as irregular forces or *francs tireurs* (free shooters), as some French citizens had during the Franco-Prussian War of 1870–71. Their retaliation against Belgian citizens was therefore often fierce and relentless. Moreover, when Germany finally conquered Belgium, it proved a ruthless occupying power. Over the four years of war, it would extract from the Belgian economy whatever it thought it needed for its own war effort. It deported 120,000 Belgians to work in German industries, stripped Belgian factories of their machinery, destroyed over 100,000 homes and laid waste huge tracks of arable land. During the whole war, perhaps half a million Belgian soldiers and civilians were killed.[67]

In the wartime culture of all Allied nations, therefore, German atrocities in Belgium played a central role in consolidating national unity. Belgium came to represent much more than a small occupied nation. It was the just cause for which to fight. As Judith Smart puts it, 'poor little Belgium' was:

> constituted in such a way as to signify Germany's guilt and perfidy. Its signification or cultural meaning for the audience was that the war was a just one for an indisputably moral cause which must in the long run triumph, and that that cause, the cause of civilisation itself, was represented by Great Britain and her allies.[68]

As the war progressed, Belgium's struggle became constructed as an engrossing narrative. At times it was a fairytale, in which the characters were starkly good and evil. At other times, Belgium was depicted as a young male hero, or a vulnerable heroine in the thrall of Germany, the bad father, the inhuman beast or the sexual violator. Alternatively, German behaviour in Belgium was represented not as a matter of harsh military necessity but as the product of a warped historical development. The Melbourne *Church of England Messenger*, for example, argued on 25 September 1914:

> Suppose in a historical examination, the question occurred, 'Trace the probable causes of the ferocity of the Germans?' the following answer might deserve some marks: — 'The ferocity of the Germans, as manifested in their devilish doings in Belgium, is traceable to these causes:—
>
> 1 Their ancestral savagery of 2000 years ago has received too little admixture of gentler breeds (contrast British culture, due partly to the Norman infusion).
> 2 To some extent the Germans are influenced by Martin Luther, whose lack of Christian meekness was shown in his brutal treatment of Zwingli at the great religious conference at Marburg, in 1529.
> 3 Modern Germany owes its existence to the heartless and bloodthirsty and perjured Frederick the Great, whom, probably, the present Kaiser is feebly trying to imitate.
> 4 German ferocity is also partly due to the highly contagious nature of the disease (blood lust), from which its foolish leader suffers.
> 5 Another Satanic influence under which Germany suffers is the memory of the hard cynic, Bismarck.'

With such intellectual nonsense being peddled seriously, the demonising of German-Australians rapidly gathered pace. In the days before the declaration of war, German clubs and consulates had been threatened by riotous crowds in the capital cities. Now, individuals, regardless of their sympathies and allegiances, were forced out of employment. German businesses were shunned and the government began a process of internment. Initially, only those who were foreign nationals of military age were deemed 'enemy aliens', but by May 1916 the net had been cast far wider to include 'naturalised' Australians and Australian-born citizens with fathers or grandfathers who had been enemy subjects. That scourge of modern war, the internment camp, sprang up in various states: at Enoggera, Queensland; Holsworthy and Liverpool, New South Wales; at Langwarrin and Point Cook, in Victoria; on Torrens Island, South Australia; on Rottnest Island, Western Australia; and at Claremont and, later, Bruny Island, Tasmania. In 1915, these state camps were broken up and the internees relocated in what Scott later called 'a great concentration camp' at Liverpool.[69]

In all, some 6890 persons were interned during the war, including 84 women and 67 children. Of these, about 4500 had been resident in Australia prior to the war, some 700 were naturalised Australians, and another 70 had been born in Australia. Some were 'voluntary internees', choosing to be interned to escape hostile neighbours or seeking a place to live after being thrown out of work. Others were sailors removed from enemy ships in Australian ports or enemy civilians captured in the Asia-Pacific region and transported to Australia. A further 4260 suspected persons were on parole under police supervision. Once under suspicion, these people had no access to judicial appeal processes, and no chance of gaining legal representation. The onus was on them to prove that they were not hostile enemy aliens, as the authorities claimed. In practice, the system of internment was arbitrary, capricious and subject to the vagaries of local authorities interpreting the regulations of the *War Precautions Act* as they saw fit. In many instances, the confinement of these Australians, and their stigmatising as 'disloyal', was a denial of the very civil and legal rights for which Australians claimed to be fighting.[70]

Stalemate on the Western Front

The harsh treatment of German-Australians might be seen as misdirected aggression—a deflection of anger from the war itself, which was rapidly slipping beyond the power of anyone to control or end. By mid-September

1914, none of the initial attempts by armies in Europe to invade and conquer their enemies had succeeded, although Germany had conquered much of Belgium and northern France, and Russia held valuable Austrian territory. Everywhere—in Belgium, France, Serbia, Prussia and Galicia—armies were confronting the terrible cost of industrialised warfare. Machine guns, with their rapid-fire mechanisms, artillery that could pulverise men and fortifications several kilometres away, and barbed wire that formed metal jungles impenetrable to infantry—all of these, it now emerged, had given a great tactical advantage to defenders. Advancing infantry were being mown down by murderous fire and, even where they made progress, they were suffering horrendous losses. Individual courage and human will—what the French called *élan*—were no longer sufficient for victory. Instead, twentieth-century warfare demanded endless quantities of munitions, complex logistical systems and casualties on a previously unimaginable scale.

On the Eastern Front, this new warfare remained relatively fluid not only in 1914 but throughout much of the war. But in France and Belgium it soon settled into the infamous stalemate of trench warfare. After some desperate and confused battles in Picardy and Artois in September—erroneously called 'the race to the sea'—the armies on both sides in France began to take cover by digging in. To their north, in Flanders, the Germans made a last attempt in late October and early November to break through and capture the Channel ports, which would prevent the British building up forces on the Continent. But in one of the most costly battles of the war, the First Battle of Ypres, they were stopped. In what became known as the *Kindermord*, or 'the massacre of the innocents', they lost perhaps 60 per cent of the young students who had been thrown into action untrained. Thereafter Flanders, too, became a static front.

By the end of 1914, then, there stretched from Switzerland to the English Channel opposing lines of trenches and earthworks, fortified month after month until they became virtually impenetrable. Thus the Western Front stayed, with only minor changes, until early 1918—by which time the belligerents had learned from their mistakes, developed new tactics, created more accurate artillery, mobilised their populations for mass munitions production and developed more integrated weapons systems—which, in combination, would secure victory for the Allied Powers.

Was there an alternative? Could the war have been ended by negotiation when the first offensives of 1914 failed? War, as Carl von Clausewitz's endlessly quoted aphorism reminds us, is a continuation of politics by other means. In late 1914, however, there was no political will, on either side, to compromise. Even though it had not won the decisive victory it needed, Germany had conquered Belgium, occupied strategic parts of industrialised France and triumphed at Tannenberg, a name that resonated with the mythic history of the Teutonic knights. France had held Paris, but had lost valuable territory in its north. It had no option but to fight until this was regained. So long as northern France and Belgium remained in German hands, Britain could not withdraw from the war. Even if there were a settlement in the west, Germany could then have turned all its energies to the east, defeated Russia, dominated Central and Eastern Europe and thus fundamentally altered the European balance of power. Russia and Austria-Hungary, for their part, though they had suffered huge losses in the first months of the war, could not accept German hegemony. With the terrible logic of war, they, like the other belligerents, had to continue fighting until they gained something commensurate with their huge losses.

So the voices calling for peace were few. The Australian Peace Alliance, an amalgam of various anti-war and pacifist associations, met on 17 December 1914 and called upon 'men and women of all nations to demand an immediate cessation of hostilities and the submission of the claims of each nation involved in this brutalising war to arbitration'. But at this stage of the war calls for a negotiated peace were few and unheeded. The *Sydney Morning Herald* spoke for far more Australians when it wrote on Christmas Day 1914 that:

> The cause for which our fellow-countrymen are fighting and preparing to fight is ... the cause which Christian teaching most strongly inculcated to a heathen world. They are fighting for justice for a people too small to protect itself, for equal rights for all men, and

for the supremacy of one moral law over the strong as well over as the weak. Their enemies . . . are the champions of force, of brute strength, of the power of terror to overcome reason, and of cruelty to drive out the love of freedom. Those parents who to-day miss our soldiers from their gatherings may recall the saying of a wise critic of Napoleon when his glory was at its height:—'It is unjust; It cannot last'.[71]

2

---·∙·---

1915

Gallipoli and
mobilisation at home

Visitors to the Australian War Memorial, Canberra, soon come across a large rowing boat in the entrance to the galleries. Faint images of moving men flicker in the half light on the wall above. Water can be heard lapping through the sound system, while inscribed on the wall above are the words of W.M. Hughes: 'Australia was born on the shores of Gallipoli.'

In this and countless other ways, the Allied campaign on the Gallipoli peninsula from April to December 1915 dominates the national memory of World War I. It would seem from this that 1915 was the decisive year of the war. Yet it was not; instead, on all fronts including Gallipoli, 1915 was a year of frustration—one of 'escalation and stalemate, both sides applying rising levels of violence yet failing to terminate the [strategic] impasse'. Realising, after stalemate had set in on the Western Front, that a titanic struggle now lay ahead of them, governments set about increasing their military manpower and retooling their industries to meet the seemingly insatiable demand for munitions. New fronts opened, with Turkey (or, more accurately, the Ottoman Empire) and Bulgaria joining the Central Powers in late 1914 and October 1915 respectively. Italy threw in its lot with the Allies in May 1915. The geographical spread and strategic complexity of this already complex war therefore increased dramatically.[1]

The strategic context

The year began with the French continuing to attack the Germans, at Champagne and the Woëvre in Lorraine, while in the east the Central Powers and Russians launched a series of massive offensives in appalling winter conditions. First, on 23 January, the Austro-Hungarians opened 'a cruel folly' of an offensive against the Russian armies in the region of the Carpathians and Bukovina. As Norman Stone has said:

> Mountains had to be scaled in mid-winter; supply-lines were either an ice-rink or a marsh, depending on freeze or thaw; clouds hung low, and obscured the visibility of artillery-targets; shells either bounced off ice or were smothered in mud; whole bivouacs would be found frozen to death in the morning.

The attack ultimately ran out of steam, and by the time the Russians had counter-attacked and the Austro-Hungarian armies gone onto the offensive once more, some 800,000 men had 'disappeared' from the Austro-Hungarian army. Another 120,000 were lost in the Russian siege of the fortress of Przemyśl (now in south-eastern Poland)—a victory that the Australian press noted with great acclaim in March 1915. Further attempts by the Russians to complete the ruin of the Austro-Hungarian armies in Carpathia, however, stalled in March and April, and prompted Germany to intervene to shore up its teetering ally.[2]

In East Prussia, meanwhile, the Germans attacked in the central plains of the Vistula in late January, using poison gas for the first time in the war. The Russian counter-attack cost them 40,000 casualties in three days. Further offensives in February and March cost each side tens of thousands of casualties for no significant strategic gain. In early March, the Germans chose to withdraw tactically to their frontiers.[3]

Thousands of kilometres to the east, the Ottoman Empire (Turkey) had entered the war on the side of the Central Powers in October 1914, after a complex period of diplomatic and military manoeuvring in which it had made no firm commitment to either camp. In December 1914 it launched an attack on the Russians in the Caucasus. By January 1915, the Ottomans had lost perhaps three-quarters of their Caucasus army—as much to illness and cold as to the battle itself, since the logistics of supplying troops beyond a railhead proved as intractable in the east as in Western Europe. Using the pretext of internal disloyalty and insecurity, the Ottoman government then turned inwards, murdering possibly a million of its Armenian subjects in a succession of massacres that remain the subject of bitter dispute to this day.[4]

Turkey's belligerence had a direct impact on the way the AIF would be deployed. When the first convoy sailed from Albany in early November 1914, it was assumed that the Australians and New Zealanders would head for the United Kingdom and then the Western Front. But British interests in the Middle East were now under threat. The Ottoman Empire stretched as far as Sinai, from where it could attack the Suez Canal, the lifeline of the British Empire, which linked the Mediterranean with India, South-East Asia and Australasia. The British were also in the process of trying to formalise their control over Egypt, which they had occupied in 1882 but which remained nominally a colony of Turkey. It was realised that any attempt to establish a protectorate would probably inflame the 70,000 Turkish nationals living in Egypt and the burgeoning Egyptian nationalist movement. Having Australian and New Zealand troops stationed in Egypt could therefore contribute to internal stability while helping the British to counter any threats Turkey might mount to the canal.

To add to this, the training camps of the British army on the Salisbury Plain in England could not cope with the number of troops the Dominions were so energetically raising in the first months of the war. The first contingents of the Canadian Expeditionary Force were being housed in tents in a sea of mud in the dismal British winter, and were falling ill. It made pragmatic as well as strategic sense, therefore, to train the Australians and New Zealanders in the warmer climate of Egypt.

Australians in Egypt

The first convoy arrived at Alexandria on 3 December 1914. From here, the New Zealanders (an infantry brigade and a mounted rifles brigade) headed to camps at Zeitoun, on Cairo's northern edge, while the Australians went to Maadi, an outer suburb on the Nile, and Mena, memorably sited near the pyramids of Giza. Contrary to popular belief, the Australians were not natural fighters and training began immediately: a mix of drill, marching through the sand, and digging and attacking trenches, six days a week. General fitness improved after weeks at sea, but the swirling sands caused throat and chest complaints. Some men died from pneumonia—hardly the heroic death they may have envisaged when they enlisted.

Training doctrine had yet to reflect the lessons of recent battles in Europe. Richard Casey, a young lieutenant who would later become Australia's Minister for External Affairs and governor-general, commented after watching an exercise involving the 1st Brigade in Egypt: 'The disregard of cover and the advancing in face of strong fire in the open will have to be remedied—or our troops will very soon be wiped out.'[5]

It was in Egypt that the Australian and New Zealand forces were formed into the ANZAC Corps, the Australian and New Zealand Army Corps. It was a wonderfully fortuitous choice of acronym. As Australian war correspondent F.M. Cutlack would later say, 'Anzac' was a war cry 'pitiless as a hurled spear', conveying 'something savagely masculine, ruthless, resolute, clean driven home'. Australians therefore should be grateful to New Zealanders for the helpful consonants. Anzac was a far stronger moniker than another title mooted in 1914, the Australasian Army Corps—or AAS![6]

At this stage, the corps had two divisions. The first, consisting entirely of Australian troops, was commanded by Bridges, who for a time also retained administrative control of the whole AIF. The second, the New Zealand & Australian Division, was commanded by a British regular officer, Major-General Sir Alexander Godley. The command of the corps itself was given not to an Australian—it would take four more years for this to happen—but to a 49-year-old British officer from the Indian Army, Major-General William Birdwood. His record as corps commander would be mixed. On the one hand, he lacked an instinctive feel for strategy and tactics, and tended to defer to his British superiors when a more vigorous assertion of Dominion interests was called for. Yet he knew how to delegate, particularly to his chief of staff (from September 1915 on), the highly competent Cyril Brudenell White. Birdwood also had two qualities of great value in a commander: an ability to maintain rapport with his troops and a reputation for personal bravery. John Monash, appointed to command the Australian 4th Brigade, met Birdwood in Egypt in late January 1914 and described him as:

> A small, thin man, nothing striking or soldierly about him, [he] speaks with a stammer and has a rather nervy, unquiet manner, but there is no mistaking his perfectly wonderful grasp of the whole business of soldiering . . . I have been around with him for hours and heard him talking to privates, buglers, drivers, gunners, colonels, signallers and generals and every time he has left the man with a better knowledge of his business than he had before.

Bean's assessment was also positive, partly because Birdwood conformed to Bean's emerging conception of the AIF as a distinctively egalitarian institution:

> The Australians might have found themselves under a commander who would have summed up a man by the boots he wore, or the roughness of his voice, or the manner in which he parted his hair, and who would have laid a horrified insistence upon the correct manner of saluting or addressing an officer, or upon insignificant points of dress. To such details of dress and manner British officers ordinarily attached great importance. It was Birdwood's nature to look past the forms at the man himself.[7]

While the Australians were training, the Ottoman forces (as the multi-national 'Turkish' armies should really be called) attacked the Suez Canal, as anticipated. Their advance across the Sinai desert in early 1915 was a considerable achievement, but as they tried to cross the canal they were slaughtered by New Zealand and Indian fire. By the time the 2nd Australian Brigade was scheduled to join the fighting, the Ottomans had been forced to retreat.

The Australians' months in Egypt have therefore been remembered not for their military accomplishments—though Bean, ever prone to hyperbole, would argue that the AIF's rapid training was one of its finest achievements—but for their behaviour while on leave. For many young Australians, this was their first experience of a foreign country and the culture shock was profound. Major Coe of the 12th Australian Field Artillery Brigade wrote in his diary on 26 December 1914:

The shops never close. The natives won't work on Friday, they say their prayers in the open. Women are beasts of burden, child marriage, harems, high palaces, and indescribably filthy stinking houses in which the donkeys, bison, fowls, sheep and goats all sleep together with the natives; camels, overloaded donkeys, Arab horses, motor cars, phaetons, pyramids, Sphinx, tents, desert, cultivation, electric trams, ploughs drawn by camel and donkey harnessed together, scorpions, huge beetles, mosquitoes, morning temperature 45, midday temperature 98, no rain, bell tents, marquees, the smell of the east, home memories, mix the lot and that is Egypt for you.[8]

Though fascinated by the Egyptian ruins, the Australians were supremely confident about their own cultural superiority. They were happy to play 'lords of the desert', exploiting the cheap labour and sexual services that were readily available. However, they took great umbrage when they were fleeced or 'gypped'. They were aghast at the poverty, the subservience of women, the servility of the market vendors, the poor health of the children, the filth in public places, the cruelty to animals and the endemic petty thieving. Monash, though his own German-Jewish background would later make him a target of prejudice, described everything as 'dirty, squalid smelly and repugnant to any refined sense'. His principal impression of a day at Memphis was 'of a yelling screaming crowd of dirty, smelly Arabs, donkey boys, Bedouins, Dragomans, donkeys, camels and mules, whirling along in a pandemonium of confusion, noise, shouting and muddled arrangements'.[9]

As products of an unashamedly White Australia, the AIF soldiers slipped easily into negative racial stereotyping. Egyptians were 'Gyppos', 'Gyppies' or 'niggers'. Collectively, they were untrustworthy, dishonest and immoral. To quote a Light Horse private, P.S. Jackson: 'There is something particularly repellent about Eastern races. All places with a large "native" coloured population are undesirable but vice and depravity are more deeply ingrained in Cairo than elsewhere.' This prejudice in turn seemed to legitimise violence and casual abuse. Hawkers in the streets had their trays of merchandise deliberately upset. Trams were commandeered and driven wildly through the streets. Soldiers would throw coins from balconies onto the street below, only to then empty buckets of water on the crowds who rushed to catch them. The Muslim call to prayer was parodied. Women were accosted, even raped. Inoffensive passers-by were attacked or verbally abused. The list could go on. It was a 'latter-day plague'.[10]

The most notorious incident was the 'battle of Wassa' in Cairo's prostitution district. There are many versions of what happened on Good Friday, 2 April 1915, but the classic story is that Australian and New Zealand soldiers sacked a brothel in revenge for the infection being spread by prostitutes working in the area. (Had they not been warned by their officers about the risk of venereal disease?) Angered also by the bad liquor they had been sold—and had eagerly downed—they threw the prostitutes, their pimps and their possessions into the street. Mattresses, furniture and clothing were then set alight. When the local fire brigade arrived, this too was set upon and its hoses cut. The military police appeared, only to be bombarded with bottles and stones when they fired above the crowd, now swelled to perhaps two thousand. More shops were looted and a Greek hotel torched before order was finally restored by the Lancashire Territorials, who, unlike the detested military police, were popular with the troops.

Of course, such violence was not typical of all Australians based in Egypt. Arguably, the Australian authorities were also at fault for not providing recreational facilities at the Anzac camps. But much of the Australian behaviour in Cairo was simply ugly. Racism was so deeply embedded in Australian culture that cruelty, violence and disrespect to non-Europeans was acceptable—even a source of fun. When troop ships berthed at Colombo and South African ports later in the war, for example, Australians would delight in tossing coins to the 'niggers' on the wharf and watching them fight to catch them:

A two-bob piece floats down from the officers' deck and the coons almost tear each other to pieces in their mad haste to get it . . . a bloke rushes forward with a red-hot two bob in a tobacco tin lid he's been busy heating up to almost white hot. The coons jump for the two bob. One tall nig catches it and, screaming, drops it. Another grabs it, another scream and the coin bounces on the boards. A third fellow thinks his luck's in and lands on it, but jumps back yelling like blazes and the two bob lies there on the wharf with twenty niggers ringed round it, waiting for it to cool. A move, and with one accord they dive together for the coin, the thud of thick skulls meeting in an awful bash brings joy and delight to us.[11]

Even years later, such behaviour was excused as endearing larrikinism on the part of the Australian digger. Bean's official history of 1921 relegated the battle of Wassa and a similar incident in July 1915 to a long footnote. These events, he said, were 'not heroic', but they 'differed very little from what at Oxford and Cambridge and in Australian universities is known as a rag'. Five decades later, in his classic *The Broken Years*, Bill Gammage concluded that the incidents in Egypt 'betrayed some of the worst aspects of the Australian character', but they were understandable:

[The AIF] had come across half a world to fight for one of the noblest causes that uplifted men. They were sustained by notions of splendour and battle and glory. They were the first and the finest of their country. And they had been dumped on bare sand among hordes of natives so persistent that a man had to buy a stick to beat them off, they were obliged to drink 'poisonous' beer or none at all, they were expected to endure heat, sand, dust, flies, and monotony without hope of alleviation, and in and out of training hours they had, as they put it, to march, drill and meander uselessly about the desert 'like a pack of bloody dills'. It was not for this that they had come. They dubbed Egypt land of sin, shit and syphilis, and set about devising their own entertainment.[12]

Australian films have also implied that the AIF in Egypt was guilty of little more than boyish pranks. Charles Chauvel's *Forty Thousand Horsemen* (produced in 1940 as part of the propaganda of the next world war) shows three mates, Red, Jim and Larry, winning the trousers of an Egyptian in a game of two-up. They ride through Cairo with this clothing draped over the rumps of their donkeys, the half-naked Egyptian running after them as an ineffectual figure of fun. Peter Weir's 1981 *Gallipoli*, the film that introduced a new generation to the mythology of Anzac, also depicts Archy Hamilton, Frank Dunne and their mates trashing the store of an Egyptian who has sold one of them a souvenir at an inflated price. Their behaviour seems uncon-scionable only because they have targeted the wrong trader.

The commanders of the AIF, however, were less tolerant of its lack of discipline. Little could be done about the cavalier attitude that many Australians were already displaying towards saluting, infuriating though British officers found this. But absence without leave, insubordination, drunkenness and assaults on military police were a different matter. By December 1914, the AIF command extended training hours, strength-ened picket lines on the road to Cairo from the camp at Mena and in February 1915 sent back to Australia 131 disciplinary cases and 24 men with venereal disease.

A news release in the Australian press explained that these men were 'losing Australia her good name in the outside world'. Bean probably wrote this under pressure from Bridges, and qualified his case by arguing that perhaps only 1–2 per cent of the AIF—and these mostly older veterans from the South African or other imperial campaigns—were troublemakers. But the moral police in Australia were unleashed. Letters to the newspapers called for the names of the 'wasters' or 'undesirables' to be published—not just to shame them, but to protect the reputation of men sent home for acceptable medical reasons. Temperance campaigners also seized the chance to make their point about the evils of drink. 'Merely a Woman' argued that the 'rotters' should be sent to the front.

> Why not give 'the rotters' a chance? They may be hopeless in society; they are useless as citizens; but they must have some glimmer of manliness, for they have offered to serve their country . . . Send them to the front to take their chance, and we women in Australia shall await—not the shameful home-coming of rejected men—but the 'rotter' with perhaps a V.C.[13]

Bean's standing within the AIF meanwhile took something of a battering. 'I suppose you have read all that rot written by his wowsership, C.E.W. Bean', wrote Lance Corporal F.C. Eric Mulvey of the 2nd Light Horse Regiment on 14 March:

> What [he] wrote is fairly true but he made it the main theme of his report which magnifies it greatly and after all was there any necessity to mention it at all . . . It would be ridiculous to expect an expeditionary force to be all members of the Y.M.C.A. wouldn't it?[14]

It was a relief, then, when on 1 April 1915 the news came that the Australasian troops in Egypt would go into action. Progressively they sailed in convoy for Lemnos, a thousand kilometres across the Mediterranean. Their ultimate destination, so Birdwood and Bridges learned on 12 April, was the Turkish peninsula of Gallipoli. As they sailed, Ben Leane wrote to his wife, Phyllis:

> In case the worst happens and I am unable to make any more entries I will take this opportunity to bid you 'goodbye' dear girl. I trust that I will come through alright, but it is impossible to say, and I must do my duty whatever it is. But if I am to die, know that I died loving you with my whole heart & soul, dearest wife that a man ever had. Kiss little Gwen and our new baby, who perhaps I may never see, and never let them forget Daddy.[15]

The planning for Gallipoli

Controversy has always surrounded the Gallipoli campaign. Ill-conceived and poorly executed, it had its origins in a request by the supreme commander of the Russian forces early in January 1915 for a 'demonstration' against the Ottomans by the British and French. From this modest appeal grew a campaign that ultimately aspired to eliminate Turkey from the war, to entice the Balkan states to join the Allied side and to gain access through the narrow Bosporus strait to the Russian ports in the Black Sea. This, in turn, would allow the Russians to export their wheat to Allied and neutral powers and thus gain the foreign exchange they needed to wage the war.

The problem facing the British and French was the geography of Turkey. The initial Allied plan was to threaten the capital of Constantinople (now Istanbul) with a combined naval force, but the city sits at the eastern end of the Sea of Marmara. This inland sea can be accessed from the Aegean only via the Dardanelles, a sea lane that is some 65 kilometres in length and at the Narrows only 1600 metres wide. The currents in the straits vary wildly, and the surrounding shores form steep cliffs. In 1915, these were bristling with forts and guns, while the sea channels were mined and fitted with anti-submarine nets.

After a period of planning—perhaps 'one of the strangest in Britain's military history'—the British government concluded that it could overcome these formidable obstacles by bombarding the fortifications dominating the entrance to the Dardanelles with long-range naval shelling, while also landing small forces of marines to neutralise the Turkish defences. Then the British and French capital ships and mine sweepers would enter the Dardanelles and force their way through the Narrows.[16]

It was a strategy that the First Sea Lord John ('Jacky') Fisher began to question as soon as it was approved, and it failed when it was progressively implemented in February and March 1915. Most critically, on 18 March, when a combined unit of British and French ships attempted to force its way through the Dardanelles to the Sea of Marmara, one-third of the fleet was sunk or put out of action even before it reached the heavily mined Narrows. The British Admiralty had no choice but to halt the operation. In Turkey, 18 March would be celebrated in later years as Victory Day. The Ottoman forces had halted the greatest fleet in the world—though, as Robin Prior has put it, 'with the force available, no admiral could have conquered the Straits defences unless the Turks threw in the towel'.[17]

In retrospect, it is clear that the Dardanelles campaign should have ended there. The Russians who had sought help in January had actually gone on to annihilate the Turkish Third Army in the Caucasus in the Battle of Sarikamish. In London, however, the enticing prospect of finding an 'eastern solution' to the war had already taken hold of the imagination of some politicians and strategists—particularly the First Lord of the Admiralty, Winston Churchill, and the Chancellor of the Exchequer, David Lloyd George. By opening a new front in the eastern Mediterranean, Britain could capitalise on its naval advantage and avoid becoming entangled in the deepening stalemate on the Western Front. How this would actually assist in defeating Germany was not clear—Turkey was manifestly a junior partner in the Central Powers alliance—but victory against the Turks also offered tempting prospects of dismembering the Ottoman Empire (as indeed the British and French did after World War I, with consequences that still haunt the Middle East).

Hence the British War Council decided to land Allied forces on the Gallipoli peninsula. Here, it was hoped, they would capture the Turkish fortifications and clear the way for another attempt by Allied naval forces to force the Narrows. What would happen then was again uncertain. Viewing the Ottoman Empire as a second-rate power and 'the sick man of Europe', the British seemed to have expected that its ramshackle structure would simply implode. The Secretary of State for War, Lord Kitchener, thought the capture of the Dardanelles forts would trigger a wider political revolution (which British agents had in fact been trying to foment). The War Office too, even after the failure of the naval operation on 18 March, expected the Turks to 'throw up the sponge . . . and clear out of the Gallipoli peninsula'. It was planning of an almost pre-modern kind. As Tim Travers says:

> In the absence of proper planning a number of prominent politicians, together with Churchill and Kitchener, simply indulged in a Darwinian

struggle for control of operations. Imaginative and grandiose ideas by a confident and optimistic ruling class, with an eye to their own reputations, were no substitute for careful planning.[18]

The assault on Gallipoli was to consist of three amphibious landings by a 70,000-strong Mediterranean Expeditionary Force (MEF) under General Ian Hamilton. At Cape Helles, on the tip of the peninsula, the British 29th Division and the Royal Naval Division would land and capture Achi Baba, a dominant feature of the landscape some 6 kilometres inland. A subsidiary landing would be launched by French troops at Kum Kale, on the opposite, Asian shore of the entrance to the Dardanelles. Meanwhile, to the north along the Aegean coast, a force of Australians and New Zealanders would land in the vicinity of the Gaba Tepe promontory. Their role was to move across the peninsula to a south-west spur on the Sari Bair range, Mal Tepe. From here they would disrupt Ottoman communications, intercept the enemy forces retreating from Helles, and prevent their reinforcements from heading south to halt the British. Eventually, it was hoped, the Allied forces at Helles and the Anzacs would converge and capture the Kilid Bahr plateau, which overlooked and dominated the Narrows. This, at least, was the plan (see Map 1). The Australian government was neither consulted nor told about it, since it had no input into high-level British strategic planning, either in 1915 or for the rest of the war.

The landings at Gallipoli

Amphibious campaigns against defended territory are some of the most difficult operations in war. While approaching the shore, the landing forces are exposed and vulnerable. They need surprise, good weather and covering fire from naval vessels if they are to get ashore safely. Once landed, they need to be rapidly reinforced with additional manpower, field artillery, ammunition, food, supplies, medical support and means of transport if they are not to be driven back into the sea. The risks of amphibious operations are so great that it is usually thought attackers need a numerical superiority of at least three to one over the defenders. They certainly need sophisticated coordination and communication between land and naval forces, artillery and logistics.

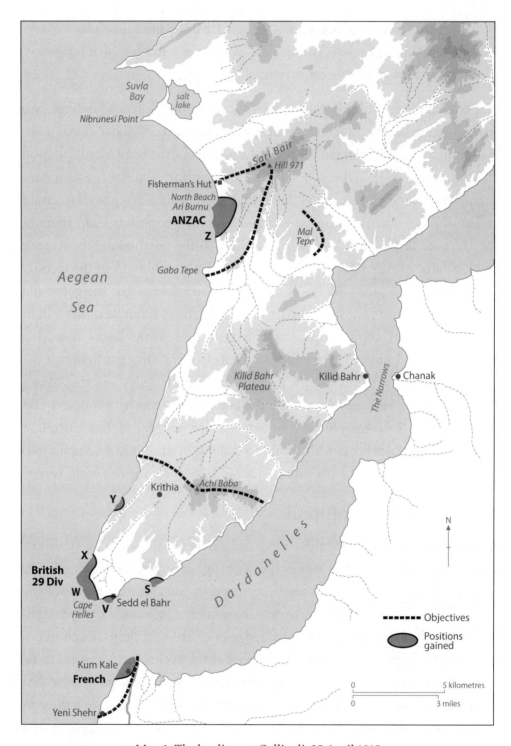

Map 1: The landings at Gallipoli, 25 April 1915

The landings on 25 April 1915 had few, if any, of these settings right. At the planning stage, the Allied commanders failed to resolve the respective roles of the army and navy. The Royal Navy thought that its task was to prepare for a combined attack on the Narrows. The army command thought the navy's role was to soften up Turkish defences and help the troops land. As for surprise, the earlier naval operations in February and March had blown that. Although the German and Turkish commanders did not know the precise timing or location of the April attacks, they did anticipate a threat in the general area where the Allied landings occurred.

In any case, the Ottomans, with the benefit of internal lines of communication, could deploy reserve forces relatively quickly to meet attacks wherever they happened to occur. There were some 40,000 Ottoman troops located on the Gallipoli peninsula and another 30,000 nearby in reserve. The MEF had only about the same number of men available—and, moreover, was short of artillery.[19]

Unsurprisingly, some British officers were pessimistic about their chances of success. However, under orders to proceed they convinced themselves otherwise. Major-General Aylmer Hunter-Weston, who was to command the 29th Division at Helles, wrote to his wife on 7 April: 'the odds against us are very heavy. However, nothing is impossible.' Birdwood, fearing that Turkish artillery would be fearsome and the logistical challenges of the landing considerable, reassured himself that once the troops were ashore, 'all will be well'. Godley thought that if the landing came off, 'it will be one of the greatest feats of arms that have ever been done'. The commander of Australian 3rd Infantry Brigade, Colonel Ewen Sinclair-MacLagan, however, warned his men of the danger of casualties and urged them to hang on to whatever land was gained 'even to the last man'.[20]

At least the weather was fine on the night of 24–25 April. Despite gales in the days before, the seas that night were calm. Off the coast of Gallipoli, a flotilla of warships and transports assembled and, after the moon had sunk, moved in to land the troops in thick darkness. Given the importance of surprise, there was no preliminary bombardment from the fleet offshore.

The Gallipoli landing, 25 April 1915. Members of No. 2 Field Company, Royal Australian Engineers, land on the beach at 6.30 a.m. (AWM P0226.014)

Steele's Post at Gallipoli, 3 May 1915, showing dugouts perched precariously on the slopes. Turkish snipers reached the gully opposite during the first week of the occupation. (AWM G00942)

As is evident from this photo, the systems for evacuating the wounded from Gallipoli were primitive. (AWM C02679)

Australian troops inside a captured Turkish trench at Lone Pine in August 1915. (AWM G01126)

The story of the landing at Anzac Cove has been told so often, and with such reverence, that it is almost a political statement not to grant it a capital 'L'. On that celebrated morning, the men of the Australian 1st Division's 3rd Brigade (9th, 10th, 11th and 12th Battalions) were the first to go ashore. Before dawn, they climbed down the rope ladders dangling from the decks of their transports into rowing boats, 30 to 40 men per boat. Steamboats then towed them towards the vague outline of the coastline before releasing them near the shore. The men waited, silent, tense and exposed. Not for them the protection of modern landing craft or even the steel-plated self-powered 'beetles' or barges that were used at the landings at Suvla Bay some months later, in August 1915. The surviving boat in the Australian War Memorial looks primitive and vulnerable. Bean later wrote:

> It had become very dark; except for the stars, sea and sky were sheer black, and it was often impossible for soldiers in any of the twelve tows to see even the tow abreast of them . . . In the silent crowded boats the tension was extreme. Did the Turks suspect? Were they posted on those invisible hills and on the beaches? Would they detect the landing? Would they resist it in force? When would the first shot come?

Captain George Mitchell of the 10th Battalion recorded in his diary:

> My breath came deep. I tried to analyse my feelings, but could not. I think that every emotion was mixed—exultation predominating. We had come from the New World for conquest of the Old . . . The price of failure we knew to be annihilation, victory might mean life. But even so whispered jests passed round.

At 4.29 a.m., the first boat grated on a shingle. The Queenslanders of the 9th Battalion leapt out on to the shore. The Ottomans almost immediately opened fire from a knoll above the beach, Ari Burnu, and from a site further north that the Anzacs would call Fisherman's Hut. As Lieutenant James Aitken recalled:

> everything went smoothly until the keels were just grating on the beach when—bang! went the enemy's signal, followed closely by two more

shots, then a whole fusillade, & so we landed under fire. I quite forgot to be frightened . . . It was a matter of getting out & rushing the Turks with our bayonets & we did.[21]

The troops found themselves confronted with a terrain different from the one they had expected. They had landed on a narrow front of 700 metres in a small indentation of the coastline between Ari Burnu and Hell Spit. Confronting them were steep hills raked with gullies and covered in tangled scrub. In the distance, a towering range of hills, Sari Bair, stretched from the sea near Gaba Tepe to the north-east, culminating in the peaks of what would become infamous as Chunuk Bair, Hill Q and Hill 971. From this highest ridge, and running roughly parallel to it, two lower ridges stretched down to the sea. Rugged spurs branched off them at various points. Over this landscape brooded a dramatic feature, the Sphinx, with precipitous sides dropping away from its narrow crumbling projection into the sky.

Was this the wrong place for the landing? A man in charge of one of the tows shouted out just before the first enemy shots were fired that 'the dam' fools' had taken them a mile too far north. This became orthodoxy: that the Anzacs had landed too far north, beyond the promontory of Gaba Tepe and the more open Brighton Beach to the south. Several factors have been blamed for this: a strong current that dragged the tows off course; the difficulty for the navigators of identifying the various headlands in the dark; their keenness to avoid Ottoman fire from Gaba Tepe; someone's mistake in positioning the marker battleship, HMS *Triumph*, offshore; the inaccuracy of the charts provided by the Admiralty; and the failure of the tows in the darkness to maintain the prescribed distance between them. However, Tom Frame has demolished the theory about the currents and, although the other factors may have played some part, there was in fact no clarity about what was the 'right' landing spot. The orders given to midshipmen guiding the landing craft were relatively flexible on the subject. Later, Birdwood and others would argue that landing at Ari Burnu, even if unintended, was fortunate since it took the Turks (as well as the Anzacs) by surprise. It also spared the landing forces the full effects of the artillery at Gabe Tape. But the beach near Ari Burnu was actually more vulnerable than Brighton Beach, since two companies of Ottoman troops were positioned there—considerable opposition for an amphibious assault force of initially only one brigade.[22]

Once on shore, the Australian troops were under orders to push on at all costs towards the heights of the third ridge, the landing force's target for the first day. They therefore dashed across the beach and scrambled up the hills and ravines through the waist-high scrub. Artist George Lambert, painting the landing after the war, imagined the men as a swarm of ants, climbing painfully and laboriously upwards. Sergeant Henry Cheney of the 10th Battalion later recalled:

> The first act ashore was to fix my bayonet, second to divest myself of my pack. Everything was disorder now, excitement running very high. No one gave a thought of [sic] what we had been told to do, we had been told we had to dig them out with as little noise as possible, but that was cold blood teaching, now we were at fever point, and they just made as much noise as they possibly could. In two seconds after, I was lost in the wild mob, in the wildest of charges, that I think was ever made . . . Straight up that rugged, rocky precipice we went . . . [The Turks] fled before us . . . It was simply our bluff that got us through, we never fired a shot.[23]

Although many men were hit by enemy fire on the beach or left hanging on the scrub, within about fifteen minutes of landing some Australians had reached the top of the first ridge, a point later called Plugge's Plateau. Some then sprinted on towards the second ridge and features that would soon be known as Johnston's Jolly, 400 Plateau and Lone Pine. Others paused to try to reorganise and wait for the rest of the 3rd Brigade, then coming onto the shore below.

This second wave was launched in rowboats direct from the destroyers offshore. With the enemy now alerted, this wave met a tirade of fire from Ari Burnu and the guns at Gaba Tepe, churning the water and thudding into the boats. All of the rowers in some boats were hit. They had to be pushed overboard to allow others to take their place. Reaching the shore at last, these troops landed across a much wider front than the first wave. In fact, at the southern extreme they landed so close to Brighton Beach that this would have gone some way to rectifying the error of the first wave's landing—if indeed this had been an error. Men of the 9th and 10th Battalions then scrambled up to the open and flat area of 400 Plateau and Lone Pine. Reaching these points at around 6 a.m., even before the troops of the first wave, who had further to travel, they captured three Turkish guns. Some men then headed for the prominent features further north, including the tactically vital land that lay at the junction of the ridges and overlooked a steep ravine later called Monash Valley.

Further to the north, other groups from the second wave scrambled up a tortuous spur projecting from the first ridge, Walker's Ridge, and reached a narrow steep-sided plateau, the Nek. Thinking that the battle might be over, some started to dig in. Others made a bayonet charge against the Turkish 8th Company, which had fallen back towards the sea along another spur, Russell's Top. Yet others headed up beyond the Nek towards Baby 700 and Battleship Hill and gained a foothold there by 7.30 a.m.

In three hours, some of the landing troops had climbed up to 2 kilometres of formidably steep terrain with heavy packs while fending off Ottoman skirmishers. This remarkable physical feat would become the stuff of legend. A young British captain on Hamilton's staff later wrote to his wife:

> regardless of losses [the Australians] stormed their way up the first hills . . . it seemed almost incredible that any troops could have done it . . . How they got up fully armed and equipped over the rough, scrub-clad hillsides one can hardly imagine.

Harry T. Bennett, a navigating lieutenant on the battleship *Canopus*, also wrote:

> It was awe inspiring to watch the brave attacks made by the Australians to take what was obviously a very difficult, in fact almost impregnable position. We could see what a fight they had had for it by the dead and wounded ashore on the beach.[24]

Back on the beaches, the 2nd Brigade (5th, 6th, 7th and 8th Battalions) under Colonel James McCay had started to come ashore at around 4.45 a.m. In the confusion around the landing area, four boats beached by mistake in front of the Turkish positions at Fisherman's Hut on North Beach. Captain Herbert Layh of the 7th Battalion recalled:

> As we got close the Turks opened fire with machine guns and rifles . . . They were cutting the water up ahead of us and we were rowing into it . . . When we got under fire five out of the six rowers were shot down . . . but others jumped to the oars . . . I saw Lt Heighway, who was at the tiller, sliding forward into the boat and starting to kick. We just hit the shingle at that moment and I sung out to the men to disembark. I threw myself down at the side of the boat and got shot through the hip.[25]

Of the 140 men in the four boats, 110 were killed or wounded by only one enemy platoon and one enemy machine gun.

Despite losses such as these, the opposition to the landing was relatively light. Most of the Ottoman defenders near the beach fled as the Australians pushed up the hills. Hence, when the 1st Brigade (1st, 2nd, 3rd and 4th Battalions) started to land later in the morning, there were fewer than 500 enemy troops directly facing over 8000 Australians. For a few critical hours, the Australians had a significant local numerical superiority.[26]

Could they have captured the heights of the third ridge at this time? Was a window of opportunity lost on the morning of 25 April? The debate on this issue continues to this day. Sinclair-MacLagan, commanding the 3rd Brigade, scrambled up to Plugge's Plateau at 5.30 a.m. and assessed the landscape. The third ridge, he decided, was too distant to capture immediately. So he chose to consolidate his forces on the second ridge. Fearing that the Turks might counter-attack from Gaba Tepe in the south, he also decided to change the original plans that envisaged McCay's 2nd Brigade pushing on towards the third ridge after landing. Instead, he persuaded McCay to reinforce the right of the Anzac positions on the edge of the second ridge above Brighton Beach, later known as McCay's Hill. In effect, this shifted the centre of gravity of the attack away from its strategic objectives. In the opinion of Chris Roberts, it was this decision 'rather than the misplaced landing which "tore the [landing] plan to shreds". While it is acceptable for a subordinate commander to take contrary action if the circumstances demand it, there was no evidence that such a drastic change was required at this point.' However, Bridges, landing at 7.20 a.m. with Brudenell White, did nothing to undo Sinclair-MacLagan's decisions, and the all-important drive towards the third ridge slowed, leaving the centre of the emerging Anzac line—at Russell's Top, the Nek and Baby 700—only weakly occupied.[27]

This was to prove critically important because it happened that the Ottoman forces in the vicinity of the landing were able to respond relatively quickly and strongly. Chance is always part of the friction of war, and the Ottoman reserves on the peninsula—the 19th Division—were under the command of Mustafa Kemal, a charismatic and talented commander who would go on to become the founder of modern Turkey and its president from 1923 until his death in 1938. Kemal arrived at Battleship Hill on the third ridge at perhaps 10 a.m. on 25 April. He concluded that the Australian landings were a major attack, not just a diversion from the operations at Helles as some other Ottoman commanders believed. Stopping the flight of the Ottoman troops from the lower slopes, he ordered up further forces and—so legend would have it—threw them into the attack down the ridge from Chunuk Bair, saying, 'I don't order you to attack. I order you to die.' He also positioned his artillery so that it could drench the Australians moving up along the first and second ridges below.

The Anzac forces were therefore soon confronted with a ferocious struggle to maintain the positions they had taken immediately after the landing. Those small groups that had rushed ahead of their own initiative to the third ridge—and who for a moment had a tempting glimpse of the Narrows in the distance—found themselves cut off and forced to retreat, if they could. Lower down the slopes, a see-sawing battle for control was played out. As the day progressed, Baby 700, positioned critically at the head of Monash Valley, changed hands six times in a sequence of attacks and counter-attacks. Henry

Cheney, trying to dig in at what later became Quinn's and Courtney's Posts, recalled:

> To call it Hell, appears to me to be very inadequate. They poured every sort of conceivable fire into us. The day seemed as though it was never coming to an end, every five minutes seemed an hour . . . As it was the Turks had the commanding heights, and any fire directed on by them [sic], simply could not miss if aimed properly. Our nerves were strained to an intense degree.[28]

From midday on, the Australians were joined in the battle for Baby 700 by units of the New Zealand Infantry Brigade, which had landed mid-morning. But at 4.30 p.m. their defences broke and Ottomans took control of both Baby 700 and the Nek leading to it. The Anzacs managed only to cling on to the heads of the valleys in small disconnected parties sheltering in niches that offered some protection from the enemy fire.

At 400 Plateau to the south it was again a struggle for the Australians, now joined by the New Zealand Otago Battalion, to hold the ground taken earlier in the day. The Ottomans were outnumbered and themselves in considerable chaos, but they had the advantage of the higher ground. As successive waves of Anzacs tried to move forward, they were trapped by rifle, machine-gun and shrapnel fire so dense that it 'seemed to pour out from whole hillsides'. Earlier, as they prepared to land, Australian engineers had been advised how to respond to shellfire:

> If . . . you are walking along quietly with a pick on your shoulder and a shell should burst nearby, for your very life don't dream of turning round and running, as fear may spread like wildfire and utter confusion as well as a victory turned into defeat, will probably result.

But on the open expanse of 400 Plateau there was no escape. Digging in meant standing up, which in turn meant courting almost certain death. Withdrawing to the cover of the gullies, on the other hand, involved surrendering the plateau to the enemy. All the men could do then was hug the earth, scratching holes in the ground as best they could. Private Phil Harrison said, 'You are lucky if you stick it half an hour.'[29]

The infantry were particularly exposed because of the lack of Allied artillery. In the rudimentary planning of artillery support for the landing, it was expected that British warships would provide the initial cover until field artillery was landed. But no one had decided clearly whether or not the naval vessels in the landing force were to provide close-in fire support for the landing. The initiative was left up to individual captains. One ship, the *Bacchante*, did come in close and stay all day, firing broadsides from near Gaba Tape. But it was the exception. The ships that stayed further offshore struggled to provide supporting fire for the troops on land. The trajectory of their naval guns was too low, the broken terrain made targeting very difficult, and the fighting was so fluid and tangled that 'friendly fire'—one of war's more absurd euphemisms—could easily cause casualties among the Anzacs. There were also serious communication problems, and range and direction were difficult to get right, given that technical issues required naval fire to be straight on.

As for the field artillery, not only were there not enough howitzers and ammunition, but Birdwood, Bridges and Colonel Joseph Talbot Hobbs, commanding the artillery of the 1st Australian Division, vacillated throughout the day as to whether to land their guns or not. Paralysed, it seems, by anxiety about operating artillery in such hostile countryside, the problems of moving guns in the steep gullies and the fear of losing their equipment if the whole landing failed, they ordered and cancelled guns, then embarked them and re-embarked them. In the end, only a single 18-pounder arrived late in the day. Manhandled by a hundred men up to Hell Spit just south of Anzac Cove, it soon shut down the Gaba Tepe battery, which had inflicted many casualties on the landing forces. However, in the interim the infantry were supported only by six howitzers of the 26th Indian Mountain battery, weapons that had limited value because of their small calibre. These came ashore at 10.30 a.m. and went into action at 11.55 a.m., but retreated to the beach at 2.25 p.m. (it seems because they were being targeted by enemy guns above them). As Tim Travers has said, 'Something had gone very wrong with the artillery staff work, no doubt made worse by conflict between Bridges and the artillery commanders.'[30]

This lack of artillery support was a key weakness of the Anzac landing. It allowed the Ottomans such dominance over the landing beaches that no reinforcements were brought onshore between noon and 4.50 p.m., when Monash's 4th Brigade finally landed. Moreover, the terror the infantry felt when facing enemy fire without support from their own artillery contributed to a collapse of morale among some Australians. From early afternoon, men who were not wounded began taking shelter in the gullies and the ravines rather than staying on the open ridges. Some even drifted back to the beaches. According to Bean, there were between 600 and a thousand of them by nightfall. Many—perhaps too many—had come down with the wounded; others, he thought, had held on until they believed they were the only survivors of their battalions. But the demoralisation was probably far more extensive than this. Most of the Anzacs were inexperienced; some had become lost in the chaotic landscape, their officers had often been killed or wounded and they were under intense shelling and sniper fire. Some officers themselves had cracked. The commander of the 9th Battalion was met by a fellow officer when he was 'in a terrible state', lamenting the fact that his battalion was practically wiped out. Other officers, on the other hand, performed well, including one Major H.G. Bennett of the 6th Battalion, who was to achieve notoriety in the next war by abandoning the 8th Division in Singapore in 1942.[31]

The Australians were also confronting for the first time the obscenity of sudden, arbitrary death—what British historian Joanna Bourke has called 'the dismembering of the male'. George Mitchell recorded meeting a grievously wounded man:

> The bullet had fearfully smashed his face and gone down his throat, rendering him dumb. But his eyes were dreadful to behold. And how he squirmed in his agony. There was nothing I could do for him but to pray that he might die swiftly. It took him about twenty minutes to accomplish this.

Ellis Silas, a signaller who landed on the afternoon of 25 April, also found the sight of injuries unnerving:

> I had no sooner vacated the position and [Captain Margolin] had got into my place, than he was struck in the mouth by a bullet. 'Good God!' I exclaimed, 'have they got you Sir? 'My God!' he yelled, 'they have caught me at last' . . . Just at that moment a shot struck the parapet close to my face; I thought my turn had come; although it was nearly dark the snipers seemed well onto this particular dug-out. A body was lifted out of the trench; . . . I asked if he was dead—then I saw the top of his head—oh God![32]

More distressing perhaps than death was the suffering of the wounded. Today's Western armies evacuate their wounded within hours, but at Anzac Cove the authorities were not ready to handle the medical crisis that rapidly unfolded. Neville Howse, now assistant director of medical services of the 1st Division, landed at 7.22 a.m. with Bridges and other senior divisional staff. Since the infantry attack had not yet advanced far inland, it was difficult for him to set up casualty clearing stations that were protected from enemy fire. Instead, he established them on the congested beach, much of which was open and exposed. At first there was only one Australian casualty clearing station in an area of about 6 square metres, at the southern end of Anzac Cove. The New Zealanders soon set up another one at the other end of the beach.

The scale of the necessary rescue and evacuation operations had also been completely under-estimated. There were only 200 stretchers for a force of 24,000 men. Henry Cheney, caught under Ottoman fire, wrote later: 'It was one long continuous cry for stretcher bearers . . . The stretcher bearers simply could not cope with the work, and many, many men laid for over a day before getting any attention.' George Mitchell meanwhile wrote that on 25 April: 'The wounded and dying had to ly [sic] in their blood and ask for things they could not have. Some begged to be shot, and others asked their mates to load and pass them their rifles so that they could end themselves!'[33]

Such was the lack of stretchers that the seriously wounded had to be carried down from the ridges on the stretcher-bearers' shoulders or lowered by improvised means. Ambulance personnel would unwind the wounded men's puttees, place them as 'ropes' under their arms and then carefully lower them down the gullies. Some wounded were never rescued. Cheney saw on the skyline:

> a wounded man staggering about, [he] would fall exhausted and then slowly rise to his feet, in his endeavour to reach help. At last his strength seemed to be put into one last effort to accomplish this end, but after reeling about 10 yards like a very inebriated man, he flung up his hands and fell to the ground, I am afraid never to rise again.[34]

Having reached the beach somehow, the wounded then waited for treatment and evacuation. On the day of the landing, only one well-equipped hospital ship lay offshore. It had the capacity to handle only 300 seriously wounded. Those who were lightly wounded were meant to be treated on the transports that had landed the troops. But in the chaos and congestion on Anzac beach, triage (or the classification of men by the urgency of their need for treatment) broke down. Seriously wounded men were left lying on the shingles exposed to enemy fire. Howse and his team worked throughout the night of 25–26 April and evacuated about 2000 wounded, but many of them received little more than first aid until they reached Alexandria in Egypt.

Not that the medical situation was better managed in Egypt. With weeks of the Gallipoli landing, the facilities at No. 1 Australian General Hospital in Alexandria—a converted hotel—were massively overcrowded. Wards overflowed into nearby Luna Park, where there were initially 'absolutely no conveniences'. As one nurse recalled:

> The *sterile?* [sic] water was brought up . . . from the Cook House—which by the way consisted of 5 or 10 large dixies with a fire under each. One day when we had almost finished one jug of sterile? water we found a large onion in the bottom. There was an absence of even antiseptics . . . There was no sterilized dressings.

It became common, at least in wartime propaganda, to describe the wounded as cheerfully or silently bearing their pain, their stoicism and courage redeeming the failings of military planning. But many men might have survived the Gallipoli campaign had they received earlier and better treatment for their wounds.[35]

By nightfall on 25 April the two divisional commanders, Bridges and Godley, feared that the landing near Gaba Tepe had failed. The Anzacs had only a precarious foothold on the first two ridges and, if the stragglers were anything to judge by, the troops were dangerously stressed. Almost certainly the Ottomans would attack again within the next 24 hours, with additional troops and artillery. Would it not be not more rational, then, to re-embark the landing force and avoid the humiliation of its being driven into the sea? The Anzac troops could then be consolidated with other Allied forces at Helles. Evacuation, of course, would be an admission of defeat and in retrospect, when the Anzacs had held on for many months, various commanders distanced themselves from any association with the idea. But late on the night of the first day, Godley and Bridges did urge Birdwood to re-embark, and Birdwood with considerable reluctance put this option to Hamilton, who had just arrived offshore on the *Queen Elizabeth* from Helles.[36]

Hamilton, woken from his sleep, decided that the Anzacs should stay. Given the number of troops ashore and the damage that had been done to the boats and lighters, there was no guarantee that re-embarkation would be feasible within a reasonable time. Moreover, some far more encouraging news had just come in, to the effect that the Australian submarine *AE2* had slipped through the Narrows into the Sea of Marmara and torpedoed an enemy gunboat there. This was a dramatic and high-risk operation. Submerged at a depth of 21 metres, the submarine had made its way at dead-slow speed through the minefield the Ottomans had laid at the Narrows. At times, its casing actually scraped against the mooring wires from the mines. Whenever it rose to periscope depth, it came under fire or was in danger of being rammed. Some days later, on 29–30 April, the *AE2* would sink and its crew would be taken prisoner, but for the moment its exploits energised Hamilton, who messaged Birdwood:

> Your news is indeed serious, but dig yourselves right in and stick it out. It would take at least two days to re-embark you . . . Make an appeal to your men to make the supreme effort to hold their ground. P.S. You have got through the difficult business, now you have only to dig, dig, dig until you are safe.[37]

In fact, the Anzacs had already begun to dig in, and as night fell they established the line that they would hold with only minor adjustments until December 1915 (see Map 2). This stretched from Brighton Beach in the south up Bolton's Ridge to 400 Plateau. Then it snaked along the second ridge to a series of precariously held positions named after various Anzac officers: Steel's, Courtney's, Quinn's and Pope's Hill. From Russell's Top on the first ridge, the Anzac line then turned to make its way down Walker's Ridge to the sea at North Beach. Importantly, the line was not continuous. Between Quinn's Post and Russell's Top there were critical gaps held by the enemy: places soon named the Chessboard, Dead Man's Ridge and the Nek. From these positions, the Ottomans could fire into the back of Quinn's, Pope's and Courtney's posts. They also controlled the dominating heights of Battleship Hill, Chunuk Bair, Hill Q and Hill 971. In the centre of the line, therefore, the critical Anzac positions—those heading Monash Valley, which provided the only line of communication to the beach—were almost untenable. They would be the focus of fierce fighting for many weeks.[38]

Holding this line for nearly eight months was a remarkable achievement—human, tactical and logistical—which explains some of the lasting hold of the Gallipoli campaign on the Australian imagination. But by failing to reach the heights of the Sari Bair range, the Anzacs had actually suffered a defeat from which they were never to recover. The landing had failed for a complex mix of reasons: the confusion about the landing site; the impromptu reorientation of the operation to the right by Sinclair-MacLagan; the impact of the scrub, hills and gullies on the cohesion, communication, discipline and

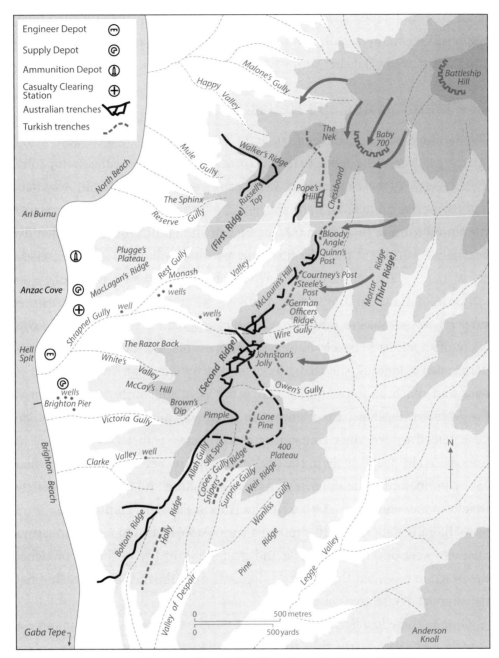

Map 2: The Anzac line, Gallipoli, at the end of 25 April 1915

effectiveness of the units as they pushed inland; the varying quality of the leadership at all levels; the failure to land field artillery; the resulting exposure of the troops to continuous and terrifying shrapnel fire; the slowness in landing reinforcements; and, perhaps most importantly, the effective enemy response. As many historians have commented, it was a wonder that the Anzacs achieved what they did.

The landings at Cape Helles

The landings at Cape Helles further to the south on 25 April were also a strategic failure, although here the outcome was not so immediately apparent. The objective of these operations was to capture the prominent hill Achi Baba and then drive on to Kilid Bahr plateau, above the Narrows. Aiming to upset the equilibrium of the Ottomans, the British and French forces landed at five beaches: V and W, at the very tip of the peninsula; X and Y, on the Aegean coast; and S beach, on the open Morto Bay just inside the Dardanelles.

Some of these landings were relatively successful, thanks to a mix of surprise, favourable terrain and valuable supporting fire from the Royal Navy offshore. At V beach, however, where an old fortress—Seddulbahir—dominated a landing site that was defended by Ottoman trenches, barbed wire and machine guns, the British plans went hideously wrong. Men of the Munster Fusiliers, the Hampshire Regiment and the Dublin Fusiliers were forced to exit their transport, the converted collier the *Clyde*, via an improvised bridge directly in the line of enemy fire. Few survived unscathed. Many jumped into the water trying to swim ashore and drowned under the weight of their full packs. Others of the Dublin Fusiliers, coming in on tows, were 'literally slaughtered like rats in a trap'. At W beach, too, the Lancashire Fusiliers were devastated by rifle and machine-gun fire as they approached the beach in tows, but they at least—in contrast to the men on V beach—had the support of effective naval fire.[39]

Despite these losses, and a collapse of morale that resulted in the force at Y Beach being withdrawn, the British managed to get a foothold on the tip of the peninsula. By 26 April they were unloading masses of stores, guns and horses at Helles. The Ottomans had withdrawn some 3 kilometres, and would face (as we now know) something of crisis of leadership during the subsequent weeks. On 27 April, the French force at Kum Kale, the 6th Colonial Regiment, which included Algerians, also joined the British on their side of the straits. It had soon been realised that they could continue their push on that side of the Dardanelles only at the expense of the main operation on the Gallipoli peninsula.

The following day, the British resumed their efforts to capture Achi Baba in what would become known as First Krithia. The attack was uncoordinated, demanded too much of the already exhausted troops and had to be halted by late afternoon. The struggle to capture Krithia would continue with great loss of life for many weeks, with further British offensives on 6–8 May (Second Krithia), 4 June (Third Krithia) and a final attack on 12–13 July. However, the chance of an Allied breakthrough at the base of the Gallipoli peninsula had really been lost within the first week of the campaign.

Consolidation and stalemate

On 26 April, Hamilton's decision to dig in at Anzac seemed to have been vindicated. That day the Ottomans launched only some disjointed attacks, not the major operation Godley and Bridges had feared. Although the British did not know it, Mustafa Kemal had his own problems of discipline and cohesion among the troops he commanded. But the respite was short and the hold of the Anzacs on the second ridge above Anzac Cove was still precarious. On 27 April, the Ottomans had stabilised enough to counter-attack and, despite being hungry, thirsty and sleep-deprived after two days in action, the Anzacs managed to hold their position. Then, on 1 May, the enemy forces attacked again, this time advancing at night to avoid the fire of the Royal Navy. Once more they failed to break the line, and for a time Esat Pasha, the commander of the Turkish III Corps, ruled out further attacks. By this stage, four battalions of the Royal Naval Division had been brought ashore as reinforcements for the Anzacs. Though Birdwood thought them 'nearly useless . . . immature boys with no proper training', they allowed the exhausted Anzacs to withdraw from the fighting line and rejoin their units, from which many had become separated in the chaos of the landing.[40]

On 2 May, Birdwood decided to try to improve the Anzacs' precarious position and ordered an attack on Baby 700 and the entire 400 Plateau.

It was an ambitious operation because it required two brigades—the Australian 4th and the New Zealand Infantry—to make their way up Shrapnel and Monash Valleys before they attacked from Quinn's Post and Pope's Hill. In the event, the 4th Brigade, supported by heavy bombardment from naval and land artillery, did manage to reach the area of Quinn's Post and then charged towards Baby 700, cheering. As Ellis Silas recorded:

> Up we rushed—God, it was frightful—the screams of the wounded, bursting of the shells, and the ear-splitting crackling of the rifles. In a very few minutes the gully at the foot of the hill was filled with dead and wounded—these poor lumps of clay had once been my comrades, men I had worked and smoked and laughed and joked with—oh God, the pity of it.[41]

However, the New Zealanders were delayed as they tried to push their way up valleys full of wounded men. They arrived at their point of attack 90 minutes late, by which time the Ottomans were expecting them. With no artillery cover, many New Zealanders were hit as soon as they stepped over the Anzac line. Two battalions of the Royal Marines were then pushed up to the heights—only to be thrown into confusion when hit by their own artillery firing from below. Almost nothing was gained by this operation, and the ground of the aptly named Dead Man's Ridge was soon strewn with corpses, which lay for days 'like ants shrivelled by a fire'.[42]

With the failure of this attack, Hamilton ordered the Anzacs to conduct only minor raids for the time being. These were intended not to break the stalemate now setting in above Anzac Cove, but rather to prevent the Ottomans from reinforcing Helles as the Allies made their second attempt to capture Krithia and Achi Baba in early May.

The New Zealand Infantry Brigade and the 2nd Australian Brigade were assigned a role in this disastrous operation. Re-embarking from Anzac Cove, they landed north of Helles to find a landscape of open and relatively flat grassland, a stark contrast to the impossibly difficult ridges, gullies and tangled shrubbery of the Anzac sector. However, this was no easier terrain on which to fight. When the attack on Krithia was launched on 6 May by British and French forces (the Australians were in reserve), the enemy machine guns and artillery inflicted terrible losses on the advancing infantry. Almost nothing was gained in the first two days of battle. However, the British commander, Hunter-Weston, insisted on continuing the attack—and in daylight, which was almost suicidal. He should have been overruled, but Hamilton refused to intervene at the operational level or to 'force the hand of an executive commander'.[43]

On the morning of 8 May, therefore, the New Zealanders and the French 2nd Division were sent into the battle, only to be stopped again by withering Ottoman fire. The New Zealand brigade commander, Colonel F.E. Johnston, thought that further attacks in daylight over open ground would destroy his brigade. But Hamilton still hoped for a breakthrough. At 4.00 p.m., therefore, the whole line, reinforced by the Australians, was ordered to storm Krithia and Achi Baba some 90 minutes later!

The men of the 2nd Brigade were eating their evening meal when they got the news at 4.55 p.m. They had no clear orders, no time to plan and little chance of succeeding. Bean, close to the front line, described them going on the attack, 'heads down, as if into fierce rain, some men holding their shovels before their faces like umbrellas in a thunderstorm'. Leading the brigade was their commander, McCay, who insisted on playing what he called the 'damned heroic act'. At one stage he stood on the exposed parapet of a British trench that the brigade had stumbled into, blowing his whistle and shouting, 'Now then, Australians! On, Australians!' Anyone who hesitated he threatened to shoot. Seeking to keep control of the operations, he continually pushed his headquarters forward, 'directing the men as if the air was full of blancmange instead of bullets'. As he wrote to his wife later: 'After a while you get fairly used to it, bullets included, and feel certain the enemy will not hit you.' So much for hubris! At 2 a.m. the following morning, a stray enemy bullet smashed McCay's leg.[44]

By daybreak, some Australians were within sight of the houses of Krithia, but it was obvious that the assault had failed. In less than 24 hours, the 2nd Brigade had suffered 1056 casualties, more than a third of its strength.

The New Zealand Brigade took 771 casualties from 2676 men. As on 25 April, the arrangements for evacuating the wounded were appalling. There were too few stretcher-bearers and only the herculean efforts of medical units in the darkness cleared the battlefield of most of the wounded before they were exposed to Ottoman fire at dawn. Even McCay took many hours to reach a hospital ship.[45]

Second Krithia was a souring experience for the troops involved. Although McCay had little choice but to follow Hamilton's orders on 8 May, he earned a reputation for being willing to sacrifice his men for personal advancement. Calling men cowards and threatening to shoot those lagging behind was not the way to lead the AIF. Hunter-Weston, in turn, was the popular caricature of a British general: vain, self-important and determined to keep attacking no matter what the cost. At Krithia, and later on the Western Front, he seemed detached from reality, lacking mental balance, 'given to extravagant and flamboyant gestures, far too interested in irrelevant detail, a romantic out of place in an industrial war'.[46]

The home front mobilises

The news of the landings at Gallipoli reached Australia on 8 May and electrified the home front. The first report came from a British journalist, Ellis Ashmead-Bartlett. Although he had not actually gone ashore with the Australian troops, Bartlett's account read as if he had. With all the seeming authority of an eyewitness, he wrote:

> The Australians rose to the occasion. They did not wait for orders or for the boats to reach the beach, but sprang into the sea, formed a sort of rough line, and rushed the enemy's trenches . . . Then this race of athletes proceeded to scale the cliff without responding to the enemy's fire. They lost some men, but didn't worry . . .
>
> The courage displayed by [the] wounded Australians will never be forgotten . . . Though many were shot to bits, their cheers resounded throughout the night . . . They were happy because they had been tried for the first time and had not been found wanting . . .

There has been no finer feat in this war that this sudden landing in the dark and the storming of the heights, and above all, the holding on whilst reinforcements were landing. These raw colonial troops in these desperate hours proved worthy to fight side by side with the heroes of Mons, the Aisne, Ypres, and Neuve Chapelle.[47]

Bean's report, which had been caught up in military red tape, followed a week later, on 15 May:

When all is said [he wrote], the feat which will go down in history is that first Sunday's fighting when three Australian Brigades stormed, in face of a heavy fire, tier after tier of cliffs and mountains . . . it is a feat which is fit to rank beside the battle of the heights of Abraham.

This, it seems, was what many Australians had been waiting to hear. It confirmed that Australian men, though reared in a young nation in the Antipodes, were as good as the fighting men of old Europe. Possibly they were even better! Bartlett's report was printed around the country under headlines such as 'Heroic Work, Holding Firm, Thrilling Narratives', 'How Australians Fight, "Extraordinarily Good Under Fire"' and 'Wonderful Dash and Bravery'.[48]

Across the nation, the news of Gallipoli was repeated at public meetings, in churches and schools. The Anglican Archbishop of Melbourne declared that 'no one doubted the spirit and courage of our men, but we waited with trembling hope in the confidence that they would not turn back on the day of battle'. A Melbourne Presbyterian, W. Borland, spoke of the landing as an event 'which nothing in the history of human bravery has surpassed'. Bartlett's despatch, all the more credible for having been written by an Englishman, was reprinted multiple times, included in fund-raising pamphlets, theatre playbills and educational materials. For school children, it was supplemented with Bean's report and an effusive tribute to the Anzacs by Ian Hamilton. It was the beginning of the process whereby the celebratory narrative later known as the Anzac 'myth' or 'legend' took hold of the Australian imagination and became the dominant national memory of World War I.[49]

Yet amid the jubilation at the AIF's feats, there was a more sobering message. Bartlett spoke of 'relentless and incessant shrapnel fire which swept every yard of ground'. Men who had pushed inland had retreated, 'after having suffered heavy losses'. Then, on 3 May, the first casualty lists were published. By that date, more than 1100 Australians had been killed or died of their wounds at Gallipoli. Families at home began to see a sight that would come to be dreaded: a clergyman at the door, bringing the news that a husband, brother or—more likely, since most men in the AIF were unmarried—a son had been killed. As a church newspaper said on 11 May:

There are sad hearts all over Australia this week. Australia is experiencing the baptism of blood. The cruel curse of war is finding us out, leaving homes desolate and hearts bereaved. There is no glamour in war for those who have to suffer or lay down their lives. It becomes a scourge, a desolation, an anathema.[50]

Letters, too, began to make their way home from Gallipoli, telling Australians—often in graphic detail—of death and injury. Charles Carthew wrote to his sister on 20 July 1915:

Did I tell you that Dr. Colin Campbell died, poor fellow—he had both legs blown off with a shell. We miss him sorely . . . We never undress and seldom take off our boots or equipment. Always ready you see. It tells on some of the fellows nerves.

Later Charles would write to his mother: 'You would hardly believe the wastage of war Mother. The last of my old Non Comms [non-commissioned officers] went away to hospital last night. Only two of them might come back.' A few months later, Charles' sister would receive another letter, from Arthur Gay:

Well I just moved sideways over the loophole [in the trench] until I could see out with one eye only, but that was enough—for then two or 3 bullets came throw [sic] the hole and got me in the top lip just under the nose and the bullet striking the top teeth broke up and travelled along the jaw and down the throat after shattering the lower jaw and cutting two arteries in my throat so you can see what a narrow escape I had.[51]

Then the wounded came home. The first shipload from Gallipoli arrived in Australia on 17 July 1915, carrying 56 wounded and another 242 sick and 103 with venereal disease. The VD patients were hurried away quietly, but the wounded rode in open cars and ambulances to Randwick hospital. Large crowds lined the streets of Sydney, waving banners honouring 'the wounded brave' and showering the procession with tributes and coins. Many of these men were visibly disfigured: injuries to the extremities accounted for nearly 65 per cent of all wounds sustained by the AIF in 1915. Some were wounded in the head, face and neck (nearly 18 per cent of wounds in 1915). These men did not have the neatly bandaged heads or the pristine white slings depicted in recruitment posters. If their injuries had been that slight, they would have been treated in Egypt and returned to battle. According to one estimate, during the war some 82 per cent of wounded British soldiers returned to duty after treatment, 64 per cent of them going back to the front line.[52]

Australians at home were no longer quarantined from the trauma of the war as it has sometimes been assumed they were: 'The men at the front might have been on another planet as far as the Australian people were concerned,' one historian later claimed. But the personal emotional impact of the mass casualties must have been profound. Perhaps it seems otherwise because the social conventions of the day demanded that the bereaved accept their losses quietly and stoically. In contrast to the 'confessional culture' of the twenty-first century, where private emotions are almost expected to be publicly displayed, grief during World War I was a private matter. Whatever the individuals' anguish, it was masked in the public language of duty, heroism and sacrifice for nation, empire, God and civilisation. When Charles Carthew was killed a few weeks after writing from Gallipoli, for example, a relative wrote to his mother: 'Poor chap, he died the bravest of all deaths fighting for his King, Country and all of us at home . . . All has happened for the best you may depend. It was his turn and the Almighty took him.'

One of the men Charles had commanded concluded his letter of condolence to the family: 'Hoping that knowing that he died in a good cause will help ease the pain of grief.' A friend, meanwhile, wrote to Charles' mother:

> It was with deep sorrow that I heard of the great loss of your noble, loyal soldier son. Try to feel that it is for the best and trust in God—He will never leave thee nor forsake thee . . . If you could only see some of the poor boys who have come back without some of their limbs, you would feel that your loved one is better off.[53]

The patriotic funds

The reaction to Gallipoli included a realisation that a more systematic mobilisation of the home front was needed. Not only would more volunteers be required to replace the losses, but the badly wounded would need medical care, and employment and financial support to help them reintegrate into Australian society. Families, particularly those of the men killed in action, would need pensions and other social services—all this at a time when the cost of maintaining the AIF was escalating well beyond that envisaged when the first offer of troops had been made in August 1914.

The Australian state was not well equipped to meet these challenges in 1915. Despite some reforms in the pre-war era, the range of social services provided by the federal and state governments was limited. In past wars, moreover, much of the responsibility for caring for the victims of war and their families had been carried not by the state but by private charities. Hence, as the federal and state governments struggled to put in place the necessary policies and institutional framework, they relied to a degree that seems remarkable—even to a generation schooled in the virtues of small government—on a volunteer mobilisation in the form of the patriotic funds movement.

This mobilisation began almost at the start of the war. On 13 August 1914, the wife of the governor-general, Lady Helen Munro Ferguson, established a branch of the British Red Cross in Australia. An indomitable woman driven by a strong sense of imperial patriotism and noblesse oblige, Lady Helen travelled the country, stirring into action virtual armies of patriotic volunteers. By 1918 there would be 2200 Red Cross branches across the country involving 82,000 women and 20,000 men and boys. In contrast, there were 55,164 women in paid employment in 1917. This massive effort of 'Red Crossing' soon generated mountains of goods, some of which filled the ballroom of Government House, Melbourne. These included 'comforts' for the troops, medical appliances, kitchen equipment, clothing, recreational equipment and many other items. Ultimately, the Australian Red Cross would send nearly 400,000 Red Cross parcels to Germany, Holland, Austria and Switzerland, including some 320,389 pyjamas, 457,311 shirts, 130,842 pairs of underpants, 1,163,049 pairs of socks, 142,708 mufflers, 83,047 pairs of mittens and 3000 cases of 'prepared old linen' for surgical dressings and bandages. To the Western Front, it would send 10,500,000 cigarettes, 241,232 ounces of tobacco, 94,007 toothbrushes, 57,691 pipes, more than 65,000 tins of cocoa-and-milk and coffee-and-milk, and even 869 Primus stoves.[54]

The Red Cross was soon joined by a plethora of other patriotic fundraising organisations, most of them staffed by middle-class women volunteers and led by members of local political and social elites. To name only some, they included the Lady Mayoress's Patriotic League (Victoria), the Citizens' War Chest (NSW), the League of Loyal Women (South Australia), the Queensland Patriotic Fund, the 'On Active Service' Fund (Tasmania), the Victorian League of Western Australia, and the Belgian Relief Committees. By 1916, many of these organisations were consolidated into the Australian Comforts Fund. Endlessly inventive in finding ways to raise money, these patriotic volunteers organised parades, crammed public spaces with market stalls and staged theatrical events, including tableaus—a now blessedly defunct cultural form that saw costumed women and children posing as a famous painting or mimicking imperial icons such as Britannia. Cooking recipes were collated and sold, books donated for libraries at the front and more than 1.35 million pairs of socks knitted. Michael McKernan has calculated that some ten million 'woman hours' went into knitting. They were children hours too. My father, Clifford, only eight years old in 1915, prided himself

Women volunteers at Government House, Melbourne, 1916, the location of the Victorian headquarters of the Red Cross for some of the war years. (AWM J00346)

Some of the many thousands of children mobilised to support the war effort through knitting socks for the troops at the front. (AWM H11581)

The extraordinary reach of the Comforts Funds is evident in this photo taken in the Somme region during the harsh winter of 1916. (AWM E00034)

Among the many inventive ideas for encouraging donations to public war loans was this replica destroyer, complete with real gun, in Martin Place, Sydney. (AWM H15959)

Allied propaganda played heavily on German atrocities in Belgium. In this case the reference is to the German execution in October 1915 of the British nurse Edith Cavell for helping captured Allied soldiers to escape from Belgium. (AWM ARTV00002)

This poster, drawn by Norman Lindsay for the last major recruiting campaign in 1918, is of a piece with the cartoons crudely vilifying 'the Hun' that the artist drew for the Sydney *Bulletin* throughout the war. The poster provoked some protest in parliament, and the Minister for Recruiting, R.B. Orchard, considered withdrawing it in October 1918. (AWM ARTV00078)

until his death in 1991 on his ability to 'turn the corner' of a heel in a knitted sock.[55]

The work of this army of volunteers was not confined to Australia. The Red Cross followed the men of the AIF to many battlefronts and bases behind the lines. First, in Cairo the Wimbledon champion Norman Brookes, rejected for military service on medical grounds, found an outlet for his patriotism as Commissioner of the Australian Branch of the British Red Cross in Egypt (a post he held from August until late 1916; in May 1917 he went to Meso-potamia). Brookes was soon joined in Egypt by Vera Deakin, the energetic youngest daughter of the former Prime Minister Alfred Deakin, who formed the Australian Wounded and Missing Inquiry Bureau in October 1915 to meet the demands of anxious families for news about their missing men. When the AIF moved to France, the bureau shifted to London. There it despatched a remarkable 25,000 answers to enquiries from AIF families in one year alone. One of Deakin's co-workers, the indomitable Mary Chomley, meanwhile ran the Prisoners of War branch of the Australian Red Cross with similar passion and efficiency from 1916 to 1919.[56]

The patriotic fund movement was a remarkable industry in its own right. Yet it is now largely forgotten. There are a number of possible reasons for this. In the first instance, the very success of the patriotic funds in attracting more women than those in paid employment reflected the fact—troubling to later generations of feminists—that World War I did not transform prevailing ideas about femininity in Australia. Rather, traditional gender stereotypes were, if anything, reinforced by the war—that is, Australian men were expected to fight while women remained at home, 'waiting and weeping' and 'keeping the home fires burning'. Whereas in Britain the war offered women new employment opportunities, in Australia women generally did not replace men in factories, transport and public administration—though there was some shift of female workers from domestic work to industrial employment, office work and jobs in sectors such as banking, insurance and the public service. By one estimate, the percentage of women in paid employment in Australia actually declined between 1911 and 1921, from 28.5 to 26.7 per cent.[57]

Moreover, volunteer work in the patriotic funds was seen by some women then—and later—as a poor substitute for working in 'the real war' with the Australian defence forces. Many patriotic women in fact tried to do more practical work, be it as cooks, ambulance scouts, stretcher-bearers, drivers, interpreters or farm workers. In September 1914, a group of Sydney women formed the Australian Lady Volunteers for home defence, aspiring to become 'real rifle women and real soldiers'. In July 1915, some 1500 women representing at least 42 women's organisations met at the Melbourne Town Hall and urged the federal government to open bureaus where women could register for service to the empire. However, ultimately it was only nursing—a profession that affirmed the traditional role of women as nurturers and carers—that Australian authorities deemed acceptable. By 1917, some 1757 nurses had been accepted into the Australian Army Nursing Service (AANS). Women doctors, on the other hand, were not admitted to the Australian Army Medical Corps— supposedly because they might not be able to cope with the conditions at the front and men might refuse to work with them. As a consequence, female doctors and other Australian women who wanted to play a more direct role in the war had to make their way to the United Kingdom at their own expense, joining organisations such as the Scottish Women's Hospitals. Those who stayed at home had little outlet for their patriotic energies other than volunteer work.[58]

Feminists, therefore, tend to see World War I as a lost opportunity. Even though the women who threw themselves into voluntary work might be deemed 'patriotic feminists'—in that they gained more independent agency, a higher public profile and new organisational skills through their ceaseless voluntary labour—they did not challenge traditional gendered roles. Even as they provided most of the labour for voluntary associations, they continued to accept patriarchy and defer to male leaders.[59]

Even more significantly, the values that these middle-class women espoused were not those of later generations. Rather, they spoke the language of imperial loyalty and militarism, and supported with a growing passion the official efforts to persuade more men to enlist. So too, for that matter, did the Red Cross, which so many of these patriotic women staffed. As Peter Cochrane has said:

> The Red Cross Society was represented at recruiting rallies, and its symbols—the cross, the nurse, the wounded soldier—were prominent in recruitment propaganda . . . The red cross symbol united the military and civilian spheres of mobilisation . . . [it] stood for the salvation of the Australian soldier and figured prominently in the idea of national salvation; it signified the enlistment of the citizenry in the battle.[60]

In effect, charity became 'militarised' during World War I, not only in Australia but in all the nations that took part. For all its humanitarian and internationalist motives, the Red Cross was appropriated for the cause of nationalism. Ironically, its volunteers actually aided the work of killing by relieving national governments of many of their obligations to provide for their citizens. As John Hutchinson has said of the Red Cross movement in Europe:

> Florence Nightingale, had she lived long enough, would doubtless have been appalled to see how much of the burden of war governments gladly transferred to the willing shoulders of Red Cross societies and how readily their citizens provided the funds that made such a transfer possible.[61]

Funding the war

Significant though the Australian patriotic funds were in providing support for soldiers and their families, the Australian government had no choice but to assume the leading role in recruiting and in funding the AIF. Initially the Fisher government had hoped to finance its wartime obligations exclusively through revenue. However, by mid-1915 this was obviously unrealistic. War expenditure in 1914–15 was almost 25 per cent higher than projected revenue. Taxation could not fully bridge the yawning deficit, given the federal government's limited taxation powers. Hence the Commonwealth had to turn to alternative sources of funding, including war loans from the British government and funds raised on the London money market. The problem was that, although the British government was willing to assist Australia in financing war expenditure, it objected to funds being raised for capital works. How, it asked, could Australia expect to raise an army by voluntary means if millions were being spent upon public works that provided attractive employment options for the very men whom the Empire needed to enlist?

This conundrum was not simply one facing the federal government, which had major capital projects that it wanted to complete—including the trans-continental railway begun in 1912 and other local defence initiatives. The state governments were also borrowers of overseas capital. For electoral reasons, they did not want to reduce expenditure or delay capital works that would alleviate unemployment and stimulate their local economies. In Queensland, for instance, a new Labor government under T.J. Ryan came to power in May 1915 with plans for 'government intervention in the economy on a scale which had not previously been seen, and which (except for the years of World War II) has not since been equalled'. Not only did Ryan aim for political reform—granting women the right to stand for parliament and abolishing the Queensland Legis-lative Council (a shibboleth of the radical left)—he aspired to create state insurance, banking and business enterprises to compete with private industry and to establish price controls in the sugar industry.[62]

The conundrum was partially resolved when, in March 1915, the British agreed to allow the Dominions to borrow on the open market such sums as were needed to complete works under construction, though not to start new capital works. The federal government also, in late 1915, managed to persuade the state governments—with the exception of New South Wales—to channel all overseas public borrowing through the Commonwealth for a period of two years. Yet state indebtedness increased significantly during the war years, while the cost of war to the federal government exploded to nearly £377 million by 1919–20.[63]

In July 1915, therefore, the government turned to the people's patriotism and launched the first of what would be seven war loans from the public.

Given the many competing demands for their money, Australians were bombarded with ever more inventive exhortations to subscribe. Posters and slogans festooned public places, banks provided advances to depositors willing to subscribe to the loans, and public 'barometers' monitored the level of subscriptions and the amounts still to be raised. In the later years of the war, the new military technologies added extra punch to the war loans campaigns: a British tank lumbered along city streets while planes swooped scattering pamphlets. Ultimately, all war loans were over-subscribed and some £250.2 million was raised via this means. For the seventh loan, practically one in every four households contributed. A further £7.4 million was raised from war savings certificates issued in 1917. As the Governor of the Commonwealth Bank saw it, this was 'a stupendous achievement for Australian patriotism'.[64]

Recruitment

The question of recruitment was to prove far more intractable, and would soon shatter the initial political consensus about the war. Prior to Gallipoli, Fisher had been reluctant to promote recruitment aggressively. This was not simply because the initial surge of recruits in 1914 seemed to make it un-necessary: he feared that the public acceptance of the principle of voluntarism might be strained if the government was too interventionist. Fisher also hoped to keep the costs of the war under control, allowing his government to fund its agenda of domestic reforms and local defence. Hence the budget his government brought down in December 1914 allowed for only 42,000 troops overseas by the end of June 1915. This caution about recruitment, it must be said, was not shared by Hughes, nor by Munro Ferguson, who kept cabling London to the effect that Australia could supply more recruits than it had done thus far. Under pressure to do more, Fisher agreed in early January 1915 to offer London an additional 10,000 troops. But again it seemed that the government could achieve this target without undue persuasion, since over 33,000 men volunteered in the first four months of 1915.[65]

Gallipoli, however, made this relatively low-key approach by the federal government redundant. The patriotic fervour generated by the reporting of

the landings meant that some 10,526 men volunteered—seemingly spontaneously—across the country in May, while from June onwards the state
governments launched formal recruitment campaigns. The first was in
Victoria, where patriots were stung by the fact that their state had contributed
only 1735 recruits to the national total in May. In June, the authorities opened
a recruiting depot in the Melbourne Town Hall with opening hours extended
until 10 p.m. The streets outside were patrolled by patriotic women handing
out refreshments while soldiers in uniform moved among the crowds. A
specially illuminated tram rode through the city complete with a brass band
playing patriotic songs, a tableau displaying Britannia with her sea and land
forces, and John Bull and his bulldog in the driver's seat. The railway stations
in Melbourne and provincial towns were plastered with posters. 'Will they
never come?' one asked. 'Enlist now!' urged the dials of town clocks.

The churches soon came on side. The *Australian Baptist* ran an editorial on
29 June titled 'Every Man Wanted!' Invoking the sacrifice of Isaac by Abraham
and of Christ for sinners, it wrote:

> It is a challenge to the physically fit in Australia who are capable of
> bearing arms, but who hitherto have either not heard the call or have
> passed it by unheeded, to present themselves, a willing sacrifice on the
> altar of their Empire's needs. It is their reasonable service. They owe it to
> the Motherland; to the nations who are linked with her in this life and
> death struggle for liberty and humanity; to the men who have already
> given their lives.

Not be outdone, New South Wales launched its own campaign. The Labor
premier, William Holman, took the lead, announcing on 2 July:

> This is not a war for Empire, for territory, or for power. The nations
> of Western Europe are like honest men who want nothing except to
> live at peace with each other and the rest of the world. It is with the
> disturbers of peace, the public robbers, the criminal nations of Europe
> that they are now at war. It is to root out this nest of criminality that you
> are called.[66]

By late July there were some 270 recruiting associations across New South Wales, and the political and religious leadership of the state and country had come out in full force. At a 'Call to Arms' meeting in Sydney on 31 July, the stage was graced with the governor, the premier, the prime minister, the lieutenant-governor, the leader of the federal opposition, the Anglican and Catholic archbishops, the state commandant and an academic professor. The meeting resolved that 'every physically-fit man, of military age, unencumbered by family ties and not directly engaged in the production of warlike supplies, should offer himself for service' in the Australian Imperial Force. However, it was a sign of the dissension to come that when Holman and the leader of the opposition spoke at another rally at the Sydney stadium they were counted out by a dissident element in the crowd. As *The Worker* reported:

> Hooting started from the back benches. It rose to a roar, and then the dissenters started to count the Premier out . . . A counter demonstration soon started from those near the ringside, but it was soon overpowered by the volume of noise from the back. A soldier with an arm bandaged stepped forward and asked the crowd for fairplay. He was cheered, but when he stopped and the Premier once more made an effort to speak the demonstration again started.[67]

In rural districts, meanwhile, enterprising patriots launched their own recruiting drives. One of the more successful, which would be repeated many times in New South Wales and to a lesser extent in other states, was a march of volunteers from country to city. With names invoking the Australian bush—Coo-ees, Waratahs, Kookaburras, Wallabies, Central West Boomerangs, Kangaroos, Men from Snowy River and Dungarees—these marches made their way from town to town, accumulating volunteers en route in a snowball effect.

Successful though many of these initiatives were, it was obvious that there was a need for national coordination to maximise impact and eliminate duplication. Some also thought it was time to introduce a more unified national leadership of the war effort. In the United Kingdom, Prime Minister Asquith had been forced to form a coalition in May by scandals associated with the shortage of shells on the Western Front. Was not bipartisan cooperation also desirable in Australia? Hence, in July, the federal government established a Federal Parliamentary War Committee (FPWC) with members from all the major political parties. The Minister for Defence, George Foster Pearce, was appointed to the chair, while Irvine—no longer in government but a committed advocate of military conscription and nicknamed 'Iceberg Irvine' by the left-wing press for his efforts—was an active member. A primary role of the FPWC, and the network of War Councils it established in each state, was to coordinate recruitment efforts, but the FPWC was also assigned the role of integrating Commonwealth and state government initiatives to provide employment, medical care and land settlement schemes for returning soldiers. Not only were these needed on humanitarian and political grounds, since veterans were already causing disruption on the streets of Australian cities, but they were assumed to be an integral part of effective recruitment strategies. How could men be persuaded to volunteer if they feared that they and their families might be left destitute in the event of their death or injury?[68]

We do not know how effective such schemes were in inducing men to volunteer. The recruiting campaigns at this stage of the war had to appeal to a mix of motives: duty, honour, loyalty to empire, hatred of Germany, patriotism and the need to replace the men lost at Gallipoli. Symptomatic of the mix was a feature film released to great acclaim in Melbourne in mid-July, *The Heroes of the Dardanelles*. Advertised as celebrating the 'imperishable glory' won by the gallant Australians at Gallipoli, 'most graphically and faithfully portrayed in accordance with Ashmead-Bartlett's historic dispatch', it depicted the hero, Will, rushing ashore (on what was in fact a Sydney beach) with the landing forces (very few of whom seemed to fall). Later in the action, Will was wounded while drowning—yes, drowning—'a Red-Cross sniping Turk'! But if its authenticity was suspect, the film's message was clear. Returning to Australia to claim the 'soldier's reward'—marriage to the girl who had waited faithfully for him—Will had 'done his duty'. 'Will you do yours?'

To give such messages enhanced emotional power, the recruiting campaigns openly exploited returned soldiers. In what has been called 'the cult of the wounded', these men became emblematic of 'the glory of wounds . . . incurred in their country's cause', as the Melbourne *Argus* put it. The press regularly featured images of bandaged men and their carers, while wounded soldiers—presumably with their consent—were paraded on public recruiting platforms. As a headline in the Sydney *Sunday Times* said on 7 July 1915, 'Our Stricken Heroes Return Bringing Their Wounds and Messages—For More Men'. One press photo depicted a soldier with a bandaged head shaking the hand of a young man in a departing railway carriage; the caption read, 'Going to Take His Place at the Front'.[69]

To this message was added the ever more powerful case that the cause for which Australians were fighting was indeed just. In the first half of 1915, the Germans had resorted to two new forms of indiscriminate warfare. The first was poison gas, introduced to the Western Front in the Second Battle of Ypres. Although the Allies too would later use this cruel weapon, the fact that Germany had initiated its use was seen as confirming their intrinsic barbarity. So too was the decision by the Germans early in 1915 to embark on a campaign of unrestricted submarine warfare. Aiming to strangle British global trade and break the Royal Navy's blockade of Germany, U-boats started sinking any shipping found in the waters around Britain and Ireland. Whether they were enemy or neutral, or carrying contraband of war or commercial cargo, was irrelevant. Almost inevitably, it was only a matter of months before a passenger liner, the *Lusitania*, was torpedoed off the coast of Ireland on 7 May 1915. Nearly 1200 passengers were lost, all of them civilians. Although the *Lusitania* was probably carrying contraband, its sinking was seen at the time as 'a cold-blooded and premeditated outrage'—yet another German atrocity. As a patriotic Australian wrote on 14 May:

> Would you have us fight with your own vile tools?
> If we've no choice we must do the same,
> But we don't sink boats with civilian crews;
> We leave that to you—'tis a coward's game.[70]

Further cause for anti-German outrage was provided by the release in May 1915 of a British report citing graphic (if sometimes exaggerated) evidence of more war crimes in Belgium. Among the depositions from Belgian refugees was one that read:

I saw eight German soldiers, and they were drunk. They were singing and making a lot of noise and dancing about. As the German soldiers came along the street I saw a small child . . . about two years of age . . . [one soldier] stepped aside and drove his bayonet with both hands into the child's stomach lifting the child into the air on his bayonet and carrying it away on his bayonet, he and his comrades still singing.[71]

Fuelled by such stories, anti-German sentiment escalated into a 'fully sustained, vitriolic crusade'. Not only did it form a recurring theme in recruitment campaigns, but labour unions ordered their members to refuse to work with employees of German extraction. German clubs were closed down, while new regulations of the *War Precautions Act* extended the powers of internment and banned German-language newspapers. Even the teaching of German in schools was prohibited on the grounds that it might train students 'intellectually, if not physically for service in the German army'. Perhaps most bizarrely, English patients in a leprosy hospital complained about having to mix with German lepers![72]

In this emotionally charged environment, some 36,575 men chose to enlist in July. The national total would prove the highest of any month of the war. Victoria's contribution—at 21,608—was more than six times the number who volunteered in May.

Among those who enlisted in South Australia was Alec Raws, the son of the minister of Flinders Street Baptist Church—the same one that Joe Russell attended. He explained his motives to his father on 12 July 1915:

My decision has not been sudden. My mind has been practically made up for a month or so . . . I must ask you not to worry, but rather to be proud that I, your son, am prepared to abandon all my comforts, all my life, all of everything, to fight for principles which, I hold, mean everything to the modern world; and also—to look at it from another angle, apart altogether from patriotism—to go out to my friends and pals—to the other fellows of Australia, to my brother already there—to help them in a business of life and death in which they are hard pressed . . . I do not think I was ever a great man for heroics, but I do believe that there are some things worth more than life. I curse the systems of governments, the hideous fraud of a civilisation, which permits this dreadful welter of blood and suffering to have enveloped the world in modern times. And yet I go to join it, believing that the only hope for the salvation of the world is a speedy victory for the Allies . . . I [claim] no great patriotism. No government, other than the most utterly democratic, is worth fighting for. But there are principles, and there are women, and there are standards of decency, that are worth shedding one's blood for, surely . . . Death does not matter.[73]

Raws was only one highly articulate individual, but—given the mood in mid-1915—it seems likely that he spoke for more than himself. His mix of emotions—obligation, identification with the men at the front and dismay at the war and the systems that caused it—throws some light on that 'mystery of second acceptance' that led men to volunteer when all illusions about the nature of the war had been dispelled.

The Ottoman attack

The situation at Gallipoli, meanwhile, had settled into stalemate. Within days of the landing, it was clear that a general offensive in the Anzac sector was beyond the Allies' capacity for a time. Yet Birdwood and Godley insisted on 'some offensive enterprise', particularly in the form of raids around Quinn's Post, the key to the Anzac line, where the Anzac hold was so precarious. On the night of 9 May, the 15th Battalion and a company from each of the 16th and 13th Battalions (4th Brigade) were ordered to attack across the short distance separating them from the Ottoman lines. Initially, they managed to break into the enemy trenches, but the predictable counter-attack soon came. Under a shower of enfilading fire and bombs, the Australians were pushed back along the trenches they had seized, over No Man's Land and back down a narrow communication trench they had dug to join their two lines. If anything, the raid worsened the Australian position at Quinn's and survivors were bitter about what they had been asked to do at such a cost of lives.[74]

Birdwood persisted. He shipped in reinforcements from Egypt: men of the Australian Light Horse and the New Zealand Mounted Rifles, without their horses, which were of no use at Anzac. Then on 15 May the 2nd Light Horse Regiment was set the hopeless task of filling the three saps between Quinn's and the Ottoman lines that had been left exposed by the earlier attack on 9 May. Under murderous fire from the German Officers' Trench and Baby 700, only fourteen of the 60 attackers returned unharmed. '[T]hey hadn't a Buckley's chance and knew it', one observer commented. The wounded lay in No Man's Land where the Turks shot them before they could be rescued.[75]

Gallipoli, like the Western Front, was proving that it was profoundly difficult to dislodge an enemy entrenched in well-developed defensive lines. This, however, was as much a problem for the Ottomans as for the Allies. When Enver Pasha, the Minister for War, decided to try to dislodge the Anzacs by launching a major offensive, this too failed with a huge loss of life. Following the most intensive bombardment since 25 April, the Ottoman infantry attacked at 3 a.m. on 19 May. All along the line, from Russell's Top in the north to Bolton's Ridge in the south, they moved up in slow waves, some soldiers silent, others chanting a rhythmic 'Allah! Allah'. Without cover, they were silhouetted against the rising sun. Bean recorded in his diary:

> The Turks did not seem well-trained. There was no attempt at covering fire, and so our men could sit right out on the traverses of the trench or even the parapet, and shoot for all they were worth. The Turks wd lead out all along the same path, one after another—simply inviting death.

As one Australian said, it was 'the best bit of sport [we] ever had . . . better than a wallaby drive'. J.M. Aitken wrote in his diary:

> Mother, it was pitiful to see it all, the Turks kept coming on & on, numbers of them together, & our orders were to allow them to come quite close before opening fire; they were simply mowed down & yet, in spite of the terrible slaughter, they still kept coming on until quite exhausted . . . I forgot to take cover, & did not notice the shrapnel while the blood-lust was on me, Mother. I'll admit a certain savage pleasure in firing to kill.

George Mitchell, on the other hand, confessed to feeling pity for his enemy: 'My rifle was in at the start blazing at those shadowy forms. "Oh you poor devils" was all I could say . . . It was a massacre.' By late morning the Ottomans had lost over 3000 dead and 7000 wounded. Only at Courtney's Post, a little to the south of Quinn's, did nine Turks manage to break through the Anzac line. But then Albert Jacka of the 14th Battalion jumped into the group, shot five of them, bayoneted two more and drove the others away. For this he earned Australia's first Victoria Cross of the war.[76]

When the Ottoman offensive finally stuttered to a halt, the ground between the trenches was so thickly strewn with bodies, and the health risk to both armies so great, that a truce was arranged to bury the dead. On 24 May the Ottoman and Anzac troops ventured curiously out from their trenches to meet in No Man's Land. Thomas Richards recalled:

> It was so strange to see a Turk and an Australian standing together on guard every 70 yards. They tried hard to exchange a few words of conversation too, but it was impossible . . . I helped to dig a few trenches but the smell was awful . . . The misery of war is brought home to one more vividly after a day like to-day. The Turk is a pretty game one to die in such numbers and in such a determined rush.[77]

During the truce, both sides surreptitiously surveyed each other's defences and the Australians took the opportunity to use enemy bodies to fill in the communication trenches that had been left exposed since the raid of 9 May.

After this, life above Anzac Cove settled into a period of relative quiet, except at Quinn's, where the pattern of raid and counter-raid continued. On 29 May, after exploding a huge mine in the early morning, the Ottomans almost captured this critical post, but the exhausted men of the 4th Brigade just held on. The following day, Godley ordered another raid—by a party from the 10th Light Horse—to show that 'the garrison still had the heart and capacity to inflict a blow in retaliation'. In June, two further sorties—intended partly to support the British, who were making yet another attempt to take Krithia in the south—were made by the New Zealand Brigade, which had replaced the exhausted Australians. Each of these raids involved elemental close combat and bombs being lobbed by hand from trenches that were only a few metres apart in places. Yet none of the raids achieved anything: 'Men get cut up and no apparent good comes of it,' one young officer commented. '[T]he men are getting pretty sick of these half-hearted side shows,' Bean conceded after the raid of 7–8 June.[78]

Life at Anzac

Yet it was the peculiarly intense quality of life at Quinn's and other posts along the Anzac line that gave Gallipoli much of its fascination, then and later. The most striking feature of the sector was its topography. One of Hamilton's staff, visiting on 24 May, wrote:

> The first impression from a boat is that of seeing the cave dwellings of a large and prosperous tribe of savages who live on the extremely steep slopes of broken sandy bluffs covered with scrub which go up from a very narrow sandy beach to a height of 300 feet . . . the place is in perpetual motion like an antheap of khaki ants.

As the months passed, the hills above Anzac Cove came to resemble 'a vast mining shantytown': 25,000 men were crammed into a complex network of trenches edged with sandbag parapets and dugouts that almost hung off the ridges. For much of the time, the men occupying these were bored, but they also lived with the constant danger of snipers, artillery fire or mines exploding in tunnels being excavated silently beneath them.[79]

Tunnelling became increasingly important as the trench lines at Anzac solidified and No Man's Land grew impossibly dangerous. Working in suffocating darkness, sappers pushed tunnels out towards the enemy lines, straining for sounds of the enemy nearby, ready perhaps to blow their own mines. Shellfire, too, would collapse tunnels, burying sappers alive. It took a particular temperament to do this work. Sergeant Cyril Lawrence of the Australian Engineers wrote on 22 July:

> Mind you, it is no pleasant sensation to feel the earth under, above and around you all of a shake, and a damn big shake too, not a mere earthquake, and then be plunged into darkness away out in a tunnel, but this is the third dose that I have had, and it did not even stop me finishing the cigarette that I was making.[80]

The logistics of maintaining the Anzac line were also a nightmare. Since the Ottomans held the higher ground and had positioned artillery at Gaba Tepe, access to Anzac Cove was restricted. Additional bases were developed at Brighton Beach and North Beach, and any space beyond the reach of enemy guns was soon crammed with ammunition, wireless stations, field ambulances, mules, donkeys, and the corps and divisional headquarters. From these beaches, everything needed by the troops above—guns and ammunition, rations and water—had to be carried via Shrapnel and Monash Valleys along narrow paths that were under constant fire. As Hamilton wrote on 3 June:

> you find notices stuck up warning you to keep to the right or left of the track. Extraordinary, one half of the road being comparatively safe, the other most dangerous. If the Turks were twenty yards nearer the edge of the cliff they would look right down into the valley.[81]

The problems of supplying the beachhead became even more difficult when, in late May, the Ottomans sank the British *Triumph* off Anzac and the *Majestic* off Helles. The Admiralty responded by withdrawing its capital battleships (including the super dreadnought *Queen Elizabeth*), cruisers and the transport fleet that had patrolled offshore.

The Anzac sector also had little natural water, although wells were dug in Shrapnel Valley. Additional water supplies had to be brought in by lighter from Alexandria, and rationed strictly. Orderlies carrying the 9-litre petrol tins up the line were often picked off by snipers, so men in the trenches—if they were lucky—received 4.5 litres a day. To wash themselves they had to bathe at the beach under enemy shellfire. Setting an example, Birdwood swam every night among the men, taking with good grace their advice to 'Duck, yer silly old fool' when the enemy artillery at Gaba Tepe lobbed shells into the sea. The food at Gallipoli meanwhile was monotonous and poor in nutritional value. There was no refrigeration and little in the way of fruit and vegetables. Hot meals became rare as the hills were stripped of firewood. Typically, the Anzac diet was tea, sugar, jam, hard biscuits, stew or heavily salted bully beef. Other food—potatoes, onions and cheese— went rancid and stank almost as badly as the rotting corpses, whose smell penetrated everything. As Cyril Lawrence said on 8 June, the food got 'absolutely unbearable'. Dental problems increased, with some 600 men evacuated for dental treatment in the 1st Division alone by the end of July.[82]

The health of Anzacs also deteriorated thanks to problems with sanitation and waste disposal. With so many men and animals in such a congested space, and the trench lines so close, refuse was buried rather than burned. But shellfire often unearthed it. Latrines, meanwhile, were partly uncovered and also exposed to enemy fire. At posts like Quinn's, where sniper fire was incessant, men used the trenches as toilets. Around them, bodies or body parts lay unburied, bloated, stinking and crawling with maggots. Due to lack of water, men also neglected to wash their 'dixies', or mess tins. To this noxious mix was added, as summer approached, the flies. By June and July 1915, gastric and intestinal infections had reached epidemic proportions. To quote the official historian of the medical services:

> The latrine poles were perpetually thronged by men, so that attempts
> at covering or disinfecting excreta became a farce. Black swarms of flies
> carried infection warm from the very bowel to the food as it passed the

lips; they contaminated the unwashed mess-tins . . . As the heat became greater and the flies and foci multiplied, intestinal disease became almost universal.[83]

By 30 July, at least 30 per cent of the force was estimated to be unfit and Howse himself had been evacuated to Cairo with acute gastroenteritis.

In addition to physical illnesses, the Anzacs grappled with range of psychological stresses—particularly the fear of a death that was often arbitrary and capricious. Cyril Lawrence wrote in his diary on 10 July:

> They were putting high explosive into us, and one shell hit just in front of his dugout and never went off. One of the boys in the dugout that appeared safer sang out, 'Come up here, you bloody fool Shep. You'll get your blasted head knocked off.' At this, and before the next shell, Sheppard bounded up to this man's dugout and got well into the corner. The very next shell hit the exact spot and blew his head off, whilst the man that called him in was not touched. And so it is in this war; some men just walk to their death. I have seen it time and time again.

The Anzacs made every effort to retrieve and bury the men who were killed, but snipers often made this impossible. Ellis Silas recalled on 2 May:

> One poor chap in a dug-out close to us was killed while preparing his meal; he has been lying there two days—his mess tin full of tea, the charred remains of the fire he was cooking by, a few biscuits scattered about, his pipe by his side—we cannot bury him on account of the snipers; it seems no place is safe from them.[84]

Many more bodies were never buried. Goldy Raws (Alec's brother), arriving at Gallipoli in September, wrote home:

> if I tell you that the smell is not so bad except when the Turks are bombing and the dead bodies round about 'get stirred a treat', and if I describe to you a particularly interesting feature just at the opening of my dug-out in the firing line which the men call 'The Lone Hand';

this is the complete hand, nails and shrunken skin of a dead Turk (the body of whom lies at the top) the hand lying open, the fingers slightly clenched as thrown out in a grasping fashion.

On 20 October he wrote again: 'I really sometimes get muddled up as to who is dead and who is alive . . . somebody says to you—"There's Col. White over there" (you are looking through a periscope of course)—well, it's not he at all—it's just what he was living in.'[85] For sappers, the encounters with the dead could be especially unnerving. As Lawrence wrote in his diary on 10–11 June:

After working for some time, managed to get through—Good God, the stink, I had been quite successful in poking my way up right under a dead body, probably—judging by the aroma—a big fat juicy Turk . . . There are hundreds of dead Turks buried just above where we are working . . . In the tunnels or saps we are constantly digging them up . . . They have a peculiar smell of oily fat flesh. Ugh.[86]

The suffering of the wounded also tormented those around them. Ellis Silas, while carrying a message to the rear during the attack on 3 May, was forced to pass through gullies 'choked with wounded':

the horrors of this night have been too much for me, I cannot get used to the frightful sights with which I am always surrounded. [Bodies were] hanging in all sorts of grotesque and apparently impossible attitudes . . . One poor fellow, a New Zealander came tearing past smothered with blood and quite delirious, kissing everyone he passed, upon whom he left splashes of blood.[87]

At Gallipoli there was little respite from these emotional and physical stresses. Although men were rotated between the front line and the support trenches, there was no systematic scheme of rest and recreation off the peninsula. At the end of June, some troops were given leave on the island of Imbros, but the scheme was halted when planning for a new offensive in August began. Not surprisingly, some men broke down. Silas admitted early in May:

I think I am about done—thank God men of my temperament are few and far between—I am quite satisfied that I'll never make a soldier—a thousand pities to have been born an artist at a time like this . . . I dread being asleep more than awake as my dreams are so frightful.

After the raid at Quinn's on 9 May, he wrote that he was 'Delirious again last night . . . I am taking morphine given me by the M.O.—I can now neither eat nor sleep.' On 16 May he was no better: 'I think if I am here much longer my reason will go—I do not seem able to get a grip of myself and feel utterly crushed and unmanned, though I shall try and stick it to the last.' A few days later, he was evacuated to Alexandria suffering from neurasthenia (shell shock) and enteric fever. Discharged as medically unfit in August 1916, he later painted evocative scenes of Gallipoli, including 'Roll Call', which depicted the survivors of the 16th Battalion after a Quinn's Post raid: 'Name after name would be called; the reply a deep silence.'[88]

One of the things that drove Silas and others like him to breaking point was the constant noise. 'The incessant cracking of thousands of rifles intermingled with the boom of the hand grenades and shrapnel, gets rather on one's nerves,' Captain Stanley Parkes noted in his diary on 5 June. After the Ottoman attack on 27 April, Captain James Durrant of the 13th Battalion wrote:

The noise was terrific—bullets always make a great noise passing over a valley but we found that each shell made a roar like an express train. Machine-guns made it worse, and the heavy shells from the ships worse still, and the echoes from the cliffs at the back of us redoubled it, until we were nearly driven mad by the racket . . . Noise is not supposed to hurt anyone but under those conditions the strain on our nerves was terrible.

Some succumbed to shell shock, though this condition was not yet understood. Thomas Richards recorded on 21 July:

At Dr. Butler's there was a fellow who complained several times of weak, nervous attacks but the doctor only grumbled and called him a shirker.

This evidently bothered the patient very much and it was a very unfair accusation also. The outcome was the fellow blowing his head off with his rifle to-day.[89]

However, the majority of men seem to have coped. In time, the violence of war became almost normalised. A New Zealand stretcher-bearer, James Jackson, wrote:

The old saying 'familiarity breeds contempt' is very true as regards shrapnel. When we landed the first two or three days if one landed 200 or 300 yards away we all ducked and hid ourselves but now we wait until they come close up and then we hide.

Others responded with black humour. Thomas Richards wrote on 2 May 1915:

A bullet dropped into the fire at which I was cooking the midday meal. It's truly wonderful how accustomed everyone gets to narrow escapes from bullets. A piece of shell landed 10 feet away to-day and the first remark was 'Who threw that tomato?'

The Australian men also gave nicknames to the enemy guns and made light of their vulnerability. Watching from the beach on 10 June, Lawrence saw:

one of the shells burst over a latrine up on the hillside. The men sit on this, which is just a beam supported at each end over a long hole, like a lot of sparrows on a perch . . . In the scatter that followed, none waited to even pull their trousers up. The roar of laughter that went up could have been heard for miles.[90]

Then there was mateship—the intense bonds that developed between soldiers as they lived, fought and survived together. These not only helped to maintain morale at Gallipoli, but also motivated men to go into combat when every instinct told them not to. As one Australian soldier, Archie Barwick, put it when caught in a hail of bullets on Gallipoli: 'I had a terrible fight with myself . . . one part of me wanted to run away & leave the rest of my mates to face it, & and the other part said no, we would stop & see it out at any cost.' Another private, F. Clune, writing in hospital at Malta on 20 August, said that when you 'think of your poor cobbers left behind in the trenches, perhaps not [eating] . . . or still worse lying wounded in some place and not able to get a drink . . . you say to yourself "I'll play the game, I'll go back and help the boys out".'[91]

In time, mateship would become a core element of the Anzac legend. In one of the most famous passages of his official history, Bean would write that the Australian soldier:

> was seldom religious in the sense in which the word is generally used. So far as he held a prevailing creed, it was a romantic one inherited from the gold-miner and the bush-man, of which the chief article was that a man should at all times and any cost stand by his mate. This was and is the one law which the good Australian must never break.

Then, when musing at the end of his volume on the Gallipoli campaign as to why it was that Australians held on to their precarious positions on the cliffs above Anzac Cove, Bean claimed that the answer

> lay in the mettle of the men themselves. To be the sort of man who would give way when his mates were trusting to his firmness; to be the sort of man who would fail when the line, the whole force, and the allied cause required his endurance; to have made it necessary for another unit to do his own unit's work; to live the rest of his life haunted by the knowledge that he had set his hand to a soldier's task and had lacked the grit to carry it through—that was the prospect which these men could not face. Life was very dear, but life was not worth living unless they could be true to their idea of Australian manhood.[92]

Yet whatever the power of mateship, it was not—as Bill Gammage has claimed—'a particular Australian virtue'. All armies, no matter what their societal origins and values, rely on small-group cohesion and the desire not to let down the group as the motivation for men to overcome their fears in battle. This may take different names—comradeship, buddy systems, brother-hood or mateship—but it is this informal source of discipline, as much as military sanctions, nationalism or even hatred of the enemy, that makes men go into action when they know that they risk death and injury.[93]

The resilience of the Anzac force at Gallipoli may also have owed something to the fact that the hardships of battle were relatively equitably shared across ranks. On the Western Front, it was the junior officers who suffered death and injury disproportionately. But in the cramped confines of the Anzac sector, the command headquarters were close to the front line and the 'privileges' of rank were few: a basic mess and a batman providing officers with 'breakfast in bed' in a primitive dugout. Moreover, the senior commanders were exposed to the risk of wounds and death. Birdwood was wounded in the head at Quinn's Post on 14 May when peering over the top of parapet through a periscope. Later his wound turned septic, and in December the bullet had to be removed. Then the commander of the 1st Australian Division, Harold Walker, was half-buried by a shell that burst in his dugout in September. A fortnight later, while inspecting a post on Silt Spur, he was severely wounded by machine-gun fire. McCay's leg injury from Second Krithia would linger throughout the war.[94]

Most dramatically, on 15 May 1915, Bridges was mortally wounded when he was hit by a sniper while crossing open land near Steel's Post. Both major blood vessels in his right thigh were severed. Although the quick intervention of a nearby medical officer stopped the rapid blood loss, the wound soon turned gangrenous. Bridges' age and condition made an amputation high on the thigh too risky, and he died on a hospital ship on 18 May. 'Anyway,' he said to those around him, 'I have commanded an Australian division for nine months.' Though he did not know it, he had been knighted that day on the recommendation of Birdwood, who, despite his annoyance at the risk Bridges had taken, urged Hamilton to recommend him for the honour.[95]

Bridges' replacement as commander of the 1st Division was Colonel James Gordon Legge, then the Chief of the General Staff in Australia. It was not a popular choice. McCay, Monash and Chauvel all saw their own ambitions thwarted, and resented the appointment of a man who had no experience at Gallipoli. Ultimately, Birdwood and Hamilton referred the matter to the

Secretary of State for War, Lord Kitchener. Legge, Birdwood argued, was 'a man of brilliant mentality' and 'probably the *cleverest* soldier in Australia', but he was regarded as 'political and a self-seeker . . . with a knack of quarrelling and writing'. Munro Ferguson also—typically—meddled in the matter. But Fisher and Pearce stuck to their decision. In the event, Legge served only a few weeks at Gallipoli. In June he was transferred to Egypt to take command of the newly formed 2nd Australian Division. The command of the 1st Division then went not to Monash or McCay, whose injured leg had snapped on 11 July, but to Walker, a British army officer, who had been Birdwood's chief of staff and had filled in at Gallipoli as commander of the New Zealand Infantry Brigade and the Australian 1st Infantry Brigade, and as acting commander of the 1st Division. At this time, too, Birdwood was given the additional role of General Officer Commanding AIF—that is, administrative control of the AIF, a position he would hold, despite the irrationality of this arrangement, until the end of the war.[96]

Planning to regain the initiative

While the news from Gallipoli inspired Australians to euphoria and greater efforts, in Britain it contributed to a political crisis for the Asquith government. Two other British offensives on the Western Front, at Neuve Chapelle and Aubers Ridge in early March and May 1915, had also failed dismally. As Gary Sheffield has described it, Aubers Ridge conformed to the popular stereotype of a World War I battle: 'soldiers [advancing] across No Man's Land only to be cut down by machine-gun fire; generals frustrated by the lack of progress ordering further fruitless attacks; minimal gains for huge losses'.[97]

These failures triggered the public scandal about the shortage of artillery shells on the Western Front that forced Asquith to form a new coalition with the conservatives. In the reshuffle that followed, Kitchener, whose performance was attracting some criticism, continued as Secretary of State for War, but munitions production was taken from him and placed under the control of the dynamic Lloyd George, who set about reorganising British industry to meet the insatiable demands of war.

In the midst of these changes, the future of the Gallipoli campaign was hotly debated. Churchill, who paid for his role in its planning by being demoted from the Admiralty to a junior ministry, continued to argue that Gallipoli offered the prospects of a 'brilliant and formidable victory'. Kitchener also thought that it was impossible to abandon the campaign. However, other politicians, such as Andrew Bonar Law, the Conservative leader and Secretary of State for the Colonies, were far more doubtful about the chances of success, while senior military officers—particularly General Douglas Haig, then commander of Britain's First Army, and Sir Henry Wilson, Chief Liaison Officer with the French Army—wanted 'to clear out of the place', allowing Britain to concentrate on the Western Front.

Eventually, the Dardanelles Committee, which had replaced the War Council as the Cabinet committee overseeing the conduct of the war, decided in early June to make another attempt at breaking the Gallipoli stalemate. Hamilton, who had asked for reinforcements on 17 May, would be sent three divisions of the New Army that Kitchener had raised from British volunteers. After further lobbying by Churchill, this offer was increased—a decision that seemed to be validated when a huge and successful Austro-German offensive against the Russians in mid-July appeared to threaten the latter's capacity to stay in the war. Once again, a rationale for Gallipoli was found in the need to support the Russians.[98]

The question now facing Hamilton and his commanders was how to use these new troops to regain the strategic initiative at Gallipoli. There were several options, including landing a force at Helles behind the Ottoman lines or continuing the warfare of attrition of May and June. The plan that was ultimately favoured had been in the minds of Allied commanders since May. Since there seemed to be few Ottoman troops north of the Anzac sector, the Allies would launch a bold flanking movement in the form of a sweeping hook from the northern edge of the Anzac battlefield to the heights of the Sari Bair range. With these peaks under their control, the Allies would then move east across the peninsula, cutting the Ottoman forces in half and destroying the Dardanelles forts and artillery that had blocked the passage of the Allied navies to Constantinople in March. For Hamilton, who was now ready to concede that a breakthrough at Krithia was not possible, this new offensive had the potential to make the Anzac sector 'the fulcrum for the lever which will topple Germany and the pride of the Germans'.[99]

The first phase of the offensive on which this great vista depended was ambitious (see Map 3). The forces responsible for capturing the heights would start their advance from sea level. First, a covering force consisting of the New Zealand Mounted Rifles, the Maori contingent and one of the New Army brigades would seize the foothills in the vicinity of Northern Beach. Then two assault columns drawn from the New Zealand & Australian Division, the British 13th New Army Division and the 29th Indian Army Brigade would pass through the covering force and move up the steep gullies, or deres, to the Sari Bair range. The left-hand column would advance via the Aghyl Dere and then attack Hill Q and Hill 971. The other column further south would approach the heights via Chailak Dere and Sazli Beit Dere before assaulting Chunuk Bair. All this would be completed at night, so that by dawn the assault forces were in their positions to attack the heights. To distract the Ottomans while this was happening, there would be a number of feints: at Helles, Lone Pine, the Nek, Pope's Hill and Quinn's Post. There would also be an amphibious landing by the British IX Corps at Suvla Bay, to the north of the Anzac area. What this last operation was meant to achieve has been a matter of continuing dispute.

In fact, the plan was too ambitious. Even though only 3000 enemy troops, or 2.5 per cent of the total Ottoman forces in the Dardanelles, were stationed north of Battleship Hill—and Esat Pasha, if not Mustafa Kemal, discounted the rumours of an attack because of the treacherous terrain in the deres—the operation was beyond the capacity of the Allies at this stage of the war. They lacked the tactical mobility, communication systems and logistical support to succeed in such a complex operation. Moreover, as events would show, the Allied troops were too ill and inexperienced to cope with the exceptionally difficult manoeuvres demanded of them. Nor were they familiar with the difficult terrain through which they would have to move.[100]

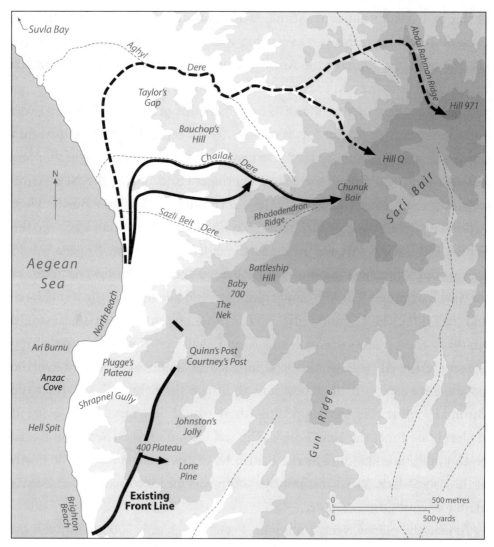

Map 3: The August offensive, Gallipoli

The August offensive

The assault on Chunuk Bair

The offensive began on the morning of 6 August, with a deluge of Allied artillery fire. A midshipman on a troopship passing Anzac on its way to Suvla Bay wrote:

> It was a remarkable sight from the sea. One large space of hillside lit up brilliantly by the destroyer searchlights and exploding shells and

star lights, at sea nothing to be seen except the numerous hospital ships anchored off Anzac with their band of red and green lights and yet the sea teamed [sic] with life.

On land, Cyril Lawrence recorded:

In less time than it takes to tell every one of our batteries was sending its screeching messages on to its target—field guns with their roar, howitzers with their mighty rushing sound and mountain battery guns with their bark, a bark too loud for a gun four times their size. The enemy were not behind in getting their guns busy and in no time the air was just a tumult of screech from flying shells, of banging explosions, the whine of flying nosecaps and fragments and the noise of empty shell cases travelling everywhere . . . the din was indescribable.[101]

As evening fell, men began to move all over the front. The covering force to the north performed its role brilliantly, thanks to good planning by its commanders Brigadier-Generals Andrew Russell and J.H. du B. Travers. By 1 a.m., they had achieved their objectives. As Bean later said—with a generosity to New Zealanders that Australians sometimes lack:

By this magnificent feat of arms, the brilliance of which was never surpassed, if indeed equalled, during the campaign, almost the entire Turkish defence north of Anzac was for the moment swept aside and the way cleared for the infantry to advance up the valleys to Chunuk Bair.[102]

However, the advance of the New Zealand Infantry Brigade towards Chunuk Bair did not proceed as smoothly. Divided into two groups, the column was slowed down by enemy resistance and growing congestion in Chailak and Sazli Beit Deres. By dawn, only one of the brigade's three battalions, the Wellingtons, had reached Rhododendron Ridge, the place where the two deres converged, and from which the attack on Chunuk Bair was meant to be launched. A second battalion, the Otagos, was still straggling behind, while a third, the Canterburys, had got lost. It had actually returned to its starting point on the beach where a furious Godley ordered it back up the valley.

The New Zealand 'advance' was not helped by the fact that its commander, Johnston, was by many accounts drunk and incoherent. Generally considered 'an absolutely terrible choice for a key commander in this offensive', he stalled on the morning of 7 August, waiting for his missing units and arguing with his officers. A 'priceless opportunity' to seize Chunuk Bair was lost when no more than 20 Ottoman infantry and an artillery battery were on the crest. However, they were soon to be reinforced from Mustafa Kemal's 19th Division.[103]

When the attack on Chunuk Bair began at 11 a.m.—Johnston having been ordered into action by Godley at the end of a field telephone line—the New Zealanders were cut to pieces. The Canterbury Battalion was so badly mauled that its commander, Lieutenant-Colonel J.G. Hughes, phoned his headquarters in tears, reportedly declaring that he was 'the most miserable man on earth'. For his part, the commander of the Wellington Infantry Battalion, Lieutenant-Colonel W.G. Malone, refused to continue the attack in daylight. Godley agreed with him.[104]

Reinforcements were rushed in, and the following morning at 4.45 a.m., a second attempt was made by a multinational force to take Chunuk Bair. This time the attacking force actually reached the crest that the Ottomans had abandoned under a deluge of Allied artillery fire. The Dardanelles were at last in sight, and the infantry dug in. Over the next two days, however, this vital high ground was lost. Caught in a nightmare of ferocious hand-to-hand fighting, enemy shellfire from Hill Q and Battleship Hill, and—almost as dangerous—their own artillery fire, the Allied units clinging to Chunuk Bair were progressively isolated. By the time the Wellingtons were relieved on 8 August, 690 of the 760 men who had attacked Chunuk Bair had become casualties. The survivors 'could only talk in whispers; their eyes were sunken; their knees trembled; some broke down and cried like children'.[105]

The assault on Chunuk Bair was foundering, thanks to failures in Allied leadership and planning. Godley, trying to manage the offensive from sea level, failed to keep a close grip on the battle. Johnston insisted on changing the route of Brigadier-General Anthony Baldwin's 38th Brigade, sending it along a ledge, the Farm, that was impossibly congested with wounded and reinforcements. The troops in advanced positions were running out of food and water.

Finally, at dawn on 10 August, Mustafa Kemal threw his last reserves into the attack. A terrifying mass of men in grey in the dawn, they surged over the crest of Chunuk Bair with their rifles and bayonets drawn. The Allied forces were engulfed, some as they slept exhausted by their piles of arms. Others panicked. For a moment it seemed that the whole line might collapse back down the valleys. But with the officers threatening to turn their guns on their men if they gave way, the Anzac line was eventually consolidated at Rhododendron Ridge. The Ottomans, however, had recaptured Chunuk Bair. They would never lose it again.

So defining was this moment in the Gallipoli campaign that Chunuk Bair became etched in the national memory of New Zealand and Turkey. Returning to bury their dead after the war ended, the New Zealanders erected a towering pylon on the peak in 1925. Its inscription invoked the memory of the men who had come 'From the Uttermost Ends of the Earth' to die at this place. Nearby, a second memorial was erected to commemorate the missing New Zealand soldiers—more than 800 of them. For years these memorials dominated the landscape. Then the Turks, seeking to reclaim Gallipoli as part of their national memory of the war, installed a large statue of Mustafa Kemal (Atatürk) next to the New Zealand pylon. The New Zealand government demurred, but the national memorials now stand only metres apart, recasting the physical battle for this peak in 1915 as a contest over 'commemorative space'.[106]

The assault on Hill Q and Hill 971

The second assault column in the August offensive also failed to capture its objectives. The task set for Monash's 4th Brigade and the 29th Indian Army Brigade—that is, advancing up Aghyl Dere to capture Hill Q and Hill 971—was impossible. The route they took on the night of 6 August was almost twice as long as that of Johnston's column, and the terrain facing them was terrible. The dere was full of boulders, the scrub was so thick it had to be hacked away, and the passages so narrow that men at times could move only in single file. There were no maps, no aerial reconnaissance—only advice from local Greek guides, who led the column along an almost impassable route. To add to this, it was dark and there were constant attacks from enemy snipers. Captain H.V. Howe, who covered the ground in 1919, concluded that 'only complete idiots could have expected it to be carried by infantry assault'.[107]

Many of the infantry were in no state to cope with this task. After months of sitting inactive in their dugouts, they had no experience in tactical manoeuvre in difficult country. Many were malnourished, racked with gastric complaints, dysentery, bronchial infections and even heart dilation. As the night wore on, the march slowed to a shuffle. A concertina effect set in, cohesion was lost and men fell asleep where they stopped. Officers, too, became disoriented. Monash, a not-so-slim 50-year-old, rushed along the column, trying to impose some order and sense of direction. But at sunrise on 7 August, his force was literally lost.

Monash and his superiors thought they had reached Abdel Rahman ridge, a long spur leading to their goal of Hill 971, but this ridge was still a valley away. Between them lay even more precipitous and overgrown terrain. Too tired to proceed, the 4th Brigade spent the whole of 7 August resting, reorganising and calling up reserves. When they finally attempted to move forward, they met such heavy machine-gun fire from the Ottoman troops on Abdel Rahman ridge that they retreated in a shambles. Sergeant Tom Smith of the 14th Battalion recalled that 'a mournful procession' limped back, 'played out, carrying and helping along the wounded, our dead left behind and in a great many cases some of the severely wounded left behind too'.[108]

With Hill 971 now beyond their reach, the 6th Gurkhas and some of the 8th Warwickshire Battalion made a dash at dawn on 9 August for Hill Q, closer to Chunuk Bair. Hoping to converge with Baldwin's 38th Brigade coming from the right, they managed to reach a saddle between Hill Q and Chunuk Bair. There, as the commander of the Gurkhas, Major C.J.L. Allanson, later recalled:

> we met the Turks; Le Marchand [1/6th Gurkha Rifles] was down, a bayonet through the heart. I got one through the leg, and then for about what appeared to be 10 minutes, we fought hand to hand, we bit and

fisted, and used rifles and pistols as clubs; and then the Turks turned and fled.

However, the Allied forces were themselves driven back. Possibly this was because their own naval fire landed among the Gurkhas, causing them to panic and flee, but this is not proven. More likely the attack on Hill Q failed because of the scale of the Ottoman reinforcements and the fact that, in the absence of strong direction from Godley, Baldwin's brigade failed to arrive and support the attack.[109]

Later, Monash would describe 8 August 1915 as one of his and the AIF's blackest days. Indeed, his leadership of the advance up the Aghyl Dere has been criticised. His most severe detractor, Allanson, claimed that on 7 August Monash 'seemed to have temporarily lost his head, he was running about saying "I thought I could command men, I thought I could command men."' Bean, too, condemned Monash for not 'pushing on in spite of fatigue till he was actually stopped by the enemy. [Instead he] stopped short of his objective without being stopped.' Neither of these accounts, it should be said, was especially credible. Allanson later contradicted himself, while Bean's judgement of Monash was clouded by personal antipathy. They had clashed earlier over Bean's reporting of the exploits of the 4th Brigade: Monash thought the coverage was inadequate, while Bean concluded that Monash was self-promoting. Bean also conceded in his official history that the terrain over which the 4th Brigade had to advance appeared to be 'more difficult than any against which Australian infantry was elsewhere sent', and that 'the attainment of Hill 971 by [the] left assaulting column was never within the range of human possibility even in those hours of August 7th when its objective may have been unoccupied except by fragments of the 14th Regiment'. Yet for all that, it seems that Monash was thrown off balance by the chaos that eventuated as the offensive unfolded. As his later success on the Western Front would show, his brilliance as a commander lay in his ability to plan meticulously every detail of a battle, bringing to bear his formidable skills as an engineer. For such a man, it must have been intolerable to be in command in a situation where control was impossible and planning redundant.[110]

Lone Pine

Given the failure of Monash's assault, Australian memories of the August offensive have been dominated by the smaller operations on 6–7 August: Lone Pine and the Nek. The assault on the enemy positions at Lone Pine, at the far right of the Anzac sector, was meant to divert attention from the left hook starting to the north. It began at 5.30 p.m. on 6 August and involved the 1st Brigade, whose turn it now was to have an especial 'honour'. The 3rd Brigade had led the landing on 25 April and the 2nd had been committed to Second Krithia.

Lone Pine was an intimidating objective. Having held the line for three months, the Ottomans had developed a complex trench system, the first line of which was covered with pine roofing. No Man's Land was bare, flat, up to 140 metres wide and overlooked by Baby 700. To reduce their exposure, the Australians had dug a tunnel shortening the distance over which they would attack, and it was hoped that the supporting artillery fire would break holes in the trench coverings. But the attacking troops still had to cross No Man's Land under heavy fire and jump into the gloom of the enemy trenches with no knowledge of what awaited them. Did they hesitate? one account asks:

No, they tore up the roof from those front trenches and leapt down into a darkness ripe with death. Then was there bloody work! In and home went their steel; it had a thirst in it for the blood of those Turks. Then did they fight like the men they were, now thrusting, now holding off, now twisting, now turning, now wrenching out their bayonets from this crush of flesh, now dropping down with their limbs shattered, with their bowels slit and torn out by the foe. Along through those trenches, dark and stinking, men fought hand to hand. Many, with clubbed rifle, spilt out the brains of others, trodden soon to mud on the floor there.[111]

Other Australians pushed on to the next, more open line of trenches. Here the enemy troops panicked. They were demoralised by the heavy bombardment—there had been three days of shell and howitzer fire preceding the attack—and their commanders were some distance in the rear. By 6 p.m., the Australians had taken Lone Pine and had set up posts, blocking the communication trenches with sandbags.

However, the Ottomans were able to counter-attack quickly. When the Australian attack began, the 1st Battalion of the Turkish 57th Regiment was being relieved after 45 days at Lone Pine. But they were still close by, and turned round to support the fresh and rested Arab battalion that had just come into the line. Soon the Australians faced a hand-to-hand struggle of exceptional horror and ferocity. In the confined, fetid maze of tunnels built by the Ottomans, it was often impossible to manoeuvre a rifle. Men resorted to killing each other with spades. They strangled each other, tore at each other's flesh, even bit each other's ears or noses off. The exchange of bombs was especially destructive. Those with long fuses could be hurled back before they exploded, while those with short fuses were smothered, if possible, with sandbags. However, they often detonated, shattering men's legs and genitals. The Ottomans had an advantage in this exchange: their German-made grenades were of higher quality than the bombs that the Anzacs had improvised out of jam tins.

In the next three days, the trenches and tunnels of Lone Pine became a charnel house. Often there was no choice but to walk over carpets of the dead. Cyril Lawrence, sent up to Lone Pine on 7 August to widen captured tunnels and trenches, wrote in his diary that day:

> within a space of fifteen feet, I can count fourteen of our boys stone dead . . . Men and boys who yesterday were full of joy and life, now lying there, cold—cold—dead—their eyes glassy, their faces sallow and covered with dust—soulless—gone—somebody's son, somebody's boy—now merely a thing . . . God, what a sight. The major is standing next to me and he says 'Well we have won'. Great God—won . . . then may I never witness a defeat.[112]

However, it *was* a victory, of sorts. Lone Pine was held and remained in Anzac hands until the end of the Gallipoli campaign. In this visceral battle, the Ottomans lost some 5000 casualties, the Australians around 2000. More than 60 per cent of the Australian 1st Brigade were casualties. Seven of the 40 Victoria Crosses awarded in World War I were won at Lone Pine .[113]

In later years, Lone Pine came to stand for something much wider than this battle of 6–7 August 1915. After the war, the Imperial War Graves Commission reburied at this site many of dead from across the Anzac area: 650 Australians, two New Zealanders, thirteen from the United Kingdom and 504 men so badly wounded that they were 'known unto God' only. In 1923–24, a white obelisk was erected as a memorial to these Allied dead. With the insensitivity that only victors can show, it was positioned over the original Ottoman tunnels. Visible from many points along the ridge, the memorial's walls list the names of 3268 Australian and 456 New Zealand 'missing' and the 960 Australians and 252 New Zealanders buried at sea. Over the years, Lone Pine became a 'keystone of memory' for many Australians. Parents and relatives of the dead and missing of Gallipoli, lacking graves at home on which to focus their grief, started to visit the site seeking consolation. As a witness to one sobbing mother who placed a wreath below a row of names at Lone Pine commented: 'Here on this very spot, peaceful enough to-day, her son had been killed. That was all she knew.'[114]

Meanwhile, an Australian soldier who had fought at Lone Pine and lost a brother there sent back to Australia a cone from a branch used as cover for the Ottoman trenches. In time, his grieving mother cultivated a tree from the seed and donated it to the national memorial then being planned for Canberra. In 1934, the Duke of Gloucester planted the tree in the memorial grounds. 'Lone Pine' trees soon proliferated, and continue to do so today. They can be found across Australia: at the Melbourne Shrine of Remembrance; at the Royal Military College, Duntroon, Canberra, where they commemorate the 71 RMC graduates who served on Gallipoli in 1915; even at Cowra, the New South Wales town where a breakout of Japanese prisoners of war occurred in August 1944. Seedlings of 'Lone Pines' can now be purchased from a Canberra nursery, and individuals, schools and veterans' associations have snapped them up. The Australian War Memorial shop also sells a range of Lone Pine memorabilia: brooches, pens, letter openers and coins. As Peter Stanley has said, the Lone Pine is no longer 'lone'.[115]

The Nek

Almost as celebrated as Lone Pine is the attack at the Nek on 7 August. In this second diversionary action, three regiments of the 3rd Australian Light Horse Brigade were ordered to attack Russell's Top and dislodge the Ottomans from the positions they had held since 25 April. From here the Australians would proceed to Baby 700 and converge with Johnston's units, who—or so the plans went—would by then have taken Chunuk Bair and be moving towards Battleship Hill and Baby 700. The delays in the New Zealand advance early on 7 August deprived the Nek attack of its original rationale, but it went ahead anyway. Like a number of attacks then being made against other positions along the enemy line—the Chessboard, Dead Man's Ridge and the German Officers' Trench—its purpose became to distract the Ottomans from the fighting at Chunuk Bair.

The Nek was a narrow ridge, 120 metres wide at the most. The terrain dropped steeply away on either side. The Light Horse, serving as infantry without their horses, therefore had no option but to attack the enemy trenches head on. They would be under intense fire frontally and also from the side, given that the Ottomans still held commanding positions to the south. The enemy positions were to be bombarded, slowly during the night and then with greater intensity from 4.00 to 4.30 a.m, at which time the charge would start.

However, the Allied artillery fell silent some minutes early—at 4.23 a.m., according to the watches of those in the Australian trenches. Why? The common explanation is that the watches of the men manning the naval guns and those at the Nek were not synchronised. However, it seems that the guns were scheduled to begin bombing other areas at 4.30 a.m., and they ceased firing to allow time to switch to their new targets. Possibly, too, they stopped firing for fear of hitting the Australians as they advanced in the confined space of the Nek. Hobbs also blamed the New Zealanders, to whom responsibility for the batteries involved at Nek had been handed on the night of 6 August. Whatever the reasons, the bombardment failed to destroy the enemy machine guns and trenches. The Ottoman troops were able to resurface and reoccupy their trenches while the Australians went over the top without any support from their own artillery.[116]

When the whistle blew and the first wave of the Victorians of the 8th Light Horse Regiment went over the top, they were immediately mown down. Many were hit as they left the trenches or some 5–7 metres beyond the rim. Men sank to the ground as though their 'limbs had become string'. 'Every one fell like lumps of meat,' recalled Sergeant Cliff Pinnock, who was wounded in the shoulder. 'It was simply murder.' As Bean wrote: 'The first line, which had started so confidently, had been annihilated in half-a-minute; and the others having seen it mown down, realised fully that when they attempted to follow they would be instantly destroyed.' Despite this, at 4.32 a.m. the second wave was ordered into the attack. The men cheered as they left the trenches but they too fell after advancing only a little further. The Western Australian 10th Light Horse Regiment was then in line to go over the top. However, its commander, Lieutenant-Colonel Noel Brazier, was now convinced of the futility of the attack and raced to brigade headquarters to call a halt to the operation.[117]

What happened next is a matter of legend. According to Brazier, the brigade commander, Colonel Frederick Hughes, was not at his headquarters. A 57-year-old militia officer, he was already ill and overwhelmed by the task of command. In his absence, the brigade major, Lieutenant-Colonel Jack Antill, was in charge. Already nicknamed 'Bullant' because of his aggressive manner, and loathing Brazier to boot, Antill refused to halt the attack at the Nek. A light horseman's red and yellow flag, he claimed, had been seen in the Ottoman line, suggesting that at least some Australians had reached the enemy trenches. When Brazier declared that 'it was murder to push on', Anthill simply roared 'Push on!'[118]

After the war, Anthill disputed this account, blaming divisional headquarters for the problems at the Nek. Hughes, in turn, told Bean years later that the attacks at the Nek had been ordered to cease but that the runner conveying this message had failed to find the regimental commander. In all likelihood, Hughes' and Antill's accounts were self-serving and invented in the intervening years—though recent access to Turkish records suggests that some Australian troops in the first waves of the attack may have reached the enemy trenches.[119]

Whatever the reasons, Brazier returned to the Nek and told his men, 'I am sorry, boys, the order is to go.' Aware that they had only moments to live, the Light Horsemen scribbled notes of farewell to their families, pinning them, along with wedding rings and other treasures, to the sides of the trenches. They said goodbye to each other and, when the whistle sounded at 4.45 a.m., went over the top cheering. Bean wrote of this moment:

> The 10th went forward to meet death instantly, as the 8th had done, the men running as swiftly and as straight as they could at the Turkish rifles. With that regiment went the flower of the youth of Western Australia . . . Men known and popular, the best loved leaders in sport and work in the West, then rushed straight to their death. Gresley Harper and Wilfred, his younger brother, the latter of whom was last seen running forward like a schoolboy in a foot-race, with all the speed he could compass.[120]

Like the first and second waves, the third line was annihilated. Brazier again tried to persuade Antill or Hughes to halt the attack, but in the febrile atmosphere at the Nek itself the impression was gained somehow that the attack had been ordered to continue. At 5.15 a.m., some men on the right of the trench, which was now crowded with dead and wounded, jumped over the top. The rest of the line followed like some terrible domino collapse. Of the 600 men in the four waves who charged at the Nek, 234 were killed immediately. The Ottomans lost scarcely anyone.[121]

This debacle owes its continuing fame not simply to its futility—the awful sense of 'what if?' that the story still invokes—but also to its depiction decades later in Peter Weir's feature film *Gallipoli*. Its memorable last scene shows the central character, Archy Hamilton, based on Bean's Wilfred Harper, dashing across No Man's Land, his chest thrust out to receive the inevitable enemy bullet. Weir had originally intended to conclude the film with Archy dying as he landed at Anzac Cove. But after reading Bean's vivid account of the Nek, he extended the plot to end with the 10th Light Horse charging into a hail of bullets. Such is the power of film as a medium that Weir's image of the young man frozen in the moment of death has become iconic, inseparable in popular memory from the wider Gallipoli campaign. Generation Y tourists turn to their companions, as did my daughter at Anzac Cove in 2007, and say: 'Show me where Archy ran!'[122]

Weir's *Gallipoli* has also perpetuated the Australian belief, fuelled not only by the Nek but by many other episodes of the war, that British commanders sacrificed Australian lives in recklessly futile operations. The filmic representation of Antill gives him a British accent, even though he and the unfortunate Hughes were both Australian. The reality was that Australian officers were as willing as their British superiors to tolerate heavy Australian casualties. As Brudenell White said when justifying another of the attacks made on 7 August, at the nearby German Officers' Trench: 'In war as every soldier knows resolution is almost invincible and the lack of it the cause of most failures. From his youth up therefore, the officer has instilled in him that he must not flinch or hesitate at loss.'[123]

The landing at Suvla Bay

By 10 August, it was clear that the 'great gamble', as Birdwood called the August offensive, had failed. All of the Allied commanders—Birdwood, Godley and their staff officers—were accountable. They failed to assess realistically the forces needed, the difficulty of the terrain or the logistical problems of such a complex operation. They asked the impossible of sick and, in the case of the newly arrived British battalions, inexperienced infantry. Godley failed to provide the necessary leadership at a critical time. While his subordinates lost control of the situation above, he remained in his headquarters at the base of the ridge with no tactical grasp of the increasingly chaotic situation. He conceded as much after the war:

> I have never ceased to regret that I did not stick to my original intention of going to see the ground for myself. I feel sure that I should have insisted on the advance [of Baldwin's brigade] being made by the high ground, and it is possible that it might have succeeded.[124]

However, there was one factor that did *not* cause the failure of the August offensive, though it has often been blamed for it. This was the disappointing landing by the British IX Corps at Suvla Bay on 6–7 August. Popular mythology has it that the landings at Suvla, in which the Royal Australian Navy's Bridging Train played a role, were successful, but then the incompetent generals and raw troops were incapable of advancing as planned towards the Sari Bair hills. In Weir's *Gallipoli*, a radio operator describes the British as 'just sitting on the beach drinking cups of tea'.

Indeed, the advance inland from Suvla Bay by the British was limited to less than 2 kilometres. Their momentum did stall, thanks to a mix of poor leadership, inadequate maps, water shortages, sub-standard staff work and an underestimation of the Ottoman response. To add to this, the corps commander, Lieutenant-General Frederick Stopford, was not up to the role: 61 years old, in indifferent health and lacking any command experience, he made an easy scapegoat. However, for all this, it was not in the plan that Stopford received from Hamilton that the Suvla operation would support the offensive further south. Rather, its aim was to establish a port—supposedly to supply later Allied operations in the winter and beyond. The idea that 'the Suvla tea party' caused the failure of the August offensive is a myth.[125]

Mourning in Australia

News of the August offensive reached Australia in late August. The press reports were a mix of euphoria, graphic detail and confusion as to exactly what had happened. Ashmead-Bartlett, though he had now become deeply critical of the Gallipoli campaign, called the landing at Suvla 'a wonderfully successful operation'. Bean also masked the losses at the Nek by describing the charge of the Australian Light Horse as being, for 'sheer self-sacrifice and heroism . . . unsurpassed in history'. However, beneath the hyperbole it was clear that the 'true objective' of the offensive had not been achieved. Bean's communiqués about Lone Pine—or, as it was often then called, Lonesome Pine—also left little doubt about the savagery of the fighting:

> The conditions in the trenches were indescribable. Over 1000 dead have
> been removed from the trenches themselves, but during the first three

days, while the fighting was acute, almost the whole time the men simply had to fight over bodies two or three dead in the bottom of the trenches . . . in the foremost trenches . . . there was taking place a constant series of desperate, often wildly adventurous, combats between parties of our men and the enemy, who were constantly bombing one another around corners and angles of this maze of trenches.[126]

In Western Australia, meanwhile, the news leaked out that the 10th Light Horse Regiment, which had been recruited locally, had suffered 'severely' at the Nek. One or two papers published the names of the dead, only to have the censors suppress them. Rumours began circulating that the 10th Light Horse had been 'practically wiped out'. The actual casualty list was published on 26 August.

The grief that these and earlier casualties caused found some outlet in a remarkable public event, the funeral of General Bridges. After his death in May, Bridges been buried at Alexandria with four other soldiers—a gesture to Australia's egalitarian ethos. But within a month it was decided to exhume his body and return it to Australia for a state funeral. In Melbourne on 2 September, Australia's political and social leaders filled St Paul's cathedral to capacity. Outside in the streets, large crowds of men and sobbing women waited to follow the cortege to Spencer Street railway station. A mourning train then carried Bridges' coffin to Canberra, through a succession of country towns where residents lined the stations. In Canberra, after a service in St John's Anglican Church, Bridges was finally buried with full military pomp on the eastern slopes of Mount Pleasant above the Royal Military College, Duntroon, which he had founded.[127]

Bridges was the only Australian soldier whose body was to be returned to Australia during World War I. All other Australian dead would be interred in cemeteries near the places where they died. Bridges' horse, Sandy, was likewise the only one of 6100 'Walers' to return to Australia, though not until 1918. Bridges' funeral was not just an occasion for honouring Australia's most senior commander: it stood as a surrogate funeral for all the dead of Gallipoli. Some of the families struggling with the lack of a body to inter could find in this ceremony a means of giving public voice to their private grief.

Significantly, this grief was not channelled—as it might be today—into any serious criticism of the Gallipoli campaign, at least in Australia. The Labor Party's National Conference had passed a resolution in June urging 'the prevention of war through the settlement of international disputes by a tribunal clothed with power sufficient to support its awards', but this was little more than an affirmation of a pre-existing commitment to international arbitration. The same conference sent birthday greetings to King George V, praying that 'during the coming years his reign will be crowned by victory for the British and Allied arms in the great war for freedom and the realisation of an enduring peace'. More widely, to quote one of Australia's prominent intellectuals and later diplomats, Frederic Eggleston, there was 'no whimpering'. Instead, there was

> no thought that we have done unwisely; done more than our duty. Nobody believes that we have conferred a favour on the Mother Country by fighting for her. We realise that the war is our war, and that we are vitally interested in its results. As a matter of fact the Dardanelles Expedition appeals strongly to the Australian imagination. The association of the place and the dramatic character of the fighting touch us.

The Australian government therefore acquiesced in the continuation of the Gallipoli campaign, even though it was not consulted and received little information about it from the British government.[128]

Debates in London

In London the failure of the August offensive intensified the long and painful debate about the future of the Gallipoli campaign. Some weeks earlier, in July, the British Cabinet had been so concerned about the situation that it sent two representatives to report on the management of the campaign. One of these, Maurice Hankey, the Secretary to the War Council, witnessed the Suvla landing and sent back 'a rather dismal report'—though he did compliment the Anzac Corps and Birdwood was subsequently promoted. Stopford, however, was sacked on 15 August and Hamilton's leadership was also coming under attack from many sources, including several officers on his own staff.

However, the Dardanelles Committee hesitated to do more, fearing the reputational damage of defeat and concerned that the evacuation of Allied forces from Gallipoli might itself be a military disaster.[129]

Their hand, though, was being forced by wider events. Gallipoli was not the only front on which the Allies' strategic position had deteriorated during the summer of 1915. In the east, the Germans had shattered the Russian army in a succession of attacks, overrunning the whole of Russian-controlled Poland, recapturing most of the Hapsburg territory lost in 1914–15 and occupying Lithuania. The Russians were forced to retreat nearly 500 kilometres and took huge losses (as, for that matter, did the Germans). On the new Italian front, from which much was hoped after Italy had entered the war on 23 May, the Italian commander Luigi Cadorna launched a series of uncoordinated attacks along the Isonzo front from 23 June. These had the effect over the next six months of tying down the Austro-Hungarian armies, but there were few strategic benefits to the Allies and the Italians suffered casualties at the terrible levels of all other armies.

On the Western Front, the Germans had managed to hold the spring offensives of the French and British even while giving a higher priority to the campaigns in the east. Therefore the British, with considerable reluctance but under pressure from the French Commander-in-Chief, General Joseph Joffre, agreed in August to a combined offensive in Artois. The Battle of Loos that followed in late September and October was a failure, but the decision to launch it meant there could be no large reinforcements for Gallipoli, as Hamilton requested after the August offensive failed.

So too did the fact that in late September Bulgaria was enticed by offers of post-war territorial gains in Serbia and possibly from Turkey and Greece to enter the war on the side of the Central Powers. When Bulgarian forces—with German support—massed to attack Serbia, the French government decided to go to that country's aid. Moreover, they persuaded the British to do likewise. To meet their commitment to this appallingly misconceived Salonika mission, the Allies withdrew, in the first instance, two divisions from Gallipoli: one Irish and one French. By November, the British would have four divisions in the line and the French, nine. In these circumstances, as Robin Prior says, the 'chances of [Hamilton's] attracting reinforcements for a new offensive at Gallipoli were practically nil.'[130]

It was these strategic developments and the onset of winter that would bring the Gallipoli campaign to an end. However, the pace of decision-making in London may also have been influenced by two journalists whose interventions are prominent in Australian accounts of Gallipoli. One was Ashmead-Bartlett, who was now deeply disillusioned with the campaign. The second was an Australian, Keith Murdoch (now possibly better known for fathering Rupert). Murdoch had lost to Bean in the ballot for the official war correspondent held by the Australian Journalists Association in August 1914, but since then he had assiduously cultivated links with Australian political leaders, including Fisher, Hughes and Pearce. When in 1915 he left for London to become managing editor of the United Cable Service, Murdoch was asked, when passing through Egypt, to investigate delays in mail deliveries to the AIF. There he gained Hamilton's permission to visit Gallipoli, and met with Ashmead-Bartlett.

Accounts of what then happened vary, but Ashmead-Bartlett seems to have persuaded Murdoch to carry a letter to Asquith in London detailing the problems on Gallipoli. When this letter was confiscated by military author-ities in France, who searched Murdoch after a tip-off by another journalist, Murdoch compiled his own version of Hamilton's handling of operations at Gallipoli. He sent this account first to Fisher, and then to Asquith and other political leaders in London.

This remarkable letter—a 'farrago of fact and gossip', as Les Carlyon has put it—described the Dardanelles campaign as 'one of the most terrible chapters in [Australian] history'. The British had bungled, leaving the Australians clinging to 'a slender perch on the cliffs' of Anzac and wasting lives in the August offensive. The Australian soldiers themselves were exemplars of 'magnificent manhood, swinging their limbs as they walk about Anzac', but the British soldiers were 'merely a lot of childlike youths without strength to endure their condition'. Hamilton, Murdoch urged, should be recalled and a replacement appointed who could command the respect of the officers he led.[131]

Despite its sensational content, Murdoch's letter had little impact in Australia. Probably this was because it reached Fisher just at the time when he decided to resign as prime minister and was being replaced by Hughes. In London, however, Murdoch's accusations had more effect. Exploiting his media connections, Murdoch lobbied the editor of *The Times*, Geoffrey Dawson, the press magnate Lord Northcliffe and politicians including Churchill, Lloyd George and the First Lord of the Admiralty, Arthur Balfour. Asquith was sufficiently impressed to order Murdoch's letter to be printed as a Cabinet paper, and it was discussed at a meeting of the Dardanelles Committee on 6 October. Ashmead-Bartlett also published his own critique of Gallipoli in the *Sunday Times*. On 14 October, the Dardanelles Committee finally acted and recalled Hamilton from Gallipoli. He was replaced by General Sir Charles Munro, who had risen to the level of army commander on the Western Front. Winston Churchill would soon be another casualty, resigning from the government on 15 November. His later World War II career would make him one of the most famous figures of British history, but for many Australians he would never cease to be 'the bungler of the Dardanelles', the man responsible not only for the Gallipoli debacle but the later equally catastrophic campaigns of Greece, Crete and Singapore in 1941 and 1942.[132]

Hughes, prices and the War Census

Fisher's decision to relinquish the prime ministership in October 1915 was caused by his finding the burden of wartime leadership increasingly unpalatable. Never entirely comfortable in the role, he was troubled by poor health and perhaps had intimations of the dementia that would afflict him later in life. He therefore decided to take up the position of Australian high commissioner in London.

The man the Labor caucus chose to replace him was the attorney-general, Billy Hughes. It is hard to overstate the importance of this change of national leadership. Although he was a Welsh immigrant—coming to Australia in 1884—and a man whose political career had been built on trade union leadership, Hughes had a passionate attachment to the British Empire. He had already shown a much greater willingness than Fisher to take political risks in prosecuting the war, and his first statement on becoming prime minister was that he would continue to do this 'with the utmost vigour until a complete and final victory is assured'. Viewing international politics as a Manichaean struggle between good and evil, in which power and force were the ultimate determinants, he never wavered in his commitment to British victory and the crushing of Germany. At the same time, he was acutely aware of Australia's vulnerability to threats within its own region—particularly from Japan.[133]

In holding this world view Hughes was not alone, but his political style—pugnacious, emotional, abrasive and at times irrational—would mean that he pursued what he saw as core national interests in a way that soon shattered what remained of the political consensus within Australia. In imperial and international politics, meanwhile, his erratic brilliance—though it raised Australia's profile significantly—would jeopardise the very goals he sought to achieve. Individuals alone cannot be held accountable for major historical change, but it is certain that Australian politics would have been radically different in 1919 if another man had led the country for much of the war.

Hughes was elected unanimously by the federal caucus and his coming to power was welcomed in the left-wing press. 'Without doubt [he is] the most brilliant member of the Federal Labor party,' *The Worker* wrote on 4 November:

> He is no half-hearted Laborite. This Billy Hughes is a man of pluck, of nerve, of brain, and skill and judgement. His heart is in the movement. It always was; and because his heart is right and because he has grim determination he finds himself to-day Prime Minister of Australia.

However, it was only a matter of weeks before two major policy issues started to erode Hughes' labour power base. The first was the question of the price of essential goods. During 1915, the cost of living and food prices had continued to rise. The government blamed the war and the drought, but the left-wing press increasingly saw the villains as the 'Huns of Commerce'—the businesses, monopolies, speculators and trusts that were committing 'wholesale robbery' against Australian workers. Throughout 1915 *The Worker* and the *Australian Worker* regularly published data on price rises and a stream of emotive cartoons depicting hungry families in the thrall of bloated plutocrats. A country that was not prepared to provide a man with three meals a day, they observed, had a 'dashed impudence' in asking him to fight. The Sixth ALP Commonwealth Conference in Adelaide in July meanwhile called for a register of national wealth: 'Who are bearing the burdens of the war? The workers. They are doing all the paying. They are doing all the slaying. The whole bitter cost of the war is laid upon their shoulders.'[134]

There were some mechanisms within the states for regulating price increases, but these—as *The Worker* put it—seemed to be 'wholly ineffective' and 'shilly-shallying'. The federal government, on the other hand, had limited powers over trade, commerce and the control of business and monopolies. In 1911 and 1913, two referenda aimed at conferring greater powers on the Commonwealth had failed, the second by only a small margin. The labour movement was therefore committed to trying again, and in June 1915 Hughes, as attorney-general, had introduced into parliament a Bill for another referendum to be held on 11 December.[135]

By the time Hughes became prime minister, however, opposition to holding the 'prices referendum' had mounted on both sides of politics. Conservatives and businessmen, detecting a socialistic attack on free enterprise, argued that divisive legislation should not be introduced at a time when national unity was essential. A petition of some 55,000 signatures, collected by the Australian Women's National League, an anti-socialist and imperial loyalist lobby group, demanded that the referendum be postponed until after the war. On the left, meanwhile, some Labor leaders had also come to have reservations about proceeding with the referendum. Holman, Ryan and the Queensland treasurer, Edward Theodore—as state politicians typically do—opposed any permanent cession of states' rights to the Commonwealth. Hence, at a premiers' conference on 4 November, Hughes was persuaded to abandon the referendum. There was no guarantee that it would succeed, and the Labor state governments promised to introduce legislation into their respective parliaments which would transfer the required powers to the Commonwealth for the duration of the war and twelve months thereafter.

This compromise deal was soon ratified by the Labor federal caucus. But the parliamentarians were given very little time to consider the proposal, and some—like the radical socialist and member for Bourke (an outer Melbourne seat), Frank Anstey—were critical of the decision. The left-wing press also quickly became sceptical. Believing that there was little chance of the state upper houses, with their property-dominated franchises, agreeing to the proposed transfer of powers to the Commonwealth—in the event, only New South Wales did so—they saw the decision to postpone the referendum as a capitulation to the interests of the dominant economic class. As the *Australian Worker* said, the premiers' word was a 'rotten reed to lean upon':

> The issue [of prices] has been shifted from the polling booths where the People prevail, to the non-elective or property-elective branches of the State Legislatures, where the Trusts and Combines, the food mono-polists, the sweaters of industry, and the whole vile crowd of Capitalistic Huns, have made their citadels.[136]

Later, in 1916, Hughes would use the *War Precautions Act* to tackle price control, establishing a commission that 'set about its task of fighting the rise of prices with the vigour and zeal of a St. George doing battle with the dragon'— at least according to Ernest Scott. But the political damage of abandoning the prices referendum had been done. To quote *Labor Call* on 9 December 1915:

> Every day that passes shows Hughes in a less favourable light, as far as the Labor Party is concerned . . . Since he threw out the Referendum, with the blushless impudence of Iscariot, the way of political ill-doing seems easy for him to travel. He has become, if we may judge him by his recent utterances, a doddering Tory.

The Victorian party meanwhile denounced Hughes as an 'Imperial sycophant', predicting that he and Holman would soon be 'right with the crowd of political snobs and Tories to whom they rightfully belong'. In January, the party convened a special meeting of the Federal Labor Executive, which Hughes had failed to consult, and almost succeeded in censuring him.[137]

The second and even more divisive issue confronting Hughes was recruitment for the AIF. As casualties in Gallipoli continued to mount, the demands on the government to abandon the voluntary principle in favour of military conscription intensified. This was political dynamite for Labor, and in an effort to neutralise the issue, Hughes secured parliamentary approval in early August for a War Census. Taking its inspiration from the British *National Registration Act*, the census required Australian males aged between 18 and 60 to complete questionnaires about their potential for military service (their age, occupation, amount of military training and state of health). Labor parliamentarians had their reservations, but they agreed to the Bill, given that the census also included a register of personal wealth, including assets, property and income. Moreover, Hughes gave assurances that the census was not a forerunner to conscription, but rather was intended to organise the forces of the country so 'that we may put forth the greatest effort of which we are capable'. However, it was ominous that he also refused to rule out future 'possibilities that might shatter preconceived ideas as to what was necessary and grind to powder every political and economic principle that Australians perceived to be sacred and eternal'.[138]

The consensus about the War Census was fragile, and it soon frayed when in September a lobby group in favour of conscription, the Universal Service League (USL), was launched in New South Wales. Modelled on the British National Service League and driven by the Round Table—a movement devoted to imperial collaboration—the USL boasted support from across the political spectrum. Its members included Holman and a number of his ministers, leading figures in the Liberal opposition, major church and business leaders, the lord mayor of Sydney, prominent academics, the president of the National Council of Women and even some union leaders. Its manifesto, published on 11 September, demanded that the federal government move to introduce legislation to allow conscription for overseas service. As the USL saw it, the principle of compulsory military service was already embodied in the *Defence Act* so far as home defence was concerned. Logically it should be extended to include the defence of the empire, since 'today Australia is being defended in the fields of Flanders and on the hills of Gallipoli. If she is to be saved at all it must be there.' Conscription, the USL further claimed, would command 'the loyal support' of Australians.[139]

As it happened, the USL did not attract the same level of support in other states, including in Melbourne, where the movement was headed by another prominent Round Table member, J.G. Latham. But its creation had the effect of bringing into the open the debate about conscription that Hughes had been trying to contain. Two days after the USL published its manifesto, a meeting of trade unions in Sydney created an Anti-Conscription League, which soon had branches in every state. The Trades Hall Council in Melbourne and a conference of Victorian trade unions also declared themselves against conscription, as did the New South Wales Labor Council unless there were a matching 'conscription of wealth'. The fact that the War Census when conducted revealed that half of the wealth in Australia was owned by fewer than 3 per cent of the population, and two-thirds of it by the top 5 per cent, added grist to their mill. In his last days in office, Fisher tried to control the situation by assuring an anti-conscription delegation that he was 'irrevocably opposed to conscription', and that it was 'for every man to decide where he will fight'. But Hughes was another matter. For him, compulsion was not a problem in principle. It was, after all, core to union solidarity. As he would say later to a union delegation: 'The temple of our Liberty is in flames, and you are asked to help put it out, and yet to come and speak to me about compulsion! You are unionists, and as such you come here to speak to me about compulsion. The very foundation of our great movement is compulsion.'[140]

No sooner had he become prime minister than Hughes raised the stakes. Pearce had already agreed in response to pressure from the British Army Council to reinforce the Australian divisions in the field by raising 9500 recruits per month (an increase from 10 to 20 per cent of the AIF's establishment) to provide reinforcements for existing divisions. Now, in November, Hughes offered a further 50,000 troops to enable additional units to be created. This would take the total number of men supplied by Australia by June 1916 to some 300,000, fifteen times that promised in August 1914.[141]

To achieve these targets, Hughes and the Federal Parliamentary War Committee adopted an approach modelled on a scheme then being trialled in Britain by the conservative politician Lord Derby. All eligible men—the War Census had identified 600,000 'fit men' between the ages of 18 and 44—would be sent a personal letter and asked to complete the following questions:

> Are you prepared to enlist now? Reply 'Yes' or 'No'.
> If you reply 'Yes' you will be given a fortnight's notice before being called up.
> If not willing to enlist now, are you willing to enlist at a later date? Reply 'Yes' or 'No' and if willing, state when.
> If not willing to enlist, state the reason why, as explicitly as possible.

Included with this letter was a 'Call to Arms' from Hughes himself. Appealing to patriotism, idealism, national pride and democratic instincts, he argued:

> If those rights and privileges for which Australian democracy has struggled long and values dearer than life itself are to be preserved, Prussian military despotism must be crushed once and for all . . . to wage this war with less than our full strength is to commit national suicide by slowly bleeding to death . . . This Australia of ours, the freest and best country on God's earth, calls to her sons for aid. Destiny has given you a great opportunity . . . If you love your country, if you love freedom, then take your place alongside your fellow Australians at the front and help them to achieve a speedy and glorious victory.[142]

For all of Hughes' undoubted powers of oratory, the Call to Arms was counterproductive. The scheme was widely criticised as being inquisitorial, invading individuals' privacy and exposing them to harassment and victimisation. In particular, it was a matter for concern that men who failed to reply to their letter, or who answered the questions in a way that authorities deemed unsatisfactory, would then be contacted by local recruitment committees. The Call to Arms might purport to be compatible with the voluntary principle, critics said, but in reality it was 'disguised' or 'veiled conscription'. The Brisbane Industrial Council, meeting with Hughes to express their opposition, even threatened to withdraw its support for the Labor candidate standing for Fisher's vacated seat unless the federal government radically amended the scheme. (The seat was in fact lost.)[143]

Hughes and Pearce did what they could to dampen the growing opposition to conscription. They met with angry union delegations and persuaded the major daily newspapers not to publish anything pertaining to conscription in the period during which Hughes was planning to be overseas in early 1916. But the unease about conscription within the labour movement was not placated—particularly when, on 6 January, the British government finally conceded the failure of voluntarism, Derby's scheme notwithstanding, and introduced conscription for single men. There seemed little doubt that Australia would come under intense pressure to follow suit.[144]

The end at Gallipoli

On 8 December, the British government finally decided to evacuate the Anzac and Suvla sectors of Gallipoli. Munro had arrived on 28 October and, under pressure from an increasingly isolated Kitchener, recommended immediate evacuation. There was little prospect of strategic or operational surprise. The British positions on the peninsula had no depth. There was no room within which reinforcements could be built up without detection. Artillery was inadequate. Frontal attacks by the infantry were the only option, and the infantry themselves were sick and exhausted. Only the Anzacs were capable of a sustained effort. The force, therefore, should be evacuated for the defence of Egypt—though this operation, Munro concluded, might cost 30 to 40 per cent of the Allied force. Confronted with this estimate, the Dardanelles Committee again dithered, and Kitchener left for Gallipoli to assess the situation.[145]

The onset of winter made the decision for the British government. Heavy rain began to fall, making the steep tracks to the ridges treacherous to negotiate. Violent storms, particularly on 17 November, then smashed the piers and the facilities at Suvla on which the supply of the Anzac sector depended. Finally, a blizzard set in from 26 to 29 November. Some 4211 men were evacuated with frostbite and 280 died from exposure. One soldier writing home compared conditions with those during Napoleon's retreat from Moscow. If this were not enough, the Germans were now able, with Bulgaria joining the war, to reinforce Turkey by rail. It was all over.[146]

The evacuation of the Anzac sector is often described as the best executed operation of the whole Gallipoli campaign. Far from causing losses of 30 to 40 per cent as Munro predicted, it went flawlessly. Between 22 November and 8 December, the troops who were surplus to holding a defensive line were withdrawn. This reduced the numbers from 41,724 to 36,001. Over the next ten nights, another 16,000 men were evacuated. The final troops were embarked on the nights of 18–19 and 19–20 December. The last man left the Anzac sector at around 4.30 a.m. on 20 December. As Goldy Raws told his family on 2 January 1916:

> Silently, without a word, at 9p.m., we moved off. Every man had his feet wrapped around with a piece of blanket to reduce sound. Without a stop we moved through saps ... to a point of rendez-vous, some 100 yds. back. There we halted for an hour, and the parties from other points of the firing line were collected. Everyone waited in expectancy. How much did the Turks know? ... If they knew they would attack now ... I shall never forget waiting in that gully; ... At last a sign was given, and we started off in single file through the last line of saps on to the beach. It was a beautiful moonlight night, too clear for our liking.[147]

The evacuation involved an elaborate game of deception. For three days in late November, the Anzacs stopped shooting in an effort to get the Ottomans to view silence in the Anzac lines as normal. In the final days fires were lit to suggest men were cooking all over the front. Men loitered in clear view of the enemy. A game of cricket was played ostentatiously on 17 December. Contrivances were also set up to fire after the troops had actually left the trenches. In fact the Ottomans almost certainly knew that the evacuation was coming, if not its precise timing. Their artillery began bombarding the beaches 90 minutes after the last man had left. Only five guns and 50 decrepit mules and donkeys remained to be hit.[148]

To the south at Helles, the Allied troops remained for a few weeks more. The Royal Navy had thought that holding the tip of the peninsula might help the operations of British submarines against the Ottomans, but this was soon clearly pointless. Helles was evacuated—again successfully—in early January 1916.

Over the years, the memory of Gallipoli has been appropriated by Australians, but throughout it was a multinational, imperial campaign. In all, some 46,006 Allied lives were lost, of which only 7825 were Australian and 2445 New Zealanders. The remainder were mostly British—some 260,544—but India also lost 1682, while the French Empire—'French' at Gallipoli often meant colonial troops—lost 8000 men. In addition to the dead, there were over 86,000 wounded. The Ottoman casualties are harder to establish, but Robin Prior judges that possibly they lost about the same number as the Allies.[149]

Remembering Gallipoli

For the Anzac troops, the evacuation brought mixed emotions. As Ben Leane said on 20 December:

> It is not that we are beaten. By jove no, don't think that for one minute. It is simply that the recent turn of events has made the further holding of the place impracticable and useless, and consequently the only thing to do is to get out. It's like buying shares that make repeated calls but never pay dividends . . . it is best to drop it without further waste of money, time and lives. But it hurts, and hurts and hurts hard to think of all those lives thrown away in the landing and during the subsequent eight months.[150]

The Australian press also struggled to find a positive spin. As the *Daily Telegraph* said, it could not be denied that the 'retirement' was 'a dramatically disappointing anti-climax to the Dardanelles campaign, so brilliantly begun and persevered in with so much heroism'. *The Argus*, too, could not deny that:

> The whole of the land occupied at Anzac and Suvla had evidently become intolerably tainted . . . It was felt that our efforts had reached a futile and wasteful stage, when they were devoted to training the prime

of our young manhood in order to transport them at a great cost to a spot where youth and strength were sapped and lives were endangered, and, in too many instances, sacrificed.[151]

However, although it was a matter for 'profound regret' that thousands of Australians were to leave their bones to mingle with Gallipoli's 'still unconquered dust', *The Argus* would not presume 'to criticise those who planned and undertook the Gallipoli campaign'. In contrast, Gallipoli

is sanctified for us by many noble sacrifices in a great cause, and enriched by memories of heroic deeds. And we shall not join in any harsh criticism or vain reproaches because all that was attempted and hoped for there has not been achieved.

For all its disappointments, the campaign was thought to have served some strategic purpose. It had prevented any serious attack by Turkey on Egypt and the Suez Canal, allowed Russia to focus more on fighting Germany and influenced Italy to join the war on the Allies' side. Beyond all that, it had given Australians the opportunity to shine. As the *Daily Telegraph* said: 'Whatever else may be said of the Dardanelles campaign, history will record it as a victory for Australian valor, and such a victory as there is nothing on the brightest scroll of fame to eclipse.'[152]

So victory was salvaged from defeat and Gallipoli began to assume a central and lasting place in the national memory of war. It is not the place here to trace the processes by which the Anzac legend would evolve over the ensuing century to become a signifier of national identity and the discourse within which all later experiences of war would be positioned. This complex journey has yet to be fully understood. Suffice to say that at the end of 1915 the essentials of the Anzac legend were already being articulated: the exceptional fighting ability of Australian men; their personal initiative and courage in battle; their superiority to their British counterparts; their resourcefulness under duress; their resilience and humour; their cheeky disrespect for formal authority—and, of course, their mateship. It matters not whether all Australians manifested these qualities in battle. It was Gallipoli that led many Australians to believe that they did.[153]

Part of this process of memory formation was *The Anzac Book*, compiled by Bean during the campaign and published some months later. Conceived as a way of boosting morale during the winter months at Gallipoli, it included a selection of writings, art and cartoons created by the men in the trenches. When published in London and Australia, it received enthusiastic reviews and sold over 104,000 copies almost immediately. Several hundred copies were given to Australian museums and libraries.

The image of the digger presented in *The Anzac Book* was a sympathetic one, emphasising those qualities of humour, coolness under fire and contempt for injury that would become staples of the Anzac legend. The less admirable behaviour of some Australians in war—cowardice, malingering, fear and bitterness—was absent. In editing the collection, Bean—according to his critics—culled, edited and even rewrote contributions in order to present 'a sanitized and idealized image of the Anzacs on Gallipoli'. Some might demur, but the fact that the Australian War Memorial chose to reprint *The Anzac Book* in 2010—a time when the Anzac 'values' had been distilled to courage, endurance, mateship and sacrifice, not the skill in killing and bayoneting of which AIF soldiers often boasted—suggests that Bean's critics had a point.[154]

The Anzac Book therefore fed the sense of a new national identity that was being constructed as a result of the Gallipoli campaign. However, it is as well to remember that its initial edition carried a message from King George V to the effect that 'The Australian and New Zealand troops have indeed proved themselves worthy sons of the Empire'. Yes, 'Empire'. Whatever the Australians' pride in the AIF's achievements at Gallipoli, and their distrust of the British commanders whose incompetence they had endured, their nationalism was still a dual one. They were Australians *and* 'sons of the Empire', and imperial loyalty would remain the lode that was tapped successfully for many more months of the war.[155]

Another memory of the Gallipoli campaign that would last down the decades was that of one member of the 3rd Field Ambulance, John Simpson Kirkpatrick. Simpson, as he was more commonly known, was only one of many stretcher-bearers at Gallipoli who used donkeys to bring the wounded down from the heights under constant shrapnel and sniper fire. He was British-born and worked for only three weeks at Anzac Cove before being killed. But in a remarkable example of how a particular memory of the past can survive to the exclusion of others, the story of Simpson and his donkey, first published in the *West Australian* on 20 July 1915, rapidly became part of Australian folklore. For a press and recruiting authorities hungry for heroic stories, Simpson represented the qualities expected of Australian soldiers at the front. He was brave yet compassionate, heroic yet tender, indifferent to danger, willing to show initiative and, above all, self-sacrificial and caring for his mates. He stood for the civilised values that Australians should fight to defend. They did not leave their wounded to die untended; nor were they brutal to the wounded they captured. They did not target medical facilities and Red Cross personnel, as the Germans allegedly did.[156]

As for Simpson's donkey, or donkeys—there were actually many— they resonated effortlessly with the Christian narratives embedded deep in Anglo-Australian culture: Jesus riding triumphantly into Jerusalem, the animals around the Bethlehem manger and the parable of the Good Samaritan. Hence, as Peter Cochrane has argued, Simpson and his donkey were appropriated almost effortlessly as a way 'to instruct and inspire [Australians] in the nature of heroic virtue, to will men to similar action'.[157]

This story served its purpose well in the war years, but it endured well beyond that. Representing non-militaristic values of duty and self-sacrifice, Simpson's narrative survived the growing disillusionment with World War I in the decades after 1918. In 1936, a statue depicting him supporting a wounded soldier on a donkey was installed in the vicinity of the Melbourne Shrine of Remembrance. Three decades later, when Anzac Day was coming under attack because of its identification with conservative nationalism and militarism, Simpson and his donkey again provided a unifying memory of war. In 1965, the 50th anniversary of the Gallipoli landing, they featured on a set of Anzac commemorative stamps, 'The Stamp of Courage'. Two years later, when Australian society was again deeply divided over the question of conscription—this time for the Vietnam War—Simpson was the choice for the Anzac Commemorative Medallion distributed by the Australian government to surviving veterans of 1915 or their next of kin.[158]

When a new wave of war memory swept Australia and the world in the late twentieth century, Simpson and his donkey continued to be invoked as the iconic image of Gallipoli. In the Bicentennial year of white settlement of Australia—1988—another, larger statue (by Peter Corlett) was installed outside the Australian War Memorial in Canberra. Many other representations and allusions to the now mythic story appeared in public rituals and popular culture. Anzac Day marches even included donkeys! The five-dollar coin cast to commemorate the 75th anniversary of the Gallipoli landing also depicted Simpson and his donkey, while in 1996 the pair found a place on the Australian $100 note—though on this they were upstaged by a brooding General Monash. In the early twenty-first century, Simpson and 'Duffy' continue to feature in educational materials, while a 2009 children's novel, *The Donkey Who Carried the Wounded*, tells the story of 'a true Anzac legend'.

The narrative of Simpson and his donkey has proved so enduring because, although many of the values of the World War I generation have become anachronistic, its core elements continue to resonate. In today's Australia, which condemns militarism and imperialism but supports the deployment of its defence personnel to peacekeeping and humanitarian operations, compassion and self-sacrifice remain values around which consensual politics can be built. Moreover, Simpson's is a story from which the killing and violence that were integral to the World War I experience are notably absent. Instead, as the Australian War Memorial website says of the Simpson statue, 'The sculpture is warm, accessible and above all, a work about humanity.'

Hence it is Simpson—not a World War I general—who has become the national icon. And he has been joined in the precinct of the Australian War Memorial and the Melbourne Shrine of Remembrance by another quintessential representation of compassion, a statue of the surgeon who tirelessly worked to save lives on the Thai–Burma railway, Sir Edward 'Weary' Dunlop.

In another Peter Corlett statue, Dunlop is depicted not as the towering medical officer who angrily confronted his Japanese captors during World War II but as a benign, non-threatening, stooped old man, wearing that symbol of remembrance inherited from World War I, the red poppy.

3

---·--·---

1916
War of a different kind

The war had not gone well for the Allied Powers in 1915. On every front—Gallipoli, the Balkans, Italy, France, Belgium and the Eastern Front—they had lost huge numbers of men and materiel for little, if any, strategic gain. There were many reasons for this, but one obvious problem was the lack of coordination between the Allied offensives launched in the various theatres of operations during 1915.

As the year ended, representatives of the Allied Powers met at the headquarters of French commander Joffre in Chantilly and agreed that their planning would be synchronised in 1916. In particular, if one ally were attacked by the Central Powers, the others would support it. Moreover, it was agreed that in 1916 Allied efforts would be focused on defeating Germany. In the previous year, Britain's leaders had been ambivalent about their commitment to the Western Front, but with the French army struggling to replace its huge manpower losses it was now conceded that Britain would have to play a major role in defeating Germany. Although this would clearly involve heavy losses, it was thought that the growing industrial production and manpower of Britain and its Empire would swing the balance of the war in the Allies' favour.

Changes in the Allied high command soon followed. The commander of the British Expeditionary Force, Sir John French—whose base of support had crumbled with the disappointments of 1915—was replaced by Sir Douglas Haig, the man whose name would become synonymous with the relentless war of attrition on the Western Front. General Sir William Robertson—another 'Westerner', in that he believed the war could be won only on the Western Front—became Chief of the Imperial General Staff (CIGS). Joffre was given command over all French armies. In Russia, meanwhile, Tsar Nicholas had already assumed supreme command in September 1915, replacing Grand Duke Nicholas, who had not only shown that he lacked the broad strategic sense and skills to command the Russian armies but was also seen by some liberals as an alternative to the Tsar, whose grasp on power was weakening.

The expansion of the AIF

Given the priority being given to the defeat of Germany, it was only a matter of time before the AIF would move to the Western Front. However, in early 1916 it was back in Egypt again. The mood of the men was reflective. As the New Year was celebrated with gongs and hooting sirens, George Mitchell wrote: 'The old year of blood, murder and sudden death went out, the new came in. And what does it hold for me? Death or life? But these are only little things. What does it hold for the nation, Glory or disaster?' Goldy Raws, writing home while en route to Egypt via Lemnos, said:

> My mind is filled with mixed feelings as I wait. For the last fortnight we have kept our minds from war. You would not have seen jollier parties than we've had at 'afternoon teas' at the hospitals, where the nurses used to entertain us. Australians have made their name at Gallipoli, and you should see the way the English officers (with all their smart clothes and tan belts, and we in our much worn out breeches and tunics) look up to us. I don't believe there is one that would not rather have been an Australian and one of the heroes at Anzac . . . But we turn our minds now to active service again.[1]

Thanks to the recruiting campaigns of 1915, some 35,000 to 40,000 new recruits were flooding into Egypt. They had to be turned into soldiers quickly. As Monash told a friend in January, he was:

refitting and recruiting and training and knocking discipline and a semblance of fighting capacity into a few thousand more Australians ... so that in a month or two they may, with all due circumstance, get blown into little pieces, or get holes drilled into themselves, for the honor of Australia and for the good of posterity.[2]

With growth came organisational change. In the first months of 1916, the AIF more than doubled, expanding from two to five divisions while the New Zealand Infantry Brigade was converted into a division. Birdwood was strongly in favour of forming the five Australian divisions into a discrete army supported by heavy artillery, mounted troops and an air component. However, the War Office would not agree. Opposed to creating 'national' armies, it promised only that it would make every effort to meet the wish for an Australian army if circumstances permitted. (They never did.) The Australians and New Zealanders therefore were formed into I and II Anzac Corps under the command of Birdwood and Godley respectively. The mounted troops, reunited with their horses after Gallipoli, became the Anzac Mounted Division, assigned to defending Egypt and the Suez Canal.[3]

Deciding that he needed cadres of experienced men for the new 4th and 5th Divisions (the 3rd would be formed in Australia), Birdwood ordered that the battalions of the 1st and 2nd Divisions be split in two. Each half would form the base on which a new battalion would be built. Since these units had formed a strong sense of identity on Gallipoli, this felt, as an officer of the 12th Battalion said, as if he were 'having a limb amputated without any anaesthetic'. There was also some tension between veteran Anzacs and the recruits arriving from Australia. Thomas Richards noted when stationed near the Suez Canal on 23 February:

On our side—Asia Minor—were a lot of 2nd Brigade men, while on the other side was a crowd of the 8th Brigade and our side commenced calling them cold footed b——and telling them across the Canal that they were driven away from Australia by shame. The late arrivals resented this very much and the insults and bad language that passed across the water was terrible.

Bean, on the other hand, would later claim that the four new divisions, with their common roots, were 'bound together by the strongest feeling'. A sense of continuity was also ensured by the new divisions adopting similar colour patches to their 'parent' division. The affiliation of units with particular states of Australia was also maintained.[4]

The choice of commanders for the new divisions was predictably contentious. Birdwood preferred British officers, arguing that it was difficult for a small army like the AIF to provide men with the experience needed for 'a really big command like that of a division'. The Australian government, however, thought that the eight months of the Gallipoli campaign must surely have produced some Australians capable of commanding a division.[5]

Monash certainly thought so. When he heard that Major-General Herbert Cox, a British officer who had commanded the 29th Indian Army Brigade at Gallipoli and was also a friend of Birdwood from his Indian Army days, would command the 4th Division, he wrote to McCay:

> Surely Australia won't stand this! I have a very live interest in the matter, because I am the only Australian Brigadier who has served continuously throughout the campaign, without a single day's absence from duty; and have secured three 'mentions', and have been recommended for special distinction in connection with the closing phases at Gallipoli . . . there will be at least two, if not three, commands of Australian Divisions vacant very shortly, and it is surely not an unreasonable aspiration, that in the light of my training and services, I should be selected for one of them.

However, Birdwood had his doubts about Monash. While conceding that he had 'very considerable ability and . . . good administrative powers', he thought that Monash had 'not shown that resolution which is really essential'. Furthermore, Legge had told Birdwood that he thought it 'very inadvisable' to promote Monash because of his German extraction. Though Monash had been born in Melbourne, his parents were Jewish migrants from East Prussia, an ethnic and cultural heritage that was doubly problematic for Monash since anti-Semitism was never far beneath the surface in early twentieth-century Australia and Britain.[6]

Monash would in fact get the command of the 3rd Division, in June 1916 when it arrived in England. The command of the 5th Division, at Pearce's insistence, went to McCay, who was in Australia recovering from his injury at Krithia. On hearing this, H.E. (Pompey) Elliott, who had been appointed to command the 15th Brigade under McCay, wrote to his wife:

> so there will be more slaughter I suppose. The opinion all the men have of McCay is that he is personally very brave but utterly selfish, and he would cheerfully sacrifice thousands of lives to get his name into the paper; but I am by no means sure this is right.[7]

Meanwhile, the command of a new Anzac Mounted Division (formed of the three Australian Light Horse Brigades, the New Zealand Mounted Rifles and some British artillery) was given to Henry (Harry) Chauvel, even though Birdwood thought him to be 'slow, but very loyal'. Brudenell White remained Chief of Staff of Birdwood's I Anzac Corps, a position he had assumed in October 1915.[8]

Three of the five AIF infantry divisions were therefore commanded by men either born or raised in Australia. At the lower levels of command, a new generation of Australian leadership was also emerging. Thirteen of the sixteen brigadiers in the infantry divisions in Egypt were Australian: men like Elliott, William Glasgow and John Gellibrand became brigadiers: Gordon Bennett, Owen Howell-Price and Humphrey Scott—all in their twenties—gained battalions. War, if you survive it, is great for the career.

Sinai

Most of the AIF would soon set sail for France, but the Australian Light Horse remained in Egypt. With the end of the Gallipoli campaign, the Ottoman threat to the Suez Canal had intensified. Rather than wait for the Ottomans to attack, the commander of the Mediterranean Expeditionary Force, General Archibald Murray, decided on a strategy of forward defence in Sinai. His aim was to deny the Ottomans the central and southern routes across the desert, thus forcing them to attack in the north where the British forces would be concentrated. The Light Horse therefore was required early in 1916 to undertake raids and patrols deep into the desert, destroying the Ottoman outposts and wells along the southern and central routes. Once this was completed, the Anzac Mounted Division was based at the oasis of Romani, from which it continued to make patrols to the east (see Map 4).[9]

These would be the first moves in a long campaign in Sinai and Palestine that would culminate in the capture of Damascus and Aleppo in late 1918. War in the desert posed radically different challenges from those confronting strategists in France and Belgium. The desert front was fluid and mobile, but the heat, dust and water shortages made logistics a nightmare. Men and animals alike required extraordinary resilience and endurance to survive and fight.

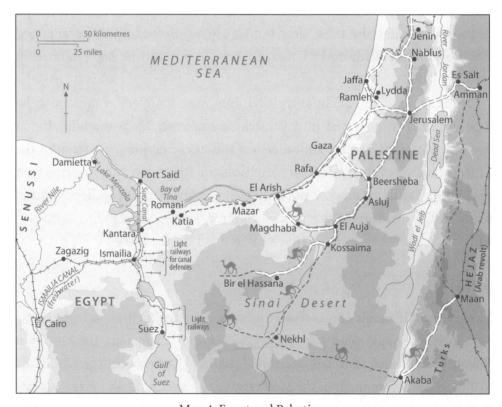

Map 4: Egypt and Palestine

This, as it turned out, was a form of warfare in which the mounted rifles of the Dominions would excel. By May 1915, Murray—who had been critical of the Australians' lack of discipline in Egypt—viewed the Light Horse and the New Zealand Brigade as 'the only really reliable mounted troops I have . . . any work entrusted to these excellent troops is invariably well executed'. Perhaps, as Bean would argue later, this was because Australians in 1914 brought to battle the skills that they had honed in an earlier outdoor life. As he saw it, Australia was a society in which the bush dominated the imagination and set the standards for Australian men—even if they lived in the city, as the majority of Australians did. If this was so, it can never be proved empirically. But the Light Horsemen certainly resonated with the centrality of the bush in the Australian cultural imagination. Riding across the sand dunes, charging at Beersheba and ultimately being captured in George Lambert's memorable 1920 portrait, *A Sergeant of the Light Horse*, they would become a quintessential image of Australians at war: the bushmen turned soldiers.[10]

To the Western Front

After the relative quiet of winter, the Western Front erupted on 21 February with a massive German attack on the French city of Verdun. In what would be the only major German offensive on the Western Front between September 1914 and March 1918, the German Chief of the General Staff, General Erich von Falkenhayn, aimed to weaken France to the point where Britain would lose the will to continue the war. With its massive forts of Vaux and Douaumont, Verdun had such strategic and emotional significance for the French that they risked everything in its defence. Over the next ten months, Verdun would become the epitome of attrition, a murderous furnace of siege warfare that remorselessly sucked in men and resources. As France almost literally bled to death, losing perhaps half a million men, all of British strategy was shaped by the need to provide relief and support.

The AIF landed at Marseilles about a month after Verdun began. To the relief of their commanders, the troops behaved considerably better than they had in Cairo. As Goldy Raws wrote to his sister on 29 March:

In coming to the country of our Ally we have been most careful in imbuing into our men the need for courtesy and good feeling. The French are a demonstrative people, easily, I guess, offended—as easily pleased. Our men are careless and happy-go-lucky.[11]

From Marseilles, the Australians boarded trains heading north to the sector of the front being held by the British. Stretching some 140 kilometres from the River Somme region in the south, near Albert and Amiens, to Ypres (Belgium) in the north, the line was little changed from where the war of movement had stopped in late 1914.

France, as it always does, wowed the visitors with its hedgerows, green fields, farmyards, vineyards, chateaux, cathedrals, abbeys and villages. Life near Armentières, the so-called 'nursery' or training sector, was delightfully different from the hardship of Gallipoli. There was plenty of beer, wine and female company in the villages in which the Australians were billeted. British bases, further back, offered libraries, canteens and YMCA recreation huts. There would also be periods of leave in the 'mother country' across the Channel. Even life in the trenches seemed better than it had in Gallipoli. Food was more varied, water was piped in, and the trenches were accessed not by scrambling up sniper-infested gullies but via long communication trenches. The men were also issued with steel helmets to protect them against shrapnel and splinters, as well as Lewis light machine guns (four per battalion) and Mills grenades, rather than the crude jam tins with which they had improvised at Gallipoli.

The positive impressions, however, were short-lived. On 7 April, the 1st and 2nd Australian Divisions and the New Zealand Division were sent to join General Sir Hubert Plumer's Second Army in the Bois Grenier sector, also known as Fleurbaix. This area had seen no serious fighting for a year, but both sides regularly launched patrols and raids across No Man's Land. The aim of the raids was to capture prisoners and gather intelligence. Goldy Raws wrote to his father on 18 April:

On the second night in the trenches I had my first patrol . . . The moon had gone down and it was fairly dark; it was very wet and muddy under foot. My object was to examine our barbed wire entanglements, and I had to creep along half on my hands and knees . . . Every half minute, at least, enemy flares are sent up and they light the whole ground tremendously. If you can see the flare just as it going up [sic] it is best to let your limbs just sink under you and drop flat. If you can't you just stand absolutely still. It is fatal to move.[12]

The Germans were soon found to be formidable opponents. Their weapons included flamethrowers, gas and highly destructive medium trench mortars, none of which the Australians had met at Gallipoli. The presence of aircraft overhead was also new, as was the intensity of artillery. On 5 May, the 20th Battalion (2nd Division) was raided by some 60 Germans in the Bridoux salient, east of Bois Grenier. Outclassed, they lost 100 casualties, ten prisoners and, mortifyingly, two Stokes mortars that were still secret technology. The cost to the Germans was nineteen men. A second German raid occurred south of Bridoux on 30 May. Again for very light casualties, they attacked 55 metres of the line the Australians were holding and caused 116 Australian losses for only eight Germans killed.[13]

On the night of 5 June, the 36th and 28th Battalions hit back in the first of a series of raids against enemy positions opposite the Australians. These were small-scale operations using rifles, bombs, knives and clubs, and culminating in 'an orgy of killing, wounding and capturing'. Thought to be useful in providing tactical experience and nipping in the bud any tendency to slackness, they were also viewed by Haig as a way of distracting the Germans from the major offensive he was planning to launch further south at the Somme, on 1 July. The men, however, came to hate raids. Not only did they seem rather random in their targets but their costs were high. Once the Germans were alerted, the infantry were vulnerable to machine-gun fire and artillery as they crossed No Man's Land. Even if they reached the German trenches, they became entangled in the jungles of barbed wire. Still, a dozen raids were launched in this sector by I Anzac Corps between 25 June and 2 July.[14]

Hughes in London

Hughes meanwhile had left Australia in late January 1916 to go to London. He would be away from Australia for some seven months—a long absence for a war leader, particularly one who had been in power for only three months and whose base of support was already showing signs of eroding. But there were several issues of core interest to Australia that Hughes felt he must discuss with the British government and other Dominion leaders. These included strategic planning, over which Australia had as yet had little influence; the sale of Australian raw materials, which had been disrupted by the war; the crushing of German economic competition now and in the future; and, pre-eminently, the containment of Japan.

Since the Japanese had occupied the Mariana, Caroline and Marshall Islands in late 1914, there had been further troubling signs that they intended to extend their sphere of interest in the Asia-Pacific during the war. Not only did the Japanese government try in 1915 to force the unstable Chinese government to make humiliating concessions, but there were alarming reports in the Japanese press in which the former German colonies were described as 'stepping stones to the South Seas' and 'certainly important and indispensable places for the future Southward expansion of the Japanese'. Throughout his term in office, Fisher had tried to persuade London to convene an imperial conference to discuss the defence of the Pacific, but neither the British nor other Dominion governments were persuaded that this was necessary.[15]

Once he became prime minister, Hughes took up the issue with his usual passionate energy. He was already deeply distrustful of Japan, and in late December received an alarming assessment of Australia's security situation prepared by the head of the Naval Intelligence Department, Captain Walter Thring. Its pessimistic conclusion was that Japan had displayed aggressive intentions for some 20 years. It was not a satiated power and might 'at some future (and not very distantly future) time put direct hostile pressure' on Australia. Seeking to relieve its population pressures, it might colonise the 'half-empty' Australian continent or force Australia to modify its White Australia Policy. Further, Japan might try to seize the wealth of the Netherlands East Indies, and from this position establish bases on the north-west coast of Australia. All that protected Australia, the report argued, was the Anglo-Japanese alliance—hardly a robust guarantee, given the recent proven fragility of treaties—or Japanese respect for the Royal Navy, though this presumably would be focused for an unknown time in the Atlantic. The British, moreover, could not be relied upon to resist Japanese pressure in relation to Australia's immigration policy, since many British politicians, publicists and missionaries—not to mention the Indian government—were critical of its transparent racism. The only way to provide adequate defence for Australia, the report concluded, was to persuade Britain to create an imperial Pacific fleet, rather than continue to assume—as did the Admiralty—that the Royal Navy was indivisible around the globe. However, this proposal, which the Australians had put to the Imperial Defence Conference in 1909, had not been accepted by the British.

If this assessment were not enough to alarm Hughes, shortly after taking office he found himself being pressured by the Japanese consul-general in Australia to agree to an Australian–Japanese commercial treaty. Since this carried the risk of Japan's gaining 'most favoured nation' status in trade (under which it could be treated no less favourably than any other country with MFN status) and its demanding 'the admission of coloured races to Australia', Hughes had no intention of agreeing. Exploiting his deafness when he met with the consul-general on 19 January, he played for time until he could consult with the other Dominions and London. His hope, like Fisher's, was that the British government would convene an imperial conference; however, even though London was now more open to this possibility, the domestic commitments of the other Dominion leaders made it impossible for them to join discussions in London.

So Hughes took up an earlier invitation issued by the colonial secretary to the Dominion leaders to go to London for consultations. On the way, he visited New Zealand and Canada to lobby their leaders about the Pacific and the structure of future imperial relations. He had mixed results. New Zealand's prime minister William (Bill) Massey seemed responsive to the idea of a common approach to Pacific defence policy, but his Canadian counterpart, Robert Borden, was non-committal about how Canada would respond should the Japanese Navy come to dominate the Pacific as a result of the Royal Navy's being defeated in the Atlantic by the Germans. The Canadians, however, did honour Hughes by making him a member of the Canadian Privy Council, the first non-Canadian to be so honoured.

Hughes arrived in London on 7 March and began a veritable Dervish dance of activities that soon gave him an extraordinary public profile—and almost broke his health. Unlike other Dominion prime ministers, he was determined to speak publicly on a range of issues relating to the conduct of the war and the future of the British Empire. He toured the country, haranguing meetings on the justice of the Allied cause, the need for a maximal war effort, the importance of mobilising imperial resources more effectively, the future of imperial cooperation and the need to exclude Germany from imperial trade during and after the war. As L.F. Fitzhardinge has said:

> What these speeches lacked in argument, they made up in vigour and in colourful and incisive phrases. They were not designed to instruct or to persuade, but to produce action; the style was that of the evangelist, not the lecturer or pleader. According to one contemporary, 'the effect upon his audiences was simply electrifying!'[16]

Hughes soon found himself the darling of the British establishment. He dined with royalty, received the freedom of a number of cities, collected a clutch of honorary degrees from British universities and was feted in his region of origin, Wales. He cultivated, and was cultivated by, senior members of the British government, including his fellow Welshman Lloyd George and the Secretary of State for the Colonies, Andrew Bonar Law. He was, as one observer said, 'scintillating very beautifully'.[17]

Hughes also wooed the soldiers of the AIF. He met them in the streets of London, at his hotel and at the AIF administrative headquarters at Horseferry Road. He visited the wounded convalescing in hospitals, and was photographed with troops in France, carried on their shoulders and hailed with coo-ees. It was brilliant populist politics by the 'Little Digger', though one officer said after Hughes and Fisher had visited France: 'God damn the politicians. They are not doing much for us and they cannot cheer us up, we are sick of talk, & long for action, anything but this weary waiting for something to turn up.'[18]

Much of Hughes' dizzying profile was managed by Keith Murdoch, who was now based in the building of *The Times* and in league with its owner, Lord Northcliffe, and its editor, Geoffrey Dawson. Fisher, now installed as high commissioner in Australia House on the Strand, was sidelined. It seems that he was not consulted on any of the issues about which Hughes spoke. Instead, Murdoch established himself as the prime minister's de facto public relations officer and confidant. He produced two hastily compiled biographies of Hughes and ensured widespread exposure of his speeches. These were published not just in the national press but also in anthologies and pamphlets. A remarkable 34,000 copies were sold. Lloyd George provided the introduction to one of the anthologies, describing Hughes as:

> a flame bearer to help us to victory. He realises the impending danger to Britain and to British ideals of freedom and right, and with characteristic intensity he is endeavouring to rouse his fellow-citizens to the same understanding of the lurking disaster.[19]

Soon there was even talk of Hughes, the 'win the war politician', being the man that Britain needed to inject new energy into the management of the war effort. However, like Robert Menzies after him—who was spoken of as a possible wartime leader when he visited London in 1941—Hughes' reputation was inflated and ephemeral. He almost certainly owed his heady prominence not to any serious possibility of his holding political office in London, but to the fact that it suited others to promote him. There was continuing disquiet in Britain about Asquith's leadership and the lack of decisive victories on any front. (This included Mesopotamia, where on 29 April 1916 an Anglo-Indian force of 13,000 men trapped at Kut after making its way up the Tigris in 1915, was forced to surrender despite relief attempts that cost 23,000 casualties.) Hughes' energy and ruthless aggression gave those intriguing against the lacklustre Asquith government useful ammunition, just as Menzies' eloquence made him a focus for dissatisfaction with Churchill's leadership after the debacles in Greece and Crete in April–May 1941.[20]

To put it into perspective: in his four months in Britain, Hughes attended only one Cabinet meeting and one War Committee meeting. His relationship with Asquith was never close. Nor, probably, was it as unnerving for the British prime minister as a 1916 cartoon by former New Zealander David Low suggested. In the cartoon, Asquith cowers at one end of a table flanked by up-ended chairs while Hughes thumps the other end and dances like a leprechaun. Asquith pleads with Lloyd George: 'Talk to him in Welsh, David, and pacify him!'

Yet if Hughes' political influence in London has been overstated, he did achieve much of what he hoped for in relation to Australian trade. One of his principal concerns was to guarantee the sale of the primary commodities on which Australia's economic stability and capacity to fund its war debts depended—as, for that matter, did Hughes' own political fortunes. The acute shortage of merchant shipping in 1914–15 had put Australia at a disadvantage vis-à-vis closer and alternative suppliers of metals, meat and wheat. German U-boats had closed the Mediterranean route, and the journey via the Cape of Good Hope was three times as long as that from Canada and the United States.

After complex negotiations, in which the Australian businessman and government consultant W.S. Robinson played a leading role, Hughes managed to secure guaranteed sales for the Australian zinc industry. He also extracted the promise of a loan from the British government for the construction of a refinery in Australia. In addition, he laid the groundwork for a satisfactory deal regarding wool—which at that time accounted for around a third of Australia's exports. When war broke out, the British government had placed restrictions on wool exports, partly to ensure its own supplies but also to prevent wool exports leaking to Germany via companies operating out of neutral countries. By October 1915, when it was clear that 'on-shipping' from neutrals was occurring, London embargoed all sales of Australian wool to countries other than the United Kingdom. This threatened to have a major impact on wool exports and prices, since the United States had bought one-third of the Australian clip in 1915, and merino wool—which formed

70 per cent of the Australian clip—was not suitable as a material for British uniforms. Before Hughes left Australia, he had been lobbied by Australian pastoralists, who then suspended wool sales in Brisbane and Sydney in mid-1916. Hughes therefore pursued the issue aggressively in London, where he was ultimately successful (though the decision would not formally be approved until November 1916) in persuading the British to purchase the whole of the Australian wool clip (including merino wool) for the remainder of the war. The price was 55 per cent above pre-war values.[21]

Shipping remained a sticking point, however. From the start of the war, the British had imposed stringent controls over the use of shipping, including vessels engaged in trade. As Lloyd George said, this was 'the jugular vein which if severed would destroy the whole life' of Britain. But London's priorities were not those of Australia. For example, in late 1915, just as a record Australian wheat crop was ready for export, the British had requisitioned fourteen Australian ships in the Mediterranean for use in the Salonika campaign. By early 1916, only 831,000 tons of the 1.18 million tons of Australian wheat that had been sold had actually been shipped.[22]

Unable to reach any agreement with the British authorities despite prolonged negotiations, in June 1916 Hughes unilaterally and secretly purchased fifteen tramp steamers (ships that did not have a fixed schedule or set ports of call) for Australia's exclusive use. Lord Curzon, who chaired the Shipping Control Committee, thought Hughes' head had been turned a little by 'all the caskets and degrees that have been showered upon him', and the President of the Board of Trade, Walter Runciman, threatened to confiscate the ships as soon as they arrived at British ports. But after a dramatic meeting at No. 10 Downing Street, the British government acquiesced in the purchase and a compromise was reached about when and how the vessels could be requisitioned by the Admiralty.[23]

With this purchase—made without consultation with the Australian Cabinet or a parliamentary appropriation—Hughes made the Australian Commonwealth a merchant shipping owner. Back home, the Labor Party accepted the purchase as an experiment in state socialism, and farming interests too were generally positive. Shipping experts, however, thought the new Commonwealth Shipping Line might make a loss, and the Liberal leader Cook described the purchase as 'something to help expropriation of capital which is Labor's policy'. Since the tonnage of wheat to be moved far exceeded the capacity of the new ships, he argued, this was no solution to Australia's wheat problems. *The Argus* of 28 June was also sceptical about Hughes' motives:

> Mr. Hughes has doubtless been kept well informed as to the state of feeling in Australia and the effect which the admiration of the commercial classes and the adoration of the duchesses, both so openly tendered to him, has had upon the members of the Caucus . . . So he asked himself in the few spare moments at his disposal: What can I do to bring those rebels back into line and once more solidify the Caucus in my favour? And in one of his many moments of inspiration the answer has come: I have it. I will go out and purchase a line of steamers. If that won't fetch them nothing will. And hey, presto! the line of steamers was purchased.[24]

Beyond these key trade issues, several other matters kept Hughes busy in London. Late in May, he tried to overturn the War Office's decision that Australia could not have its own army under the command of Birdwood. However, Haig—though he warmed to Hughes—was not convinced. Even if Australia raised a sixth division, as it was considering doing, the Australian forces would not be large enough to form an army. Birdwood, it was agreed, could retain administrative control over all AIF forces, while their operational deployment would be a matter for the British high command.

Hughes also struggled to achieve all he wished in relation to Japan. Even though the British government shared many of Australia's concerns about Japanese intentions in Asia, it was worried that Germany might entice Japan into the war with promises of post-war gains. Hughes was therefore put under intense pressure to make concessions to the Japanese, including the commercial treaty that he had opposed so strongly while in Australia.

Hughes fought hard, but finally conceded that he would place Japan on a 'most favoured nation' status in any tariff regime Australian might make. He also indicated that he would accept Japan's retaining control of the Pacific islands north of the equator if Australia were allowed to do the same with the German colonies it had occupied to the south. White Australia, however, was another matter entirely. As he told Foreign Secretary Sir Edward Grey, 'Australia would fight to the last ditch rather than allow Japanese to enter Australia'. Even if the Japanese wanted equal treatment in immigration, and if this suited British diplomacy and strategy, Hughes would make only minor concessions, allowing visas for Japanese students and tourists and temporary residence for selected groups. London did not press him further.[25]

The Allied Economic Conference, Paris

All of Hughes' dealings in London reflected the fact that the relationship between Britain and Australia was changing as a result of the war. Hughes was the quintessential dual nationalist: committed without reservation to the British Empire and its victory in the war, but at the same time proud of Australia's distinctive achievements and convinced that Australia's and Britain's interests were not always one and the same. Be it on Japan, trade or military command, Australia had a right to be heard in London and to be given the respect due to a people making a significant contribution in blood and money to the imperial war effort. In feeling this, Hughes was not alone. Other Dominion leaders—like Borden in Canada—were beginning to demand a greater voice in imperial affairs as the quid pro quo of their military effort. In essence, the war—which Britain could fight only by mobilising the resources of its global empire—was reshaping relationships within that empire.

Nowhere was this clearer during Hughes' visit to London than in the debate about who should attend an Allied conference on post-war economic issues that was scheduled to be held in Paris in June 1916. There were few subjects on which Hughes had stronger views. He had already moved to crush any German commercial interests within Australia, and was now keen to be part of any Allied planning for post-war economic policy towards Germany. The

British, however, were reluctant to allow Australia—or, for that matter, any other Dominion—to have independent representation at an international conference. If the existing practice, whereby British ministers spoke on behalf of the whole empire in international forums, were to change, this would affect constitutional arrangements within the empire itself. It was also politically difficult to take to Paris one Dominion prime minister, Hughes, simply because he happened to be in London. For Hughes, however, it was a matter of principle: 'the present system: under which the Parliament of Great Britain determines our destiny—we having no voice, cannot (ought not to) continue'.[26]

Such was Hughes' public profile at this time that he was eventually included in the British delegation to Paris. His cause was taken up by Lloyd George and the British press. In France, where his speeches had been reported daily, there was also support for his being a delegate to the conference. Borden too, when asked by Bonar Law, approved 'entirely' of Hughes going to Paris. Asquith therefore conceded the point: Hughes was included in the British delegation— but as part of the British contingent, not as a representative of Australia. The fact that he was an Imperial Privy Councillor provided the technical rationale.

In fact, the British government had considerable reservations about the value of the Paris conference, and hoped that an invitation would be enough to placate Hughes. Bonar Law told him: 'Of course there will be no need for you to speak! There will be but one spokesman for the Empire, and he will express its policy!' To which, so Hughes recounts, he replied:

> 'What is your Policy? You have no Policy! . . . I have a very definite policy, and if I am not to be allowed to put it forward, there is no sense in my going to Paris!' [Bonar Law] looked at me very hard for a minute, and then said: 'It would never do to speak with a divided voice at the Conference. Perhaps you had better not go!' . . . 'Oh, very well!' I replied. 'I won't go! But I shall tell the people of England why I failed to go!' That alarmed him.

Predictably, Hughes was not silent at the conference. Although he could not speak French—he was one of only two of a total of 76 delegates who could not—he contributed to debates when given the chance and played a role in drafting resolutions. The views he articulated were some of the most extreme voiced at the conference. With unwavering conviction, he advocated draconian restrictions on direct and indirect trade with Germany during the war and for an undefined period after it. As he told the conference:

> It is known ... that the Germans intend to begin after the war an economic campaign which will be even more implacable, more harmful, than the military campaign they are waging to-day ... Why hesitate to say that the Allies, who represent, without counting the population of India, an agglomeration of 300,000,000 inhabitants, intend to defend themselves by every means against the Germans. To hesitate is already to be lost, especially when one is concerned with an enemy who respects only strength.

Despite Hughes' efforts, the conference ended by adopting resolutions that he thought mild. But they still caused something of a storm by declaring that the Allies intended to prohibit trade with Germany after the war and to take permanent measures to guarantee their own access to the raw materials they needed for their future economic development. To Germany and neutral countries alike, it seemed that the Allies were aiming at a closed post-war economic system, with preferential treatment for themselves. The prospects of a peace if this were to be the Allied position seemed bleak.

As it happened, it did not matter all that much. The decisions of the Paris Economic Conference were soon to be overtaken by events, and when the United States entered the war in 1917 there would be a very different agenda for peace. Hughes, however, had at least put Australia on the international map in Paris. His closing address, for example, was a masterful exposition on Australia's commitment to the war:

> Although Australia has been protected by a vast ocean against the furious aggression of a barbarian enemy, she has entered this war obedient at once to the voice of blood, to duty, to the instinct of self-preservation, and to the passion for freedom. Thus it is that she finds herself henceforth united with the Allies in a just and glorious cause.

This cause of the Allies is the cause of civilization and of humanity. When we saw in what manner Germany waged war, when we learnt of the savage massacres of non-combatants, the outrages on women, the ravages carried out in Belgium and the north of France, the destruction of the most noble monuments, our blood began to boil in our veins. When we learnt that the Teuton stretched out an arrogant hand to take possession of the world, our national pride reared up at once . . . [Australia] has sworn to continue the struggle until we have freed the world of the pestilence that is German militarism.

Hughes had also, less positively, positioned himself as a leader whose advocacy of a draconian peace was implacable. Though this was not yet evident, his realism would put him on a collision course with the liberal internationalism of the Woodrow Wilson administration. The US Secretary of State, Robert Lansing, would say later of the 1916 conference, 'How sensible men acting deliberately ever committed such a folly is beyond my comprehension . . . Hughes of Australia and the French seem to me chiefly to blame.' And when in 1917 Hughes wanted to mobilise American support for Australia's peace aims, he would meet with a cool reception in Washington. It was not so much Australia that was being put on the international map in Paris, but Hughes—with all his inflexible and somewhat idiosyncratic views about the future world order.[27]

The first Anzac Day

Hughes was in London when the first anniversary of the Gallipoli campaign in April 1916 came round. It was celebrated in a remarkable imperial event that did much to establish 25 April as the key date on the commemorative calendar that was taking form in Australia during the war. From their camps outside London, some 1300 Australians and 700 New Zealand soldiers were taken by train to Waterloo Station and then marched to Westminster Abbey via the Strand, Trafalgar Square and Whitehall. The crowds that greeted them were estimated to be the largest in London since the King's coronation. Some two-thirds of them were women. Such was the enthusiasm that in various places the march's formation broke down—men walked in groups and girls threw garlands of flowers from the tops of London buses. As Lieutenant George Makin told his mother, 'We got a wonderful reception, the people were almost besides themselves with excitement . . . Our boys can do no wrong in the eyes of most English people & the English Tommies are fearfully jealous.'[28]

At Westminster Abbey, the service of commemoration was attended by a galaxy of the British establishment: King George V and Queen Mary, Kitchener, the imperial statesman Lord Milner and Generals Hamilton, Robertson and Birdwood. Asquith could not attend because Dublin was erupting in the Easter rebellion against British rule. After the service, the Australian troops marched on to Buckingham Palace, the Mall and Trafalgar Square, stopping at the Hotel Cecil, where Hughes eulogised them:

> We who knew the Anzacs never doubted how they would comport themselves amid the horrors of modern war. Yet their acts outshone our expectations, but the world stood thrilled in wonder. You have won a place in the temple of the immortals, the world has hailed you as heroes, the British Army has claimed you as brothers-in-arms, the citizens of the Empire are proud to call you kinsmen, your glorious valour has lifted up your fellow-citizens to heights not seen before, and is inspiring them with a newer and more noble conception of life.

Fisher was permitted only a few words, as was Birdwood, who lapsed into anecdotes.[29]

Anzac Day is now so central to the Australian political culture that all this seems natural—almost inevitable. But it was not. The event was organised by Fisher and Murdoch, who mobilised their contacts in the newspaper industry. Possibly the size of the street crowds owed something to the fact that the *Daily Mail* encouraged its readers to seize 'the chance to cheer'. *The Times* also announced the march on three occasions, and on 25 April itself the *Daily Telegraph* featured the march in its leader and published a map of the route.[30]

It seems clear that Anzac Day served a political purpose for the British government. At a time when the news of the war was bleak, it turned the failure of Gallipoli into a kind of triumph. It also gave public recognition to the role the Dominions were playing in the imperial war effort. As the *Daily Mail* said on 24 April, 'After all, we do feel deeply our gratitude and love for these brave sons of proud mothers across the seas. Why should we not let them see how we feel?'

Yet if the celebrations in London can be seen as 'an astute and cynical propaganda exercise', as Eric Andrews has put it, the first Anzac Day was more than that. In Australia, where ceremonies were held throughout the land, it was an occasion on which government mobilisation and private grief converged in powerful collective acts of remembrance. The lead was taken by the Queensland government, which, notwithstanding its being a reforming Labor adminis-tration, identified strongly with 'the ceremonial and ideological aspects of Anzac commemoration'. At the instigation of its State Recruiting Committee, Queensland went direct to the Colonial Office in early February, requesting a message from the King for the anniversary of the Gallipoli landing. This irritated Munro Ferguson, who saw his monopoly over communications with London being infringed; however, the King obliged, replying:

> Tell my people of Australia that to-day I am joining with them in their solemn tribute to the memory of their heroes who died in Gallipoli. They gave their lives for a supreme cause in gallant comradeship with the rest of my sailors and soldiers who fought and died with them. Their valour and fortitude have shed fresh lustre on the British Arms.

In New South Wales, Holman appointed the theatrical entrepreneur J.C. Williamson to manage the Sydney celebration. Thinking that the Gallipoli landing might be overtaken by other more glorious events later in the war, the federal and Victorian governments were more hesitant about marking the anniversary. But the press thought otherwise, and the federal government granted public servants a holiday.[31]

On 25 April itself, a crowd of between 50,000 and 60,000 people gathered in Sydney. Munro Ferguson and his wife—not, it seems, in a reverential mood—took umbrage at being pushed and dragged through the crowds while having to meet the lord mayor of Sydney and others of dubious social standing. The mayor, so Munro Ferguson claimed, was a failed lawyer whose wife had kept a house of ill repute. Lady Helen referred to Governor Sir Gerald Strickland as 'The Dago' (his mother was Maltese). After the event, Munro Ferguson told Bonar Law that he would never attend another march unless the army organised it, and he thought Holman was 'bossing the Returned Soldiers Association for political purposes'. No doubt the vice-regal couple would have preferred to be at Westminster Abbey![32]

As in London, the message of Anzac Day was imperial loyalty inter-mingled with national pride and exhortations to do more. The acting premier of Queensland, E.G. Theodore, said: 'When the Empire was called upon to protect the weak against the oppressor . . . the overseas dominions would not hesitate for one moment in springing to arms to protect the motherland.' From this, it was a short step to recruitment. The best way to honour the heroes of Gallipoli was to replace or join them. The headline of the *Sydney Morning Herald* on 24 April read 'Tomorrow's Commemoration, Big Recruiting Effort'. In Sydney alone, there were nine recruiting rallies on Anzac Day.[33]

Yet, for all this, the first anniversary of Anzac Day was for many Austra-lians a day of mourning. Women in the crowds were dressed in black and those lining the Domain in Sydney were overcome by emotion when the returned soldiers from Gallipoli marched by. As George Black later recalled in the New South Wales parliament:

> It was as though the crowd was swayed by a great wind, and sobs and sighs went up on every hand. Then suddenly somebody . . . began to sing 'Abide with me, fast falls the even tide' and the great crowd took it up . . . it was one of the most emotional moments of my life.

In Brisbane, too, the hearty 'outburst of cheering' that greeted the returned soldiers died away to a hush as the 'pathetic figures' of the disabled wounded were carried from motor cars to the saluting podium.[34]

A few communities also honoured their soldiers by unveiling war memorials. These were the first of many thousands that would be installed in

Australian cities and towns over the next two decades. In Balmain, Sydney, on 23 April 1916, a memorial was unveiled at a busy intersection in the presence of politicians, church leaders and military officials. In Newcastle, the foundation stone of a soldier statue (a form that would prove to be immensely popular) provided the focal point for an Anzac Day march led by men wounded at Gallipoli. One of them told the crowd that he was sure that 'every man that could do so would go forward and take part in the battle'.[35]

The fact that in 1916 Anzac Day happened to fall two days after Easter Sunday invested its rituals with a semi-sacred quality that it retains to this day. Easter provided Australia's largely Christian population with the cultural forms within which to express mass grief. As Jay Winter has argued, when searching for an appropriate language of loss, communities bereaved by World War I turned to traditional motifs, which took on 'new meaning and new forms'. Christianity not only offered the hope of resurrection and reunion with the dead in the next life, it also provided a theology of atonement and redemption within which the deaths of so many young men could be given deeper meaning. Just as God's only son had died to save a sinful world, so the innocent of Australia were now sacrificing their lives for the sake of guilty mankind. As the *Australian Baptist* wrote some months later:

> The war has opened [our] eyes to this possibility—that one dying for all and the innocent suffering for the guilty may be precisely the most powerful force in all the world for redeeming men and uplifting them to higher levels . . . [the soldiers] are doing what Christ did, and the greatest love that man can show is to do what He did—to lay down their life for their friends.

Hence, as Richard Ely has said, Anzac Day at home was 'not so much invented, as effortlessly discovered'. Even those whose faith was weak could find comfort in texts such as 'Greater love hath no man than this, that a man lay down his life for his friends.' Resonating as it did with the values of mateship and self-sacrifice, this text would soon be inscribed on many sites of public commemoration around the country.[36]

In the first Anzac Day, then, could be seen that mix of public commemoration and private grief that would ensure it retained its hold on the Australian imagination for many decades. Official orchestration of the day certainly existed, but the public honouring of the dead and wounded, and the celebration of their achievements, resonated with individual citizens' need for affirmation of their loss.

The wider war

The war meanwhile continued with no side gaining a decisive advantage, despite massive offensives and counter-offensives across multiple fronts. Though the focus of Australians was on France and the titanic struggle at Verdun, in the east the front now stretched from Riga on the Baltic Sea to Romania on the Black Sea. This was more than double the length of the Western Front, and in the northern sector alone more than 20 Russian divisions of over 350,000 men faced four and a half German divisions of 75,000 men. Capitalising on their superiority and giving effect to the Chantilly agreement to support the French, the Russians launched an offensive on 18 March against a combined German-Austrian force in the region of Vilna-Narotch (now Lithuania). However, their infantry was poorly supplied and outclassed tactically, and they became bogged down in the spring mud. The attack failed, and in April the Germans counter-attacked and retook what ground they had lost, even without diverting troops from Verdun.[37]

In May, the Italian front also exploded, with an attack by the Austrians on the Trentino front in the Venetian Alps. Initially they were successful, pushing the Italians back to within 30 kilometres of Vicenzia and the railway line that supplied the whole of their front along the Isonzo. But then, as so often happened in World War I, the offensive stalled, partly because the Austrians diverted troops to the east and the Italians were able to push them back to their starting line.

Then, on 4 June, the Russians went on the attack again, this time on a 300-kilometre front extending from the Pripet marshes (in today's Belarus and Ukraine) to the Romanian border. The massive Brusilov offensive, as it was called, after the Russian commander who had been appointed in April to lead the Russian forces in the south-west, was a dramatic success. Over the next five to six months, the Russian armies would destroy half of the Austro-Hungarian army on the Eastern Front, force the Germans to intervene over Austrian objections, and trigger Romania's entry into the war on the Allied side in August 1916. Ultimately, too, the crisis in the east would compel Falkenhayn to suspend German attempts to capture Verdun. However, the cost to the Russians was huge—possibly over a million casualties— and their initial brilliant successes could not be sustained by their poor logistical systems.

The British, in contrast, did not launch any major land campaign in the first half of 1916. Despite the desperate situation of the French and Italians, Haig refused to fritter away his troops, many of whom were untrained, in *batailles d'usure* (battles of attrition). It was not until 1 July that the British would launch the 'big push' in the form of a joint operation with the French at the Somme.

However, the British were also waging a global naval campaign, a fact that is often forgotten in histories dominated by infantry operations, especially on the Western Front. Britain's naval strategy had two main goals. The first was to impose a tight blockade on the Central Powers with the aim of strangling their trade and denying them the imports and food they needed to survive. The second was to protect the sea lines of communication that were vital to Britain's own economic survival and the imperial war effort. To guarantee this, the Royal Navy had to prevent the German High Seas Fleet, whose growth had been the cause of so much anxiety in the years before 1914, from dominating the North Sea and the Atlantic.

Ultimately, the British blockade would have less of an impact on the economies of the Central Powers than the British hoped—or as the Germans later claimed. Though it necessitated considerable adjustment for enemy economies, it was not the sole cause of the tremendous decline of the Central Powers during the war years; nor was it the single reason why their civilian populations faced starvation in the later years of the war. Rather, this was attributable to the profound distortions within the Central Powers' economies as they tried to meet the excessive economic demands of the war.[38]

Furthermore, to the frustration of naval strategists, the titanic clash of the dreadnoughts never happened. The only major battle between the British and German navies occurred between 31 May and 1 June 1916 off the Jutland peninsula of Denmark. Some fourteen British ships and eleven German vessels were sunk with great loss of life, but the battle seemed indecisive. Neither side managed to cripple the other. Since there was no other major naval battle in the war, it seemed that the massive pre-war investment in naval power had been wasted. The merits and failings of the British admirals John Jellicoe and David Beatty were debated fiercely for decades afterwards. Yet in retrospect Jutland can be seen as a British victory for the simple reason that the strategic balance of naval power remained unchanged. The Royal Navy continued to control the approaches to the British Isles, assisted from late 1916 by two of the Royal Australian Navy's cruisers, the *Sydney* and *Melbourne*, which kept a 'ceaseless vigil' in the often stormy North Sea. The German Navy, though it forced the British to keep their ships concentrated in the North Sea, could not venture unchallenged into the North Sea and the Atlantic. In particular, the German Navy could not break the British blockade.[39]

Germany had increasingly to resort to other options for destroying British merchant shipping—namely, mines and torpedoes launched from U-boats. Mines made their most famous 'kill' when, on 5 June 1916, they sank the ship on which Kitchener was travelling to Russia. His drowning shocked an empire attuned to seeing his accusing finger in recruitment posters as the embodiment of the will to make war. The *Broken Hill Miner*, at one of the most remote—and more radical—ends of the British Empire, lamented on 8 June:

> The commanding personality of the man who crystallised everything that stands for the British military eminence marked him as the supreme ruler of Britain's might in the coming cataclysm. And now that he is gone, struck down as by a thunderbolt from the god of war . . . there seems a gap in the Empire's line of battle that may for the moment cause millions of hearts to quail.

U-boats, in contrast, were not such a major threat—at least in 1916. In the previous year they had sunk some 750,000 tons of British merchant vessels. But when the sinking of the *Lusitania* was followed by the loss of more American lives in another British passenger liner, the *Arabic*, in August 1915, the US government had issued an ultimatum to the Germans. In October 1915, the Germans had stopped all U-boat warfare on the west coast of Britain and in the Channel. However, U-boat operations continued in the Mediterranean, where there was less chance of American lives being lost.[40]

The Somme

If the war was going to be won in 1916, then it would be decided on the land. By mid-year the British were ready to make their contribution in the form of a major offensive in the region of the river Somme, north-east of Amiens. The point of attack was chosen partly because this was where the British and French armies joined. The terrain was relatively flat, free of hedges and trees, and had no particularly dominating physical features controlled by the Germans. Nor were there any built-up areas like those that had complicated earlier British operations around Loos. Moreover, the soil at the Somme was chalky and topped by loam, so there was not the high water table that had reduced the landscape around Ypres to a quagmire when it was bombarded. Finally, the Somme had not seen major fighting in 1915 and was not associated with failure.

The very quietness of the front, however, meant that the Germans had had the time to develop formidable defences. Opposite the British Fourth Army, which would spearhead the Somme attack, there were three lines of trenches 90 to 180 metres apart, a succession of fortified villages and deep, well-fortified bunkers. This defence system was protected by two jungles of barbed wire, 27 metres wide and 14 metres apart.[41]

The Somme was planned to be a joint Anglo-French operation, but by the time it was launched the French were forced by their losses at Verdun to reduce their contribution of divisions by about half. Haig's plan of attack continued to be ambitious, however. While the commander of the Fourth Army, General

Henry Rawlinson, favoured a 'bite and hold' approach, in which modest gains of territory would be consolidated before the troops moved forward, Haig insisted on trying to penetrate the first and second German lines across much of the attack frontage on the first day. As he conceived it, the British infantry would attack along a front stretching from Beaumont Hamel in the north to the river Somme in the south. The French Sixth Army meanwhile would launch a subsidiary attack further south. Once the British had broken through to the German lines of defence, the cavalry divisions of General Hubert Gough's Reserve Army would move in, advancing on Bapaume, turning north and driving the Germans out of the Arras salient. Although in popular memory Haig is irredeemably associated with pointless attrition and stalemate, here at the Somme—and later—he aspired to a war of movement. Long after the experience of the Western Front proved this to be anachronistic, he imagined his beloved cavalry delivering a decisive coup de grâce.

The success of Haig's plan depended on the Allied artillery smashing the German opposition before the infantry attacked. All previous battles on the Western Front had shown that if the infantry were to survive crossing No Man's Land, the preliminary bombardment would have to cut the barbed wire in front of the enemy trenches and kill or drive out the German troops manning these defences. If possible, the Allied artillery also had to destroy the German guns, since these would rain metal on the infantry as they advanced and attempted to consolidate their hold on whatever enemy positions they captured. If none of these preconditions was met, the infantry would be slaughtered or overwhelmed by the counter-attacks that the Germans inevitably launched.

The British command was confident that all this would be achieved by the bombardment that began on 24 June, seven days before the offensive began on 1 July. But even the massive artillery that the Fourth Army had at its disposal—the greatest concentration of guns and howitzers yet used by the British army—could not inflict enough damage on the German guns and wire. The front over which the British guns were dispersed was too long. Moreover, it happened that some of the British guns, rushed into production as Britain was forced to improvise a mass munitions industry, had defects—as did a high proportion of the 1.5 million shells they fired. Possibly a quarter or even a third of British shells did not explode. Those that worked were not capable of destroying the earthworks and the German defences located deep in the ground. Nor did the British guns have the range and capacity to hit German defences in the second and third lines, or enemy strong points that were located on the reverse side of ridges, as they were at Thiepval.[42]

Most seriously, British artillery was still relatively inaccurate. It could not pinpoint targets such as machine-gun posts and gun emplacements. Counter-battery fire (that is, fire that destroys enemy artillery positions) was not to be perfected until later in the war. In mid–1916, it was simply hoped that enemy guns would be hit by blanket fire. To add to this, not all of the British artillery at the Somme had mastered the more sophisticated technique now beginning to be used on the Western Front: the creeping barrage. This was a precisely targeted curtain of artillery fire that moved slowly in front of the infantry as they advanced to within reach of the enemy lines, sweeping the ground in front of them and preventing the enemy from emerging from his dugouts until the last minute.

Finally, the weather was bad in the last days of June: there was low cloud, mist and rain, all of which prevented the four squadrons of aircraft that were available from reporting on the position of enemy guns. In fact, the British pre-battle bombardment had to be discontinued on two of the seven planned days. As a result, most of the German artillery survived the British bombardment and awaited the infantry attack.

The first day of the Battle of the Somme, 1 July, was a catastrophe (see Map 5). When British troops to the north of the Albert–Bapaume road advanced towards Thiepval, they met a hail of German machine-gun and shell fire. Around 20,000 men were killed and a further 40,000 wounded. The figures are almost incomprehensible. About half the British troops who attacked had become casualties by nightfall. For the English, Northern Irish and Newfoundlanders—all of whom suffered terrible losses—1 July became a tragedy comparable to 25 April for Australia. The first day of the Somme

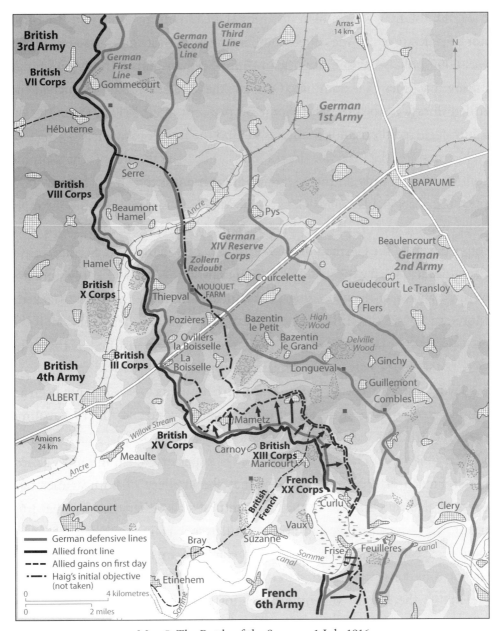

Map 5: The Battle of the Somme, 1 July 1916

entered popular memory as the quintessential example of criminally unimaginative British tactics: men burdened with 30-kilogram packs advancing at walking pace in an easily targeted line. In fact, many battalions used more varied tactics, but in the great majority of cases it made no difference. Whatever

187

they did, infantry were mown down by the German machine guns that had not been destroyed by the Allied bombardment. The rate of fire in some places was 6000 bullets per minute. Meanwhile, German guns—those long-range killing machines that dominated war on the Western Front—drenched the Allied lines well into the rear. Some 30 per cent of all British casualties on 1 July occurred thousands of metres behind the trench parapets.[43]

Yet despite the massive losses on 1 July, the Battle of the Somme continued—not only on the next day but for months to come. This may now seem unconscionable, but as Gary Sheffield says, 'Great battles cannot simply be turned on and off like a light switch.' For one thing, British troops were trapped behind the German lines and could not be abandoned. Second, heavy casualties had been expected and, as Haig saw it, the losses of 1 July were not 'severe in view of numbers engaged, and the length of the front attacked'. Moreover, severe casualties had a depressing logic of self-perpetuation: if the gains from an attack were significant, large losses were justified. If the gains were not, then the battle must continue until they were.[44]

Beyond this, there was the fact that 1 July, for all its losses, had not been an unmitigated failure. To the south of the front, beyond the Albert–Bapaume road, the British XV and XIII Corps and the French XX Corps had taken all of their objectives. Their success was due to superior French infantry tactics, better French artillery and the fact that the artillery of both armies had concentrated on eliminating the German first line rather than bombarding field fortifications further back. From this success, Haig concluded that there were prospects of the Allies pushing forward towards the Bazentin Ridge if the focus of their attack shifted to the south.[45]

Finally, there were the imperatives of coalition politics. The Somme had been launched to support the French at Verdun, and this goal had not changed. Indeed, the willingness of the British to suffer huge losses at the Somme was proof of their commitment to assuming an increased burden on the Western Front. As Robertson said with good reason, it was impossible for the British to 'tell Paris that we had had enough and meant to stop'. So the Somme continued.[46]

Fromelles

The AIF was thrown into this haemorrhaging warfare on 19 July—not on the Somme itself, but further north at Fromelles, about 20 kilometres west of Lille. This sector of the Western Front was relatively inactive, with the result that German troops were being transferred from here to the Somme. Haig concluded that these diversions might be stopped if an attack were launched towards Lille, an important industrial centre and rail junction in German hands.

Fromelles (or, as it was often called, Fleurbaix) was not a promising place to attack. It was a flat, marshy area through which a small river meandered. Since the soil was waterlogged, the British lines were formed not of trenches but rather of passages between parapets of earth and sandbags raised 2–3 metres above the ground. They were prone to flooding and provided poor protection against shellfire. Even worse, the Germans (the 6th Bavarian Reserve Division) controlled the dominant physical feature of the area, the Aubers Ridge. From here they could look down into the British lines and observe all movements and preparations for an attack.[47]

To add to this, since the front line in this sector had moved little since late 1914, the German defences were well developed. Barbed wire was everywhere, and the so-called Sugar Loaf, a small fortress of concrete machine-gun emplacements and underground chambers, jutted out into the British lines as a kind of elbow. From here, the Germans could fire on advancing troops from both the front and the sides. Previous British attempts to capture these positions in the spring and summer of 1915 had failed dismally.

The only advantage that Fromelles offered was, to quote John Bourne, that 'it was on the front of a corps that wished to make an attack'—or, more precisely, the front of a corps commander who wished to make an attack. Lieutenant-General Richard Haking, the commander of IX Corps, was one of those generals who had remained convinced of the power of the offensive and 'the spirit of the bayonet' despite all the evidence to the contrary over the past two years of war. Frustrated by the dull routine of holding the line and 'something of a loose cannon', Haking was keen to oblige when Haig called for action to pin the Germans down.[48]

The planning for Fromelles was rushed and confusing. Its focus changed several times, and in the end it was a re-run of tactics that had proved disastrous in the past. Recognising this, Walker, who was commanding the Australian 1st Division, refused to allow his troops to take part in the attack, an act of 'rank insubordination' that was probably tolerated only because Dominion troops were involved. But if Walker refused to be profligate with Australian lives, McCay did not. Gratified that his 5th Division would be 'the first Australians to have a big fight in France, and so get a big splash', he accepted their being involved.[49]

The plan of attack was for the British 61st Division to assault the Sugar Loaf head on while the 15th, 14th and 8th Brigades of the 5th Division, in that order, moved forward on their left (see Map 6). Elliott, commanding the 15th Brigade, took one look at the battlefield and concluded that the attack had 'not an earthly chance of success'. Not only did the Germans at the Sugar Loaf overlook all approaches, but No Man's Land was over 365 metres wide at the point of the 15th Brigade's attack. Previous experience on the Western Front had shown that 180 metres was about the maximum width over which infantry could successfully attack. The troops assigned to this perilous task were also inexperienced. The 5th Australian Division had arrived in France only two to three weeks earlier, as had the British 61st Division. The 61st, moreover, was a Territorial unit, intended to be a second-line division providing reinforcements for other units.

Deeply pessimistic about the operation, Elliott confessed his fears to a staff officer from Haig's headquarters, Major H.C.L. Howard, who inspected the front on 14 July. Howard agreed that the attack would be 'a holocaust', and triggered some new scrutiny of the attack by Haig and Haking's superior, Monro (now commanding the First British Army). But Haking remained adamant that he would succeed, and the attack was allowed to proceed.

Success, as always, depended on the enemy positions being shattered by the pre-attack bombardment, but at Fromelles this was ineffective. Although there was no shortage of artillery, the British guns were old, worn and inaccurate. The Australian artillerymen were also inexperienced; some of their guns had

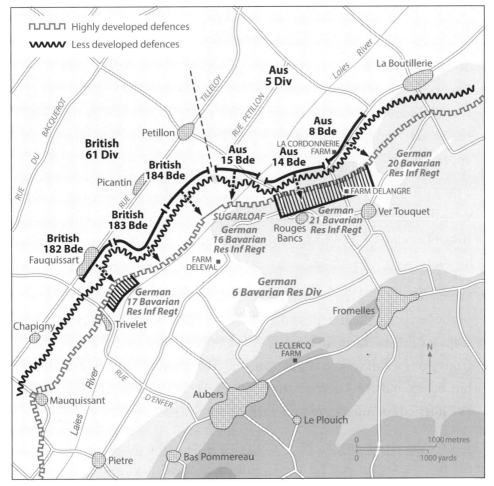

Map 6: The Battle of Fromelles, 19 July 1916

never been fired in action and, thanks to poor weather and haste, had not been adequately registered—that is, had not been accurately sighted in so they could fire repeatedly on the intended point. To make matters worse, mist and heavy cloud cover in the days before the attack made it difficult for the Royal Flying Corps' spotter planes to identify artillery targets. Consequently, the artillery fire failed to destroy the Sugar Loaf defences, although this was not to become clear until the battle began.[50]

The Germans, holding the higher ground, were well aware that the attack was coming. The Australians, in turn, knew that their chances of survival

191

were poor. Major Geoffrey McCrae, a 26-year-old who would die leading the 60th Battalion, wrote to his family on 19 July:

> Today I lead my battalion in our assault on the German lines and I pray God I may come through alright and bring honour to our name. If not, I will at least have laid down my life for you and my country which is the greatest privilege one can ask for. Farewell, dear people, the hour approacheth.[51]

The Australians started to suffer serious casualties to German artillery even as they assembled in the communication trenches on the afternoon of 19 July. Lieutenant Percy Chapman of 55th Battalion (14th Brigade) recalled in his diary:

> We marched along the road in single file keeping to the right under cover of the hedge as much as possible . . . till we got to the Communications Gaps leading to the main trench . . . In the gap a shell landed among our front party—but we could not stop, one poor chap was blown to a pulp, bits of legs and arms were scattered about. I trod on his head by mistake as I hurried by and it gave under my foot like a sponge.[52]

Before the attack began, Elliott told his men, 'You won't find a German in the trenches when you get there.' But when the British moved forward at 5.30 p.m., they were drenched with shrapnel and machine-gun fire. Funnelling through exit points cut into the parapets (known as sally ports), they made a perfect target. They had no chance of taking the Sugar Loaf, which remained largely undamaged by the Allied bombardment.

Hence, when the Australian 15th Brigade followed a few minutes later in successive waves, it too was mown down. W.H. Downing of the 57th Battalion watched the men of the 60th moving out from the parapet, heavily laden with their packs and equipment.

> The air was thick with bullets, swishing in a flat lattice of death . . . The bullets skimmed low, from knee to groin, riddling the tumbling bodies before they touched the ground. Still the line kept on.

Hundreds were mown down in the flicker of an eyelid, like great rows of teeth knocked from a comb, but still the line went on, thinning and stretching. Wounded wriggled into shell holes or were hit again. Men were cut in two by streams of bullets. And still the line went on.

Corporal T.C. Whiteside remembered the scene as if it were 'cardboard nine-pins in a hurricane only it was human beings who were facing up to it'. For all this, a few men of the 15th Brigade seem to have survived long enough to reach the wire in front of the Sugar Loaf. Pieces of Australian uniform were found there after the war.[53]

Further along the line, where No Man's Land was only 100–200 metres wide and the German fire less intense, the 14th and 8th Brigades did manage to capture the German first line. But the intelligence on which they were operating was faulty, and they soon moved into a confusing landscape of water-filled ditches rather than well-demarcated second and third lines of German defences. With the Sugar Loaf still in German hands on their right, they were exposed and vulnerable to counter-attacks.

Three hours into the attack, Haking ordered another attempt to take the Sugar Loaf, but he later cancelled it when he learned how badly mauled the 61st Division was. However, in a lamentable failure of communications, the 58th Battalion of the 15th Brigade were not told of the cancellation. At 9 p.m. they charged Sugar Loaf again, in what Bean has called 'one of the bravest and most hopeless assaults ever undertaken by the Australian Imperial Force'. Few men came back unharmed.[54]

As the night continued, the troops that had made some progress on the left came under fierce counter-attacks. In danger of being cut off by Germans infiltrating behind them, they tried to retreat to their own lines. Raked by fire from every direction, they dashed from shell hole to shell hole, in what to those watching them seemed 'an eternity of time until the lucky ones reached our parapets to be pulled in by willing hands'. Many others were killed, wounded or taken prisoner. The prisoners were paraded next day in the town of Haubourdin, where it is said the population gave them chocolates.[55]

In less than 24 hours at Fromelles, the 5th Division suffered 5533 casualties, of whom 1917 were killed or died of wounds, 3146 wounded and 470 taken prisoner. When the roll call was held for the 60th Battalion after the battle, only 106 men of 887 answered to their names. The British 61st Division's casualties were 1547 dead and wounded, and the Germans 1444. Corporal Hugh Knyvett of the 59th Battalion wrote:

> The sight of our trenches that next morning is burned into my brain. Here and there a man could stand upright, but in most places if you did not wish to be exposed to a sniper's bullet you had to progress on your hands and knees. If you had gathered the stock of a thousand butcher-shops, cut it into small pieces and strewn it about, it would give you a faint conception of the shambles those trenches were . . . It were folly to look over the parapet, for nearly every shell-hole contained a wounded man, and, poor fellow, he would wave to show his where-abouts; and though we could not help him, it would attract the attention of the Huns, who still had shells to spare.[56]

The losses devastated Elliott and Brigadier-General Tivey, commander of the 8th Brigade, both of whom wept as they confronted the dead and the shattered survivors on the morning after the attack. Bean, who arrived at the battlefield on 20 July, recalled that he felt when meeting Elliott 'almost as if I were in presence of a man who had just lost his wife. He looked down & cd hardly speak—he ws clearly terribly depressed and overwrought.' Elliott himself wrote to his wife:

> The battle is over. My brave boys have done all that man could do . . . I think over 2000 of my own Brigade alone are killed, wounded or missing, and very very [sic] many of these will be killed, as the Germans fired at them as they lay all night and all today . . . many many [sic] must perish slowly and miserably of starvation and want of attention in that no-man's-land. God help us all, it is cruel indeed.[57]

Three days later he wrote to his cousin in Britain with a degree of indiscretion that was remarkable for an officer of his rank:

God knows why this enterprise was ordered, apparently as a feint to distract the enemy's attention from the Somme area. However . . . the Division was hurled against the German trenches without anything like adequate preparation, and although we broke the German line and captured two hundred prisoners the slaughter was dreadful and at length we were ordered to retire . . . I presume there was some plan at the back of the attack but it is difficult to know what it was.[58]

Elliott's anger never died. In 1930—on the fourteenth anniversary of the battle and only eight months before he committed suicide—he would tell the Returned Sailor's and Soldier's Imperial League of Australia (RSSILA) in Canberra that Fromelles was 'so incredibly blundered from beginning to end, that it is almost incomprehensible how the British staff, who were responsible for it, could have consisted of trained professional soldiers of considerable reputation and experience . . . and why, in view of the outcome . . . any of them were retained in active command'.[59]

Haking, of course, disagreed. He blamed the failure at Fromelles not on leadership but on the inadequate training of the Australians and the lack of 'offensive spirit' in the 61st Division. He even declared that the action had done both divisions 'a great deal of good', and issued a congratulatory order to the survivors for having driven back the enemy 'with true British vigour'. The 5th Division thought this fatuous, and Haking became known as 'the Butcher'. Yet he retained command of IX Corps, even though he was never to be promoted beyond the rank he held in July 1916.[60]

The British high command also won no respect among the Australians when they masked the scale of the disaster at Fromelles. The official communiqué released after the battle described it as 'some important raids' in which Australian troops took part. Privately, Bean called this 'deliberate lying', and made a point in his cable to the newspapers at home of calling Fromelles an 'attack' in which Australians suffered 'severe' casualties. The troops, meanwhile, were reportedly disgusted at the way in which their efforts had been consigned to a few paragraphs in the British press.[61]

A further casualty of Fromelles was McCay's reputation—at least with his men. He was overheard saying of his division that 'they'll get used to it'—'it' being the slaughter of the Western Front. To the troops with whom he met after the battle he said, 'The Boche beat us today, but very shortly we will attack again when there will be a different tale to tell.' Perhaps most damagingly, he refused to tolerate negotiations with German officers for a truce that would allow the Australian and German wounded to be brought in from No Man's Land. In his defence, the British command's position on local truces was inflexible, but the survivors of Fromelles were tormented by the suffering of the wounded lying untended and crying for help and water, sometimes for days. Although an arrangement was reached at the local level allowing the wounded to be taken out at night, McCay's veto on any formal truce confirmed his reputation—perhaps unwarranted—as an unfeeling and cold commander, as good at killing Australians as any British officer. [62]

Remembering Fromelles

Fromelles is now one of the most famous battles in which Australians fought during World War I. But it was not always so. After the war, the ground of No Man's Land on 19 July 1916 became the site of one of the thousands of cemeteries created by the Imperial (later Commonwealth) War Graves Commission in honour of the dead of the British Empire. Here, at VC Corner, the remains of 410 unidentified Australian dead were interred and the names of the 1299 Australian missing from Fromelles inscribed on the memorial walls. In Australia, meanwhile, survivors of Fromelles would gather in Australia on the anniversaries of 19 July in the inter-war years and lay wreaths at local war memorials. Families who had lost men in what they called Fleurbaix would also insert 'In Memoriam' notices in major newspapers for many years after the event.

However, most of these acts of remembrance were at the individual and local levels, and Fromelles did not become a 'national memory', in the sense of being a battle whose anniversaries were the occasion for national commemoration and ritual. Perhaps this was because Fromelles was soon eclipsed by other, more costly battles on the Western Front, such as Pozières at the Somme and the Third Battle of Ypres in 1917. Perhaps also it was because survivors of World War I preferred to see themselves as heroes, not—as is the vogue in twenty-first-century war commemoration—as victims. The 5th Division, for instance, when asked in 1919 where it wanted the memorial celebrating its wartime achievements to be located, chose not Fromelles but Polygon Wood, the site of one of the more successful actions during the Third Battle of Ypres. Whatever the reason, if newspaper records are a reliable indication, it seems that anniversaries of Fromelles passed unnoticed at the national level for decades in the post-1945 era.

All of this changed in the 1990s. As the extraordinary resurgence of interest in war memory occurred not only in Australia but globally, Fromelles was one of the memories to be rediscovered. As is often the case with the construction of public memory, this was the result of both government intervention and individual agency. The government of John Howard (1996–2007) engaged in a spate of new war-memorial building overseas, and in 1998—the 80th anniversary of the end of World War I—opened a memorial park at Fromelles. At its heart was a statue of a man staggering under the weight of a wounded soldier draped across his shoulders. Called Cobbers, it immortalised a Victorian farmer, Sergeant Simon Fraser of 57th Battalion, who in the days after the Fromelles battle joined small groups scouring the battlefield for the wounded. As Fraser himself recalled:

> It was no light work getting in with a heavy weight on your back, especially if he had a broken leg or arm and no stretcher-bearer was handy. You had to lie down and get him on your back; then rise and duck for your life with a chance of getting a bullet in you before you were safe. One foggy morning in particular, I remember, we could hear someone over towards the German entanglements calling for a stretcher-bearer; it was an appeal no man could stand against, so some of us rushed out and had a hunt. We found a fine haul of wounded and brought them in; but it was not where I heard this fellow calling, so I had another shot for it, and came across a splendid specimen of humanity trying to wriggle into a trench with a big wound in his thigh . . . I got a stretcher. Then another man about 30 yards out sang out, 'Don't forget me, cobber'.

It was a story of compassion and mateship waiting to join Simpson and his Donkey and 'Weary' Dunlop. Indeed, the sculptor of Cobbers, Peter Corlett, had already created the statues of these two iconic figures that stand outside the Australian War Memorial. Of Cobbers, Corlett said, 'I think the bravery of men who went out to rescue their injured comrades, against orders, is incredibly moving . . . I hope my work represents a wider spirit among our troops.'[63]

In the decade that followed, Fromelles was positioned even more firmly within national remembrance thanks to the efforts of a small group of Australians headed by retired schoolteacher Lambis Englezos, who became intent on finding the burial site of the missing of Fromelles who were not interred at VC Corner. At first they fought some official scepticism, but in 2007–08 a geophysical survey commissioned by the Australian government identified a mass grave at Pheasant Wood near Fromelles. On excavation, it was found to contain the remains of 203 Australians, 3 British and 44 soldiers of indeterminate nationality buried by the Germans in 1916.[64]

There the remains might have lain undisturbed, with a new memorial erected to mark the location and the presumed dates of death. Mass graves are not uncommon in the European culture of war death. The French cemetery at Rancourt contains an ossuary of 3240 men; the German *Soldatenfriedhof* nearby has two mass graves with 7492 bodies. Langemarck near Ypres has an even larger mass grave, of 24,917 remains. These cemeteries can invoke in the visitor no less powerful an emotional response than do the individual crosses and headstones typical of the British way of burial.

However, the tradition established by the IWGC was to give every soldier an individual grave. The remains found at Pheasant Wood were therefore reburied with great official ceremony in 2010. Moreover, rather than their being interred—as was normal practice—in an existing cemetery nearby, they were buried in a specially created cemetery, the first to be built by the Commonwealth War Graves Commission (CWGC) in 50 years. Even more unusually, a search was launched to identify the missing individually. With access to modern medical science, these men of Fromelles became the 'as-yet-unknown soldiers'. DNA samples taken from Pheasant Wood remains were matched, where possible, with living descendants in Australia and the United Kingdom.[65]

Few questioned why at least $15 million ($6.2 million from each of the Australian and British governments and $2.3 million from CWGC) was spent on this exercise. Nor was there a public questioning of the precedent of using DNA to identify the missing. Rather, the media featured stories of families who needed 'closure', even though they had never known the men who fought at Fromelles nor experienced the grief of their loss. It seemed enough that they claimed that they had never stopped wondering about Uncle Jack or had passed down stories about a missing great-great-uncle over the years.[66]

The missing of Fromelles, it seems, spoke to a phenomenon that has fuelled the growth of war memory globally in recent decades: the explosion of genealogy and, with it, the desire to 'locate family stories in bigger, more universal, narratives' of the past. As the former head of the French army, General Bruno Cuche, said when the first Fromelles soldier was buried on 1 February 2010, 'Memory is only alive when nations are brought together. Memory is only alive when it unites generations.' Or, as historian Jay Winter has said of war museums:

> Such imaginings of war are attractive because they rest on the contemporary link between generations, and in particular between the old and the young, between grandparents and grandchildren, at times over the heads of the troublesome generation of parents in the middle.[67]

The new rituals of Fromelles also testified to the continuing salience of the implied contract between citizen and state that underpins a voluntary system of enlistment for military service. In a liberal democracy, where the rights of the individual are a core value, those who choose or are required to die in the defence of the state are deemed to be entitled to individual honour. This was the ideal that informed the work of the IWGC in the years after World War I, one of the first mass conflicts in which rank-and-file soldiers were granted a grave and headstone personalised with their name, age and date of death.

In conflicts of earlier times, officers had been honoured individually but the other ranks were thought too numerous to list by name.

It is a message that still resonates in a society that, for all its individualism and intolerance for the death of the young, requires some individuals at least to be willing to die in defence of the nation. Be that service in Afghanistan, Iraq or United Nations humanitarian interventions, these men and women must be assured that their deaths will be honoured, as those who served before them were. Hence, press accounts of the reburials at Fromelles invoked the high diction of war—'devotion' and 'honour'—and spoke to the need for 'a proper send-off' and 'a fitting farewell at last' for the 'fallen sons' who 'can finally be laid to rest with honour'. At the same time, the Battle of Fromelles itself was reclaimed from its relative obscurity. It is no longer a 'raid' or even an 'attack', but 'the bloodiest 24 hours in Australia's military history before or since'.[68]

Pozières and Mouquet Farm

Within a few days of Fromelles, the other three Australian divisions on the Western Front—the 1st, 2nd and 4th—were thrown into the main battle of the Somme. (The 3rd Division was training in the United Kingdom and would not arrive in France until December 1916.) After 1 July, Haig had ordered a series of attacks in the hope that the Fourth Army would push to within striking distance of the German second line on the Bazentin Ridge. Once this was secured, he planned for another powerful attack to be launched from the new starting line in mid-July. The attacks between 2 and 13 July were hurriedly mounted, poorly coordinated and lacked adequate artillery support. They cost the British possibly another 25,000 casualties. But since they kept the Germans from regaining their balance, and the German army had suffered over 40,000 casualties in the first ten days of the Somme, they were, in Western Front terms, something of a success.[69]

The major attack on 14 July, launched on a much narrower front than on 1 July and with a more concentrated artillery barrage, also had some success. Since the distance to be covered was dangerously long, the infantry crept out towards the German positions in the dark and attacked at dawn. When the intense British barrage lifted, some men were within 90 metres of the German positions, able to assault them in seconds rather than minutes. By the end of the day, they had captured the villages of Bazentin le Petit and Bazentin le Grand, as well as most of Longueval. However, this success was not exploited— partly because the cavalry could not function on the slippery and broken ground or were mown down by machine-gun fire when deployed later in the day. The Germans brought in reserves and, with considerable improvisation, converted the woods that confronted the British—High Wood and Delville Wood—into nodes of formidable resistance. Still, by nightfall the British had advanced into what had been, on 1 July, the German second lines.

Believing that the British might be on the point of a dramatic breakthrough, Haig now ordered the Fourth Army to keep pushing on to High Wood, Ginchy and Guillemont, while General Hubert Gough's Reserve Army was focused on capturing the village of Pozières on the Albert–Bapaume road. Standing on high, open ground, this was one of the most strongly fortified points of the German defences and blocked the way to Bapaume. Although Haig hoped that further advances to the east might ultimately outflank Pozières, capturing the village itself would open the way for the British to assault Thiepval not from the front, as had proved so catastrophic on 1 July, but along the ridge from the south-east. The British therefore launched a series of attacks on Pozières between 13 and 17 July. Haig described them as a steady, methodical step-by-step advance, but in fact all attacks failed.

It was at this point that I Anzac Corps was deployed to the sector, marching up to the front through French villages, including Albert, where the statue of the Virgin Mary hung precariously from the spire of the shelled church. Gough, impetuous and loath to lose the momentum of the attacks on Pozières, bypassed Birdwood and White and immediately told Walker that the 1st Division should prepare to attack the village on the 19 July. Since the Australians were not yet even in the area, Walker protested vehemently and, with Birdwood and White weighing in, Gough deferred the date of the attack for a few days. This allowed time for 'jumping-off trenches' to be prepared, narrowing the distance the infantry had to cross in No Man's Land, and for Walker to persuade the British command that the attack should be launched not from the south-west of Pozières, as previous attacks had been, but from the south-east.[70]

An awe-inspiring artillery barrage preceded the attack, now scheduled for 23 July (see Map 7). While incendiary rounds set fire to trees and buildings, the barrage—which grew in power over some days—culminated in a massive round of 'hurricane fire'. Every gun fired as fast as its crews could load it. For the Australians waiting for the assault to start, the tension was excruciating. As Sergeant B.W. Champion of the 1st Battalion said:

> it seemed as if the earth opened up with a crash. The ground shook and trembled, the concussion made our ears ring. It was impossible to speak to a man lying alongside. It is strange how men creep together for protection. Soon, instead of four paces interval between the men, we came to lying alongside each other, and no motioning could make them move apart.

For the Germans, who were the target of the barrage and already hungry and thirsty, the barrage became 'almost unendurable'.[71]

The attack on Pozières by the 1st and 3rd Brigades was tactically more innovative than the one at Fromelles. Instead of the whole force trying to push through to the final objective, becoming increasingly exhausted as they did so, the plan was for a first wave of infantry to creep as close as possible to the German trenches, even though this risked their being hit by their own barrage. Once they had captured the first line of German trenches, a second wave would pass through them, taking the second line. A third wave, in turn, would leapfrog the second.

When the attack began, at 12.30 a.m. on 23 July, the first German trench was captured quickly. As Archie Barwick of the 1st Battalion recalled:

> Nothing stopped us and we swept into their front line like a torrent, shooting, bayoneting and clubbing everything like fury. It was all over in a few minutes and we dashed on to the next line . . . The Germans seemed thunderstruck at the violence of the attack.

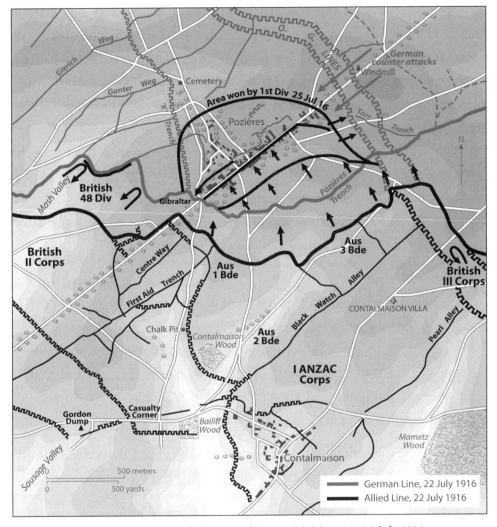

Map 7: Pozières, attack by Australian 1st Division, 23–25 July 1916

By daybreak, Australians were in the ruins of Pozières itself. There, according to Bean, they engaged in the 'grim sport' of:

> 'ratting' occasional fugitives from the rubble heaps, chasing terrified and shrieking Germans and killing them with the bayonet, or shooting from the shoulder at those who got away, and then sitting down on the door-steps to smoke and wait for others to bolt from the cellars. Occasionally parties of prisoners, in some cases numbering nearly a score, were brought in by two or three men.[72]

However, as always on the Western Front, initial success was only part of the story. The Germans were under orders never to abandon territory. Any enemy breakthrough must be met with an immediate counter-attack. Soon German troops began to reappear from the bunkers and ruins of pulverised Pozières, intent on taking back what they had lost. Since the British 48th Division and III Corps had not made the same progress to the left and right of the line, the Australians were exposed as a spearhead into the German lines.

A wave of German counter-attacks took place on 23 and 24 July. H. 'Squatter' Preston of the 9th Battalion later wrote of an attack coming from the direction of the Windmill:

> The enemy came over the ridge like swarms of ants, rushing from shell-hole to shell-hole. Our men, full of fight and confidence, lined the parapet and emptied magazine after magazine into them. Some of the men, anxious to get a shot at the Germans, pulled one another down from the fire-step in the midst of the fight. Under this fire and that of our machine-guns and the artillery, which tore great gaps in the advancing lines, the enemy attack withered.

The German artillery fire at this time was more intense than anything the Australians had ever experienced. To quote Archie Barwick:

> As the day wore on the shelling became heavier and heavier. The earth rocked and swayed like a haystack. Our heads were aching like mad, men were being buried by the falling trenches and hastily dug out again. Others were crying like children, crouched in the trench, their nerves completely gone. Some went mad and rushed out of the trench to certain death . . . By nightfall our trenches had practically ceased to exist.[73]

Within four days the 1st Division had lost 5285 officers and men and the battlefield was strewn with decaying corpses. The wounded could be evacuated only by heroic stretcher bearers who were themselves shot down. When the division was relieved on 27 July by the 2nd Division, the survivors seemed like men who had 'been in hell'. E.J. Rule later said:

> Almost without exception each man looked drawn and haggard, and so dazed that they appeared to be walking in a dream, and their eyes looked glassy and starey. Quite a few were silly, and these were the only noisy ones in the crowd . . . In all my life I've never seen men so shaken up as these.[74]

The 2nd Division under Legge was brought in to capture the German second line, so-called O.G. (Old German) lines north and north-east of the village (see Map 8). From here, the advance along the ridge towards Mouquet Farm and Thiepval could be developed. However, Legge lacked Walker's touch, and the attack—which began just after midnight on 29 July—was a failure. No jumping-off trenches were dug and the element of surprise was lost when

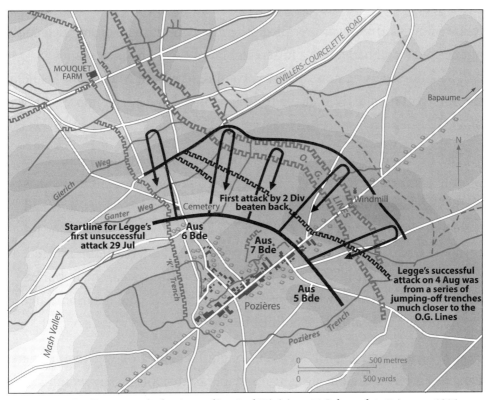

Map 8: Pozières, attacks by Australian 2nd Division, 29 July and 4–5 August 1916

the Germans saw the 7th Brigade moving up to the line. As Corporal Peter Gaffney recalled:

> Fritz had heard or saw us moving. They at once gave the alarm and opened up a most awful m. Gun and artillery fire on us where we lay . . . We charged through a most hellish fire and were cut down in hundreds. On arriving close to his trench we found that his barb [sic] wire had not been touched by our shells, and it was an utter impossibility to get through it, as it was a thick uncut entanglement, after a vain attempt to get threw [sic] and being literaly [sic] mown down all the while, we were forced to retire to the centre of no mans land and there made an attempt to dig ourselves in, the shelling the whole time was intense.[75]

Unable to find distinguishing features in a landscape pockmarked with craters and shattered soil, the troops became disoriented in the darkness. The attack failed, with the loss of 3500 officers and men. Days of intense shelling followed. As Gaffney again recalled, 'there were hundreds of wounded could not be got at, and had to die a miserable slow death in no man's land'.[76]

The landscape was now almost beyond description. Major B.B. Leane of the 48th Battalion arrived at the front line on 3 August. His impression was of 'Hell'.

> The dead are lying everywhere, some of them several days old, some only today or yesterday. The stench is terrible but that is nothing. It is the sight of the poor fellows huddled up there—gruesome, unsightly and bloodied—that makes you realise to the full the beastly side, the awful side of war. The charges, the taking of villages and ridges, all this is heroic and glorious to read of—but afterwards the rotting dead, the unburied dead, the fine fellows who a few days ago were brave, and handsome and full of life and health, now nothing but horrible, putrid masses of flesh.

Bean's reaction when he wandered through the desolation was that 'Pozières has been a terrible sight . . . [an] insatiable factory of ghastly wounds. The men are simply turned in there as into some ghastly giant mincing machine.'[77]

Haig, however, had little sympathy. He noted in his diary of 29 July that the attack by the 2nd Division had failed, so it seemed, from 'want of thorough preparation . . . Some of the [Anzac Corps] Divisional Generals are so ignorant and (like many Colonials) so conceited, that they cannot be trusted to work out unaided the plans of attack.' To Birdwood he said, 'You're not fighting Bashi-Bazouks now . . . This is serious, scientific war, and you are up against the most scientific and most military nation in Europe.' It was patronising and callous, but Haig at least listened when Brudenell White corrected his interpretation of events.[78]

When the 2nd Division attacked again on 4–5 August, with the British 12th Division to their left, they were better prepared. Their artillery support was greater and jumping-off trenches had been dug, despite appalling conditions in which men and trenches alike were buried by the constant German bombardment. This attack also started at dusk so that the infantry, increasingly disoriented by the lunar landscape, could see the German lines ahead of them. Gaffney, back on the front line again, recalled:

> we charged for the two lines of enemy trenches and captured the first line with little trouble the next objective 700 yards distant gave us a rough time bombing the Hun out from his strong posts his shell fire playing on us, as we advanced. The barb wire this time was cut to ribbons by our previous shelling, so gave us no trouble after clearing the Hun out and taking a number of prisoners, we set to work to dig ourselves in and put in the night thus . . . Fritz resighted his artillery on to our new positions and gave us hell all night.[79]

Finally, on 5 August, the 2nd Division captured the highest point of the ridge: the Windmill. From here, Bapaume—the goal of the British cavalry on 1 July—could be seen 9 kilometres away. Some men set out for the O.G.2 line but the inevitable German counter-attacks started, one after the other, accompanied by the heaviest bombardment of the campaign.

Now completely exhausted (it had lost over 6600 casualties since 27 July), the 2nd Division was relieved by the 4th Division under Cox. What awaited

The village of Pozières some months after the battle of July 1916. (AWM E00532)

The memorial erected to commemorate the Australian soldiers of the 1st Division killed during the capture of Pozières in July 1916. It no longer exists. (AWM EZ0131)

An Australian soldier on the Somme front trying to obtain a drink under a frozen tank during the harsh winter of 1916–17. (AWM E00171)

A wave crashes over the bow of HMAS *Melbourne*, seen from HMAS *Sydney*. Both ships were taking part in patrols of the North Sea with the Royal Navy. (AWM EN0344)

these reinforcements as they came through the lines was 'gruesome, horrible'. Edmund Sullivan, who was to die on 2 September, wrote on 9 August: 'We are in a half made Fritz dug out . . . Dead men half buried everywhere. As I walked along the ground "gave" underneath me and I discovered that it was dead bodies with just a few inches of earth covering them.'[80] The Australians' task was to push along the ridge from Pozières to Mouquet Farm (see Map 9). Gough thought the Germans had evacuated the area, but he was wrong. Beneath the rubble was a honeycomb of defensive works, which the Germans fought ferociously to retain. The attacking troops were at a huge tactical disadvantage. Forced to advance along the crest of a narrow ridge, they created a salient that became progressively more vulnerable to fire from various directions. All their movements could be observed by German forces around Courcelette and, because the attacks were always small in scale, the German artillery was free to concentrate its fire on them. As Robin Prior and Trevor Wilson have

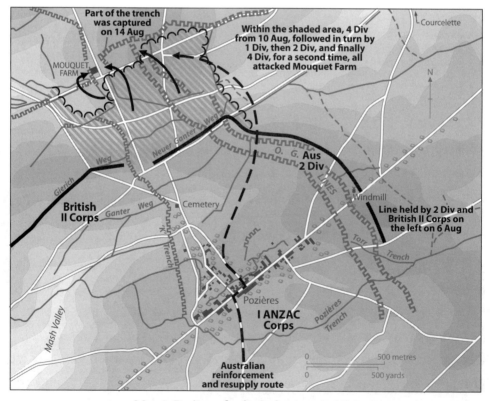

Map 9: Pozières, final attacks, August 1916

said, 'Of all the tactical nightmares on the Somme this has some claim to be considered the worst.'[81]

Over the next three weeks, the Australians—in turn, the 4th Division, the 1st, the 2nd, and again the 4th—fought desperately to capture the farm, but although they got to within 200 metres of the Germans' positions, they could not completely dislodge them. E.R. Rule's later account captures some of the intensity of the fighting:

Some Huns showed up in front and we pelted bombs into them as hard as we could throw, and they ran for their lives . . . One man shot a Hun who was almost falling on him. Anyway we had captured this part of the place; but when I looked round I discovered that I had only about four men left . . . as I turned I found that the Huns were flowing back, pelting bombs at us. One almost hit my foot and I had barely moved a yard when the bomb went off. I had the impression that someone had stabbed me with hot pins along my legs, and I felt blood running down my hand. It knocked the breath out of me, and I remember staggering around for a while. But the fight became so willing that we had to get out . . . My ears were ringing with the row of the bombs, but about it all I could hear the Huns yelling 'Ja! Ja!' as they heaved them.[82]

Finally, on 5 September, the exhausted I Anzac Corps was taken out of the line. Its casualties since 19 July totalled 24,139. After their relief, Gough reverted to the idea of taking Thiepval frontally. A major attack launched on 26 September with a huge concentration of artillery on a front wide enough for the infantry to present a dispersed target resulted, at last, in the capture of Thiepval and the Zollern Redoubt beyond it. Mouquet Farm fell the next day.[83]

Whether these 'successes' were worth the cost must be questioned. In retrospect, the British operations to this point of the Somme campaign seem piecemeal, poorly directed and disproportionately costly in terms of casualties. In what J.P. Harris has condemned as 'a breakdown of command and control', Haig and his headquarters seem to have lost their grip on the battle and on the armies of Rawlinson and Gough. The campaign was allowed to drift without clear strategic purpose, even though between 15 July and 14 September the Fourth Army advanced only about 900 metres across an 8-kilometre front.[84]

Even then Haig continued to plan for another major attack, on 15 September. Convinced that the Germans must now be near breaking point, he thought that the Fourth and Reserve Armies, together with the French Sixth Army, could break through north-east of Flers. Then the cavalry could flow through behind the rear of the Germans. It was, as ever, an illusion. However, Haig had a new weapon at his disposal: the tank. Though as yet primitive, these armoured vehicles promised to bring some mobility back into warfare. Clad in steel and advancing on caterpillar tracks, they could grind their way across No Man's Land, crushing the barbed wire, demolishing the trenches and opening the way for the infantry.

In fact, when they were used on 15 September, many of the 48 British Mark I tanks proved mechanically unreliable, vulnerable to shellfire and unable to keep up with the infantry (they could travel at only 3 kilometres an hour). In addition, since the British artillery did not lay down a barrage on the corridors along which the tanks lumbered, German machine-gun fire was completely unsubdued on some sections of the front, with terrible conse-quences for the infantry. When grouped together, the tanks did have some positive effect, but generally their contribution to the battle was marginal.

Yet the Battle of Flers-Courcelette, as it became known, was a major success—at least compared with the first day of the Somme. More than twice the ground taken on 1 July was captured for perhaps half the British casualties: in all, some 8000 metres of the German first line and 3650 metres of the second line. From this point, the British XV Corps, including the New Zealand Division, would push on in the following week to capture the villages of Flers, Courcelette and Martinpuich. In the opinion of one military historian, September was by far the worst month of the Somme battle for the Germans. As it ended, they were 'closer to collapse than they would be again any time before 1918'.[85]

The human cost

The Somme saw a dramatic escalation in the rate at which Australian troops were killed and wounded. In the seven weeks after 19 July, the AIF lost at least 23,000 casualties, of whom more than a quarter were killed or died of their wounds. At Gallipoli, it had taken some eight months to incur 26,111 casualties, including 8141 deaths.[86]

It was the intensity of artillery and machine-gun fire that made the difference. The vast majority (85 per cent) of battle casualties suffered by the AIF on the Western Front were caused by missiles—shrapnel, shell fragments and high-velocity bullets—rather than the bayonets (0.28 per cent) that are popularly associated with trench warfare. The wounds these projectiles caused were grievous. As the official medical historian said of high-velocity bullets, 'The close range of attrition warfare made common some degree of the "explosive" effect or severe disruption [of soft tissue and flesh]'. Of high-explosive shells, he said:

> The great variation in the shape and size of the fragments from these, and their comparatively low velocity, resulted in a very wide range of wound. Fragments often lodged and lacerated severely . . . they almost invariably carried portions of clothing and other matter . . . The wounds inflicted were often multiple, and of a truly 'shocking' nature.

Constant shellfire also made it difficult to give the wounded the rapid treatment they needed. Within a few hours in the mud and filth of the battle-field, infection could set in. E.J. Rule recalled that 'Lots of the boys that were being found at this time had their wounds all fly-blown.' In a matter of hours, the deadly bacterial infection gangrene could take hold.[87]

Modern warfare also drove men mad. The deafening noise of artillery and its all-pervasive threat shattered the nerves of many men already exhausted by terror and lack of sleep. As the British author Eric Leed has said, noise created 'the altered state of consciousness' that many soldiers described. Combined—as it so often was—with the constriction of vision on a shattered battle landscape, it:

eliminated most of those signs that allow individuals to collectively order their experience in terms of problems to be solved in some kind of rational sequence. The sheer volume of noise that dominated the front was experienced as supremely disorienting . . . noise meant nothing but chaos; it caused nothing but fear, stupefaction, and dull resignation . . . the barrage most often effected a transition into neurosis, breakdown, and mental disorder.

Close-quarters fighting could have a similar effect. Rule again wrote of Pozières:

One poor beggar . . . was out of his mind with terror, his eyes were staring out of his head, blood was splashed all over his face and tunic; he could only mumble; and he came up and tried to take hold of me . . . He was always a very nervous man, and the work of bombing platoons was a terror for him.[88]

Initially, military authorities refused to recognise shell shock as a 'genuine' injury, suspecting its victims of being cowards, lacking self-control and even having a hereditary weakness. But in time the evidence of the psychological trauma inflicted by industrialised war became too compelling. The symptoms were physical as well as psychological: exhaustion, delirium, confusion, hysteria, depression, amnesia, obsession and even loss of speech. A soldier on medical detail, Sergeant J.R. Edwards, who was buried alive by shelling at La Boiselle, recalled:

I tried to raise a cry but the earth was over my face, and my hands were pinned across my chest by the weight [of earth] . . . I struggled like hell but could do nothing. All of a sudden the pressure became heavier; it was irresistible, and I was blotted out. I recollect thinking 'I'm gone'. [When rescued] something had been jarred inside my tough old nut, and my memory was affected . . . I would recognise the boys, but for the life of me could not remember their names.

By early 1916, shell shock was officially recognised, and over the next three years some 1624 Australians would be identified as suffering from it (55 per cent of the cases occurred in 1917). However, the stigma of cowardice and the suspicion that these men had failed to conform to masculine ideals were never entirely dispelled.[89]

Some victims recovered, but many did not. John Forsyth, who commanded the 2nd Brigade at Pozières, was hospitalised and sent back to Australia with his health broken. The 4th Division commander, Cox, would suffer a breakdown in January 1917, and the 6th Brigade commander, Jack Gellibrand, though he stayed on to endure the disasters of Bullecourt, would also relinquish command for a time in 1917.[90]

The growing trauma affected Australians at home, too. For every man killed or wounded on the Somme, there was a family struggling to cope—not just with the scale of the casualties, but with the gnawing doubt about their value. The authorities tried to suppress details of the losses on the Somme, but letters from the front told a more realistic story. The Raws family in Adelaide, for example, lost two sons within a matter of weeks in July and August 1916. Goldy Raws went missing near Pozières, possibly blown to pieces by a shell that landed near him as he charged a German trench. His brother Alec wrote home on 19 August 1916:

> His death has proved a far greater shock to me than I thought possible, since we came out of the line—probably due to nerves . . . I want to tell you, so that it may be on record, that I honestly believe that Goldy and many other officers were murdered . . . through the incompetence, callousness, and personal vanity of those high in authority. I realise the seriousness of what I say, but I am so bitter, and the facts are so palpable, that it must be said.

This was the man who had volunteered a little more than a year earlier to fight for principles and things that were 'worth more than life'.[91]

Alec himself was killed four days later, on 23 August. What did his parents make of his last letter home, with its indictment of the Allied command? It would have reached them after he died. Would they have found consolation in the letters of condolence that poured in, invoking the high diction of duty that Alec himself once espoused? 'They were good fearless soldiers, and were lost in bravely and devotedly doing their duty. To give one's life for King and country and the principles of humanity and righteousness is the supreme sacrifice. They made it.' Perhaps the Rawses found consolation in their faith and church. They dedicated a room to their sons at Flinders Street Baptist Church. But it seems that even the power of faith to console was becoming strained. As the *Australian Baptist* lamented on 27 June 1916:

> Ministers are finding it hard to preach, as though there were a stone wall in front of them, instead of responsive hearts. People in the pews are finding it hard to listen. It is as though God had sent . . . famine in the land . . . This awful holocaust is in itself a challenge to Christianity. It has exploded like a bomb at our feet, at the very base of our religion, and with many has shaken the foundations of their faith.[92]

Remembering Pozières

Not surprisingly, Pozières soon acquired the status of 'Australia's most sacred acre' outside of Gallipoli. The commemoration of the battle began early. Close to the first anniversary, a white Celtic cross was unveiled in honour of the 1st Division. The site of the Windmill was also marked during the war with a wooden cross remembering the 2nd Division. Then, when the 1st Division came to choose a site for its permanent memorial in 1919, it selected Pozières. Even though the division went on to fight at Bullecourt, the Third Battle of Ypres and in the triumphal 'Hundred Days' of 1918, this battle remained the defining moment of its wartime record. As the 1st Division veterans saw it, Pozières was their first major operation on a large scale in France, and one in which they were 'unmercifully shelled from 7 in the morning to 11 at night, but in spite of this bombardment the troops held onto the positions until relieved'.[93]

The permanent divisional memorial, taking the same austere obelisk form of other divisional memorials on the Western Front (though flanked, for a time, by field guns), was installed at the western end of Pozières village in 1919. Hopes that further areas of Pozières—some trenches and an infamous German pillbox, Gibraltar—might then be preserved as memorials were thwarted when the local landowners and town authorities had reservations about so much of their land being appropriated. However, after the 2nd Division's wooden cross was destroyed by a storm in 1930, the Australian War Memorial managed to purchase in 1935 the land on which the increasingly iconic Windmill had stood. As Bean would say in 1946, in one of his most-quoted passages:

> At Bullecourt, Messines, Ypres and elsewhere Australian infantry after-wards suffered intense bombardment, but never anything comparable in duration or effect with this . . . The Windmill site . . . with the old mound still there—marks a ridge more densely sown with Australian sacrifice than any other place on earth.[94]

Today the Windmill is a quietly evocative place. A path leads to a plaque that paraphrases Bean's tribute to the Australians' sacrifice. Australian and French flags flutter overhead and the landscape beyond reveals, even now, the pulverised soil and concrete detritus of battle. In the distance can be seen the massive Thiepval monument to the 73,000 missing of the Somme and the seemingly innocuous ridge to Mouquet Farm that cost so many Australian lives in August and September 1916. The Windmill has none of the drama of the heights of Gallipoli, and in recent years it seems to have lost ground as a site of national memory to Villers-Bretonneux, which since 2008 has been the site of an official Dawn Service on Anzac Day. But it was from Pozières that a handful of soil was retrieved in 1993 to be scattered on the coffin of the Unknown Soldier interred in the Australian War Memorial on the 75th anniversary of the end of World War I. The soil of Pozières is therefore literally at the heart of Australian national commemoration.

Romani

The terrible news from France in August 1916 was briefly offset by events on the Italian front and in the Middle East. From 4 to 17 August, the Italians under General Luigi Cardorna attacked along a 240-kilometre front in the region of the Isonzo river and advanced nearly 5 kilometres (the Sixth Battle of the Isonzo). It was their first major offensive success of the war, though later battles in September to November would fail to exploit it. On 28 August, Italy also declared war on Germany (to that date, it had been at war only with Austria-Hungary and Turkey).

In Sinai, meanwhile, the Ottoman Army under its German commander, General Friedrich Freiherr Kress von Kressenstein, made another attempt to capture the Suez Canal. On the night of 3–4 August, it attacked Romani with the aim of outflanking the British positions on the coast by taking the high ground to the south-east (see Map 10). At first the Australian and New Zealand mounted troops were driven back from the forward positions they had taken up. But the Ottoman attacks eventually lost momentum and, as the British yeomanry and the New Zealand Mounted Rifles were brought in, the Ottomans were driven back by a line of Anzacs advancing across

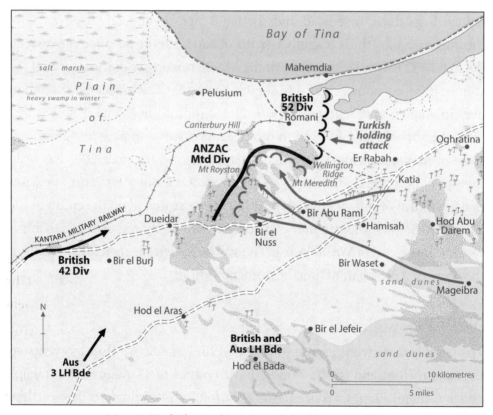

Map 10: Turkish attacks on Romani, 3–4 August 1916

the dunes with bayonets drawn. Some 4000 Ottomans surrendered. By this stage, their forces were strung out around Romani and might then have been themselves outflanked, but a breakdown in command and communications meant the opportunity was lost. Romani was a victory nonetheless, and would prove to be the last Ottoman forward movement in this theatre of operations. Thereafter, the Ottomans would be on the defensive in Sinai.

Though few Australians today know of Romani unless they happen to have come across its diorama in the Australian War Memorial, in 1916 it was hailed in a provincial newspaper as 'one of the most brilliant operations ever performed [which] has taught the Turks a lesson they will long remember'. Here was war as it was meant to be! A contributor to an Adelaide newspaper later enthused:

Romani! Our day has come at last
Romani! Our furious fight and fast.
While echoing wide o'er the desert drear,
Rolls the rollicking, roaring light horse cheer.
With dominant, daring and strafing strife,
Each galloping moment is pulsing life . . .
Romani! Ah! Life was not lived in vain.

Chauvel meanwhile was assured by a colleague, Edward Hutton, after the battle that 'all the world has complimentary remarks to make upon the Australian Light Horse'. It was unlikely, but no doubt gratifying.[95]

Conscription

However, the general strategic situation for the Allies in August 1916 was depressing, and the scale of the casualties on the Somme brought to a head the debate within Australia as to whether voluntary recruitment was sufficient to replace them. While Hughes had been overseas, the issue of conscription had not stayed under control as he had hoped it would. In January, the British government passed legislation allowing it to conscript single men and childless widowers between the ages of 18 and 41. Although there were initially a number of exemptions (the ill, married men, conscientious objectors, ministers of religion and those in essential occupations), within months conscription had been extended to almost all males. The Asquith government was also considering plans to require compulsory service— either military or economic—of all adults, male and female. In May 1916, New Zealand followed suit, introducing legislation for the conscription of non-Maori males (this would be extended to Maoris in June 1917).

Hughes was on record as saying in July 1915 that he would 'in no circumstances . . . send men out of the country to fight against their will', but rumours abounded in Australia that he would follow the British and New Zealand examples on his return. The forces for and against conscription therefore continued to mobilise. The Universal Service League, which had agreed to go into recess during the War Census, swung back into action when enlistments declined in early 1916 after peaking at 22,000 in January. It was joined by the Australian Natives Association, a nationalistic friendly society started in 1871, which also lobbied for the government 'to take immediate steps to fully utilise the services of every citizen and the resources of the Commonwealth'.[96]

Opposing conscription was the labour movement—though the strength of its opposition varied from state to state and the industrial and political wings of the movement were divided on the issue. In Queensland, the Labor-in-Politics Convention passed a resolution in March, sponsored by the Australian Workers' Union, which opposed conscription, while the Brisbane Industrial Council formally moved in April to repudiate the views Hughes was expressing in London. *The Worker* thought it was time he came home: 'you have been keeping bad company lately, company which once wouldn't "tolerate" you, and which (once upon a time) you couldn't stand at any price'. In Victoria, meanwhile, where the militants gained the upper hand during early 1916, members of parliament found themselves being threatened with loss of preselection if they refused to sign a pledge to oppose conscription. Queensland parliamentarians were under similar pressure.[97]

In New South Wales, Holman and most of his Cabinet were supporters of the Universal Service League and conscription. But they were increasingly in a minority. At the Easter Labor Conference, the parliamentarians only just held off an attempt to strip them of any control or influence over the wider labour movement. Some weeks later, in May, delegates at the interstate conference, which claimed to speak nationally for 280,000 unionists, declared by an overwhelming majority of votes their 'uncompromising hostility' to conscription.[98]

Conscious that the situation was slipping out of control, Pearce, as acting prime minister, called a secret session of parliament in May and appealed to both sides to wait until Hughes could personally report on the situation in Europe. But the debate was acrimonious, and simply reinforced existing battle lines. On 6 July, the Liberal Party's National Conference committed itself to the principle of compulsory military service overseas, while the Melbourne Trades Hall and *Labor Call* offices got busy printing thousands of copies of an anti-conscription manifesto—only to have Pearce order their confiscation on the grounds that the proofs had not been submitted to the censor prior to publication.

Everyone was poised for Hughes' return. As soon as he landed at Fremantle on 31 July, he was bombarded with exhortations to act from newspaper editors, ministerial colleagues and the governor-general, who assured him that 'public opinion is for conscription'. Hughes himself did not reveal his cards for some weeks, but he was now convinced that conscription was essential. Not only had Britain and New Zealand introduced it, but it seemed impossible to replace the AIF's huge losses on the Somme through voluntarism. In August, enlistments had been only 6345—well below what the British Army Council estimated was required. According to its calculations, the AIF needed an immediate special draft of 20,000 troops and a further 16,500 troops for each of the next three months if the 3rd Division were not be cannibalised to keep the other divisions in operation.[99]

As Hughes saw it, conscription was something that the Australian state might legitimately command of its citizens. 'The State has power to take away the liberty of those who break its laws,' he said to a meeting at the Sydney Town Hall; 'it has power to take away life itself.' However, it was patently obvious that he could not expect the support of all the parliamentary Labor Party, and particularly not of the industrial labour movement. As one of his colleagues wrote to him on 12 August, 'Conscription will, in my opinion, split the political labor party into fragments.'[100]

Hence the option of amending the *Defence Act* of 1903 to allow conscription for overseas service was precluded. Even if the lower house were to pass legislation with the help of the Liberal opposition, the Senate—with its large Labor majority—would almost certainly reject it. Nor could Hughes introduce conscription by regulation under the *War Precautions Act*. This would require the concurrence of the Executive Council (in fact, his Cabinet, which was already divided on the issue) and could again be disallowed by the Senate. In any case, the Chief Justice, Sir Samuel Griffith, considered that this course of action would be unconstitutional.[101]

So Hughes decided to take the matter to the people. Given his rapturous welcome in the southern capitals as the imperial statesman who had put Australia on the global map, he was confident that he could win the campaign. And although a popular vote would have no legal force, it would at least give him a mandate with which to confront his opponents in the labour movement. As Kevin Fewster commented later:

> It seemed a masterful tactic. Few Laborites could object to what appeared the most democratic of decision making processes. Skilful campaigning coupled with hegemonic assertion of the 'national interest' were thought likely to bring about a 'Yes' victory.[102]

After stormy meetings with his Cabinet and the federal Labor caucus over some four days, Hughes announced to parliament on 30 August that there would be a referendum on conscription for overseas service on 28 October. The case he made was partly pragmatic, partly an articulation of his passionate conviction that core national interests were at stake. The voluntary system of recruitment, he claimed, had failed:

> The great offensive, in which our troops have covered themselves with glory, has cost a fearful price; yet it is, and must be, pressed forward with implacable resolution. To falter now is to make the great sacrifice of lives of no avail, to enable the enemy to recover himself, and, if not to

defeat us, to prolong the struggle indefinitely, and thus rob the world of all hope of a lasting peace . . . Our national existence, our liberties, are at stake. There rests upon every man an obligation to do his duty in the spirit that befits free men.

This obligation, Hughes conceded, must also extend to the wealthy. In deference to the long-standing demand within his own party for a 'conscription' of wealth, he said:

Wealth has its duties; it owes all that it has to the State, and must be prepared, if necessary, to sacrifice that all to the State. Many wealthy men have responded nobly to the call of duty, others have not. But they cannot be allowed thus to evade their responsibilities.[103]

With this began a public debate that has never been rivalled in Australian political history for its bitterness, divisiveness and violence. For the next two months, Hughes toured the eastern states working for the success of the referendum 'as if it were the only thing for which I live'. Proponents and opponents of conscription, in turn, formed organisations, convened mass public meetings, campaigned in the press and, in the case of the government, mobilised various instruments of repression and censorship in an effort to win the majority of Australians to their view.[104]

The question to be put to the Australian people was rather opaque: 'Are you in favour of the Government having, in this grave emergency, the same compulsory powers over citizens in regard to requiring their military service, for the term of this war, outside the Commonwealth, as it has now with regard to military service within the Commonwealth?' What was at stake, it soon emerged, was not simply a disagreement about the military need for conscription, but an irreconcilable conflict of views about core values: the nature of citizenship and national security; equality of sacrifice in times of national crisis; and the legitimate exercise of power within Australia's democracy. These are contentious issues at any time, but against the backdrop of the Battle of the Somme, with its endless toll of dead and wounded, the debate about conscription became infused with the passion and hysteria of mass grief.

The case for yes

The faultlines along which Australian society divided on conscription were complex, and are still not entirely clear, given the lack of sophisticated psephology in 1916. However, with some important exceptions, Australians voted in ways that reflected their class, religion and gender, with class perhaps the dominant variable. The 'yes' vote was generally championed by the political and social elites, including the leadership of the Protestant churches, the majority of the press, business leaders and the Liberal Party. For these largely middle-class Australians, whose voice was channelled through a newly created National Referendum League, the military case for compulsion seemed irrefutable. They accepted the British command's view that there was no other way of supplying the AIF with the reinforcements it needed. Put simply: 'The surest way and the quickest way of ending this war is to throw every ounce of our strength and resources into the conflict.' Australia had promised two years earlier to commit itself to 'the last man and the last shilling'. Now was the time to prove its people meant this by embracing conscription.[105]

For such Australians, the case for conscription was also a moral and principled one. The war remained a just cause—a noble struggle in defence of the British Empire and the values for which it stood. The enemy was a brutal one, whose atrocities and war crimes continued to be given prominence in the daily press. As Hughes said in his manifesto to the Australian people on 18 September:

> Europe has been drenched with blood, innocent non-combatants foully murdered or subjected to unspeakable outrages, millions of helpless men, women, and little children driven from their homes, their beloved country ravaged by fire and sword . . . This is a war to the death, a fight to the finish . . . Our only hope of national safety, of retaining our liberties, lies in decisive victory by Britain and her Allies over the hosts of military despotism.[106]

Leaders of the Protestant churches also continued to see the war as a righteous struggle between 'the interests of the Kingdom of God' and the satanic forces of Germany led by the Antichrist Kaiser. To quote the *Australian Baptist*:

> Some of us . . . advocate fighting this war to the bitter end because we conscientiously and righteously object to the triumph of German 'kultur', and the perpetual reign of German militarism, which victory for Germany would involve . . . this is not a war of aggression in the case of Britain and her Allies . . . it is primarily a war of defence, and a war which could not be avoided . . . [conscientious objection would mean] the sacrificing of France to German barbarism, the annihilation of our soldiers in Flanders, the subjugation of England, the loss of all her Dominions, and the setting back of the clock of civilisation for centuries. Is conscription too big a price to pay for the aversion of such horrors and calamities as these?[107]

For some Protestant leaders, the war was also a blessing—terrible but positive in that it was purifying the people of Australia through their suffering, sacrifice and self-abnegation. Christians, it was said, should repent of their sins and follow Christ's injunction to 'Render unto Caesar the things which are Caesar's, and unto God the things that are God's' (Matthew 22:21). Though there was not a shred of biblical authority justifying it, one clergyman even concluded that Jesus would have voted 'yes'. This, it must be said, was not a universal view. Some Christians believed that 'Warfare was not Christ's way of gaining human progress', and a small group of Protestant clergymen issued their own manifesto condemning the new 'religion of the State'. 'In this new religion patriotism is the virtue which takes the place of Christian Brotherhood: the State replaces God, and the National flag replaces the Cross. Its supreme law is not the law of God, but the military safety of the country.'[108]

However, if sacrifice and hardship were to be embraced as moral goods in themselves, the advocates of conscription also insisted that the suffering of war must be shared equitably. It was invidious that only those who volunteered took the risk of injury and death. One federal member of parliament argued:

I can take honourable members into street after street and show them families, every son in which has gone to the front, whereas in the same street there are families with more sons, not one of whom has volunteered. It is the inherent selfishness of human nature that has made me a conscriptionist.[109]

Australia also owed it to those who had already volunteered and died to ensure that others followed them: 'our own boys, those brave young men whom we have sent over there, are calling us to come and assist them', one of the fathers of Federation, Sir John Forrest, argued. A handbill appealing to 'Women of Australia' also pleaded:

WILL YOU JOIN OUR BATTALION?
It is the largest Battalion in the world.
It consists of Women who will vote 'YES' on October 28th.
It includes the Mothers, Wives, Sisters, and Sweethearts of the men who have gone to fight for everything in the world worth fighting for.
It will not allow these heroes to perish in the trenches from utter weariness and heartbreak for want of reinforcements . . .
It is a line of defence behind the men in the trenches.[110]

Equality of sacrifice was an argument rooted partly in the agony of bereavement and loss: Why should my son, father or husband die while yours lives? But it was also a debate about the obligations of citizenship. Conscription was a great social leveller. Military service should not be a matter of individual choice. As one church leader said, the principle of voluntarism

is wrong in conception, unfair in its incidence and inadequate in its results. It is wrong in conception because it treats the supreme question of the preservation of the nation as if it were purely a matter of private inclination instead of being the inalienable duty of each individual.

Hughes also argued that 'The supreme duty which a democrat owes to his country is to fight for it . . . Unless a nation fights for its liberties, it can neither earn nor deserve them.' These were powerful arguments, highlighting the contradiction at the heart of any democratic state which enshrines individual freedom and choice but requires for its survival that its citizens be willing to die in its defence.[111]

For the 'yes' case, voluntarism had a further flaw in that it weakened the future viability of the Australian race. If only volunteers—who were assumed to be the fittest, the most virile and the most morally sound of the male population—were willing to die, the race might become degenerate. As Lieutenant Thomas Richards wrote from the front,

> the fathers of [the coming generation of Australia] will be medical rejects and cold footer malingerers . . . Australia should take the lesson from France, and not allow her bravest and her best to be killed off: take them home, they have proved themselves and replace them with untried men. We have plenty of them.[112]

Even more alarming than the impact of war on the Australian race would be the vulnerability of the continent to external threats if Britain were defeated in Europe and the Royal Navy no longer a presence in the Pacific. Who then would restrain Japanese influence in the region?

All of these arguments were positioned within the unquestioning affirmation of the British Empire that had validated Australia's initial commitment to the war. The sense of national pride in the AIF's exploits as a result of Gallipoli and the Somme had done nothing to challenge the view of many Australians that British interests were their own. 'Nothing could be more glorious than Britain drawing the sword in defence of right and justice,' the *Daily Telegraph* trumpeted. Only if Britain triumphed could Australia's security be ensured. As one federal MP argued:

> Where is Australia now being defended, if not on foreign soil? What on earth will be the use of our democratic institutions if the Empire goes down in this struggle? . . . everything we have enjoyed up to the present is based upon the strength of the Empire, and if the Empire goes down we go down with it.

'Just as a mother throws a mantle of protection over her child,' another parliamentarian argued, 'so Great Britain, the mother of the Empire, has thrown her flag about Australia, and has defended us during every moment of our existence. For that reason, if for no other, we ought to respond ungrudgingly, unselfishly, to her call.'[113]

Loyalty to Britain therefore became the quintessential test of civic virtue in the rhetoric of the 'yes' case. Those who opposed conscription and the unequivocal commitment to the imperial cause that it represented were not nationalists with a different understanding of Australia's interests. Rather, they were 'disloyal', stigmatised with insinuations of treason, treachery and pro-Germanism. 'Nothing could be more certain than this fact,' one pamphlet said: 'if you vote "No" you will help the Kaiser and his infamous Huns.'[114]

The case for no

The opponents of conscription had their own powerful logic, matching each of the arguments for conscription with a competing view. Dominated by the trade union movement but not limited to them, the anti-conscription groups also spoke of loyalty and equality of sacrifice. But for them it was loyalty to class as well as to nation, and equality meant the 'plutocrats' as well as the workers bearing the economic cost of the war. After two years of conflict, the union movement's disillusionment with the government was explosive. Despite many government assurances, there was no 'conscription of wealth'—whatever that might mean—and no serious commitment to protecting workers' conditions by controlling war profits and prices.

Military conscription was feared as a harbinger of industrial conscription. The rights that the union movement had wrested from capital by bitter industrial action over the past 20 years would be in jeopardy, and the very existence of the male working class put at risk. The *Australian Worker*, under the editorship of the brilliant wordsmith Henry Boote, warned on 7 September that 'unscrupulous capitalists, waxing fat on the ghastly profits of war, will have the multitudes at their mercy'. With men drafted overseas, women would take their place on half the pay as 'cheap-labor competitors with the men': 'Unionism is to be ground beneath the Iron Heel. The door is to be thrown wide open for the sweating of women and children robbed of their bread winners.'[115]

Even worse, conscription would almost certainly lead to Australian workers being replaced by cheaper Asian labour. The referendum, the radical parliamentarian Frank Anstey said, should be called the 'Coloured Labour Referendum', since a 'yes' vote would result in coloured workers displacing white ones. This was a theme on which Boote waxed lyrical:

> If . . . the white workers are drained away from our industries and shipped away like cargoes of meat, a labor famine will be created, and this MUST mean the influx of labor from that colored ocean by which Mr. Hughes himself, in an unguarded moment, warned us that we are surrounded. There is one way, and only one way, to avert this cataclysm of color which would utterly destroy us as a White Nation—Vote 'No'.[116]

These fears were inflamed in the midst of the conscription debate by the arrival in Australia of two groups of Maltese workers. The first 98 immigrants arrived at the end of September; another 200 were known to be heading for Australia on a French ship, the *Gange*, which was expected to arrive on 28 October—the very day of the vote. The labour press saw in this a dark plot to introduce what it described as 'sullen, dark intruders with Negroid features or . . . turbanned coolies flooding across the land'. The threat they posed was not only to jobs but to Australian women. 'If you want to preserve your women folk from the contamination of the black man,' *The Worker* said, 'be careful to vote "No".'[117]

Fearing that this issue would 'kill the referendum', Hughes put the British government under pressure to stop issuing passports to single Maltese men. The captain of the *Gange*, meanwhile, was urged to delay the ship's arrival until after the referendum. When the boat eventually reached Melbourne, the Maltese passengers were required to take the dictation test that was the regulatory mechanism of the White Australia Policy. The language that the authorities chose to test their language skills, and hence eligibility for admission to Australia, was Dutch! Predictably, the Maltese failed and were pushed on to the French colony of New Caledonia. Eventually they were allowed to settle in Australia, but a visceral racism had been unleashed into the conscription debate. 'Australia bids fair to be a white man's paradise; do not run the risk of turning it into a black man's hell' was the advice of the *Australian Worker* to its readers on 26 October, two days before they voted.[118]

Racism, of course, struck a chord well beyond the labour movement, as did many other arguments mobilised by the 'no' case. Conservatives and radicals alike feared that stripping Australia of all its adult males might leave it more vulnerable to the threat from Japan. Seven of the nine parliamentarians speaking against conscription when the referendum bill was debated in September mentioned in some way the threat to Australia from the north. But beyond this, the 'no' case had other demographic and economic cards to play. Australia's resources and population were not infinite. At some time the country would reach breaking point, and national bankruptcy and economic 'ruination' might follow. Small businesses would collapse if the domestic market were to shrink and the male population of breadwinners be depleted further. Rather than provide more men to 'pump lead into the Hun "Somewhere in France"', Australia should do more of what it did best: exporting food and raw materials to maintain the armies already in the field.[119]

Opponents of conscription also challenged the accuracy of official estimates of the number of reinforcements needed to replace the AIF losses. 'Too many men were asked for,' the *Australian Worker* argued on 24 September, maintaining that the Army Council's calculations were based on recent very severe losses on the Somme, not on the average wastage across the two years of war. It was not necessary to recruit 16,500 men per month to maintain Australia's five divisions in the field. Rather, 'this queer manipulation of figures drawn by a conjurer's hand out of the darkness' was a ploy behind which lurked plans to create a new army. As it happened, the critics were right. Australia's five divisions were maintained in the field (though with ever-declining numbers) until late 1918 without the recruitment targets of Hughes and the Army Council ever being met.[120]

Like their opponents, those advocating the 'no' case also claimed the high moral ground. Invoking civil liberties, anti-conscriptionists claimed that it was a violation of democracy to force men to fight and kill against their will. 'Society cannot compel an individual to love, Society cannot compel the individual to hate,' Boote argued on 7 September. 'Society goes outside its moral jurisdiction when, against his will, it compels the individual to caress another; or when, against his will, it compels the individual to fight another.' *The Worker* continued to elaborate this point on 14 September:

> To permit a majority to vote to resolve such a question is, we say, a prostitution of the democratic system . . . There are matters beyond the jurisdiction of the ballot box. This is one of them. There are issues which only the individual conscience can rightly adjudicate upon. This is one of them . . . You cannot, by counting heads, dispose of a question that belongs to the province of the soul. In this respect the personal will is supreme and sacred.[121]

Censorship, surveillance and repression

These arguments were given weight by the fact that it seemed the country might well be heading towards a form of despotism. Despite Hughes' and Pearce's assurances in parliament that complete freedom of speech would be allowed during the referendum campaign, the government resorted to partisan censorship and severe repression of opposition. Censors were instructed to discreetly suppress all discussion of conscription in the press except official statements made by Hughes. Newspaper editors were deluged with instructions about what they could—or, more often, could not—publish. Permissible material was that which was not offensive to Britain or any of its allies, which did not incite any breach of federal or state law or any strike, and which did not contravene the already comprehensive regulations of the *War Precautions Act*. Given that the censors were middle-class and professional men, and intolerant of anyone who questioned Australia's commitment to the war, their discretion was usually used to the benefit of the 'yes' case. The radical press were forced to play 'a cat and mouse game' with the censors, repeatedly submitting drafts of articles for mauling and revision. At first, the fact that a news report had been censored was flagged by blank columns where the offending text would have been, but eventually the authorities demanded that there be no indication that any material had been excised.[122]

At the same time, the government's regime of surveillance and control was becoming more intrusive. In January 1916, the censors and state police forces had been joined by the first Commonwealth agency dedicated to security, the Australian Special Intelligence Bureau (established as a branch of the Imperial Counter Espionage Bureau). Anti-conscriptionists found their correspondence being monitored and their homes being raided for potentially treasonable material. Socialist and anti-war organisations, such as the Peace Alliance and the Women's Peace Army, established by Vida Goldstein, Adela Pankhurst and Cecilia John in July 1915, were also denied access to public spaces for their mass meetings. Since the civic authorities controlling these venues were elected on a franchise determined by property qualifications, they usually identified with the 'yes' case, as did the police—at least in Victoria. Even where meetings were disrupted by returned soldiers and pro-conscriptionists, it was the 'no' supporters who were arrested, usually on charges relating to property and public order.[123]

The most vicious repression was reserved for the Industrial Workers of the World. With a membership of about 2000 across Australia, the 'Wobblies' were not a serious threat to the Australian political order, despite their ideological commitment to Marxism, class warfare and the destruction of capitalism. But from August 1914, they had been implacably opposed to a war in which, as they saw it, the working class had no stake. As the IWW newspaper *Direct Action* said soon after the war commenced:

> Workers you have nothing to 'gain' by volunteering to fight the battles of your masters . . . Make class before country your motto. Your class have made the Empire for the few to live in and to enjoy the fruits of your labour. When the Empire is in danger, let those who own and control it, fight for it.

Naturally the IWW opposed all recruitment, be it voluntary or compulsory, and even encouraged workers to sabotage the war effort by 'go slows'.[124]

For Hughes and the pro-conscriptionists, the IWW could easily be represented as the epitome of disloyalty and subversion. The *Sydney Morning Herald* described the movement as a 'viper in our bosom which must be killed or it will strike when we can least guard against it'. Hughes also declared that 'You have to go for them with the ferocity of a Bengal tiger. They have no nationality; they have no religion. There is only one thing they understand and that is force.' There was in fact no clear evidence that the IWW was practising sabotage, but this did not really matter. After a number of suspicious fires broke out in Sydney, twelve IWW leaders in New South Wales were arrested in late September on charges of forgery, treason, felony, conspiracy and arson.[125]

Their trial was deeply flawed. The only evidence against the accused was provided by police informers, and it was uncorroborated. The defendants' alibis were disallowed. Yet all twelve IWW leaders were found guilty on all or some of the charges and received prison sentences of five to fifteen years. Two sentences were reduced in February 1917 on appeal. The IWW 'Twelve' soon became martyrs of the working class, but their treatment also troubled civil libertarians concerned about the erosion of the very freedoms that Australia was supposedly fighting to defend. As Anstey said, 'What is the good of victory abroad if it only gives us slavery at home?'[126]

Sectarianism

To the already febrile mix of the conscription debate was added Protestant–Catholic sectarianism. Some 22 per cent of the Australian population were Catholics, most of them working class and of Irish extraction. Their religious leaders were also, with few exceptions, Irish by birth or training. In contrast to the Protestant leaders, the Catholic hierarchy—at least in 1916—did not adopt a formal position for or against conscription. In fact, it was divided on the issue, with some of the 22 Catholic bishops, such as Archbishop Kelly in Sydney and Archbishop Clune in Perth, publicly favouring conscription. Others opposed it, the most notable case being the co-adjutor (and later archbishop) of Melbourne, Daniel Mannix. The formal position the hierarchy adopted was that conscription was a secular rather than a moral issue, which parishioners should resolve according to individual conscience.[127]

The Catholic laity, it seems, largely opposed conscription—though whether this was because of their class, ethnicity or religion has been much debated. Almost certainly it was a mixture of these. Professional and better-educated Catholics tended to favour conscription, believing that Christian values were at stake in the war. Working-class Catholics experiencing economic hardship as a result of the war identified with the messages that Boote and others promulgated so effectively through the labour press. But class loyalties may have been mitigated by a more general anxiety that Catholics shared about their place in Australian society, including their long-standing sense of grievance at the Australian state's attitude towards aid for Catholic schools. Their Irish extraction also made many Catholics naturally distrustful of the imperial history of Britain that so entranced the Anglo-Australian loyalists.

Probably many Catholics were also radicalised by the uprising of Irish republicans in Dublin in Easter 1916, in an attempt to end British rule. The initial response of the Catholic leadership to the rebellion was conservative. Archbishop Carr called the rebellion 'an outburst of madness, an anachronism and a crime' paid for by German gold, while Kelly described it as 'anti-patriotic, irrational and wickedly irreligious'. But when the British government court-martialled and executed fifteen leaders of the rebellion in early May, and then failed to reach a negotiated agreement with Irish leaders about Home Rule, Catholic opinion in Australia soured. British repression in Ireland seemed a mockery of the values for which the war was being fought. As the Melbourne Catholic newspaper *The Advocate* said on 26 October 1916, 'It is useless to come to the Irish people and say, "We want you to help us to fight the battle of the small nations".' The Sydney-based *Catholic Press* meanwhile wrote on 5 October:

> The base betrayal of the Irish Party by the Asquith Government, the broken promises with regard to Home Rule, coupled with recent events in Ireland, have created such a feeling of disappointment and resentment

in the minds of Irish-men, that it is bound to assert itself in connection with the referendum campaign.

In Queensland, too, Cabinet minister John Fihelly caused a storm on 2 September by publicly denouncing 'the mailed fist of Prussianism operating in Ireland'. In the resulting furor, he was forced to apologise, but 'Fihellyism' entered the language of the loyalists as a synonym for support for the Sinn Fein rebels, pro-Germanism and disloyalty.[128]

The first Labor split and the call-up

As the conscription campaign began to spin out of Hughes' control, the Labor movement imploded at the national and state levels. Hughes rushed from state to state in early September, trying to persuade each of the local labour executives to support conscription, but he met with an often-hostile reception. The New South Wales parliamentary caucus was split on the question, while the Western Australian and South Australian movements agreed to allow their members the freedom to support conscription. For many Laborites, however, Hughes' credibility was in shreds: cartoons in the left-wing press would later depict him as a pie with a crust that, like promises, was 'made to be broken'.[129]

When on 14 September Hughes submitted the bill for the referendum to parliament, his Minister for Trade and Customs, Victorian member Frank Tudor, resigned from the federal Cabinet in protest. In both houses, a bloc of Labor parliamentarians also opposed the bill on the grounds that conscription was a matter of conscience and that no majority had the right to impose its will on a minority. In the days that followed, Hughes was expelled from the various trade unions that had formed his power base for many years. At the same time, he was expelled from the labour movement by the New South Wales Political Labor League. So too was Holman. Other New South Wales Labor parliamentarians were meanwhile put under pressure to declare that they would oppose conscription. When they refused to do so, over half of the sitting members lost their future endorsement by their local leagues. In Queensland, the only state where under Ryan the Labor government was united in opposing conscription, the executive of the Labor Party also announced on 13 September that any federal members who did not vote against the conscription bill would be denied endorsement in future.

With voluntary recruitment reaching only 9325 in September, well below the number the British Army Council had requested, the government proceeded on 29 September to implement a partial call-up. Using its powers under the *Defence Act* (which could require all Australian males between 18 and 60 to perform militia service within Australia), the government ordered that all single and childless 'male inhabitants of Australia' aged from 21 to 35 years should present themselves at camps for training. Supposedly this was meant to ensure that there would be a body of troops partially trained and ready to embark in the event of the referendum approving conscription. But the tactic misfired. To pro- and anti-conscriptionists alike, it seemed a pre-emptive and arrogant pre-judging of the result of the referendum. The impression of an overweening state was also fuelled by the fact that all men registering were fingerprinted, supposedly to stop trafficking in exemption certificates.

In protest, the trade unions called a one-day general strike on 4 October (the call-up began on 2 October). The labour press also ran a dramatic scare campaign, arguing that married men would soon follow. Since only 70,000 of the 'eligibles' were single, the *Australian Worker* calculated, by Christmas every single man would have 'been gobbled up, and the married men may begin to mumble their unavailing prayers'. A number of cartoons played on this anxiety, one depicting a widow dressed in black telling her young son that she voted 'yes' because she relied on Hughes' promise that married men would be exempt.[130]

In the event, there was widespread non-compliance with the call-up—only 178,197 of the 600,000 'eligibles' responded—and most of the men declared fit applied for exemptions. The grounds for exemption were wide, including medical conditions, employment in essential occupations, conscientious objection, membership of a family where half of the males had already enlisted and being the sole supporter of parents or siblings under sixteen. However, the tribunals convened to review applications for exemptions placed the onus of proof on the applicants, who were denied legal representation. The resulting decisions were often resented—'a sample of Prussian military methods', one rural newspaper in Victoria called them.[131]

For a brief time, voluntary enlistment rose, as men eligible to be called up chose the seemingly more honourable course of volunteering. (Joe Russell was not one of them!) But in retrospect, the call-up seemed to have inflicted decisive damage on the 'yes' campaign. Not only workers but farmers were alienated—in their case because the call-up reduced the supply of labour for shearing and harvesting. As the survival of individuals and their families was threatened, the momentum shifted inexorably to the opposition.

It was a long campaign, lasting eight weeks, and public order soon disintegrated. Each side held mass rallies, often in the open. Crowds numbered up to 100,000 in Sydney. Physical violence and crude disruptive tactics became common on both sides. Hecklers brought pro-conscription meetings to a halt by stamping, chanting, booing, catcalling, counting down, singing the socialist song 'The Red Flag' and invading the speakers' platforms. Effigies of Hughes were burned. Three women speakers for the National Referendum Council were pelted with mud as they left a meeting of factory workers in Melbourne. Much of this violence dismayed the leadership of the 'no' case. Some, it was rumoured, was the work of provocateurs. But the cycle of violence escalated. Pro-conscriptionists threw rotten eggs and broke banners, for example, during the march of the United Women's Anti-Conscription Committee through Melbourne on 21 October.[132]

Returned soldiers featured prominently in this often officially sanctioned thuggery. By the end of 1916, there were more than 23,000—most of them wounded or ill. Many presumably were suffering from what today we would call post-traumatic stress. In Brisbane, between 50 and 100 men in uniform attacked a 'no' rally even though military pickets were present ostensibly to maintain order. The meeting collapsed into a 'free fight of knuckles and boots, riding whips and curses'. One of the pickets was shot, with each side blaming the other for the assault.[133]

The appeal to women

Notably, this violence often targeted women, as did the propaganda on both sides. The 'yes' case exhorted them to fulfil their traditional biological role as wives and mothers by providing husbands and sons as a sacrifice to the nation. 'Any right-minded woman would rather be the mother of a dead hero than a living shirker,' the *Brisbane Courier* argued. 'If we fail in our duty by wanting to keep our men at home then we do not deserve the name of British women.' Hughes, in a manifesto aimed specifically at women, also declared that:

> A man who does not love his country, and when she is in danger will not risk his life on her behalf is like a woman who will not give her life for her child. Both are decadent, both are unworthy . . . Will you be the proud mothers of a nation of heroes, or stand dishonoured as the mothers of a race of degenerates?

By supporting conscription, the 'yes' case argued, women would also have the chance 'to demolish the final argument against the right of women to the fullest citizenship'. To quote Hughes again:

> Women in this Commonwealth are endowed with the full rights of citizenship; they are the equals of men. They are consulted on all question [sic]—even on this, the greatest question of all. In Germany women are not only denied the franchise; they are regarded as mere household chattels.[134]

The 'no' case turned the biological argument on its head by arguing that women, as mothers, should protect their offspring from the ravages of war. In possibly the most famous Australian cartoon of the war, 'The Blood Vote', a doubtful woman was depicted as voting 'no', with a vampire-like figure resembling Hughes hovering in the background. The verse read, in part:

> Why is your face so white, Mother?
> Why do you choke for breath?
> I have dreamt in the night, my son
> That I doomed a man to death.[135]

Doggerel though it was, 'The Blood Vote' was a winner. The *Australian Worker* ran it twice, the second time as a full-page on the day before the referendum vote. The 'yes' case was provoked to reply:

> Why is your face so white, brother?
> Why are your feet so cold?
> Are you afraid to fight, brother?
> To guard that Mother old?[136]

Two further verses condemning the cowardice of those who 'cling to your Mother's skirts' followed.

Women on both sides of the campaign were therefore catapulted into the public sphere that had traditionally been dominated by men. Middle-class leaders of the Australian Women's National League, the National Council of Women and the Woman's Christian Temperance Union spoke from public podiums and organised petitions. Socialist women also became regular speakers at public gatherings, though behind the scenes they—like their conservative counterparts—continued to bear most of the 'women's' duties in their organisations. Working-class women, in turn, used local meetings as the forum for expressing their frustration, anger and grief. As Judith Smart has said of Melbourne:

> Localised demonstrations were both more accessible and more meaningful to working-class women, whose consciousness was defined differently from that of most men in terms of space and 'mental maps' of the city. Their domestic duties and working experiences usually did not take them far from home and their horizons were consequently limited to a geographical area that did not extend much beyond their own suburban enclaves ... The direct expression of feeling and the outright disruption that characterised most of the meetings also encouraged greater involvement of women than the more formal debating procedures required in the unions and political party forums, into which workers' discontent had largely been channelled by 1916.[137]

The passion that Prime Minister 'Billy' Hughes brought to promulgating the war is evident in this photo of him addressing a rally in Martin Place, Sydney, probably in 1916. (AWM A03376)

One of the most famous anti-conscription posters, 'The Blood Vote'. (*Australian Worker*, 12 October 1916, Noel Butlin Archives Centre, ANU)

"I'LL HAVE YOU!"

A 1917 anti-conscription cartoon of Hughes, echoing the accusing finger of Lord Kitchener of earlier British recruitment posters. (*Australian Worker*, 13 December 1917, Noel Butlin Archives Centre, ANU)

"MOTHER, HOW DID YOU VOTE ON THE GREAT REFERENDUM?"

THE WIDOW: "I relied on Mr. Hughes's promise that married men would not be needed, and voted "yes.""

The 'no' case played skilfully on fears that married men would be called up as well as single men. (*Australian Worker*, 19 October 1916, Noel Butlin Archives Centre, ANU)

All of this public contest became deeply personalised and bitter in suburbs and rural districts where everyone knew each other. Small-town communities were riven by the public naming of families who had or had not sent their sons to the war. Friendships were left in tatters by personal abuse, the labelling of men still at home as 'shirkers', and accusations of cowardice, dishonesty, treachery, and betrayal of men at the front. It was raw emotional violence of a kind rarely seen in Australian public life.

The result

On 28 October, Australians finally voted. The result was 'no'—but by a margin of only 72,456 votes, or 3.2 per cent of the valid votes cast. Given that the whole apparatus of the state and most of the media had been campaigning for 'yes', it was a remarkable victory for grassroots activism, trade-union organisation and the brilliant invective of the left-wing press. As the president of the Political Labor League in New South Wales said at a public meeting in the Sydney Town Hall, 'You will see here no Prime Ministers, no Premiers, and no Lord Mayors, but you will see the people's representatives, who will tell you there is no need of conscription in Australia.'[138]

The states were split: Victoria, Western Australia and Tasmania voted 'yes'; New South Wales, Queensland and South Australia voted 'no'. New South Wales was most strongly 'no'. Many words have been written analysing the result. It seems that class was a strong influence, with the working class and trade unionists largely voting 'no' and the middle class 'yes'. So too were gender, birthplace and religion. Catholics voted strongly against conscription; women ('The Blood Vote' notwithstanding) generally for it. Those born in Britain tended to vote 'yes', a fact that may help account for the 'yes' vote in Western Australia, where 21.54 per cent of the population had been born in Europe—6 per cent more than the national average. Primary producers, in contrast, often voted 'no', presumably fearful of the impact of conscription on their labour force and angry over the impact of the call-up and the wartime control of wheat and other primary goods.[139]

However, none of these variables was exclusive. Some voters defected from their class or usual political allegiances. The 'no' vote in New South Wales, for example, was much greater than Labor's electoral base of support, and nationally the country vote was unpredictable. Wheat growers in Queensland supported the 'yes' case, and Victorian country electorates also recorded a 10 per cent majority for 'yes'. But fifteen of sixteen traditionally conservative rural electorates in New South Wales voted 'no'. It seems that primary producers probably voted according to whether they were employers or employees.[140]

The one conclusion we can reach with confidence is that, after a complex and intensely passionate debate, each Australian cast his or her vote in a way that was personal and idiosyncratic. Local and national issues, reason and emotion, economic interest, ideology and personal experience of the war were layered on each other, at the individual level, in ways that can never be definitively understood.

One cohort whose vote was of particular significance was the AIF itself. Hughes was so sure that the soldiers with whom he felt such a rapport would vote 'yes' that he scheduled their polling day more than a week before 28 October. The AIF's support for conscription, progressively released during the campaign, would then set an example for Australians at home. By early October, however, it appeared that a majority of soldiers in France might vote 'no'. Hughes went into overdrive, seeking through a campaign organised by the London-based Murdoch to sway the soldiers' vote—even when a reluctant Birdwood believed that the troops should be allowed to vote according to their consciences. In the end there was a small majority for 'yes': 72,399 votes versus 58,894. According to Murdoch, this 'victory' was attributable to two groups: the men in the 3rd Division training on the Salisbury Plains and the Light Horsemen in Egypt who '[enjoy] the fighting'. In contrast, the men who had experienced war on the Western Front, Murdoch thought, voted three to one against compulsion.[141]

What were their reasons? It is impossible to generalise across many thousands of personnel, few of whom left us their thoughts. Probably some believed it was time to force the 'shirkers' to do their duty: Lieutenant-Colonel George Short, for example, wrote in his diary on 23 August:

Compulsion seems to be coming soon in Australia, The Premier has the people with him, and the unions will have to bow to the people's will.

Both things good. The national sentiment is right . . . the shirkers will be where their betters are, on the battlefield, and not in the snug, selfish, luxurious ease of pleasure, when their superiors are daily laying down life and limb for the Empire's existence.

But others were ambivalent. Captain Henry Davis of the 46th Battalion wrote in his diary on 17 October 1916:

We are trying to take the vote on conscription but it is an ass of a thing to do. The men in many cases are against it as they say that they don't want conscripts. The fools can't see that we must have them otherwise our men have died in vain.

Lieutenant George Makin, for his part, speculated that 'The spirit of unionism is deep rooted in some of [the men] & they said "Oh I wouldn't bring a pal over here. Let them stay where they are well off".' Munro Ferguson, who was hardly in a position to know, thought the volunteers in the AIF were disinclined to associate themselves with conscription, were concerned about inadequate welfare for those who were discharged, and nurtured 'fancied grievances by comparison with soldiers of the British Army'. To these arguments, Bean—who mingled with the troops—added that the men of the AIF wanted sufficient men left in Australia to develop the country after the war; thought Australia was already 'doing enough'; feared that units brought up to strength would be more likely to be sent back into battle; and believed that conscription might bring with it the death penalty for disciplinary offences. Some were also Labor voters and followed the lead of the left-wing movement. Finally, they would not force others to endure the horrors they had experienced.[142]

Deeply disappointed, Hughes refused to publish the soldiers' votes as a discrete cohort. Instead, they were buried in the totals of the states from which the soldiers had originated. Moreover, Hughes made it an offence, under a special regulation, to disclose details of the AIF votes. Only when the Labor Party attempted to make political capital from this cover-up the following year were the figures finally made public, some five months later.[143]

The split widens

The political fallout from the referendum result was rapid and profound. On the day before the vote was taken, a further three members of Hughes' Cabinet resigned in protest at his plan to empower all returning officers at polling booths to interrogate men aged 21 and 35 about whether they had enlisted under the September call-up or been exempted. In this 'crude piece of intimidation', any voter whose reply was unsatisfactory would have his vote set aside for further consideration as to whether it counted.[144]

Then, on 14 November, the federal Labor caucus met and the 'now triumphant and exulting opponents', as Pearce called them, moved in for the kill. A vote of no confidence in Hughes as party leader was moved, and a disorderly and bitter debate followed. But Hughes, rather than waiting for his enemies to unseat him, stopped the debate after lunch and left the room, calling on those 'who think with me to follow me'. Twenty-four members did. Most were members of the generation who had worked with Hughes in shaping the ALP in its earlier days, when it was still struggling for parliamentary dominance.[145]

Perhaps the party members left behind expected that they would form government, but they misjudged their man. With astonishing resilience, Hughes and his group of defectors met excitedly in the Senate clubroom and agreed to create a new political party, the National Labor Party. A new Cabinet was thrown together, and later that night, with the support of Munro Ferguson, Hughes formed a new government, anticipating that he could govern with the support of the Liberals. The remainder of the federal Labor Party—some 40 parliamentarians—elected Tudor as their leader.

In the next months, the ALP continued to unravel at the state level, too. Even though many in the party hoped that after the furor of the referendum debate had subsided it might be possible to rebuild unity, the fight had been too personal and divisive. As with families, the previous intimacy made the betrayal all the more bitter. In New South Wales, Holman quickly moved to form a coalition National government with the former opposition. In Tasmania, pro-conscription premier Earle was deposed from his leadership of the Labor

Party, vilified as 'a time-server, a seeker after place and pay, a traitor to his class'. On 4 December, at a special interstate conference convened in Melbourne to consider the party's future, the radicals pushed through a motion expelling not only those who had followed Hughes but all federal members who had favoured conscription.[146]

Progressively, any pro-conscriptionists remaining in the state labour movements found their position untenable. In South Australia, where most of the federal and state Labor parliamentarians had supported conscription and Hughes, the rump drove them out of the party in early 1917. They formed a branch of the National Labor Party. Even in Western Australia, where the Labor government had not made opposition to conscription an article of faith, it was impossible to avoid the split. Only in Victoria and Queensland was the party left relatively unscathed by defections.

Hughes blamed this rending of the ALP not on the referendum or his own confrontationist politics, but on the pre-existing tensions within the labour movement. He wrote to Murdoch:

> The Labor Party is now split into two camps and can never come together again. Do not think that the Referendum is the cause of this unhappy division—it is not, it is only the occasion for it. The seeds of disruption were there. The Syndicalist element has grown until it has quite diverted the development of the movement from the lines along which it has been progressing this quarter of a century . . . if the split had not come now it would not have been delayed for more than a few months at most.[147]

He may have been right. Even before the referendum, the rift between the industrial and political wings of the labour movement was deep, and militants were probably waiting for an opportunity to purge the political leadership. But a different leader might have managed to control the centrifugal forces. As it was, Hughes' political style—his transparent use of state power to his political advantage, his intemperance, abrasiveness, dictatorial style and intolerance for his critics—played into his opponents' hands. Munro Ferguson concluded that:

Possibly the Labour split might have been avoided, or at least moderated, by the employment of more tactful and conciliatory methods ... there are those who think that had he possessed more savoir faire, the Prime Minister might have aroused less hostile feeling and secured a better result.

Instead Hughes was vilified for the rest of his political career, demonised in Labor mythology as the traitor or 'rat', a devil replete with cloven hooves, horns and tail, who had destroyed the very movement he had been instrumental in founding.[148]

The damage to the ALP would last for decades. As subsequent elections at the federal and state level would show, the vote against conscription was not a vote against the war. The vast majority of Australians continued to support the war effort. Hence the coalition Hughes would form with the Liberals in early 1917 was able to claim a patriotic mantle as the 'Win the War party'. It would win power federally in May 1917 and continue to dominate federal politics in the inter-war period. Hughes himself would remain prime minister until 1922. Labor, in contrast, would hold power federally for only 26 months between 1917 and 1941.

At the state level, it was a more mixed record. As is often the case, Australians voted differently at federal and state levels. In the 20-year inter-war period, the ALP held power in Victoria for a cumulative total of four years and three months, and in South Australia, for a total of five years and ten months (followed by a record 27 years of conservative rule by Thomas Playford). In New South Wales, where Holman remained in power until April 1920, Labor had three terms in the inter-war years, totalling five years and ten months. In contrast, in Queensland Labor dominated all but the period 1929–32, while in Western Australia, it was in office for six years from 1924 to 1930 and a further fifteen years from April 1933 on. Tasmania, too, had Labor rule from 1923–28 and a long 24-year period after June 1934.

There were many reasons for Labor's eclipse federally, but the legacy of 1916 was critically important. The split left the ALP a much more identifiably Catholic party: according to one estimate, the proportion of federal

Labor parliamentarians who were Catholic rose from 21 to 45 per cent. As the Protestant majority saw it, this made the ALP inherently unreliable as the national government charged with ensuring Australia's security and defence. Not only had the Catholics within the party seemingly voted against conscription, but apparently they owed their allegiance to a papal authority that transcended any national one. Hence, for years to come, the ALP would be tarred with the brush of disloyalty and would struggle to be seen as worthy of being trusted with managing the foreign and defence policies of the nation.[149]

The Somme again

Much of the bitterness of the conscription debate can be attributed to the fact that it was played out against the backdrop of the Somme campaign, which continued to drag on through October and November. This was despite the fact that some within the British government were deeply concerned about the high casualty rates and the lack of the strategic victory that Haig had promised. Churchill, for instance—though confined to the back bench after resigning in November 1915—had no hesitation in telling the Cabinet and War Committee in a devastating written critique that he thought the Somme a failure. Lloyd George, too, was keen for Britain to turn its attention away from the Western Front again to the east, encouraging Romania to enter the war with promises of support if it attacked Bulgaria (with which Romania had unresolved disputes as a consequence of the 1913 Second Balkan War).

However, when Romania entered the war on the Allied side in late August, it proved not to be the asset that Lloyd George hoped for, but a catastrophe. Its armies rapidly collapsed in the face of intervention by the Germans, who would soon control the country's valuable oil and food supplies. With the crisis in the Balkans unfolding, Lloyd George argued acrimoniously with Robertson, who thought that Britain should support Romania not by renewed action in Salonika, Greece, but by continued attacks in France. Haig, of course, agreed, and assured the Cabinet that even now the Somme offered the prospect of a far-reaching success that would give 'full compensation for all that had been done to attain it'. Almost by default, the British government allowed him to keep trying.[150]

Haig's plan at the start of October was to push on in the hope of capturing the high ground still controlled by the Germans, thinking that this would form the base from which further offensives could be launched in the spring of 1917. On 29 September, he ordered yet another massive attack by three British armies. The Third would take the high ground east of Gommecourt, the Reserve Army the remainder of the Thiepval spur, Serre and Beaumont Hamel, while the Fourth Army would capture the German position called the Transloy lines before pressing on towards Cambrai.

Almost incredibly, however, Haig had not taken the weather into account. October was always a wet month on the Somme, and on 2 October the rains began. The valley that the Fourth Army had to cross became a quagmire. High-explosive shells thudded into the ground before bursting in puffs of steam and smoke, while the aerial observers, so essential to the targeting of artillery, were grounded. The German defenders, on whom the rain had a less damaging effect, were meanwhile reinforced by new troops and artillery.

Three attempts to capture the Transloy lines—on 7, 12 and 18 October—failed. But the French Sixth Army attacking on the British right reached Sailly-Saillisel, on the same ridge as Bapaume, and Joffre kept pressuring Haig to repeat the attacks in the hope of achieving something greater by the end of the year. It seemed impossible to Haig and Rawlinson to leave the Fourth Army to spend the winter where it was, at the bottom of a valley.

I Anzac Corps, which been recuperating after Pozières in the sector around Ypres, was brought south on 21 October to join the Fourth Army. It was to be one of the most difficult times experienced by the AIF. By now the ground conditions were truly appalling. The territory that had been fought over in the previous weeks was a wasteland full of craters that blocked the drainage. The roads used to supply ammunition, food and medicines from the railhead near Albert collapsed, becoming impassable to wheeled vehicles. To get to the front line, the infantry faced long marches through deep mud that left them utterly exhausted. W.H. Downing recalled:

> We entered a waterlogged sap where one or two duckboards (planks laid over mud) were uselessly floating. Then there were no more duckboards but mire, to the thighs at best, to the middle at worst. There men were caught as in a vice . . . [at the firing line.] All the time shells and rain fell from the leaden, pitiless skies . . . What few dugouts there were were full of water . . . The dead lay everywhere. The deeper one dug, the more bodies one exhumed. Hands and faces protruded from the slimy, toppling walls of trenches. Knees, shoulders and buttocks poked from the foul morass, as many as the pebbles of a brook.

To add to the misery, the nights were bitterly cold.[151]

A number of the Allied commanders—Elliott, McCay and the commander of the British XIV Corps, Lord Cavan—thought the conditions were too bad for operations to continue. Elliott said that to attack across such ground was 'sheer madness'. Cavan described it as the worst his staff officers had seen and insisted that Rawlinson come and see it for himself. But Haig, initially inclined to cancel the operations, ordered them to proceed after meeting with the French commander of Northern Army Group, Ferdinand Foch. Another attack by XIV Corps to assist the French was launched on 23 October, again with no success, and then on 5 November, after some postponements due to the rain, it was the turn of the Australians.[152]

Just after midnight, the 1st Battalion and some bombing parties of the 3rd Battalion (1st Division) attacked a German position, the Bayonet Trench, which protruded into the Allied line 450 metres north of Gueudecourt. Later in the morning, in a freezing gale, the 7th Brigade (2nd Division) attacked a network of trenches called the Maze, almost 2 kilometres north of Flers. A brigade from the British III Corps to the west assaulted a large ancient mound, the Butte de Warlencourt, 180 metres south-west of the road to Bapaume. None of the attacks succeeded in gaining ground. Only a small foothold in the Maze was gained, but it would be lost again a few days later. Even then, Haig ordered the attacks to be repeated at the earliest possible moment, but the continuing bad weather meant that they were postponed until 9 November, and then 14 November.

Winter on the Somme

Throughout this time, the troops had to man the trenches in the bitter cold, mud and wet, with little, if any, shelter, no fires (these were prohibited) and almost no hot food. The normal period spent as the garrison of the firing line was 48 hours, but even the reserve position, where another three days might be spent, was 'an open muddy drain'. Bean's description is unforgettable:

> At first the men tried to shelter themselves from rain by cutting niches in the trench-walls, but this practice was forbidden, several soldiers having been smothered through the slipping in of the sodden earth-roof, and the trenches broken down. If, to keep themselves warm, men stamped or moved about, the floor of the trench turned to thin mud. At night the officers sometimes walked up and down in the open and encouraged their men to do the same, chancing the snipers; but for the many there was no alternative but to stand almost still, freezing, night and day.

Trying to make light of their misery, the troops sang a song to the tune of a well-known hymn:

> Cold feet, cold feet, cold feet,
> Always bloody well cold feet
> Cold feet in the morning
> And cold feet in the night.[153]

In these conditions, the troops suffered from a particularly ghastly torment: trench foot. With the circulation in their legs stopping, their feet started to swell, turned red, burned with excruciating pain and then went numb. Gangrene set in. Unable to fit their boots on, men dragged themselves on their hands and knees to treatment at the Regimental Aid Posts or Advanced Dressing Stations behind the lines. In the worst cases, their putrefying toes were amputated.

Sometimes a whole foot was taken, perhaps both. Military authorities chose to view trench foot as a problem of discipline, blaming men for failing to observe the approved procedures for wrapping their feet in sandbags and loose boots, regularly drying them and rubbing in whale oil. But these precautions were impossible in the semi-frozen mud and slush of October and November 1916. One battalion of the 7th Brigade had 90 per cent of its men affected to some degree when it was relieved after the battle of 5 November. A 5th Division medical officer described trench-foot sufferers at Bernafay Wood:

> To me it was perhaps the most harrowing scene of the war. Scores of the same fine men who were seen silently suffering the most awful wounds writhed and groaned and wept as children. The men experienced, besides, a curious physical and mental loathing of the disease, as of a rottenness or putrefaction.[154]

For those wounded by German fire, conditions were even worse. Some lay in the open for many hours without blankets. Stretcher-bearers struggled to reach them. They worked in relay teams, wading through the mud, which initially was not bridged by duckboards. At times, it could take over six hours for one wounded man to be carried to the Advanced Dressing Station. Sledges were improvised on which the wounded could be dragged in by men and horses, but these also bogged in the glutinous mud.

Then the frost and snow came. This at least had the advantage of freezing the roads, but for the troops it meant further hardship. Colonel A. Sutton of the Australian Army Medical Corps wrote on 14 November:

> Cold—very heavy frost—ground covered with snow ... frost all over clothing—Rotten... Will they not realise we Australians who have worked to a stand still & need complete rest right away from the line, if not we shall go to pieces. The awful weather added to the continuous work is slowly doing us up [sic] & personally I think is breaking the hearts of men.[155]

In the midst of this, the men had to fight. On 14 November the 5th Brigade attacked the Maze again, supported by two battalions from the 7th Brigade and with British forces alongside. The 7th Brigade had scarcely recovered from the attack of 5 November. Corporal Peter Gaffney later described the charge:

> Our guns opened up with a tremendous roar and the first heavy shells dropped and exploded right beside our post partly blowing it in and wounding two of our small party. The Battalions which were about 100 yards behind us started to charge, and were chopped about by our own artillery fire which was falling fearfully short, the Hun fairly mowed them down with m. gun fire, and shells. When the remnants of the infantry got near in a line with our post we pulled the m. gun off the parapet, where we had been firing it on the Huns and charged out with our men dropping down and firing bursts into the enemy, but again our attack failed as his barb wire was untouched by our artillery and Fritz was four to our one.

Despite the chaos, the Australians managed to take some 450 metres of the Maze—only to lose them when the Germans counter-attacked two days later. The November attacks cost the Australians another 2000 casualties.[156]

Morale and survival

In retrospect, we can only wonder how the soldiers stood this 'time dreadful beyond all comparison', as George Mitchell later called it. Why did they not mutiny when the impossible was asked of them—when they were forced to endure mud, cold, hunger, fatigue, the desolation of the blasted winter landscape as well as the fear and danger of battle? In Bean's assessment, the morale of the AIF reached 'the bottom of the curve' in November 1916. But it never broke.[157]

Military morale is a complex phenomenon, closely linked to the discipline of a fighting unit. Both depend on a mix of negative and positive variables: in popular terms, sticks and carrots. No army exists without coercion, a formal system of military law that punishes miscreants, deserters, mutineers and cowards. The British Army's disciplinary regimes were harsh, including punishments that dated from the Napoleonic era. During World War I, it executed 266 men for desertion, even though some may have been suffering severe psychological trauma.[158]

The men of the AIF, however, did not live with the threat of capital punishment hanging over them. This was not for want of trying on the part of the British commanders, who despaired of the Australians' lack of discipline. Their refusal to salute officers, their sloppy dress, their irreverence for military rank and their drunkenness on leave were irritating enough, but Australian divisions also had very high rates of being absent without leave (AWOL): 130 of the 182 AWOL cases in the Fourth Army in December 1916 were Australians. But the Australian government would not permit the execution of any Australian offenders. Although Australian soldiers could be *sentenced* to death—and 121 were—the government blocked these sentences being endorsed by the governor-general in council, as was required under the *Defence Act*. In 1917, Birdwood, Godley and the British government all tried to change Hughes' and Pearce's mind, but they refused to allow executions.[159]

Fear of punishment therefore is unlikely to have influenced many Australians to remain in the trenches in the early winter of 1916. What of the carrots? These were scarce. The conditions on the front line, and particularly the breakdown in supply, meant that there were few, if any, of the short-term comforts—good rations, rest, decent accommodation, warm clothing, alcohol and tobacco—that, as Niall Ferguson puts it, 'kept men going' in World War I.[160]

Perhaps, then, we can only explain the remarkable endurance of the troops in terms of what sociologists have called 'legitimate demand' and 'primary group' loyalty. Even in the trenches, many soldiers retained some underlying commitment to the legitimacy of the war's aims and of the military authority that controlled them. They believed 'in the worth of the socio-political system to which they belong[ed], the necessity for its defence, and the legitimacy for the commands which they [were] called on to obey as a means for that defence'.[161]

Moreover, their immediate social group commanded their loyalty. As at Gallipoli, mateship kept Australians functioning, As Bill Gammage has said: 'War makes soldiers comrades, because comrades sustain hope in battle, mitigate despair in adversity, and relieve a monotonous existence.' Captain

Mark Cotton wrote after Pozières that 'between all of us who had been through the experience together seemed to be a bond quite unknown before . . . we had all faced the big things together and were comrades rather than officers and men'. In the midst of the winter of 1916, Private Edgar Thompson was able to write: 'Sing song in hut around five—good fellows— I shall never regret the past eleven months experiences for they have given me friends—chums & cobbers—& it has been soul stirring—some of it—& good.' And George Mitchell would later write:

> We Diggers were a race apart. Long separation from Australia had seemed to cut us completely away from the land of our birth. The longer a man served, the fewer letters he got, the more he was forgotten. Our only home was our unit, and that was constantly being decimated by battle, and rebuilt by strangers.[162]

Perhaps too many soldiers accepted the appalling privations of trench warfare because they felt they could do nothing else. World War I, with its vast technology and weapons of mass destruction, acquired the character of a monstrous maw that devoured human beings in a way beyond human control. As Eric Leed has said:

> The war assumed an awesome autonomy from the motives and purposes of combatants. Increasingly it was spoken of in anthropomorphic terms, or described as an automaton—an organization that authored and authorized actions no longer attributable to individual motives.

If the politicians who aspired to control events felt this, then Australians at the front must have had no sense of personal agency. How could they change anything? What would they achieve if they threw down their arms, mutinied or deserted? Where, even, would they go? Home was 15,000 kilometres away, across the oceans—not, as was the case for the French and Russian soldiers who mutinied in 1917, a distance that a desperate man might walk.[163]

Surrender, of course, was a way out. Bean records one young Australian who crossed to the enemy side in search of warmth and comfort. Perhaps there were others. But surrender involved high risk. Many men were killed at the moment of, or shortly after, their capture: in Niall Ferguson's words, these were the 'forgotten atrocities' of World War I. With little formal protection under the international legal conventions, their treatment in captivity was also often poor.[164]

Self-harm was another possibility. Injuries could be self-inflicted in an effort to escape a battle. Between 1916 and 1918, 700 Australian soldiers were convicted of this offence, over half of them in the last year of the war. Soldiers could also fake illness—what the official historian of Australia's medical services called a 'conscious escape into disease' (as opposed to the 'unconscious escape' of hysteria). Medical officers were therefore constantly on the alert for men who suddenly discovered they were deaf or blind, who added egg white to their urine to mimic kidney disease, chewed on cordite to produce an irregular heartbeat or drank picric acid to imitate jaundice, to name only some of the options for faking symptoms. If detected, malingerers could be punished: sentenced to prison, denied pay or allowances for their families, or confined to barracks with odious jobs. In the absence of official data, we cannot know the prevalence of malingering, or what the soldiers called 'swinging the lead', but it seems to be have been something of a tradition in the AIF. Australian doctors also had a reputation for being sympathetic to men who were showing signs of being the 'war-weary warrior'.[165]

The ultimate 'escape' was suicide. One soldier of the 24th Battalion, told to make the nightmare journey back to the line through the cratered battlefield, took out his gun and shot himself. Presumably many others put themselves in positions in which they would be killed. It was not difficult to do so in the firing line on the Western Front.

In the absence of reliable statistics, it is impossible to know how many of these 'escape' attempts there were, but it seems they were not endemic. Rather, a fatalistic resignation set in among the troops, mediated through black humour and mutual support. One Australian was to write later:

> The mud well you know the nastiest thing you can get used to and we also look back to some other place and say, Oh well, its [sic] not as bad as that joint anyhow and there you are. A joke and a laugh at every poor beggar who goes up to his neck (yourself included) a hand out and there you are.[166]

The Somme balance sheet

The Battle of the Somme finally puttered to an end when, on 13 November, the British Fifth Army (as the Reserve Army was now called) attacked on a more northerly part of the front around Gueudecourt. Here, because there had been no advance after 1 July, the terrain was easier and the problems of supply were less acute. The operation was also well planned, amply supported by artillery and had very limited objectives. Hence Beaumont Hamel, to the north-west of Thiepval, was captured, although Serre was not, because men sank up to their waists in mud and became separated from the protection of the creeping barrage. Beaumont Hamel was, of course, one of the objectives of the 1 July attack, but on that subject there was a kind of collective amnesia. It was success enough for Haig to call the Somme offensive to a halt, on 19 November.

Historians are divided on what the Somme contributed to the war, or who even won. In terms of territory conquered, the gains for 141 days of fighting were slight. At its furthest point, the British line was about 10 kilometres further advanced on 19 November than it had been on 1 July. And these proved to be ephemeral gains. Within three months, the Germans would choose to evacuate the lines they had defended so passionately in late 1916 and withdraw to a new defensive line, the Hindenburg Line.

Who lost the most troops is not known conclusively. Figures for German losses range from 230,000 to 500,000. The British lost some 432,000 (killed, wounded and taken prisoner) and the French suffered 200,000 casualties. As Robin Prior and Trevor Wilson, whose figures these are, have said, if statistics are the measure then there is no doubt who won the Battle of the Somme.[167]

However, raw casualties do not tell the full story. What mattered was which side in the long term could better tolerate such losses. This again is difficult to judge. Each of the belligerents on the Somme was not fighting alone. They had allies who could compensate for their losses—or more often place a further strain on them. The Germans were already underpinning the Austro-Hungarian military effort, and the Italians—who had launched another three unsuccessful attempts to break the stalemate at the Isonzo from September to

November—would become an increasing drain on Allied resources in 1917. But since Germany was critical to the victory of the Central Powers and did not have the capacity to outlast its enemies if it kept losing casualties at the rate of 1916, the Somme probably weakened the Central Powers more than the Allies. Or, to put a slightly more positive spin on it, it was 'a gruesome kind of limited victory for the Allies'.[168]

The Somme arguably shifted the strategic balance of the war. It tipped Verdun in favour of the French, weakened the German army and, in particular, convinced the German military leadership that Britain was committed to winning the war, even at a huge cost. In response, the Germans would make some critical strategic decisions in early 1917, including the reintroduction of unrestricted submarine warfare that would trigger the entry of the United States into the war.

None of this was known at the time. In Britain, the sense of frustration at the meagre results of the Somme contributed to the final collapse of the government of Asquith, who himself was reeling from the death of a son on the Somme in September 1916. 'Whatever pride I had in the past, and whatever hope I had for the future—by far the largest part was invested in him. Now all that is gone,' he wrote, as any of the millions of bereft parents worldwide might have done. Unable to reach an agreement with the ambitious Lloyd George over management of the war effort, Asquith resigned on 5 December. After complex cross-party negotiations, Lloyd George formed a coalition government committed to more vigorous prosecution of the war.[169]

The aftermath of conscription

In Australia, it was also time for building 'some degree of order out of the prevailing chaos', as Munro Ferguson put it in the aftermath of the conscription campaign. Superficially, life resumed its normal rhythms. The Melbourne Cup proceeded as usual in early November, though it was delayed a week by rain and had to justify its continuance by committing its profits in 'the spirit of patriotism' to the patriotic funds. Presumably it was attended by those same men who, as Hughes had put it a few weeks earlier, flocked to pony races and 'shriek and hoot because they are asked to do their duty'.[170]

In many ways Australian society was now divided into oppositional camps. Heady with the defeat of Hughes, the coal unions called a strike on 1–2 November in New South Wales, Victoria, Tasmania and Queensland. Their log of claims was long-standing, and the dispute had been brewing through October. As they now resorted to direct action, they threatened to close down civilian industry, transport, public services, troop transports and wheat exports. The conservative press was outraged. To take industrial action at this time was a 'public scandal', providing the world with 'still another striking example of the inability of a free democracy to so govern itself as to combat successfully a foe like Germany'. With years of union experience behind him, Hughes pulled out all stops to find a settlement. Invoking the *War Precautions Act*, he called a compulsory conference of all parties and, bypassing the Arbitration Court, where Justice Higgins quite reasonably refused to be instructed as to what his findings should be, established a special tribunal that conceded the key demands of the miners.[171]

The conservatives were also galvanised by the referendum defeat to overhaul the machinery for voluntary recruitment. With enlistments falling to 5055 in November and a miserable 2617 in December, responsibility for recruiting was taken from the overworked Department of Defence and placed, as of 29 December, under an able Victorian barrister and politician, Donald Mackinnon. The tone of public appeals continued to verge on the hysterical, however. A letter from a wounded soldier that was circulated publicly:

'Give us liberty and freedom', you scream, and wave flags, thinking that liberty and freedom can be bought for nought. We, poor, miserable fools that we are, are giving you the liberty asked for. My blood boils at the thought of dear, sweet, free Australia having its fair name dragged in the mud. Australia, the laughing stock—and justly so—of our enemies! Was it for this that Australia's sons left their bones on the Peninsula! . . . If there is any man in Australia with an ounce of sense and an ounce of patriotism . . . he will leave no stone unturned until he has helped to free Australia from the clutches of the fiends that are choking her. If not, farewell peace, farewell liberty.[172]

Hughes also moved to smash the IWW. The arrest and imprisonment of the 'Twelve' was not enough for him, and on 18 December 1916 he introduced legislation to ban the movement itself. In addressing parliament, he declared war against the IWW, which he claimed had 'declared war on society, upon the people of this country': 'This organization holds a dagger at the heart of society . . . As it seeks to destroy us, we must in self-defence destroy it.' It was as if Hughes, the long-time unionist, could not tolerate the almost personal betrayal that the radicalisation of Australian workers represented:

> their [IWW] agents have poisoned the well from which some of the workers of this country drink, and made them believe that it is by setting all law at defiance, by destroying machinery, by retarding the wheels of production, that their salvation alone can be achieved.

The *Unlawful Associations Act* did not make membership of the IWW per se a criminal act—that would come later—but it criminalised the organisation and proscribed any other association which, 'by its constitution or propaganda, advocates or encourages, or incites or instigates to the taking or endangering of human life, or the destruction or injury of property'. Tudor thought that the bill would be better described as an attempt 'to try and entrap the Political Labor Party', but he feared that by opposing it the ALP would damage its standing in the electorate. It was an indication of the new political alignment after the conscription vote that the Liberals also supported Hughes, who continued to set the agenda.[173]

Australians had little to celebrate as Christmas approached. To counter the bitter domestic political conflict and the fearful loss of life in France, there was only a glimmer of peace—and that was soon extinguished. On 12 December, the German government, in the glow of its victory over Romania, put out feelers for a negotiated peace. The offer was ambiguous and haughty in tone, but it triggered an effort by President Woodrow Wilson of the United States to mediate an international settlement. On 18 December, he asked both sides of the conflict to state their terms on which the war might be concluded and the means by which this might be achieved. However, by implying that there was no moral difference between the war aims of the belligerents, he infuriated the Allies, whose moral outrage was dutifully repeated in the Australian press and, it seems, at the front. Edgar Thompson noted in his diary on 29 December that peace talk was 'prevalent': 'everyone desires peace—longs for it—expects it—but not a word about giving in or giving up'.[174]

On 10 January 1917, the Allies replied to Wilson with a public statement of war aims, which was 'neither very precise nor corresponding very closely with their real objectives', as David Stevenson has put it. In fact, they had no intention of settling for peace on any but their own terms. Nor, for that matter, did Germany. Although Chancellor Bethmann Hollwegg had many disputes with Germany's military leaders, across the political spectrum there was consensus about the need to retain after the war a German-led Mitteleuropa—that is, a colossal customs union of dependent states stretching from Belgium to Turkey, which would enable Germany to compete globally with the British Empire and the United States. With such war aims, there could be no compromise.[175]

Magdhaba

The only positive news as the year ended came from Palestine. During 1916, the British railway line and water pipeline, which were so essential to logistics in the theatre, had inched their way across the desert. On 21 December, the Anzac Mounted Division—now part of the Desert Column under Lieutenant-General Sir Phillip Chetwode—moved to occupy El Arish, a post on the Mediterranean coast that the Ottomans had already abandoned. Accompanied by the Imperial Camel Corps, they rode 37 kilometres across unknown country in the dark of night. Charles Cox recalled:

> That night will always seem to me the most wonderful of the whole campaign. The hard going for the horses seemed almost miraculous after the months of sand; and, as the shoes of the horses struck fire on the stones in the bed of the wady, the men laughed with delight. Sinai was behind them.[176]

Then, on 23 December 1916, they attacked Magdhaba, an Ottoman position that lay a little inland at one of the wadis or streambeds that cut deep across the landscape. A multinational force of infantry, camels and their drivers assembled chaotically and set off after midnight. In the morning, the aircraft of No. 1 Squadron Australian Flying Corps bombed the Ottoman positions, demonstrating the growing role that aircraft were playing in projecting firepower beyond the range of artillery.

Some of the Ottoman positions were difficult to locate, however, and the ground attack ran into difficulties. Worried about the lack of water for the horses, Chauvel ordered the force to retreat back to El Arish, but the 1st Light Horse Brigade attacked at virtually the same time. Eventually, a major Ottoman redoubt was captured and the garrison surrendered. The implacable logistics of the desert then dictated that the exhausted column, with men falling asleep and hallucinating in their saddles, make its way back to the water of El Arish that night.[177]

The casualties at Magdhaba were 97 Ottoman dead and 1282 prisoners, as opposed to only 146 casualties (including 22 killed) for Chauvel's force. The Australian press reported the battle as a 'brilliant achievement' in which the enemy was 'practically destroyed' by the 'fine work of the Anzacs'. It was the usual overstatement, but it was understandable, perhaps, given the unremittingly depressing news from the Western Front—and the fact that in late December nature struck another blow.[178]

On 27 December, a cyclone swept across the Queensland coast between Townsville and Mackay, bringing torrential rain. The small town of Clermont, nearly 300 kilometres inland, was deluged by a wave of water that to survivors seemed like the sea. Whole families were swept away and stock losses were great. Fifty buildings were smashed by debris, lifted off their blocks and carried downstream. A horse, in its fear and desperation, climbed the staircase of the hotel and was found on the second floor. When the waters retreated, 61 residents of a town of 1600 had died. It was 'a disaster compared with which previous troubles were trifles', and Australians had yet another reason, as 1916 closed, to be 'struck dumb in grief and pity'.[179]

4

---·•·---

1917
The worst year

As 1917 began, it seemed to many Australians that the end of the war was 'as far off as ever, unless the end should come in a stalemate'. Yet the strategic balance was shifting. Germany had failed at Verdun to break the stalemate on the Western Front and had suffered huge losses on the Somme—losses that were becoming increasingly difficult to replace, given the need to prop up the Austro-Hungarian armies. The impact of the war on the German economy was also now severe, with German civilians suffering terrible deprivations during the 'turnip winter' of 1916–17 (so called because the potato crop had failed, forcing Germans to depend on turnips as a staple food). Germany's successes in the east, conquering Romania and parts of Russian Poland, had gone some way towards redressing this situation by providing new sources of raw materials and agricultural land. However, German industry was struggling to produce munitions at the level that the war demanded, even when in 1917 it became totally mobilised for war production. Its allies, meanwhile, gave Germany little strategic benefit. Indeed, the Austro-Hungarian Empire was now a liability, needing to be propped up by a joint command system with German officers distributed throughout the Austrian army.[1]

At the same time, Britain was showing an increasing commitment to supporting France and defeating Germany. With its war economy shifting into full gear and its political leadership rejecting peace initiatives, it was now the power that Germany had to defeat if it was to win the war. However, with global imperial resources to draw on, Britain had the capacity to outlast Germany.

Germany's strategic dilemma

This was apparent to the German commanders Paul von Hindenburg and Erich Ludendorff, who became the dominant force in strategic decision-making and German politics from late 1916 on. Seeing the only solution to their strategic dilemma as being the destruction of Britain's offensive capacity, they decided to resume unrestricted warfare against British merchant shipping in February 1917. There were huge diplomatic risks in this decision, since unrestricted submarine warfare was certain to antagonise the United States, as it had in 1915. But the German command calculated that with its increased torpedo capacity it could destroy 600,000 tons of British shipping a month, and since neutral shipping would not risk sailing into waters patrolled by U-boats, Britain would be compelled to sue for peace within six months.

At first the German gamble seemed to be paying off. From January to April 1917, the shipping tonnage sunk by German U-boats, mines and surface raiders combined rose from about 330,000 to 870,000 tons. It seemed that Germany might succeed in strangling the trade on which the British war economy depended. However, despite the dramatic shipping losses, Britain's global trade was never completely stopped and, more significantly, a number of American ships were sunk. This, together with an astonishingly maladroit attempt on the part of the Germans to enlist Mexico in a war against the United States, persuaded Woodrow Wilson to bring his country into the war on 7 April. 'The world,' he said in a phrase that would echo down the twentieth century, 'must be made safe for democracy.'[2]

It would be nearly a year before American troops arrived in France in any numbers, but the Allies gained immediate benefits from US belligerency. About half a million tons of German shipping, trapped in US harbours, was seized and used in the Allied cause. Destroyers from the US Navy were also immediately deployed on anti-submarine warfare in the Atlantic. In addition, US credit to finance Britain's war purchases—which had all but dried up by 1917—became available again. As Trevor Wilson puts it, the U-boat campaign would accomplish 'in a sense quite contrary to the intentions of its originators, its most considerable contribution to the outcome of the war'.[3]

The irony was that just as Germany had transformed the strategic balance in the west to its disadvantage, the Russians began to collapse in the east. Although the Russian military leaders began 1917 full of fight, their home front was disintegrating. The development of heavy industry for munitions and war production had created a large industrial workforce in 1914–16, much of which had been drawn from peasants migrating to urban centres. But by 1917, the inflation of the currency, the dislocation of agricultural production and the inability of the railway system to adjust to multiple new demands meant that these workers could not translate their wages into food. They were hungry and angry, and in the winter months of 1916–17 they began rioting and looting in Petrograd.

On 15 March, Tsar Nicholas II abdicated, bringing to an end the 300-year-old Romanov dynasty. The provisional government that then assumed power remained committed to Russia's continuing in the war, but there would be little serious fighting on the Russian front in 1917. Instead, virtually the whole of the country went on strike, the food crisis in the cities intensified and soldiers at the front mutinied. Progressively, the Soviets, the revolutionary committees established during the March revolution, gained the political ascendancy. On 7 November, the Bolshevik faction under the leadership of Vladimir Lenin, who had returned to Russia with German support in April, seized power. Unlike its predecessors, the new Soviet government was intent on implementing a truly revolutionary program, waging unremitting class war at home and negotiating an immediate peace on the Eastern Front.

The Allies' strategic dilemma

The strategic dilemma facing the Allied Powers as 1917 opened was scarcely less difficult than Germany's. They had no doubt of the need to maintain pressure on the Central Powers, but where and how? The fact that, in the aftermath of the profoundly costly battles of the Somme and Verdun, the French and British leaders were feuding among themselves made the resolution of these questions acutely difficult.

In Paris, Joffre was removed from command on 13 December 1916 and replaced by General Robert Nivelle, who had achieved some dramatic successes in the last months of Verdun. But the French military and political leadership remained deeply divided about the conduct of the war, and the government of Aristide Briand would fall in March 1917. In Britain, meanwhile, Lloyd George's appointment as prime minister triggered a crisis of civil–military relations. Appalled at the casualty rates of 1916, Lloyd George distrusted Haig and was determined to avoid more battles of attrition on the Western Front. 'Haig', he said privately, 'does not care how many men he loses. He just squanders the lives of these boys. I mean to save some of them in the future.' Haig and Robertson, in contrast, wanted to keep British efforts focused on the Western Front. Their preference was to end the lamentable Salonika campaign and resume operations in Flanders or along the Channel coast, with the aim of capturing Ostend and Zeebrugge.[4]

In a remarkable attempt to mobilise his allies against his own generals, Lloyd George tried in January 1917 to persuade the Italians to launch a new offensive against Austria-Hungary, supported by generous amounts of British artillery. This proposal collapsed, however, thanks partly to intriguing by Robertson but also because the Italians would have nothing to do with Lloyd George's plans. The focus of Allied planning therefore, almost inevitably, turned back to the Western Front. The French thought they had found a new saviour in Nivelle, who argued with great assurance and eloquence that the French armies were not exhausted and that Britain did not need to assume the major burden on the Western Front in 1917. Instead, he would lead a new Allied offensive that would break through the German line using 'violence, brutality, and speed'. Haig and Robertson had their reservations, but Lloyd George was captivated. Here was a general who had imagination and promised quick victories with an economy of losses. The Allied leaders therefore agreed that the French would launch a new offensive in the spring of 1917 at Chemin des Dames, the scene of earlier fighting in 1914 and 1915. The British would play a supporting role, holding German forces away from the main battle by attacking out of Arras, to the north of the Somme region.[5]

Still lacking confidence in Haig, Lloyd George tried clumsily at a conference at Calais in February to place the British armies under Nivelle's control for at least the duration of this coming campaign. But Haig and Robertson had influential networks in London, including King George V, who made it clear to the prime minister that he did not expect to see his army under foreign control. Ultimately, Lloyd George was forced to confirm that Haig possessed the full confidence of the British government, and that his status was that of a fellow commander of, not a subordinate to, Nivelle. Since he had so openly sided with Nivelle against his own commanders, however, Lloyd George had much riding politically on the success of the coming spring offensive.[6]

Political realignments in Australia

As ever, the British government did not consult Australia during these tortuous discussions, even though the AIF would be involved in the planned operations. Hughes' attention in early 1917 was therefore more on his own political survival. The split in the ALP in late 1916 had left an unstable and fluid political situation. Hughes had managed to remain prime minister, but he could govern only with the support of the opposition. Initially, he hoped he could build a power base for his new National Labor Party from unions across the country that had not supported the expulsion of pro-conscriptionists from the ALP. Instead, he found himself in late 1916 and early 1917 being courted by his erstwhile political opponents. Among them was William Watt, a former Victorian premier who had entered federal parliament in 1914 with the credentials to be prime minister, only to find himself confined to the opposition with Labor's victory in September 1914. Now Watt, together with prominent pro-conscriptionists from the National Referendum Council—including Irvine—proposed a new cross-party coalition of Hughes' National Labor and Cook's Liberals. The program to unite them would be winning the war.

Hughes was cautious. He distrusted coalitions and he had no wish to play second fiddle to the Liberals and Cook, the latter of whom he called 'the biggest damn fool in creation'. But after discussions with all state premiers bar Ryan in mid-December, he came round to the idea of a coalition. On 9 January 1917, a new nationwide National Federation was formed. Its platform was winning the war, maintaining empire solidarity and free trade, providing effective repatriation for soldiers and sailors, settling disputes by concilia-tion and arbitration, upholding the White Australia Policy and developing Australia's natural resources. The Federation was not a political party per se, and it would take some weeks of further negotiation and jockeying for position before a new government emerged.[7]

A key issue to be resolved was the leadership. Should the prime minister be Hughes, Cook, or even the prominent Western Australian Sir John Forrest, who threw his hat into the ring in late January as a consensus candidate? A second question was whether the ALP should be included in the coalition, making it a truly national government. Eventually, on 7 February, the ALP caucus resolved this issue by refusing to join three-party discussions, provoking Hughes to declare: 'The official Labour party is no longer master of its own actions. It is a mere pawn in the hands of outside bodies. It does what it is told to do. If a member dares to murmur, to speak as he thinks . . . he lives with the sword of excommunication suspended over his head.' The way was open for the fusion of the Liberals and Hughes' National Labor in a new National Party.[8]

The leadership went to Hughes, but he had to concede to the Liberals six Cabinet places out of eleven. Cook took second place in the Cabinet while Forrest, disappointed in his hope of being prime minister, was compensated with the Treasury, which Hughes had wanted to give to Watt. Pearce fell to fourth place in Cabinet seniority. He almost lost the portfolio of Defence, since he was thought to be ineffectual and his department was criticised as being extravagant and inefficient, but he was allowed to retain the role on the condition that there be a formal inquiry into his department's administra-tion. The new government was sworn in on 17 February.[9]

The creation of the National Party represented a major shift to the right in federal politics, one that would last for most of the inter-war years. It was, of course, welcomed by the non-Labor press. The left-wing press, however, was scathing about this 'mushroom party'. *The Worker* warned on 18 January 1917 that:

> Nothing but overwhelming disaster can be expected from association with such a gang as this. For it is a party that is neither fish, fowl nor good red herring . . . it is the sort of party Hughes deserves—and it is the sort of party that deserves Hughes for its leader!

'WE HAVE TO KEEP THIS BASIC FACT IN MIND,' it continued: 'THERE ARE ONLY TWO PARTIES: THE ROBBERS AND THE ROBBED.'[10]

The new government had a majority in the House of Representatives, but not in the Senate. Hughes could do 'not a darn thing' while ALP senators policed his beat, as a *Worker* cartoon rejoiced. This included his not being able to extend the life of the current parliament. Elections were due for both houses in 1917, and Hughes—as pugnacious as ever—was willing to face the electorate. But the Liberals wanted to defer elections until October 1918, or six months after the end of the war—whichever was sooner. They made this a condition of the coalition.[11]

However, the term of a parliament could be extended only if both houses of parliament requested this of the imperial parliament. The House of Representatives did pass the necessary resolution, despite the strong opposition of the ALP, which wanted to force Hughes to face the electorate, but the Senate did not follow suit. On 6 March, therefore, the governor-general approved the dissolution of parliament and elections were scheduled for 5 May.

To his dismay, the timing of the federal election meant that Hughes was unable to attend the Imperial War Conference being convened in London from March onwards. This was a significant gesture on the part of the British government. Whereas Asquith had kept the Dominions at a distance, fearing that Britain's freedom of action in determining war and peace aims would be compromised if London shared power, Lloyd George was prepared to

Some six thousand Victorian schoolchildren spell out Anzac on the Melbourne Cricket Ground in December 1916, creating an effect *The Argus* described as 'thrilling'. (AWM H16097)

Melburnians demonstrating their loyalty in February 1917. The gathering was addressed by the Minister for Defence, George Pearce. The memorial was temporary. It was erected 'not only as a reminder of the heroes who had fallen', Pearce said, but to show 'the way to duty to those who remained, who could and should take their place'. (*The Argus*, 26 February 1917; AWM 19379)

Design or chance makes others wive, But Nature did this match contrive.
—Waller (1042).

THE NUPTIALS.

The *Australian Worker*'s view on the coalition between Hughes and Cook's Liberals. The officiating priest is bloated 'Capitalism', while the onlookers are an angry Labor worker and an approving 'Tory press'. (30 November 1916; ANU Noel Butlin Archives Centre)

THE RAT TRAP.
J. T. Cam, 336-338 Elizabeth Street, Brisbane.

The labour movement's profound sense of betrayal by Hughes is evident in this 1917 election campaign cartoon. (*Australian Worker*, 26 April 1917; ANU Noel Butlin Archives Centre)

concede that the Dominions deserved a greater role in decision-making, given their significant contribution to the war. He therefore offered to create an imperial conference that was 'a special and continuing meeting'—in effect, an expanded session of the British War Cabinet, dealing with the great issues of war and peace. In Irvine's view, this was 'the most important constitutional development since the grant of self-government' to Australia. What was being proposed was 'for the first time an Imperial Cabinet in the fullest sense'. Certainly the creation of the Imperial War Cabinet (IWC) revealed that relations between London and its Dominions were being transformed by the war.[12]

Hughes, of course, wanted to attend the conference. Not only was he keen to make Australia's voice, and his voice—he seems to have viewed them as one and the same—heard again in London. He was also anxious to get the question of Irish Home Rule elevated to centre stage of imperial politics. The British believed this was simply a domestic matter, but for Hughes the Irish question was fundamental to sustaining the Australian war effort. As he wrote to Lloyd George on 12 March 1917 (using Keith Murdoch rather than Munro Ferguson as his channel):

> Present position in Ireland now rendered acute makes neutrals regard our cry that we are fighting for rights small nations [sic] hypocritical. Effect of present position in Ireland upon manpower most serious throughout Empire. In any case Australian recruiting is practically at a standstill. Irish National Executive here has carried resolution to effect that until Home Rule granted no Irish Catholics shall join forces. This is being acted on and in such a way that the non-Irish population are going out of Australia to fight or as railway workers, carpenters etc. The Irish remain behind and in any election their voting strength is greatly increased.

The resolution of the Irish Home Rule issue, Hughes thought, was essential if he were to appease the Irish-Catholic element in the ALP.[13]

However, there was no bipartisan support for Hughes going to London. The ALP was not in principle opposed to imperial cooperation, but it distrusted anything that smacked of imperial federation—that is, a single federal state of all parts of the empire, governed from London, an idea that various leaders across the empire had been championing for some decades. Risking any of Australia's self-governing powers in return for a voice in the empire's foreign policy would, as Labor saw it, be 'disastrous for Australian ideals'. An imperial cabinet, one Labor parliamentarian suggested, might even impose conscription on Australia. If Hughes went to London, he 'would win the war and damn Australia'![14]

Since the election promised to be bitterly contested, Hughes knew that it would be political suicide to leave Australia. The Imperial War Cabinet therefore went ahead without him. Australia was the only Dominion not represented—something Hughes would find worked against him when he did finally manage to get to London in 1918.

Into Palestine

There were, at least, further positive developments in the Middle East in early 1917. After taking Magdhaba in late 1916, the Desert Column continued its push towards Palestine by attacking another Ottoman outpost on the Egyptian–Palestine border, at Rafa. Advancing during the night of 8–9 January 1917, the mounted forces took the enemy forces by surprise. As Lieutenant-Colonel Guy Powles of the New Zealand Mounted Rifles Brigade later wrote:

> The great wonder of the desert is its all-embracing silence—all sound is swallowed up—and so in silence they go by, each troop riding in line with its troop leader in front . . . noiseless they go—no song, no laughter, no talking, not a light to be seen; no sound but the snort of a horse as he blows the dust from his nostrils; or the click of two stirrup irons touching as two riders close in together; or the jingle of the links on the pack horses; or perhaps a neck-chain rattling on the pommel.[15]

The battle that ensued was finely poised. The Ottomans were entrenched in defensive positions that overlooked the approaches of the attack. The mounted troops were also at a disadvantage, in that they were lightly armed. Since they needed mobility in the desert, their horse-drawn artillery carried only light field guns and relatively little ammunition. Consequently, this 'slender striking force', when dismounted, lacked the power and depth that infantry attacks normally had.[16]

By early afternoon, with a number of Allied guns ceasing to fire for lack of ammunition and Ottoman reinforcements moving in from the north, Chauvel and Chetwode discussed withdrawing. But then the New Zealanders were seen to have stormed the highest point of the wadi. Under fire from this vantage point, and shaken by a wild charge from the Imperial Camel Brigade, the Ottomans escaped or surrendered (1635 were taken prisoner).[17]

The Desert Column was now poised to enter Palestine as part of what was becoming a three-pronged assault on the Ottoman Empire. In January 1917, the Mesopotamian campaign—which had stalled with the humiliating surrender of Kut in April 1916—was renewed under the command of General Frederick Maude. The imperial forces, now re-equipped with flying machines, river craft and artillery, retook Kut and proceeded up the Tigris. On 11 March, Baghdad was captured and the British forces moved forward to control key points on the Euphrates and Diyala rivers at which flood control around Baghdad could be managed.

To the west, a revolt of the Arab tribes against Turkish rule, which had begun in mid-1916, was also gathering momentum. A mix of irregular Arab forces and a more formal Arab Army had been supported in 1916 by British and French officers, of whom the charismatic T.E. Lawrence—immortalised in the 1962 film *Lawrence of Arabia*—was just one, albeit the most important. Arab attacks on Turkish ports on the Red Sea in 1916 had been also been assisted by the Royal Navy providing firepower and aircraft. Now, in early 1917, the Arabs, British and French started a campaign of sabotage of the Hejaz railway, the lifeline supplying and providing an escape for the Ottoman forces in Medina.

The German withdrawal to the Hindenburg Line

On the Western Front, the first weeks of 1917 found I Anzac Corps still operating, as part of Gough's Fifth Army, in the vicinity of Gueudecourt to the south of Bapaume. From here they launched a series of small operations, capturing the trenches they had failed to take in the last phases of the Somme campaign. Three changes of senior command occurred around this time. Brigadier Nevill Smyth, a British officer who had commanded the 1st Brigade at Lone Pine, Pozières and Mouquet Farm, replaced Legge at the 2nd Division. Ostensibly this was because Legge was unwell, but he had in fact lost Birdwood's confidence. 'Legge [Birdwood wrote to a colleague] does his best according to his likes . . . but he has an unfortunate manner of rubbing people the wrong way, and I fear he does not inspire complete confidence.' Holmes, the commander of the AN&MEF in New Guinea in 1914 and the 5th Brigade in 1915–16, succeeded Cox as commander of the 4th Division, becoming the third citizen soldier after McCay and Monash to be given divisional command. McCay, having developed neuritis in his Gallipoli leg injury, had broken down in December 1916. He was replaced at the 5th Division by Talbot Hobbs, an architect in civilian life who had led the 1st Division's artillery at Gallipoli and the Somme. Few seemed to regret McCay's going, although Elliott was generous enough to say that, whatever his faults, McCay 'does know his job and . . . is a wonderfully brave man, as brave as anyone I have ever seen'.[18]

Then, on 23 February, the position on the Western Front was transformed. All along the line from Arras in the north to Soissons in the south, the Germans began to abandon their trenches and withdraw. Ludendorff had decided that, as part of Germany's strategic repositioning, it should consolidate its western armies behind a heavily fortified line of defences: the Siegfriedstellung, or, as the Allies called it, the Hindenburg Line (see Map 11). When completed, this would consist of line after line, some 8000 metres deep, of concrete bunkers, machine-gun emplacements, barbed-wire belts, tunnels, trenches, dugouts and command posts. As they withdrew, the Germans surrendered soil that had been defended passionately in 1916, but they remained entrenched deep within French territory. Moreover, by flattening out two bulges in the line near Bapaume and Noyon that were of little strategic advantage, they freed up a major reserve of divisions for flexible deployment elsewhere.

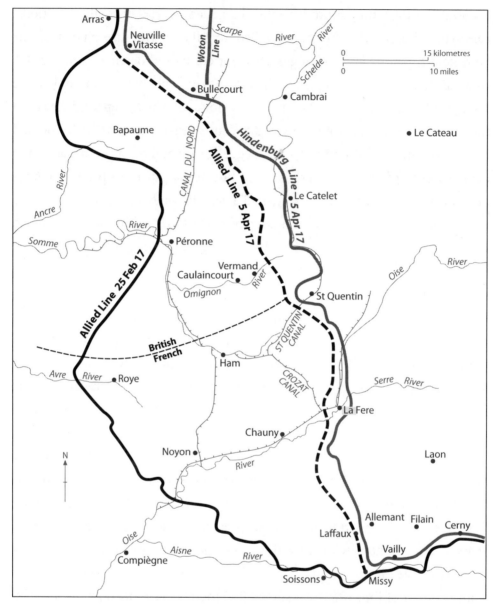

Map 11: German withdrawal to the Hindenburg Line, February to April 1917

When they began to discover German trenches abandoned, the Australian troops were 'electrified'. Lieutenant Thomas Miles noted in his diary: 'this retreat is I think the beginning of the end although it may take months to beat him yet, he knows he is beaten and it is only a matter of time, he is getting weaker everyday and we are getting stronger.' However, the Germans were not

276

beaten, and they fought fierce delaying actions as they withdrew. Sometimes they were glimpsed retreating into the distance, but more often they contested control of the very villages and soil they were surrendering. They also left a wasteland behind them: trees levelled, buildings destroyed, roads mined, sites booby-trapped, bridges detonated, telegraph communications destroyed and water supplies poisoned.[19]

By 17 March, the pursuing Australians had reached Bapaume, the grail of the Somme battle of 1916 but now a set of smoking ruins. Lieutenant Albert Edwards recalled:

> It was with a curious eerie feeling that I marched through the now vacant French villages, and saw the way of life led by the men who had been trying to kill me. There was something unreal in handling the things they had so recently handled, in picturing the manner of men they were, and then again to see the effect of our shells, shells that one had more or less watched being fired.[20]

Beyond Bapaume, however, was almost untouched green country. Tempted by this, Gough was keen to continue the pursuit right to the Hindenburg Line, positioning his Fifth Army in the optimal position to support the Third Army's offensive at Arras, now scheduled for 9 April. Haig, too, wanted take advantage of the opportunities that were arising from the German withdrawal, but he was more cautious. For him, the Arras offensive had the higher priority, and the pursuit of the Germans had to be strictly limited to avoid provoking major retaliation.

In this context, two columns of Australians set off on 18 March to harass the German withdrawal (see Map 12). Headed by Elliott's 15th Brigade and Gellibrand's 6th Brigade, and including artillery and light horse, they took a number of villages relatively easily in the first three days. Elliott's column was soon well ahead of the Fourth Army. On 20 March, however, Gellibrand's troops failed in an attempt to capture the village of Noreuil, and since a chain of more strongly defended villages lay ahead, Hobbs ordered Elliott to stop.

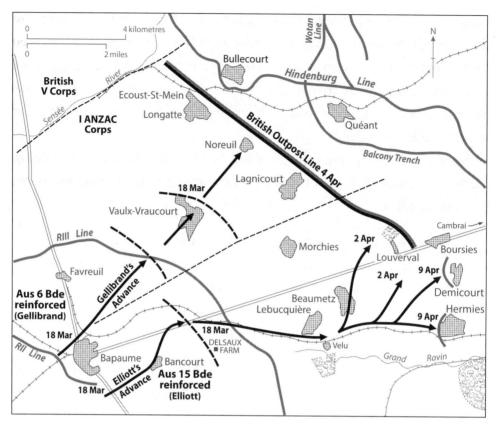

Map 12: Australian pursuit to the Hindenburg Line, March to April 1917

Elliott had been in his element directing mobile warfare and outflanking villages held by the Germans. As he said in a letter home:

It is lovely to see [the troops] fight. They go out as if they were going to a parade, never a check or halt, and then . . . the old Bosches jump out and run for their lives when we get a few hundred yards from them and our guns open up on them and smash them as they scoot for cover. It is just the fun of the world.

He now found the restrictions imposed on his operations profoundly frustrating, and made no effort to hide this from his superiors. He further incurred the wrath of Birdwood when, on 20 March, he ordered one of his platoons to occupy a village, Bertincourt, in a zone beyond his brigade's area of responsibility. Not for the last time, Elliott decided that since the British were doing a poor job in the role assigned to them, he needed to take unilateral action to remedy the situation. Brudenell White concluded that Elliott was inclined to 'Napoleonic ideas', imagining 'the whole German army was retiring before him'. It was a damaging perception of Elliot's temperament that would become more pronounced as the war continued.[21]

The pursuit of the German withdrawal continued into April, with more costly operations by the British V Corps and I Anzac Corps. Progressively, villages still in German hands in front of the Hindenburg Line—Lagnicourt, Noreuil, Doignies, Louverval, Boursies and, finally, Demicourt and Hermies—were wrested from German hands. By 9 April, the British faced the Hindenburg Line just as the Arras offensive was scheduled to begin to the north.

First and Second Gaza

The British push into Palestine also continued with an attack on Gaza on 26 March (see Map 13). The plan was to encircle the town, positioned on the Mediterranean coast beyond El Arish, using the mounted troops of the Desert Column and the camel brigade as a covering screen. These would cut off the Ottoman garrison from outside relief and block their withdrawal, while the infantry of 53rd Division attacked the town itself. The terrain in which the British were now operating was very different from that of Sinai: undulating grass, crops, orchards and fields, with herds of sheep and goats grazing as they had in biblical times.[22]

On the morning of the battle, fog poured in from the sea and the infantry attack, lacking adequate artillery support, proceeded ponderously. By the afternoon, the British had suffered 3000 casualties and the mounted troops had to be ordered to join the fight. Still, the day ended with Gaza in British hands—but then it was given back to the enemy! Commanding the Desert Column, Chetwode had become concerned—unnecessarily, as it happened—about the lack of water for the horses. It seemed also that Ottoman reinforcements were converging on Gaza from a number of directions. Hence, to their great frustration, the infantry who had taken vital ground were ordered to withdraw from Gaza and victory 'was effectively handed' to the Ottomans.[23]

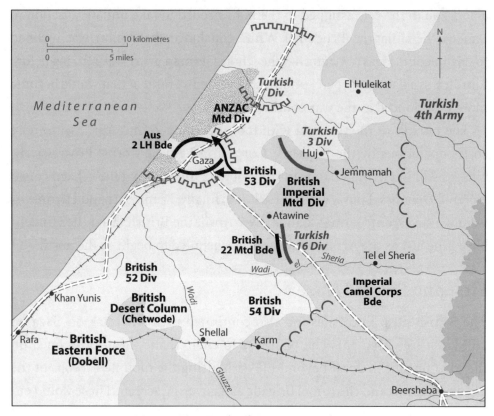

Map 13: First Battle of Gaza, 26 March 1917

For all that, Gaza was reported by Murray as a success that fell just short of disaster for the enemy—an interpretation that verged on the misleading. He was therefore encouraged by London to try again. By this time, however, the Ottomans had reinforced their defences and, thanks to German aerial reconnaissance, were aware of the British preparations. Hence the second attack on Gaza from 18–20 April was far less successful (see Map 14). Three British infantry divisions and the Imperial Mounted Division were supported by six old tanks, only light field guns, and poison gas, which dissipated in the hot air. The Anzac Mounted Division was consigned to a relatively minor role, securing the right flank of the attack. In this 'mismanaged, poorly planned and costly battle against prepared defences [which] would not have been out of place on the Western Front in 1915 or 1916'—to quote Jean Bou—the Ottoman hold on Gaza was never really threatened. Official British casualties

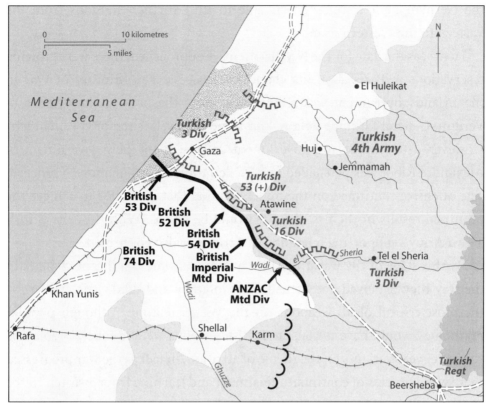

Map 14: Second Battle of Gaza, 18–20 April 1917

for the day were 6500, of whom 5000 were infantry. When the missing were taken into account, the figure was much higher. Most seriously, the force that might have advanced into Palestine was frittered away as the British had no choice but to dig in ahead of Gaza.[24]

Arras and First Bullecourt

On the Western Front, many of the assumptions underpinning the Nivelle offensive and the supporting Arras offensive, scheduled for early April, had been made redundant by the German withdrawal to the Hindenburg Line. Not only had the Noyon and Bapaume salients on which the Allied attacks were to be focused been flattened out, but the Germans were now entrenched in even stronger defences than before, and had greater operational flexibility thanks to their strategic reserve. Moreover, as Russia slipped into revolution, the German high command was able to shift further divisions from the Eastern to the Western Front.

Hence, as the date for the Nivelle offensive approached, there were growing reservations in Paris about its chances of success. The Minister of War in the Briand government was sceptical, as were the hero of the defence of Verdun, General Philippe Pétain, and some of Nivelle's senior commanders. However, after the Briand government collapsed, the new government of Alexandre Ribot was persuaded by Nivelle's threat of resignation to proceed. The offensive continued on the understanding that if it failed to achieve the promised results in the first days, it would be halted. With this, the British Third Army's supporting operation at Arras was also confirmed.

By this stage of the war, the Allies had made some significant changes in the way they deployed and armed their infantry and used their artillery—the most critical of all weapons on the Western Front. Although popular mythology would have it that the British generals were 'donkeys', replaying year after year variants on the theme of attrition, in fact as the war progressed there was a process of continual adjustment and learning from disaster. In the case of artillery, this involved the systematic application of scientific methods to planning and targeting. In particular, new techniques were developed to locate the positions of enemy artillery and improve the accuracy of fire. 'Flash spotting' established the position of guns by observing the flash of their firing from a number of different locations. Sound ranging used sets of microphones to determine a bearing from a gun's explosion. Aerial patrols also flew low across enemy lines, photographing defensive systems and giving army commanders, for the first time in history, the capacity to see over hills.[25]

None of these methods was foolproof. Rain and mist could limit the effectiveness of aerial reconnaissance and flash spotting, while strong winds could distort sound ranging. Aircraft were also vulnerable to attack, since the skies above the battlefields had become the stage for spectacular wheeling dogfights. But at any given time, at least one of these methods was able to provide the British artillery with some information about the position of German guns. No longer did they have to surrender surprise before an attack and give away their own position by preliminary firing. They were also able to compensate, with the aid of trigonometrical surveys, for any variations in the range of their guns caused by worn barrels. Most importantly, they were able to shift the focus of their firing to counter-battery work. Whereas in 1916 artillery bombardments before major battles were intended largely to destroy the enemy wire and trenches, and provide cover for the infantry as they advanced, now the artillery could target the enemy guns themselves. If these were silenced, then the infantry would not be annihilated by enemy fire once their own barrage had lifted.

As Allied artillery became more accurate, Allied gunners were also able to provide closer cover for infantry as they advanced across No Man's Land. Progressively, the artillery refined the 'creeping barrage'—the curtain of fire landing just in front of the infantry as they advanced. This forced enemy defenders to stay under cover until the infantry attack was almost upon them. Finally, the number of guns and quantities of ammunition available to the British army were increasing thanks to the mobilisation of British industry. Some of this ammunition was fitted with new fuses that detonated the shell's explosive charge on impact, thus destroying barbed-wire entanglements more effectively. In addition, mathematical calculations ensured that the weight and number of shells provided bore an appropriate relationship to the length of the front being attacked.

By mid-1917, too, the British armies, with a generation of 'tougher and younger' leaders emerging, were adopting new infantry tactics reflecting the lessons of the earlier disastrous battles. Rather than the infantry being seen, as they had been in the Victorian era, as riflemen in lines, they were now conceived as flexible, manoeuvrable and self-contained small groups, armed with their own firepower: Lewis guns (light machine-guns), rifle-grenades (which could project grenades a greater distance than if thrown by hand), and the more traditional rifles, bombs and bayonets. Thus armed, the platoon became an independent fighting unit with the capacity, in theory and increasingly in reality, to fight its own way forward and complete the work of the artillery by assaulting enemy defences.[26]

When the attack at Arras by the British Third Army (under General Edmund Allenby) began on 9–10 April, it was at first a resounding success. The Canadian Corps to the north of the line emerged from laboriously built tunnels and, under the cover of a creeping barrage, captured a dominant escarpment, Vimy Ridge. This was, at least in terms of national memory, Canada's Gallipoli. Church bells were rung across the country and a flood of congratulations poured in, including a message from the King. Vimy was later to become a 100-hectare memorial park and the site of a powerful 1936 memorial where a towering brooding woman faces out across the plains of Douai.[27]

However, the advance could not be sustained. The British command did not allow sufficient time for the guns to be hauled into new positions and to locate the sites of the more distant German trenches and defences. The Germans brought in new units to stem the Third Army's attack. The progress of the British and Canadians troops faltered, and the battle slipped into the slogging match typical of the Western Front.

The role of the Fifth Army, holding a line from Ecoust through Noreuil to Lagnicourt further south, was to assault the Hindenburg Line on the Third Army's right. As Gough planned it, the 4th and 12th Brigades of the Australian 4th Division and the British 62nd Division would capture the fortified village of Bullecourt; not by attacking it frontally, but rather by squeezing it out as the British attacked towards the village of Hendecourt and the Australians towards Riencourt. This was a daunting task. Four battalions of the 4th Division would have to advance over 1600 metres on a 2700-metre front, stretching across an indentation pointing into the Hindenburg Line (known as a re-entrant). Their line of attack would be overlooked on three sides by higher German positions, and the German barbed wire was 30 metres thick in some places. However, Gough—one of Haig's most controversial generals, disliked for his bullying command style and abrasive personality—believed that the Hindenburg Line was not strongly defended at this point. He assumed that the line could be broken by a combination of infantry attack and artillery.[28]

As he envisaged it, the 4th Cavalry Division would then push through the gap in the line, joining up with three cavalry divisions of Allenby's forces, which—having also broken through the German line further north—would be 'trotting down the Cambrai road', as Les Carlyon puts it. Assuming Nivelle's offensive to the south was also successful, the Allies would then be in a position, as Gough explained in his post-war memoirs, 'to cut off all the German forces holding the front of about 70 miles' between the British and French attacks. Whatever it turned out to be, Bullecourt was not meant to be 'bite and hold'.[29]

Things soon started to unravel. On 8 April, aerial reconnaissance and patrols showed that the artillery bombardment at Bullecourt, which had begun in a serious way only on 5 April, had scarcely broken the wire in front of the Australians. Since the railway lines stopped short of the front and the roads had been badly sabotaged by the Germans during their withdrawal, the British had not been able to bring up enough heavy guns and ammunition to destroy the enemy wire. In Brudenell White's opinion, another eight days of wire-cutting were needed before the attack could be launched.

Gough, however, was so keen to have his army's attack coincide with that of the Third Army that he seized on an offer of twelve tanks, which were stationed to the rear of the line. According to their commanding officer, Major W.H.L. Watson, if concentrated in a formation that moved ahead of the infantry, the tanks would be able to achieve what the artillery had not: suppress the machine-guns, crush the German wire, trample the trenches and lead the infantry as they mopped up what remained.

This was a high-risk gamble for a number of reasons. First, the plan involved the infantry approaching the formidable Hindenburg Line without the support of an artillery barrage. Second, the tanks—which were still a novelty on the Western Front—had never worked with the infantry, and would have no time to assemble prior to the attack (as would become the norm in later conflicts). Third, the tanks themselves were fairly primitive Mark IIs, clumsy, thinly armed training vehicles with a maximum speed in battle of 3 kilometres an hour. Their engines generated immense heat, fumes and noise, making conditions inside the cabins unbearable and exhausting their crews within two hours. Finally, the tanks were located several kilometres behind the front line and, since it was snowing and dark, they might not even arrive at the front line by the time of the attack.[30]

Nonetheless, Gough approved the plan, and set the time of the attack for 4.30 a.m. on 10 April (see Map 15). This was only twelve hours away, and there

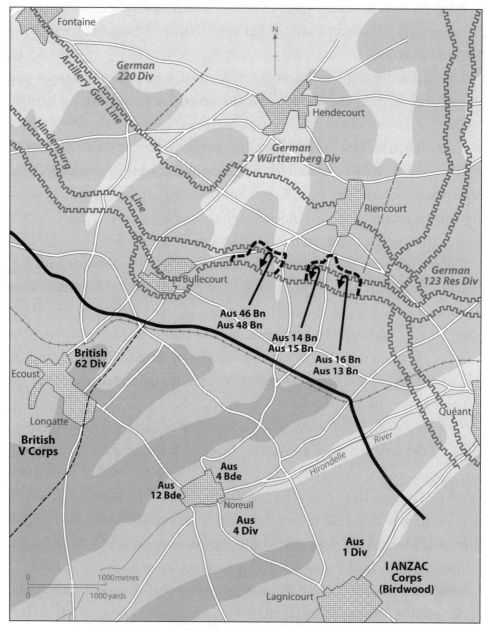

Map 15: First Bullecourt, 11 April 1917

was little time to adjust the existing battle plans. Holmes, commanding the 4th Australian Division, protested that it was all too risky—especially as the Third Army's attack to the north was now known to be running into trouble. But he was overruled by Birdwood, who, under pressure from Gough's headquarters, swallowed his earlier reservations—arguably too readily.

Holmes was right. By 4.15 a.m., the tanks had not reached the infantry and the Australian attack had to be aborted after the infantry had lain for hours in the snow in advanced positions beyond their trenches. The men of the 48th Battalion, according to their unit history,

> got up stiff and cold and cramped, damning the tanks, and the stupidity of the higher command that backed the tanks. They returned to their own trenches just as does a crowd disperse after a football match, no pretence at taking cover, no care for an enemy.

As Captain N.G. Imlay wrote later: 'The lads were too disgusted to worry about anything just then, and did not seem to care a continental cuss as they meandered back, although the enemy put over some hate.' The British 62nd Division, however, thinking that the action was still on, sent patrols out towards Bullecourt and lost 162 men.[31]

Although this fiasco had alerted the Germans, Gough rescheduled another attempt for early the next morning, 11 April. Birdwood protested but again buckled under pressure from Gough, who insisted—possibly disingenuously—that Haig thought the operation was urgent. Once more the troops, many of whom had spent another night scarcely protected from the snow—moved forward. Private Gallwey of 47th Battalion, who was new to battle, wrote:

> I carried my rifle in my left hand, just holding it by the sling and trailing the butt through the mud. It was too much energy to carry it any other way. Knees were giving way, and I was plodding on like in a dream . . . Of what use would I be to fight to-night? My body was in a wretched state of weakness.[32]

The plan now was for the tanks to advance some fifteen minutes ahead of the infantry, at 4.30 a.m. But by the appointed time only four tanks had made it to their position in front of the 4th Brigade. One tank had reached the gap between the two brigades while the four tanks that were supposed to lead the 12th Brigade on the left of the attack were all late. This delayed the infantry attack until after the Allied bombardment of the German line had stopped. In the confusion, one tank managed to open fire on the Australian 46th Battalion as it waited to move forward. After being abused by the Australians, the commander of the tank emerged to ask for directions to the enemy positions![33]

Once in action, the slow-moving tanks were soon overtaken by the infantry. Some developed mechanical problems. George Mitchell, now a corporal in the 48th Battalion, looked across No Man's Land and saw them: 'Dark black against the snow. They lined up and moved slowly, oh how slowly. I cursed them and cursed them for their sloth.' Continuing on their lumbering journey, some tanks got tangled in the wire or were hit and immobilised. Silhouetted against the snow, they made easy targets. One crew was incinerated, emerging from their tank aflame and screaming. Perhaps four tanks eventually made it to the German wire. One reached the village of Bullecourt, only to be abandoned because the infantry had not kept up with it. Gough admitted later that the tanks 'failed completely to fulfil the great expectations we had cherished'. Over 50 per cent of their crew were killed.[34]

The infantry of the 4th and 12th Brigades were therefore largely unprotected as they made their way across 'a machine-gunners' paradise' towards the forest of partially cut barbed wire. Since the tanks were meant to be preceding the troops, there was no British creeping barrage. There was, however, a rain of German fire. Mitchell later recalled:

Countless great shells rushed and crashed into our midst. Shrapnel burst, and the concussion jostled and knocked us over. Maxim bullets made the air a crackling inferno, to be heard even above the roar of shells. Men were dropping like flies. Some lay still, some were crawling to cover. No one yelled. The human voice was too insignificant a thing there.

Men became entangled in the barbed wire, hanging 'like scarecrows wounded and helpless only to be riddled with bullets . . . They were like birds in a snare and had to just stand there until bullets ended their suffering'. As Lance-Corporal Bert Knowles recalled,

> The enemy machine guns were having it all their own way. Anywhere, where men were grouped together trying to penetrate the barbed wire, the machine-guns simply wiped out 50 per cent with a swish, but men lay on their sides and hacked at the wire with their bayonets. Some few had cutters; others tried to cross the top, leaping from one strand to another. Many slipped and became hopelessly entangled in the loosely bunched wire.

So thick was the wire that men could not even see through it.[35]

Despite all this, the infantry of both brigades, particularly the 4th, managed to penetrate two belts of wires by 7 a.m. and reach the German trenches. A vicious exchange of bombs and bayonets followed. To quote Knowles again:

> things seemed to be a sort of nightmare, consisting of throwing Mill's bombs over a traverse of the trench or sap, waiting for them to explode, and then rushing into the next portion of trench with a bayonet, and shoot or chase any Hun who was not wounded . . . we would see a shower of enemy bombs come over, and we would get back round the corner until they had exploded, and then rush forward again.

Having broken into the Hindenburg Line, the Australians were soon exposed to fierce counter-attacks. As the German 27th Württemberg Division sought to drive into the gap between the two brigades, the infantry tried to call on their artillery to lay down a barrage, but their SOS rockets were ignored. The Fifth Army artillery commander and Birdwood, influenced by faulty reports from artillery observers and aerial reconnaissance (very few runners could get through the blanket of machine-gun fire), thought the attack had succeeded. If the Australian troops were beyond the German front line, then they might be hit by their own 'friendly' fire.

Without a supporting barrage and isolated in the German trenches, the Australians began to run out of ammunition. They had the choice of surrendering or making a desperate dash back to their own lines across No Man's Land. Many set off, hopping from shell hole to shell hole under fire from all sides. This included their own guns, which were at last allowed to fire when it was thought that the positions on the Hindenburg Line had been lost. Sergeant Max McDowall of the 48th Battalion later wrote:

> I ran at top speed and as soon as my speed slackened dived into a shell hole. After a short rest I started off again. Top speed was not possible for long and I slowed to a walk. Shortly after that I saw two figures on my right, one supporting the other. I went over and found a corporal helping [Lieutenant] Dennis, who was badly wounded. I caught hold of Dennis's left arm to put it over my shoulder, but the movement made him gasp with pain. He urged us repeatedly to leave him, stating we would surely be shot. But Fritz was a good sport and let us go![36]

By early afternoon, it was all over. The Germans had regained everything they had lost, the surviving Australians were back where they started and, to add to their misery, another blizzard blew up. In less than 24 hours, the 4th Division lost some 3500 men, with the 4th Brigade, numbering 3000 men, suffering 2339 casualties. By one estimate, 1164 Australians were taken prisoner of war—the largest number in any single action during the war. Among the dead of the 48th Division was a Private Mark Cummings: not a notable death in itself, except that eight days later his brother would die in the equally mismanaged attack on Gaza. A third Cummings brother had already died at Quinn's Post, Gallipoli, in June 1915. Just one brother remained to post 'in memoriam' notices in the press many years after the war.[37]

The survivors of First Bullecourt, as the action on 10–11 April became known, were devastated. When Birdwood congratulated the Australian troops for being the first to break through the Hindenburg Line, assuring them that their losses had 'not been in vain ... Officers—hard-faced, hard-swearing men broke down'. The men were also filled with an 'icy, contemptuous anger', as even Gough's biographer concedes. They railed at the 'useless and worse than useless' tanks, and also blamed the British 62nd Division, which they thought had sat idly by, although its orders had actually been to move forward only after the tanks and the Australians had entered Bullecourt.[38]

Gough's performance has been universally condemned. Bean's official history concludes that:

> with almost boyish eagerness to deliver a death blow, the army commander broke at every stage through rules recognised even by platoon commanders. He attempted a deep penetration on a narrow front, and that at the head of a deep re-entrant. When, despite impetuous efforts, he was unable to bring forward his artillery and ammunition in time to cut the wire, he adopted, on the spur of the moment, a scheme devised by an inexperienced officer of an experimental arm, and called the attack on again for the following morning. Finally, after the tanks, on the first trial, had confirmed the worst fears of his subordinates, he insisted on repeating the identical operation next day.

The British official historian was equally critical: 'In the whole course of the War few attacks were ever carried out in such disadvantageous circumstances against such defences.' Gough himself conceded in his memoirs that the attack had been launched on too narrow a front, though he praised the Australians for their 'display of courage worthy of all praise'.[39]

Birdwood and Brudenell White must also share some of the responsibility for Bullecourt—not so much for poor staff work, since they had so little time in which to adjust to Gough's haphazard planning, but more for their failure to stand up to him. A tearful Birdwood assured the Australian troops that none of the officers 'had anything to do with the arrangements for the stunt', and it was certainly difficult for him to contest the orders of a superior army commander. That said, however, Birdwood and Brudenell White could have voiced their reservations more firmly. As E.M. Andrews concludes in a persuasive critique, they 'compare unfavourably with the independent Currie, the Canadian Corps commander, who was not afraid to stand up to either Gough or Haig'.[40]

Within days of First Bullecourt, the Germans attacked further along the line between the villages of Noreuil and Hermies. Here the 1st Australian Division was stretched thinly across a front of nearly 12 kilometres and the Germans still held a number of 'outpost' positions beyond the Hindenburg Line. The Germans' aim on 15 April was to capture or destroy as many men and guns as possible before returning to the security of their new defences. Attacking at night with four divisions, 16,000 Germans streamed silently through the point near Noreuil where the 1st Division met with the 2nd (only just brought up to the front line to replace the battered 4th Division). They surged up the valley leading to the village of Lagnicourt and captured the guns of the 1st and 2nd Australian Field Artillery.[41]

However, the Australian infantry were now becoming skilled at 'defence in depth'. While their piquets (or troops placed forward of the line to warn of an advance) took the initial brunt of the attack, the support troops and reserves moved up from behind to retake the territory the Germans had gained. Though outnumbered four to one, the Australians pushed the Germans back, inflicting 2313 casualties and taking only 1010 casualties themselves. Importantly, the Australian guns survived almost intact because the Germans, during the time they held the position, busied themselves with finding food and souvenirs. By afternoon, 31 of the guns that had been taken by the Germans were back in action.[42]

The Nivelle offensive

Further south, at Chemin des Dames, Nivelle's offensive began on 16 April. Although so much was hoped of it, it failed dismally. Poor weather, the enemy's superiority in the air and supply difficulties all reduced the impact of the massive artillery bombardments in which Nivelle had placed such faith. With the German defences left relatively intact, the advance of the French infantry was uneven. At best they progressed some 6–7 kilometres; at other points, they hardly moved. Moreover, their casualties were huge. Between 16 and 25 April on the Aisne, some 30,000 were killed, 100,000 wounded and

4000 captured. This was the largest total of any month in the war, apart from November 1914.[43]

Although the Germans also lost heavily, and at a different stage of the war the balance sheet for the Allies might have been read as positive, the contrast between the miserable gains of the offensive and Nivelle's extravagant promises was intolerable. Throughout France, there was a pervasive sense of failure and despair. In mid-April, the French troops began to mutiny. In 44 divisions, the soldiers refused to enter the trenches, smashed property, got drunk, shouted revolutionary and peace slogans, and even assaulted or killed their officers. Their anger was fuelled by a mix of battle fatigue, the lack of leave, pacifism and revolutionary sentiment inspired by the news of events in Russia. Essentially, the French soldiers felt betrayed by their leaders: 'fiasco', 'lynching', 'massacre', 'butchery' and 'failure' were words used in their letters home to describe the Nivelle offensive.

This was a critical moment for the Allied Powers. If the French army had disintegrated, the entire British position to the north would have become untenable. Perhaps, as in 1940, they would have had to withdraw across the Channel, hoping that with American aid they might one day return to expel the Germans from Belgium and France. However, the mutiny—or, in the language of the day, the acts of 'collective indiscipline'—was contained. On 28 April, Pétain was appointed French Chief of Staff to counterbalance Nivelle. Systematically, he set about addressing the soldiers' grievances: improving their food and leave opportunities, and insisting on officers being more visible in the trenches. He personally visited 90 divisions, explaining the wider war situation to the troops, assuring them of the value of their contribution and guaranteeing that there would be only limited offensives in the immediate future. At the same time, Pétain made examples of a few soldiers in each of the mutinous regiments. In a matter of weeks, some 3427 soldiers were convicted of offences. Probably 632 of these were executed. Order was restored in the French army, but it was clear that the British would have to assume much of the burden on the Western Front in the future.

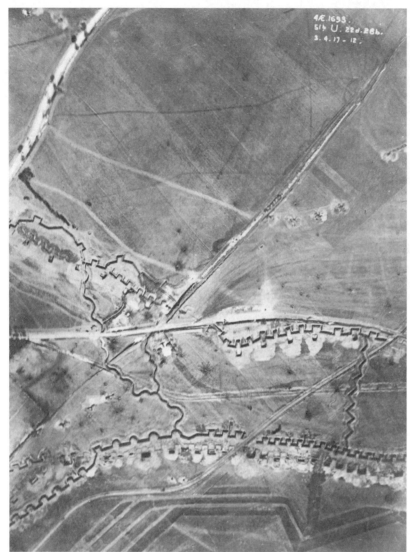

An aerial view of the Hindenburg Line, illustrating the strength of these defences at the time of the first attack at Bullecourt by the 4th Division. The dark rectangular bands are belts of barbed wire. (AWM A01121)

German officers with a British Army Mark II tank disabled during First Bullecourt. (AWM G01534J)

One of the conventions of mourning for bereaved families was a Roll of Honour card, this one for Private William Quinn, 20th Battalion, killed during Second Bullecourt. (AWM P06560.005)

A crater caused by the massive explosions on Hill 60 near Messines, Belgium, in June 1917. (AWM E00580)

Second Bullecourt

With the French needing every support possible, the British First and Third Armies continued the Battle of Arras throughout April. The gains were minimal and the losses high, but another major offensive was scheduled for 3 May. The Fifth Army was assigned the role of trying again to take Bullecourt. Ominously, the battle plan was almost a repeat of 11 April, though the 62nd Division and the 2nd Australian Division would attack at the same time. The 5th and 6th Brigades, in an act of 'sheer folly', were allocated the task of charging the Hindenburg Line across a section of exposed land between Bullecourt and Quéant, a spur that overlooked the attack on the right. Then, after joining with the 62nd Division, which was supposed to have taken Bullecourt, they would advance to the Fontaine–Quéant road and capture the villages of Hendecourt and Riencourt (see Map 16).[44]

At least the weather was much better than the snow of early April and the preparations were more thorough than for First Bullecourt. The ammunition dumps were well stocked and, with extra batteries of heavy guns, the German lines were bombarded from mid-April onwards. The infantry had rehearsed the attack carefully, and were provided with mats of netting to throw over any uncut wire. The Australians could also have had the support of ten tanks but, distrusting them after 11 April, they allowed these to go the British 62nd Division.

The preparations for the attack, however, were detected by the Germans, whose artillery targeted the British ammunition dumps and drenched the Noreuil Valley with gas shells. Even more seriously, the Allied artillery supporting the attack, in a major failure of Australian staff planning, did not target the strong German defences to the west of Quéant. Instead, they pounded Bullecourt itself, the villages that were meant to be captured and the German front line directly in front of the attack.

As a result, when the 5th Brigade set off at 3.45 a.m. on 3 May behind a creeping barrage, they were deluged from their side and rear with machine-gun fire and shrapnel, which burst at head height, shredding men's upper bodies. The attack rapidly disintegrated. Officers and NCOs suffered heavy

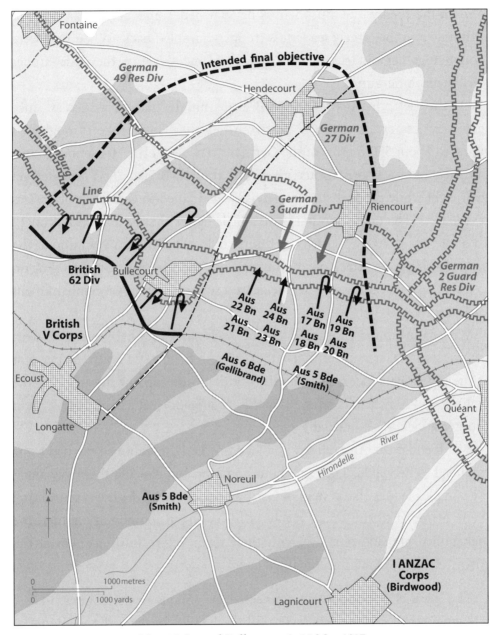

Map 16: Second Bullecourt, 3–15 May 1917

losses and the 5th Brigade ceased to be an effective fighting formation. The fact that the brigade commander, Brigadier-General Robert Smith, had positioned his headquarters more than 2000 metres to the rear, in the village of Noreuil, did nothing to help the situation. Despite everything, some men did manage

297

to reach the enemy line. But then, as day dawned, someone gave an order to withdraw and the largely leaderless troops scrambled back. When they were brought together and tried again to take their first objective, they failed under terrible machine-gun fire.

On their left, the Australian 6th Brigade initially had more success, since they were less exposed to the fire from Quéant. They broke through and captured about 550 metres of the German trenches in the Hindenburg Line. But their hold was precarious, given that the 5th Brigade had retreated on their right while the British 62nd Division had failed to gain their objectives on the left. (The tanks had performed little better than in First Bullecourt.) To quote Bean, 'like a mushroom on its stalk, deep in enemy ground at the head of a single long track of communication', the 6th Brigade had to cling on to what they had captured, with the nearest support at a railway embankment 1.2 kilometres to their rear.[45]

With hand bombs, rifle grenades and Lewis guns, they managed to hold off a succession of German counter-attacks. But in the first 24 hours, 53 per cent of the 6th Brigade became casualties—killed, wounded or missing. On the night of 3–4 May, it was relieved by the 1st Brigade, just as another German counter-attack was launched.[46]

The toehold the Australians now had on the Hindenburg Line had to be extended to be viable. They set about bombing and clawing their way along the complex ladder-like system of German trenches and dugouts confronting them. Stripped to the waist, revolvers in one hand, bombs in another, the men pulled grenade pins out with their teeth before hurling them at the enemy. As W.H. Downing explained later:

The parallel trenches were connected by oblique 'switch' lines, like swinging gates; so that wherever any breach might be made the assailants would inevitably find themselves trapped in a deadly salient . . . There were trenches where the struggle never ceased, where bomb fights raged for hours of every day. These trenches were filled with corpses, over which men trampled and stumbled and fought like demons until the enemy were driven back a few yards and we could make a sandbag 'block' in the trench. And then the enemy would come again in force and drive us away; and so it would go on.[47]

The Germans were now deploying a new weapon: flamethrowers. Sergeant P. Kinchington of the 3rd Battalion recalled:

When the Germans were about 40 yards away I saw a fellow shoot a jet of flame into the bank . . . I fired and shot the carrier through the belly . . . my bullet went through the *flammenwerfer* can, and it caught fire at the back. You could hardly see for smoke. There was a hole in the road; the man fell into it, and about a dozen men on top of him—they all appeared to catch fire.

This intense fighting, under constant German barrage, demanded huge supplies of ammunition. Carrying parties struggled across the exposed access routes, bringing up bombs, trench-mortar shells and rifle grenades, along with other supplies.[48]

The wounded had to be evacuated across the same naked landscape. To quote Bean:

a wounded man was observed waving a bandage or handkerchief. The troops next saw two of their own stretcher-bearers climb out and walk over to pick him up. As they did so, German riflemen and a machine-gun to the left front of the captured position opened fire on them. With the bullets pecking the dust all round them, the stretcher-bearers . . . laid the man on the stretcher and began to carry him back, when one of them . . . fell. The other laid down the stretcher and bent over his mate, but found him dead. A third stretcher-bearer . . . was then seen to climb from Pioneer Trench, run across to the little group, ignoring the fire which was kept up, take the dead man's place and bring in the stretcher.[49]

The battle continued for some two weeks. The Germans launched counter-attack after counter-attack—seven general attacks and at least a dozen local ones—and the battle descended into fighting that was, in the opinion of the German general commanding the 27th Würtemmberg Division, much more bitter than on the Somme. After four days of this, the Australian 2nd and the British 62nd Divisions were used up and the Australian 1st and British 7th Divisions that replaced them were also badly mauled. Yet the Australians had extended the piece of the Hindenburg Line they controlled to nearly a kilometre.[50]

This position was immensely vulnerable as long as the Germans held the village of Bullecourt to the rear and left. On 7 May, the British 7th Division attacked Bullecourt, aiming to connect with the Australians still bombing their way along the trenches. The 'village' was now a desolate landscape of rubble and corpses. The trenches were barely recognisable and the Germans occupied deep dugouts, the entrances of which were hidden under heaps of debris. Entombed in this subterranean world, they were protected from the full impact of Allied bombardments and could emerge to drench any attackers with machine-gun fire and trench mortars nestled in the craters. But for all this, the British and Australian 9th Battalion did manage to link up, if not to capture the village—now more accurately described as 'a heap of dead'.[51]

On the night of 8–9 May, the shattered 1st and 2nd Divisions were replaced by the Australian 5th Division. The battle was winding down. Haig was already planning his next step in Flanders, and from mid-May the troops around Arras went on to the defensive. However, the struggle to capture Bullecourt staggered on. Eventually, after a final German counter-attack on 15 May had been beaten off, the Germans decided that this heap of rubble was not worth any more lives. The British and Australians were left in control of Bullecourt and the small length of the German line to its north that they had captured two weeks earlier.

Given that the Arras offensive had been a failure almost everywhere else along the line, even these pitiful gains were celebrated in a succession of British military communiqués in the first weeks of May. Praises were heaped on the Australians. Haig sent a congratulatory message after a German counter-attack on 6 May had been stopped, saying:

> The capture of the Hindenburg Line east of Bullecourt, and the manner in which it has been held . . . against such constant and desperate efforts

to retake it, will rank high among the great deeds of the war and is helping very appreciably in wearing out the enemy.

Even one of the labour newspapers in Australia described First Bullecourt as 'the most smashing defeat inflicted on the enemy'.[52]

However, the two battles of Bullecourt cost the Australians about 10,000 casualties, each a personal tragedy for his loved ones. As the Leane family received the news that their son Allan had been killed, his brother Geoff wrote:

You will note Dad that I do not speak much of Allan but please understand that he is in my thoughts day & night & I have not had a nights rest since I got the news on 13 April & I am hanging on to myself for all I am worth to prevent myself from breaking down. I have some terrible fits of the 'blues' but one hope still lives with me & that is, to hear from him as prisoner of war as there are a hundred chances for him because I have spoken to men who were with him to the last & they swear that he was hit in the leg & thigh and <u>not</u> badly. Oh Dad it eased the pain a lot to hear how these boys spoke of him.

When the family of Captain Henry Davis received news of their son's death, his commanding officer hoped that 'the glorious nature of his last act and his great sacrifice will help to soften the grief that must surely be with you'.[53]

At the government level, Bullecourt forced some rethinking about the role and structure of the AIF. In February, Hughes and Pearce had decided to approve the creation of a sixth division, but the losses of April and May, combined with the slow rates of enlistment at home, now made this impossible. If recruitment did happen to pick up, the higher priority would be reinforcing the five existing AIF divisions. Bullecourt also fuelled a suspicion among AIF commanders and troops that the Australian infantry was being over-used—a view that persists even today. Munro Ferguson typically had little time for these suspicions, writing in June that:

the 'Special correspondents' at the front give the impression that the Australian troops do the bulk of the fighting and win most of the important battles, consequently the picture left in the public mind is that the Australians are always engaged while other units do 'Gallery' or are taking their ease in rest camps . . . undoubtedly these one sided accounts lead to the idea that Australians have done more than their fair share. There are still many quite educated people in Australia who do not know that there were any other troops than Anzacs at Gallipoli, and we run the risk of their thinking the same about the Somme.[54]

Whatever the governor-general might think, any suspicion that the AIF was being over-used was potentially political dynamite. Hence the men of I Anzac Corps were given four months' rest after Bullecourt. Returning to the region around Amiens, they enjoyed one of the longest periods of leave given to a corps in the British forces.

Revisiting the battlefields of 1916, the Australians had mixed emotions. Sergeant Rupert Baldwin wrote in his diary on 16 May:

> Four of us walked all over the place [Flers] . . . There are bodies all over the place. Now the warm weather has set in, you can see the bodies just under the ground as they fell. The sun has made a black mark the shape of the bodies. Of course we could not tell one from the other but some of us knew just about where some of the boys fell. So we had a good afternoon looking around talking of different ones that went under on that eventful morning.

Lieutenant J.T. Maguire, in contrast, experienced the intense joie de vivre that survivors often feel. He wrote home on 14 May:

> Well Mum dear I am in the best of health and spirits. I think your prayers must have something to do with it. I have been very very lucky in the line. The bullets & shells seem to miss me somehow, Thanks be to God. Today is absolutely perfect . . . I feel as happy as larry. This life suits me. Oh its grand the exciting tramping life. Free and untramelled. Nothing to worry about.[55]

Prisoners of war

Some 1170 Australians who had fought at Bullecourt, however, were not enjoying rest and leave but rather were adjusting to being prisoners of war. This was the largest number of Australians captured in any single engagement during World War I. It constituted nearly 30 per cent of all Australian prisoners taken in France and Belgium in the years 1916–18. In contrast, in the Gallipoli and Middle Eastern campaigns, only 217 Australians were captured by the Ottomans.[56]

Like all prisoners of war, these men were at profound risk in the first days after they surrendered. In this fluid time, they might be killed—either for revenge or because it was too much trouble for their enemy to keep them alive. If wounded, they might wait days for treatment, perhaps being given a lower priority by enemy medical personnel than the wounded of their own army. If their injuries seemed terminal, they might even be shot. If being evacuated from the front line, they were also in danger of being exposed to their own artillery fire.[57]

All prisoners of war during World War I had limited protection under international law. The prevailing regulations were the Hague Conventions of 1899 and 1907. These stated the general principle that prisoners should not be punished for having borne arms, but specific guarantees of prisoners' rights were relatively rudimentary. There were also significant gaps in the conventions' coverage. There was, for example, no precise definition of the work that prisoners could be ordered to undertake by their captors. In any case, the Hague Conventions technically did not apply in World War I since they came into force only if all belligerents were party to the conventions. Out of necessity, therefore, wartime governments negotiated bilateral agreements to regulate the treatment of the five million prisoners taken on all sides.

However, the conditions of many prisoners still fell far short of the standards codified later in the 1929 Third Geneva Convention relative to the treatment of prisoners of war. The 13,000 British and Indian troops captured at Kut, for example, were marched some 1100 kilometres across the desert after being captured; most died in captivity, some while building a railway through the Taurus mountains. These deaths included nine mechanics from the Australian Flying Corps, only two of whom survived the forced march. In addition, the death rate of Australians captured at Gallipoli was possibly 36 per cent (many estimates are much higher)—though in their case it was the epidemics that ravaged the Ottoman Empire during World War I, as much as overt maltreatment, that accounted for many deaths.[58]

The men captured at Bullecourt were initially interned in the notorious Fort MacDonald in Lille. Here the cells were small, crowded and unsanitary. As one prisoner recalled:

> There were about 95 of us altogether. We were very overcrowded and were made to sleep on the bare floor and were not given any blankets. The sanitary arrangements consisted of tubs in the room. There were no washing facilities . . . The food was very poor and consisted of a slice of bread and a drink of water for breakfast, hot greasy water—without any nourishment whatever—for dinner, and a slice of bread again in the evening.[59]

Despite a prohibition in the Hague Conventions on prisoners being employed on tasks connected with the operations of the war, many Australians were forced to bury German dead or build roads and ammunition dumps. This was dangerous work, often within range of Allied artillery. The Germans, however, claimed that the British had refused to agree to withdraw the prisoners in their hands some 30 kilometres behind the lines. The Allied POWs were therefore treated as 'prisoners of respite' and denied many basic necessities. One prisoner recalled of a 30-kilometre march to Douai that:

> The men were in a very weak condition and many of them were suffering from diarrhoea. Stragglers on the march were roughly handled by the guard. Civilians who tried to give us food also got a rough time. Our guards would not allow us to accept anything from them. During the march the men were pulling up turnips in the field and eating them raw.[60]

Ultimately, Allied prisoners were transferred to one of the 167 prison camps (*Gefangenenlagers*) and associated work camps in Germany. Here conditions were generally better, although they varied according to the location, the attitude of the camp commander and the number of prisoners in the camp. In accordance with international norms, the Germans respected the right of officers to be exempted from manual work. There was time—at least for them—to plan escapes, hold concerts and suffer profound boredom. Other ranks, in contrast, worked on farms, in factories and down mines.

Most importantly, Australian prisoners in Germany received letters from home and parcels prepared by the patriotic funds and delivered by the Red Cross. This meant that they had ample supplies of tinned food, soap, sugar, biscuits, clothing and cigarettes with which to survive the bitter winters and the growing food shortages of Germany. In fact, they were better off than many German civilians, with whom they sometimes shared their supplies. Hence, although their treatment was often harsh and many prisoners suffered what has been called 'barbed-wire psychosis', only 310 Australians—or one in twelve—died as prisoners of the Germans.

Remembering Bullecourt

Having survived Bullecourt, W.H. Downing concluded that the battle represented for Australians 'a greater sum of sorrow and of honour than any other place in the world'. Recognising this, the 4th Division—which took nearly 10 per cent of its total wartime casualties at First Bullecourt—came close in 1919 to choosing Bullecourt as the site of its divisional memorial. But then it opted instead for Bellenglise. This was the site where in late 1918 the division broke the Hindenburg Line, earning from a German battalion commander the accolade: 'Your men are so brave and have so much dash that it is impossible to stop them.' It is not recorded why the 4th Division leaders relegated Bullecourt to second place after two 'long and worrying meetings' discussing the subject. Perhaps they wanted to be remembered as victors, not victims—a status that became central to war remembrance only later in the twentieth century.[61]

As the decades passed, however, the memory of Bullecourt came to eclipse that of Bellenglise, at least in terms of public commemorative activity. This was partly because of the agency of local French individuals. In the 1970s, a French schoolteacher living in Bullecourt translated Bean's account of the 1917 battles for the benefit of his students. Inspired by the narrative, he then initiated the building of a memorial commemorating the British and Australian dead. With funds raised locally and the support of the Australian embassy in Paris, the memorial was unveiled in 1981 near the local church. Soon Australian authorities had capped it with a distinctively Australian digger's slouch hat in bronze, funded by the Australian War Memorial, the RSL and the Department of Foreign Affairs.[62]

In 1981–82, the residents of Bullecourt erected another memorial, to the missing of 1917. They had been sensitised to this issue by the persistent inquiries of an Australian woman whose brother had gone missing at Bullecourt. Taking the form of a cross, this memorial was located at the point where one of the main German trenches had cut across the road in 1917. Among the plaques attached to the cross was a tribute to a missing Australian officer, Major Percy Black, whose death while leading his men through the gaps in the wire on 11 April had been immortalised in 1923 in an oddly stilted painting by Charles Wheeler. In the early 1980s, too, Bullecourt began to host Anzac Day ceremonies, while the town mayor, Jean Letaille, oversaw the creation of a museum that housed, among other artefacts, remnants of the infamous tanks from 11 April 1917.[63]

The Australian government became increasingly woven into the tapestry of commemoration at Bullecourt in the 1990s. A new Australian memorial park on land donated by the town was approved in 1990 and opened in 1992. At its heart stood a stone pedestal. However, when this was thought to lack 'a certain something', the government commissioned a bronze statue by Peter Corlett—the same sculptor who would create Cobbers for Fromelles, the Light Horse at Beersheba, and Simpson and his Donkey and 'Weary' Dunlop in Canberra. The Bullecourt Digger now stands erect and confident, looking over the 1917 battlefield with the 'fresh face of a young man about to set off on a great adventure'. It is, in fact, the face of Corlett's father, who he discovered had served at Bullecourt in the 4th Field Ambulance. Private and public memory converged as he became the inspiration for Corlett's tribute to the men of Bullecourt.

Bullecourt is now an integral part of official Australian commemoration in France. Its museum has been refurbished and included in the Australian Remembrance Trail developed for the centenary of World War I. Anzac Day is also commemorated each year at Bullecourt, in a ceremony promoted by government and commercial tour companies. The ceremony is scheduled at 2 p.m., allowing Australians visiting France, in what former prime minister Julia Gillard has called Australia's 'memory season', the time to attend an earlier dawn ceremony at Villers-Bretonneux, another French town that has shaped its present identity around its wartime past.[64]

Anzac Day 1917

In 1917, First Bullecourt fed directly into the emerging rituals of Anzac Day. The second anniversary was a similar mix to 1916: triumphalism and exhortations to the population for ongoing sacrifice, intertwined with individual grief. One South Australian, Mrs Willett Bevan, poured her emotions into a prayer published in the Adelaide *Register*:

> Lord God, this Anzac Day
> With one accord we pray,
> Send us Thy peace
> From fear by day and night,
> For those gone forth to fight,
> Grant us release . . .
> To those who mourn their dead
> Come Thou, beside the bed,
> Whereon they weep.
> And where those, wakeful lie
> In mental agony,
> Grant them sweet sleep!

Officials at the federal and state level, meanwhile, made sure that Anzac Day was marked with appropriate public ceremony. The grand imperial event of 1916 was not repeated, but Hughes wrote to all religious leaders— Protestant, Catholic, Jewish and Salvation Army—encouraging them to hold memorial services on or near 25 April (which fell that year on a Wednesday). Marches were scheduled for returned soldiers and the militia in capital cities and major provincial towns. Trams, trains and traffic were stopped for one minute at 1 p.m. Since Anzac Day had not yet been declared a public holiday— this occurred progressively across the states over the next ten years—public servants were granted leave from 11.30 a.m. to 2 p.m. In France, meanwhile, Birdwood sent a message on behalf of all Australian troops to the wounded and sick in British hospitals and congratulatory messages were exchanged between the divisions.[65]

The rituals of Anzac Day seem still to have been fluid and improvised at the local level. In Beaulencourt, near Bapaume, one of the units marked the day by having sports and a rowdy 'good time', with the officers and men working 'hand in hand'. In Perth, 'Beer flowed' after an 'immense number' attended a ceremony and street march. 'Gallipoli man' reflected: 'If any excuse is needed for a man to get drunk, Anzac Day should surely furnish it. Sorrow for the dead, pride in the living, exultation in the anticipation of being able to do one's own little bit in the future.' This was a mix of emotions shared by many veterans, to the point where, over the years, Anzac Day would become notorious as 'one long grog-up', to quote the veteran's son, Hughie, in the controversial Alan Seymour drama *The One Day of the Year*, first performed in 1960.[66]

What is striking is the degree to which in 1917, only two years after the Gallipoli landing, the public discourse was already articulating an 'Anzac tradition' that drew strongly on classical and chivalric imagery. The *Sydney Morning Herald* thought the second anniversary of the Gallipoli landing was 'especially memorable' because it affirmed that the 'vital qualities of the race' had persisted beyond 1915:

the standard for all future action was set at Gallipoli . . . The story of the peninsula will be read with the famous description of the retreat from

Syracuse, or with the song of Roland. The men who took part in the landing may claim a place similar to that which the men who fought at Marathon held in the history of Greece.

The *Brisbane Courier* also claimed that the battles of 1916–17 had 'added to the unfading laurels of the men who landed at Anzac Cove on April 25, 1915'. The Anzacs, it declared, were 'the representative of the best manhood of the Commonwealth and the Dominion'. 'Always,' the *West Australian* added, the Australians 'have been in the forefront of battle, and always the thinned ranks of the enemy mourned the ill fate that brought the reckless warriors of the South against them.'

As in 1916, this rhetoric was used to stimulate flagging enlistments for the AIF. The Adelaide *Advertiser* declared that Anzac Day was not 'a mere tribute of veneration' for the AIF, but the dedication of those at home to the 'unfinished business' of the war: 'If we cannot all fulfil the first duty of citizenship by entering the trenches, let us perform all the more heartily those secondary duties of labor and sacrifice for which the struggle affords only too wide a scope.' It is not surprising, then, that the left-wing press let Anzac Day 1917 pass without comment. They focused rather on local labour issues, including the sacking of 2000 workers after the suspension of public works on the North Coast railway line in New South Wales. Their war was closer to home, and its goal was the defeat of Hughes.[67]

The federal election

The weeks leading up to the federal election of 5 May were torrid and marked by scandal. With his political future at stake, Hughes lobbied for numbers in the parliament, resorting to tactics that at times verged on the corrupt. In March 1917, an anti-conscriptionist Tasmanian senator resigned on grounds of ill-health—only to be replaced within 24 hours by a *pro*-conscriptionist, the former Tasmanian premier John Earle. This manoeuvre required Earle to resign his lower-house seat in Tasmania and be appointed by the state Executive Council to the federal Senate vacancy—all before the matter became public.

It was easy to see the hand of the 'the conjuror of Wales', Hughes, in this, and *Labor Call* declared the business 'about as fishy as a staff Newmarket favourite. It wants buckets of phenyle to wash out the odor.' Other Tasmanian senators were sufficiently annoyed to withhold their support for the prolongation of the parliament.[68]

Then an official Labor Party senator, David Watson, alleged that he had been offered bribes by Hughes to support the coalition. The Senate demanded a royal commission, but the government blocked this in the lower house. Munro Ferguson suggested that Hughes had done no more than 'attempt to prevail on a wavering Senator to have the courage of his opinions, coupled with an assurance that he would not lose by so doing', but a David Low cartoon of 25 March put it more acerbically. Hughes was depicted as being 'Acquitted without a stain' in a courtroom in which all the jurors, barristers, police officers and the judge wore his face![69]

The question on everyone's mind was whether the vote against conscription seven months earlier would translate into a vote against Hughes and the Nationalist coalition he now led. The fact that Holman's new non-Labor coalition had won the New South Wales election in February 1917 suggested that it might not, as did the narrow majority for the 'no' vote nationally in 1916. First, however, Hughes had to find himself a new seat, since he had lost endorsement for his own electorate, West Sydney. After declining several safe seats, he finally chose Bendigo. It was an electorate in which majorities either way had never been large, but it was relatively close to the federal seat of government and Hughes' own home in Melbourne. Leaving his supporters to campaign locally, Hughes set off on a punishing tour of the eastern states and South Australia, travelling by train or cars jolting along dirt roads. As his biographer says:

> It was almost as if, having cut himself off from his industrial base in the big cities, he was trying to recover some of the atmosphere of those far-off days in the early nineties when he was organizing the little towns of the central west of New South Wales for the Labor Party.[70]

For Hughes and his Nationalist colleagues, it was a single-issue election. Branding themselves the Win-the-War Party, they insisted that they alone could lead Australia to victory in the imperial cause. As the 'National' in their title implied, they were 'not a rich man's government, not a poor man's government', but 'the people's government'. Their commitment to the British Empire was unqualified. Hughes said repeatedly during the campaign that 'We are loyal to the Empire first and foremost because we are of the British race.' Britain was Australia's sword and shield, 'the greatest guarantee of the world's peace' and the source of the nation's material wealth. Britain's wartime purchases of Australian wool, wheat and base metals, and its war loans to Australia, demonstrated this. This was a message about the indivisibility of Australian and British interests that had hardly changed since August 1914, when Australians rushed to join the war.[71]

In contrast, Hughes claimed, the Labor opposition could not be trusted with national leadership. This was not because Tudor and his colleagues were personally anti-war or even anti-empire, but because the ALP had been captured by a 'narrow-minded disloyal section'. Extremists such as the IWW and Sinn Fein were now manipulating and controlling the more moderate leadership. With brilliant scaremongering, Hughes claimed in early April that the workers of Australia

> were following in the wake of . . . men who, like pirates, had captured the ship, thrown the pilot overboard, murdered the crew, and were now masquerading under the guise of honest sea men . . . caring nothing for the Empire, nothing for the flag, and leading the working men to destruction. Many of them say they know no God, no country and no flag. They are, save at election time, hand in glove with IWW-ism and every extreme section in this community.[72]

The Labor leadership tried desperately to set a different agenda, depicting the election as a 'battle of the classes'. But the 'Message to the Australian People' by the party's leader, Tudor, was limp and lacklustre compared with Hughes' impassioned rhetoric. While assuring the electorate that the Labor was 'determined to see the present great struggle through to a successful issue', Tudor promised to do everything to support repatriated soldiers and the dependants of the men who had died. Moreover, he would ensure that all the gains Australian workers had secured through past Labor legislation would not 'crumble to the ground'.[73]

The commentary in the labour press was more trenchant. Cartoons depicted Hughes as a snarling rat with his nose about to be crushed in a trap primed to be set off by the people. At other times, he was shown as a thief robbing chests of money saved for maternity allowances and old-age pensions in order to fund repatriation. In the *Australian Worker*, the prime minister was labelled 'a glib liar' who 'lies as simply as he breathes'. He had reneged on his pledge to have a prices referendum, to hold a royal commission into corruption, to maintain freedom of the press, and above all not to attempt to introduce conscription. *Labor Call* became almost apoplectic, calling Hughes a mountebank of political corruption and intrigue who 'has no equal as a preposterous blatherskiting bounder'. His colleague, George Pearce, was 'a dull commonplace individual who has brought a great State department to ridicule and a place of pilfer and plunder'.[74]

It took little to provoke Hughes at any time, and he was now roused to invective and vitriol of an unusual intensity. 'Sometimes he seemed to confuse the Imperial cause with his own,' the ever circumspect Ernest Scott wrote in his official history, 'as though in breathing forth fire against his own enemies he was assisting in the defeat of the enemies of the Allied Powers.' Insisting that he was the custodian of the Labor tradition, Hughes promised that he would 'not destroy one stone in the temple of Labor legislation'. He would 'protect the interests and promote the welfare of the old and unfortunate, the widow and the fatherless, the mothers of our future citizens, the returned soldier and his dependants, and the great mass of workers of the country'.[75]

The elephant in the room was, of course, conscription. Hughes tried to claim that it was not an issue in the election, but with Irvine openly pressing for its introduction, his opponents could easily claim that a vote for Hughes was a vote for compulsion. Mannix, soon to be elevated to the archbishopric of Melbourne, had already outraged loyalists in January when he referred to the war as 'simply a sordid trade war'. Now he warned that 'As they previously said that conscription was necessary then they, if elected to power, would find the very ready excuse that conscription was still necessary and would put a referendum to the people again.' On the defensive, Hughes and his colleagues stressed that they accepted the people's verdict in October 1916, but—and it was a crucial caveat—if national safety demanded it in the future, they would refer the question of conscription again to the people.[76]

When Australians finally voted on 5 May, they delivered a stunning victory for Hughes and the Nationalists. In the House of Representatives, the coalition won 53 seats, the ALP just 22. In the Senate, the Nationalists won all eighteen vacancies. Even in Queensland, where Ryan's Labor government had not split, the Nationalists gained a majority of Senate votes. Hughes himself won a substantial majority in Bendigo. The electorate, it seems, agreed with the Nationalists that the ALP had 'blown its brains out' when it expelled Hughes and his followers. Even more, the result showed that the rejection of conscription in 1916 did not equate with opposition to the war. In voting for Hughes, the majority of Australians endorsed a leader whose commitment to victory was absolute. They confirmed their will to continue the fight. The values and emotions that had led them to support the war in 1914—a sense of shared destiny with the British Empire and a belief in the superiority of its 'civilisation', politics and culture—still retained their resonance and emotional power.

Hence, whatever the divisions and rancour within the Australian home front, it was not—like Russia—about to collapse. Recruitment was certainly sluggish, and this was already imposing constraints on the actual contribution that Australian forces could make to the war. But this did not imply a wish on the part of most Australians to withdraw from the war. Those within the peace and industrial labour movements had been energised by the rebirth of internationalism with the Russian revolution, and were beginning to demand an end to the war, but they were still a minority of the Australian population in mid-1917. They would remain so even in 1918, when a negotiated peace became the majority position within the trade union movement.[77]

With his new mandate, Hughes moved quickly to crush what remained of his bête noire, the IWW. The *Unlawful Associations Act* of late 1916 had not completely silenced the Wobblies. Even though they were under constant surveillance, they avoided prosecution under the *War Precautions Act* by not commenting directly on the war and recruitment. When police seized their own presses, they continued to publish *Direct Action* using a commercial press. They also collected money to support the families of the imprisoned twelve leaders, and held public meetings that attracted crowds of over 10,000 during the federal election campaign.[78]

For Hughes, even this level of activism was intolerable. On 18 July, he introduced federal legislation amending the *Unlawful Associations Act* to make membership of an 'unlawful association' of itself an offence. The penalty for Australian-born members would be six months' imprisonment; for foreigners, deportation. Moreover, no member of an unlawful association, after a period of one month's grace, could be a member of the Common-wealth public service. This legislation extended further the arbitrary powers of a government whose record showed it would not use them impartially, and one Labor parliamentarian warned that the Bill revived:

> all the rigours of past autocracies, and [applies] them to those who happen to have different opinions, and the courage to express them . . . Like the Germans in Belgium, [the Nationalists] say to the people, 'We are anxious for your welfare, but if you do anything against us, you will be shot.'

However, the ALP leadership was focused on ensuring that the trade unions were protected from the discretionary powers of the Act. Once suitable guarantees were given on this matter, they were willing to give Hughes 'any power' to deal with the IWW. Like many political parties on the defensive, they let their opponents' rhetoric define them. Having been tarred with the IWW brush during the May election, they were at pains to prove their loyalty. As the member for West Sydney said, 'We are quite prepared to assist in winning the war. No one can say that organised labour in Australia has not done as well as others in this direction.'[79]

Over the next few months, the destruction of the IWW proceeded. Its records and publications were seized and its meeting halls sealed. One hundred members were arrested and sentenced to six months' hard labour. Those who were born outside Australia were deported, with eight deportees in 1917 being shipped to Chile, where they were harassed by police and faced destitution. Some determined IWW members tried to fight back, mounting public speaking boxes and courting arrest by declaring their membership in a 'free speech fight'. The last issue of *Direct Action* trumpeted: 'We will go to Long Bay [Gaol]. We will go through hell and fire and water, and insects like Hughes and all his slimy crawling satellites will never stay us. We will answer the call in our hundreds and our thousands.' However, as Ian Turner says, 'The movement which had declared politics impotent and the state a fraud was crushed by politics and the state.' The IWW was finished as a force in Australian politics.[80]

The decision for Third Ypres

The failure of the Nivelle and Arras offensives confronted the British government with another excruciating debate about strategy. Given the state of their Allies, their options were limited. The fragility of the French army's morale meant that their leaders were tempted to revert to a defensive stance, waiting for American troops to arrive in force and tip the balance on the Western Front in the Allies' favour. The Italians, for their part, failed to make any progress in yet another offensive in the region of Slovenia (the Tenth Battle of Isonzo), launched on 10 May. In Russia, the political situation was highly unstable and the state of the army totally unreliable. Although Alexander Kerensky, who became Minister for War in early May, would manage to launch another attack against the Austro-Hungarians and Germans in Galicia on 1 July, it would end with the final disintegration of the Russian army. All of this meant that if the war was to be taken to the Central Powers in the remainder of 1917, it would be Britain that would have to do it.

There were also domestic political reasons why Britain needed to remain on the offensive. The Russian revolution had transformed the ideological landscape of the war by giving new inspiration to socialist movements in Britain, as in Australia. It seemed that international class solidarity might again triumph over the nationalism that had proved so irresistible to the working classes in August 1914. Moreover, the Bolsheviks were undermining the moral authority of the Allies' cause by calling for a peace without punitive indemnities or territorial annexations. As yet, the peace movement in Britain was in the minority—as it was in Australia—but when the British socialist and pacifist George Lansbury told a meeting at London's Albert Hall in early April that 'when the working classes of all nations refuse to shoot down the working classes of other countries, Governments won't be able to make wars anymore', he was greeted with tremendous applause. The British War Cabinet therefore had to factor into its strategic calculations the need to achieve victory before 'a peace atmosphere' eroded the national will to fight.[81]

It was also critical to keep the pressure on the Central Powers, since they too were confronting serious problems of morale and internal cohesion after nearly three years of war. In March, the young Austro-Hungarian emperor, who had come to the throne after the death of the 86-year-old Franz Joseph in November 1916, put out peace feelers to the Allies (without Germany's knowledge). It was a desperate effort to end the war before his empire disintegrated into its centrifugal parts. In Germany, meanwhile, thousands of workers went on strike in April, demanding higher wages and better food. German socialists, liberals and Catholics also campaigned for democratic reforms such as those it seemed Russia had achieved with the overthrow of Tsarist authoritarianism. In the Reichstag, there were open demands for an end to the monopoly of political power by the property- and land-owning classes, and for 'a peace of reconciliation'. Ludendorff and Hindenburg retaliated by effectively blackmailing the Kaiser with threats to resign, and the civilian chancellor, Bethmann Hollweg, was forced out of office. But still the Reichstag passed a resolution in favour of 'a peace of understanding and the permanent reconciliation of the peoples', without forced territorial annexations or political and economic oppression. In effect, the German government was now at war with itself.[82]

It therefore seemed that the Allies must maintain the pressure on the Central Powers—but how and where? Haig, as before, favoured attacking in Flanders. Lloyd George, still desperate not to squander British troops in more costly battles on the Western Front, again promoted alternative strategies. Either Britain should support the Italians or invest more effort in the Balkans and Palestine. However, so damaged was Lloyd George's credibility after he had backed Nivelle that he lacked the capacity or will to overrule Haig.

Hence, after long debates over May, June and July, the British War Cabinet (and its War Policy Committee, created on 19 June) finally decided to approve Haig's plans for Flanders. There was a caveat, however: the offensive would be halted if at any time it was proving too costly. At the same time, the British decided to reinforce the Palestine campaign with two divisions taken from Salonika, given that the implications for British imperial interests in the Middle East would be dire should the war against Turkey be lost.

The Flanders campaign, known as Third Ypres, was to become the most controversial of Haig's battles on the Western Front. Its final weeks in November, when Allied troops struggled through an utterly desolate landscape of mud and mire to capture the ruins of the 'village' of Passchendaele, became synonymous in popular memory with futile attrition. However, this was never what Haig intended. As he saw it, the Flanders offensive had two grand strategic elements. The first was a sweeping attack that would start from behind the town of Ypres and push through to the Channel coast. Since the Germans would not surrender Belgium without a bitter fight, this was likely to inflict heavy casualties on them while also liberating the occupied territory. The second attack, consisting of an amphibious landing and a land advance along the Channel coast, would capture the Channel ports of Ostend and Zeebrugge. The benefit of this would be the elimination of the bases from which German U-boats, mine-layers and destroyers were able to threaten British shipping.

In fact, this second goal was somewhat redundant even before the campaign actually began. From early 1917, the crisis in British shipping had receded—thanks largely to the British Admiralty's belated decision in May to introduce a system of convoy. Rather than merchant vessels travelling alone, a situation in which they were easy targets for U-boats, they sailed in formation covered by a screen of destroyers. For reasons to do with its hidebound naval tradition, the Admiralty had opposed introducing convoys for months, but by April 1917 the depredations of unrestricted submarine warfare had forced its hand. Convoys were an immediate success. The first one, which sailed from Gibraltar for England in May, lost only one of its twelve ships. However, the challenges of organising a convoy system were huge. Merchant ships had to be assembled into units of comparable speed, captains needed training in the skills required to keep formation when sailing, and there were log jams in the ports where the convoys assembled and arrived. Finding enough naval escorts was also problematic. On 9 May 1917, the Royal Australian Navy was called upon to provide a flotilla for escort operations in the Mediterranean. This meant reducing the Australia Station's capacity to defend local trade, but from August 1917 RAN vessels patrolled the Adriatic Sea from a base in Brindisi, Italy, hunting enemy submarines, rescuing the crews of sinking ships, chasing enemy ships and bombarding Albanian ports.[83]

Given all these complexities, by the end of 1917 only a little more than half of British overseas trade had been brought under convoy. Merchant shipping losses had declined substantially, but another 2.25 million tons were sunk between August 1917 and January 1918. Capturing the Channel ports therefore still seemed to Haig, in mid-1917, to offer considerable strategic advantages.[84]

Messines

The Ypres salient on which the British offensive was to be focused was a bulge projecting into the German lines to the east of the medieval town of Ypres. Formed when the British, French, Canadians and Belgians stopped the German advance in 1914, the salient had already been the site of a major battle in 1915. The topography of the area was not dramatic, but the Germans held an arc of ridges edging the salient. Even though these slopes hardly require a change of gear in the car today, they were high enough to give the Germans a kind of ringside seat from which they could observe and fire on the British armies moving around and behind Ypres.

Well before the decision to proceed with the major Ypres offensive was finally approved, Haig decided to clear the Germans from the ridge that stretched from Messines to Ploegsteert Wood, south of Ypres. This task was assigned to three corps of the Second Army under the command of General Hubert Plumer. Among them was Godley's II Anzac Corps, including the 3rd Australian Division under Monash, which had arrived on the Western Front in late 1916.

In contrast to Bullecourt, the attack on the Messines ridge was superbly prepared. Plumer, who with his red face and white walrus moustache may have inspired David Low's caricature Colonel Blimp, was actually one of the more competent British generals of the war, a 'sound, methodical and sometimes outstanding army commander', as Peter Simkins has put it. He and his staff officer, Charles Harington, had a reputation for preparing clear and sensible plans and briefing their subordinates through regular conference meetings. In addition, Plumer had had many months to plan the attack, since the British had held the line outside Ypres since late 1914 and Messines had been a possible target in 1916.[85]

Monash, too, planned the 3rd Division's role meticulously. This was his first test as a divisional commander, the occasion on which he could display to brilliant effect his civilian training as an engineer and his skills in administration and planning. He devoted countless hours to honing the plan of battle that he called his 'Magnum Opus'. With almost excessive micromanagement, he listed details of tactical objectives and procedures down to the level of platoons and sections, discussed his plans at length with his brigade commanders, arranged practice attacks in training areas, studied aerial reconnaissance photographs, worked out barrage timetables for the artillery, organised the formation of ammunition dumps, coordinated the building of roads and railways, and arranged the camouflaging of gun emplacements. Monash even observed the Canadian attack on Vimy Ridge in April to learn what he could from this operation. Haig, who arrived on 24 May, was impressed. Monash, he said, was a 'clear headed determined Commander. Every detail had been thought of. His Brigadiers were equally thorough. I was much struck with their whole arrangements.'[86]

The pre-battle bombardment at Messines lasted some seventeen days. With 635 medium and heavy guns and 600 lighter weapons, Plumer had the highest concentration of artillery yet achieved in the British army, and more than double the number of German guns in the area. The British also had a two to one advantage in aircraft. This, together with the fine weather in May, ensured that the artillery received accurate intelligence and aerial photography of German gun emplacements.[87]

The British had also prepared an intricate network of tunnels running deep and far under the German lines. This work had begun more than two years earlier, when British and Canadian tunnellers started excavating and packing tunnels with over 20 mines containing more than 450,000 kilograms of TNT. They had been joined in late 1916 by the 1st Australian Tunnelling Company. Assigned to the mineshafts under Hill 60, a protuberance at the northern-most end of the German bulge that had already changed hands several times during the war, the company's main task was to keep intact two great mines. This meant maintaining effective drainage and ventilation, and ensuring that the Germans did not discover the tunnels.

Even by the standards of the Western Front, this was a dangerous war: claustrophobic, subterranean, exhausting and full of tension. When extracting the soil, the tunnellers would lie in adjustable seats, driving their spades into the clay with both feet. Each side monitored the other's activities, sending out exploratory shafts, listening through the soil for sounds of digging and then 'blowing' the enemy tunnels and galleries when they edged too close. Suffo-cation and entombment were constant threats.[88]

So dramatic was the experience of these men that their story was one of those that survived the selectiveness of post-war memory. The 1st Australian Tunnelling Company was commemorated in a memorial placed on Hill 60 in 1919. When the original monument rusted and cracked, it was replaced by a granite obelisk in 1923. It still stands today in the cratered landscape of Hill 60, its plaque scarred with bullet holes from World War II and flanked by signage from the Australian Department of Veterans' Affairs. Other memorials have joined it over the years (including one for French Resistance martyrs killed in World War II). Indeed, Hill 60—like the wider Ypres salient itself—is a multinational site of memory.[89]

Yet in cinematic memory Australians have claimed Hill 60 as their own. A 2010 feature film, *Beneath Hill 60*, features the 1st Australian Tunnelling Company almost exclusively, save for the stereotypically toffee-nosed British officer and the soon-to-be-defeated German enemy. Its promotional blurb says of its central character, Captain Oliver Woodward, who was based on a real-life Queensland mine manager:

> men with Woodward's underground skills are desperately needed to counter a deadly German offensive. After two years of claustrophobia and bloodshed, of triumph and heartbreak, it all comes down to a single moment. As infantrymen quietly fix bayonets in the darkness, Oliver Woodward crouches in a muddy bunker preparing to press a detonator that could change the course of the war.[90]

When all the Oliver Woodwards actually detonated the mines at Messines at 3.10 a.m. on 7 June, they did not so much change the course of the war as produce a spectacular explosion. Two of the mines failed to detonate, but the other nineteen generated such huge force that the sound was reportedly heard in London, perhaps even Dublin. As George Mitchell recalled: 'The earth shook shook and shook again . . . We saw Messines in a boiling cauldron of flame smoke and dust. The thunder of our guns surpassed imagination.' The detonations immediately killed some 10,000 Germans, who were buried alive in the mass of displaced soil. Those who survived were so disoriented that they could hardly resist. Six weeks later, when the Australian photographer Frank Hurley visited Hill 60, the devastation was still complete:

> Way down in one of these mine craters was an awful sight. There lay three hideous almost skeleton decomposed fragments [sic] of corpses of German gunners. Oh, the frightfulness of it all. To think that these fragments were once sweethearts, may be, husbands or loved sons, and this was the end . . . Until my dying day I shall never forget this haunting glimpse down into the mine crater on Hill 60.[91]

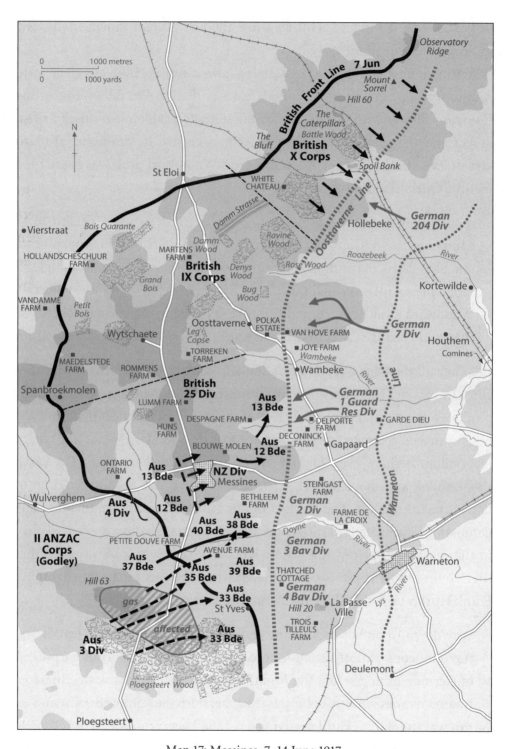

Map 17: Messines, 7–14 June 1917

As the explosions died down, the British and Anzac infantry moved forward behind a creeping barrage to capture the German front line (see Map 17). The crest of the Messines ridge fell quickly with few Allied casualties. The only misadventure happened, despite all Monash's planning, when the 3rd Australian Division, marching through the Ploegsteert Wood to the starting line for the attack, entered an area that the Germans had recently shelled with gas. They suffered 10 per cent losses before even going into action.

Days of tense fighting followed as the 4th Division was brought in to continue the push beyond the summit and the Germans, in turn, counter-attacked. However, by 14 June the whole of the German bulge had been straightened out along what was called the Oosttaverne Line. Then, over the next six weeks, the Allied troops continued to creep forward towards the new front line the Germans had created, the Warneton line. In eighteen exhausting days, the 11th Brigade created a new trench system under constant German fire and bombing.[92]

This same German fire caused the death on 2 July of the 4th Divisional commander, Holmes. The New South Wales premier, Holman, was visiting the battlefield as politicians did, and while being escorted by Holmes along what was normally a safe route, his party was hit by a random German shell. Holman survived unhurt—although, according to one account, he was knocked flat by the force of the blast. Holmes, however, died of his chest wounds. He was replaced as commander of the 4th Division by Ewen Sinclair-MacLagan, who had led the 3rd Brigade at Gallipoli, and at Pozières and Mouquet Farm, before commanding the AIF depots in Britain in early 1917.[93]

Messines has been heralded as a classic illustration of what could be achieved on the Western Front when an operation was well planned by competent leaders and the infantry were asked to advance no further than the distance covered by their own artillery. Yet for all its brilliance, the Allies' Messines success could not be repeated. The massive underground detonation that started it was possible only because the British had held the line at Ypres for years. It should also be remembered that Messines cost 26,000 British casualties, of whom almost 14,000 were from II Anzac Corps, many of them victims of gas. Moreover, it is rarely acknowledged how little Messines actually achieved. As the British historian A.J.P. Taylor said pithily:

> It was a remarkable success, and a beautiful exercise in siege warfare. But it had disquieting aspects. Two years of preparation and a million pounds of explosive had advanced the British front at most two miles. How long would it take at this rate to get to Berlin?'[94]

Planning Third Ypres

If Plumer had had his way, Messines would have been followed immediately by another attack towards Ypres while German morale was still weak. Haig, however, called a pause. Remarkably, he had already appointed Gough to command the next phase of operations. Although Gough's record at Bullecourt had been disappointing and he had no knowledge of the Ypres salient, he had qualities that appealed to Haig. First, he believed in the rapid advance rather than the 'bite and hold' approach of the other contenders for the command, Plumer and Rawlinson. (Rawlinson, who was 'very much disgusted and disappointed' at Haig's decision, had to settle for command of the Channel coast attack.) Second, Gough's very lack of experience at Ypres meant he was unlikely to challenge Haig's conception of the campaign.[95]

Gough needed time to plan the battle and, true to character and Haig's expectations, he planned on a large scale (see Map 18). Third Ypres was to involve three armies attacking along a front of around 13 kilometres, stretching from Steenstraate in the north to St Ives in the south. Gough's own Fifth Army was to be positioned in the centre, Plumer's Second on the right and the French First Army under General François Anthoine on the left. In the first two days of the attack, the infantry would make a series of jumps, pushing the Germans in the centre back to a line stretching from Gheluvelt and Becelaere in the south through Broodseinde to Langemarck. This was, in fact, a kind of 'bite and hold' approach—but these were big bites. Their scale was dictated not so much by what was feasible but by Haig's orders to clear the Passchendaele ridge, nearly 13 kilometres distant, by 8 August—the date

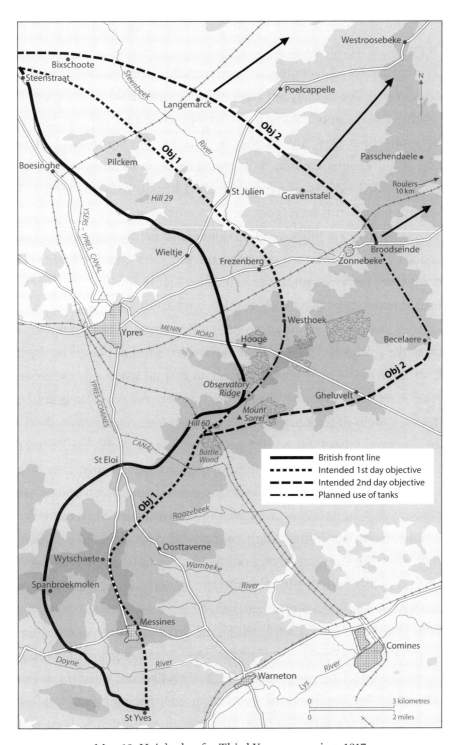

Map 18: Haig's plan for Third Ypres campaign, 1917

on which the high tide in the Channel would allow the planned amphibious operation on the coast to proceed.

As Gough laboured over his plans, seven critical weeks passed. Haig thought the delay would not matter, but days of precious fine weather slipped by in July. In these weeks, too, the Germans strengthened their already formidable defences on the ridges around Ypres. Shaken by Messines, Ludendorff brought in an expert, Colonel Fritz von Lossberg, to develop a system of 'elastic defence'. Under his supervision, the German defences around Ypres were strengthened with even more trenches and breastworks, more machine-gun posts and scores of pillboxes. Distributed in a dense chequerboard system and made of thick reinforced concrete, the pillboxes could survive all but a direct hit from heavy howitzers or tank fire. Secure in these mini-fortresses and armed with one or two machine guns, a relatively small number of troops in the front line, it was assumed, would endure a preliminary bombardment and slow the initial attack. Then the far stronger forces poised in the battle zones to their rear would counter-attack at a time when the enemy troops were overextended and vulnerable, struggling to consolidate their hold on an unfamiliar system of trenches.

The Germans also took advantage of the clearly visible Allied prepara-tions in July to launch some spoiling operations. On 10 July, they attacked the bridgehead across the River Yser, the point from which the subsidiary attack along the Channel coast was meant to be launched. Most of the 50 men of the 2nd Australian Tunnelling Company who had been stationed there, mining under the German strong points in the sand dunes, were captured. Some of them hid in their tunnels until the air was so foul with mustard gas and smoke bombs that it drove them out.[96]

Within the Ypres salient, meanwhile, the British artillery were systematic-ally targeted by the German guns positioned around the rim and behind the Passchendaele and Gheluvelt ridges. High explosive and mustard gas rained down on gun emplacements and the routes used for bringing up supplies. The Menin Road leading south-east from Ypres became a kind of 'Valley of Death', strewn with dead horses, shattered lorries, overturned gun carriages and other detritus of war. One of its junctions, Hellfire Corner, became especially notorious for its constant fire and danger. Among the gunners at risk were Australian artillerymen extracted from the 1st, 2nd and 5th Divisions on the Somme to work with the British artillery. At Ypres, they would suffer the highest rate of casualties they had experienced in the war—losses of 1375 by the end of August.[97]

The British were actually dominant in artillery at Ypres. They had twice as many guns as the Germans, and the pre-battle bombardment—which lasted fifteen days—delivered an almost unimaginable 4.3 million shells on to the German lines and guns. But even this was not enough to eliminate all the German guns deployed along the long front on which Gough had chosen to attack, particularly as the variable weather in July hampered aerial reconnaissance and sound ranging. The result was that the bombardment destroyed the German defences on the left and centre of the front of attack to a maximum depth of 2.7 kilometres. However, many blockhouses, machine-gun posts and gun batteries further to the rear were left operating. Most seriously, the German strong points on and behind the Gheluvelt plateau to the right of the front remained active. From here, the Germans could dominate the battlefield by firing from the flanks onto the advancing troops.

Third Ypres

The first months

The first day of the Third Ypres offensive, 31 July, therefore saw mixed results. In the north, the French advanced over 2 kilometres with relatively light casualties. To their immediate right, the Fifth Army's XIV Corps also advanced some 2.7 kilometres, capturing two German defensive lines and the Pilckem Ridge. These successes meant that the northern flank of the offensive was secure. In the centre, XVIII and XIX Corps also had some success, although they soon met more serious resistance.

However, the attack on the Gheluvelt plateau further south failed. A small section of the plateau east of Battle Wood was captured, but along the rest of its 1.2-kilometre front Plumer's Second Army stalled in the face of shelling from the German guns and strong points that had not been taken out. By Western Front standards, the gains of 31 July were substantial, but there was no sign that the Germans were crumbling—and the weather was dreadful.

It began raining on 31 July and hardly stopped over the next month. There was almost double the average monthly rainfall in August 1917. Only three days were without rain. Soon the complex irrigation system of the region, which had already been destroyed by the artillery bombardments of this and earlier battles around Ypres, turned the ground into a quagmire. The infantry could not move quickly. Tanks sank in the slime. Shells failed to burst in the mud. Guns were almost impossible to relocate and reposition on new targets, and the constant cloud cover prevented systematic aerial observation for the targeting of artillery.

Gough, however, would not wait for the ground to dry out. Throughout August and into September, he pushed on—at Haig's insistence—with a succession of narrow attacks at various points along the front. Some limited gains were made. Langemarck, for example, was captured on 16 August. (It is now the site of a poignant German war cemetery in which 44,000 remains are interred, including nearly 25,000 in one mass grave.) Generally, however, these penny-packet attacks were failures as the Germans, with many of their strong points and artillery unsubdued, inflicted huge losses on the wretched infantry. By the end of August, the British had lost nearly 70,000 casualties and the Gheluvelt plateau was still in German hands.

Remarkably, Lloyd George and the British War Cabinet allowed the offensive to continue. Having approved it on the understanding that they would not tolerate 'protracted, costly, and indecisive operations as occurred in the offensive on the Somme in 1916', they now deferred to Haig's judgement that there was no alternative but to press on. With the French and Italians faltering and the Russians collapsing, he claimed that the British army was the only one that could be relied upon to wear down the Germans. He was actually right.[98]

Yet Haig knew that Gough's meagre gains had left him politically exposed. He therefore transferred the main responsibility for capturing the Gheluvelt plateau from Gough to Plumer and the Second Army. With this, the Australian infantry were drawn into the battle. Only the 3rd Division (42nd and 43rd Battalions of the 11th Brigade) had been involved to this point, in a diversionary attack on 31 July against the Warneton line east of Messines. They captured the defences they had been attempting to reduce since 23 June, suffering some 550 casualties as they did so.[99]

The general strike

As if in reaction to this huge battle at Ypres (though Australians knew little of it as yet), the Australian eastern states erupted into industrial warfare in August 1917. The beginnings of what became known as 'the great strike' lay in a dispute in the New South Wales Government Tramways Workshops in Randwick, Sydney. The railway management had been facing growing losses as result of rising interest bills, the increased cost of coal and the need to provide free transport for troops and war materials. In an effort to cut costs, it decided to introduce a 'card system' whereby it could more precisely record the cost of each job and measure the performance of each worker. The labour force saw this change of work practices as heralding lower wages and longer hours, and some 5780 railway and tramway men downed tools on 2 August. The unrest then spread rapidly throughout New South Wales, Victoria and Queensland. Within five weeks, 69,000 workers had struck, many in sympathy: coal miners, waterside workers, painters and dockers, railway men, meatworkers, sugar mill workers, carters, drivers, to name only the most important groups. At the height of the strike, more than a quarter of all New South Wales unionists were on strike, even though the Australian Workers' Union, the state's biggest union, was not involved at any time. The number of working days lost in 1917 was to be the highest of any year of the war.[100]

The issues in dispute were not especially significant: the card system was not an unreasonable way of recording jobs. But it was as if all the war weariness and grievances of the past three years combined to trigger spontaneous combustion: the erosion of living standards, the increased cost of living, the 1916 uprising in Dublin, the anger at the abuse of executive government

Table 4.1: Industrial disputes, 1914–19

	Number of disputes	Working days lost
1913	208	623,528
1914	337	1,090,395
1915	358	583,225
1916	508	1,678,930
1917	444	4,599,658
1918	298	580,853
1919	460	6,308,226

Source: Ernest Scott, *The Official History of Australia in the War of 1914–1918*, vol. XI, p. 665.

powers and the fury generated by the conscription campaign. The strike was a call to arms that in its enthusiasm and naïveté had some of the qualities of the rush to join the AIF in August 1914. Its early days were marked by an 'almost millennial enthusiasm, tinged with more than a touch of larrikin energy'. In Sydney and Melbourne, the strikers took to the streets in almost daily demonstrations, and there were crowds of 100,000 in Sydney and 30,000 on the Yarra Bank in Melbourne. Henry Boote was ecstatic:

> I never hoped to live to see the workers so united . . . This revolt against governmental tyranny is a spontaneous manifestation of feeling. The men took matters into their own hands. The officers had nothing to do but voice the demands of the rank and file . . . One after another the Unions rushed to the assistance of their mates who were attacked . . . With a passion for class loyalty as grand as unparalleled they took the field and swept to battle.[101]

Thoroughly alarmed, Munro Ferguson concluded that Australia was in 'the same boat as Russia', and Hughes and the Nationalists saw the hand of the IWW still at work. This was not entirely fanciful. Although the IWW had been crushed by legislation, many workers remained influenced by its ideology of direct action. Radicalised by the perceived inequities of the war years, they had lost faith in the ability of the arbitration system—set up only a decade earlier—to protect their standard of living, and saw in the strike the chance for 'a great class-wide confrontation with the employers'. Everywhere, strikers sang the IWW song from the United States, 'Solidarity for Ever'.[102]

However, the direct influence of the IWW on the strikes was minimal. In Queensland, where some the IWW members from New South Wales had relocated in an effort to escape prosecution by the less inquisitorial Ryan government, they retained some agency. But in New South Wales, the movement had been decapitated: the last show trial of its leaders started on 31 August. In Victoria, meanwhile, the IWW had never been as influential as other socialist movements.

In Victoria, it was rather sympathy with the unions interstate and concern about the cost of living that underpinned much of the industrial unrest. Since 1914, the retail price of food and groceries in Melbourne had risen by 28.2 per cent. The attempts of the state governments to hold prices down had failed, and the agreements Hughes had negotiated with London to export wheat and frozen meat were distorting local supplies and prices. Given the lack of shipping, wheat was actually rotting on the wharves and supplies of frozen meat were accumulating in warehouses.

Food was a highly emotive issue that galvanised into action not only the labour movement but also women. As the socialist and feminist leader Adela Pankhurst said, it was 'sinful to waste, to fill storehouses with meat and wood, and warehouses with clothes and boots, while human stomachs are empty and human bodies want clothes'. For the unions, high food prices were a form of economic conscription—'the most cowardly form of recruiting', forcing men to enlist to escape unemployment and the high cost of living. The Wharf Labourers' Union therefore decided in late July to ban the shipment of foodstuffs overseas until the cost of essential items had been brought back to pre-war levels. The labour movement in Melbourne also launched a campaign to protect workers' standards of living. 'Winning the war did not mean starving the people,' the president of the Political Labor Council told a meeting at the Melbourne Town Hall. A Women's Peace League was also formed to campaign for reductions in the cost of living.[103]

As the public pressure mounted, Hughes referred to the Interstate Commission the questions of price rises, the impact of exports on commodities, and market manipulation by combines. But the working-class women of Melbourne took to the streets. As wives and mothers, they were the ones who struggled with the daily challenge of feeding families, who denied themselves meals so their children could eat. Their husbands were on low wages, the value of which was declining. They could not tighten their belts, as the conservative Australian Women's National League had urged them to do in an economy campaign launched earlier in the war. Instead, working-class women were inclined to see thrift as a ploy of capitalism, as the Labor paper *Vanguard* put it.

Inspired by the Women's Peace League, the Victorian Socialist Party and the Women's Peace Army, and female leaders such as Pankhurst, Jennie Baines, Lizzie Wallace and Alice Suter, the women of Melbourne demonstrated in their thousands (one estimate for August 1917 was 15,000). They congregated in Treasury Gardens and on the steps of Parliament House. They chanted 'We want food and fair play', sang 'The Red Flag' and cheered their leaders as they denounced profiteers and those who allowed children to starve while exporting food for higher prices. They also turned to violence, smashing windows in the city streets and pelting the police with gravel. The police, in turn, broke up demonstrations with batons or mounted charges.[104]

With the strikes disrupting the flow of goods around Australia and creating panic about food supplies, the state and Commonwealth governments went on the offensive. As the Nationalists saw it, industrial action was more than an intolerable threat to the war effort: it was 'an organised attempt to take the reins of government out of the hands of those duly elected by the people to carry on the affairs of government . . . [and] a belated effort by those who were defeated to set aside the will of the people'. In fact, there was no serious challenge to state authority, but the Nationalists were determined to smash the strike and break the grip of what they saw as 'the revolutionary and extreme element of the trade unions'.[105]

The loyalists seemed almost to welcome the showdown. Perhaps it was a payback for the defeat of conscription. State employees were threatened with loss of seniority and other rights, even dismissal, if they did not return to work. The four unions most directly involved in the New South Wales railway strike were deregistered by the New South Wales Industrial Court on 23 August, never to be reinstated. Newly created unions of the kind favoured by the authorities took their place. Meanwhile, leading unionists— including members of the Defence Committee, an ad-hoc body set up to run the strike with delegates from each of the striking unions—were arrested in mid-August on charges of conspiracy. Pankhurst and other women leaders in Melbourne were also arrested on a number of occasions, charged with various civil offences and then breaches of the *War Precautions Act* and the *Unlawful Associations Act*. Although Hughes claimed to 'hate punishing women', he considered deporting the 'damned nuisance' Pankhurst. Ultimately, however, she served only some weeks in prison.[106]

Determined to keep the economy running while they sat out the strike, the state and Commonwealth governments commandeered coal stocks, shipping and motor- and horse-drawn vehicles in order to keep essential power and transport services operating. Gas and electricity were rationed. The Commonwealth government also recruited a volunteer force of strike breakers—or 'scab labour', as the unionists saw it—to keep the mines operating and the waterfronts manned.

Responding to patriotic calls from the conservative press, volunteers from the regional areas, which were solidly behind the government, streamed to the cities, wharves and coal mines. Improvised barracks sprung up in locations like Taronga Park Zoo and the Sydney Cricket Ground—which strikers promptly renamed Scabs Collecting Ground. Some of the volunteers were middle-class loyalists: students from private schools or universities who had 'the time of their lives' working on the wharves of Melbourne, for example. But many were blue-collar workers seeking employment, a fact that was to make the resolution of the industrial unrest deeply problematic. In all, the governments were able to organise some 170,000 man days of strike-breaking labour, far fewer than the three million strike days lost but still enough to keep essential services going.[107]

Soon the strikes began to falter and fail. The union officials, far more timid than the workers who had sometimes downed tools without their approval, lacked a strategy for responding to the mobilisation of non-union labour. The Defence Committee hesitated to take on the 'scab' workers if this meant violence, and at times restrained the rank and file rather than encouraging them to continue the fight. In addition, the work stoppage was far from universal: at no time were more than half the railwaymen on strike. Progressively, the union leadership began to call off strikes, only to find that they had turned into lockouts.

As strikers tried to return to work, they discovered they had to apply for their former positions individually. In those workplaces where there were now significant numbers of loyalist volunteers, unionists had to accept humiliating terms of re-employment. On the Sydney waterfront, for example, men wanting work had to declare that they were not members of the Waterside Workers' Federation (some 2000 did). The future prime minister, Ben Chifley, a striking railway engine driver, was reinstated at a lower level than he had previously held, and forced to report to former subordinates who had risen through 'scabbing'.[108]

This victimisation of the strikers inflamed the already violent situation. On two nights in September, the city and inner suburbs of Melbourne erupted in more window smashing. Targets included the offices and prestigious shop fronts of Collins, Russell, Bourke, Flinders and Elizabeth Streets; the inner suburb of Richmond; and the Dunlop factory in Montague, where the management was adopting a particularly intransigent attitude to returning workers (it accepted back only 50 of the original 1104 strikers). Enraged by these 'evil disposed and seditious persons', the city authorities banned public meetings and organised a force of volunteer constables to roam the streets with batons.[109]

Yet power ultimately rested with the state and the employers it backed. During September and October, the food riots stopped and strikes at each workplace across the eastern states collapsed in almost unconditional surrender. The effect on the union movement, as Ian Turner says, was 'shattering':

The railways and tramways unions were impoverished, internally divided, and almost defunct; the wharflabourers' [sic] union was rendered impotent . . . the front of the A.W.U. and the other mass unions, created in the 1916 political crisis, was seriously weakened by the refusal of the A.W.U. to be drawn into the struggle. The unions were far from happy about the timid role played by the Labor Party; but in their weakened condition there was little they could do about it.[110]

The 'great strike' has been described as 'arguably, the most cataclysmic event in the class struggle in the early twentieth century in Australia'. Yet for all the passion and polarisation that it generated, it has largely been forgotten, except perhaps within union circles. As David T. Rowlands said in 2008:

While Australians are routinely exhorted to remember the 'mateship' of the 'diggers', they are seldom encouraged to reflect on the solidarity displayed by working-class Australian civilians who banded together in a collective effort to resist a campaign of acute industrial oppression.

In no small part, this is because the dominant narrative to emerge from World War I was Anzac—which, as Marilyn Lake reminds us, has worked to 'to sideline different stories of nation-building, oriented not towards military prowess, but to visions of social justice and democratic equality'. But the erasure of the 1917 strike from modern memory is also a confirmation of how the present defines our understanding of the past. At a time when neoliberal economics is triumphant, and only one in five full-time employees in Australia is a member of a trade union, class warfare and millenarian visions of the collapse of capitalism seem to be tales from a past that is indeed a 'foreign country'.[111]

Third Ypres: 'step by step'

Menin Road

Planning of the Ypres campaign changed for the better when Plumer took over responsibility for capturing the high ground east of Ypres in late August. Methodical and painstaking, Plumer and the competent Harington insisted

Artillerymen loading a 15-inch howitzer near the Menin Road, in the Ypres sector. Superior firepower was essential to the infantry's advance in September–October 1917. (AWM E00921)

A photograph of the Menin Road, near Hooge, on 20 September 1917 taken by Australian photographer Frank Hurley. The wounded on the stretchers are waiting to be taken to the clearing stations. Shortly after the photograph was taken a shell landed in the area, killing most of the wounded. (AWM E00711)

A group of Australian soldiers at one of the formidable German reinforced-concrete pillboxes near Zonnebeke, 29 October 1917. (AWM E01069)

A 1917 postcard depicting the Battle of Polygon Wood and the planting of the Australian flag on the so-called Anzac Redoubt. This postcard was produced for sale, with all profits being directed to the Australian Comforts Funds. (AWM H00563)

A photograph showing dead and wounded Australians and Germans in the railway cutting on the Broodseinde Ridge, in the Ypres sector, on 12 October 1917. (AWM E03864)

The desolate water-soaked battlefield near Passchendaele in late October 1917. (AWM E04591)

on having three weeks to prepare for the next stage of the campaign. This would consist of a series of attacks—'step by step', as Bean later described it—against the Gheluvelt plateau and beyond. Key to the planning was the principle that the infantry would be set only objectives that fell inside the range of British artillery.[112]

The first 'step' scheduled for 20 September was an attack across the road that ran from Menin to Gheluvelt. Eleven divisions of Plumer's Second Army and Gough's Fifth Army were assigned the task of capturing the strong points and woods on the Gheluvelt plateau that the Germans had managed to hold against all attacks in August. 'Woods' was by this time a misnomer, since the destruction on the Gheluvelt plateau was almost complete. As Bean recalled:

> At Hooge . . . all marks on the original surface were completely erased . . . Westhoek, on the second spur, was marked only by the line of pillboxes which the Germans had built in its ruins. On the main ridge the woods had been shredded to stubble, and the slight depressions of the Polygon Wood plateau on the crest, as well as the hollows on either side, had been turned into bog.[113]

The 1st and 2nd Divisions of I Anzac Corps were to fight side by side at the centre of the attack. They spent weeks in training, learning the latest tactics for capturing pillboxes, studying models of the landscape and rehearsing, both day and night, attacks over land that resembled the battlefields. Aiming to achieve maximum punch, Birdwood and Brudenell White decided that the infantry would attack on two narrow fronts in three distinct waves, each of which would pass through, or leapfrog, the others. The first wave would be relatively light, since it was assumed that the German first line would be wiped out by the Allied preliminary bombardment. Later waves of infantry would be stronger, but would advance progressively shorter distances. In essence, the further the attack advanced into the German lines where resistance would be strongest, the greater its concentration. In addition, the infantry were by now skilled in fighting in teams armed with portable Lewis machine-guns and rifle grenades. While some elements of a platoon would assault a pillbox from the front, others would work their way around the flanks and attack it from the rear. Yet more groups would follow, consolidating the gains of the first waves.

The attack by the infantry at Menin Road would be preceded and supported by the fiercest concentration of British artillery yet seen. The bombardment would begin weeks before, blasting the German strong points and guns. When the attack itself began, the German batteries would be drenched with gas while the creeping barrage would provide a moving curtain some 1000 metres in front of the infantry. The barrage would continue for nine hours after the attack, protecting the infantry from German counter-attacks and giving them time to consolidate their hold on the ground they had gained. Never had what Wilfred Owen called the 'Great gun towering towards Heaven, about to curse' been so dominant on the battlefield. Bean wrote later of the Battle of Menin Road:

> The advancing barrage won the ground; the infantry merely occupied it, pouncing on any points at which resistance survived. Whereas the artillery was generally spoken of as supporting the infantry, in this battle the infantry were little more than a necessary adjunct to the artillery's effort.[114]

Yet this is too simple. Despite their significant superiority in artillery, as on 31 July, the British did not manage to eliminate all the German guns facing them. Low cloud and rain limited the accuracy of the British fire and the Germans moved their guns around frequently. A proportion of their artillery also held their fire at first, thus escaping British sound ranging and flash spotting. As the troops moved up to the line of attack, therefore, there were some heavy losses. 'Fritz has killed nearly all the horses in our Battalion,' Rupert Baldwin noted in his diary for 21 September. Cyril Lawrence wrote to his sister on the day of the attack:

> The roar and shaking of the artillery is simply awful. The biggest fight of the war has just commenced & we are waiting to go at any time. The bombardment has been going on for some days now & and during the last two it has got terrific. Our heads are just throbbing. No one can imagine what it is like. Just a continuous crashing & banging, blast of hot air, concussion & terrific spurts of earth and flying metal.

One battalion of the 1st Division lost all its company commanders and half its junior officers even before it reached the front line.[115]

Still, when the infantry went into action at 5.40 a.m. on 20 September, the creeping barrage provided enough protection for them to push forward (see Map 19). They penetrated between and around the formidable pillboxes and strong points. Gerald Douglas of 59th Battalion later wrote in his diary:

> when rushed by us [a pillbox] becomes a veritable death trap for the Germans. When close against the structure the machine guns are of course useless, and then all that needs to be done, unless Fritz surrenders in a body, which usually happens, is to take the pins out of a couple of Mills grenades and throw em thro [sic] one of the holes. They will settle all arguments and any hun that is left alive wont [sic] be fit for much.

In the face of this onslaught, many Germans chose to surrender, stunned by the bombardment. Others were not given the chance. One non-commissioned officer recalled:

> Fritz was only too eager to cry 'Mercy *Kamerad*' and in most cases got it. There are some who do not get mercy, they get in a blockhouse and fire on our chaps with machine-guns, but when we get up with them, they throw up their hands and ask for mercy but very rarely get it, which is quite right.[116]

By midday on 20 September, all but one of the objectives in the centre of the attack had been achieved. On the left of the Anzac front, the Fifth Army had also managed to gain its goals, even though it had been attacking on a wider front and with less artillery support. When the Germans tried later in the day to counter-attack, they were crushed by the ongoing artillery deluge. Pompey Elliott wrote home: 'Our boys . . . have made a glorious advance and captured a whole lot of Boches and driven [them] back a long way . . . That will be another feather in our boys' cap for the British troops have been blocked along this line for about a month.' Yet even 'glorious' success came at a huge cost: up to 21,000 British personnel were killed or wounded on 20 September; 1250 were from the Australian 1st Division and 2500

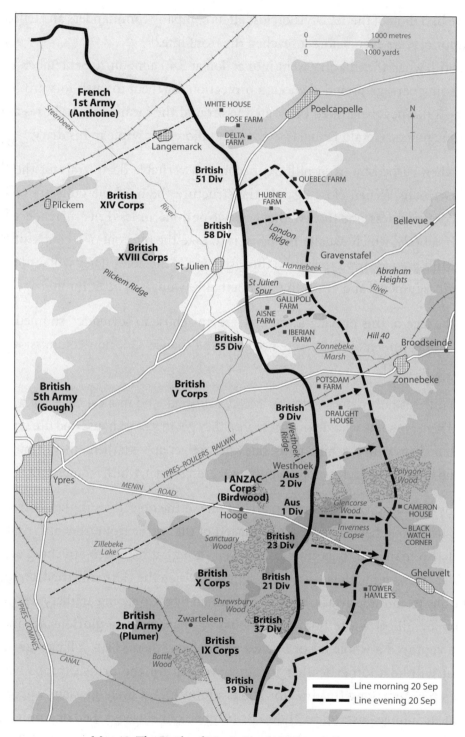

Map 19: The Battle of Menin Road, 20 September 1917

from the 2nd Division. For these losses, some 1425 hectares were gained. In contrast, on 31 July Gough's forces suffered 27,000 casualties and took 4660 hectares.[117]

Polygon Wood

The next step in Plumer's campaign followed only six days later, on 26 September. Haig was energised by the successes of Menin Road and ordered the final clearing of the Gheluvelt plateau by an attack on Polygon Wood and Zonnebeke. At the same time, he revived the plans for the seaborne landing on the coast that had receded during the disappointments of August. What *was* he thinking? The grand sweep to the coast from Ypres that was the precondition of the coastal attack involved advancing some 80 kilometres in weather that was bound to deteriorate as the autumn set in. In the past seven weeks, the British had advanced only 5–6 kilometres at the cost of 86,000 casualties. The only explanation seems to be what Haig himself articulated to Plumer and Gough at the time: that he believed 'the enemy is tottering, and . . . a good vigorous blow might lead to decisive results'.[118]

Polygon Wood was a less ambitious operation than Menin Road because it was impossible to assemble the same weight of artillery in the conditions and time available. The front of attack was narrower (7.7 kilometres as opposed to 13 kilometres) and the targets were set at a distance of a little over a kilometre. The Australian 4th and 5th Divisions were brought in to relieve the 1st and 2nd Divisions and positioned towards the centre of the attack. Their task was to capture the wasteland of charred and splintered stumps that now constituted Polygon Wood and the plateau to its north. The British X Corps (with the 33rd and 39th Divisions) on its right would seize the high ground around Tower Hamlets. Meanwhile, V and XVIII Corps of Gough's Fifth Army would secure the northern edge of the attack, overrunning the ruins of Zonnebeke and the high ground around Hill 40.

The British plans were thrown into disarray when, on the morning of 25 September, the Germans launched their own pre-emptive attack at the point where the Australian 5th Division and the British 33rd Division linked up south of Polygon Wood. Attacking in the mist, two regiments of the German 50th Reserve Division caught the British just they were taking over the front. With the support of ferocious artillery fire and low-flying aircraft firing machine guns, they pushed the British back for some 650 to 700 metres. The Allied attack scheduled for the following morning was in jeopardy.

However, as the skies cleared, the British artillery were able to bring down their own furious barrage on the Germans. Elliott's 15th Brigade and the still-functioning elements of the British 33rd Division also swung round to face the Germans, thrusting between them. With considerable improvisation, Elliott then threw into the battle three battalions (the 57th, 58th and 60th) committed to attack the following day. They moved forward along a single track through the cratered battlefield under the intense German shelling. W.H. Downing wrote later:

> By the red and flickering light of the shellbursts men could be seen running and staggering, bent low. They dropped into what had been a trench, into shellholes, enduring, enduring with tautened faces, lying close to the ground, crouching as they burrowed for dear life with their entrenching tools, while the storm of steel wreaked its fury on tortured earth and tortured flesh. There were on all sides the groans and the wailing of mangled men.

One company of the 60th battalion lost over 60 men, including two officers.[119]

The German attack was stopped. The next day, an Australian stretcher-bearer could see 'the Fritz stretcher bearers carrying their wounded from their counterattack . . . he was badly cut up'. But somehow the Germans managed to cling to the land they had recaptured, meaning that the right of the 15th Brigade's planned advance on 26 September would be dangerously exposed. Since practically all the supply dumps for the operation had also been destroyed by German shelling, Elliott wanted to call the whole operation off.[120]

However, too much was at stake. His divisional commander, Hobbs, 'with deep anxiety' ordered him to proceed. Elliott therefore rapidly overhauled his plan of attack during the night of 25–26 September. The two battalions that had been shattered by holding the German attack were replaced by two reserve battalions (the 29th and 31st), whose men knew nothing of the territory over which they would attack. Fortunately, the Germans—thinking that they had succeeded in delaying the attack—lessened their shelling of AIF positions during the night. The new troops were somehow able to reach their jumping-off places, literally minutes before the attack began.[121]

The attack on Polygon Wood, launched at 5.50 a.m. on 26 September, was a success (see Map 20). It began with an artillery barrage that Bean famously described as 'the most perfect that ever protected Australian troops. It seemed to break out, as almost every report emphasises, with a single crash . . . Roaring, deafening, it rolled ahead of the troops "like a Gippsland bushfire".' The 4th and 5th Divisions captured their key objectives with relative ease. These included the Butte, a large mound at the centre of Polygon Wood that was riddled with bunkers and tunnels, seized with the loss of only two Australian officers and ten other ranks. One battalion commander later recalled:

> On reaching the Butte the two platoons which had been previously detailed to occupy it rushed the position and established themselves on the top after slight fighting. Sentries were placed on all entrances to the dug-outs and bombing parties were organised and worked down the passages, several of these were met with fire from inside the dug-out and retaliated with grenades, eventually driving the occupants into one compartment, and as they still continued firing grenades were thrown amongst them and several wounded; the remainder consisting of two officers and 56 others then surrendered.[122]

It was here, not at Fromelles, that the 5th Division chose to place their divisional memorial after the war. Like the 4th Division, they chose to be remembered by victory, not catastrophe. They crowned the Butte with an obelisk while boasting that their success on 25–26 September was 'largely due to the vigour with which the troops of the Division snatched complete victory from an almost desperate situation'.[123]

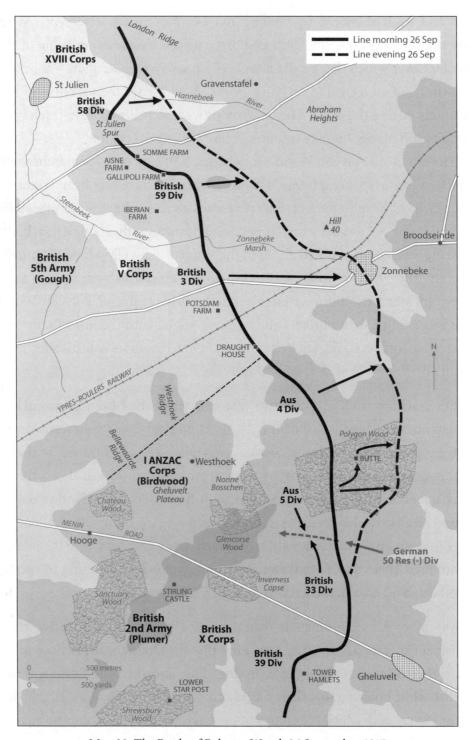

Map 20: The Battle of Polygon Wood, 26 September 1917

However, not everything went quite according to plan on 26 September. In the north, heavy morning mist caused the British 3rd Division to become lost, stumbling around the Zonnebeke marsh and falling behind its barrage. It managed to capture its objective, Hill 40, only late in the day at the cost of heavy casualties. At the southern end of the front, the boggy ground meant the British 39th Division also lost contact with its barrage and its men were shot down in large numbers. Tanks sent to support them sank in the mud, and Tower Hamlets, at the southern end of the Gheluvelt peninsula, remained in German hands.

The 33rd Division, on the Australian right, also failed to recapture the front-line sector that had been lost to the Germans on 25 September. Finally, Elliott ordered his own troops to intervene and capture some of the most resistant German strong points in the British sector. In vintage Elliott style—impulsive, foolhardy but courageous—he even went to the front line himself at dawn on 27 September to find out what was happening. His presence astonished the British. 'Was one of [our generals] ever within the shelled zone when there was the greatest need for him to know how things were being done, and what might be needed?' an officer of the 2nd Royal Welch Fusiliers commented. Elliot's appearance also energised the Australian troops and gave direction to the operations needed to ensure that the objectives in the British sector were taken in the following days.[124]

Elliott was showered with congratulations by Birdwood, Hobbs and Plumer. The 5th Division was deemed to have saved the British army from disaster. As ever, Elliott paid tribute to his 'boys', but it was a personal triumph, too. At the very time Elliott was managing the crisis on the battlefield, he learned that his brother George had been killed nearby. A letter from home added to his turmoil by telling him that he was facing financial ruin because of his business partner's accumulation of massive debts. Elliott wrote to his wife:

> I cannot tell you what I went through that night . . . After I knew Georgie had died I would have gladly welcomed a shell to end me. I walked twice from end to end of our zone and along the front line in front of the enemy's machine guns and never a shot came near me. It may be your prayers that protected me.[125]

For all its success, Polygon Wood had some troubling lessons for those who could read them. First, the 'bite and hold' approach worked only when visibility was good, the ground was dry and the artillery was effective. Most of the nine counter-attacks that the Germans launched on 26 September were halted by British artillery able to target accurately as the mists lifted. Where the ground was a quagmire—as much of it was—the artillery struggled to bring its guns up to a new starting line and the infantry became as vulnerable as ever. Second, since the depth of the attack was shallow, the British did not capture the German guns. Positioned to the rear, these were still able to exact terrible revenge on and beyond the British front line. Finally, like Menin Road, this was not a cheap success. Total British and Australian casualties at Polygon Wood were over 15,300; the Australian 4th and 5th Divisions lost 1730 and 3730 dead and wounded, respectively. According to Robin Prior and Trevor Wilson, this represented a cost of nearly 4400 casualties per square mile—50 per cent higher than at Menin Road.[126]

The wounded

Among the wounded at Polygon Wood was Joe Russell, whose story began this book. On his journey to the casualty clearing station, he was reportedly buried alive on two occasions by the torrent of German fire. He was one of countless others to suffer such trauma. Leonard Bryant of the 2nd Field Ambulance wrote on 21 September:

> having a very busy day getting the wounded back. Fritz shelling heavily all day dropped three at the mouth of our dugout killing four and wounding six, one of our 'B Boys' killed was only standing near him a half minute previously and both of us were blown on our backs with the two previous shells.

Photographer Frank Hurley also observed five German prisoners some days earlier, 'carrying one of our wounded in to the dressing station, when one of the enemy's own shells struck the group. All were almost instantly killed, three being blown to atoms . . . How ever anyone escapes being hit by the showers of flying metal is incomprehensible.'[127]

The work of the stretcher-bearers, already perilous, was rendered more torturous by the fact that the duckboards across the mud were now shattered by the shellfire. Bryant again recalled: 'Received a case at midnight had a very rough carry through a swamp, trenches and around crater holes getting bogged once and sinking up to my knees having to get pulled out.' In these conditions, even minor wounds could become fatal. Infection would set in during the hours or days that men awaited treatment. One Australian nurse, May Tilton, wrote on 4 October 1917:

> We hated and dreaded the days that followed this incessant thundering, when torn, bleeding and pitifully broken human beings were brought in, their eyes filled with horror and pain; those who could walk staggering dumbly, pitifully, in the wrong direction. Days later men were carried in who had been found lying in shell-holes, starved, cold, and pulseless, but, by some miracle, still alive. Many died of exposure and the dreaded gas gangrene.[128]

Nurses and other medical personnel at Casualty Clearing Stations were themselves in danger, inhaling mustard gas and working within range of German artillery and aircraft. No. 3 Australian CCS, at Brandhoek near Ypres, was shelled on five occasions in one week in mid-July 1917. On 4 August, a shell case fell through the theatre roof, landing on the operating table during surgery. Nurse Alice King recalled:

> Captain Calson had been giving an anaesthetic and had lifted the patient's head while orderly lifted feet to place him on stretcher on the floor, otherwise it would have caught both anaesthetist and patient in the head. Captain Calson very shocked and had to go off duty. I wet my pants.

On another occasion, King rushed to lift a patient on a stretcher only to find that the leg she grasped had been blown off the body: 'a loose leg with a boot and puttee on it'.[129]

Like the men they tended, medical personnel also suffered psychological trauma. There was not only the tension of being under fire but the horror of nursing mutilated and disfigured young men racked with pain and fear. Some of these were men they loved. Nurse Elsie Grant received a letter on 20 October:

> It is with regret I take up my pen to write these few lines telling you that your Brother A.H. Grant was killed in action on the 12:10:17; but Sister is it not just consolation to know that he died a grand and noble death fighting for his God; King; Country and dear ones. I had not met your brother prior to his joining our Battn (40th) but he was so jolly; full of sport; and good natured that he was soon known and loved by all the boys, in fact his platoon used to just idolise him.

May Tilton read in a newspaper on 16 October that her fiancé had been killed:

> An overpowering sense of desolation swept through me. I felt I could endure no more. That night I wrestled with myself all alone in my tent, unable to face the work in the theatre . . . Next morning, Captain Wilson came and sat beside me, and talked of things that made me realise my own selfishness in forgetting for a moment the needs of our poor men, dependent on us. The comforting kindness and consideration of those about me helped me to restore my balance again. But something had happened to my head, which was all tight inside.

Within three months, both May and Elsie were close to nervous collapse and were sent back to Australia.[130]

Broodseinde

Haig, however, was ebullient, convinced by Polygon Wood that decisive results were at last within reach. As he judged it, the Germans were demoralised, had no answer for the new British tactics, and would soon collapse. So confident was Haig of an imminent breakthrough that he ordered Plumer and Gough to prepare by 10 October reserves of infantry, tanks, cavalry and mobile artillery, all poised to exploit the planned advances on the Passchendaele ridge. Cavalry in the mud of Flanders seems an absurdity. As Geoffrey

Serle says, 'they probably could not have got through even if the Germans had laid down their arms'. But by this stage Plumer seems to have become infected with Haig's optimism.[131]

The next 'step' in the campaign—an attack on 4 October against Brood-seinde—fed these illusions. In the centre of the front were the two Anzac Corps, going into battle—so Bean would have us believe—with their spirits soaring because they were fighting at last side by side. Protecting their flanks were the British X and IX Corps to the south and XVIII and XIV Corps to the north (see Map 21). The hours before the battle were wretched. It was raining (though as yet only lightly) and the infantry had to lie in water-filled crater holes as they waited to go into battle. Then they were caught by German fire, which poured down on the 1st and 2nd Australian Divisions even before their own attack had started.[132]

This happened because the Germans decided to launch an attack of their own, at almost exactly the time that the British attack was scheduled, in an effort to regain the land lost near Zonnebeke on 26 September. Lieutenant Thomas Miles wrote later:

> Fritz's shells fell heavy and not a gun of ours replied, could our lads 'stick it' for a quarter of an hour? I took out my watch, the minutes seemed to crawl, it seemed like hours, our infantry were suffering heavily, of my three guns waiting to open up with the barrage, one was blown to pieces, the other two partly buried, but the crews stuck to their posts, our infantry stood steady waiting, not a murmur. Who says Australians haven't got discipline? . . . exactly on the stroke of six, our barrage burst with one long roar, which I will remember to my last day, it was magnificent.

But one man in every seven of I Anzac Corps was lost before they even started their attack.[133]

As they finally went into action at 6 a.m., the infantry met Germans advancing from a front line that was more heavily defended than in recent battles. Since elastic defence seemed to have failed at Polygon Wood, the

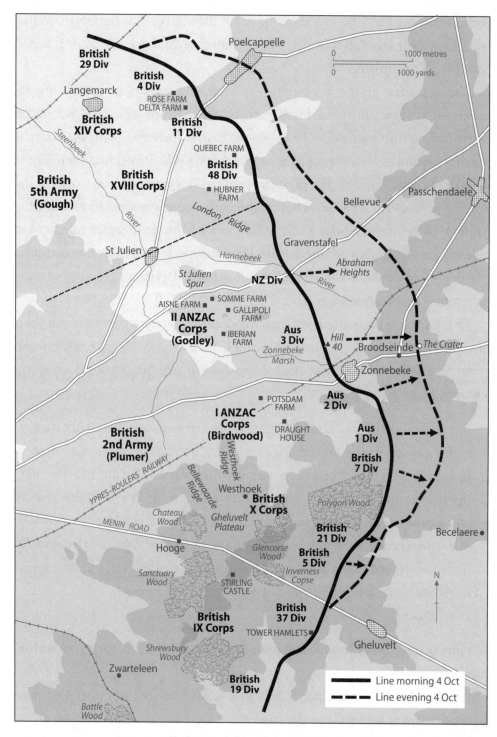

Map 21: The Battle of Broodseinde, 4 October 1917

German command had concentrated more troops and machine guns in its front line, holding the counter-attack forces back until the second day. The usual desperate close hand-to-hand fighting followed. Soon German prisoners were coming back in their hundreds. 'If ever men had fear in their faces these men did,' Miles said. 'They were pitiful to look at. I collected them in a group, and "shooed" them to the rear as you would "shoo" sheep.'[134]

At most points along the line, the attack succeeded. Where the ground was boggy—as it was in the north and in front of the New Zealand Division—attacks slowed or faltered. But I Anzac Corps captured Broodseinde ridge, while most of the village of Poelcappelle was taken by XVIII Corps, assisted by a small force of twelve tanks. The New Zealand Division captured its goal of Abraham Heights and the 3rd Division reached a point on the ridge only 800 metres from the village of Passchendaele. As always, the losses were huge: some 20,000, of whom at least 6500 were Australian. But at last almost all of the Gheluvelt plateau was in British hands and the lowlands beyond the ridge stretched out before them, undamaged and enticing. Monash exulted: 'Great happenings are possible in the very near future, as the enemy is terribly disorganized and it is doubtful if his railway facilities are good enough to enable him to re-establish himself before our next two blows, which will be very severe.'[135]

Poelcappelle and Passchendaele

Broodseinde, like Menin Road and Polygon Wood before it, was a victory in Western Front terms, and had Haig stopped in early October 1917 Third Ypres might have been remembered as one of his greatest achievements. But Haig was like a gambler who cannot rest until he hits the jackpot, the contestant on a quiz show who risks the $500,000 he has already won in the hope of $1 million. Broodseinde only fed his conviction that the Germans were on the point of collapse. Five thousand Germans had been captured in that battle, adding to the 'swarms' taken in the previous weeks. According to Haig's intelligence officer, who did not serve him well, there were no German reserves within easy reach of the battlefield able to replace these losses.[136]

The British War Cabinet, having reserved the right to halt the Ypres offensive if it stalled, did not intervene. In an almost inexplicable dereliction of leadership, in August and September it hardly questioned Robertson's optimistic accounts of the campaign or debated the progress in Flanders. Instead, it focused its attention on some old favourite sideshows, supporting the Italians and increasing the pressure against the Ottomans in Palestine. While Lloyd George continued to proclaim the futility of Haig's offensive, he 'failed to raise a finger to stop it'.[137]

Hence another attack along the Passchendaele ridge was set for 9 October. The short time lag of five days was intended to keep the Germans off balance, but it was too little time for adequate preparation—particularly as 30 millimetres of rain fell in the five days after 4 October. Everywhere the ground turned to bog or lakes. Roads and duckboard walks collapsed, making it almost impossible to bring up supplies. The men laying communication cables spent days in the wet, sleeping in waterlogged holes and succumbing to influenza, dysentery and trench foot. Struggling to the front line, the infantry risked drowning if they slipped off the duckboard pathways into the mud. As Thomas Miles said, 'Our worst enemy was the mud, it is beyond description. I really think soldiers dread mud more than shells.' Everyone was exhausted and debilitated well before they went into battle. Bean noted that the men struggling along the Menin Road were 'white and drawn and detached, and put one foot slowly in front of the other, as I had not seen men do since the Somme winter . . . but these men looked whiter'.[138]

The worst impact of the foul weather was on the artillery. It took huge physical efforts and many hours to move guns to within effective range. Then they sank into the mud as they fired. Horses and pack animals bringing in the ammunition floundered and panicked as their drivers tried to keep their heads above the mud. As James Carthew wrote to his mother on 23 October:

> We had a terrible time getting our guns into position on the last occasion, at times they were almost out of sight in the mud and the horses that were trying to pull them were almost as bad. It is almost impossible to find a patch of ground without a shell hole, in fact it has been turned over and over, and as soon as a drop of rain comes it is turned into one

huge bog. We used to have twelve horses and about thirty men pulling on ropes.[139]

Shells became coated with mud and had to be cleaned of slime before they were usable. No aerial spotting was possible because of the weather. Hence guns were often firing blind, and the barrage became ragged and thin. The artillery weapon that had been so critical to success at Menin Road, Broodseinde and Polygon Wood was becoming blunted, particularly as the Germans brought up new divisions and artillery and inflicted huge casualties on British gun emplacements in the days after 4 October.

The attack on Passchendaele village on 9 October was therefore a failure (see Map 22). II Anzac Corps attacked along two spurs while British and French troops to their left made diversionary attacks. Despite the fact that the artillery support was nowhere near that provided for earlier attacks, the 2nd Division and later the British 66th Division did make some initial progress. However, they were soon driven back. Meanwhile, the 1st Australian Division, which had been assigned the task of diverting German fire from the main attack, also met with disaster. A raid by the 10th Battalion on Celtic Wood cost 71 of the 85 men involved. No trace of the missing was ever found.[140]

Only on the extreme edges of the attack did the British and French forces manage to creep forward, taking the ruins of Poelcappelle from which this battle was to take its name. Generally, however, the battle ended with the troops almost at their starting line. Colonel Alfred Sutton, of the Australian Army Medical Services, wrote: 'Thus all our work is for nothing & our victory of the 4th is dimmed by this defeat. The task was too much for worn out men exhausted by much rain. When will the Generals realize that we are but men?' Thomas Miles lamented that 'some more of the old Gallipoli boys "went under" it seems hard after three years to go under now'.[141]

However, Haig and Plumer managed to convince themselves that some gains had been made on 9 October. They ordered a second attack towards Passchendaele to be launched three days later, on 12 October. The goal set for II Anzac Corps (now incorporating Monash's 3rd Division and the New Zealand Division) and the 9th Division of XVIII Corps was to capture

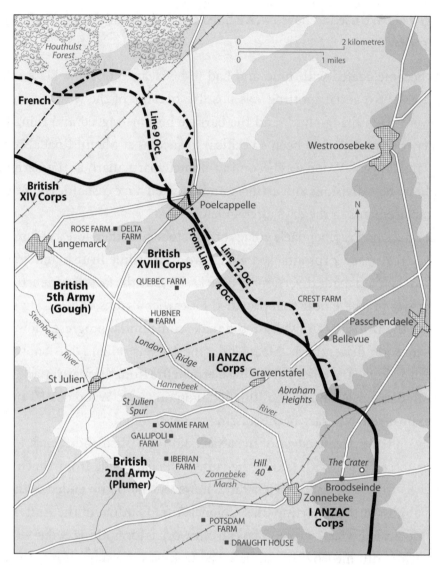

Map 22: Passchendaele, 9–12 October 1917

Passchendaele village and a section of the ridge to its north. This was a distance of 1800 to 2300 metres, 900 metres more than the infantry had covered in any of the battles of Menin Road, Polygon Wood or Broodseinde! To the north, the Fifth Army would provide support and in the south I Anzac Corps, which Birdwood insisted was approaching exhaustion, would protect II Anzac Corps' flank by moving along an adjacent spur. The burnt-out 1st and 2nd Divisions were replaced by the 4th and 5th Divisions.[142]

There was almost no time to prepare, and the rain continued to pour down. Even the normally bullish Gough recommended that Plumer delay the operation, and Monash also requested a 24-hour postponement. But Haig insisted that 'every hour's postponement gave the enemy breathing time'. Hurley wrote:

> God knows how those red tabbed blighters at headquarters (60 miles from the front) expect our men to gain such a strong position when they have to drag themselves through mud. Curse them! I'll swear they were not within 20 miles of the firing line when this attack was arranged, the ground is impassable.[143]

In the short time available and the terrible weather conditions, the artillery could neither eliminate the German batteries, barbed wire and machine-gun posts nor provide an effective creeping barrage for the infantry. Even before the attack began, the German guns—positioned on undamaged ground beyond the line—had drenched the front-line troops with high explosive and mustard gas mixed with a 'sneezing gas' that forced men to remove their gas masks. Though mustard gas did not necessarily prove fatal, whole units were incapacitated as they succumbed to its effects, sometimes hours after contact. Their eyes burned and streamed, their skin blistered and they lost their vision and voices. Internal bleeding corroded their respiratory and digestive systems. To quote an Australian nursing sister:

> It was a very deadly gas and the patients suffered terrible pain, one would not recognise a patient who had been badly gassed, they were so disfigured with burns and swollen, the eyes very swollen and closed. The skin was always burnt worst in the axillas under knees, groins or in any parts where the skin rubbed against the skin, also the membrane of the mouth and throat, some patients were unable to speak the voice having completely gone.[144]

The attack on Passchendaele of 12 October was a catastrophe. As the infantry moved forward at 5.25 a.m. beyond the slimy duckboards they had to wade through often knee- or waist-high mud. They struggled to keep up with the barrage—which was in any case so thin that, according to Bean, 'the attacking troops had difficulty in judging whether the scattered shells that burst fitfully around them were their own or the enemy's'. Unsubdued German machine-gun posts and pillboxes mowed the troops down. Communications collapsed as wires were destroyed, pigeons were stopped in flight by the wind and runners were killed, wounded or delayed for hours. It was the worst of 1915 and 1916 again.[145]

Despite everything, the 3rd Division moving up the Passchendaele ridge towards the village reached its first objective by working from shell hole to shell hole and rushing the German guns with suicidal courage. However, the troops were forced to withdraw almost to their starting line later in the day by annihilating fire. The New Zealand Division, which was meant to capture the Bellevue Spur to the left, had meanwhile been slaughtered in the swamp of the Ravebeek valley and the approaches to the uncut wire. To the right, the 4th Division—which had managed to progress along the Keiberg spur—was 'left in the air' by the 3rd Division's retreat and had no alternative but to fall back to its original starting line. The British XVIII Corps on the Australians' left had also been halted in the mud and ruins of Poelcappelle. Only on the extreme left had XIV Corps and the French advanced a few hundred metres into the Houthulst 'forest'.

The cost of what little was gained was terrible. The 3rd Division lost 3200 men, 62 per cent of those engaged, and almost as many as the New Zealanders. As Lieutenant-Colonel L.J. Morshead of the 33rd Battalion said, things were 'bloody, very bloody': 'It is a fact that four men in the Brigade on our left were drowned in the mud & it was quite usual for men to be bogged up to their armpits.' Monash lamented:

> Our men are being put into the hottest fighting and are being sacrificed in hare-brained schemes like Bullecourt and Passchendaele, and there is no one in War Cabinet to lift a voice in protest. It all arises from the fact that Australia is not represented in the War Cabinet, owing to Hughes, for political reasons, having been unable to come to England.

> So Australian interests are suffering badly, and Australia in not getting anything like the recognition it deserves.[146]

The battlefield was covered with the dead and wounded. In a gesture of humanity, the Germans held their fire, even pointing to the wounded so that the stretcher-bearers could collect them. But countless soldiers had simply disappeared, shredded by shellfire or swallowed up in the shell holes in which they were left while awaiting evacuation. They joined the already huge lists of the 'missing'—that category of casualty that was of particular torment to families waiting at home, desperate for certainty.

Astonishingly, the battle for Passchendaele continued even after the failure of 12 October. For Haig, capturing the village seemed to have become an obsession. The Australians were exhausted, and Birdwood insisted that they could do no more, but the Canadian Corps was still relatively fresh after carrying out diversionary attacks at Lens. It was brought in to complete the task. Currie protested with a vehemence that might have meant his being 'sent home had I been other than the Canadian Corps Commander', as he later admitted. But he could extract from Haig only a two-week pause. Then, in five excruciating slogging actions—26 October, 30 October, 6 November, 10 November and 12 November—the Canadians crept slowly and painfully forward through the desolate wilderness until Passchendaele and a little of the ridge beyond it was at last taken. In a supporting role, the Australian infantry participated only on 26 October, while Australian artillery provided supporting fire. Even then, many became casualties—particularly to mustard gas.[147]

Finally, the terrible Third Ypres campaign stumbled to a close. By mid-November it was clear—even to Haig—that nothing more of significance could be gained. In fact, the land taken at such cost in the final attacks was almost a liability. It formed such a sharp projection into the German lines that it was likely to be indefensible in the future. The British armies, of whom so much had been demanded, were also showing signs of nearing their breaking point.

In any case, there were no further troops to commit. Haig was already turning his attention to another offensive by the 3rd Army—at Cambrai, south of Arras. Using tanks for the first time *en masse*, and fourteen squadrons

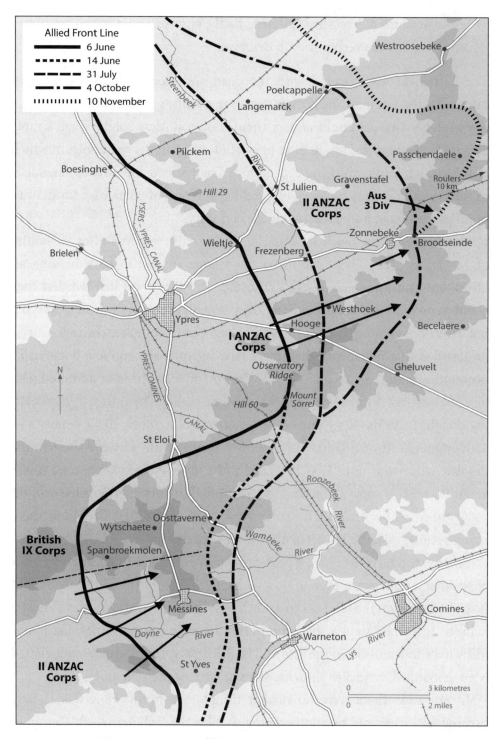

Map 23: Overview of Third Ypres, June to November 1917

of the Royal Flying Corps (RFC) in a foretaste of later warfare, this attack on 20 November was initially a spectacular success. The Australian Flying Squadron's No. 2 Squadron, deployed for the first time on the Western Front, flew only metres above the trenches in the dense fog, bombing and strafing the enemy positions and supply trains in a way described by the commander of the RFC, Major General Hugh Trenchard, as 'really magnificent'. But it lost seven of its eighteen aircraft, and the attack as a whole stalled when the cavalry failed to break through late on the first day. Thanks to Ypres, there were too few infantry reserves to exploit the initial brilliant success at Cambrai. On 30 November, the Germans counter-attacked, neutralising earlier gains.[148]

The Third Ypres balance sheet

Third Ypres had proved not to culminate in sweeping breakouts across Belgium, but rather a bitter slogging match of attrition. What did it achieve? Certainly not what Haig had hoped. The Germans did not collapse, and Belgium was not liberated. Nor were the Belgian ports gained (see Map 23). Perhaps the French were given time to recover from their crisis of late spring by the German reserves being drawn to Flanders. A senior German commander suggested as much after the war. But the worst of the French troubles seem to have been over by the time Third Ypres began, and it is doubtful whether such a huge and prolonged offensive was needed to distract the Germans' attention from the French. Even if it was, there were many more suitable places along the Western Front than the quagmire of Ypres at which to fight.[149]

The balance sheet of casualties is also ambiguous. The British forces (which included the Australians) lost at least 250,000 men (some estimates are as high as 310,000), of whom 70,000 were dead. The Germans incurred possibly 200,000 casualties. This was in fact a better ratio than at either the Somme or Arras, but it is clear that many thousands of lives were squandered in the last terrible weeks of the campaign. The realisation of this damaged the morale of the British armies. As J.P. Harris puts it, it is possible that 'Haig had done proportionately very much more damage to his own army than to the Germans'.[150]

As with the Somme, the key question was who had the greater capacity to absorb the losses of Third Ypres. With the Bolsheviks seeking peace, the

Germans would soon be able to replenish their forces on the Western Front with armies from the east. The British and French, in contrast, were being forced to send eleven divisions to prop up the Italians, who had suffered a stunning defeat at the hands of the Austrians at Caporetto on 23 October. Yet to offset this, the Allied Powers were soon to be strengthened by the arrival of fresh US divisions in Europe.

On balance, it seems that the situation for the Allies was less favourable at the end of Third Ypres than it had been at the beginning of 1917. Sensing their disadvantage, the British and French governments in early November took some tentative steps towards creating a unified command. On 7 November, at a conference in Rapallo, Italy, they created a Supreme War Council. This, however, was still something of a toothless tiger, and it was not until the Allies were staring defeat in the face in spring 1918 that they appointed one supreme commander, the French General Ferdinand Foch, charged with coordinating the efforts of the Allied armies on the Western Front.

Whatever the strategic balance sheet of Third Ypres, its impact on the Australian home front was devastating. The *Sydney Morning Herald* might have declared with astonishing insouciance that the capture of Passchendaele was 'a striking British success', 'a brilliant feat . . . the culminating stroke of a series of successes beginning on July 31', but few Australians would have believed this. In eight weeks of fighting in the Ypres salient, the AIF had suffered around 38,000 casualties. This was 15,000 more than during the seven weeks of fighting around Pozières and Mouquet Farm in July and August 1916, and 12,000 more than during the eight *months* of the Gallipoli campaign. Any thinking Australian must have questioned how long this bloodletting could go on, and what it had achieved. The implications of the Bolshevik revolution for the Allies' prospects were also dire. As the editor of the *Australian Baptist* wrote on 13 November:

> This has been the blackest week in the whole hundred and seventy-three weeks of the war. Everything seems to be falling to pieces. The end appears to be farther off than ever, unless the end is to be disastrous . . . we seem to be up against a great black wall of darkness as high as the clouds and as deep as the bottomless pit.

The 'in memoriam' notices inserted by the bereaved in the daily newspapers told a similar story of despair, though some seemingly found consolation in their faith in an afterlife. As Agnes Bird wrote of her husband, David, on 27 October 1917:

> He was my all.
> The best, kindest, truest, dearest, most unselfish,
> and most devoted husband who ever lived.
> Our love is stronger than death, and our reunion sure.

Another 'sorrowing and broken hearted wife', Lena Blyth, wrote of her husband, killed in action on 4 October:

> Far away on yon great battle field
> My beloved husband lay;
> A husband hard in this world his equal to find,
> A father loving, true and kind.
> How we longed for his home coming.
> And his little sons would say,
> Muma, when is dada coming
> From the big war home again.
> Behind all shows standeth God.

But other expressions of grief were stark. The mother of John Foley, who died on 26 October, wrote:

> A mother's love is deepest
> And so her grief is greatest.

She had already lost another son, James, at Pozières in August 1916. The sister of Hugh Dentry wrote simply, 'Oh! my brother.'[151]

Beersheba

At least a spectacular victory was won in the Middle East in late October. This came after six months of relative inactivity following the failure in April of the second attempt to take Gaza. The British command had used these

363

months to retrain and reorganise as reinforcements arrived from Salonika. The changes in force structure, which Murray began earlier in 1917, were soon to be overtaken by events, but they were notable for raising the hackles of a number of Australian officers. In March, for example, the command of the newly formed Imperial Mounted Division, made up of two Light Horse Brigades and British yeomanry, was given to a British officer, Major-General Sir Henry Hodgson. This decision fuelled 'a simmering belief' among some Australian officers that their forces, who had been 'doing much of the fighting . . . had not been receiving the credit due to them'. In particular, Major-General Granville Ryrie, who commanded the 2nd Light Horse and was ambitious for promotion, maintained that the four Australian Light Horse brigades should be formed into an exclusively Australian division. Ryrie and the commandant of AIF Administrative Headquarters in London, Brigadier-General Robert Anderson, lobbied Birdwood on the matter, and the Australian government protested to Murray.[152]

Their objections were not entirely reasonable. The forces in Palestine were, after all, multinational, and an Australian, Chauvel, was promoted after Second Gaza to command the Desert Column. Though less widely known than Monash, he was in fact the first Australian to command a corps. In addition, even though Hodgson's staff were predominantly British, qualified Australians were appointed to key administrative positions in Chauvel's corps. Murray stood his ground about Hodgson, although he conceded his political mistake and consulted the Australian government about further command and organisational changes in June 1917, including the reforming of the Imperial Mounted Division, which included the 3rd and 4th Light Horse Brigades, into the Australian Mounted Division (still under Hodgson).

Then Murray was himself removed from command. Having lost the confidence of London in the aftermath of Gaza, he was replaced in late June by Allenby. Although his performance at Arras had not impressed Haig, Allenby—known to his troops as 'The Bull'—would bring a new energy and dynamism to the Middle East (even as he coped with the news of the death of his son—his only child—on the Western Front). Moving his headquarters from Cairo to the front, he dashed from camp to camp in his car, consulted with his subordinates and imprinted his personality on his forces. He also initiated another reorganisation from which two new infantry corps emerged: XX Corps under Philip Chetwode and XXI Corps under Edward Bulfin. Chauvel's Desert Column, known as the Desert Mounted Corps from mid 1917 on, now consisted of three mounted divisions—the Australian and New Zealand Mounted Division, the Australian Mounted Division, and the Yeomanry Mounted Division—and various small and specialist units.[153]

The summer months in Palestine were a torment of dust, flies, lice, intense heat, fierce winds and boredom, alleviated by periods spent on rotation on the Mediterranean coast. But by late October 1917, the EEF was ready to attack again. Allenby now had a superiority of eight to one in mounted troops and Lloyd George, desperate for some morale-boosting news, had told him to take Jerusalem as a Christmas present for the British nation. This meant breaking the Turkish Eighth Army, which now held—fairly thinly in places—a line stretching from the coast near Gaza to Qawuka, and then facing a gap of 13 kilometres to Beersheba.

Gaza itself was now something of a fortress, but at Beersheba the Ottoman defences were less well developed. The town's wells, famous since Old Testament times, were a critical source of water, but the Ottomans thought the British were unlikely to attack the town, given the arid terrain around it and the lack of roads. However, Allenby adopted a bold plan, some elements of which had been drafted earlier by Chetwode, which envisaged capturing Beersheba as a way of neutralising Gaza. While Bulfin's XXI Corps fooled the Ottomans into thinking that Gaza was the main focus of attack, Chetwode's XX Corps would assault Beersheba from the south-west. Two divisions of Chauvel's Desert Mounted Corps would then move in to capture Beersheba from the east. Once Beersheba's wells were in British hands, the main assault on Gaza by XXI Corps would proceed, while the Desert Mounted Corps and XX Corps would move forward to cut off the escape route of the retreating Ottoman forces.

The bombardment of Gaza began on 27 October, with British and French naval vessels positioned offshore enhancing the artillery on land. Three days later, Chauvel's mounted forces assembled within striking distance of Beersheba, at Khelsa and Asluj, where British engineers had managed with considerable ingenuity to locate and develop the all-important water supplies. Then, on the night of 30 October, the Desert Mounted Corps made the long ride to take up its attacking positions east and south-east of Beersheba.

On the morning of 31 October, XX Corps opened its bombardment of Beersheba and the infantry moved in from the south-west (see Map 24). By early afternoon, they had taken their objectives; however, they then halted, since the task of capturing the town and its wells had been assigned to Chauvel's forces. On the right of the attack, however, progress had been slower. The 2nd Light Horse Regiment had quickly captured the small hill of Tel el Sakati and cut the road from Beersheba to Hebron. But the New Zealand Mounted Rifles had found it more difficult to control Tel el Saba, the feature that was the linchpin of Beersheba's defence. Their 13-pounder guns—chosen partly

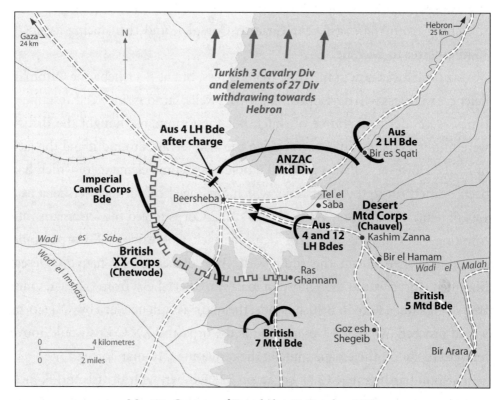

Map 24: Capture of Beersheba, 31 October 1917

because they were more mobile than 18-pounders—lacked the weight of fire needed to destroy the entrenched tiers of enemy defences. Not until 3 p.m. did the Auckland Mounted Rifles, reinforced by the 1st and 3rd Light Horse Brigades and supported by British artillery, take Tel el Saba.

With this, the Ottomans' position in Beersheba became untenable, and they decided to withdraw. However, Chauvel, who was watching the battle anxiously some 6.5 kilometres away on a hill at Kashim Zanna, did not know this. Under acute pressure to capture the Beersheba wells intact, and with only two hours of daylight remaining, he decided, probably at the urging of the commander of the 4th Light Horse Brigade, Brigadier-General William Grant—ownership of the decision is moot—to launch a cavalry attack on the town. An agonising hour passed during which the 4th and 12th Light Horse Regiments formed up side by side in lines some 500 metres apart. Then, supported by two batteries of horse artillery, they trotted off at 4.30 p.m. across 3 kilometres of open ground to the south-east of Beersheba. When they were about 2.5 kilometres from the Ottoman trenches, they drew their bayonets and broke into a gallop, yelling wildly. An eyewitness recalled:

> it was a most inspiring sight. It was growing dark, and the enemy trenches were outlined in fire by the flashes of their rifles. Beyond, and a little above them, blazed the bigger, deeper flashes of their field guns, and our own shells burst like a row of red stars over the Turkish positions. In front the long lines of cavalry swept forward at racing speed, half obscured in clouds of reddish dust. Amid the deafening noise all round, they seemed to move silently, like some splendid, swift machine.[154]

Ottoman artillery tried to stop the charge with high explosive and shrapnel, while two German planes dropped bombs and fired machine guns. The panicking troops in the trenches also opened up with machine-gun and rifle fire. But the gunners seemed to fail to estimate the range and drop their elevation fast enough, and the Light Horse reached the trenches, where there was no barbed wire. Some of them charged through the gaps on horseback. Others dismounted and engaged in hand-to-hand fighting. When darkness fell, Beersheba was in Australian and British hands. All but two of the seventeen precious wells remained intact, over a thousand Ottomans were taken prisoner and nine field guns were captured. The 4th Light Horse Brigade lost 32 men killed and 36 wounded.[155]

Beersheba provided some joy for an Australian public wearied by the casualties of Flanders. While the official communiqué reported the charge as 'a wide turning movement through the desert [which] approached to the town from the east', the Australian press spoke of glory and the Light Horse's 'characteristic dash and valor'. One country newspaper enthused:

> No branch of the army has done more magnificent work than these men; their sacrificial charges on Gallipoli will live in immortality . . . their glorious deeds of the past must act as an inspiration and incentive to the eligible man left in Australia. MEN! if you respect the sacred word of mateship, you will go to your mate's help in Palestine. [He] needs you, your country needs you and your honor must compel you to enlist.[156]

Remembering Beersheba

Almost a century later, Beersheba would be described as 'Australia's forgotten war' (one of many candidates for this title, it seems, in today's memory politics), but it was hardly that. On the contrary, it was a dominant memory of the Middle Eastern war throughout the twentieth century, if those influential agents of cultural memory—art and film—are any indication. In 1920, the official war artist George Lambert chose to make the charge at Beersheba the subject of one his four largest canvases of the war (the others being the Gallipoli landing, the charge at the Nek and Romani). The painting went on display in Melbourne (1921–22) and Sydney (1922), then was hung in the Australian War Memorial when it opened in 1941. It remains there today.[157]

The memory of Beersheba was also enshrined in the now classic 1940 film *Forty Thousand Horsemen*, released at a time when Australians were again facing war in the Middle East. With Charles Chauvel, the nephew of Harry Chauvel, as its director and Frank Hurley as a cameraman, the film makes little pretence to historical accuracy. The Germans, not the Turks, are the primary enemy, as the opening titles make clear:

> When Germany stretched greedy hands towards the Middle East a great cavalry force came into being. The Anzacs, the bushmen, the men from Down Under: Call them what you will—their glories can never dim. The great cavalry force of modern times.

The Turks are relegated to a supporting role, praising Australian military prowess with compliments such as, 'We broke two armies trying to push a handful of these men back into the sea at Gallipoli', 'After Gallipoli we do not underestimate the Australians', and the Australian uses 'cold steel . . . nothing stops him'. Even the French heroine in the improbable love story exclaims, 'There is Australia' when she meets Red, the central Australian character. Meanwhile, the quintessential Australian digger—played by the young Chips Rafferty—muses that Australians are fighting in the desert for core national values: 'the right to stand up on a soap box in the Domain; the right to tell the boss what he can do with his job if we don't like it; the right to start off as a roustabout and finish off as a prime minister.' What, one wonders, would the workers who could not get their jobs back after the 1917 great strike and who faced prosecution under the *War Precautions Act* and *Unlawful Associations Act* have made of this?

Nearly half a century later, a similarly mythic view of Beersheba was promulgated in another feature film, *The Light Horsemen*. In this case, the historical details about the campaign were generally accurate but the British—as so often in Australian popular culture—provided the foil for Australian brilliance. Allenby is dismissed as 'typically bloody idiot Pommy brass' and Murray as a 'dunderhead' who has captured Gaza but not known it. The British 'don't know how to use' the 'formidable [Australian] soldiers'. They are 'good troops . . . wasted'. The DVD's blurb leaves no room for doubt:

> The British campaign in Palestine is stalemated—the Turco-German army holds a formidable line from Gaza on the coast to Beersheba . . . In a final attempt to save the attacking British Army from disaster,

everything depends on the 800 young Australian horsemen who obey the seemingly impossible order to gallop their horses across three miles of open desert into a hell of shell fire and machine gun cross fire. Smashing their way through Turkish defences to win the precious well of Beersheba they change the history of the Middle East.

Rather than being 'forgotten', then, the charge at Beersheba has served over the years to affirm a narrative of Australian exceptionalism. The ninetieth anniversary in 2007 was marked with a re-enactment of the event and celebrated as 'the last great cavalry charge'. Six months later, Australian Governor-General Major-General Michael Jeffery, when unveiling a statue (again by Peter Corlett) in a new peace park in Beersheba funded by the Pratt Foundation, would describe the Desert Mounted Corps as 'among history's finest warriors', renowned for 'courage, initiative and a pervasive sense of humour'. The charge itself was again recalled as an event 'that changed the course of World War I'.[158]

Third Gaza and Jerusalem

In fact, the capture of Beersheba did not change the course of the war—or, for that matter, the strategic outcomes of the Palestine campaign. By late 1917, Allenby had such a preponderance of forces over the Ottomans that his armies would have broken their line sooner or later. As Jean Bou concludes, 'the Beersheba attack was just one element of the greater third battle of Gaza, which, in its totality, decided the outcome in southern Palestine'.[159]

Moreover, Beersheba was not followed by the immediate destruction of the Ottoman armies facing the British in Palestine. The plan was that XX Corps and the Desert Mounted Corps would go on the attack only two days after taking Beersheba. But the much-vaunted wells were not as plentiful as expected, and Chauvel and Chetwode pleaded for four days to allow their troops to recover. Then the Turkish Seventh Army launched a counter-attack aimed at recapturing Beersheba. This tied down several British formations for five days in a bitter fight around the bare, flat-topped hill of Tel el Khuweilfe. 'Khulweilfeh [sic] was a horrid show,' Trooper Kempe of the 3rd Light Horse Regiment recalled, 'the sort of fear that is hard to throttle.' Men and horses went without water for many hours, and the Ottomans fired on stretcher-bearers and the carts carrying the British wounded.[160]

Hence, when XXI Corps finally captured the now empty Gaza on 7 November and the Turkish Eighth Army fell back, the Desert Corps, dispersed along the front, was in no position to pursue them. Chetwode's forces did break through at Tel el Sheria on 6–7 November, but the chronic problems with water, the dispersal of the British forces and the sheer exhaustion of the men and horses meant that critical time had been lost. The Ottomans slipped through the net and retreated northwards (see Map 25).

When the various British forces finally joined up on 11 November, they set out on a multi-pronged pursuit of the Ottoman armies—the so-called 'Great Drive'. One cohort swept up along the coast through orange groves and vineyards to capture Jaffa in mid-November. Inland, a second force rapidly pushed on to take Junction Station, where the railway from Jerusalem met the north–south railway line, on 14 November. In this 'remarkable military operation' between 31 October and 18 November, Chauvel's Desert Mounted Corps advanced about 290 kilometres, fought five major engagements and captured nearly 7000 prisoners and 60 guns. No. 1 Australian Flying Squadron and other aircraft added to the demoralisation of the enemy, dominating the air by bombing and providing the land troops with excellent aerial reconnaissance. The Ottoman armies were now split, with the Seventh Army retreating towards the hills around Jerusalem and the Eighth moving north along the coast (see Map 26).[161]

The great prize of Jerusalem—home to Christianity's Calvary, Islam's Al Aqsa Mosque and the Jewish Temple Mount—was within Allenby's grasp. Under instructions not to destroy the city, he hoped to force the Ottomans out by isolating them, but they fought tenaciously in the rocky and steep terrain of the Judean Hills. The rains fell and temperatures plummeted. Horses were useless in these conditions, and the men of the Egyptian Expeditionary

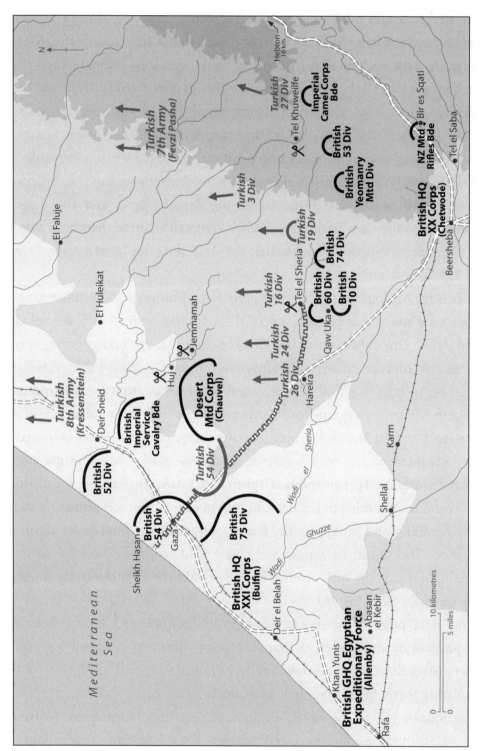

Map 25: Third Battle of Gaza, November 1917

Force (EEF) were exhausted by weeks of fighting and constant movement. Not until 9 December, after a final Ottoman attempt to strike back collapsed, did Jerusalem finally fall to XX Corps. The British line in Palestine, which only two months earlier had been stalled, now stretched across central Palestine from just north of Jaffa on the coast to just north of Jerusalem.

The conquest of Jerusalem was more than a major military victory in the Palestine campaign of World War I. For Christians, it was an inspirational end to a centuries-old crusade against Islam. As the Adelaide *Advertiser* editorialised on 12 December 1917:

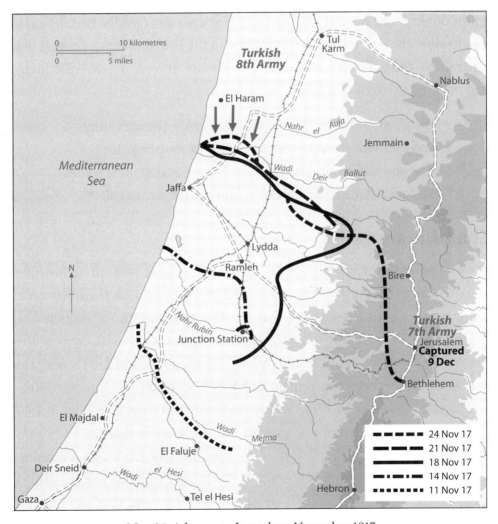

Map 26: Advance to Jerusalem, November 1917

Deferring speculations as to the military consequences of a victory, certain in any case to affect the moral [sic] of the Turks, the mind for the moment is naturally absorbed in the more spiritual aspects of this recovery by Christendom of the cradle of its faith . . . It is like the closing of a great gulf separating the present from the past to have wrested from Moslem hands with next to no bloodshed the treasures which hundreds of thousands of believing soldiers in the middle ages perished in vain to secure.

To add to the joy, Australians were there, trotting into Jerusalem like Christ on the donkey. The Australian 10th Light Horse was, in fact, the first mounted unit to enter the city, having been attached to the British Corps to ensure that Australians took part in the triumphal event. It was a powerful image that inspired a citizen of Adelaide to verse:

> The glamour of the far Crusades has down the ages rung,
> And ever will the story of their deeds in song be sung;
> And now their valour lives again, fierce flaming in its pride,
> As slouch-hat Anzac horsemen into old Jerusalem ride.[162]

Conscription again

It was against the backdrop of Jerusalem, Beersheba and, pre-eminently, Passchendaele that Australians were asked to vote again on the question of conscription. Given the damage that the 1916 referendum had inflicted on Australian politics, it was remarkable that Hughes would risk putting this issue to the vote a second time. But by late 1917 his options had narrowed, and almost against his better judgement he felt he had to go to the people again.

The first reason, as in 1916, was the shortage of troops. Throughout 1917, voluntary recruitment continued to fall below the levels that the authorities claimed were needed to replace the losses on the Western Front. According to the government, in June 1917 some 7000 recruits a month were needed to maintain the five Australian divisions in the field. This was far fewer than the 16,500 per month that Hughes had claimed to be the minimum in late 1916, a discrepancy quickly noted by Mannix and other anti-conscriptionists. Indeed, in May 1917 the British Army Council conceded that only 20,000 men were required over five months, or 4000 per month—but this was not made public.[163]

However, even this modest target was reached only in July 1917. This was despite the continuing efforts and ceaseless ingenuity of the government authorities and patriots. By mid-1917, it seems that there was no public place free of recruitment propaganda. Restaurants, hotels, cafes, cinemas, public transport and box kites flown over race courses all carried the patriotic message. City footpaths bore huge footprints leading 'eligibles' to recruiting depots. There were recruiting trains, more route marches and military displays of every kind. Open-air meetings in Sydney paraded horses with empty saddles, inviting recruits to fill them.[164]

Cohorts of patriotic women continued to inveigle men who had yet to volunteer. They distributed literature on trams and trains, and threw scones and cakes containing exhortations to enlist—a kind of recruitment fortune cookie—from 'travelling kitchens' in the streets. In a particularly noxious campaign by the 'one woman, one recruit' league, potential recruits were targeted 'even if [they] were the poor, unfortunate but eligible tradesman who knocked at the back door each day'. To the joy of the league, one baker enlisted after 'two years of unremitting effort' on the part of a determined woman. If 'persuasion' such as this failed, there was always ostracism and coercion. Single women were encouraged not to socialise with eligible men, while some Sydney retail stores sacked 'shirkers'.[165]

In September 1917, the government also finally moved to restrict public sports meetings in an effort to 'concentrate the minds of the people on the more serious aspect of the War'. The continuation of spectator sports during wartime had long been an affront to loyalists, who thought it intolerable that some Australians should enjoy leisure while others were dying in battle. As the *Sydney Morning Herald* put it, the love of sport and ease and luxury was 'laying deadly hold' on Australians and 'sapping the national character'. From 1915 on, many sporting clubs had closed of their own accord under patriotic pressure. These included Rugby Union, polo, interstate and inter-club hockey, amateur athletics, cricket, interstate tennis, rowing and most of amateur and country football. All states but Queensland and Western Australia had also restricted the consumption of another indulgence, alcohol, in 1915 and 1916 by legislating for the early closing of hotels. Not only was this seen as a necessary gesture to a mood of national sobriety, it was thought to promote the well-ordered, self-disciplined and morally upright home front required for the successful prosecution of the war. As Cecilia Downing, one of the leading campaigners of the Woman's Christian Temperance Union—an organisation that had been campaigning for the abolition of alcohol since 1887—put it, 'The truest patriotism [lay in] engaging in the world-wide war against the drink evil to secure national and personal efficiency.' However, for all the patriotic moralising, some sporting activities had continued to operate in 1916 and 1917, particularly those with largely working-class audiences. Now the government finally intervened. Boxing matches were restricted to one contest per state per fortnight, and almost all weekday horse races were eliminated. Football in Melbourne and Sydney, however, remained relatively exempt since, as Michael McKernan says, 'what government would have dared to prohibit football finals in Melbourne?'[166]

Even the landscape was transformed in the cause of recruitment. In Victoria, some 128 local committees started to plant 'avenues of honour', with each tree representing an enlisted man. In Ballarat, where the funds were raised by the women employees of the Lucas clothing factory, the avenue would ultimately include more than 3700 trees and stretch for more than 22 kilometres. A distinctively Australian phenomenon, these avenues are now assumed to be memorials—as indeed they were—but in 1917 they were also a means of mobilising men. The tree planting in Ballarat, for example, started in June 1917. The Arch of Victory that crowned the avenue was installed later, in 1920.[167]

However, all these efforts made little difference to the final recruitment figures. Although there was a slight increase to 4155 in July—in response, it seems, to a focused attempt to repeat the recruiting success of the June 1915 campaign—by October the number volunteering had fallen to 2761. This was at a time when, according to the Commonwealth statistician, there were some 140,000 single and 280,000 married men between the ages of 18 and 40 still outside the forces. Whether this was a negative reaction to the losses of Third Ypres is not known. Probably many Australians were simply tired of the war and resistant to the well-rehearsed arguments of the recruiters. Perhaps the ban on public entertainment was counter-productive. Since the choice of sports to be restricted was to some degree class-based, the bans may have worked to increase working-class antipathy towards enlistment.[168]

Loyalists, however, saw in the stagnation of recruitment 'sinister influences at work', to quote the infuriated Donald Mackinnon. Irvine and other pro-conscriptionists, who had held their fire for a while at the request of the recruiting authorities, finally broke their silence. At a series of meetings in the eastern capital cities, Irvine demanded that the government, which now had a parliamentary majority, should immediately introduce conscription by legisla-tion. In Sydney, conscriptionists also started a petition for a fresh referendum, declaring that 'a choice must be made between a Government that is prepared to stake its existence on conscription and a Government that is not'.[169]

Hughes was caught. He thought conscription was 'quite impossible', and possibly doubted whether—given the United States' entry into the war—it was necessary to again 'throw the country into turmoil', as Munro Ferguson put it. But Hughes' power base in the National Party was not secure. Despite his massive electoral endorsement in May, he was isolated from his Nationalist Cabinet colleagues, most of whom he did not trust and with whom he shared little other than a passion for winning the war. His private secretary, Percy Deane, thought there were moves within the Nationalist Party to unseat him, and Hughes himself felt, as he confided to Murdoch in July, 'like a swimmer in a vast ocean without the friendly shelter of even a dilapidated hen coop', 'as one in the wilderness, with every man's hand against me'. For domestic political reasons, then, as much as strategic necessity, Hughes felt compelled to act.[170]

He could have used his majority in both houses to force conscription through, but he decided early in November, after consulting with Pearce and

Cook, to risk a second referendum. Legislation would be a slow option, Pearce calculated, with the first conscripts possibly reaching Europe only in October 1918. Moreover, Hughes had promised in the May elections to refer the matter to the people if the strategic situation deteriorated. Cabinet approved the decision for the referendum on 7 November.[171]

The campaign

The question to be put to the people was short but imprecise: 'Are you in favour of the proposal of the Commonwealth Government for reinforcing the Australian Imperial Force overseas?' However, the conscription scheme being proposed was elaborate. The number of men to be recruited each month was set at 7000. Conscription—a word not mentioned in the question, as critics noted—would be used only to bridge the gap between numbers volunteering and the 7000 needed. If conscription turned out to be needed, men would be selected by a ballot of single men, widowers and divorcees without children dependent on them, between the ages of 20 and 44. There would be many exemptions: married men, the physically unfit, ministers of religion, judges, police and magistrates, conscientious objectors, those working in industries necessary to food and war production, and those for whom service would impose undue hardship on their dependants. To ensure equity of sacrifice, families that had already provided servicemen would be exempt until all others eligible had been balloted. In no case would the sole remaining eligible male of a family that had already contributed men to the war be called up.[172]

It was a more modest proposal than that of 1916, but the debates it triggered were perhaps even more bitter and divisive. All the arguments for and against conscription were rehearsed again, but the tone was more strident, irrational and hysterical. As John McQuilton says in his study of rural Victoria, 'Speakers no longer sought to persuade—they preached to the converted.' It was if all the despair and grief about a war that seemed beyond human control, unable to be ended yet devouring more and more lives in its monstrous maw, was displaced onto enemies at home. Despite the rhetoric of democracy, those with dissenting views were demonised. As in 1916, it was not a rational debate about the military need for conscription, but a deeply personalised contest of values and ideology. Paranoia and suspicion invaded public discourse, eroding the trust that is central to civil society and bringing the country—in Queensland at least—to the point of serious civil violence.[173]

For the 'yes' case, conscription continued to be the litmus test of imperial loyalty and Australia's willingness to 'do its share' in the war—a moral value almost in its own right. The United States had introduced conscription immediately after declaring war earlier in the year. Canada, too, had approved conscription in July, although Prime Minister Borden had previously opposed it and the French Catholic minority was opposed. Why should Australia not follow these examples of unqualified commitment?

The answer, according to Boote, was that Australia alone, 'in the midst of universal madness', had preserved its sanity. But for the loyalists it was the subversive forces within the Australian state that made this policy option impossible. Russia and Italy had been undermined by internal enemies; now Australia's war efforts were being white-anted by a sinister and treacherous trio: Sinn Fein, German-Australians and the IWW. As Hughes said, 'They, upon whom Italy relied, betrayed her. Treachery, mark that word, and apply it to our own circumstances. The agents of Germany within the gates of Italy, and not the valour of German arms, brought about the Italian debacle [at Caporetto].'[174]

It was against these 'enemies within' that much of the energy and vitriol of the 'yes' case was directed. Persecution of German-Australians reached an apogee in this period as the Anti-German League held a monster rally in Sydney and successfully lobbied the government to disenfranchise not only naturalised citizens of enemy origin but Australians of enemy parentage. Only German-Australians who had served in the AIF or had sons serving in the forces retained the right to vote in the referendum. The Commonwealth Statistician wrote to Hughes: 'Whether naturalised or not, the average German is so strongly pro-German that he *cannot* (and in many cases his children cannot) give a patriotic (Australian) vote on "conscription" or any other "defence question".'[175]

Daniel Mannix

The menace of Sinn Fein was more elusive, but for many loyalists it came to be embodied in the figure of Mannix. Relatively silent in the debates of 1916, he now emerged as the voice of working-class Irish Catholic disaffection and opposition to conscription. His meetings drew huge crowds, reaching an estimated 100,000 people in November. At the Richmond racecourse, according to the Catholic *Advocate*:

> Like a roar of distant thunder, the wave of wild cheers grew in strength, and thousands shouted 'Here he comes!' In the distance, the Archbishop could be seen making his way, with much difficulty, through the immense assemblage, that would fain have carried him shoulder high.

With beautifully modulated oratory and an acerbic wit, Mannix castigated those who urged Australia to fight for the rights of small nations while denying independence to the Irish. He openly supported Sinn Fein, which sought to 'wrest from English hands the government of their country and to set up in Ireland a government with Irish ideals and for Irish interests'. As for conscription, 'it was nonsense,' Mannix declared, to say that Australia had not done enough. The government had not even had 'the ordinary honesty, or even decency, to put a fair straight question. A straight question on conscription would get a straight answer.' Like the Irish, Australians should give primacy their own country. Playing also on Australians' fear of Japan, Mannix claimed that there were 'enemies nearer to Australia than Germany, and the day may not be too far distant when Australians will be required to defend their own interests at home'. It was perhaps time 'to get out of the war', using the offices of the Vatican to negotiate a compromise peace.[176]

Mannix's motives and appeal were complex. His sympathy for Ireland was no doubt genuine. He had left Ireland only four years earlier, and strongly identified with its political struggles. As Patrick O'Farrell puts it: 'Mannix's loyalties were, in this order, Catholicism, Ireland, Australia, the Empire and Britain—and he regarded Britain as having been disloyal to Ireland in its failure to implement a Home Rule Act which had already been passed.' Mannix, however, was also speaking to a wider Catholic agenda and a long-standing sense of injustice on the part of Catholics in Australia. They had always been a minority exposed to prejudice from the Protestant majority. The lack of state funding for Catholic education had rankled for decades. Now it seemed that Catholic religious and ecclesiastical students, essential to Catholic schools and sacramental life, might not be exempt from conscription. Hughes assured the Catholic hierarchy that they would be, but he was not believed.[177]

Mannix also tapped into the class identity of his parishioners, many of whom were workers angry at the crushing of the general strike and the perceived inequity of the economic burden of the war. The Catholic hierarchy acknowledged this. Whereas in 1916 the leadership had been divided on conscription, in 1917 it found itself forced by the laity to adopt a far stronger position against compulsion.[178]

Mannix reduced the loyalists to apoplexy. Pro-conscription meetings passed resolutions condemning his sedition and treachery and those of other Catholic prelates. Some Melburnians suspected him of being in league with another prominent Catholic, the notorious entrepreneur John Wren. As Patrick O'Farrell puts it, this supposed Mannix–Wren axis seemed to link 'priestcraft, sedition, moral corruption and underworld power [in a way that was] utterly scandalous and most seriously threatening'. Other Protestants suspected Mannix of plotting to place Australians 'under the rule of Rome'. Yet others called for his deportation. According to *The Argus* of 7 November 1917, Mannix was 'an arrogant Irish ecclesiastic, openly vaunting his disloyalty in the most intensely loyal dominion'. The Baptist minister at the Collins Street Baptist Church, the Reverend, T.E. Ruth, meanwhile took up the cudgels against him publicly:

Dr. Mannix [Ruth declaimed] is engaged in this country in a sordid, ecclesiastical traffic, destructive of manhood, destructive of patriotism, destructive of Christianity, and as a man, as an Englishman, as a Christian, I fling back into his teeth the offensive slander he has hurled against my country and the Empire that gives him protection. It is he who is engaged in a sordid trade war, a sordid trade war with the souls of men, with the free institutions of a free country, with the doctrines and principles of a free Gospel. He is fighting to reduce mental and moral manhood to terms of ecclesiastical machinery, patriotic politics to the level of sordid bargaining, and Christian truth to a ceremonalised and commercialised paganism ... But there is one thing this ecclesiastical commander-in-chief of a sordid trade war forgets—Australia is not Ireland. The average Australian is not priest-ridden. The Australian patriot is a British patriot.[179]

Like Mannix, Ruth drew passionate crowds—so large that they had to be accommodated in an auditorium across the road from his Collins Street sanctuary. Ruth himself had to be protected from Mannix supporters. To some, it seemed that in Melbourne the conscription debate had become a contest of 'Ruth versus Mannix'.[180]

Hughes, too, found Mannix utterly infuriating. He tried to block his nomination as a Chaplain General to Australian military forces, and even sought to have him restrained by the Vatican. But Hughes was no Henry II, and no one would rid him of this 'troublesome priest'. Mannix not only survived the 1917 campaign with his power base intact, but remained Archbishop of Melbourne until his death at the age of 99, in 1963. He outlived Hughes by eleven years.

Ryan versus Hughes

Hughes also found another bête noire in the form of Queensland Premier Ryan. Already deeply irritating because of his championing of state rights, his economic radicalism and his refusal to use scab labour in the general strike, Ryan in fact supported voluntary enlistment. However, he opposed conscription as an abuse of government power. Like Mannix, he was an accomplished orator and more than a match, both tactically and temperamentally, for the short-fused Hughes. Throughout Australia, Ryan's reputation soared 'as the one man capable of standing up to Hughes'.[181]

In a celebrated incident, Ryan spoke at an anti-conscription rally in Brisbane on 19 November. Challenging the Hughes government's statistics on military manpower needs, he accused it of bad faith in the wording of the referendum question, warned that married men would soon be called up and argued that Australian industry would be crippled by conscription. Predictably, the censor excluded vital sections of this speech before it was published in the press. Not to be foiled, Ryan responded by using parliamentary privilege to read the censored sections into the *Hansard* of the Legislative Assembly. His treasurer, Ted Theodore, also read into the parliamentary debates a banned anti-conscription pamphlet. As Raymond Evans says, 'it now seemed as if *Hansard* was the only medium still free from extravagant censorship action'.[182]

Ryan's plan was to then print 10,000 copies of *Hansard* with the censored passages highlighted in bold face. However, Hughes happened to arrive in Brisbane on 26 September and ordered copies of the offending *Hansard* to be seized from the government printing office, the *Worker* building and the General Post Office. By some accounts, he even led the military raid on the printery! Now determined on confrontation, the Ryan Cabinet in turn printed 50,000 copies of a government gazette outlining the incursions of the 'intolerable' censorship. As the print run was proceeding, armed Queensland police guarded the printery, government offices and even Ryan's home and person. The situation seemed set for an open clash between Commonwealth and state authority, but Hughes showed uncharacteristic restraint. Although he dispatched the censor, who arrived at the government printing office just after midnight, he did not use force to seize the gazette. Had he done so, John Fihelly, Ryan's Assistant Minister for Justice and Minister Without Portfolio, is reported to have said, it would have been 'a declaration of civil war'.[183]

The immediate crisis ebbed, but later in November Ryan and Theodore were charged with a breach of the *War Precautions Act*, which made it an offence to promulgate misleading information. In turn, Ryan issued an action against Hughes for contempt of court. Ultimately, the case against Ryan was dismissed on the grounds that he had based his case on government estimates of the number of recruits needed—not misleading information, at least officially! The Queensland case was also lost. A third case, for the possession of seized material, ended in a compromise.

In retrospect, this cat-and-mouse game between federal and state politicians seems surreal, but it was indicative of the highly volatile state of Australian political life in late 1917. Queensland police noted a large number of firearms being purchased and carried at public rallies, and there was talk by some unionists of physically expelling Hughes from the state. For his part, Hughes thought that Queensland was 'ripe for revolution' by left-wing groups preparing to seize Brisbane. When he returned south, he authorised the despatch of some rifles hidden in piano cases and machine guns in crates marked 'Furniture' to trusted loyalists in Brisbane to 'prepare for eventualities'. He also instructed the commandants of all military districts to ensure that contingency plans drawn up a year earlier to put down riots and insurrections be ready to be 'put into force without the smallest delay'.[184]

Fihelly and Hughes notwithstanding, it seems unlikely that Queensland—or, for that matter, Australia—was on the verge of civil war, at least in the sense of what was occurring in Russia. But the ideological conflicts were profound, and violence kept erupting in the public sphere. Speakers at mass meetings were jostled, heckled, shouted down or pelted with eggs, rocks and other missiles. Fist fights broke out between members of extended families. Women were set upon. At a Brisbane meeting of a newly formed Women's Compulsory Service Petition League, a young pacifist named Margaret Thorp was 'rolled on the floor, kicked and punched and scratched' by a 'seething mass of struggling women'.[185]

What was remarkable about this last attack was not that it targeted a woman—such assaults had become increasingly common—but that it was perpetrated *by* women. Expected to be 'sedate, reserved and respectable in their public demeanour, in keeping with their ostensibly passive and peaceable biological natures', women were now directing their repressed grief against accessible scapegoats. As Raymond Evans says:

Wrenching grief at the suddenness and permanence of war loss was rapidly transmuted into an ungovernable 'display of fury' and brute force . . . home front conventions of behaviour . . . discouraged relatives, lovers and friends of the war dead from expressing their anguish publicly, but rather impelled them to accept their loss 'for the Empire's sake' soberly and graciously, perhaps thankfully, or even to glory in this act of military sacrifice. Public rage thereby became the Janus face of covert private mourning.[186]

The most celebrated act of violence of the whole campaign was against Hughes, who was hit by an egg when addressing a meeting in the Queensland town of Warwick on 29 November. In the ensuing melee, Hughes rushed into the crowd, demanding the arrest of the assailants and, according to one witness, reaching for the gun that he normally carried in his pocket. Order was restored enough to allow Hughes to deliver a tirade against all and sundry, and then to remonstrate with a local police officer who insisted on applying Queensland rather than Commonwealth law. Hughes would later demand the officer's suspension and prosecution under Commonwealth law.[187]

An official inquiry into the Warwick incident exonerated the police and concluded that Hughes had not been assaulted (apart from the egg). But ever one to make political capital, Hughes seized the opportunity to strengthen federal power by creating a Commonwealth Police Force. It seems that he hoped it would intervene where a state did not enforce Commonwealth law. As he told Munro Ferguson, 'there's going to be *great fight*. Glory be to God for that! I'm trying to make Ryan Fihelly and Co. realise that this is *not* Ireland as the Sinn Fein would have it.' However, the new police force's powers were initially limited to intelligence, counter-sabotage and protecting federal property—activities that had been identified earlier in 1917 as needing nationwide coordination.[188]

The result

By the time Australians went to the polls on 20 December, the campaign had become hysterical. Nothing captured the febrile climate more effectively than 'The Anti's Creed', which was issued by the Reinforcements Referendum Council. Consciously parodying the Nicene creed used over the centuries by Christian denominations, including Catholics, it merits quoting as a collage of loyalist fears and hysteria:

I believe the men at the Front should be sacrificed.

I believe we should turn dog on them.

I believe that our women should betray the men who are fighting for them.

I believe in the sanctity of my own life.

I believe in taking all the benefit and none of the risks.

I believe it was right to sink the *Lusitania*.

I believe in murder on the high seas.

I believe in the I.W.W.

I believe in Sinn Fein.

I believe that Britain should be crushed and humiliated.

I believe in the massacre of Belgian priests.

I believe in the murder of women, and baby-killing.

I believe that Nurse Cavell got her deserts.

I believe that treachery is a virtue.

I believe that disloyalty is true citizenship.

I believe that desertion is ennobling.

I believe in Considine, Fihelly, Ryan, Blackburn, Brookfield, Mannix, and all their works.

I believe in egg power rather than man power.

I believe in holding up transports and hospital ships.

I believe in general strikes.

I believe in burning Australian haystacks.

I believe in mine-laying in Australian waters.

I believe in handing Australia over to Germany.

I believe I'm worm enough to vote No.[189]

Yet on 20 December, the majority of Australia did prove to be 'worms' and voted 'no'. The vote was 1,181,747 'no' and 1,015,159 'yes'. The patterns of voting seemed to have been similar to those of 1916, but the 'no' margin was slightly larger, and Victoria joined New South Wales, Queensland and South Australia in rejecting conscription. Not surprisingly, given Ryan's confrontations with Hughes, Queensland's 'no' vote rose by 22,000. Yet, even in loyal Western Australia, the 'no' vote increased. Only in South Australia did the 'no' vote decline—perhaps because of the disenfranchisement of German-Australians.[190]

The soldiers of the AIF, whose votes were so important to the legitimacy of the government's case, again voted 'yes'. In the weeks leading up to the vote, Pearce had told Birdwood that it was imperative that the AIF be kept out of the firing line and given the best possible conditions. Murdoch, too, was again active in trying to promote Hughes' message to the troops. Even so, the 'yes' vote's margin in the AIF was slight, and it was thought to have come more from men in camps in Britain and on transports rather than those at the front. As Hughes' personal secretary, Percy Deane, wrote, 'Even the soldiers [sic] vote, from which we hoped so much, went adrift, and brought only a narrow majority.' It was probably just was well that it did. Had the soldiers been strongly in favour of conscription, they might have felt betrayed by the home front's rejection. The ambivalence of the AIF to conscription— together, obviously, with the fact that Australia emerged victorious from the war—ensured that the AIF was not susceptible to anything resembling the 'stab in the back' mythology which took hold among German veterans.[191]

Victoria's conversion to the 'no' case was assumed by loyalists to be the work of Mannix. As George Steward, head of the Special Intelligence Bureau, wrote in January 1918:

> I attribute the defeat almost entirely to the Roman Catholic element in this country; particularly do I attach the greatest blame to Dr. Mannix . . . His conduct in Australia would not have permitted him to have lived in Berlin more than twentyfour hours after the mildest of his utterances in this country . . . It may be accepted without the slightest hesitation that ninety per cent. of the Roman Catholics in this country voted 'No', and did all they could to induce others to do likewise . . . I am perfectly satisfied that the chief object before Dr. Mannix is a cherished dream of the Roman Catholics to one day see this country under the rule of Rome.[192]

Percy Deane also wrote:

> Mannix ... practically took charge of the Opposition. All the new
> arguments advanced, were first advanced by him. And underneath it
> all was a crafty sinister appeal to all that was bad—sectarianism, class
> hatred, and the like. He solidified the Irish vote into a wall of Opposition;
> and altogether raised that damnable feeling of bitterness which comes
> always when rival religions face each other at the polls.[193]

However, this was too simplistic. Mannix was based in Melbourne and, while
he did travel to country districts and other states, he was never as prominent
there as he was in his own city. Possibly his provocative rhetoric may even have
persuaded some wavering Protestants to vote 'yes'. Nor was there, whatever
the pro-conscriptionists might have said, a necessary correlation between the
percentage of Catholics or Irish in the population and the 'no' vote. Western
Australia, with almost the same percentage of Catholics as across the Commonwealth, voted 'yes'. Although this might be read as confirming the influence
of the Catholic hierarchy, in that the archbishop of Perth, Dr Clune, and the
Irish Catholic Senator Paddy Lynch supported conscription, there were other
variables at work shaping voting patterns in Western Australia.[194]

Keith Murdoch was probably closer to the mark than Steward when he
attributed the defeat of conscription to a mix of factors: 'the great block vote'
of the trade unions; the Irish vote (which was not 'solid', however); the feeling
that Australia had already done 'her full share under the voluntary system';
the dearth of labour in Australian industry; the need to 'keep an eye on the
Asiatics' and 'a certain distrust' of British policy in the Pacific; local consid-
erations such as the farmers' vote; and women's dislike of 'sending their own
and other people's menfolk into battle', which 'amounted to a moral inability
to vote "yes"'. To this, Murdoch added the fact that Australians had a 'different
view of the war' from the British. There was, he argued,

> the feeling that Australia's duty to Great Britain does not include an
> extreme act of self-denial—i.e. that conscription for European fighting
> does not come within its sphere. No one doubts that Australia would

conscript every man for a war in the Pacific . . . Australia entered the war and continues in it more in support of Great Britain and the Empire than for dislike of Germany. Though Germany is now abhorred, she is so far away that she does not come directly and massively into Australian affairs.

If there was something to be learned from the 'no' vote, Murdoch concluded, it was that Australians thought their troops were being 'overworked'. Letters home and the stories of returned soldiers told of divisions under 'prolonged and intense strain' in 1917. Such stresses would have been tolerated better if the Australian army were being treated as 'a distinctive national effort', with Australians and Birdwood given full authority to command an Australian Army.[195]

The Australian government agreed. In October 1917 it had made its strongest request yet for the grouping of the five Australian divisions in a single command under Birdwood. At last, on 1 November, the Australian Corps came into existence: I Anzac Corps was subsumed into it while II Anzac Corps, containing the New Zealand Division, became the British XXII Corps.

The defeat of the referendum not only meant conscription was dead as a policy option; it also left Hughes with a crisis of legitimacy. During the campaign, he had declared 'that the Government must have this power; it cannot govern the country without it, and will not attempt to do so'. This was a concession to the conscriptionists within his party, but it had the effect of converting the 'no' vote into a vote of no confidence in the government. Some, like Holman, thought Hughes should step aside, making way for Tudor. But Christmas Day was only a few days away, and for Hughes and the nation there was a short breathing space before this issue had to be confronted.[196]

Remembering 1917

In retrospect, it is clear that 1917 was the worst year of the war for Australia. Not only did the conscription debate shatter what remained of civility and consensus at home, but the casualty rate was far higher than in any other year of the conflict. In 1917, over 76,000 Australians were killed, wounded and missing on the Western Front. This was almost twice the number of casualties in France in 1916 and close to three times that of the Gallipoli campaign. The 40,000 Australian deaths in 1917 amounted to two-thirds of all Australian deaths during the war. What made these losses so terrible was not just their scale, but the fact that they occurred three years into the war and seemed to advance the Allied Powers' cause very little. If anything, as the year closed the general strategic situation seemed worse than before.

For many families, this misery was compounded by the fact that so many of the casualties of 1917 on the Western Front were missing: men whose bodies were pulverised by large-calibre shells or swallowed by the mud of Flanders. The fact that they had literally disappeared intensified the anguish of loss. Mothers, wives, siblings and lovers waited, craving for certainty, desperate to learn that their soldier was not dead, but rather captured or wounded.

Not surprisingly, then, it was a monument to the missing that became the dominant site of memory of 1917 in the post-war years. On the outskirts of Ypres, at the point where millions of men set off to battle, the British government erected the Menin Gate in 1927. A huge arch designed by Reginald Bloomfield, its walls were inscribed with the names of 54,896 Allied soldiers who had been lost in the Ypres salient *before 15 August 1917.* So numerous were the missing that the British forces lost after that date were recorded at the nearby Tyne Cot Memorial, which carries the names of a further 35,000 missing.

The Menin Gate soon became a place of commemoration and pilgrimage for many nations. Visitors were drawn by its awesome scale, the heart-rending lists of names it contained and by a ritual that was established soon after 1927. Moved by the playing of the Last Post at the Gate's opening, a local Belgian police superintendent organised a repeat performance of this bugle call every night. With some interruptions, the ritual has continued to this day. Suspended when Germany occupied Belgium in 1940, the playing of the Last Post resumed on the day of Ypres' liberation in September 1944.[197]

Given the distance and cost of travel, many Australians were unable to make the physical journey to the Menin Gate in the 1920s. Yet it became a focus for their mourning too. Some gained consolation from knowing that their relative's name was recorded on such a grand imperial monument.

In May 1928, for example, a friend of a mother of a missing man asked the Australian War Graves Commission for a photograph of the Menin Gate:

> His mother is very old and feeble and it would give her great pleasure, or at least great comfort, to know her son's name is inscribed among those heroes and not forgotten as she now thinks, he was all she had and it was a terrible blow to her.

His name, it eventuated, was on Panel 25, Column 14.[198]

Menin Gate also became a focus for Australians' grief when an official war artist, Will Longstaff, released the painting 'Menin Gate at Midnight' after attending the opening ceremony in 1927. Depicting 'a host of ghostly soldiers' marching before a starkly illuminated Menin Gate towards soil strewn with that quintessential symbol of remembrance, the Flanders poppy, the painting resonated powerfully with bereaved populations. After being displayed in the United Kingdom, where its viewers included the Royal Family, it returned to Australia. Touring the capital cities and regional towns in 1928–29, it attracted record crowds. Thousands of Australians bought copies for charitable purposes, and ultimately it became one of the best-known paintings in the collection of the Australian War Memorial. It now hangs in a darkened room in an environment consciously intended to inspire 'a meditative and spiritual response'. It also adorns hotels in Ypres (Ieper) frequented by battlefield tourists and 'pilgrims'.[199]

The positioning of Menin Gate at the heart of official Australian memory was also aided by the donation by the city of Ypres to the Australian War Memorial in 1936 of two 'Menin Gate lions'. In a reciprocal gesture of friendship, Australia gave Ypres a sculpture, 'Digger', by a wartime member of the Australian War Records Section, C. Web Gilbert. Originally installed on plinths on either side of the Menin Gate and damaged during the war, the lions were ultimately placed at the entrance to the Australian War Memorial. They will be returned temporarily to Ypres during the centenary commemorations of World War I.[200]

Yet for all this, the clashes on the Ypres salient and the other battles of 1917 have a strangely ambiguous place in Australian national memory today. Anecdotally, it seems that few Australians know that the towering cross of sacrifice at Tyne Cot, the largest British cemetery on the Western Front, sits on a pillbox captured by the Australian 3rd Division on 4 October 1917. A dedication inscribed in stone tells the visitor this, but Tyne Cot and 4 October are not central to the national calendar of commemoration. Nor is 12 October, the second and more terrible battle of Passchendaele. Rather, in 2011 the ABC noted the day as the anniversary of the 2005 Bali bombings.

Beyond that, it seems that many battles of 1917—Bullecourt, Messines, Menin Road, Polygon Wood, perhaps even Passchendaele—elude popular cultural imagination. Ghastly though they were, they lacked the form, drama and sense of place that shape a strong heroic narrative. They presented no scaling of cliffs, no climactic moment like the charge at the Nek. They gave centre stage not to courageous individuals—though there were plenty of these—but to artillery, poison gas, air power and all the other lethal technology of mass industrial warfare. If Peter Weir were to make a sequel to *Gallipoli* called *Broodseinde*, we can only wonder what its dramatic climax would be.

Moreover, no battle in 1917 could be constructed as 'a baptism of fire', as were Gallipoli, Fromelles, Pozières and, in the Vietnam War, Long Tan. Instead, the 'bite and hold' operations of September and October 1917 were episodes in the middle of a long war of attrition. The fact that they were successful episodes has been forgotten. Rather, they have been subsumed into a dominant discourse of futility, in which Haig—the supreme British 'donkey'—sacrificed countless of Australian and other 'lions' in a terrible campaign that achieved very little.

Yet there is a contradiction. If the details of the battles of 1917 are vague in the minds of many Australians, the visual imagery of Third Ypres dominates the contemporary representation of the war. Some of the most haunting and well-known photographs of World War I are drawn from late 1917: Australian soldiers marching past the ruins of the Ypres Cloth Hall on 25 October 1917; dead and wounded soldiers huddled in the railway cutting at Broodseinde on 12 October; and five lonely men in single file negotiating a duckboard track through the mud, water and gaunt bare trees of the desolate Chateau Wood near Menin Road. The location may be obscure, but it is these images that have come to stand for all the horrors of the Western Front.

5

1918
Crisis and victory

The year 1918 is routinely described as the year of Allied victory, a victory so comprehensive that a punitive and humiliating peace could be imposed on the Central Powers in 1919 and beyond. Yet this seemed an unlikely outcome as 1918 began. To be sure, the Central Powers were under severe strain. Germany had lost heavily in the campaigns of 1917, and continued to be plagued with economic hardship and political and industrial unrest at home. In January 1918, half a million German workers went on strike over a catalogue of demands including democratic reforms and an end to the war.

By this time, too, the Austro-Hungarian Empire had lost any serious capacity to support its ally. Even though it had cleared its territory of invaders with the defeat of Russia and the routing of the Italians at Caporetto, its heavy industry began to shut down over the winter of 1917–18. With over 70 per cent of its eligible men conscripted, the Hapsburg army could do 'little more than wait passively for the larger conflict to end'. Further east, Bulgaria had fended off the Allies in Macedonia, but internal opposition to its government was growing. The Ottoman economy was sliding into hyperinflation, the central government was losing control of the provinces and, as trade collapsed and agriculture was disrupted by conscription, near-famine conditions and huge refugee movements developed in some regions of its empire.[1]

Yet for all this, the Germans had won the war on the Eastern Front. In early March they would impose a draconian peace, the Treaty of Brest-Litovsk, on the new Soviet Russia and secure massive gains of territory and raw materials. With the German armies invading deep into Ukraine and on to Crimea, Lenin agreed to forfeit over a third of Russia's population (mostly non-Russian speaking) and much of its heavy industry, coal production and best agricultural land. West of the Brest-Litovsk–Riga line, Germany and Austria-Hungary were left controlling Poland and the Baltic states of Courland and Lithuania. If it chose, the German command had the flexibility to move more than half a million soldiers to the Western Front. It had a window of opportunity to defeat the British and French armies before American troops arrived in force.

The Allied Powers, in contrast, had lost Russia as an ally and suffered huge casualties in 1917. Australia was not alone in finding it difficult to replace this manpower. To offset this, there were a number of positive developments: the mastering of the U-boat threat, the growth in British war production and the belligerency of the United States. But these were medium- to long-term advantages. Therefore, 1919 seemed the earliest year in which the Allies might win the war.

This was the point at which the war might have ended with a mutual recognition of exhaustion. Indeed, in the winter of 1917–18, there were some further attempts to negotiate a peace. The South African leader General Jan Smuts, acting on behalf of the British government, met with a former Austrian ambassador to London in December 1917. The German and Austrian foreign ministries also, to the fury of Hindenburg and Ludendorff, issued a declaration on 25 December 1917 offering to negotiate a general peace without annexations or indemnities if the Allies would do likewise. However, like all previous peace feelers, these initiatives faltered and withered. Despite nearly three and a half years of slaughter, there was still no possibility of compromise or consensus between the warring powers.

Allied war aims

However, the question of what the Allies would demand in any peace settlement was becoming a matter of public debate, both domestically and internationally. This was partly because, in late 1917, the Soviet government of Russia published the secret treaties that the Tsarist government had signed with various Allied powers. Since these detailed predatory territorial annexations and deals regarding spheres of influence in the post-war world, their release was a public relations disaster for the Allies. It shattered their moral authority among liberals at home and within the United States, where Woodrow Wilson was formulating a very different view of the post-war order.

Feeling obliged to articulate Britain's war aims more clearly, Lloyd George addressed a meeting of trade unionists at Caxton Hall on 5 January 1918. Britain, he said, was not seeking to destroy Germany. However, the independence of Belgium and the restoration of Alsace-Lorraine to France were non-negotiable elements of any post-war settlement. Austria-Hungary should grant self-government and democracy to those of its nationalities that wanted them. Poland should become independent. Turkey might retain the genuinely Turkish parts of its empire, but no more. Germany's former colonies, meanwhile, might be placed under governments acceptable to their inhabitants and an international organisation should be established to reduce armaments and the probability of wars in the future.[2]

Within days, Lloyd George was trumped by President Wilson, who issued his Fourteen Points on 8 January 1918. A fundamentally important document in twentieth-century history, the Fourteen Points included the need in the post-war world for open diplomacy (no more secret treaties); 'absolute' freedom of navigation on the seas in war and peace (in contrast to the blockade and unrestricted submarine warfare of the war years); the removal of economic barriers to trade; the reduction of armaments to the 'lowest point consistent with domestic safety'; the impartial adjustment of all colonial claims; the evacuation of occupied Russia and 'the independent determination' of its political development; the creation of an independent Poland with secure access to the sea; the evacuation and restoration of Belgium; the return of Alsace-Lorraine to France; the 'autonomous' development of the peoples of Austria-Hungary and the Ottoman empire; and the creation of a 'general association of nations'—that is, a League of Nations—for the purpose of guaranteeing political independence and territorial integrity to all states. It was an ambitious liberal internationalist agenda for the peace, serving notice on the Allies as to what the United States would tolerate, enticing the Bolsheviks to stay in the war and appealing to liberals and progressive elements in all belligerent countries.

This, it must be said, was a vision of the peace that was emphatically not shared by Hughes. For him, the world was not one of idealism, self-determination and altruistic negotiation but of realism, raw power, ceaseless conflict and Manichaean oppositions. He had nothing but contempt for Wilson's 'sermonising', particularly since the United States had entered the war so late. Moreover, he had no intention of renouncing Australia's right to annexations or indemnities. On the contrary, as he saw it, Australia was entitled to share in the fruits of a total victory. It deserved to keep German New Guinea as a guarantee of its future security, while Germany itself should be crippled economically and militarily, forced to pay the costs of the war and be crushed so profoundly that it could never again threaten global peace. Even the peace terms implied in Lloyd George's Caxton Hall speech were too liberal for Hughes and his Nationalist colleagues. Indeed, during the conscription campaign, they had denounced similar views as disloyal and dangerous.[3]

Hughes, the great survivor

For much of 1918 and 1919, Hughes would devote his formidable energies to fighting those who sought to impose Wilson's world-view on the peace process, but for the moment in January 1918 his focus was on keeping hold on power at home. Having promised during the conscription campaign to resign if the vote was 'no', he was now under considerable pressure to do so. Even though his government still commanded a majority in parliament, Hughes himself, exhausted and frustrated by the second defeat of conscription, was tempted for a time to stand down.

However, as in late 1916, the question was who would replace him. Should there be a Labor government led by Tudor? A Nationalist government led by someone less divisive than Hughes? Or even a coalition government of

Nationalists and Labor? The Cabinet, meeting on 27 December 1917 and 2 January 1918, agreed to refer the matter to the Nationalist Party. However, when the Nationalists met on 3 January they struggled for two days without finding a solution. The option of calling another election—something that Irvine favoured—was rejected, supposedly because it would be treachery to the Allies to allow Labor to come to power since it might withdraw from the war. This was not as self-serving as it might sound, given the growing demand within the labour movement for a negotiated peace. Eventually the Nationalists passed an almost unanimous vote of confidence in Hughes (63 votes to two, the two being from Western Australia). But the vote was possibly 'une politesse', as Forrest called it, and it seemed that some in the party thought that Hughes should resign even if there were no obvious alternative. (The fact that a backbencher, Austin Chapman, was proposed in a second resolution as the leader of the government confirmed this!) The matter was returned to the Cabinet to resolve.[4]

After two more inconclusive Cabinet meetings, Hughes presented his resignation to the governor-general on 8 January. As it happened, relations between the two men had deteriorated during 1917 and Munro Ferguson was tiring of the prime minister's chaotic and confrontational style of leadership. He thought Hughes should stand down to 'avoid any suspicion of trickery or equivocation', but he asked him to continue to lead the administration until a new commission was issued.[5]

A frenetic day of lobbying and manoeuvring followed as Munro Ferguson consulted with a succession of politicians at Government House, Melbourne. Tudor assured the governor-general that he had as good a prospect of governing successfully as Hughes had had when Labor split in late 1916. However, Labor lacked the majority in parliament to govern in its own right, and it seemed impossible for Tudor to persuade his Labor caucus to join a coalition government. The Nationalists, then, would have to continue in power—but under whose leadership? Cook and Watt claimed that Hughes was the only person able to hold the two elements of the Nationalist Party together, even though there was a widespread desire for change on the back bench. Forrest, on the other hand, denounced Hughes' autocratic ways and muttered repeatedly during a two-hour interview with Munro Ferguson that it was a case of '*aut Caesar aut nihil*' (either Caesar or nothing). As Forrest saw it, *he* was a compromise candidate. He was, he claimed, popular with all classes of society, including Catholics, was more acceptable than Hughes to Labor parliamentarians and had the necessary experience in the public sector. Munro Ferguson thought this was 'one of the most promising solutions of the problem', but then found that Forrest was blackballed by Cook and Watt, who had often clashed with him in Cabinet. Forrest, they argued, would not be able to command a majority in parliament, and had lost rather than gained support.

So it fell to Hughes, the great survivor, to form a new government. However, Munro Ferguson took the opportunity to lecture him on the merits of including some Labor politicians in his administration and on the need to reform the chaotic management of government business.

> I reminded him [Munro Ferguson reported to London] that ... the Prime Minister's Department was becoming a 'dead-end' into which important business of all kinds was switched but from which little or nothing issued. I have often urged on the Prime Minister that he should attach a polite letter-writer to his office so that Ministers and others who write to him might at any rate be placated by the receipt of a civil answer. He has, however, never had the elements of a business training and his naturally secretive, accaparative [hoarding] nature makes it difficult for him to let any single thing go out of his own hand.[6]

The next day, Tudor moved a vote of censure in the House of Representatives, claiming Hughes should have honoured his pledge to resign 'not in the breach but in the observance', even if this meant Labor coming to power or parliament being dissolved. But the motion was lost 43 to nineteen. Hughes' domination of Australian federal politics was now secure. He would remain prime minister until 1922, while Forrest—thwarted in his dream of being prime minister—had to settle for a peerage that was bestowed on him a month later. In March, he resigned from office, allowing Hughes to reconstruct his cabinet as Munro Ferguson had advised and to give Watt the Treasury. Late in July Forrest set sail for London to seek medical treatment and to take up his seat in the House of Lords. However, he died on 3 September 1918 while the ship on which he was travelling was anchored off Sierra Leone.

The political crisis was resolved, but Hughes' credibility with the Australian public had taken a further hammering and he was shattered emotionally. He wrote to Keith Murdoch in London:

> The [referendum] result was a bitter bitter pill to swallow—the soldiers' vote the most bitter of all . . . I have been through many Hells [sic] since I last saw you but in some respects the last month or 6 weeks has been the bitterest and worst of all. How *do* you account for the soldiers' vote? How *do* I account for the Australian vote say you? Well Sinn Fein I.W.W. selfishness and sentimental vote of the women: AND WAR-WEARINESS!!! *War-weariness* of a people who have escaped all the consequences of this awful war! But there it is. And upon my head these rotters have visited the consequences of Australia's failure to do her duty.
>
> What I felt when the result was beyond doubt I cannot tell you now—some day when I see you face to face when I can pour out the anguish and anger seething within me, and in burning words into your very ear I can make you understand what I feel . . . Damn everyone and everything!![7]

Jericho and Amman

During these first months of 1918, the Australian Corps was positioned in the region of Armentières and Messines. Haig was expecting the Germans to attack in the spring, and the focus of all British forces during the winter was on honing their skills in defence in depth, since their experience on the Western Front thus far had been in taking the offensive. The Australians also maintained patrols and, when the numbers of enemy facing them seemed to warrant it, launched raids.

Members of the 4th Australian Light Horse Regiment on the way to water their horses at Auja, in the Jordan Valley, May 1918. The need for water was a constant constraint on operations in this theatre. (AWM B00032)

The controversial photograph purportedly of the charge of the 4th Light Horse Brigade at Beersheba on 31 October 1917 is almost certainly of a re-enactment. (AWM A02684)

The 1st Australian Light Horse Brigade making its way from Judea to the Jordan Valley prior to the attack on Jericho in February 1918. (AWM B01468)

The main action at this time was in the Middle East. Keen as ever to find some alternative to the Western Front, Lloyd George's government decided in early 1918 to reinforce the British forces in Palestine, wind back the Mesopotamian campaign and concentrate on Allenby's advancing from Jerusalem to Aleppo in Syria. This campaign would involve Allenby's armies first pushing up the Jordan Valley to a line stretching from Haifa on the coast to Tiberius on Lake Tiberius (the Sea of Galilee). The Arab forces operating near the Dead Sea would meanwhile cut the Hejaz railway supplying Arabia where it passed along the high plateau to the east of the Jordan at Amman.[8]

In a preliminary adjustment of the British line, Chetwode's XX Corps, including the Anzac Mounted Division, set off from near Jerusalem on 19 February to capture Jericho and the bank of the Jordan. This was the wilderness of biblical fame, barren and stony and with tracks across the hills that were steep and narrow. Men had to dismount and lead their horses in single file and there was no chance of bringing up artillery support on the sides to dislodge the Ottomans from their well-entrenched positions. Eventually, however, the infantry fought their way through and the horsemen were able to advance onto the Jordan River plain. The Ottomans withdrew from Jericho, leaving the British imperial forces controlling the west bank of the Jordan from the Dead Sea to the Wadi Auja.

From this point Allenby planned to strike eastwards to take Amman and destroy the strategically important tunnel and viaduct of the Hejaz railway. On 21–23 March, the 60th Division, the Anzac Mounted Division and the Imperial Camel Brigade fought their way across the Jordan despite strong enemy fire and the river being swollen by floods. Once on the east bank, they headed up the bare, precipitous hills towards Es Salt and Amman. Es Salt was taken without difficulty, but the approach to Amman proved slow and difficult. Again the tracks were too narrow to bring up any significant number of guns. When the rain started, they became impassable. The wadis flooded and the ground froze. Even worse, because local Arab tribes had been told of the attack in the hope that they would join it, all security was lost.

By the time the British forces had reached Amman, the Ottomans had brought in reinforcements and were waiting for them relatively well armed. The attack on Amman on 27 March failed, and subsequent attacks over the next two days—when reinforcements had come in from Es Salt—went no better. It even seemed that the Ottomans might cut the British forces between Amman and Es Salt. Hence on 30 March, the British command decided to withdraw. By 2 April, the entire force—swollen with refugees from Es Salt whom the retreating Light Horsemen and cameleers carried on their saddles through the freezing night—was back on the west bank of the Jordan. One important bridgehead across the Jordan, at Ghornaiye, remained in the hands of the EEF. It had suffered more than 1300 casualties, half of whom were Australians or New Zealanders. It was the first defeat since Second Gaza.

The German spring offensive

Frustrating though this setback was, it was immediately eclipsed by dramatic events in France. On 21 March, the Germans began the first of a series of offensives on the Western Front that almost won them the war (see Map 27). This was Ludendorff's high-risk gamble, an attempt to use the troops liberated by Russia's collapse on the Eastern Front to defeat the British and the French while the strategic balance was perhaps still in Germany's favour.

The first offensive, code-named Michael, was launched in the region of the 1916 Somme battlefields. Its aim was to drive a wedge between the British and French armies at their point of junction, forcing the British back towards the Channel ports and the French towards Paris. Three German armies—the Seventeenth, Second and Eighteenth—would attack the Third and Fifth British Armies between Cambrai and St Quentin. The Seventeenth Army under Otto von Below, who had recently defeated the Italians at Caporetto, would drive for Bapaume while the Second Army under Georg von der Marwitz, who had planned the successful German counter-attack at Cambrai, would head for Péronne. Both armies would then swing right and roll up the British line that stretched north.

The offensive started at 4.40 a.m on 21 March with an intense and concentrated bombardment of 6473 guns (including 2435 heavy pieces)

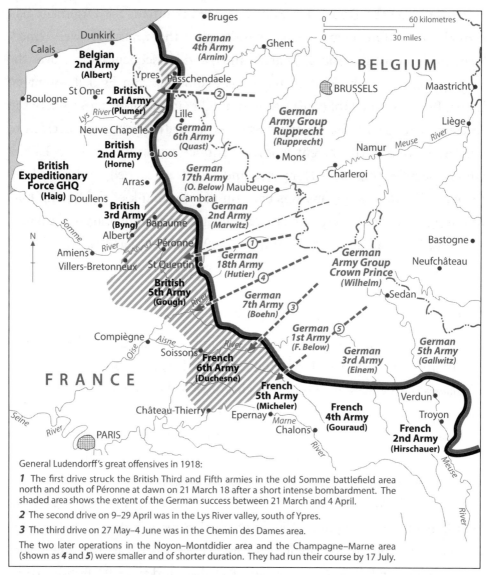

General Ludendorff's great offensives in 1918:

1 The first drive struck the British Third and Fifth armies in the old Somme battlefield area north and south of Péronne at dawn on 21 March 18 after a short intense bombardment. The shaded area shows the extent of the German success between 21 March and 4 April.

2 The second drive on 9–29 April was in the Lys River valley, south of Ypres.

3 The third drive on 27 May–4 June was in the Chemin des Dames area.

The two later operations in the Noyon–Montdidier area and the Champagne–Marne area (shown as **4** and **5**) were smaller and of shorter duration. They had run their course by 17 July.

Map 27: German offensives, March to July 1918

and 2532 trench mortars firing 1.16 million shells in some five hours. In contrast, the British had fired 1.5 million shells over seven days in June 1916. Taking the Allied armies by surprise, the barrage moved relentlessly between front- and rear-line targets, drenching the Allied forces with high explosive, shrapnel and gas. The infantry attack that followed was spearheaded by stormtrooper units, many of whom were veterans of the war in the east. Experienced in a war of movement, they dashed across the battlefield in small groups, sheltering under the deep fog that lasted until noon, the creeping barrage or any other cover they could find. Penetrating deep into the enemy lines and eliminating opposition with grenades or light machine guns, they moved constantly onwards, even if their flanks were uncovered and pockets of enemy resistance remained behind. These they left to be destroyed by follow-up 'battle unit' divisions, armed with heavier machine guns, flamethrowers, field artillery and engineering equipment.[9]

These tactics were not radically new, nor unique to the German army, as has often been thought. By this stage of the war, the Allied Powers had also developed small-group tactics as a way of penetrating dense German defences. But on 21 March, Gough's Fifth Army simply collapsed under the tidal wave of men and metal that engulfed it. His fifteen divisions were outnumbered, spread too thinly and positioned too far forward. In fact, across the Western Front in spring 1918, the British had about 75,000 fewer troops than at the start of 1917, a situation that was attributable in part to manpower shortages, but also to the fact that Lloyd George was restricting Haig's supply of manpower for fear he would waste it on new futile offensives. In addition, the British decision to reinforce the Middle East meant that the Empire now had, to quote J.P. Harris, 'a surplus of troops in peripheral theatres . . . and was dangerously weak where it really mattered, on the Western Front'. Beyond that, Haig was expecting the German offensive to come in Flanders, not the Somme, and was therefore holding his eight reserve divisions in the north. Assuming that the British armies in the line would be able hold any German attack for up to eighteen days, Haig had also granted 88,000 troops leave in Britain on the eve of the attack. Finally, a reserve of 120,000 troops was also being held in Britain, partly because it was thought that this would simulate the British economy.[10]

Hence, by nightfall on 21 March, the Germans had achieved the unthinkable. They had broken through the British lines into open territory while the Fifth Army was retreating to the Somme, the only natural defensive line behind it. Further north, the Third Army—which held better positions and faced less fog—managed to hold its line for a while. But the collapse of the Fifth Army left it exposed on its right.

In the following days, the Germans maintained the momentum of their attack—again, something not seen on the Western Front for years. By 23 March, a breach 64 kilometres long had opened up in the British front. Desperate military police and officers threatened troops at gunpoint in an effort to staunch the collapse, but the withdrawals continued all along the line. The British were pushed back across the land won at such terrible cost in 1916 and 1917—Thiepval, Pozières, Mouquet Farm, Bullecourt—until by 4 April they were within sight of Villers-Bretonneux. This small town was only 20 kilometres to the east of Amiens, a vital centre of Allied road and rail communications. If Amiens were lost, supplying the British armies in the Somme region would be impossible.

With the military situation reaching crisis point, the British and French at last conceded the need for a more unified inter-Allied command. Meeting in the elegant Hotel de Ville of Doullens, 30 kilometres north of Amiens, on 26 March, they agreed that Foch should become Generalissimo of Allied Forces, a kind of supreme commander with responsibility for coordinating the action of the Allied armies on the Western Front. Energetic and decisive, Foch was committed to covering Amiens at all costs—unlike Pétain, who proposed withdrawing the French armies to protect Paris. Two days later, the unfortunate Gough was replaced by Rawlinson. The shattered Fifth Army, in turn, was renamed the Fourth Army on 2 April.

Though Allied leaders did not know it as they met so close to the front at Doullens, the momentum of the German attack towards Amiens was actually slowing. There were several reasons for this. First, the spectacular speed of the stormtroopers slicing their way through the British lines was ultimately a source of vulnerability. They soon outran the support of their artillery and were forced to rely for protection on the light weapons they carried. Exhaustion set in and they began to suffer heavy casualties. Second, the Second Army's rapid advance took it into the battlefields of 1916, a landscape scarred and pitted with shell holes and trenches. The German supply system could not keep up with the troops, particularly as Ludendorff had expected to have more success against the Third Army, towards Arras, rather than against the Fifth Army. After two days of rapid pursuit, the advance troops began to run out of essential supplies. Looting and drunkenness broke out as hungry and thirsty German soldiers raided stores left behind by the retreating British.

More fundamentally, the German military leaders had failed to give due thought to how to exploit the dramatic breakthrough that their armies had achieved. In a dangerously simplistic formulation, Ludendorff had declared that his armies would tear a hole in the enemy line and everything else would follow. But wars are won not by taking land but by destroying armies. Having broken through the British lines, the Germans needed to encircle and destroy them. Yet for this they needed pursuit forces, and what remained of the German cavalry was still deployed in the east, while German war industries had not produced the tanks and armoured vehicles that could have given their armies strategic mobility. Even more seriously, Ludendorff failed to focus his armies' attacks in a strategic way. Rather than consolidating the gains made by the Michael offensive and concentrating on exploiting the breakthrough near Amiens, he chose instead early in April to launch another offensive to the north in Flanders.

Hébuterne and Dernancourt

The AIF was drawn into the fighting in the Somme region within days of the German attack. On 25 March, the 3rd and 4th Divisions together with the New Zealand Division were ordered to move south from Messines. Approaching the battle zone, they came across scenes of chaos and panic: French villagers fleeing homes that were under threat for the first time in the war and British soldiers retreating, exhausted and disheartened. Finding villages stocked with food and wine, the Australians took the chance to indulge themselves. Whether this was resourcefulness—a characteristic for which the Anzac digger has been celebrated—or looting is a matter of perspective. As Bean saw it, it was not easy 'for the authorities to determine ... where reasonable "salvage"—or use of abandoned property—ended and reprehensible looting began'.[11]

Once in the battle zone, the Australians were immediately deployed to points where the British lines were close to breaking. The 4th Brigade was rushed to the vicinity of Hébuterne, between Doullens and Bapaume, where the British 19th Division (IV Corps) was close to collapse after being reduced to only 2000 men during the previous days' fighting. Some of them wept on learning that they were to be relieved.

Once in position, the Australians held off a succession of German attempts to break through over the next few days. Then, as the situation settled into more static warfare, they began 'nibbling' at the Germans. Battalions or companies acting on their own initiative seized a sap here, a length of sunken road there. So successful were they in these roles that, at the request of the IV Corps commander, they stayed at Hébuterne for another month. The New Zealand Division, which had filled the southern part of the gap, remained with IV Corps for the rest of the war.[12]

A little to the south, the 4th Division's other two brigades (the 12th and 13th) and the 3rd Division were tasked with stemming another potential break in the British lines. A triangle of critically important land formed by the convergence of the Somme and its tributary, the Ancre, had been left open when the British 9th and 35th Divisions (VII Corps) had started to withdraw after misinterpreting their orders. They left a gap of about 16 kilometres through which the Germans, who occupied Morlancourt on 26 March, could drive to Amiens. Adding to the urgency was the fact that, on the afternoon of 27 March, the Germans pushed past the left edge of the British Fifth Army and crossed the River Somme at the town of Cerisy, a little further to the east. Potentially, they could now move westwards, re-cross the Somme and attack the British Third Army from the rear.

After an exhausting 34-kilometre march over the night and day of 26 and 27 March, the 4th Division took up positions at Dernancourt along an almost indefensible railway stretching south from Albert. That same night, 5000 men of the 3rd Division (10th and 11th Brigades) were bussed to occupy a line of old trenches across the enemy path stretching from the Ancre to Sailly-Le-Sec on the Somme. The timing was exquisitely tight. Looking down from

Franvillers at daybreak on 27 March, Monash could see the Germans pushing back scattered troops of the British cavalry near Morlancourt: 'It was really a question of an hour one way or the other whether we could intercept him or not. You can imagine the state of my mind,' he wrote later. He almost expected any minute to 'be mopped up by Bosch armoured cars'.[13]

The precarious situation was stabilised over the following days as the Australians and the British 35th Division stopped wave after wave of sometimes desperate German attacks. The Australian 12th and 13th Brigades at Dernancourt were under-strength and significantly outnumbered. On 5 April, for instance, about 4000 Australians faced an attack by some three German divisions of 25,000 men. But with the skilful leadership of Brigadier-Generals John Gellibrand and William Glasgow, and battalions mounting local counter-attacks that kept the German attackers off balance, the Australian line was held. Just as the brigades seemed to be at the limits of their ability to resist, the Germans called off their attack. Although the Australians then failed in their own efforts to recapture the villages of Dernancourt, Morlancourt and Sailly-Laurette, a little further along the Somme, the situation in the triangle to the north of the Somme was under control by 30 March. The line from the Somme to the Albert–Amiens road was now held by the 3rd and 4th Divisions, while the crossings of the Somme a little to the east, at Corbie, were being defended by the 15th Brigade of the Australian 5th Division, which had also been rushed to the Somme region in the last days of March.[14]

Monash was immensely proud of the 3rd Division's achievements at this critical time. His post-war account of the Australian victories in 1918 described the arrival of the 10th and 11th Brigades in their buses early on 27 March as a 'spectacle that . . . will be ever memorable to me, as one of the most inspiring sights of the whole war':

Here was the Third Division—the 'new chum' Division, which, in spite of its great successes in Belgium and Flanders, had never been able to boast, like its sister Divisions, that it had been 'down on the Somme'— come into its own at last, and called upon to prove its mettle. And then there was the thought that they were going to measure themselves, man to man, against an enemy who, skulking behind his field works, had for so long pounded them to pieces in their trenches, poisoned them with gas, and bombed them as they slept in their billets.[15]

Presumably others in the 3rd Division, like Monash, thought that the Somme, rather than Flanders, was the ultimate validation of their courage and reputation. When it came to choose the site of its memorial after the war, the division settled on Sailly-le-Sec, not Messines or Passchendaele (Third Ypres), which are more renowned battles today. Its austere obelisk was placed just north of Sailly-le-Sec on the side of a road between Corbie and Bray-sur-Somme, the point that, to Monash at least, represented 'literally, the end of the great German advance in this part of the field'.[16]

Villers-Bretonneux

In fact, the Germans were still advancing south of the Somme in the hope of capturing Amiens. Even though the main focus of their offensive was turning to Flanders, Hindenburg still saw Amiens as worth capturing. If this nodal point of communications fell into German hands, the Allied armies would be 'cleft in twain and the tactical breakthrough [of Michael] converted into a strategic wedge, with England on one side and France on the other'. Throughout April, therefore, the Germans made a number of attempts to capture Villers-Bretonneux. Despite its strategic importance, the town's defences were in a poor state, given that the Somme sector had been quiet after the Germans withdrew to the Hindenburg Line in early 1917.[17]

The first German attack came on 30 March, when eight divisions attacked on either side of the Roman road that stretches east–west through the town. To the north of the road, the attack was contained, as was an assault that the Germans launched at noon against the 3rd Division across the river at Morlancourt. However, to the south of the road the exhausted British infantry fell back towards the woods less than 2 kilometres from the town. Villers-Bretonneux was in danger of falling, and the 3rd Division's 9th Brigade was transferred to the British 31st Division with orders to counter-attack to the south-east of the town that afternoon.[18]

Although they knew little about the position of many of the British troops and had no artillery support, the 33rd Battalion attacked at 3.10 p.m. with the 34th Battalion supporting it and the British 12th Lancers riding ahead of them, complete 'with their gleaming lances and swords'. Passing 'several bodies of troops peculiarly and uselessly entrenched in queer places, and large bodies of stragglers', the 33rd managed with heavy losses to reach the German line and dig in along the edge of the Bois de Morgemont. Leslie Morshead, its commander, later wrote:

> together with the 12th Lancers we made an attack on nearly a three mile front . . . The cavalry acted as an advanced guard and cleared the way for our attack. The odds were very great—we had no artillery— the greatest that I have ever experienced, but our fellows got there. I was never so proud a man as on that day. They fought magnificently . . . But of course we had to pay the price. Still it was worth it for the good it did can never be estimated. It did much to stop the rot and very much to stop the advance on Amiens.

In recognition of the role the Lancers played in clearing the Bois de Morgemont, Australians called it Lancer Wood thereafter.[19]

The German assault on Villers-Bretonneux paused for a few days while their exhausted troops rested. This offered the Australians the chance to empty the now devastated town of food and wine, confirming for the British their reputation for poor discipline. But Talbot Hobbs and Charles Rosenthal thought the British troops were more guilty of looting, and Pompey Elliott was scathing about the quality of the British troops in his area. Apprehending a British captain with a mess cart full of champagne in Corbie, he issued an order stating that the next officer caught looting would be summarily hanged in the Corbie square, where his body would dangle as a deterrent! Anglo-Australian relations, already strained, were not improved by this soon infamous order.[20]

One Australian officer was breakfasting on chicken and champagne when the Germans next attacked Villers-Bretonneux with fifteen divisions on 4 April (see Map 28). To the north of the Roman road the British line was now held by the 14th Division—men who had been on the move for the previous two nights and had never seen in daylight the ground they now had to defend. They were soon forced back by the German 4th Guard Division past Hamel to Hill 104, a vital shoulder about a kilometre east of the town overlooking Neuville, Corbie and Fouilly. Some stragglers crossed the river and seeped through Elliott's 15th Brigade, defending the bridges on the Somme. Elliott was not surprised:

> As I expected from the manner in which they [14th Division] were holding the line, they gave way very badly . . . great numbers flung down their arms and ran away. The cavalry . . . were consequently forced to give ground, and the situation looked disastrous.[21]

To the south of the Roman road, the situation was also precarious. The German assault cut through the Allied line, capturing the woods south of Villers-Bretonneux and even reaching the monument to the Franco-Prussian war of 1870–71 on the town's outskirts. However, the situation was stabilised in the late afternoon, when the Australian 36th Battalion, supported by

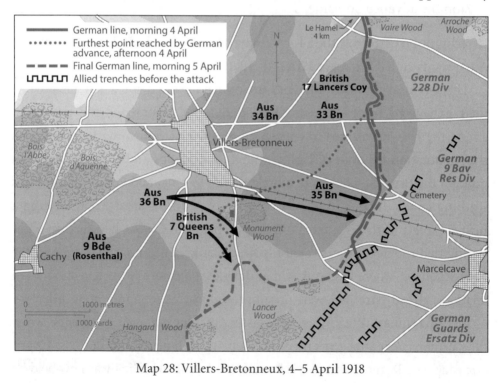

Map 28: Villers-Bretonneux, 4–5 April 1918

the 35th Battalion, and British cavalry, counter-attacked south of Villers-Bretonneux. Losing a quarter of its strength as it swept forward into intense machine-gun fire, the 36th clawed back some of what had been lost earlier in the day, including Monument Wood. The 35th pushed the Germans back to where they began the day. Meanwhile, Elliott to the north was allowed his head and the 15th Brigade crossed the Somme to join the British cavalry in retaking Hill 104. For the moment, Villers-Bretonneux was safe.[22]

Still the Germans kept trying to force their way forward. On 5 April, they tried three times to recapture Hill 104 while also attacking north of the Somme at Dernancourt. Here the 12th Brigade of the 4th Division was trying to hold its precarious position along the railway embankment running close to the town. Under intense fire, including gas—one officer thought the barrage the heaviest since Pozières—and with no artillery support because of the mist, some sections of the Australian line crumbled. The German infantry poured through, forcing the 47th Battalion—whose dead and injured were 'everywhere underfoot'—to withdraw through the 48th Battalion's positions. George Mitchell recalled that:

At 1.15 p.m. a bunch of men suddenly burst over the hill. Some were wounded. Some fell as they ran. Went to meet them. Asked one man what had happened. He pointed to his face. Rags of flesh were all that was left of his lower jaw . . . The world had fallen. The Australian line had been broken. Not even pride was left. Tears of grief ran down my face.[23]

Yet the German intrusion was narrow and, with the higher ground still in Australian hands, the ugly situation was somehow contained. In the afternoon, the 13th Brigade joined the survivors of the 12th to counter-attack and push the Germans back.

Flanders

Intense though these see-sawing battles for Villers-Bretonneux were, the main thrust of the German spring offensive was shifting to Flanders. On 9 April,

Ludendorff launched Operation Georgette (known to the British as the Battle of the Lys), an attack by his Sixth and Fourth armies across a 17–18-kilometre front to the south of Ypres. The British forces in this sector were now relatively weak. Not only had Haig creamed off the best forces to stem the crisis further south, but many of the troops in Flanders had been retired there after their mauling around the Somme in March. In the vicinity of Neuve Chapelle, the line was held by three brigades of the Portuguese Corps, who were about to be relieved after a year in the trenches.[24]

Hence, when the Germans attacked after drenching the front with phosgene and mustard gas, and shellfire from some 900 guns (the British had only 200), they penetrated some 5–6 kilometres within the first day. The Portuguese troops gave way almost completely. On 10 April, Armentières had to be abandoned and the Germans were threatening Hazebrouck, a rail junction as vital to the Allied position in the north as Amiens was further south. From this point, supply lines radiated out to the channel ports of Calais, Dunkirk and Boulogne. If Hazebrouck fell into German hands, their artillery could target the vast complex of depots and reinforcement camps lying between Ypres and the English Channel.

It was a moment when the war's outcome seemed to hang in the balance. So important was Hazebrouck to the British war effort that the usually imperturbable Haig was moved on 11 April to issue a *cri de coeur* to all ranks in the British armies in France and Flanders:

> Many amongst us now are tired. To those I would say that victory will belong to the side which holds out the longest. The French Army is moving rapidly and in great force to our support. There is no other course open to us but to fight it out! Every position must be held to the last man; there must be no retirement. With our backs to the wall, and believing in the justice of our cause each one of us must fight on to the end. The safety of our Homes and the Freedom of mankind alike depend upon the conduct of each of us at this critical moment.

Supposedly, some British troops thought this appeal insulting—a reflection perhaps on the high command's morale rather than their own—but according to Bean it brought the usually cynical Australians to 'the highest pitch of determination'.[25]

On 11 April, the Australian 1st Division, which had recently arrived on the Somme and was on its way to relieve the 3rd Division, was turned around to join the battle in Flanders. Delayed by the shelling of Amiens railway station, it arrived in time to relieve British forces who were exhausted after successfully holding the Germans about 8 kilometres from Hazebrouck. With a self-assurance that bordered on arrogance, the Australians shouted, 'Mind you don't get drowned in the Channel' at some British troops drifting back.[26]

The Germans continued to attack on 13, 14 and, finally, 17 April. But the forces against them were mounting. Foch, proving more supportive than Pétain, sent two corps of his Détachement d'Armée du Nord while British reinforcements were rapidly extracted from Italy, Palestine and Egypt. The British command was also willing, having learned the lessons of 1917, to withdraw from territory that was indefensible. Painfully, in mid-April they surrendered to the Germans the Passchendaele ridge and other wastelands that so many men had died to take only months before. As a British officer lamented:

> the elements of five divisions holding the line outside Ypres trailed back over the greasy duckboard tracks, past the loathsome stagnant pools, the rusting wrecks of tanks, the still unburied bodies. Four out of the five divisions of the withdrawing troops had participated in the gruesome attacks to seize this unspeakable wilderness, and now the survivors of the earlier disasters covered in two nights the ground that had taken them three months to win.[27]

Finally the Germans were stopped 8 kilometres short of Hazebrouck. Although on 25 April they captured Mount Kemmel, an important high feature to the west of Messines, by 29 April Ludendorff had to conclude that this offensive too had failed, at a huge cost, to achieve any strategic benefit or decisive result.

Recruitment battles

With the Australian divisions again suffering major losses on the Western Front, the question of recruitment flared up once more at home. Voluntary enlistment had sunk to record lows in January, February and March 1918: 2344, 1918 and 1518 respectively. This was despite the fact that since April 1917 the minimum height for recruits had been 5 feet (1.52 metres), as compared to 5 feet 6 inches (1.67 metres) at the start of the war. Height restrictions had been lowered progressively: to 5 feet 4 inches (1.63 metres) in February 1915; 5 feet 3 inches (1.60 metres) in May 1915; and 5 feet 2 inches (1.57 metres) in July 1915.[28]

Those responsible for recruitment agonised over the reasons for their failure. Was the pay for soldiers' dependants too low? Were men deterred by the news that recruits who were passed as fit in Australia were rejected when they reached the front? Were reports that ex-soldiers were begging on the streets of Newcastle accurate? Were under-age recruits and men with minor disabilities being sent back to Australia only to be denied their deferred pay and their discharged soldier's badge? Would enlistment be more attractive if men were able to sign on for a fixed term of 18 to 24 months rather than the current 'endless nature of the term'? Men recruited in 1914 had not yet had any home leave.

As the despairing Director-General of Recruiting, Donald Mackinnon, saw it, the real problem was the poisonous legacy of the two conscription debates. Recruitment, he believed, had to be quarantined from bipartisan politics and placed in neutral hands. Sceptical Australians had to be persuaded that conscription had finally been renounced as a policy option and that the government's estimate of the numbers of recruits required was credible. The Chief Justice of Australia, Sir Samuel Griffith, was therefore charged with making a definitive ruling on the enlistment needed to maintain the current five Australian divisions in France and other Australian forces overseas. Unhelpfully, he concluded in March that ideally an average of 8233 volunteers per month would be required. This was clearly unrealistic, and the authorities compromised on a target of 5400 per month—still more than triple the March 1918 figure.[29]

When, on 1 April, Lloyd George pleaded with the Dominions to reinforce their troops 'in the fullest possible manner, and with the smallest possible delay', Munro Ferguson was inspired to intervene. He had always taken a keen interest in recruitment, which—as a matter of prime concern to the British Crown, which he represented—he deemed a 'fit subject for the Governor-General to take under his care'. Agreeing with Mackinnon that the issue should be above party politics, he convened a conference at Government House with the aim of generating a bipartisan consensus. Everyone with political or industrial influence was invited: the leaders of all federal and state political parties, employer associations, trades and labor councils and senior union representatives. Only the Queensland Industrial Council and the Tasmanian Trades and Labour Council refused to come.[30]

The conference began on 12 April with Munro Ferguson paraphrasing Dante's *Inferno*: 'Abandon strife all ye that enter here!' But the proceedings rapidly became 'somewhat heated'. Tudor was still smarting at his vilification during the conscription debates: 'I am as good an Australian citizen as any other man in the community,' he said. Ryan predictably criticised the use of the *War Precautions Act* and censorship to stifle debate. As a group, the Labor leaders tabled a log of issues that had to be resolved if they were to support even voluntary recruitment: military conscription must be renounced absolutely as a policy option; there could be no economic conscription; unions deregistered in 1917 must be re-registered; victimised unionists should be reinstated in their jobs; war profiteering should be controlled; any *War Precautions Act* regulations not vital to the conduct of the war should be repealed; partisan political and industrial prosecutions under the Act should cease; and all constraints on free speech and the press, other than the publication of military news, should be abolished.[31]

The Nationalists resisted giving any assurances on these issues. Instead, the relatively new Assistant Minister for Recruitment, Richard Orchard, suggested that there be a ballot of men eligible for recruitment using numbered marbles. It might be months or years, Orchard said, before a man was required to actually serve. Possibly he would never be required to. In any case, 'The Australian lad is prepared to take a sporting risk and there is an element of chance about a ballot which we hope will appeal to men who have not seen fit to enlist.' This was drawing a long bow. Men in 1918 were no more likely to welcome taking a 'sporting risk' in a conscription ballot than were Australians five decades later during the Vietnam War. In the event, only one draw—of a hundred names—was conducted in Sydney before the war ended.[32]

Hughes missed the first days of the conference through illness, and then stormed out when his attempt to read a cable from the British government about the seriousness of the military situation elicited the response 'We've had enough of your forgeries.' However, he was under pressure from Munro Ferguson and he needed to secure the labour movement's continued support for voluntary recruitment. So ultimately he made some concessions. Unions would be re-registered so long as the men who had taken the place of dismissed unionists were not victimised. Anyone confined because of the 1917 conscription campaign and general strike would be released, and the use of the *War Precautions Act* in relation to free speech and political and industrial prosecutions would be reviewed.

Even then, the conference could agree only on an anodyne resolution about recruitment. Brokered by Holman, it committed the participants 'to make all possible efforts to avert defeat at the hands of German militarism', and urged the Australian people 'to unite in a whole-hearted effort to secure the necessary reinforcements under the voluntary system'. Hughes snorted that this was 'piffle'. 'I do not why we have come here at all, if we pass that.' His parting shot to the conference was: 'If I were still a leader of Labour, and if we were conducting a strike as in the old days, would we not tear to tatters a man who tried to force on us such a meagre and in fact emasculated motion?'[33]

However, there was no chance of a more substantive agreement. Labor politicians and union leaders alike had little room to manoeuvre politically. As the refusal of the Queensland and Tasmanian Councils to attend the conference showed, there was not just opposition within the grassroots labour movement to recruitment of any kind—be it voluntary or compulsory—but also a growing demand that the war be ended through negotiation. Tudor and Ryan ran the risk of Labor splitting again if they moved too far towards Hughes.

In the wider community, the political situation was febrile, thanks in part to the continuing activities of Mannix. On 16 March he presided over a 'deliberatively provocative' St Patrick's Day march in Melbourne, in which all floats were decorated in Sinn Fein's green and gold. When a Young Ireland Society tableau representing 'The men of Easter Week' passed by, he removed his biretta—but he ostentatiously left it on when 'God Save the King' was played. Outraged, 3000 loyalists convened a counter-demonstration in the Melbourne Town Hall, where Mannix was denounced as an agent of Sinn Fein who stood 'shoulder to shoulder with the Hun and the hosts of Satan'. Demanding that he be deported and that disloyal processions be banned from public display, a deputation marched to the Commonwealth Offices to lobby Hughes for action. The Council of Churches (Victoria) also condemned Mannix for hindering recruiting, promoting disloyalty and lawlessness and promoting 'religious animosities to an extent unparalleled in the history of the Commonwealth'.[34]

Needing little encouragement, Hughes issued new *War Precautions Act* regulations, making it an offence to incite disloyalty to the British Empire by word or deed, or to display flags or emblems that were symbols of either an enemy country or groups disaffected from the British Empire. Irish National Associations in the eastern capitals were also raided, their newspapers seized and a number of their leaders arrested.

Hughes also resumed his diplomatic efforts to get Mannix recalled by the Vatican. He would not succeed, but behind the scenes the Vatican was moving to restrain Mannix's inflammatory behaviour. It served the Catholic Church no good to have all Catholics stigmatised as disloyal 'because an Archbishop is suffering from swelled head [sic]', as one letter writer to the press put it. The Apostolic Delegate (the representative of the Vatican in Australia) contacted Rome, and on 3 April Mannix was reminded by the Sacred Congregation of Propaganda that the office of the pastor was intended 'to pacify souls, to allay discords and to prevent their arising or becoming embittered'. A meeting of Catholic archbishops was also convened by the Apostolic Delegate in May to discuss 'how to restore calm' and avoid further trouble.[35]

Presumably bowing to the authority of Rome, Mannix moved a resolution at this meeting that urged the clergy to 'use prudence and caution in dealing with public questions', especially conscription, recruiting, Ireland and the war. Yet for all this, Archbishop Kelly in Sydney proceeded with issuing a pastoral letter in May that linked support for voluntary recruitment to changes in British policy in Ireland and policy towards Catholic schools in Australia. When challenged by the press, he claimed that these were the 'two glaring obstacles to Catholic enthusiasm in the matter of voluntary enlistment'. He was probably right.[36]

The recruitment campaign that followed the governor-general's conference therefore had little chance of success, even though Labor leaders Tudor and Ryan kept to their cross-party pledge to support it. Tudor, for example, sat on the platform at the Melbourne Town Hall when the campaign was launched on 8 May. Munro Ferguson exhorted the capacity crowd to take the prompt action needed to reinforce the five AIF divisions, 'Otherwise it might be said that Australians were driven out of the field not by the enemy, but by the defeatism of their own country-men.' Tudor, in turn, said: 'I am bitterly opposed to any militaristic system of German or Prussian birth . . . I urge every man of fighting age to ask himself: should I remain here or go over there and do my bit in this great struggle. (Cheers).'[37]

In the following weeks, Tudor also addressed a number of other recruitment rallies and issued a letter to the press, affirming that he supported harmony in relation to the prosecution of the war. Ryan, too, backed the recruitment campaign in Queensland, Sydney and Melbourne. Assuring the public that he supported voluntary enlistment, if not conscription, he even lent his name to 'The Ryan Thousand', the next thousand recruits in Queensland.[38]

As ever, the politicians' calls to arms were backed by a range of desperate inducements and incentives on the part of the recruitment agencies. Mackinnon commissioned the artist Norman Lindsay, already renowned for his lurid anti-German cartoons in *The Bulletin*, to produce a series of leaflets promoting the recruitment ballot, 'The Gospel of Frightfulness'. Intended to persuade or terrify the potential recruit, they included typical Lindsay images of the German monster atop piles of corpses, his sword dripping with blood, while disrobed females looked desperately on. Other Lindsay cartoons played on the emergency in France: 'Quick!', for example, depicted an Australian soldier lying on the ground, his finger pointing accusingly at the reader while his mate was being bayoneted by Germans in the background. Perhaps most memorably, 'Shameless' depicted a fit hulk of an 'eligible' standing proudly on an Australian beach, oblivious to the wounded soldiers on crutches and in a wheelchair behind him.[39]

Recruiting regulations meanwhile were amended to allow men under 21 years of age to enlist without their parents' or guardians' consent. More 'snowball marches' were arranged, including one—a 'March to Freedom'— beginning at Armidale, New South Wales. Complete with 18-pounder field guns, searchlights and contingents of engineers and reinforcements who had already enlisted, it managed to net only 120 recruits. However, a 'Sportsman's Thousand', aimed at recruiting athletes, did meet its quota in Victoria. Scottish-Australian associations also thought men might be encouraged to enlist if promised the right to wear kilts in service. This was too much for Brudenell White. The AIF's fame, he said, had been 'made by the Australian soldier as a man distinctively Australian'! Monash, too, thought it would be 'a trespass upon the solidarity of the A.I.F.'[40]

Finally, as in 1916 and 1917, the celebration of Anzac Day—especially sober because of events on the Western Front—was grasped as an opportunity to promote the message that more men were needed to replace those who had died. Munro Ferguson issued a public statement reminding the Australian people that:

> it will be an empty ceremony, unworthy of the deeds we commemorate, if unattended by a great increase in recruiting whereby the famous divisions which fought at Gallipoli can be reinforced, and the Australian Army made fit to take as glorious a part in the last, as it did in the first phase of the war.[41]

It all made little difference. Only in May, when the crisis situation on the Western Front sent a frisson of fear through Australia, did recruitment increase—to 4888. But as the situation in France stabilised, the number of volunteers slipped back, to 2540 in June. The *Sydney Morning Herald* might intone on 23 May that 'more than ever this summer must the Allies offer the last man and the last shilling', but the well of recruits was almost dry. As an alderman in Maryborough, Queensland, lamenting the low attendance at a recruiting meeting in May, said:

> Oh where oh where are the men tonight! Eligible men at less than 10 and never more than 40, ladies, children and old men . . . It seems almost a degradation, a scandal, a disgrace and a shame that we should have to come before a British audience time and again and beg and plead in order to get British men to realise their duty.[42]

Ryan, meanwhile, found himself in an increasingly untenable position, poised between loyalists who thought his recruitment efforts facile and the left who condemned him for supporting the war. The search for 'The Ryan Thousand' became chaotic, ultimately raising only 478 men, and in September Ryan had to retire from a recruiting platform at the Brisbane Post Office after heckling from conscriptionists made it impossible for him to finish his speech.[43]

Nothing, it seemed, could revive recruitment to the levels needed to replace the losses on the Western Front. The gap between casualties and enlistments became ever wider in 1918 (see Figure 5.1), and had the war not ended later that year there would have been little option but to cannibalise one of the AIF's five divisions to keep the others in the field.

Villers-Bretonneux again

The battle to control Villers-Bretonneux continued throughout April. After a series of inconclusive actions between 7 and 15 April, the Germans deluged the town and the surrounding areas on 17–18 April with some 20,000 shells of a potent mix of mustard gas, 'sneezing gas' and phosgene. Removing their gas masks too early, the British and Australians suffered streaming eyes and

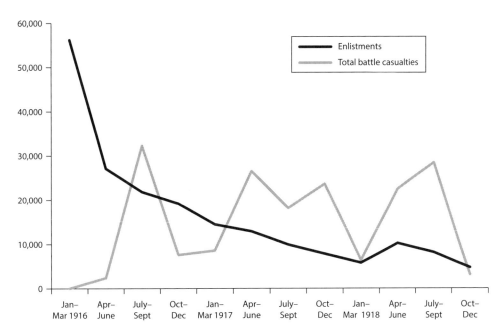

Figure 5.1: Enlistments and battle casualties, 1916–18

Sources: Ernest Scott, *The Official History of Australia in the War of 1914–1918*, vol. XI, pp. 871–2, and A.G. Butler, *The Official History of the Australian Army Medical Services, 1914–1918*, vol. III, p. 911.

painfully inflamed skin and crotches from clothing impregnated with gas. Over a thousand men of the British III Corps were affected, together with some 50 Australian officers and 600 men. Leslie Morshead was one of them: he almost lost his sight and a promising military career (he would command the 9th Division and I Corps in World War II).[44]

Another German attack followed in force on 24 April. By this stage, Villers-Bretonneux was being held by the British 8th Division under the command of Major-General William Heneker. The Australian brigades detached to defend the town during the first battles of April had returned to the Anzac Corps, which now sat astride the Somme. The German attack began on a misty morning with a massive barrage of high explosive, yet more gas and, for the first time, a contingent of thirteen new A7V tanks. North of Villers-Bretonneux, the Australian 5th Division brought the attackers to a halt. To the south, too, British tanks engaged the Germans in what is commonly seen as the first tank battle in history. But in the centre of the line, the 8th Division—which included many young and inexperienced raw recruits—collapsed. By mid-morning, the Germans had captured Monument Farm, the rest of Hangard Wood—and the town of Villers-Bretonneux itself.

Elliott, scathing as usual about the British, had expected that this would happen and was itching to launch his brigade into a counter-attack. He even issued an order on the morning of 24 April telling his 59th and 60th Battalions to rally any British troops they came across en route and shoot those who hesitated! Hobbs, probably on instructions from White, countermanded this extraordinary order, another lapse of judgement for which Elliot would soon pay.[45]

Not surprisingly, Heneker and his superior, British III Corps commander Lieutenant-General Richard Butler, insisted that they could handle the crisis that was unfolding; however, Rawlinson, under orders from Foch to retake Villers-Bretonneux as soon as possible, had already intervened. At 9.30 a.m. he ordered the Australian 13th Brigade (4th Division) billeted north of the Somme to march nearly 13 kilometres south and join the 8th Division in a counter-attack later in the day. Rawlinson also asked the Australian 5th Division to assist—as if Elliott needed any asking!

The plan of attack, thrashed out during a frenetic afternoon, was to encircle Villers-Bretonneux. Glasgow's 13th Brigade and the British 54th Brigade would attack from south of the Bois l'Abbé while the 15th Brigade would sweep down from the north. The forces would converge east of the town while the 8th Division was clearing it of the German troops trapped there. It was a complex manoeuvre with significant risks. The distances to be covered were considerable, and many of the troops—particularly the 13th Brigade—were already exhausted and hungry. Glasgow got his first chance to reconnoitre the ground only early in the afternoon, and Hobbs did not know until 3.30 p.m. that the 15th Brigade would be involved. Details of the attack were still being sorted out between Glasgow and Elliott as late as 8 p.m. Moreover, the attack was scheduled for 10 p.m. when there was still some light, not at 10.30, as the Australians wanted. Bean, close to the action, went to bed 'thoroughly depressed feeling certain that this horrid attack would fail hopelessly'.[46]

However, the attack was a spectacular success (see Map 29). At 10.10 p.m., the 13th Brigade charged off through heavy machine-gun fire and a landscape lit up by tracer bullets and enemy flares—a scene recreated in a dramatic painting by the official war artist Will Longstaff in 1919. To the north, Elliott's troops, delayed by the German barrage and a company being forced to detour around gas, went on the attack two hours later. Across the line, the men of the 15th Brigade sprang forward with a 'raw spontaneous roar'. Then, according to Bean, 'the restraints of civilised intercourse' were thrown off. The 60th Battalion became 'what the bayonet instructors of all armies aimed at producing by their tuition—primitive, savage men'. Elliott's intelligence officer recalled:

> The Boche was at our mercy. They screamed for mercy but there were too many machine-guns about to show them any consideration as we

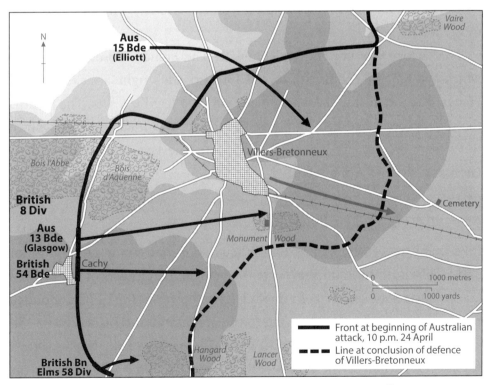

Map 29: The counter-attack, Villers-Bretonneux, 24–25 April 1918

were moving forward . . . in very few instances did the enemy put up a fight and when he did he was quickly dealt with . . . Here and there a Fritz would hop out of trench or shell-hole only to fall riddled with bullets and then to be bayoneted by the boys as they came up.

By this stage of the war, the 15th Brigade had perfected the 'throat jab'—a thrust of the bayonet up through a man's throat into his spinal cord. As Elliott put it, this killed a man 'easily, quickly and painlessly, often without a cry or movement'. Clearly by 1918 these Australians were highly efficient killers, a fact that twenty-first-century commemoration with its high diction of 'sacrifice' and 'deeds of valour' elides.[47]

Early on 25 April, the British forces began to clear Villers-Bretonneux of Germans trapped there. By 1 a.m. on 26 April, the Australian 15th and 13th Brigades had completed the town's encirclement meeting up on its eastern side. The cost to the 15th Brigade was 455 men; to the 13th, 1009. The British III Corps lost 9500 men, including 2400 taken prisoner, while German losses were 7500.[48]

The victory was not entirely complete. The French Moroccan Division, which had relieved the British on the 13th Brigade's right, attacked towards Hangard Wood during the daylight and suffered terrible losses. The line that the British forces had held earlier in the month was therefore not regained. But Villers-Bretonneux was secure and would never again be taken by the Germans. Nor did Amiens fall.

Remembering Villers-Bretonneux

Like many successes, Villers-Bretonneux soon had many fathers. Elliott and Hobbs both thought they were the principal architects of the brilliant counter-attack of 24 April. To their chagrin, however, the GHQ announcement gave credit for the planning to the command of III Corps. The 13th and 15th AIF brigades were deemed only 'deserving of the highest praise' for the execution of the attack. Elliott fumed: 'Some who opposed my request [to counter-attack] in the beginning are now unblushingly trying to usurp the entire credit.' His biographer concludes that he probably had good cause to feel aggrieved, but Hobbs, too, believed that he 'really planned [the night operation of 24–25 April], but I feel I should never get the credit of it'.[49]

However, if credit for the planning of the attack was disputed, no one quibbled about the fighting skills of the AIF. Foch spoke of the Australians' 'altogether astonishing valiance', while a British officer with senior GHQ responsibilities concluded that 'Even if the Australians achieved nothing else in this war, they would have won the right to be considered among the greatest fighting races of the world.' The adjutant of the 2nd Northhampton-shires serving at Villers-Bretonneux also spoke of 'the personal ascendancy of the Australian soldier on the battlefield which made him the best infantry man of the war and perhaps of all time'. Heneker, however, uttered no word of thanks or praise.[50]

With accolades such as these, Villers-Bretonneux rapidly assumed a central place in Australian memories of the war in France. More than nine decades later, it remains a—possibility *the*—dominant site of commemoration of the Western Front, overshadowing even Pozières and Fromelles. Why is this so? To some degree, we must look to Bean. As so often, his account of the AIF's journey south to the Somme in March 1918 was memorably evocative. Of the Australians' arrival near Barly, he wrote:

Australian infantry had never been stationed in that region, but before long—spontaneously, as it seemed—they were recognised. The gazing villagers could be heard calling from one house to the other, 'Les Austra-liens'. A few minutes later, as spontaneously, they began unloading their carts, and the furniture was carried indoors again. An old man said to one of the 13th Battalion, whose lorries halted there for a while, 'Pas necessaire maintenant—vous les tiendrez.' [Not necessary now. You will hold them.]

His account of the 3rd Division making its way along the road from Franvil-lers to Heilly was also eminently quotable:

Women, who during the past night had seen the flashes of the enemy's guns, like summer lightning on the horizon, coming closer to their homes, and for the first time had heard the swish and crash of enemy shells, now in a revulsion of pent-up feeling burst into tears and raised a thin cry of 'Vive l'Australie!' ... Some who had left their homes turned back, and others, who had not left, stayed on. 'Fini retreat, Madame,' said one of the 'diggers' gruffly, when the leading battalion was halted, and sat cleaning its rifles along the side of the Heilly street. 'Fini retreat—beaucoup Australiens ici.' [Finished retreat—many Australians here.][51]

These vignettes actually described the approach of the AIF to the Somme rather than Villers-Bretonneux, but such fine distinctions tend to be lost in popular memory. Even though they are the recollections of an avowedly sympathetic eyewitness, they have become a staple of Australian historiography of 1918.

Villers-Bretonneux also assumed a central place in Australian commemoration of the war thanks to those who experienced its loss and recovery in 1918. Memories are not agents in themselves. They require individuals to preserve and promote them. In the case of Villers-Bretonneux, as in Bullecourt, these were French as well as Australian. No sooner had the town started to recover from its 'desolation' (as one visitor described it in 1919) than its citizens raised funds for a plaque in memory of the Australian forces who had liberated it. In July 1919, this was presented to the Australian Graves Detachment, which was exhuming and re-interring the dead in the region. The mayor of Villers-Bretonneux said:

The first inhabitants of [the town] to re-establish themselves in the ruins of what was once a flourishing little town have, by means of donations, shown a desire to thank the valorous Australian Armies, who with the spontaneous enthusiasm and characteristic dash of their race, in a few hours chased an enemy ten times their number . . . Soldiers of Australia, whose brothers lie here in French soil, be assured that your memory will always be kept alive, and that the burial places of your dead will always be respected and cared for.

In 1920, another tablet remembering the Australian dead was unveiled in the Amiens cathedral by no less than Foch. Praising 'that wonderful attack' at Villers-Bretonneux, he said, 'You saved Amiens, you saved France. Our gratitude will remain ever and always to Australia.'[52]

Australians, for their part, remembered Villers-Bretonneux. When a scheme was established in 1920 for British cities to adopt and support devastated French towns, a patriotic Melbourne woman, Charlotte Crivelli, mobilised prominent citizens—Monash, Elliott, Gellibrand, Munro Ferguson and his wife, and the mayor of Melbourne—and persuaded the city to adopt Villers-Bretonneux. Despite many competing demands on charitable funds, some £22,000 was raised in the next two years to support the town's reconstruction. This was the largest sum raised for a French town under the British League of Help for the Devastated Areas in France scheme.[53]

Almost half of the total, £10,000, came from the Victorian Education Department's War Relief Organisation, a patriotic fund that had accumulated a significant surplus during the war thanks to the energetic fundraising of students and staff of Victorian state schools. As the Director Frank Tate now saw it, the school in Villers-Bretonneux was a fitting and lasting means of recognising this war work. Opened on Anzac Day in 1927, the school still carries a plaque, designed by Tate, which reads in English and French:

This school building is the gift of the school children of Victoria, Australia, to the children of Villers-Bretonneux, as proof of their love and good-will towards France. Twelve hundred Australian soldiers, the fathers and brothers of these children, gave their lives in the heroic recapture of this town from the invader on 24th April 1918, and are buried near this spot.

Even more significant in making Villers-Bretonneux a dominant memory of 1918 for many Australians was its being chosen after the war as the site for the national memorial to the dead and missing in France. It was not an automatic choice, given the relatively small number of Australian casualties suffered in the town's defence. But by a remarkable coincidence, the Second Battle of Villers-Bretonneux had fallen on Anzac Day—as, for that matter, did two other important events in the national narrative of war: the starting of work by Australian prisoners on the Hellfire Pass (Konyu cutting) on the Thai–Burma railway in 1943 and the Battle of Kapyong during the Korean War in 1951. Villers-Bretonneux was therefore ready-made as an anniversary and a site of national commemoration.

In addition, it can be surmised that Villers-Bretonneux recommended itself as a site of memory to Hobbs, who—as an architect in civilian life—was chosen by the Australian government to manage the building of the national memorial after the war. Private and public memory may have converged as Hobbs, smarting from the neglect of his role in the battle for Villers-Bretonneux, nominated the hill, which, as he said in 1922, was:

> the spot where the 14th Australian Infantry Brigade stood their ground—under the most trying conditions—on the 24th April 1918, and were the direct means of defeating the last German attempt to take Amiens; and enabled the famous counter attack to be made which led to the recapture of Villers-Bretonneux.[54]

The fact that this hill was already the site of a wartime cemetery which would in time hold some 779 Australian dead (of a total of 2142 burials) also recommended it.

It would take nearly two decades for the Australian national memorial at Villers-Bretonneux to be completed. A design competition was held in 1925–27, with applicants restricted to Australians who had served in the war or who had children who enlisted. But then little progress was made for some years. Perhaps this was because by the mid-1920s the French authorities were becoming uneasy about the 'colossal dimensions' of some of the British and Dominion memorials planned for the Western Front. As a meeting of an Anglo-French committee on 25 June 1926 was told, some memorials would be 'about as large and as high as the Arc de Triomphe de l'Etoile at Paris'. A French representative explained:

> It is not a question of drawing a comparison in any way in regard to the human sacrifices of the two allied nations, nor of wishing to have on the battlefields lasting Monuments showing the extent of such sacrifices, but nevertheless it appeared that the British Government came to the help of France who was attacked with so much loyalty at the beginning of the war, not to feel that there would be a certain number of French people, not at once, but perhaps in 100 or 150 years who would make an unkind comparison between the Monuments erected by France and those erected by Great Britain on French soil.[55]

Not until May 1929 did the French government approve an Australian memorial at Villers-Bretonneux. The Great Depression then made the original budget of £100,000 impossible. Finally, the Australian government turned to a cheaper (£30,000) option designed by the British architect Edwin Lutyens. Although not Australian, Lutyens had already created the gates at the Villers-Bretonneux cemetery and scores of other war memorials, including the impressive Thiepval on the Somme and the Cenotaph in Whitehall, which had been replicated around the imperial world. Lutyens had also designed New Delhi, the acme of imperial hubris. The 'national' memorial was becoming decidedly imperial—but so too was the nationalism of many Australians at that time.

The final design was a tower some 31 metres tall, diplomatically shorter than the Arc de Triomphe's 50 metres but high enough to gaze out across the sites on which Australians fought around the Somme in 1916 and 1918. The tower was flanked by walls inscribed with the names of more than 10,000 Australians missing in France. Aesthetically, it was Australian only in the rising sun crest above the tower's doorway and the stone flags draped on the pavilions flanking the walls.

As befitted the mood of the times, the memorial was unveiled in 1938 by King George VI, with Queen Elizabeth and the French President Le Brun in attendance. Since budgets were tight, the Australian prime minister did not come—an absence almost unthinkable at any major commemorative ceremony today. Instead, the Australian delegation included the high commissioner in London and former prime minister, Stanley Bruce, the deputy prime minister, Earle Page, and Cabinet ministers Robert Menzies and T.W. White, who happened to be in Britain on government business. Birdwood, too, was present, invited by the King to be his Gold Stick in Waiting! Hobbs, however, died at sea on his way to the ceremony. Elliott, another major Australian protagonist at Villers-Bretonneux, was also missing. He had committed suicide in 1931.

Some 400 veterans and nurses also made the journey to Villers-Bretonneux. The only government financial assistance they received was for travel from London. (Fully government-funded 'pilgrimages' of veterans from Australia would come only decades later, in the 1990s.) A representative of the Returned Sailor's and Soldier's Imperial League of Australia (the RSSILA, later the Returned and Services League) brought with him from Australia an urn containing ashes from wreaths laid at the Melbourne Shrine of Remembrance and the Sydney Cenotaph on Anzac Day. Thirty thousand people meanwhile lined the road to the site. 'Thousands were knee-deep in the golden corn. Countless larks for which this district is famous, kept up a constant trill, sweeping down frequently as if to view the military,' the *Canberra Times* reported on 23 July. The proceedings were broadcast to Britain, Australia and New Zealand, and the King's speech was quoted fully in the Australian press. The memorial was, he said,

> more than a tribute to the gallant services of a splendid army—it is a symbol marking the entry of the young nation—the gateway through which Australia passed from youth to nationhood . . . At Gallipoli [the Australians] won their spurs and henceforth they were veterans whose quality was unquestioned by friend or foe. The long glorious record of their latter achievements holds none more resounding than those which link their name to Villers-Bretonneux.[56]

Earle Page, for his part, spoke of how Australians 'had proved that they were worthy to sacrifice life itself for their fellows and the ideals they held': 'They sacrificed themselves in the belief that the cause they upheld was the cause of peace. They were men of peace, trained for peace, loving peace. Yet they died in war.' This was not actually what he had planned to say. The draft of his speech was much longer and spoke as much to the war that was coming as to that which was past. It remains of interest, however, for its reflections on the 'mixture of motives' that had led Australians to serve in the war:

> Strongest with many, especially at first, was the knowledge that the Old Country was in danger. Then there was a very general and impelling love of adventure; and then, with most thoughtful Australians, there was a belief that an attempt was being made by the rulers of the Central Powers to base international relations on a rule of force which to these freedom-loving men and women was intolerable. Later, perhaps, the most powerful motive was the realisation that, if Great Britain and the Allies went under, then the Australian nation would also go down; and finally, all were moved by the conviction that this struggle must be fought out and definitely settled once and finally, or it would all have to be fought out again by the children of the men who were then striving—an eventuality which they desired at all costs to avoid. Whatever the motive of each one, in this, the most important decision of their lives, they were acting without thought of material profit or even of personal glory.[57]

With the national memorial in place, Villers-Bretonneux was certain to hold a central position in Australian public commemoration, but its particular prominence owed much to the ongoing efforts of the local French population. Throughout the twentieth century, they continued to shape the identity of this otherwise unprepossessing provincial town around its shared history with Australia. The entrance doors to the town hall are now flanked by the Australian and French flags and painted kangaroos. The street leading off the main square is Rue de Melbourne. Rue Victoria houses the school, funded with Victorian money, which declaims 'Do Not Forget Australians'.

The school's attic also houses an Australian-French museum established in the 1950s by a local businessman, Leon Rinet, with the support of a Victorian parliamentarian and winner of a Military Cross at Villers-Bretonneux in 1918, Sir William 'Bill' Leggatt. Elsewhere in the town, a restaurant advertises itself as Restaurant Le Kangourou. Kangaroos in the shape of the letters VB also form the town's logo, adorning its website and the road signs that advertise Villers-Bretonneux as 'L'Australie en Picardie'. Other public signs celebrate a sister-city relationship established in 1983 with Robinvale, a soldier-settler town in Victoria that was named after Robin Cuttle, who died in a dogfight near Villers-Bretonneux in 1918.

It is not surprising, then, that it was to Villers-Bretonneux, and specifically the Adelaide cemetery west of the town, that the Labor government of Paul Keating turned when it decided that it should mark the 75th anniversary of the end of the war with the burial of an Unknown Soldier in the Australian War Memorial. Until that time, the 'British' soldier interred in Westminster Abbey in 1920 had been deemed to be sufficient, but with the growth of an Australian nationalism that had shed its imperial associations, it was thought that a more indisputably Australian body was needed. The remains of an unknown soldier were therefore disinterred and, to quote Ken Inglis:

> put into a coffin supplied by the Australian Funeral Directors' Association, flown home by Qantas, exhibited in the King's Hall of the old Parliament House, and given the first Australian funeral of a soldier who had died on service in the Great War since General Bridges in 1915.[58]

Fifteen years later, Villers-Bretonneux would also host the official Australian government commemorations on the 90th anniversary of the end of the war. More than 5000 Australians attended the Anzac Day dawn service, and in its aftermath it was decided to institute an annual official dawn service. 'For years,' an Australian tour operator explained, 'Gallipoli has been the destination on Anzac Day, but this year the focus has changed to the place where five times as many Australians fought and died, and where we contributed so significantly to the ultimate victory . . . We planned the dawn service as a private event for our tour members, but interest has been so great that the government stepped in and offered to take over arrangements and make it an official event.'[59]

Official commemoration, battle tourism and commercial benefit are now seamlessly interwoven in a shared transnational memory as Villers-Bretonneux is promoted by French and Australians alike as 'The other Anzac Day'. This is positioned within a wider Australia Week, the program for which in 2008 included not just the rituals of Anzac Day but also flights over battlefields, battlefield tours—and a performance by the Orchestre de Picardie of an all-German program![60]

Peaceful penetration

By early May, the German attacks on the Somme and in Flanders had run their course and for a short time the Australians found themselves facing enemy forces that were relatively weak. Since Ludendorff was planning another offensive against the French in the south on 27 May, the German line in the Somme was left manned by troops who were tired and often very young. Under constant attack from Allied artillery, gas shells and aerial bombing, and expecting fluid warfare to resume, they did not develop strong defensive lines.

This gave the Australian and New Zealand troops the chance to refine a style of tactics known variously as 'nibbling', 'winkling' or 'peaceful penetration' (the latter term being borrowed from the methods used by the Germans before the war to penetrate British trade). Small groups of infantry would attack enemy outposts, ambushing the Germans, capturing prisoners for intelligence about morale and future plans, and robbing them of stretches of land—all without incurring significant casualties. It was, in Bean's words, a ceaseless 'private war' on the Germans.[61]

These were tactics that gave free rein to initiative, improvisation, opportunism and bravado. Companies competed with each other for the most daring raid. In one celebrated incident on the Somme, an Australian officer whose troops were dozing on a hot summer day concluded that the Germans too might be sleeping. Crossing No Man's Land with his scouts in broad daylight, he brought back alive almost a whole German garrison and their light machine gun. The nearby German posts knew nothing of the raid until the company commander, doing his rounds that night, found the neighbouring post missing.[62]

Between these often spontaneous raids, the Australian divisions took part in more formal set-piece attacks aiming to seize sections of the enemy line before the Germans had fully dug in. On 4–9 May, the 3rd Division pushed along the high triangle between the rivers Somme and Ancre towards Morlancourt, capturing the new German front line and holding it when the Germans counter-attacked on 14 May. Five days later, the 9th Brigade of 2nd Division captured the town of Ville-sur-Ancre just south of Dernancourt.

Then, on 10–11 June, the 7th Brigade (2nd Division) attacked on part of the Morlancourt spur overlooking Sailly-Laurette, a feature that Australian forces had failed to take on 28 March and only partially retaken on 7–8 May. The attack, launched at dusk with the support of 7000 artillerymen, was an immediate success. Within a few minutes, according to the German divisional commander, a complete battalion was 'wiped out as with a sponge'. For only 400 casualties, the Australians advanced 800 metres, killed 230 Germans and took 325 prisoners of war.[63]

Es Salt

The crisis on the Western Front in March had an immediate impact on the Middle Eastern campaign. Desperate for additional manpower in France and Belgium, the British government rapidly withdrew from Palestine over 60,000 officers and men. While the Australian and New Zealand divisions were left intact and the EEF was given replacements from Mesopotamia and India, in effect, as Alec Hill later put it, Ludendorff's offensive on the Western Front had 'not only smashed the Fifth Army in France, [it] had emasculated the E.E.F., which must now wait and work until the autumn before it could be hurled against the enemy'.[64]

Fortunately for the imperial forces, the Ottoman high command failed to realise the strategic opportunity open to it. Instead, taking advantage of the chaos in Russia, it diverted many of its best troops to reclaim territory lost to Russia in 1877–78 and to gain control of the oil supplies on the Caspian Sea—an operation that might have supported long-term strategic interests but which would seriously detract from the Ottoman defence of Palestine in the coming months.

Despite these disruptions, Allenby was tempted to launch another operation across the Jordan River. The Ottomans had tried on 11 April to dislodge the British bridgehead that had remained at Ghoraniye after the abortive March attack on Amman. They failed, but had established a garrison of 4000–5000 troops between the Jordan River and Amman, in the foothills of Shunet Nimrin. This meant that they barred the British way to Amman, and when a local tribe of Arabs offered their help, Allenby decided to attack Es Salt again. If this were in British hands, he calculated, Shunet Nimrin could be encircled from the north, cutting off the Ottoman retreat, and the British could then strike northwards to the vital rail junction of Deraa.

The Es Salt raid came at a time when the EEF was in a state of change. Chetwode later called it and the earlier Amman raid 'the stupidest things [Allenby] ever did'. In fact, it was almost a disaster. On 30 April, the Australian Mounted Division, reinforced by the 1st and 2nd Light Horse Brigades, pushed north on the eastern bank of the Jordan while the 3rd Light Horse Brigade and a train of 360 camels dragging six guns scrambled in single file up a path that was little more than a goat track to seize Es Salt by nightfall. The 4th Light Horse Brigade was positioned to hold any enemy west of the river. Unknown to the British, however, the Ottomans—now under the command of the German Liman von Sanders, of Gallipoli fame—had recently constructed a crossing of the Jordan just to the north of the 4th Light Horse's covering position. They had also reinforced the area with some extra divisions, including German units, with the aim of making their own attack down the Jordan Valley.[65]

On the morning of 1 May, over 4000 Ottoman troops attacked the 4th Light Horse. Outnumbered and thinly stretched, the Australians were forced back over steep and broken ground and abandoned nine of their twelve 13-pounder guns. With reinforcements rushed in by Chauvel, they managed to establish a defensive line to the north of the only track that connected Es Salt to the Jordan. Had this been cut, the troops in Es Salt—the 1st, 2nd and 3rd Light Horse Brigades, the yeomanry of the 5th Mounted Brigade and the headquarters of the Australian Mounted Division—would have had to fight their way out or face annihilation or captivity. The majority of the Australian forces in Palestine and a large part of the Desert Mounted Corps would have ceased to play a role in the war.

The operation had also gone badly at Shunet Nimrin, where the attack by the 60th Division and the Australian Mounted Division on the Ottomans failed. Aerial reconnaissance showed significant enemy reinforcements converging on the area, and the Arabs—sensibly from their perspective if not that of the British—had gone on their way without completing their role of capturing a village east of Shunet Nimrin. On 4 May, therefore, the whole operation was called off. As the air force harassed the enemy with bombs and machine-gun fire, the units at Es Salt nervously pulled back down the single track to the west bank of the Jordan.

Allenby claimed that the operation had been a great success. It was hardly that, although his forces had inflicted perhaps 2000 casualties on the Ottomans and captured 980 prisoners for a loss of 1649 men. In addition, the raid had the benefit of persuading the Ottoman leadership that it was Trans-Jordan, not the coastal strip of Palestine, where the British threat was greatest. Hence, when Allenby next went on to the attack, in September on the coast, one-third of the Ottoman forces would be positioned to the east of the Jordan.[66]

Hughes in the United States

The war situation remained highly volatile when the leaders of the British Empire met in London in June for the second Imperial War Cabinet and War Conference. In contrast to 1917, Hughes was in a strong enough position domestically to go—though to ensure that nothing untoward happened in his absence, he took the Liberal leader, Cook, with him. Hughes also included in his delegation two competent advisers: his solicitor-general, the former activist for federation Sir Robert Garran; and J.G. Latham, a Melbourne barrister and naval intelligence officer with expertise in the Pacific who would later become a Commonwealth attorney-general and Chief Justice of Australia. Hughes also insisted on his wife and daughter accompanying him (even though women were not meant to travel through war zones or on war ships), together with his personal physician (he continued to be chronically ill).

The Australian party's plans were to leave in late April and travel to Britain via Canada and New York. In Vancouver, Hughes would inspect ten wooden ships that were being built under contract to alleviate the shipping shortage that continued to impede the export of Australian raw materials. Collecting Canadian government representatives en route, Hughes would then reach London in time for the opening of the Imperial War Cabinet on 11 June.

Hughes threw these plans into disarray by insisting that he go to Washington to meet President Woodrow Wilson. The American entry into the war had shifted the balance of international power, and with the publication of the Fourteen Points, it was clear that Wilson's liberal internationalism might shape the post-war settlement. If Hughes was to guarantee his radically different vision of the post-war world—security for Australia, a strong and self-sufficient British Empire, the exclusion of Germany from imperial trade and harsh indemnities from the enemy powers—he needed to 'persuade [Wilson] that the Democracies of the Pacific must stand by one another'. In particular, he had to convince the US president to accept Australia's claim to retain control of the former German colony of New Guinea, captured in 1914. Hence, even though going to Washington meant that he would arrive late in London for the imperial meetings, Hughes scheduled a visit to the United States in late May.[67]

If success is judged by positive influence on key policy-makers, this foray into the citadel of American power was probably a failure. Well before he arrived in Washington, Hughes had antagonised senior members of the US administration by sending in mid-1917 a startlingly undiplomatic message when it seemed that the Americans might commandeer fourteen ships being built in the United States on order from Australia. Forgetting that he was not berating Mannix, Boote, Tudor or the IWW, Hughes had referred to the possible seizure of the ships as 'an unfriendly act' against a country that had been 'fighting gallantly for three years'. He refused to countenance even leasing the ships back to the United States, since 'to carry American flags and crews' would be 'a blow against the naval and maritime supremacy of the British Empire'. This was strong diplomatic language, trampling on American sensitivities about the rights of neutral shipping in wartime and implying that the United States had been slow to enter the war—something that Hughes was in fact on record as thinking. Wilson's close adviser, Colonel Edward House, concluded that Hughes was 'unfitted for the place he occupies'.[68]

Still, when Hughes arrived in Washington in 1918, he was granted a meeting with the president on 29 May. It did not go well. As Hughes recalled it, he rushed to explain Australia's case for post-war territorial gains while Wilson listened to him in silence, 'as unresponsive as the Sphinx in the desert':

> He sat there like a stuffed image, never betraying by word or gesture the slightest interest in what I was saying. If he had even said 'Pooh' or 'Bah', or even 'Ah', I could have struggled on; but as it was, I gave it up and, thanking him for according me the honour of a personal interview, I tottered down into the outside world where, thank God, ordinary human beings were going about their lawful occasions.

The recollection of the British ambassador Lord Reading, who witnessed the meeting, was less negative. He thought that Wilson was sympathetic. But if the president was, he seemed utterly non-committal.[69]

Hughes was nothing if not resilient and, as he had in London in 1916, he sought out audiences for his views among the wider political and social elites. As Neville Meaney has put it:

> Hughes was able to take advantage of an Anglophile movement that had sprung up at the end of the nineteenth century in reaction to the mass migrations from southern and eastern Europe. It stressed America's British origins and . . . advocated closer ties between the British Empire and the United States and closer Anglo-American co-operation in world affairs.[70]

Speaking at a dinner of the Pilgrims Society held in his honour in New York on 1 June, Hughes explained that Australia looked to the United States to support it 'around the peace table' in its quest for guarantees against future aggression. An 'Australasian Monroe Doctrine' was needed in the southern Pacific, he said, invoking a concept familiar to an American audience. The islands to Australia's north must be controlled either by Australia or other 'friendly and civilized nations', since they stood in the same relation to Australia as 'Mt Kemel does to Ypres, Amiens to Paris, or as Calais and the Channel Ports do to England'— names carefully chosen to resonate powerfully with the current military crisis in Belgium and France. It was not that Australia wanted an empire, Hughes said, but it did demand security 'against all predatory nations'.[71]

Hughes spoke in a similar vein to other high-profile gatherings: one at the Harvard Club with members of a secret US government inquiry set up to study post-war territorial issues; and the other with the Association of Foreign Correspondents in America. To the journalists, he spoke also of his determination to exclude German economic interests from Australia after the war.

Perhaps these public appearances did something to offset the cool reception from Wilson. The US press gave Hughes wide publicity while the government inquiry later reported that Australia and New Zealand had 'a distinct and national point of view which must be taken into account' in any peace settlement. However, beyond the United States—and notably in Japan— Hughes' attempt to mobilise American support against future (if unspecified) threats in the Pacific generated only suspicion and irritation.

Before leaving the United States, Hughes made the decision to appoint an Australian trade commissioner in New York. This may not seem much today, but it represented an early step on the road to Australian diplomatic representation abroad. The war had confirmed what Australian politicians had known well before 1914: that the Dominions, while reliant on British imperial power, had interests distinct from those of Britain. As Hughes wrote to Treasurer Watt on 3 June 1918, British diplomats 'haven't the remotest idea of what Australia is like nor of its importance'. Even when well intentioned, the British represented Australia in 'a casual sort of way'. A trade commissioner therefore, as Hughes saw it, would give Australia the independent voice that it needed in an increasingly important seat of power.[72]

The Imperial War Conference, London

Hughes arrived in London on 15 June, by which time the meetings of the British and Dominion leaders were already underway. The machinery of imperial consultation that had been established at the 1917 imperial conference was cumbersome. First there was an Imperial War Cabinet, chaired by the British prime minister, which included eleven members of the British War Cabinet, two representatives each from India and the Dominions (Australia, Canada, New Zealand and South Africa) and one representative of the small island of Newfoundland, which had Dominion status until 1949, when it joined Canada. Since this cabinet dealt with issues ranging from military strategy and post-war peace to Japan and the League of Nations, other officials attended its meetings as required. A second body, the Imperial War Conference, was chaired by the Colonial Secretary and considered internal empire matters. Each of these bodies met twice a week, and on 20 June a third group—a kind of inner cabinet called the Committee of Prime Ministers—was created by Lloyd George. Since the Dominion prime ministers also consulted each other regularly, the volume of business and documentation confronting Hughes was immense. As he put it: 'the Dominion Prime Ministers, but lately complaining that they had been kept in the dark, were dazzled by the fierce glare that now beat upon them. But yesterday they had known nothing; now, alas! they knew everything, and their last state was worse than the first.'[73]

Hughes had his own agenda for the meetings, which he had cabled through from the United States. What he wanted to discuss were post-war problems including trade and tariffs, the Pacific question, the reform of the Privy Council and the improvement of communications between Dominion and British prime ministers. However, the first meetings of the Imperial War Cabinet were dominated by the continuing crisis on the Western Front. On 27 May, Ludendorff and Hindenburg launched yet another offensive, against the French and four British divisions resting in the region of the Chemin des Dames ridge. By eliminating the Allied threat in the south, the German command hoped to clear the way for a final decisive attack against the British in Flanders. The morale and effectiveness of the German troops was declining, but, as so often, they had spectacular success at first. They advanced further on the first day of the attack than they had on 21 March. Within three days they had seized Soissons, and by 29 May they were once more on the River Marne, site of the iconic battle of 1914. It was, as French Prime Minister Georges Clemenceau said later, 'a lamentable rout'. Paris was only 80 kilometres away and within range of German guns. A million people fled the capital in panic, and the British Cabinet discussed on 5 June the possibility of evacuating the British Expeditionary Force from the Continent. Hughes wrote to Pearce on 2 June that 'the war is simply awful this morning and I feel rotten'.[74]

In time, the crisis was checked. The American Expeditionary Force was at last becoming a presence on the Western Front, with the equivalent of fifteen American divisions (each twice the size of a British division) arriving between April and June. Foch was also able to move reinforcements from Flanders. Hence, on 2 June, 25 French and two American divisions counter-attacked and the German drive forward was halted. In the weeks that followed, half a million German troops contracted influenza, in the first wave of the pneumonic illnesses that would sweep across the Western Front in 1918 and later devastate the world and Australia. When on 9 June the Germans attacked again, trying to extend the salient that their earlier successes had won, they were halted within 10 kilometres in what the French called the Battle of the Matz. On 11 June, the Allied forces counter-attacked once more and Ludendorff abandoned the operation.[75]

In mid-June, the Italian front also erupted with an Austrian attack on two fronts above Venice: the Piave River and the Monte Grappa massif. Under pressure to support the Germans on the Western Front and needing to secure further resources, the Austrians were keen to guarantee a share in what they still thought would be a German victory. However, the Italians were supported by three British and one French division, and had a clear superiority in aircraft and artillery. Within a week, the Austrians had been halted. Over the next three months, disease and desertion would reduce the Hapsburg armies by more than a third.

None of this, however, was certain when the Imperial War Conference first convened in early June. Rather, the Dominion leaders were told by a deeply concerned Chief of the General Staff Wilson that the defensive line in France was so fragile that he could not predict what would happen in the next two months. This, he said, would be a 'very, very anxious time'. Lloyd George also discussed what Britain might do if France fell: would it join with the Americans in blockading Germany as the British had France during the Napoleonic Wars?

This was too much for Borden, Massey and Smuts—Hughes was still in transit. Why, the leaders of Canada, New Zealand and South Africa demanded to know, were the Allied armies still in such dire straits after all the appalling casualties of the past year? How had such failures in planning, organisation, command and leadership been tolerated? Borden even warned Lloyd George that if there was a repetition of Passchendaele, 'not a Canadian soldier will leave the shores of Canada'.[76]

Hughes added his voice to the chorus of criticism when he arrived in London. Despite the contributions made by the AIF, he complained, Australia had never been given explanations for the reverses on the Western Front, 'never a scratch of a pen'. Hughes, it should be said, had hardly been insistent on this subject. He had told the British government only in December 1917 that he was 'seriously disturbed' by the military situation and then failed to pursue the matter when the British failed to respond. But this did nothing to mitigate his sense that the British had treated the Dominions with disdain.[77]

Threatened with a serious fracturing of the imperial unity that was essential to the war effort, Lloyd George created the Committee of Prime Ministers to investigate the military situation and canvass alternative strategies. Possibly he hoped also to co-opt this group against Haig, whom, for reasons that remain profoundly difficult to explain, the prime minister still allowed to continue as commander-in chief.[78]

However, the imperial leaders found that they faced a devil's choice when it came to strategic options. No one wanted to keep squandering more of their citizens' lives on futile offensives on the Western Front. Such endless blood-letting would destroy 'the flower of your nation', as Hughes put it, leaving the British Empire so weakened that it could not compete with the United States and Germany after the war. With their 'manpower having gone', the Allies might approach the peace settlement with no choice but 'to accept the crumbs from the table'. Yet Hughes at least remained convinced that the war must be prosecuted until total victory over Germany was gained. The Empire could 'only get what we wanted by giving them a thrashing'.[79]

What, in any case, were the alternatives to the mass infantry attacks of the past? Churchill (now back in government as the Minister of Munitions) and Hughes thought the Allies could exploit their superiority in the new technologies: tanks and aircraft. Another option was to try to reactivate the Russian front. But there was no obvious Russian leader to lead the anti-Bolshevik cause—Kerensky, now an exile in London, only asked for British help—and Allied military intervention in Russia would be politically and logistically difficult. Not only did the Allies have little capacity to intervene (though they would eventually do so), but the option of Japan's attacking from Vladivostok was opposed by the Americans. The 'yellow races', they argued, would be 'unpopular in a white country', and Japanese intervention might even drive the Russians into Germany's arms. In any case, intervention in Siberia was hardly likely to change the situation on the Western Front, some 8000 kilometres away. The torturous debate ground on through June and July and was resolved only when, to the Allies' surprise and relief, they started to win the war on the Western Front.[80]

Imperial relationships

Meanwhile, the Imperial War Cabinet turned its attention to other questions, including how they should manage internal imperial affairs. With all the Dominions gaining a new national consciousness as a result of the war—Australia was not alone in this—the pre-war *modus operandi* of imperial relationships was clearly anachronistic. Borden had already raised the question of changing the constitutional arrangements within the empire at the Imperial War Conference in 1917, but given its complexity the issue had been deferred until after the war.

Hughes, however, wanted some immediate changes, notably in the way Dominion prime ministers dealt with the British government. Although inclined to favour evolutionary rather than radical change in imperial arrangements, Hughes had lost patience with the system whereby he dealt with London through the governor-general and the Colonial Office. In part this was because of the strains in his relationship with Munro Ferguson. A stickler for protocol and jealous of his vice-regal prerogatives, the governor-general had come to disapprove of Hughes' unorthodox style in domestic and inter-national affairs. He had refused, for example, to let Hughes use the official cipher to cable direct to the British embassy in Washington when Hughes decided to protest against the American decision to commandeer Australian ships. (Hughes had gone ahead anyway.) Munro Ferguson also thought that Hughes was careless with the security of official confidential papers and offhand in his approach to the Executive Council, which provided ministerial advice to the governor-general. As mentioned, the governor-general had also seen fit to lecture Hughes on his leadership style and chaotic administration at the time the new government was formed.[81]

Hughes, in turn, accused the governor-general of seeking to act as a 'supervisory power' and as 'the *de facto* Government of the Commonwealth which under our Constitution and that of Britain he is not'. Increasingly, he kept Munro Ferguson in the dark—refusing, for example, in April 1918 to tell him until the last minute who would be in the Imperial War Conference delegation and acting prime minister in his absence. He also failed to notify the governor-general of the decision to appoint a trade commissioner in New York—an omission that almost triggered Munro Ferguson's resignation. Once in London, Hughes even proposed that in future governors-general should be appointed by the national government of the country in which they served.

Even if there had not been clashes of personal style—and, presumably, class—between Hughes and Munro Ferguson, there were pragmatic reasons for procedural reform. The convoluted process of sending messages from the Dominions through the Colonial Office no matter what sector of the British government they were intended for was incompatible with the pace of wartime decision-making. Before forwarding any matter even to Lloyd George, the Colonial Office would seek opinions from other areas of government—a process that in one instance had taken up to six months to complete. Beyond this, as Hughes saw it, the new status that the Dominions had achieved during the war justified their being treated as 'participants in the councils of the Empire on a footing of equality'. He demanded the right to communicate directly with the British prime minister.

Colonial Secretary Walter Long took offence at the implied criticism of himself and his department, but Borden and Smuts supported Hughes in principle. After considerable debate, it was agreed that Dominion prime ministers could communicate directly with their British counterpart on 'matters of cabinet importance'. Long's suggestion that the Dominions allow resident ministers in London to represent their country on the War Cabinet was also adopted. Hughes presumably never intended to let any of *his* ministers play this role. Fisher, although high commissioner, had been consistently sidelined and had not been allowed to attend the 1917 Imperial War Conference in Hughes' absence, even though this had meant that Australian views were not represented at all.

Hughes may have achieved his goal in this matter, but he had less success when he proposed to the Imperial War Conference that the judicial committees of the House of Lords and Privy Council be integrated into a single Imperial Court of Appeal. Dominion judges would be appointed on their own merits and be available continuously rather than when they chanced to be in England. Hughes believed these changes, by ensuring a common final court of appeal for residents of the United Kingdom, the Dominions and India, would again recognise the changing status of the Dominions. However, none of the other Dominions shared this view, and although the Lord Chancellor claimed to find the idea attractive in principle, he also saw great practical difficulties. The matter was referred to the next Imperial Conference.[82]

The post-war order

Hughes also found himself in a minority in the imperial meetings on the question of the post-war order. His views on economic matters had not changed since 1916. He wanted the British Empire to become an autarkic economic system, freed from reliance on external countries for raw materials and giving preference to each other's goods. Germany, whose drive for economic dominance had been shown by the Treaty of Brest-Litovsk to be undiminished, should be excluded from all trade, investment and economic influence within the empire after the war. As Hughes saw it, trade was simply one element of the ruthless struggle between races that shaped the international order. There was 'no middle way . . . You have either to be for your own race or against it'. He supported the New Zealand suggestion that citizens from enemy countries should be denied naturalisation, and political and economic rights, by the British and Dominion governments for a period after the war.[83]

Seeking wider audiences for his views, Hughes addressed public meetings across the country with a passion that ultimately did his cause little good. Speaking to the British Empire League, for instance, he denounced those who 'held out the right hand of fellowship to the Hun, these pacifists, these defeatists, these little Englanders, these little Navy men'. He reserved particular venom for the metal-dealing firm Henry Merton and Co., the London agency through which the German combine had controlled the sale of Australian base metals. Although the company had been reorganised at the start of the war to exclude German control, Hughes claimed on 24 July that it was English in law but German 'in essence and character', 'a tentacle of the great German industrial and financial *corpus* which held the world in its grip before the war'.[84]

It was vintage Hughes, and a style of oratory that seemed to have worked on his previous visit to Britain, in 1916. But the British political scene of 1918 was changed. Those such as Lloyd George who had been happy to use Hughes against Asquith were now in power, and some in London (so Murdoch claimed) thought Hughes should have made more effort to have Australia's views represented at the 1917 Imperial War Conference. As he now lashed out wildly on various subjects, he gained the reputation for being impossible. Rawlinson called him a 'self-advertising ass'. The influential *Manchester Guardian* referred to one of his speeches as 'stupid vulgar abuse, unruffled by anything even faintly resembling an idea, an argument or . . . a positive suggestion'. The liberal press supporting free trade also judged him 'intellectually incapable of understanding the elements of the problem on which he presumes to dictate'. Henry Merton & Co. meanwhile sued Hughes for libel (the case was settled out of court in 1920, costing the Commonwealth £6500). Most seriously, Hughes' standing with Britain's political elite was damaged. Lloyd George, in particular, concluded that it was too much trouble to accommodate his inflammatory views in Allied decision-making councils. Hughes started to be bypassed.[85]

Perhaps, as Eric Andrews has suggested, Hughes struggled for subtlety and adroitness in debate because of his increasing deafness. Missing the point at meetings, he would explode with misdirected anger and dogmatism. The cost of this style was particularly evident in the most important debate of all: that about the position of the British Empire in the peace negotiations that at last seemed to be imminent.[86]

The final session of the Imperial War Cabinet, from 13–15 August, was devoted to this issue. Hughes took an uncompromising position on the question of the future of the German colonies and seemed to have the support of British ministers and the other Dominions. South Africa, after all, wanted to keep control of German South-West Africa and New Zealand of Samoa. However, Borden warned of the need to consider the position of the United States, and Reading suggested that Woodrow Wilson would not tolerate territorial annexations. Hughes exploded: 'If you want to shift us [from New Guinea], come and do it; here we are: J'y suis, j'y reste [Here I am, here I stay].' He denied that Australia had ever agreed to the Japanese retaining control of the islands they had occupied north of the equator, though in fact Australia had done so, in February 1917. Nor would he give Australian support to the creation of the League of Nations, even though the British government had approved it in principle.[87]

As the discussion of war aims became increasingly vague and inconclusive, Hughes' interjections became 'tart and testy', and probably ineffectual. As Neville Meaney has said:

> There was almost an air of heroic recklessness or, some might say, egotistical perversity about [Hughes'] advocacy. But, as in the conscription campaigns, his simple-minded certainties tended to alienate more than to persuade . . . [when] he had to consider war and peace not from the distance of Australia but at the centre of the Empire where hard choices, governed by the limits of military power and dependence on allies, had to be made, he became not reasonable and accommodating but querulous and quarrelsome.[88]

So notorious did Hughes' opposition to Wilson's liberal internationalism become that when he suggested that he might visit the United States on his return to Australia, Wilson instructed the American embassy in London to deny him a visa. The State Department made the point that it was unprecedented to deny entry to the head of an Allied government, but Wilson let it be known that, should Hughes make speeches in the United States similar to those he was making in Britain, the American government would publicly dissociate itself from him.

Issues of command

One other issue with which Hughes wrestled while in London was the command of the Australian Corps. After Gough's dismissal in late March, the command of the reformed Fifth Army was offered to Birdwood. Although his preference was to lead an army that included all the Dominion troops, Birdwood accepted the position—but on the condition that his replacement at the Australian Corps should be an Australian. He also asked that he be allowed to continue to administer the AIF as General Officer Commanding (GOC), even though it was possible that no Australian units would be included in the Fifth Army under his command.

The prize of the Australian Corps command was of course highly coveted. McCay, with a distinct lack of self-awareness, assumed that it was his. But his peers thought his abrasiveness disqualified him, not just from corps command but also from the role of GOC in London. This left three contenders: Monash, Hobbs and Brudenell White. Monash was the most senior of the three, and had the most impressive credentials: he had successfully commanded the 3rd Division at Messines and Third Ypres; he had earned the admiration of Haig and was judged by General W.N. Congreve of VII Corps to be the best divisional commander on the Western Front.[89]

Hobbs, the next in seniority, also had a record of successful command, and Birdwood considered him 'thorough, able, loyal and courageous'. However, he suspected that Hobbs had leant upon him for support and 'might find difficulty in standing alone'. Brudenell White, on the other hand, was renowned for his exemplary organisation and administration of the Australian Corps—skills that many thought had actually been the key to Birdwood's success in his corps command. Moreover, White had integrity and moral courage. For example, he had stood up to Haig in July 1916 when he thought the commander-in-chief had unjustly criticised the Australian performance at Pozières. However, White had no experience in field command and, with a self-effacement that was unusual among his counterparts, he subordinated his personal ambitions to the interests of the AIF. Already in July 1917, he had refused Haig's offer to command the Anzac Corps, arguing that Birdwood's rapport with the Australian troops was too valuable to lose.

Birdwood therefore recommended to the Australian government on 12 May that Monash be made corps commander. As he said: 'Of his ability, there can be no possible doubt, nor of his keenness and knowledge. Also, he has had almost unvarying success in all the operations undertaken by his division, which I know has the greatest confidence in him.' There was, Birdwood conceded, the issue of Monash's German background, which had caused some 'feeling' against him in Australia, but this had been 'entirely lived down, as far as the A.I.F. is concerned, by his good work'.[90]

The Australian government agreed, and Monash's promotion was promulgated on 23 May. Immensely gratified, he wrote to his wife: 'To be the first native born Australian Corps Commander is something to have lived for, and will not be forgotten in Australian history.' However, not only had he overlooked Chauvel's earlier appointment to corps command but his elation was premature. In the next few weeks, an extraordinary imbroglio followed during which his appointment was challenged by none other than Charles Bean. During the Gallipoli campaign, Bean had come to dislike Monash, seeing him as self-promoting and publicity-seeking. Bean had also come to idolise Brudenell White, and was appalled at the prospect of his leaving the Australian Corps to accompany Birdwood as his chief of staff in the Fifth Army. Bean therefore joined forces with the official war artist Will Dyson and another self-styled king-maker, Keith Murdoch, to lobby to get the command changes reversed. Brudenell White, as this improbable trio saw it, should have the corps command, while Monash should be compensated with the administrative leadership of the AIF in London. What *was* Bean thinking? Many years later he would write:

> That Monash was in some respects an outstandingly capable commander was well recognised in staff circles, but though a lucid thinker, a wonderful organiser, and accustomed to take endless pains, he had not the physical audacity that Australian troops were thought to require in their leaders, and it was for his ability in administration rather than for tactical skill that he was then reputed. Moreover, a few of those who knew both men doubted whether Monash's judgment would be as resistant as White's to the promptings of personal ambition or whether he was as well equipped to overbear a wrongly insistent superior or the strain of a great disaster.

Such measured arguments probably masked a latent anti-Semitism on Bean's part. He would later describe Monash as 'the elderly Jewish-Australian'.

Dyson, less inhibited, would say, 'Yes—Monash *will* get there—he must get there all the time on account of the qualities of his race; the Jew will *always* get there.'[91]

During May and June, Bean and Murdoch lobbied against Monash at the highest political and military levels: Birdwood, Pearce, Hughes, Secretary of State for War Lord Milner, CIGS Wilson, and finally Lloyd George himself. Murdoch even wrote to Monash on 6 June, clumsily suggesting that he might be tempted to assume the role of administering the AIF in preference to the corps command. Being GOC, Murdoch suggested, could attract a full general-ship and give Monash access to a publicity network (via Murdoch himself) of 250 press outlets.

In retrospect, it seems bizarre that anyone should have listened to these journalists—one of whom was only 31 years old—on a question of senior military command. But Bean and Murdoch claimed a kind of authority as the voice of the AIF. They unnerved Hughes at least with their assertions that the AIF was opposed to Monash's appointment. The prime minister cabled Pearce from the United States, urging that the matter be held over until he arrived in London. Birdwood's appointment was also declared by the Army Council to be temporary. So the matter stood for some weeks. In the interim, Monash took control of the Australian Corps and started planning for its next operation, Hamel.

Ultimately, Monash was confirmed in the corps command. Brudenell White, embarrassed by his backers, withdrew from the race, telling Birdwood that he would not accept the corps command if offered it, because it would appear that he had been 'intriguing with Murdoch'. Birdwood also came to Monash's support. With his own authority for judging who was suitable for promotion being questioned, he told Hughes of his confidence in Monash. He also wrote to Munro Ferguson, denouncing Murdoch's underhand inter-vention and aspirations to be 'an Australian [press baron Lord] Northcliffe'. When Fisher spoke contemptuously of Monash, Birdwood simply told him that he did not know what he was talking about. Hobbs, for his part, wrote to Defence Minister Pearce assuring him that, contrary to what Bean and

Murdoch were saying, Monash enjoyed 'absolutely the complete confidence and respect of the A.I.F. as a fighting leader'.[92]

The situation moved some way towards being resolved when Hughes visited France early in July. His timing could hardly have been less convenient—it was only days before the Battle of Hamel—but Lloyd George had scheduled a meeting at Versailles for the Dominion prime ministers with the Supreme War Council, including Clemenceau and Foch. Hughes seized on this chance of visiting the troops, whose company—as ever—delighted him. He wrote later to Munro Ferguson:

> I can't tell you how splendid [the Australian troops] were: words are poor things to describe them but as they stood there thousands of them armed cap-a-pie: helmets full kit ready for action their bayonets glistening in the sun: an enemy aeroplane overhead being attacked by our anti-aircraft guns . . . I thought that with a million of such men one could conquer the world.

At times, Cook recalled, Hughes lay full length on the ground, looking into the faces of the soldiers and chewing a stalk of grass. He 'seemed wrapped up in the men, and was gazing into their faces all the time'.[93]

Though inclined to defer the issue of the corps command, Hughes did take the opportunity in France to consult with the divisional commanders and other senior officers. They assured him that they supported Monash's appointment, while Monash himself told Hughes that his removal from the corps command would be 'a degradation and humiliation'. Within days, Hamel would demonstrate that Monash was more than fit for the role; however, Bean and Murdoch continued to intrigue, in what Geoffrey Serle has described as 'perhaps the outstanding case of sheer irresponsibility by pressmen in Australian history'. It was not until late July that Hughes finally decided in favour of Monash.[94]

The question of administrative control of the AIF still remained unresolved. Hughes, like many others, thought that Birdwood could not retain the role of GOC AIF. For one thing, managing the repatriation of the AIF at the war's end would be a complex and demanding task. For another, Birdwood was now charged with commanding an army—and a British one at that. As Hughes cabled to his government:

> No man can serve two masters. Remember Birdwood is now commanding an English Army. He looks to War Office for his orders and preferment for the maintenance of his position. Where interests [sic] of Australia and Britain clash—and that they do clash and have clashed in military matters is certain and that interests Australia [sic] have suffered—for which will he stand?

Preferring the Canadian model of separating field command from administration, Hughes tried on 12 August to force Birdwood to choose between the two roles. However, since the British armies were then engaged in a major offensive beyond Amiens, it was agreed that Birdwood should not relinquish the AIF administration until 30 November. By this time, the war's end had made the question redundant.[95]

With the command changes of mid-1918, the senior commanders of the AIF were at last all Australian—or nearly all so. William Glasgow, who had served on Gallipoli with the 2nd Light Horse Regiment and led the 13th Brigade at Pozières, Mouquet Farm, Messines, Passchendaele and most recently, in the liberation of Villers-Bretonneux, was appointed to the command of the 1st Division, replacing Harold Walker, who went to the 48th British Division in Italy. Charles Rosenthal took over the 2nd Division from Nevill Smyth, who also returned to the British Army. Rosenthal was another veteran of Gallipoli who had gone on to command the artillery of four Australian divisions and the 9th Brigade on the Western Front—only to be badly gassed at Passchendaele. Monash was succeeded as commander of the 3rd Division by John Gellibrand, another veteran of Gallipoli, Pozières and Mouquet Farm, and commander of the 6th Brigade at Bullecourt. He had returned to command the 12th Brigade, after taking leave from the front and overhauling the depots of the AIF in the United Kingdom. Ewen Sinclair-MacLagan and Hobbs continued to lead the 4th and 5th Divisions respectively. Sinclair-MacLagan was, in fact, Scottish-born but since he had served in Australia from 1901 to 1904, had taught at Duntroon from 1910 to 1914, and landed with the AIF at Gallipoli on 25 April 1915, he was considered an honorary Australian.

In all these changes, one man was *not* promoted to divisional command: Pompey Elliott. Although his 15th Brigade had earned countless accolades at Polygon Wood and Villers-Bretonneux, Elliott's reputation for poor judgement, lack of self-control and indiscretion counted against him. He was thought to be 'prone to go it alone, to act independently without heeding superiors' instructions or the exigencies of the overall tactical situation'. As Brudenell White put it, Elliott could 'break out like a volcano' if things did not go the way he wanted.[96]

Elliott was devastated at being passed over. He formally protested, and even threatened Brudenell White with appealing to Pearce. White, however, called Elliott's bluff, telling him he would send him back to Australia 'without the least hesitation if calmly and deliberately you repeated yr assertion to seek political aid—and if you managed to raise a dozen "Politico-military" enquiries I wd fight you to a standstill on them!' Forced to back down, Elliott then wrote a long account of the controversial incidents that were being held against him. To make sure this apologia was included in the historical record, he sent a copy to the young director of the Australian War Records Section in London, Captain John Treloar. It made no difference, however. Even though Elliott's claim for divisional command was, in the measured opinion of Ross McMullin, 'as compelling' as those of Gellibrand, Glasgow and Rosenthal, he never gained the promotion he thought he deserved. For the rest of his life, Elliott would remain tormented by 'a profound sense of injustice' about his 'supersession'.

Peace demands at home

Throughout his time overseas, Hughes claimed to be speaking for 'Australia' as prime minister. This was—and remains—the diplomatic convention. However, it is debatable how representative he was of wider Australian opinion by this point in the war. Although Hughes consulted his Cabinet while overseas, he was prone to acting first and seeking cabinet advice later.

Alternatively, when it suited him, he simply ignored his colleagues' advice. As for the Australian public, many loyalists agreed with Hughes' support for the British Empire and his demands that Germany be ruined. But the way in which he pursued these causes, and the damage inflicted on imperial relations by his combative style, would come to trouble many loyalists later in 1918.

What is clear is that Hughes could no longer claim to speak for Australians on the left of politics. Before his departure from Australia, Opposition leader Tudor tried to move an amendment in parliament to the effect that the prime minister and his deputy 'could not represent Australian opinion' at the forthcoming imperial meetings. The views that Hughes had expressed at the 1916 Paris conference had 'done more to prolong the war than anything else'. Beyond that, Hughes had been repudiated twice by the electorate on the important question of conscription. Another Labor parliamentarian argued that Hughes' 'hysteria would incite the Germans to the bitterest possible resistance'. He was 'not a proper person to represent Australia'. The Victorian Branch of the ALP also recorded in late April that it entered 'an emphatic protest against the Prime Minister (Mr. Hughes) visiting Europe as a mouthpiece of Australian political thought'.[97]

The wider labour movement was now openly advocating an end to the war through a negotiated peace—a peace very different from the total victory Hughes was demanding in London. When the ALP met in Perth at its seventh Commonwealth Conference in mid-June, it unanimously adopted 'peace resolutions' submitted jointly by the New South Wales, Victoria, Queensland and South Australia conferences. These condemned the governments of Europe, 'founded on class rule and adopting the methods of secret diplomacy', for their failure to end the war and called for an end to the 'capitalistic system of production for profit [which] compels every nation constantly to seek new markets to exploit, inevitably leading to a periodic clash of rival interests'. What was needed, the resolutions claimed, was an immediate international peace conference incorporating representatives of working-class organisations, women, the Dominions and Ireland: '[P]eace can only be accomplished by the united efforts of the workers of all the countries involved.' The principles that should inform this peace were the very ones that Hughes despised: self-determination for, or international control of, colonies; the freedom of the seas; open diplomacy; the abolition of armaments; and a 'world-wide parliament'. To this agenda, the ALP added the rights of all small nations— including Ireland—to their independence and the abolition of conscription in all countries.[98]

In the debates that followed, the political leadership of Labor was increasingly exposed, particularly since the ALP conference also tried to make any participation by Labor leaders in future recruitment drives contingent on two conditions: first, that the Allies declare their readiness to enter peace negotiations on the basis of no annexations and no penal indemnities; and second, that there be an inquiry into Australia's manpower needs for home defence and industrial requirements. When the beleaguered Tudor argued that this was a mistake and would place Labor in a weak position politically, the matter was referred to a referendum of the grass-roots branches, scheduled for November.[99]

Fortunately for what remained of the unity of the ALP, in the weeks before the planned ballot the more moderate elements of Labor distanced themselves from the Perth conference. The New South Wales parliamentarians declared in September that they were opposed to conscription but that:

> To abandon voluntary enlistment now would mean pulling out of the war, and leaving those trade unionists who are in the trenches without the help we should give them. [The Perth proposals] may be interpreted to mean that as a party we shall take no further part in the war. This would be a distinct breach of faith with the electors and a base desertion of our soldiers.

The federal Labor caucus was also divided on the matter, and in October various trade unions voted against the Perth resolution. By this time events on the Western Front had turned dramatically in the Allies' favour and the referendum on recruitment had become redundant. But had the war not ended then, the ALP might well have undergone another damaging split and yet more haemorrhaging.[100]

Hamel

Though no one knew it at the time, June and July 1918 were the pivotal months of the war. In the so-called Kaiser's battles of the previous four months, the Germans had made dramatic gains. They had captured ten times more territory than the Allies had done in 1917 and had extended the length of the Western Front from 390 to 520 kilometres. Yet for all their tactical brilliance, they had not won a strategic victory. Moreover, they had lost nearly a million men. The British and French had also lost heavily, but by 20 July there were over a million American troops in France. By November, there would be nearly 1.9 million.[101]

The door was now ajar for the Allies to take the offensive. Typically, Foch had been planning for this since he became generalissimo. His original vision was for multiple offensives in France, Salonika and Italy, but with the Austrian attack at Piave in June this became impossible. Focusing on France, then, Foch aimed to attack the three large German salients that were now protruding into the Allied line—at the Marne, in the vicinity of Amiens, and at Saint-Mihiel. If these objectives were captured, the Germans would be denied the railway systems on which the future supply of their armies depended.

Given the succession of German offensives in the spring, and the fact that Haig was nervous about diverting reserves from Flanders, it would take time for Foch's plans to unfold fully. However, in the interim he encouraged local attacks in an effort to prevent the Germans from reinforcing their troops in the south. It was in this context that Monash and his divisional commanders decided that the Australian Corps should clear the Germans from Hamel, a spur that extended from the plateau north-east of Villers-Bretonneux to the Somme opposite Sailly-Laurette. This was the highest point in the area, from which the Germans overlooked the Australian positions while their guns in the woods near the village of Hamel could fire into the flank of the Australian 2nd Division. This formation, after its success at Morlancourt in early June, held positions along the north bank of the Somme, extending beyond those of the AIF on the opposite bank. In addition, if the Germans were cleared from Hamel the British field of defence east of Villers-Bretonneux would be widened, positioning them well for future actions.

There had been an earlier plan to attack Hamel when it fell into German hands in April, but this had not proceeded given its poor chances of success. By June 1918, however, the German troops in the area were weak and the British Fourth Army had access to 60 of the most up-to-date tanks, the Mark V. Faster and more manoeuvrable than earlier models, these tanks were reliable, had stronger armour and needed only one man from a crew of eight to drive them.[102]

Both Monash and Rawlinson realised—who was first has never been determined—that with these tanks Hamel might be taken with relatively few infantry casualties. Monash even thought, on the advice of the commander of the 5th Tank Brigade, Brigadier-General Anthony Courage, that the attack could be primarily a tank operation. The infantry could be consigned to a follow-up role and the creeping barrage dispensed with, since it would slow the tanks down and, if it fell short, hit them. However, his commanders were not so sure. Sinclair-MacLagan and the 4th Division had not forgotten Bullecourt, and Monash's Chief of Staff, Thomas Blamey (later to command the 2nd AIF in World War II), also doubted the wisdom of placing so much trust in armour. A senior commander of the corps artillery, Walter Coxen, also—indeed, naturally—advocated retaining a creeping barrage. Monash therefore reverted to a more traditional plan of attack, in which the infantry were assisted by tanks rather than the reverse.

Yet Hamel was far from a traditional battle. With tanks, infantry, artillery and air power at his disposal, Monash had the good fortune to command a recognisably modern integrated weapons system. As he said famously in his post-war account of the battle:

> A perfected modern battle plan is like nothing so much as a score for an orchestral composition, where the various arms and units are the instruments, and the tasks they perform are their respective musical phrases. Every individual unit must make its entry precisely at the proper moment, and play its phrase in the general harmony.[103]

A critical element of this new weapons system was air power, in which the Allies were now increasingly dominant. In the lead-up to Hamel, Allied aircraft bombed German positions, located enemy guns, radioed aerial intelligence to artillery crews and flew 'noise patrols' to drown out the sound of the assembling tanks. When the battle began, aircraft kept the advancing infantry supplied by parachuting in boxes of ammunition, using a technique pioneered by the Germans in their earlier 1918 offensives.[104]

As at Messines, Monash planned Hamel meticulously. Every detail of the operation was rehearsed at conferences of the commanders and staffs of all the services involved in the attack. At the final meeting on 30 June, 250 officers were present; the agenda included some 133 items and the meeting lasted for four and a half hours.

> The underlying principle of the conference [Monash explained to Rawlinson] was that everybody that mattered was present, and had to explain his plans and proposals; and that, where there was any conflict or doubt or difference of opinion, a final and unalterable decision was given, there and then, and no subsequent 'fiddling' with the plan was permitted.[105]

As Eric Andrews and B.G. Jordan put it:

> Those who rather sourly remark that Monash stole other men's ideas . . . completely miss the point; the conference system was designed to steal ideas—or, more positively, 'pool' ideas—so that all possible problems could be foreseen and all possible solutions considered.

Even Bean later conceded that Monash was 'a master of lucid explanation'.[106]

The approach cascaded down the command chain. Brigade and battalion commanders worked through the plans with their subordinates, while the tanks and infantry spent hours practising together. The infantry clambered over the tanks, took joy rides and developed much-needed confidence in the capability of the machines and their crews.

The preparations for Hamel were almost derailed when, a few days before the attack, the US Commander-in-Chief, General John Pershing, learned that ten companies of the US 33rd National Guard Division, then training with the Fourth Army, had been assigned to the battle. This conflicted with his aim of maintaining the integrity of his national force by not using it piecemeal, and he insisted that six companies be withdrawn. Then, on the very eve of the battle, Monash learned that the remaining American troops were not available. He gave Rawlinson an ultimatum: either the American troops took part or the battle would be cancelled. At 7.20 p.m. on 3 July, he received the approval from Haig to launch the attack *with* the American troops included.[107]

The battle began early the next morning, at 3.10 a.m. (see Map 30). The sky erupted with the fire of 302 heavy guns, 326 field guns and a machine-gun barrage (the latter an idea borrowed from the Canadians). Then 7500 infantry 'at once rose and, lighting their cigarettes and with rifles slung, as if on a march, moved up to the line of shells', as Bean put it later. In fact, each battalion also carried light and heavy machine guns to increase its mobile

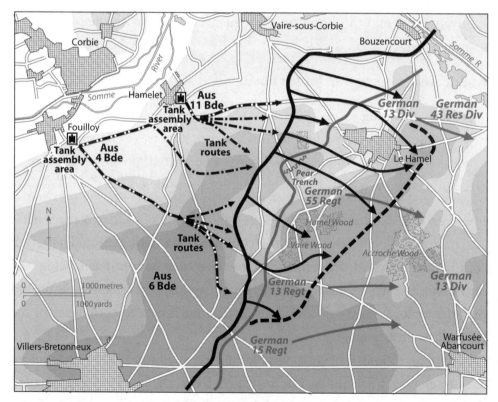

Map 30: Hamel, 4 June 1918

firepower. The 60 tanks lumbered into action, moving forward to crush the wire and destroy German machine gunners and strong points. Four carrier tanks supplied the infantry with ammunition that in previous battles would have taken 1250 men to shift.

> It was a weird sight [one private recalled] to see these ungainly objects waddling up at the toot, in response to signals from the infantry and approach a machine gun possie with blazing guns. If they did not manage to put the machine gun out of action with their fire they continued straight on and went right over the gun and crew and emplacement and flattened the whole lot out![108]

Thanks to intense efforts to ensure secrecy, the surprise was complete. However, in the darkness, smoke and heavy ground mist, some things went wrong. At Pear Trench, a well-defended German position between the village of Hamel and Vaire Woods, for example, the tanks lost contact with the infantry, who suffered heavy losses. Some Australian units were hit by their own shells falling short (the need for secrecy meant that most of the guns had set their range by map-based calculations, not registration). The inexperienced American troops also had difficulty keeping close behind the barrage.

Yet for all this, the attack was 'a perfection of team work', as Monash called it. In only 93 minutes all objectives were gained. The Germans suffered 2000 casualties, 1600 of their men were taken prisoner, and they lost 177 machine guns, two field guns and 32 trench mortars—for some 1200 Australian and 176 American casualties. None of the tanks was lost, although three came back disabled temporarily.[109]

Across the river in the Ancre Valley, a battalion of the 15th Brigade had also retaken a slice of land to the east of Ville-sur-Ancre in a diversionary action. 'My Brigade only had a small part [in Hamel],' Elliott wrote, 'but what they did do they did magnificently. We did not know that there were three times as many Boches in their trenches as we had, but notwithstanding that we hunted them out and killed about 120 of them, captured 17 machine guns from them and 64 prisoners, whilst the rest bolted like rabbits.'[110]

Hamel was over, but in the days that followed Monash kept his forces on the attack, 'feeding them on victory' as he liked to say. All along its front, the Australian Corps had 'a high old time, peacefully penetrating and nibbling, advancing the line by hundreds of yards and capturing prisoners and machine-guns'. In this way, they came to dominate the plateau around Villers-Bretonneux at minimal cost.[111]

Remembering Hamel

The victory at Hamel was much praised at the time and later. Lloyd George and the Dominion prime ministers in London asked Hughes to congratulate Monash, while Clemenceau, who had a habit of visiting a French unit every weekend, descended on the 4th Division headquarters on 7 July. To the assembled Australian soldiers, he said:

> When the Australians came to France, the French people expected a great deal of you because they had heard what you have accomplished in the development of your own country. We knew that you would fight a real fight, but we did not know that from the very beginning you would astonish the whole continent. I shall go back tomorrow and say to my countrymen: 'I have seen the Australians. I have looked in their faces. I know that these men will fight alongside of us again until the cause for which we are all fighting is safe for us and for our children.'

A steady stream of British commanders also made their way to Monash's headquarters at Chateau Bertangles to study his methods, while his orders for the battle were published by General Headquarters in two instructional pamphlets.

Hamel also did much to establish Monash's reputation with later military historians. It was 'the perfect battle', J.F.C. Fuller wrote in 1936. 'In rapidity, brevity, and completeness of success, no battle of the war can compete with [it].' Fuller, it should be noted, was hardly a disinterested commentator: he was chief of staff of the Tank Corps in 1917–18. But Major-General H. Essame would write much later, in 1972: 'A war-winning combination had been found:

a corps commander of genius, the Australian infantry, the Tank Corps, the Royal Artillery and the RAF.'[112]

Yet the significance of Hamel can be overrated. Although it manifestly demonstrated the power of an integrated force of infantry, armour, artillery and air power, it is fanciful to see it as a harbinger of the blitzkrieg of World War II, as one Australian journalist has claimed. For one thing, its objectives were limited: the attack frontage was 5.5 kilometres, to a depth of 2 kilometres. Moreover, there was no exploitation of the success. The battle was over in an hour and a half, and Hamel in no way resembled the sweeping, deep penetrations of the Wehrmacht's panzer drive across northern France in 1940. Nor was Hamel, as some Australians like to think, the Allied success that 'turned the tide against the Germans on the Western Front'. Weeks before the battle, the German army's offensives from Hazebrouck in the north to the Matz in the south had stalled. Hamel was more an exploitation of the Germans' growing exhaustion than a cause of their collapse.[113]

Despite its fame, Hamel did not become a site of official Australian commemoration until late in the twentieth century. While the 3rd Division obelisk and the national memorial rose nearby at Sailly-le-Sec and Villers-Bretonneux, the battlefield of Hamel remained unadorned. Decades later, in 1960, the military historian John Laffin began a campaign to redress this situation, but it was not until the 80th anniversary of the battle that the government of John Howard, in a flurry of new memorial building at overseas sites, funded a $1.3 million memorial to the Australian Corps and the 100,000 Australians who had served in France. For what, one might ask, did the national memorial stand?[114]

The dedication of the Hamel memorial on 4 July 1998 spoke more to the politics of late twentieth-century memory than to the 1918 battle. The French government marked the anniversary by bestowing the Legion of Honour on four Australian veterans at the nearby Villers-Bretonneux memorial. All of these men had served in France in 1918, and their longevity—three of the four were 100 or older—made them stand for more than themselves. The Battle of Hamel, in turn, was transformed in the speech of the Australian Minister for Veterans' Affairs, Bruce Scott, to a 'key to understanding ourselves and the world around us', an exemplar of 'essential human truths, as constant as nature itself, which ignore time'. Hamel proved that:

> amid uncertainty and possible defeat, a spark—although small—can be struck by determined, well led men. And from that flicker, a blaze can be fanned into life. Hamel was such a spark, a turning point . . . Hamel told an exhausted and war weary world to hold on.

Given the multinational audience at the dedication, Hamel was also translated—almost as improbably—into a fusion of the Anzac and French revolutionary traditions:

> In another of life's great lessons, Monash proved that using men's minds as well as their bodies, trusting their intellect and initiative, would achieve results. No long cannon fodder, sheep driven into the bloody slaughter of years past, but free men, partners in the enterprise before them. In the fight for France's liberty, equality and fraternity found new form at Hamel.[115]

However, if the 1998 ceremony was a triumphalist occasion, the memorial to the Australian Corps at Hamel proved a disappointment. A set of three overlapping curved walls, standing 4.5 metres high and 6 metres long, it was clad with Australian black granite. Onto this was sandblasted the rising sun badge of the AIF, images of men of the 29th Battalion ready to fight a later battle, that of 8 August 1918, and the figure of Monash flanked by the weapons of war. The glue used to fix the tiles, however, could not cope with the harsh Somme winters. Tiles began to fall off and the site was vandalised. It was even rumoured that visitors mistook Monash for Hitler![116]

Within three years, therefore, the Hamel memorial had to be redesigned, at the cost of a further $A7.9 million. Dedicated a second time on the 90th anniversary of the end of World War I in 2008, the memorial retained its original shape but the Australian granite was replaced by Canadian stone. Gone too were Monash and the diggers. (Did the choice of Monash, though obvious from the perspective of the Australian Corps' history, sit uneasily with the 'democratic' tradition of Australian military history, which prefers soldiers to generals?) The memorial now carries Clemenceau's panegyric to Australian troops of 7 July 1918, inscribed in both French and English. Monash and his men are relegated to 20 bilingual educational panels that line the path from the car park—rather like sacred stones on some Neolithic site. Here the visitor can read of VC recipients, tactical innovation, the shooting down of the German aviator the 'Red Baron' Manfred von Richthofen on 21 April 1918, and the wider strategic context of Hamel. A trench near the memorial, meanwhile, marks the site where a German strongpoint, 'Wolfsberg', was captured by elements of the 44th Battalion on 4 July 1918.[117]

The 'turning point' of the war

Within days of Hamel, the Germans launched what would be their final offensive on the Western Front. Although there were some within the German government now conceding that the war could not be won by military means and many army commanders wished to pause before striking again, Ludendorff was determined to keep attacking. His final assault, known to the Allies as the Second Battle of the Marne, was launched to the south of the Somme on 15 July, with the aim of encircling the city of Rheims, establishing bridgeheads across the Marne, threatening Paris and cutting the railway between the capital and Nancy. Another attack on the British in Flanders would follow, forcing the Allies to submit.

Despite all the losses of the previous months, the Germans could still throw 52 divisions into battle against 34 Allied divisions. But the French knew the attack was coming and deployed their forces in depth. Six divisions of the German Seventh Army managed to cross the River Marne, along which the front extended to the east of Rheims, but they then became marooned on the southern bank of the river. Their artillery could not keep up with their infantry, and French artillery was pounding the bridges to their rear. To the west of Rheims, the infantry of the German First and Third Armies also penetrated beyond the Marne, but they found themselves sucked into a trap as the French withdrew from their front line, allowing the German bombardment to fall on almost empty ground.[118]

Then, on 18 July, the French counter-attacked with the support of four American divisions. Outnumbered and with few—if any—tanks, the Germans were pushed back to within 3 miles of Soissons, the railway town that supplied their salient at the Marne. Ludendorff raced to reinforce the area with troops from the north—thus abandoning, forever as it turned out, any plans to attack the British again in Flanders. By the time Friedenssturm stalled, the Germans had lost around 250,000 prisoners and 400 guns.

It was this Allied attack of 18 July, even Bean conceded, that was 'the turning point of the war'. Never again would the Germans regain the initiative on the Western Front. Moreover, with the enemy being checked in the south, Foch and Haig were able to proceed with their plans for launching an attack east of Amiens. This would open the famous '100 days' during which the German forces were pushed to the point of final collapse.

Amiens

The idea of Amiens had been in gestation for some time. Haig had asked Rawlinson, Birdwood and Brudenell White in May to develop plans for an attack using Australian and Canadian troops to the east of Amiens. The operation had to be put on hold when the Germans attacked at Chemin des Dames on 27 May, but Rawlinson revived it soon after Hamel. Haig approved it on 19 July when it was clear that the German attack at Rheims had been held. Foch confirmed the decision to proceed on 24 August.

Later it would become 'a commonplace of patriotic journalism' and an article of faith among Australian returned soldiers, to quote Geoffrey Serle, that it was Monash who was the driving force behind the decision to attack at Amiens. Monash himself implied as much in his 1920 memoir, where he wrote that it was the 'electric' effect of Hamel that:

> stimulated many men to the realization that the enemy was, after all, not invulnerable . . . It marked the termination, once and for all, of the purely defensive attitude of the British front. It incited in many quarters an examination of the possibilities of offensive action on similar lines by

similar means—a changed attitude of mind, which bore a rich harvest only a very few weeks later.

However, as Serle concludes, it is more accurate to say that Monash was thinking along the same lines as Foch, Haig and Rawlinson in regard to Amiens, and was allowed to believe that he was the instigator of the plan. What Monash *could* claim credit for was the success of his corps at 'peaceful penetration' in the days after Hamel, which meant that both he and the corps were assigned a leading role in the Battle of Amiens.[119]

Yet the Australians were only one element, if a central one, in what was to be a multinational operation at Amiens. To the north of the Somme on 8 August was a division of the British III Corps supported by parts of the 33rd American Division. South of the river was the Australian Corps, covering the line to the point of the railway between Amiens and Chaulnes. Next was the Canadian Corps, which in turn linked with the French First Army. The attack would be spearheaded by four divisions—one British, one Canadian and two Australian—whose task was to push the Germans back to the Inner Amiens defence system constructed by the French in 1916. After this Green Line had been reached, four more divisions of the same national armies would leapfrog the first formations. They would capture the Red Line some 2700 metres ahead before advancing to take the old outer line of the Amiens defence system.

Amiens was Hamel on a larger scale. The infantry were supported by some 2000 guns, armoured cars, cavalry and the entire Tank Corps of 552 tanks, which included the new lighter Whippet tanks. With 24 tanks supporting each division, it was the largest tank battle of the war thus far. The Allies also had a four to one dominance in the air. Many German planes were still in Champagne, and the Allied aircraft—including No. 3 Squadron of the Australian Flying Corps—were able to conduct reconnaissance, blanket the noise of the tanks assembling behind the line, and support the ground attack with bombing, strafing and supply drops. The artillery, which identified the vast majority of German gun sites before the battle, silenced the enemy batteries and provided a creeping barrage.[120]

With an acute sense of occasion, Monash issued a message to his troops on 7 August:

> For the first time in the history of this Corps, all five Australian divisions will tomorrow engage in the largest and most important battle operation ever undertaken by the Corps . . . The full resources of our sister Dominion, the Canadian Corps, will also operate on our right, while two British divisions will guard our left flank. . . I earnestly wish every soldier of the Corps the best of good fortune, and a glorious and decisive victory, the story of which will re-echo throughout the world, and will live for ever in the history of our home land.

The night before the battle was full of tension, excitement and organised chaos. One soldier recalled:

> Guns were moving from all directions. Tanks were crawling about and one had to be careful he wasn't run down as it was terribly dark. Planes were flying overhead to drown the noise of the tanks and the gun limbers moving about. There was men [sic] everywhere and one had to keep close to his next man in case he lost his company.[121]

Then, at 4.20 a.m. on 8 August, the British guns opened up in 'a titanic pandemonium' and the infantry and tanks moved out into a mist so heavy that one platoon had to hold hands to stay together (see Map 31). South of the Somme, the Australians' attack made dramatic progress. The Germans facing them were blinded by the mist, unable to fire accurately and crushed by the weight of the artillery barrage and the rush of tanks and infantry. As one tank driver recalled:

> The tank crushed the German wire defences like so much paper, and left a clear pathway through which the infantry followed. As we cruised over No Man's Land several erratic strings of bullets flashed across my driving window plate as some enemy machine-gunner blindly traversed our front . . . as I straddled the bus across the main [German] trench my machine-gunners got busy from both sides and caught several of the enemy scuttling for cover. We climbed right over and went blindly on.[122]

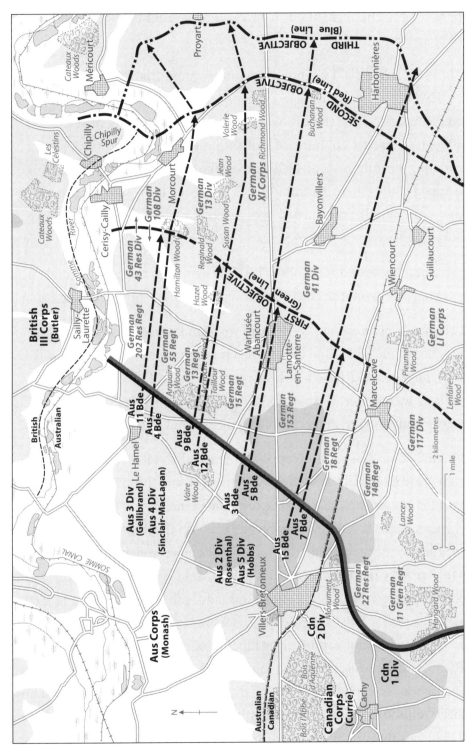

Map 31: Amiens, 8 August 1918

Then, at 8 a.m., the mist lifted to reveal a panorama best described in the words of an eyewitness:

> [The mist] rolled right up into the sky in one piece, like a theatre curtain . . . Beyond the river a miracle—*the* miracle—had begun . . . Across the level Santerre, which the sun was beginning to fill with a mist-filtered lustre, two endless columns of British guns, wagons, and troops were marching steadily east, unshelled, over the grounds that the Germans had held until dawn. Nothing like it had ever been seen in the war. Above, on our cliff, we turned and stared at each other. We must have looked rather like Cortes' men agape on their peak.[123]

At 8.20 a.m., the second stage of the battle began, with tanks and mobile field guns taking over from the creeping barrage. W.H. Downing recalled:

> it was fairly plain sailing. Whenever we found ourselves in trouble, we signalled to the tanks, and they turned towards the obstacle. Then *punk-crash, punk-crash!* As their little toy guns spoke and their little, pointed shells flew, another German post was blown to pieces. *Punk-crash!* A brick wall tottered and crumbled amid a cloud of red dust.[124]

By 10 a.m., some Australian troops had reached the Red Line and an hour later an Australian flag was reportedly flying from the church spire of the village of Harbonnières, close to the final Blue Line.

The Canadians to the right had kept pace with the Australians and by the end of the day all their objectives had been achieved. Hence in one day, the Fourth Army, while losing 9000 casualties, captured 13 kilometres across a 13.5-kilometre front, seized 400 guns and caused the Germans 27,000 casualties. Some 12,000 of these were prisoners of war. The French First Army to the south, while not capturing as much ground, had forced its way across the River Avre and was positioned to encircle Mondidier the next day.[125]

The battle was not without its difficulties. Some German machine gunners refused to give ground easily, and where the German artillery held their positions they damaged the British tanks. The use of the cavalry in combination with the Whippets also proved 'a predictable fiasco', with the horses in some cases outstripping the tanks and proving yet again that horseflesh was no match for modern weaponry. To the north of the Somme, too, III Corps did not make good progress since its 18th and 58th Divisions were rebuilding with raw recruits and had already been fighting for two days. Moreover, the terrain they faced was a series of spines and peninsulas at right angles to the advance. This was not good tank country and, as it was, they had only 36 of the available tanks. The Chipilly spur, which overlooked the battlefield, therefore remained in enemy hands, leaving the left of the Australians across the river exposed to German machine-gun fire. In the extreme south, meanwhile, the 4th Canadian Division had been halted when they had outstripped their artillery and met two recently arrived regiments of the German Reserve Division.[126]

However, the day as a whole, as Rawlinson said, was 'as fine a feat of arms as any that this war can produce'. 'The Canadians have done splendidly and the Aussies even better.' The flawless leapfrogging of divisions, Rawlinson concluded, was attributable to the 'discipline and high organization of the Australian Corps'—high praise indeed from a command that had constantly criticized the AIF's lack of discipline.[127]

For the Germans, in contrast, 8 August was 'the greatest defeat which the German army had suffered since the beginning of the war', as the German official history put it. Ludendorff famously described it as 'the black day of the German Army in this war', telling Hindenburg on 13 August that the only thing Germany could now do was go on the defensive, with occasional limited attacks aimed at wearing down the enemy and forcing them to make terms.[128]

Yet if this is known in retrospect, at the time the aftermath of 8 August was disappointing. On 9 August the Allies' momentum slowed. This was partly because their tank losses on the first day were severe: only 155 of the 430 that had gone into action on 8 August were serviceable the following day. The tank crews were exhausted after a hot summer day in stifling metal boxes, and the artillery was struggling to keep pace with the rapid advance and to register on new targets. More importantly, the Allied commanders—including Monash—failed to manage the transition to open warfare, which for many of them was a novelty. Surprised and delighted with their success, they underrated the difficulties of communicating with their units without the elaborate telephone networks of static trench warfare. They misjudged the time needed to bring up reserve forces. And as always, the Germans showed remarkable powers of recovery, mobilising six new divisions—one more than the Allied planners anticipated.[129]

The operations that followed after 8 August were therefore, as Bean would later say, probably 'a classic example of how not to follow up a great attack'. The plan was to resume the advance on the morning of 9 August, with the Canadians pushing to the south-east towards Roye while the Australian 1st Division took Lihons. (The Australian 2nd Division would be positioned to the right of the 1st, relieving the 5th Division.) But Rawlinson's staff, busy congratulating themselves on their victory, did not issue formal orders to Currie until near midnight on 8 August. Currie, in turn, transmitted these to his own subordinates at 1 a.m.—for a battle scheduled to start at 11 a.m.! Monash, too, although he had warned his divisional commanders of the possibility of exploitation some days earlier, issued formal orders to the 1st and 2nd Divisions after midnight on 8–9 August. Not until early to mid-morning were these instructions passed down the chain to the battalion commanders.[130]

The 1st Division therefore arrived at its jumping-off point just west of Harbonnières two hours late, though this was still within twelve hours of its receiving its warning order when it was stationed some 16 kilometres away! The battle procedure for 2nd Division was also 'shambolic'. Its battalion commanders received their marching orders only at 10 a.m. on 9 August, and the field artillery supporting them was initially not told which brigade it should support. The division could not start its attack until 4.30 p.m. To add to this, there were poor communications and coordination laterally between the various national forces. On 9 August, sixteen attacking brigades employed thirteen different start times.[131]

In this chaotic situation, the 15th Brigade (5th Division), which was still holding the line next to the Canadians, had to fill the gap left unfilled by the 1st Division on the morning of 9 August. With no artillery support and just one tank, the brigade moved beyond Harbonnières through heavy fire with no clearer aim than 'to push on until the First Division materialised'. In typical style, Elliott went to the front himself and directed operations—even when wounded in the buttock and with his pants around his ankles as his injury was inspected![132]

Once in action, the 1st and 2nd Australian Divisions pushed on with a series of improvised operations against increasing German resistance. With little coordinated artillery support and their few tanks knocked out quickly, the infantry relied on their tactical skills of fire and movement. The Germans they met were in many instances exhausted and committed to the battle piecemeal, without artillery support. By 11 August, Lihons and nearby Raine-court had been taken and the advance was entering the French sector of the 1916 Somme battlefield, pitted with trenches and shell holes.[133]

Meanwhile, Monash had turned his sights to Péronne, located strategically at the bend in the Somme some 30 kilometres ahead (by road). On 9 August, he persuaded Rawlinson to give him responsibility for the northern bank of the Somme. Then, when the Chipilly Spur was finally cleared by the 2/10th London regiment with some help from an intrepid six-man patrol from the Australian 1st Battalion, Monash launched an attack, on either side of the Somme, aiming to trap the Germans in the U-shaped bends of the river.[134]

The Somme at this point was not so much a river as a series of lakes and marshes. As Bean put it, with his usual knack for description:

> Here for about ten miles as the crow flies, the northern riverside is keyed into the southern by a succession of peninsulas, four on the north side, four on the south. Most of the northern ones are almost precipitous along the eastern side, into which the river eats, but slope gently on the western. It [sic] all cases the northern peninsulas overlook the southern, some of the latter being barely above the flats. The villages of Chipilly, Etinehem, Bray and Suzanne lie successively in the northern bends, each of the last three overlooked by the cliffs of the peninsula west of it.[135]

As Monash planned it, the attack would take place at night on 10/11 August with two brigades attacking along the north and south of the river respectively. Each unit would have some tank support, but this was only the second time tanks had been used at night. The tank officers said of the southern bank operation that 'the job was mad', and other officers received their orders 'with some amazement'. In the event, the 13th Brigade managed to push the Germans to a point above Bray at the end of the Etinehem Spur. But the 10th Brigade, trying to fight its way along the Roman road towards Proyart and Froissy, encountered land crisscrossed with trenches from 1916. Under heavy fire and bombing, the infantry and tanks became separated. The attack ended in 'a sharp, almost complete repulse', leaving animals, men and equipment strewn along the road. However, since the Germans were now outflanked on the other side of the Somme by the 13th Brigade, they evacuated Proyart, allowing it to fall into Australian hands in the following days.[136]

Remembering Amiens

Monash meanwhile basked in the glory of victory. On 11 August, he met his five divisional commanders and their staff on the outskirts of Villers-Bretonneux. Nearby was dramatic evidence of their success: over 3000 German prisoners in a cage. Progressively, a galaxy of Allied leaders joined them: Clemenceau, Foch, the French Minister for Finance Louis Klotz, Haig, Wilson, Rawlinson, Currie, Godley, Lieutenant-General Charles Kavanagh, commander of the Cavalry Corps, Major-General Hugh Elles, commanding the Tank Corps, and Major-General Lionel Charlton, commanding the 5th Brigade Royal Air Force. As Monash wrote to his wife:

> Of course there was no thought of serious work or discussion for some twenty minutes, while everybody was being presented to everybody else, and I was personally, naturally—with General Currie—the leading figure in the show, for everybody was highly complimentary and marvelled at the completeness of our success.

The following day Monash was knighted by King George V at the Château de Bertangles. Not everything went quite as Monash might have planned, however. He tried to rise from his knees before the regal sword had rested on his second shoulder, and the guard of honour, which had been hastily conscripted to drag German guns to adorn the driveway, was lukewarm when cheering the monarch. Bean, too, privately added a sour note. But nothing could detract from Monash's justifiable pride in reaching a pinnacle of professional success and imperial recognition.[137]

The Australian press also exulted in the news of Amiens. 'Best Situation Since War Began', the Adelaide *Register* headlined on 10 August. Lloyd George was quoted on 12 August as saying that 'We are smashing our way through, and have won a great victory.' The rededication of Amiens cathedral less than two weeks after the battle also inspired celebration:

> Allied soldiers stood or sat between the sand-bagged columns. The choir was composed entirely of dusty, uniformed soldiers. Allied flags fluttered over the altar to the wind [sic], which blew freely through the shattered windows. The floor was littered with fragments of ancient masonry.[138]

However, Monash and Hughes thought the press coverage failed to give due credit to the Australians. As was often the case, the Dominions were subsumed under the descriptor of 'British' and the Australian Corps' distinctive contribution to the battle was unclear. Hughes therefore arranged for cohorts of journalists to visit the Australian sector on 12 September, while Murdoch cabled to the Australian press on 23 August that 'It is now permissible to say that the brilliant victory at Amiens was largely Australian . . . The fact is that the Australian Corps today is the pride of the Allies' armies.' It was a version of Amiens that proved resilient over the years and persists in some quarters today. But then Australians are not alone in their chauvinism. Canadians, for their part, claim that Amiens was 'chiefly a Canadian battle' in which the Canadian Corps was 'the decisive instrument of victory'.[139]

Péronne and Mont St Quentin

While the success of 8 August was very fresh, Foch and Haig agreed that the Fourth Army should continue to push east of Amiens to the line between

Chaulnes and Roye. At the same time, the British Third Army to the north of the Somme would advance on Bapaume. Foch's grand vision was to link up all the French armies from the Somme to the Oise and into Champagne, a prospect that offered 'enormous possibilities'.[140]

However, by 13 August it was clear that the momentum of the Fourth Army was slowing and that the 'possibility of further cheap exploitation of the success of 8 August had to come an end', as Monash put it. Moreover, Currie—whose Canadian Corps was integral to the planned advance east—protested at its continuing to fight in the difficult conditions now confronting it. He recommended that the Canadians return to their normal base of operation around Arras, and since he was a Dominion commander whose prime minister was delivering ultimatums at the Imperial War Conference in London, his wishes could not be ignored. Hence Haig decided to suspend the plans for further major operations by the Fourth Army. Foch was furious, but was advised that while he might have responsibility for the strategic coordination of Allied military operations, Haig was ultimately accountable to his government for the security of British and Dominion armies.[141]

The main focus of British and French operations therefore shifted away from the area due east of Amiens in the second half of August. To the south, the French pushed forward in the region of the Oise River and Soissons, breaking the main German line of resistance between the Oise and the Aisne on what Ludendorff would call another black day for the German army. By 29 August, Noyon had been captured. The British Third Army, meanwhile, attacked towards Bapaume on 21 August. Advancing across the battlefields of 1916, they captured the deeply symbolic Albert on 22 August. The 3rd Australian Division supported this operation on the right, attacking towards the line between Albert and Bray, capturing a valley above Bray and in effect encircling the town. On the other bank of the Somme, the Australian 1st Division advanced over 3 kilometres to take the Chuignes Valley, seizing many German prisoners and the largest naval gun that had been firing on Amiens as they did so. On 26 August, the British First Army joined the attack, extending the operations over the Scarpe River past Arras.[142]

Given that the role of the Fourth Army was meant to be subsidiary, Monash received instructions on 25 August to 'mark time and await events elsewhere'. However, he was also advised by Rawlinson that troops should maintain contact with the Germans, seizing any opportunity to move towards Péronne. This was enough of a loophole for Monash. Believing on the basis of prisoners' intelligence that the Germans ahead of the Australian Corps in the bend of the Somme river were 'on the run', he allowed his troops to go on what he called 'a merry and exciting three days of pursuit'. In the last days of August, they captured the towns of Suzanne, Vaux and Curlu, and hundreds of German prisoners. By 29 August, according to Monash, 'not a German who was not a prisoner remained west of the Somme between Péronne and Brie'.[143]

Péronne itself lay before the Australians. It was a glittering prize, since in Allied hands it would render the line of the Somme useless to the Germans and perhaps force them to retreat to the Hindenburg Line. But Péronne was a formidable obstacle. Sitting on the east bank of the Somme at a major bend, it was protected not just by the river but by a thousand metres of marshes. A natural strategic site, it was fortified by a massive seventeenth-century Vauban fortress boasting 20-metre-high ramparts. The town had already changed hands three times during this war: captured by the Germans on 24 September 1914; retaken by the French during the German withdrawal to the Hindenburg Line on 18 March 1917; and then reoccupied by the Germans on 23 March 1918. The troops now defending the town in August 1918 were the 2nd Prussian Guards, one of best divisions in the German army.

However, Monash was convinced that the Germans were withdrawing across the Somme and ordered a direct attack on Péronne across the river from the west on 29 August. It failed. The bridges had either been destroyed or were under intense fire, and while the 2nd Division did manage to capture the high ground between Briaches and Orme de Barleux, it could not take the causeway at Halle. Without this, it was unable to proceed to attack the vital hill that overlooked Péronne to its north, Mont St Quentin.

Monash changed plans, shifting the axis of his forces to attack the town from the north. In an ambitious operation that demanded self-reliance and flexibility at all levels of command, the 3rd Division was set the task of capturing Cléry on the north bank of the Somme bend, opening the bridges there, and then heading to the Bouchavesnes Spur. At the same time, the 2nd Division would cross the river wherever possible in the vicinity of Cléry, swing east and assault Mont St Quentin. If the 5th Division operating further south had forced a crossing of the Somme, the 2nd could use that. Rawlinson thought it was a 'presumption' to attack Mont St Quentin with three battalions—but it turned out to be a brilliant success.[144]

The capture of Cléry took longer than planned, but by the afternoon of 30 August it was in the hands of the Australians, together with the knoll above it from which an attack on Mont St Quentin could be launched. At 5 a.m. on 31 August, therefore, the 5th Brigade (2nd Division) set off to take the hill (see Map 32). After many days of fighting, the brigade was exhausted and below strength: it was down to only 1320 men, or an average of 330 per battalion. But it was supported by five field and four heavy artillery brigades and armed with some 20,000 rifle grenades, which had recently been issued to the division. With these, the infantry could drive the enemy out of shell holes at a distance of about a hundred metres.[145]

As they attacked, the Australians made as much noise as possible, giving the impression that their numbers were greater than they were. With great skill, they then fought their way under heavy fire to the crest of the mountain, and at 8 a.m. reports (now known to have been incorrect) were received of an Australian flag flying at the summit. However, the attackers' hold on the warren of trenches and ruins on the slopes of the hill was tenuous, and as the day progressed the Germans counter-attacked five times.[146]

The next morning, at 6 a.m., the 6th Brigade was sent in with increased artillery support. The battle that followed was close fighting at its most murderous: chaotic exchanges of bombs and machine-gun fire, the dead lying thick on the ground and the wounded crying out for help. Few prisoners were taken. One Australian was reported as shooting every German he came across, saying as he did, 'There's another bastard—got him!' and 'another'. There were 'more German dead . . . on the slopes of the hill', a Scottish journalist visiting

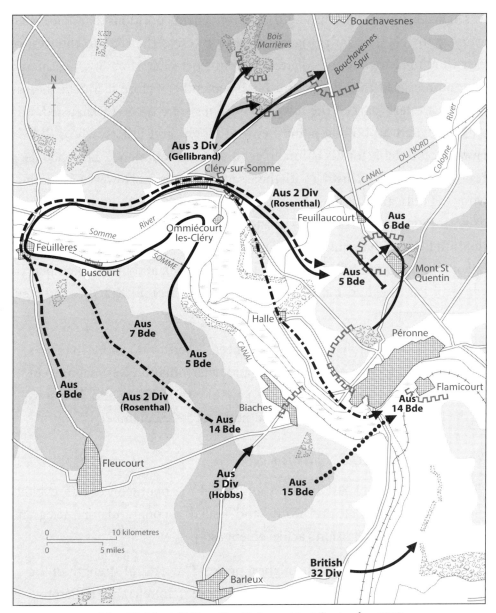

Map 32: Mont St Quentin, 31 August to 1 September 1918

the battlefield after the war wrote, 'than in any equal surface area in the course of the war'. Yet by the end of the day the 6th Brigade had established itself 500 metres beyond the summit of Mont St Quentin.[147]

The battle being fought to capture the town of Péronne below was equally ferocious. On 31 August, the 15th Brigade tried to get across the Somme but was halted by intense machine-gun fire from enemy positions that dominated every approach. The 14th Brigade, ordered to cross the river to the west of Cléry and to swing around to attack Péronne between Mont St Quentin and the Somme, also met savage fire on 1 September before it fought its way into the western part of the town. The troops were by now exhausted, and tensions flared 'to boiling point' between Hobbs and Elliott (who still held Hobbs accountable for his failure to get divisional command). Both had deep reservations about persisting with the assault on Péronne. However, Monash—who was critical of Hobbs' handling of the attack, thinking he lacked the drive the operations needed—insisted that it continue. On 2 September, the 15th Brigade did manage to get a battalion across the river (Elliott having fallen into the water fully clothed in the meantime), and by 3 September the whole of Péronne and most of the high ground around it had been taken. Hobbs later wrote:

> Never have Australian Troops [sic] been asked to do more than was asked of these men, their gallantry and determination was magnificent . . . never have I had to face such an awful responsibility and danger as the position I had to deal with that night [of 1–2 September].[148]

Remembering Mont St Quentin

The capture of Mont St Quentin soon joined the pantheon of AIF exploits in 1918. Rawlinson ate his words and issued a congratulatory telegram, describing the 2nd Division's achievement as:

> a feat of arms worthy of the highest praise. The natural strength of the position is immense, and the tactical value of it, in reference to Péronne and the whole system of the Somme defences, cannot be over-estimated. I am filled with admiration at the gallantry and surpassing daring of the Second Division in winning this important fortress, and I congratulate them with all my heart.

A bevy of politicians, war artists and journalists arrived to inspect the battle site: Cook, Hughes, even Sir Arthur Conan Doyle, whom some soldiers took to be Sherlock Holmes. The press in Australia took up Rawlinson's theme: the battle was 'the finest single feat of the war'—though whether the New South Welshmen of the 5th Brigade or the Victorians of the 6th Brigade deserved the greater credit was a matter for debate.[149]

Even Bean was willing to concede that Monash had triumphed. In his official history, he wrote that Mont St Quentin and Péronne were 'held by many Australian soldiers to be the most brilliant achievement of the A.I.F.':

> Among the operations planned by Monash it stands out as one of movement rather than a set piece; indeed within Australian experience of the Western Front it was the only important fight in which quick, free manoeuvre played a decisive part. It furnishes a complete answer to the comment that Monash was merely a composer of set pieces.[150]

There were, in fact, many contenders for the title of 'the finest single feat of the war' and for Peter Stanley, writing in 2010, Mont St Quentin's reputation is undeserved. Australians, he argues, 'have been the unwilling victims of a confidence trick' for more than nine decades. But memory and historical accuracy are not one and the same, and these were heady days on the Western Front. Like Gallipoli, Mont St Quentin lent itself to celebration because of its timing, its topography and the contours of its battle. Planting flags on summits is a powerful trope—as Joe Rosenthal's World War II photograph 'Raising the Flag on Iwo Jima' amply testifies—and even if this happened at Mont St Quentin a little later than claimed, the summit was ultimately conquered.[151]

Moreover, those who took part in the conquest of Mont St Quentin did see it as one of their greatest achievements. Within days of the battle, Rosenthal had decided to plant a memorial to the 2nd Division on the summit. By late 1918, Australian sculptors living in Britain had been contracted to prepare designs, and funds were raised from the men of the division. Unveiled by Foch on 30 August 1925, the memorial was not the austere obelisk of other divisions. Rather, it portrayed a digger thrusting his bayonet into an eagle

Hughes where he loved to be, with the Australian 'digger', in 1918. (AWM P03155.004)

A Flight of Sopwith Camels of No. 4 Squadron Australian Flying Corps (AFC) at the Pas-de-Calais, March 1918. (AWM E01878)

The AIF 2nd Division memorial at Mont St Quentin during its unveiling ceremony in 1925. The statue was removed and destroyed when the Germans occupied France during World War II. (AWM H11698)

lying on its back beneath him. Bas-reliefs on the pedestal depicted Australian artillery and infantry bombing their way down a trench. A more triumphalist image of the slaying of imperial Germany is hard to imagine, and it did not survive the next war. When Péronne was reoccupied by the Germans in 1940, the statue disappeared.

It was never found again, and the site remained empty until 1971, when a new memorial was installed as a result of lobbying by the Returned and Services League. This time, it took a less aggressive form: a 3-metre-tall digger wearing a slouch hat with his head cast slightly down. This reflected modern sensibilities about transnational reconciliation, but a memory of the original statue remains at the site in the form of a photo in one of the interpretive panels erected by the Australian Department of Veterans' Affairs.

Battle fatigue

By the time Péronne fell, the German high command had decided it needed to withdraw its forces to the Hindenburg Line. Bapaume was taken by the New Zealanders on 29 August, and five days later the Canadians smashed the Drocourt–Quéant line, a formidable defensive system that ran from the west of Cambrai to Armentières. Then, on 10 September, the US Army, with the support of French troops, eliminated the German salient at Saint-Mihiel, south of Verdun. All the gains the Germans had made in the spring were now lost, and the Allies began to sense that they would win the war. Hughes therefore decided to stay in London to ensure that he had some influence on the peace settlement. Even though the British government was full of assurances about imperial consultation, alarmingly it had not told Hughes of the 8 August offensive until the day it began.

By this stage, there was reason to be concerned about the AIF's morale. This was not just the usual carping by British officers about the Australians' lackadaisical attitude towards discipline. The statistics confirmed that a disproportionately large number of disciplinary offences were being committed by Australians. In the first six months of 1918, there were more

Australians in military prisons than men from all other British armies in France. Across the year, Australian units had about nine times more men per thousand incarcerated than did British units, and almost six times the number of other Dominion formations. Haig attributed this to the continuing refusal of the Australian government to allow capital punishment. More likely, it was a symptom of the AIF troops' exhaustion.[152]

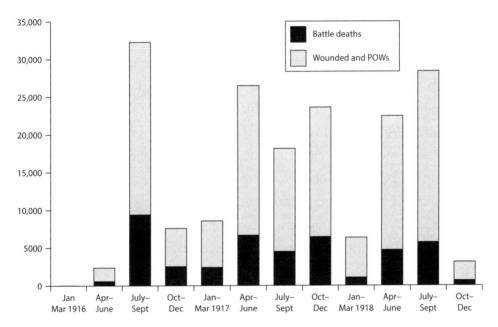

Figure 5.2: AIF battle casualties, 1916–18
Source: A.G. Butler, *The Official History of the Australian Army Medical Services, 1914–1918*, vol. III, p. 911.

The casualties of the Australian Corps between April and October 1918 had been very high: almost 10,500 men killed or died of wounds and more than 40,000 wounded or captured. Each division had lost at least 9000 casualties; the 1st Division nearly 11,000. Victory, it seemed, could be as costly as failure on the Western Front. Even though Monash rotated the divisions regularly, his commanders thought their troops were at the limits of their endurance. Bean, too, concluded that by September 1918 the Australian units were 'pretty well played out'. The impression was growing among Australian troops that their very success meant they were being used more often than the less capable British infantry:

> Battalions are going into some of these fights 150 strong (wrote one observer); 300 or 350 seems to be a big number in the fighting line nowadays. They are not as done as they were after Pozières, but they certainly are feeling that they have had more than their share of fighting ... There is a feeling that 'there won't be any dominion army left soon'. 'There'll be no more A.I.F. before long'.[153]

In fact, it would seem that the AIF had suffered proportionately higher casualties than any other army in the British Empire. Reliable comparative data are difficult to find, but War Office figures from 1920 (Table 5.1) show that although Australia provided less than 5 per cent of the British imperial troops, it suffered 6.9 per cent of all empire deaths, and the highest percentage death rate (14.2 per cent) of any empire force. Whether this was because the men of the AIF were asked to 'do more than their fair share of fighting', as many believed, is beyond empirical verification. Certainly the fact that the AIF was largely an infantry force, drawing on the British armies for most of its artillery, tank support, airpower and logistics, helps explain the high rate of losses.

The impact of this attrition on the troops' resilience was possibly accentuated by the fact that Australians may have had unusually strong emotional ties to their units. The shipping shortage throughout the war meant that none of the AIF and other units had taken home leave in all the years of war. Those who had volunteered in 1914, the 'original Anzacs', had not seen their families for nearly four years. The sense of loss, of relationships atrophying and children growing up without knowing their fathers, must have been corrosive. In turn, the deaths of so many men who had become surrogate families over the years was especially demoralising.

Hughes, to his credit, was sensitive to this issue, and since June had been working to give at least the longest-serving personnel a period of home leave. In September, he ordered the immediate repatriation of 800 soldiers and

Table 5.1: The British Empire's military effort: British, Dominion and colonial troops

	Total troops	Approximate total killed or died of wounds	Troops as % of total troops	Deaths as % of total empire dead	Deaths as % of national troops
British Isles	5,704,416	662,083	66.4	77.8	11.6
Canada	628,964	56,119	7.3	6.6	8.9
Australia	412,953	58,460	4.8	6.9	14.2
New Zealand	128,525	16,132	1.5	1.9	12.6
South Africa	136,070	6928	1.6	0.8	5.1
India	1,440,437	47,746	16.8	5.6	3.3
Other colonies	134,837	3649	1.6	0.4	2.7
Total	8,588,202	851,117	100	100	n/a

Source: Statistics of the Military Effort of the British Empire During the Great War 1914–1920 (first published London: War Office, 1920; London: Stamp Exchange, 1992, p. 756. Like all statistics, these vary from others. A.G. Butler, *The Official History of the Australian Army Medical Services, 1914–1918*, vol. III, p. 880, has different data but is not substantially at variance with the above.

instructed Monash that the Australian Corps must be withdrawn from all action by 15 October at the latest. He also began to tell the men of the AIF that they would spend the winter in southern France or Italy.

Monash protested that the corps could not afford to lose the experience and talent of the men being granted leave. Some 450 of those to be repatriated would come from the 1st and 4th Divisions, which were about to be used in the attack on the Outpost Line the Germans held in front of the Hindenburg Line. Moreover, such sudden repatriation—without farewells or time to retrieve kit from base-camp stores—would be unpopular with the troops. Elliott said his brigade would be crippled for the next year. 'If Mr Hughes had been in the pay of the Germans,' he said, overstating his case as usual, 'he could not have dealt us a more paralysing stroke.' However, Hughes gave them no choice. Monash was told that his position as corps commander depended on his meeting the 15 October deadline. The original Anzacs went home.[154]

The morale of the AIF, however, remained fragile—and it broke down on 14 September. The 59th Battalion (5th Division) arrived exhausted at its bivouac, only to be told to go back into action to follow the retiring Germans. Three platoons refused to go, saying this was the only way they could make the authorities aware of their needs. Eventually they were persuaded to cooperate.[155]

A week later an even more serious incident occurred. The attack by the 1st and 4th Divisions on the Outpost Line at Hargicourt and Le Verguier, 20 kilometres east of Péronne, had proceeded on 18 September, in cooperation with the British IX and III Corps. In deep mist and pouring rain, the Australians overran the German Alpine Corps, taking 4300 prisoners and 76 guns—a third of all the men and equipment captured by the Third and Fourth Armies that day. Their pride in this action, scarcely remembered today, was such that the 4th Division chose this battlefield as the site of its post-war divisional memorial.[156]

However, in the aftermath of the battle, on 21 September, the 1st Battalion (1st Division) was ordered to take over a section of the line where the British III Corps had failed to keep level with the Australians in the previous days. Expecting to be relieved rather than go back into action, some troops refused to obey. More than 120 men set off towards the rear of the lines. Perhaps, as Bean and their commanding officers thought, they were influenced by a few 'bad characters'. But it seemed to others that the men's nerves were 'just about gone to shreds'. Fifty per cent of them had returned to the front from hospital in the preceding six months. The cohesion of the unit was delicate: there had been constant changes of personnel; more than half of the 'mutineers' had joined the unit after Bullecourt in mid-1917; and some of the non-commissioned officers were inexperienced. They actually joined the men as they left the line. But the 'mutineers' got little sympathy from the authorities. All but one were convicted of desertion and sentenced to prison terms of from three to ten years in the United Kingdom—though most had their sentences suspended some seven to eight months later.[157]

Another 'mutiny' followed in late September, this time when orders were given to disband certain AIF battalions. Chronic manpower shortages and the continuing attrition of battle meant that 46 of 57 battalions were now under the establishment strength of 900. Earlier in the year, the Australian government had refused to reduce its battalions from four to three per brigade as the British armies had done—although after the German spring offensive they had agreed to disband the 36th, 47th and 52nd battalions. In August, however, the Army Council insisted that the AIF follow the British example more widely. The withdrawal of the original Anzacs also forced Monash's hand, and eight battalions were ordered to disband, to be cannibalised into other units.[158]

Seven of the eight battalions refused to obey. They went 'on strike', insisting on continuing to fight as they were. Elliott, whose 60th Battalion was one of the units marked for extinction, told them not to blame their commanders: 'Blame the politicians in Australia,' he said, 'who, when we enlisted, promised to support us to the last man and the last shilling, [but failed to provide] the reinforcements to keep our splendid force going.' However, he also told the battalion that he would not command a mob. After a tense confrontation, in which he claimed (wrongly) that the AIF would execute the ringleaders if large numbers of men mutinied, he managed to bring the 60th Battalion around to compliance.[159]

Monash also listened. Although—like Elliott—he had 'no intention whatever of allowing the men in any way to dictate' to him, he offered the affected troops the option of forming their own companies in their new battalions. He also persuaded Rawlinson to defer the changes until after the next round of fighting. With these concessions, the disbanding of the battalions proceeded, and by mid-October only one battalion, the 42nd, had failed to acquiesce.[160]

It is not known how widespread these incidents of 'combat refusal' were. There were probably more, although mutiny was never a statistically significant crime within the AIF. It generated only 0.9 per cent of the total number of court martials. Individual acts of resistance—absence without leave (38 per cent) and desertion (9 per cent)—were far more prevalent than collective resistance. Yet if the AIF was not disintegrating, the signs of battle fatigue were obvious in September 1918. Counterfactual history is a dangerous game, but had the war continued into 1919, the AIF might well have lost the will to keep fighting, at least at the levels it had in 1918.[161]

Breaking the Hindenburg Line

In late September 1918, the Allies launched the massive offensive that finally defeated Germany. There were actually three offensives: in the south, the Americans and French attacked on 26 September between Rheims and Verdun along the Meuse and through the Argonne Forest. It was a battle that continued until the armistice of 11 November, and ultimately captured Sedan—the place where the French had suffered humiliating defeat in the Franco-Prussian War. In the north on 28 September, a multinational force of Belgians, French and British launched the final and fifth battle around Ypres, recapturing Mount Kemmel, Messines and Passchendaele Ridge and driving towards Ghent. In the centre, where the Australian Corps was positioned, the Allies attacked the most powerful section of the Hindenburg Line between Cambrai and St Quentin.

Stretching from Verdun to virtually the Channel coast, an estimated twelve armies of about six million men simultaneously attacked the German line. It is a statistic that should temper any chauvinistic claims that Australians won the war in 1918. With its five under-strength divisions, the AIF had perhaps between 40,000 and 50,000 men in the field at this time.[162]

The Hindenburg Line now facing the Australian Corps was formidable, even by Western Front standards. The usual jungles of barbed wire, pillboxes, trenches and underground bunkers incorporated another major obstacle in the form of the St Quentin Canal. This was 30 metres wide and 15 metres deep, with a water depth of 2–3 metres and sides too steep for tanks to negotiate. Although the tunnel went underground for 5500 metres south of the village of Bellicourt, this simply gave the defenders a natural bunker. Here the Germans could shelter from the Allied bombardment, wait for an attack to pass over them and then emerge from air shafts and concealed passages to counter-attack. The surface 'bridge' above the tunnel was itself heavily fortified with multiple lines of defences, including anti-tank guns.

The Australian Corps was assigned the dominant role in attacking this formidable landscape. Since the 1st and 4th Divisions were resting, two fresh American divisions (the 27th and 30th from II Corps) were transferred to Monash's command. The plan was for the Americans to attack across the tunnel surface, capturing the villages of Nauroy and Le Catelet. The 3rd and 5th Australian Divisions would then leapfrog them, taking the final (Beaurevoir) line of the German defences 4 kilometres further on. At the same time, the British IX Corps would cross the open canal to the south, using collapsible boats, 3000 life jackets, ladders and even floating bridges. If all this succeeded (and the crossing of the canal was added to Monash's original plans by Rawlinson against his advice), the advance would be exploited with cavalry, still awaiting their moment in the war.

The planning of this operation was complex and difficult, and despite Monash's usual meticulous efforts, the 'fog of war' (in this case literally) almost brought disaster. Things started to go wrong when the British III Corps failed to straighten the line to the north in the action against the Outpost Line. This left the 27th US Division short of its assigned start line for the main attack. It was therefore ordered to capture the critical points of the Knoll, Gillemont Farm and Quennemont Farm before the main assault began. Going into action on 27 September, the Americans met such heavy opposition and became so disoriented by fog that they splintered into small groups. They became stranded in the very area where the creeping barrage for the main attack two days later would fall. Their precise location was unknown, and it would have been 'repulsive to the mass of officers and men' to voluntarily run the risk of killing them. So the barrage had to be targeted a thousand metres ahead.[163]

The three-day bombardment preceding the main attack mixed high explosive, shells with instantaneous fuses that could cut wire and, for the first time, mustard gas. There was no element of surprise—but then, as Trevor Wilson says, the target was 'just too obvious'! Finally, at 5.55 a.m. on 29 September, the remainder of the US troops set off, with the 3rd and 5th Divisions following (see Map 33). Having to advance a thousand metres without the protection of a creeping barrage, the Americans soon faltered well short of their objectives, Nauroy and Le Catelet. All their tanks were knocked out by German guns, or by mines of a former British minefield that had not been detected. As a result, the 3rd Division, instead of leapfrogging the Americans and driving for the second-stage targets, became caught up in confused and difficult fighting without artillery or tanks—and in broad daylight.[164]

Ahead of the 5th Division, things were a little easier, since the 30th US Division, having the support of a creeping barrage, captured the southern entrance of the tunnel. But as they pushed on, the Australian 5th Division got ahead of the 3rd Division and met German reinforcements streaming down from positions that the 27th US Division was meant to have captured.

Only in the south was real success achieved. Helped by the fog and the artillery's demolition of German defences, the British 46th Division stormed the St Quentin canal and captured the Riqueval Bridge intact. Crowding on to the steep banks rising from the water, they provided one of the greatest photo opportunities of the war. By mid-afternoon, the Hindenburg Line in this sector had been breached and the 32nd Division had moved through and was pushing on.

With progress stalling in the centre and north, however, Monash had to change his plans. He directed the Australian divisions to swing to the north along the main Hindenburg Line system, with the goal of capturing Bony and

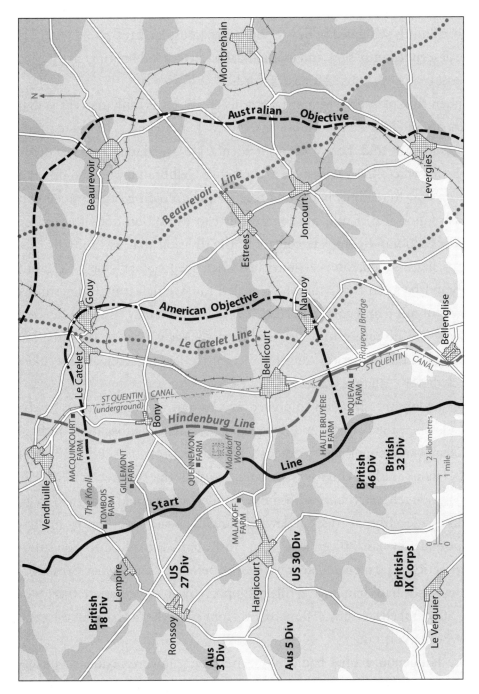

Map 33: Attack on the Hindenburg Line, 27 September to 5 October 1918

the northern end of the tunnel. The redeployment that this required during the night of 29–30 September was 'horrific'. Infantry, tanks and ammunition supply columns struggled in heavy rain to get across land full of old wire. The battle descended into 'slow and methodical hand to hand fighting, in a perfect tangle of trenches', to use Monash's words.[165]

Under this pressure, Monash became erratic and bullying. He sought scapegoats and blamed the Americans: they 'sold me a pup . . . They're simply unspeakable', he told the war correspondents. He issued inappropriate orders and dismissed contrary views. He argued with Gellibrand, who had different views on how to read the battle and react to the unfolding situation. Perhaps Monash found it difficult, his commitment to delegation notwithstanding, to allow Gellibrand complete control of the division that was initially 'his'. Perhaps, like his men, Monash flourished when 'feeding on victory'. Certainly, Gellibrand believed that Monash struggled to 'face defeat with determined coolness of mind and conduct'. His Chief of Staff, Blamey, also lost his cool. Not only did he refuse to accept Gellibrand's assessment of the situation, but he abused an American divisional commander, swearing at him 'like a bullock driver'. Alliance warfare is never easy.[166]

Fortunately the situation improved as German resistance began to ebb. On 1 October, the British 32nd Division across the canal began to outflank the Germans, forcing them to evacuate the tunnel. Bony fell and the 3rd and 5th Divisions pushed their way through towards the Beaurevoir Line. The 2nd Division relieved them and, although undermanned and weakened by gas attacks, made a frontal attack at dawn, taking the Beaurevoir Line by midday. A captured German officer said, 'You Australians are all bluff. You attack with practically no men and are on top of us before we know where we are.' In fact the Australians had huge artillery support: by one calculation, there were some 50,000 shells for any 450 metres of front from the far bank of the canal to the Beaurevoir Line.[167]

The Hindenburg Line had now been taken. However, Monash pushed the 6th Brigade on to the village of Montbrehain, beyond the Beaurevoir Line (see Map 34). It was probably not an essential operation. The Germans were

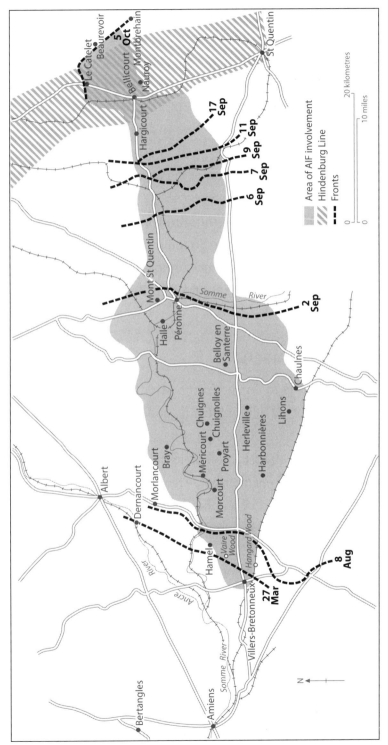

Map 34: Territory captured by the Australian Corps, March to October 1918

expecting the attack, the supporting tanks were late and the Australians lost some 460 casualties. Those who died on 5 October and whose graves can be found in the small—and, to judge by the faded Australian flags, rarely visited—cemetery at Montbrehain had the sad distinction of being killed on the last day of the last battle of the AIF in France. After the capture of the Hindenburg Line, all five divisions of the Australian Corps were withdrawn for rest, as Hughes had demanded.

In what proved to be the last month of the war, then, no Australian infantry were fighting the Germans. However, those often overlooked forces— the Australian artillery, logistics units and engineers—supported British operations to the very end of the war. So too did the Australian Flying Corps, which accompanied the British advance almost up to the Belgian border (in the case of Nos 2 and 4 Squadrons) and into Belgium itself (in the case of No. 3 Squadron).[168]

Megiddo and Damascus

The war was also coming to an end in the Middle East. The summer of 1918 had seen yet another period of reorganising and retraining, and, in the Jordan valley, the holding of a large Ottoman offensive in July. Life on the Jordan during the summer was almost intolerable thanks to the heat, blinding dust and endemic disease, but by September, Allenby's forces were ready to go back on to the offensive. The aim of the Battle of Megiddo that followed was to attack and destroy the Turkish Army Group F along a line from the Mediterranean coast to the Jordan. Contrary to what the Ottomans expected, the bulk of the imperial forces—35,000 infantry, 384 guns and 24,000 cavalry— were concentrated on the coast. The plan was for Bulfin's XXI Corps to break through to the Plain of Sharon before heading north-east towards Tul Karm and Sebustiye. Chauvel's Desert Mounted Corps would also drive through the gap and head across the Plain of Esdraelon (or Armageddon), capturing the railway and the crossings of the Jordan beyond. Chetwode's XX Corps, further along the line, would attack north towards Nablus, while Chaytor's Force, a mixed collection of troops including the Anzac Mounted Division, would prevent the enemy forces across the Jordan from intervening and chase them if the opportunity arose. In essence, the goal was to trap the Ottomans in a sack around Nablus and against the Jordan. Meanwhile, the Arab Northern Army, a polyglot force drawn from a number of tribes under the leadership of Emir Feisal, would tie down Ottoman forces further to the east.[169]

It was a plan that relied on surprise and the now complete British dominance of the air. The Ottomans were fighting almost blind, since the Royal Air Force's Palestine Brigade, which included No. 1 Squadron of the AFC, shattered the enemy communications systems. Before the battle began, the telephone exchanges at Afule, Tul Karm and Nablus had been destroyed, while a standing patrol of fighters over Jenin airfield prevented the Germans from carrying out aerial reconnaissance. To add to this, the Ottoman forces were poorly supplied, undernourished and outnumbered two to one. Their morale also seemed to be low: in one week, 52 deserters arrived at the British lines.[170]

The British attack, beginning early on 19 September with a barrage that was 'ferocious by the standards of Palestine', was a stunning success (see Map 35). XXI Corps shattered the Ottoman line and the imperial cavalry flooded through the gap, moving deep into northern Palestine with their swords and lances drawn. As a British official historian put it: 'The great column streamed northward without even its vanguard being checked. For once, it seemed, the clock had been put back and warfare had recovered in this splendid spectacle the pageantry whereof long-range weapons had robbed it.'[171]

It was warfare that would have made Haig salivate. Covering more than 80 kilometres in less than 24 hours, the 5th Cavalry Division charged up the coast and turned towards Nazareth, the site of the Ottoman headquarters. On 20 September, they entered the town, almost capturing Liman von Sanders in his pyjamas. Further inland, the 4th Cavalry Division moved through the Musmus Pass and onto the Plain of Esdraelon, overwhelming an Ottoman battlion there. Reaching Afule, the division split, with one group galloping north to seize the river crossing at Jisr el Majami and the other heading south to Beisan. The Australian Mounted Division, following through the Carmel

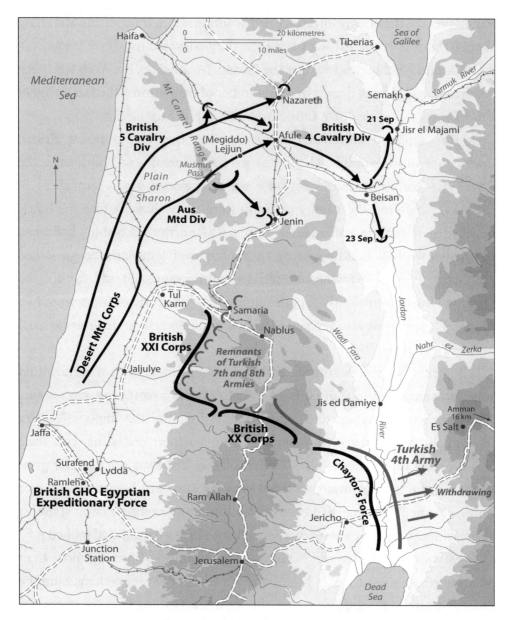

Map 35: The Battle of Meggido, 19–25 September 1918

Range, sent its 3rd Brigade south to confront the mass of enemy troops pouring north to Jenin. By morning, 8000 of the Ottoman troops were prisoners, and Jenin was being looted by the Arabs. The Ottoman armies west of the Jordan were now caught in a trap, pushed up against the hills of Nablus from both sides. With escape routes through Jenin, Afule and Beisan closed, only a gap of about 40 kilometres south of Beisan was open for the retreating forces to slip through.[172]

On 25 September, the 11th and 12th Light Horse Regiments pushed on, capturing the strategic rail town of Semakh at the base of the Lake of Galilee. In a ferocious close-quarters battle, the Light Horsemen, facing a torrent of machine-gun fire, overpowered 100 Germans and many more Ottoman troops defending the railway buildings. Later in the day, Tiberius also fell to the 3rd Light Horse Brigade. To the west of the Jordan, the Turkish Fourth Army was also withdrawing from Amman to avoid being cut off. Chaytor's Force pushed into Transjordan, taking Es Salt for the third time in the year, on 23 September. By mid-afternoon on 25 September, Amman had also been captured, though many of the enemy troops managed to escape via rail—only to find that the line to the north had been damaged by the Arabs and that they had no choice but to continue on foot. The remaining Ottoman forces south of Amman surrendered to the 2nd Light Horse Brigade at Ziza on 29–30 September. Such was their fear of the Bedouin forces circling them that the Ottoman prisoners sought shelter with the Australians, who allowed them to keep their arms and camp among them overnight. In nine days, Chaytor's Force had captured 10,300 prisoners and 57 guns at the cost of 139 casualties.[173]

Exhilarated by their success, Allenby and Chauvel decided to push on to Damascus. The pursuit continued on various axes from 26 September. Bulfin's Corps advanced along the coast road towards Beirut while the 7th Indian Division moved to Baalbek with its Ottoman depots and spectacular Roman ruins. The 5th Cavalry (formerly Mounted) Division and Australian Mounted Division pushed over the Golan Heights towards Damascus. The 4th Cavalry (formerly Mounted) Division meanwhile headed east from the Lake of Galilee to Deraa, linking up with the Arabs under Feisal before pursuing the Ottomans fleeing to the north.

Damascus was taken on 30 September. The 3rd Light Horse Brigade, led by the 10th Light Horse Regiment, was the first Allied unit to enter the city, with the Arabs following soon after. According to the journalist and official historian of this campaign, Henry Gullett:

Scores of thousands of the gaily-dressed population thronged the streets, clapping their hands, and as their excitement grew hotter they surged after the scattered horsemen. The appearance of the swarthy-looking Arabs, beautifully mounted on black and white horses and camels, aroused the wildest enthusiasm . . . The Arabs galloped in circles, firing their rifles in the air in marked contrast to the stolid bearing of the tired Australian and British cavalrymen.[174]

For a few days the city descended into looting and lawlessness while the Ottoman wounded died in misery in the appallingly inadequate hospital. When order was finally restored, malaria and pneumonic influenza started to cut down the men of the Desert Mounted Corps too.

Megiddo and Damascus were unqualified triumphs for the British forces. 'Such a complete victory [as Megiddo] has seldom been known in all the history of war,' Allenby told his troops. Chauvel wrote to his wife that he had had a 'glorious time. We have done a regular Jeb Stuart ride.' The fact that Palestine was so steeped in biblical history gave the victories added piquancy. Allenby and his men were easily imagined as the last in a long line of conquerors, dating from the Old Testament through Paul the Apostle to Richard the Lionheart and the Crusaders.[175]

However, victories so complete have a particular cruelty. Soldiers are never so vulnerable as when they are retreating, demoralised, bereft of air support or trying to surrender. As with the 'Highway of Death' in Iraq in 1991, the routes along which the Ottoman forces retreated in 1918 were littered with the dead and the debris of defeat. The plain of Esdraelon was scattered with men 'harpooned' by the Indian cavalry. The Barada Gorge, in which a column of fleeing Ottomans was trapped and machine-gunned from above, became 'a ghastly spectacle of dead Turks and animals in a welter of broken and overturned vehicles', as Gullett put it.[176]

The Arab forces, moreover, had few inhibitions about looting and slaughter-ing the wounded and prisoners. Most infamously, in the town of Tafas, north of Deraa, they exacted merciless revenge for an earlier Ottoman massacre of civilians. T.E. Lawrence, who gave an order to 'take no prisoners', later wrote,

'In a madness born of the horror of Tafas we killed and killed, even blowing in the heads of the fallen and of the animals; as though their death and running blood could slake our agony.' The boundary between legality and illegality in war, always fine, had been crossed.[177]

The political aftermath of the campaign also tarnished the triumphalism. Feisal rode into Damascus expecting to be installed as the leader of Syria. But he was soon told by Allenby that the British and French had other plans. Under the Sykes–Picot agreement of 1916, they had agreed on their respective spheres of influence after the war: Syria was to be French. Feisal would be responsible for the administration of the country, but only under French guidance and with French financial backing. 'Syria' would also be confined to the hinterland, not a greater Syria including Lebanon and Palestine. Feisal protested strongly, arguing that Lawrence (whose motives will always be debated) had assured him that the Arabs would control Syria and Lebanon. He was told that the matter would be settled after the war. In the interim, he would 'have to obey orders . . . [and] accept the situation as it was'. This did not promise to be a peace of self-determination.[178]

The war in the Middle East was nearly over. In late October, two cavalry divisions captured Aleppo, the railway junction some 300 kilometres north of Damascus that formed the hub of the railway network linking Anatolia with Syria, Palestine and Mesopotamia. Then, in a coup de grâce for the Ottomans, Bulgaria—facing internal revolution and under attack from an Allied force that included Greeks—requested an armistice on 28 September. With only a few Ottoman divisions holding the border with Bulgaria, the road to Constantinople was now open to the Allies from the north. Turkey concluded an armistice on 30 October.

The armistice negotiations

Some weeks earlier, the German and Austrian governments had also started to sue for peace. On 4 October they approached Woodrow Wilson, seeking an armistice on the basis of his Fourteen Points and subsequent statements. Although these required concessions that were far from acceptable, the Central Powers thought it was preferable to deal with Wilson rather than with the British and French. Not only was he likely to be less embittered by war; he was known to pride himself on his moral distance from Europe, as evidenced in the fact that the United States had not become an ally of the British and French when it entered the war, only an 'associated' power.

It would take some weeks for the armistice to be negotiated. During this time, the Germans continued to fight in Belgium and France, trying to establish a defensive line that would give them more bargaining power. In October, the British took a further 120,000 casualties—the same rate as for August and September. The fighting continued on other fronts, too. The Italians, supported by the British and French, broke through the Piave line in late October, causing both the Austro-Hungarian armies and the Hapsburg monarchy to disintegrate. Under American pressure, the Germans called off the U-boat campaign against merchant shipping, but they still planned a last-ditch sortie by their High Seas Fleet into the North Sea, hoping to entice the British Grand Fleet into battle.[179]

This finally brought peace. When the German crews learned of the planned sortie, they mutinied, refusing to die at this stage of the war. The wartime governance structures of Germany were also disintegrating. In the hope that a civilian government would be treated more sympathetically by the Allies, Ludendorff and Hindenburg relinquished their powers to the Reichstag and on 30 September a liberal, Prince Max of Baden, became chancellor. Moving quickly to introduce responsible government incorporating the political parties of the Reichstag, he made a raft of concessions to the union movement in the hope of stopping the contagion of a radical revolution spreading from Bolshevik Russia. Finally, on 9 November, that symbol of Prussian militarism, Kaiser Wilhelm II, abdicated, bringing to an end another of the great monarchic dynasties of Europe, the Hohenzollerns. It was therefore a civilian government that finally negotiated an armistice on 11 November, and which—tragically for Germany's and Europe's future— had to cope with the stigma and aftermath of the country's defeat.

As the armistice negotiations proceeded, Hughes became increasingly anxious about the terms on which the Central Powers would surrender. The prospect that Wilson's Fourteen Points would form the basis of the armistice, as the Germans and Austrians had requested, remained anathema to him. Although an armistice was not the same as a peace settlement, Hughes believed that the terms of any ceasefire 'must approximate to the basis of the conditions of peace', since it would be impossible to resume fighting once an armistice had been declared.

During October, therefore, Hughes did his utmost to influence the armistice negotiations. But for all his efforts, he would find himself excluded from the key Allied discussions of the matter. By now Lloyd George had tired of Hughes, seeing him as a troublemaker and demagogue. Hughes' very public opposition to Wilson's Fourteen Points also made him a liability in the delicate negotiations that were being conducted with the enemy. As a consequence, he was not invited to the meetings of the British War Cabinet, held from 18 October on, during which the terms of the armistice were discussed. As it happened, Hughes was on a speaking tour in the north of England for some of October, urging his audiences to oppose the 'Peace babble centred on President Wilson's Points which was designed to rob the Allies of victory'. But he had left details of how he could be contacted. No one in the British government, it seems, tried very hard to find him. Nor was he informed about or invited to a meeting of the Supreme War Council at Versailles late in October, where representatives of Britain, France, Italy and the United States debated whether the Allies would make peace with Germany on the basis of the Fourteen Points.[180]

Lloyd George and his Cabinet themselves had reservations about some of Wilson's Fourteen Points. Point 2, which specified 'absolute freedom of navigation upon the seas . . . alike in peace and war', was unacceptable to the British, which insisted on the operational freedom of the Royal Navy. They also had difficulties with Point 8, which implied that Britain and its Empire would have little or no right to reparations, and Point 3, which specified 'the removal of economic barriers'. Point 5 was also problematic, in that it required 'the free, open-minded, and absolutely impartial adjustment of all colonial claims, based upon a strict observance of the principle that in determining all such questions of sovereignty the interests of the populations concerned must have equal weight with the equitable claims of the government whose title is to be determined'.

However, the British and French were presented with something of a fait accompli. The fact that the Central Powers had approached Wilson gave him the upper hand, as did the fact that the United States could, if it wished, negotiate a separate peace. Hence the Supreme War Council agreed late in October to an armistice being called on the basis of the Fourteen Points and Wilson's subsequent statements. The British, however, reserved complete freedom on the issue of freedom of the seas, and specified that the 'restoration' of the invaded territories must be understood to include compensation for 'all damage done to the civilian population of the Allies and their property by the aggression of Germany' on land, sea and from the air. This clause would allow Britain—if not the Dominions, who suffered no civilian casualties—to claim some compensation.

When Hughes learned on 5 November about the Versailles conference, he exploded. This was exactly the exclusion from key decision-making that he had anticipated and stayed in London to prevent. At a meeting of the Imperial War Cabinet on 6 November, he weighed into Lloyd George, attacking him for his failure to consult with the Dominions, and for treating Australia and the other Dominions as subordinate colonies. Just as the British government had declared war in August 1914 without consulting the Dominions, so now it was settling the peace terms without reference to them. It made a mockery of the Imperial War Cabinet, which seemed to be merely a channel for informing the Dominions of British government decisions after the event. (He would later tell Watt that the Imperial War Cabinet was 'a farce and sham'.)[181]

As for the Fourteen Points, with which the Allies now seemed saddled, Hughes took issue with many of them: the limitations of the clause on reparations; the possibility of Point 3 shutting the door on differential tariffs and preferential trade within the empire; the potential control by the League of Nations of trade in raw materials and the threat it might pose to imperial self-sufficiency. Point 5, with its statement that Germany should not recover its colonies, was too weak: the Dominions, he said, expected that they would keep what they held. As for the League of Nations, this was a scheme 'so nebulous . . . [and] fraught with danger to the Empire'. If it were intended to usurp the right of the empire to govern and protect itself, Hughes was 'absolutely opposed to it'.[182]

Hughes demanded of Lloyd George that Australia be represented at the forthcoming peace conference. The prime minister had supported the claims of the Japanese to attend the conference on the grounds that they were 'a very sensitive people'. Lloyd George needed to recognise, Hughes said, that Australians too were very sensitive. They viewed Japan as a 'daily menace'. Japan, moreover, had made no sacrifices in the war: in fact, 'the number of the Australian dead was actually greater than the army Japan had in the field in Siberia where she was looking after her own interests'.[183]

It was a broadside attack, and Lloyd George went into damage control. He denied that the Dominions had been excluded from discussions about peace terms. These had been canvassed at the meetings of the Imperial War Cabinet in 1917 and 1918, and nothing decided at Versailles violated these earlier decisions. (This was, as Neville Meaney says, strictly speaking true since the Imperial War Cabinet had made no binding decisions.) As for the German colonies, Lloyd George assured Hughes that he had told Clemenceau and Colonel House 'very strongly' at Versailles that Britain would not consent to their being surrendered by the Dominions. The demand for Germany to carry the full cost of the war, on the other hand, had not been pursued because it was unfeasible. With reparations expected to cost between £1000 million and £2000 million, Germany would struggle to pay more. It could not pay in gold, and if it were to increase its export revenue in order to pay reparations, it would need access to those very raw materials that Hughes' proposed autarchic British imperial trade system would monopolise.[184]

Hughes was not placated. After the stormy Cabinet meeting, he wrote angrily to Lloyd George and, true to form, went public with the dispute. On 7 November, he vented his grievances about the Fourteen Points and the lack of consultation with the Dominions to a meeting of the Australasian Club at the Baltic Exchange, knowing full well that his speech would be reported in the press. Forced to respond, the British government published an official answer in *The Times*, arguing inter alia that there was a substantive difference between the terms of an armistice (which had been decided at Versailles) and a peace (which had not). *The Times* tended to agree with the government—Hughes' case, it said, was 'not unanswerable'—but in the same issue it carried a letter from Hughes saying: 'Had the conditions of peace as set out left no room for criticism, the mode of their settlement would still be quite incompatible with the relations which ought to exist between the self-governing Dominions and Britain.'[185]

Undeterred, Hughes continued to escalate the dispute into a debate about Lloyd George's honesty and the effectiveness of the Imperial War Cabinet as a means of managing consultation within the empire. He kept giving press interviews, including one to the *New York Times*' London correspondent in mid-November, in which he said 'Australia had been fighting for the rights of small nations, and as a small nation she wanted her own rights.' He could not see why Australia should be crippled by a huge war debt when Germany would have not hesitated to exact punitive indemnities if it had won the war.[186]

In his embittered reaction, Hughes had the support of Cook, Garran and Latham (the latter of whom normally did not hold Hughes in much esteem). As they saw it, the British government had breached the explicit promise at the 1917 Imperial War Conference and, in Garran's words, made 'an extraordinary blunder . . . [which] may do untold harm to the Empire, and is altogether inexcusable and damnable'. Both Garran and Latham registered their indignation at British high-handedness at a public moot, declaring that the lack of consultation over the armistice was a breach of the Imperial War Conference decision of 1917 and reflected a breakdown in the existing system of imperial cooperation.[187]

However, Hughes' campaign never took off in the British press. Only three newspapers noted his crusade, and two of these were unsympathetic. The *Daily Mail* accepted the British government's account of events, concluding that it 'robs Mr. Hughes's complaint of any semblance of reasonableness which it ever had'. The *Manchester Guardian* questioned whether Hughes actually had a mandate to pronounce on Australia's post-war fiscal policy, 'much less on that for Britain or her Allies'. Only the *Morning Post* supported Hughes, deploring the fact that:

> the Prime Minister of one of the great dominions should have been driven to protest against this slight on a great occasion which should have symbolised the greatness and unity of the British Empire. It is a blunder which may have calamitous and far-reaching results.[188]

However, the *Morning Post* was a populist paper, which in 1919 would organise a collection of £18,000 for General Reginald Dyer, the perpetrator of the Amritsar massacre in India, for his services to the British Empire. With friends like these, Hughes hardly needed enemies.

In Australia, too, Hughes' protests began to backfire. It was not so much a matter of what he was saying as of how he was saying it. After his confrontation with Lloyd George in the Imperial War Cabinet, Hughes cabled to get the Australian Cabinet's endorsement. (He also tried to recruit the support of state governments through lobbying the agents-general in London.) Watt assured him that the Cabinet shared his 'surprise and indignation' and viewed the failure of the British to consult with the Dominions on the armistice as a 'painful and serious breach of faith'. The Cabinet also agreed that Australia should not accept any limitation of its rights to frame its own tariffs or sell its goods where it wished. The retention of the German colonies was also 'essential to the future safety of Australia and British interests in these isolated seas'. However, Watt said, the Cabinet was 'greatly embarrassed' by Hughes' speech to the Australasian Club. They had expected him to wait for their comments before he went public and, with Lloyd George's version of events available to them, they were not entirely in accord with the views Hughes was presenting.[189]

The Australian press was critical of Hughes' style as well. Journalists across the nation described his behaviour in London as petulant, peevish, piqued, rude, splenetic, carried away in the heat of the moment, displaying a penchant for lecturing and obsessed with his own importance—traits the Australian public knew all too well. *The Queenslander* (admittedly writing in a state where Hughes' standing was not high) described the neglect of Australia's claims to representation as 'a slight or neglect of Mr. Hughes's personality, which we have come to learn is an unforgivable crime in the opinion of our Prime Minister':

> his vanity has been wounded and his pride punctured in its most windy places. Had he been considered worthy of a place as an all-British representative, doubtless he would have been appointed just as he was appointed to attend the Paris Conference during his previous trip to England.

In South Australia, *The Register* wrote on 14 November:

> Our Prime Minister is proving an undesirable representative of Australia during the peace rejoicings in the Motherland. He is exhibiting the species of bad temper which on a noteworthy occasion caused him to involve the Commonwealth in the expense of establishing a Federal Police Department—as though the existing constabulary forces of the States could not be trusted to execute Federal decrees or to afford him and his Ministerial colleagues adequate protection while on electioneering 'stunts'.

There was also some opposition in the press to Hughes' demand for independent representation at the forthcoming peace conference. Not only would this require constitutional change, it was unnecessary given that the British Empire needed to speak with one voice. Proceedings would become unworkable if 'each portion' of the empire attended conferences such as Versailles.[190]

What Hughes had managed to achieve for the first time as prime minister was a consensus within Australian politics. No one approved of his generating an imperial crisis in London. For the Nationalists, loyalty to Britain was not only an ideology, rich in emotional power and resonance, but the principle on which they had staked their right to govern in contrast to Labor. A Nationalist member of the federal parliament, Sir Robert Best, protested on 15 November:

> The Empire should be absolutely united, having regard to all the difficult problems ahead, and the many questions to be settled between our Allies and ourselves and I protest against the British Government being wantonly harassed at such a time and the strands of Empire being unnecessarily strained.

The Brisbane *Courier*, too, declared on 12 November that it was 'regrettable' that at this momentous time there should be 'even an appearance of friction' between the British government and Australia: 'Unitedly we have fought. United we must face the peace problem.'[191]

Hughes' opponents, meanwhile, thought he was simply translating to the international stage the worst of the intemperate behaviour and machinations that had done so much damage to domestic politics in the last three years. Some thought he should be recalled home, since he was bringing 'discredit on Australia'. Mannix, on the other hand, passed a public motion at a Bendigo meeting that Hughes should *stay* in the United Kingdom 'as long as he deemed it necessary'![192]

Trying to mediate between Hughes and his critics, Watt moved a motion in parliament affirming that it was essential to Australian security that the Pacific colonies not be restored to Germany at the end of the war: Australia and New Zealand should be consulted about their future. Both houses passed the motion, although there was some debate about whether this might be construed as a 'land grab' by Australia. Labor members, sensing the 'vain and foolish and costly ambition of Imperialism', cautioned against capitalist exploitation of the people of New Guinea in the future.[193]

Privately, however, Watt and the Cabinet remained critical of Hughes. While assuring him that they thought it essential that Australia be consulted on peace terms, they were convinced that the nation's interests were best left in Britain's hands. The Cabinet would not support Hughes' bid for independent representation of the Dominions, either at the recent Versailles Conference or the peace negotiations to come. Watt even warned Hughes on 14 November of the political risks at home of his public crusade: 'You will remember that opinion here is in a molten state and though community overjoyed at armistice a slight mistake concerning such delicate and important relation-ships might seriously prejudice yourself and the Government.' When Hughes did not reply, except to cable the twelve pages of the speech he had just given to the agents-general in London, Watt followed up with another letter, clarifying the points on which the Cabinet agreed with Hughes. He concluded that it would be impossible to get parliament to support independent representation at future conferences, and that Hughes' current vociferousness was harming, not promoting, Australia's interests:

> We [the Cabinet] consider that Australian and general Dominion interests would be best served by strong representations being made by the Prime Minister on behalf of his Government to the British authorities in the usual way and not in the form of a series of public protests or complaints. The latter form is equivalent to hanging the British family linen on the line for the information and amusement of other nations, including enemies. It also means that Dominion ambitions are likely to be exaggerated and misunderstood, and the ties of Empire are likely to be injured, if not broken.

Pearce, a longstanding colleague of Hughes, also wrote to him recommending that he accept Watt's advice and abandon the campaign for separate representation at the peace conference. The danger at home was that the disaffected would use the issue of imperial loyalty to bring Hughes down.[194]

Predictably, Hughes did not agree, but for the time being he made no further public speeches on the subject of the peace settlement. As his critics had recommended, 'his mouth had been closed'. But his silence was a tactical retreat only, and he would return to his campaign for Australia's rights, as he—not his colleagues—saw them, in 1919.[195]

The armistice

The war in Europe finally came to an end at 11 a.m. on 11 November 1918. Across the fronts, the guns stopped firing and silence fell—a silence that would be repeated ceremonially in the Allied nations on every anniversary of the armistice thereafter. The Germans, after failing to negotiate better terms with Wilson, relinquished all means of reopening hostilities. Their army withdrew to the east bank of the Rhine, and their submarines and naval vessels surrendered to the Allies. In a truly awe-inspiring scene, 370 British vessels, including the RAN's *Australia*, *Melbourne* and *Sydney*, and units of the French and US navies, steamed out in full battle array to meet the German High Seas Fleet in the North Sea. The enemy vessels were almost totally unscathed, given the lack of major naval action in the war. Seven months later, when its commander feared that his ships would be divided among the Allied powers, the whole German fleet would be scuttled at Scapa Flow.[196]

The news of the armistice was greeted in Allied countries with delirious joy. In London, Australian soldiers joined the celebrations in the streets and filled the galleries of Queen's Hall for a triumphal 'demonstration'. Hughes, addressing them, praised 'the valorous and glorious deeds of the Australians in various theatres of war'. The last shots fired by Australians, he said, were probably those of the 10th and 11th Brigades of the Australian artillery supporting the British infantry near Landrecies in France (see Map 36). When he mentioned Gallipoli, Pozières and Villers-Bretonneux—the triad that continues to dominate Australian memory today—there were loud cheers. Cook, as Minister for the Navy, gave the Royal Australian Navy its due and Hughes, never missing an opportunity, warned that the aggressor must pay for 'the almost unbearable burden of debt' that would otherwise fall on the next generation of Australians.[197]

In Australia, celebrations started prematurely in Sydney, where rumours circulated that the armistice had been signed on 8 November. When the news was actually confirmed three days later, the streets of cities and country towns across the nation were filled with excited crowds. People shouted, danced, waved flags, sang patriotic songs, blew whistles and beat tin cans. Factories blew their sirens and churches rang their bells. Effigies of 'Kaiser Bill' were hanged, pelted with fireworks and burned. Returned soldiers were showered in Sydney with seemingly limitless quantities of confetti. Blind and 'crippled' veterans were driven through the streets in cars. Businesses closed and churches held services of thanksgiving. The federal parliament sent messages of congratulation to the AIF and loyalty to the King, the latter appropriately forwarded through Munro Ferguson, who received it on the steps of Parliament House in Melbourne before a large crowd. As acting prime minister, Watt declared

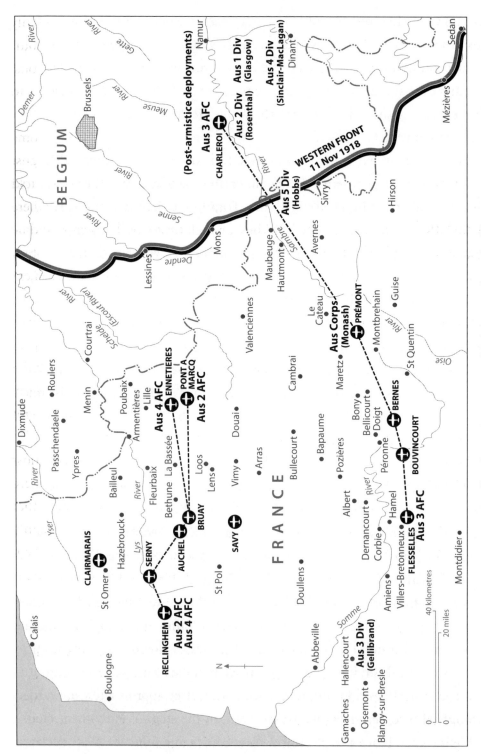

Map 36: Australian forces in France and Belgium at the end of the war

Tuesday, 12 November to be a public holiday. New South Wales mistakenly took Wednesday as well, extending its celebrations 'with unabated vigour' from 8 to 14 November. Much of this rejoicing was completely spontaneous, leading *The Argus* to complain about 'the pathetic failure of the authorities to rise to the occasion' with appropriate official events.[198]

However, if the crowds on Australian streets were euphoric and larger—some thought—than those that greeted the outbreak of war, the unanimity of August 1914 was gone. In Brisbane, the leader of the opposition, E.H. Macartney, told the crowd on armistice night that, 'We must bury all personal anger. Let there be no bitterness and no quarrelling.' Ryan, too, hoped that 'bygones would be bygones', and joined hands with his opponents in a gesture of reconciliation at a rally of some 60,000 Queenslanders at the Exhibition Ground the next day. But a section of the crowd tried to count Ryan out, and later his home had to be placed under police guard to protect him from threats of violence. Elsewhere, too, the loyalists were unforgiving. At Rockhampton, a group of returned soldiers invaded the local Trades Hall and hoisted a Union Jack on the building. As Raymond Evans says of Queensland: 'Behind all the motions of gay rejoicing, the mood remained divisive, vengeful and ugly, as loyalists, in thought and deed, demanded capitulation and atonement rather than reconciliation.'[199]

What did the soldiers think—the ones who had the starkest and most confronting experiences of war? We have no way of knowing, given that there was no systematic recording of their reactions. We can assume, however, that they experienced a range of emotions, intense and bewildering. Certainly there was excitement and intoxicating joy. There was relief at having survived, but there was also a sense of loss, anti-climax, dislocation and anxiety about the future. Thomas Miles, based in France, wrote in his diary:

> I couldnt describe how we all felt about [the armistice], in fact we didn't realize that it was over, I know in London and other places people went mad, but here in a ruined village not many miles from the firing line we couldnt realize it and didnt rejoice, I never heard a cheer and never saw anyone shake hands on it, it is strange, but I suppose that it was such a big thing and meant such a lot that we couldnt grasp it.

In Oxford, Captain Reginald Fry joined in the public celebrations but found himself troublingly detached:

> It has left us with a most peculiar feeling. We have been in this war and away from home for such a long time, that our present life seems to be the natural life . . . in fact, I dont think that we expected or thought that the war would end for a long time . . . As a matter of fact, our chaps, diggers, did not do much shouting or noise making at all, we feel rather too much thunderstruck or stunned or subdued to be noisy. Also, I think, most of us had our thoughts centred round those good pals of ours who would never return to Australia, and that made us rather sad . . . we will have to re-orient our thoughts and actions and get used to another life, almost a forgotten kind of life, as it was lived before the war began.

Cyril Lawrence, who had survived the war from Gallipoli to the end, wrote to his mother on 10 November:

> People pray for peace and I wonder if they realize what pain it is going to cause so very many. Peace—the boys will come marching home—happy, radiantly happy and victorious—upon the doorsteps and at the gates there will be loving hearts and arms to gather them in. Just think of it—the pure joy of it all, the tears of happiness—*but,* think again—there will be empty doorways and gateways. There will be tears of sorrow and behind many and many a blind will be a mother whose boy is not coming up the street, there will be wives and little children to whom the word Daddy can only be a memory—for ever and ever.

George Mitchell, who had also enlisted in October 1914 and survived the whole war, also recalled that the armistice brought 'an indefinable sadness':

> The battalion [which was] our father and our mother of unforgettable years, was drifting to pieces. The links that connected us with the unforgotten dead seemed to be snapping one by one. As each draft left, mateships were sundered, too often never to be renewed in the stress and fierce demands of civilian life.

For these men and the families to whom at last they would return, peace promised to be as difficult in its own way as the war had been.[200]

Australia's contribution to victory

How much did Australia contribute to the victory that brought such mixed emotions? It is difficult to judge conclusively. In Australian popular history, it is often implied that the AIF played a central role in the Allied victory, particularly in March–April and August 1918, when the German offensive was stalled and the Battle of Amiens launched so successfully. Over the decades, it has also been widely claimed that the AIF was an exceptionally competent fighting force. As Bean said in 1938, 'it has been referred to by at least some competent authorities in Germany, England, and America as being—at any rate towards the end of the War—the most effective of all the forces on the side of the Allies'. There were also many occasions during the war—only some of which have been cited in this book—on which the performance and courage of Australians in battle attracted the praise, even awe, of their contemporaries. The tactical skill of the AIF was also affirmed by later military historians. For example, Allan Millett and Williamson Murray's 1988 study of military effectiveness in World War I concluded that the tactical innovations, which required small-group initiative and cohesion and a less hierarchical relationship between officers, non-commissioned officers and soldiers, worked best among elite troops, or in 'forces whose social backgrounds did not cramp individualism [like the formidable Australian Corps]'.[201]

There is therefore little doubt that the AIF was a well-trained and highly effective fighting body by the end of the war. However, the case for Australian exceptionalism has to be qualified. As the war progressed, other armies also embraced tactical innovation and—like the Canadians at Vimy Ridge and the German stormtroopers in March 1918—achieved dramatic success as a result. Moreover, it is difficult to find valid measures to prove any one army's superiority over another. The data that Australian historians sometimes cite as evidence of the AIF's achievements—the numbers of tanks, prisoners or territory that Australian units captured as a proportion of totals taken by the

British Expeditionary Force in a particular battle, for example—are not robust. They fail to take into account the many variables involved, including the nature of the terrain, the strength of enemy units, the complexity of defences and even the weather in different sectors of the battlefield.[202]

Beyond that, it must be recognised that the AIF, however effective it was tactically, was largely an infantry force. The reality of World War I, proved time and time again on the Western and Eastern Fronts and in Palestine, was that artillery was the essential precondition of success by the infantry. In the imperial armies of which the AIF was a part, this artillery was largely provided by the British. So too was much of the technological innovation that led to improvements in artillery accuracy and the logistical support on which the AIF depended. Likewise, when the new integrated weapons systems that made such a contribution to the breaking the Western Front stalemate were developed in 1917–18, the aircraft and tanks that formed their key elements were again provided by the British.

Hence Australia's role in World War I must be seen as a small part of a much larger British imperial effort. This in turn was part of a massive multinational war. Victory for the Allies came after years of exhausting slogging matches on multiple fronts in which the French, the 'British', the Russians, the Serbs and the late-arriving Americans all played a role. Perhaps a quarter of German deaths occurred on the Eastern Front. Victory also depended on many things other than land battles, critical though these were: the neutralising of the German U-boat campaign; the containment of the German High Seas Fleet; the achievement of Allied air superiority in multiple battle zones; and, underpinning everything, the mass production of munitions and armaments. To all this Australia, with its small economy, navy and air force, made little contribution. Even the value of the raw materials that it could contribute to the imperial war effort was diminished by the lack of shipping to transport them to Europe. To single out any one army, or indeed any one of these multiple variables, as the factor that 'won' World War I is to ignore the immense complexity and scale on which this war was fought.[203]

6

1919
Peace and memory

Many World War I honour boards and memorials list 1919 as the last year of the war. Hostilities had ceased in 1918, but this was the year in which peace was concluded with Germany in the Treaty of Versailles, and it was when the men and women who had served in Europe and the Middle East at last came home. It was also the year in which a virulent pneumonic influenza killed another twelve to fifteen thousand Australians. Though not strictly part of the war, the fact that the 'Spanish' influenza came to Australia with the returning troops meant that this 'major demographic and social tragedy' seemed to many Australians to be the final episode of this terrible conflict.[1]

Coming home

When the war ended, there were 167,000 Australian servicemen overseas: 87,000 in France and Belgium; 63,000 in the United Kingdom (many in hospitals and convalescent homes); and 17,000 in Egypt, Syria and other minor theatres. The logistics of transporting these men—and the wives they had married and children they had fathered while overseas—back to Australia were formidable. The French and Belgian railway systems were choked with traffic, and the demand for shipping was greater than ever.

519

Crowds in Martin Place, Sydney, on 8 November 1918, waiting for bells to be rung to mark the German agreement to an armistice. (AWM P01102.001)

An Australian sapper comes home, 1919. (AWM P05328.001)

Two soldiers and three Voluntary Aid Detachment (VAD) nurses at the Randwick Military Hospital in 1919. The nurses are wearing masks for protection against the 'Spanish' influenza virus. (AWM P02789.001)

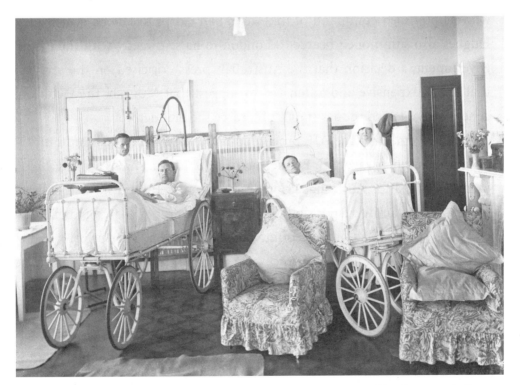

Nurses and residents at the Anzac Hostel, Brighton, Victoria. Opened by the Repatriation Department on 5 July 1919, the hostel provided a less institutional style of care for permanently disabled veterans. (AWM P03098.005)

All Allied countries were competing for troop ships to repatriate their servicemen and women as quickly as possible.[2]

Hughes was initially willing to accept some delay in repatriating the AIF, given that the Australian employment market might not be able to absorb the many thousands of veterans. However, Keith Murdoch ran a campaign in the Melbourne *Herald* and, with a federal election scheduled for the first half of 1920, it became politically expedient to bring the troops home with minimal delay. This was what they and their families wanted. As Ralph Bourne wrote to his father on 8 January 1919, 'all that people can think and talk about now is "getting home"'. Lieutenant Percy Scrivener told his mother: 'we all came over here for a certain purpose & found some degree of happiness in carrying on but now the reason for one being here has ceased to exist we none of us & the men particularly—have the heart for the same old routine work.'[3]

The planning and organisation of demobilisation were assigned to Monash, who relinquished command of the Australian Corps to Hobbs in late 1918. Hughes also summoned Pearce to London to liaise directly with the British government, a decision that the Australian press criticised on the grounds that it was expensive and 'offensive' to suggest that Monash, the victorious general, would need the assistance of 'Pearce the blunderer'.[4]

The movement of the AIF proceeded remarkably smoothly and quickly, given the numbers involved. By the end of 1918, fifteen ships carrying 13,312 men had sailed for Australia. Priority was given to those who had enlisted earliest, with family responsibilities and opportunities for employment at home also being taken into account. Those who had a lower priority had to wait their turn in England, France and Belgium, where they were offered vocational training and local employment. By the end of August 1919, almost all Australians had left Egypt, and only 10,000 members of the AIF remained in Britain. All these had sailed by the end of 1919. As Monash saw it, this massive operation—for which Pearce took much of the public credit— was the best example of staff work with which he, Monash, was associated during the war.[5]

The influenza pandemic

However, the arrival of the AIF in Australia brought catastrophe with it. In January 1919, the first case was reported of the pneumonic influenza that had already wreaked havoc among the armies of Europe in 1918. Spread by air, this virulent virus rapidly infected perhaps two million Australians. In Sydney alone, almost 40 per cent of the population contracted influenza in 1919. Across the world, it would kill between 50 million and 100 million people—many times more than World War I itself.[6]

The pandemic caught Australian authorities unprepared. Desperately attempting to contain the outbreak, they installed quarantine stations at state borders and isolation depots in the cities. All public life was controlled. Streets were sprayed with disinfectant and the use of public transport was restricted. Schools, theatres, dance halls, churches and hotels were closed—although Anzac Day was still celebrated, particularly by returning soldiers. When in public, people were required to wear masks. At home, they were exhorted to observe strict personal hygiene and ventilate all rooms.

A vaccine was developed and ultimately given to 819,000 Australians. But the death toll soared. The onset of the disease was often rapid, with victims reportedly feeling well in the morning and dying later the same day. At first they would experience muscular pain, fever, severe headache, dry cough and possibly a bleeding nose. Then, in fatal cases, their lungs would fill with fluid and they would suffocate. Hospitals and their staffs were soon overwhelmed. In New South Wales, where there were only 2000 hospital beds at the start of 1919, more than 25,000 people sought admission with influenza between January and September. Temporary hospitals were cobbled together in schools, showground buildings, drill halls, courtrooms and other public spaces. In Melbourne, the Exhibition Building was converted into a vast public hospital. Meanwhile, doctors and nurses themselves fell ill—800 in Sydney alone—and lay volunteers had to be mobilised to take their place.

As the panic spread, cooperation between state and Commonwealth authorities broke down, with each state organising its own containment policies. People shunned each other. The waterside workers refused to load ships for fear of infection and old political faultlines reopened. When Catholic nuns were proposed to serve as nurses in the Melbourne Exhibition Building, a leading Methodist minister objected that they were 'a sacerdotally trained band of anti-Protestants'. As a letter-writer to the press replied, there had been 'no distinction of sects on the battlefields of France, and there should not be here on this battlefield of disease'. But some saw 'the pushfulness of Dr Mannix' at work.[7]

Eventually, the pandemic exhausted itself after two major waves, but its impact on a population that was already ravaged by grief must have been almost intolerable. Unusually, the virus targeted the relatively young. More than half the dead in New South Wales were between 20 and 39 years of age. Moreover, young males died in greater numbers than females. Perhaps this was because they were more active in the workforce and spent more time in public places and at sporting events. But this was the same age bracket as that of the men who had been killed and wounded in the war. Even those who had stayed at home were not safe.

'Repatriation'

This public health crisis was superimposed on the problems of integrating many thousands of veterans into Australian society. It had been clear well before 1919 that repatriation in the broadest sense—of meeting veterans' needs and caring for the dependants of the dead—would be very challenging. Some 93,000 men had come home while the war was in progress, 75,000 of whom were invalids 'unfit for military service'. Their physical and economic needs were obvious, but in addition, they threatened to be a disruptive and subversive force in Australian society. Returned soldiers in 1915 and 1916 soon alarmed the authorities and the press with their anti-social behaviour, 'lounging about city streets and undermining their strength by excessive drinking'. Some clashed with police, assaulted strangers and, as we have seen, disrupted anti-conscription rallies across the country. Although with peace they could no longer harm recruitment—as authorities had feared they would by giving soldiers a bad name—their potential for radicalism, both on the right and the left, had if anything increased. The Bolshevik revolution in

Russia had provided a model for revolution at home for disaffected veterans, and as *Labor Call* warned in June 1918, the returned soldiers

> are not going to quietly slip back into their pre-war life of constant worry, grind, want and semi-starvation. On the contrary they are going to demand a decent living in this grabbed [sic] world of Capitalism. They are going to reform the world of labour and demand decent conditions for themselves and their loved ones.[8]

Hence the federal government started early in the war years to put in place the system of benefits that became known colloquially as 'Repat'. It was a monumental task, and one for which the Australian state was ill-prepared. There was no comprehensive social-welfare scheme, and the tradition dating from the Crimean War of 1853–56 was for individuals and volunteer organisations, not the state, to provide relief for soldiers and their dependants. However, it was soon clear that, however prodigious their efforts, the patriotic associations could not cope with the scale of veterans' needs, and the state would have to assume an unprecedented role. Starting with a pensions scheme in October 1914 (much amended in later years), the federal parliament then entrusted to the Federal Parliamentary War Committee and the associated state War Councils responsibility for finding employment for veterans and land on which they could settle. But confusion about the respective roles of government and the patriotic funds continued to force the Commonwealth government to adopt a more structured national approach. In 1917, a federal Department of Repatriation was created, the first Minister of Repatriation—Senator Edward Millen—was appointed and, on 28 September, the *Australian Soldiers' Repatriation Act* was passed.[9]

Forcing the pace of the repatriation agenda were the ex-servicemen's associations that sprang into being from 1915 on. Initially, there was a plethora of these—some radical and linked with the labour movement, others more conservative. They competed for membership, but ultimately one would emerge as dominant: the RSSILA. Having managed to develop a national base between 1917 and 1919, the RSSILA struck what Marilyn Lake has called a 'political compact' with the Hughes government. In return for defusing the radical potential of the returned soldier cohort—for example, by instructing members not to engage in industrial disputes—it was granted the status of their official voice. With this agreement, the RSSILA would become a uniquely powerful lobby group. Granted direct access to the Cabinet, it would campaign ceaselessly for the rights of the veterans over many decades. Thanks to this advocacy, another division would emerge in Australian society as a legacy of the war: between those who had served overseas and those who had not. The returned soldier, by virtue of his willingness to serve the nation, became the superior citizen with an 'inalienable right' to pensions, medical care and employment.[10]

Pensions and medical care

The repatriation benefits, as they were hammered out over the years, were generous. By 1920, for example, more than 90,000 incapacitated soldiers were receiving a war pension, as were nearly 49,000 dependants of those who were killed. But the need was such—and the cost so great—that there were inevitably disputes and unmet demands. Eligibility for pensions would be a subject of ongoing and often difficult negotiation between veterans and the state. How should a veteran's level of disability be assessed? How could he prove that a medical condition that presented itself after the war was war-related? Should pensions be conceived as compensation or should they be set in relation to the income a veteran formerly earned, thus facilitating his return to his pre-war social and economic position? Who were the bona fide dependants of a soldier who had been killed? Should the pension be reduced if a veteran's health improved? Should war widows and female dependants of the dead retain their pensions if they remarried? (It was decided they should not.) Struggling to secure what they deemed to be their entitlement, many of the disabled had to turn to the patriotic funds and other sources of support to supplement their income.[11]

The needs of the wounded and sick also far outstripped the capacity of the authorities to provide for them. From mid-1915, a nationwide system of military hospitals was established by the Defence Department, supplemented by Anzac hostels run by the Red Cross. Their infrastructure and facilities were, of necessity, improvised. The author George Johnston, then a child, recalled that,

> in the big military hospital [in Melbourne] where Mother worked temporary wards were added to temporary wards, and beds were shifted out on to verandas or even crowded into hastily erected canvas marquees—there were some parts of the place where one would get the odd impression that a circus or a garden fête was going on—and what had once been no more than an old mansion set in spacious grounds began to have the look of a swiftly developing city. Even so, things finally got to such a pass that any of the earlier patients who seemed capable of existing on their pensions in the civilian world outside were quickly discharged and repatriated to make room for the newcomers.[12]

The medical challenges were also unprecedented: multiple amputations; lungs corroded by gas poisoning; complex intestinal wounds; the obliteration of facial features by shell blasts and injuries from gas and fire; and the hysteria of shell shock—to name only some of the more serious conditions. Many thousands of men died of their injuries shortly after the war—casualties not recognised in the official figure of more than 61,000 dead—and for some there was no sophisticated medical support in Australia. Men with serious facial disfigurement, for example, had to spend many months in Britain at Queen Mary's Hospital in Sidcup to access such facial reconstruction and cosmetic surgery techniques as were available at the time.[13]

Australia also had limited capacity to deal with the many thousands of men with psychological trauma. There were no trained psychoanalysts in 1914, and few medical practitioners familiar with Freudian theories. There were also, at first, no facilities for the mentally ill other than asylums for the insane. Moreover, some doctors and officials continued to see shell shock not as an injury but as evidence of malingering, cowardice and lack of moral fibre. In their view, the men with 'nerves'—not the war—were to blame for their condition. Perhaps they had a hereditary predisposition to mental illness? Despite all this, by the 1930s there were nearly 13,000 returned servicemen receiving pensions on psychological grounds.[14]

The system also could not cope with the fact that many soldiers' injuries were permanent. With many men enduring pain, disability and lung damage for the rest of their lives, the responsibility for their care fell to families. Wives, sisters but mostly parents—around 80 per cent of the AIF troops were unmarried and 52 per cent were aged between 18 and 24—nursed these men. They tended to their wounds, spoon-fed them, if necessary, endured their erratic and violent behaviour, and bore the brunt of the alcoholism to which some succumbed. This 'unpaid labour of kin', as Marina Larsson has called it, 'provided an important tier of welfare that propped up the formal repatriation system'. But carers got little formal recognition or support. Suffering 'a different kind of grief', some had breakdowns. Some walked away from their marriages (the divorce rate jumped significantly after the war). Others committed suicide. Many survived only by turning to charitable organisations.[15]

Where a veteran had no family to support him, compassionate strangers and friends stepped in. George Johnston grew up with the men whom his mother brought home from hospital. There was:

> Aleck, who had been blinded early, at Gaba Tepe . . . and 'Stubby', who was really only a trunk and a jovial red face in a wheel-chair, the German whizzbang having taken both his legs and both forearms at Villers-Breton-neux . . . Then there was Bert . . . [who] lost his right leg on the first and only day of action he ever saw in France . . . [and] was still only about eighteen when he came to our house on a pair of French crutches . . . The nightmarish one in this remembered gallery is Gabby Dixon, because he kept in the background and was never seen much, and I don't suppose he wanted to be seen because he had suffered terrible facial burns with mustard gas and his face was no longer really like a face at all. He used to frighten me with his staring silences . . . sometimes at night through the thin partitions of the wall we could hear him sobbing in his room.[16]

Preferential employment and soldier settlement

Such men could not be made 'whole again', as the authorities administering the repatriation system hoped that they would. They could not regain their 'manly independence' or resume what was seen to be their rightful role as breadwinners and heads of families. (Whatever had changed in wartime Australia, traditional understandings of gender roles had not.)[17]

However, for those who could work, the government offered a range of options: vocational training, fees for educational expenses, financial assistance to purchase tools and professional equipment, and loans for small businesses, plant and livestock. There were also careers in the public service. In August 1917 the federal government amended the *Public Service Act* to give veterans preference in recruitment for the Commonwealth public service. It was not a scheme that everyone endorsed. Private companies, most of which promised to follow the government lead, disliked hiring workers on any criteria other than efficiency. The union movement also resented the challenge to the time-honoured principle of the closed shop for their members. But preferential employment was one of the rights most jealously guarded by the RSSILA, and recruitment to the Commonwealth public service was dominated by veterans well into the inter-war period.[18]

If public service did not appeal, then veterans could opt to become farmers. Very early in the war, the state and Commonwealth governments developed a scheme of soldier settlement, providing land and financial assistance for veterans to engage in mixed farming, small-scale agriculture, and other rural industries. The scheme seemed to have much to recommend it. It would be an incentive to men to enlist, and Australia's cities would be protected from becoming 'congested with idle men', with all that this implied for public order. Rural life was also thought likely to appeal to men who had experienced 'the healthy, if somewhat dangerous outdoor life' of battle, while improving the health of those who were wounded. Finally, soldier settlement was a realisation of an ideal that Australians had cherished for decades: closer settlement of the vast continent by a yeoman class.[19]

However, the gap between aspiration and need again proved to be immense. In a mood of 'undiscriminating generosity', the authorities approved the applications of some 40,000 soldiers to take up the offer of land and loans. In every state, this was more than the original quota. Some of the soldier settlers already had rural skills, but many others were urban dwellers enticed by the prospect of carving out a new life in the country. At least half would fail in the 1920s and 1930s. Many lacked adequate capital, had high levels of debt and had been granted unproductive or small tracts of land. Others were struggling with poor health or had large families, and then had to contend with low prices for primary products. Successive royal commissions in the 1920s tried to deal with the humiliation and distress of the returned soldiers, who themselves mobilised politically. The Country Party, now the National Party, was created in 1920 and a number of other lobby groups were formed by farmers disillusioned with the government and the RSSILA. However, the problems of soldier settlement proved intractable. By 1943, the accumulated losses of the scheme across Australia were a staggering £45 million. Public sympathy—always an ephemeral emotion—dissolved and from 'pitiful tolerance the attitude passed quickly to one of irritation and resentment'. This was not, as one journalist put it, 'a country fit for men to live in'.[20]

The Paris Peace Conference

The costs of repatriation were huge, and Hughes—who had stayed in Europe to attend the peace conference held in Paris in the first half of 1919—was determined to ensure that Germany would foot the bill to some degree. This, together with guaranteeing Australia's post-war security, was his chief goal in any peace settlement.

Initially, it did not seem that Australia—or any other Dominion—would be a full member of the Paris conference. Rather, as had been diplomatic practice until that time, a delegation of the British Empire would represent the interests of all. However, for the Canadian Borden and of course Hughes, this was unacceptable: 1919 was not 1914, when the British government had spoken for the whole empire when it opted for war. The imperial relationships had changed over the past four years, and the Dominions—who had contributed so much to victory, at least in proportion to their own populations—were entitled to have their voices heard in peace negotiations. Hughes in particular had no faith that the British would represent Australia's interests adequately.

Given the very public airing of imperial differences at the time of the armistice, the British government accepted the Dominions' claim in principle. If it were not heeded, there might be serious implications for future imperial unity. As the Under-Secretary of State for Colonies, Leo Amery, said, 'with a quarrelsome and vain person like our little friend [Hughes], and with a very touchy and possibly swollen-headed public behind him . . . mischief may be caused if the breach is allowed to continue'.

> The extent to which the Dominions are given a really effective voice in the Peace Settlement [he wrote to Balfour] will determine their whole outlook on Imperial questions in future. If they consider that they have been treated in the full sense of the word as partners and have had an equal voice in the decisions not merely of such questions as affect them locally but in the whole peace settlement, they will be prepared to accept the idea of a single foreign policy for the British Commonwealth directed by the machinery of an Imperial Cabinet.[21]

The question was how to include the Dominions in the peace process. Independent Dominion representation at international forums was a constitutional novelty; and one that at least the French and the Americans thought would give the British Empire undue numbers at the conference table. As the French argued in late 1918, the Dominions stood in the same relation to the British Empire as the individual American states did to the United States—a point that Lloyd George, who thought it was 'impossible to treat the Dominions as separate from the British Empire', conceded.[22]

A number of options were canvassed in the last weeks of 1918. The Dominion prime ministers might be represented within the British Empire delegation by one of their number. Lloyd George, still frustrated with Hughes, thought this should be Borden. Or they could take turns on rotation, an option suggested by Smuts. Or they might attend sessions of the conference when their 'special material interests' were being considered, as other 'small powers' such as Belgium and Serbia would do. The last option, however, risked the exclusion of Canada, and Borden told the British Cabinet secretary Maurice Hankey that if this were adopted he might well have to 'pack his trunks, return to Canada, summon Parliament, and put the whole thing before them'.[23]

The matter was resolved by the Supreme War Council in Paris early during the conference in January 1919. Lloyd George, now converted to the arguments of the Dominions, presented the case that they were 'entirely autonomous', had interests of their own that were quite separate from those of Britain and deserved to be placed on an equal footing with the lesser Allied powers. Wilson, who had previously objected to the British and the Dominions having ten to twelve votes between them, conceded the point. The Dominions and India would have their own representatives at the conference. Australia, like Canada, South Africa and India, would have two.

This was not a fundamental change in the international status of the Dominions. Hughes would later say that representation at Paris meant that Australia 'became a nation, and entered into the family of nations on a footing of equality', but Australia did not gain full sovereignty at this time. The constitutional changes that would make the Dominions truly independent international actors came only in the inter-war years, with the negotiation of the Balfour Declaration of 1926 and the Statute of Westminster of 1931. Even then, Australia remained reluctant to embrace independence. Clinging to imperial loyalty and the cultural imagination of empire more tenaciously than some other Dominions, Australia did not ratify the Statute of Westminster until 1942.[24]

Fighting for German New Guinea

Dominion representation at Paris did mean that Hughes could pursue specific Australian interests with single-mindedness and tenacity. However, he soon found that Australia's actual power to influence the outcomes of the conference was limited. The Paris Peace Conference, which opened with great ceremony in mid-January 1919, was a vast international gathering. There were thousands of delegates from the 32 states or political units that at some time between 1914 and 1918 had been at war, or had broken off relations, with the Central Powers. This included states that have played little, if any, role in this historical account of the war: Brazil, Belgium, Bolivia, Bulgaria,

China, Costa Rica, Cuba, Ecuador, Greece, Guatemala, Haiti, Honduras, Liberia, Montenegro, Nicaragua, Panama, Peru, Poland, Portugal, Romania, San Marino, Serbia, Siam and Uruguay. As Hughes later recalled, it was 'the Greatest Show on Earth', 'a little like the Tower of Babel brought up to date'. The British delegation alone numbered 500. The American contingent was even larger, and there were around 500 journalists.[25]

The Australian delegation was dwarfed. It included Hughes and his secretary Percy Deane; High Commissioner Cook and his secretary; and three advisers, Garran, Latham and Frederic Eggleston, another member of the Australian Round Table and an associate of Garran. There were also two journalists, Henry Gullett and the ubiquitous Keith Murdoch, whom Eggleston described as 'worms simply crawling around'. Since Australia had no professional foreign service at this time, there were no diplomats with the experience of the Foreign Office or the Quai d'Orsay, but in Garran, Latham and Eggleston Hughes had the advice—if he wanted it—of some of the best minds of Australia at the time.[26]

The agenda of the Paris Peace Conference was as huge and complex as its membership. In a matter of months, the conference had to resolve the details of the peace settlement with the defeated Central Powers—including reparations, indemnities, future armaments and the disposal of colonies—as well as addressing the political situation in Russia, the control of Arab lands in the Middle East and the boundaries of the new states emerging from the chaos of imperial collapse in Central and Eastern Europe. Shaping all discussions—at least as far as Wilson was concerned—was the creation of the League of Nations. Confronted with these breathtakingly portentous issues, the conference became not so much an ordered meeting of all parties in plenary session as a vast and unwieldy network of committees and commissions, or conferences within conferences. Some of the deliberations stretched over eighteen months. While the Treaty of Versailles with Germany was signed on 28 June 1919, negotiations regarding Austria (Treaty of Saint-Germain), Bulgaria (Neuilly), Hungary (Trianon) and Turkey (Sèvres) continued until August 1920.[27]

Integrating the whole proceedings, in principle, was a Council of Ten—the successor to the Supreme War Council. This consisted of two representatives each of Britain, France, Italy, the United States and—to Hughes' chagrin—Japan, but in practice it was the Council of Four—Clemenceau, Lloyd George, the Italian Prime Minister Orlando and Wilson, and their foreign ministers—who became the locus of power. Hughes and the other Dominion leaders needed Lloyd George to refer matters to this body if they were to gain any traction.

It was in this byzantine environment that Hughes set about trying to protect what he saw as Australia's interests. It was already clear that he faced a battle on the question of post-war control of German New Guinea. During the armistice discussions in 1918, Wilson had made it clear that he thought the German colonies should not be annexed outright but rather be placed under the control of the League of Nations, which might devolve administration to states as trustees. Hughes, however, still hoped to persuade Wilson otherwise. As he wrote to Munro Ferguson on 17 January:

> I hope we shall convince him. I think we shall for he is a man firm on nothing that really matters. He regards the League of Nations as the great Charter of the World that is to be and sees himself through the roseate cloud of dreams officiating as the High Priest in the Temple in which the Sarcophagus or Ark containing the body or ashes of this amazing gift to Mankind is to rest in majestic seclusion for all time. Give him a League of Nations and he will give *us* all the rest. Good. He shall have his toy![28]

Lloyd George, too, hoped that the question of the German colonies might be resolved quickly, and persuaded the Council of Ten to meet with the Dominion leaders on 24 January. Opening the proceedings, he indicated that Britain was willing to accept the principle of League mandates for the enemy territory that it had seized, but supported the claims of Australia, New Zealand and South Africa to annex the colonies they had occupied. Hughes then took the floor. Armed with a large map of a hemisphere centred on Australia, which Garran had scoured London to locate, he went straight to the strategic arguments for annexation. Australia needed to control German New Guinea, the Bismarck archipelago and the Solomons, since these islands encompassed Australia 'like a fortress'. The policies of nations changed, and 'friends in one war were not always friends in the next'. (The fact that the representative of Japan, Baron Makino, was present did nothing to inhibit Hughes!) Beyond this, it would cause administrative confusion if German New Guinea were under a League mandate while Papua, already governed by Australia, was not. Assuming, it seems, that Australia would not be the mandatory power, Hughes concluded that another power in New Guinea might be seen as 'a potential enemy' for Australia.[29]

Hughes was not alone in arguing for annexation (Smuts and Massey also made their case for control of South-West Africa and Samoa), but it was Hughes—paying the price for his earlier outspokenness—who bore the brunt of Wilson's opposition. When the leaders convened again on 27 January, Wilson conceded that South Africa was a logical choice as mandatory power in South-West Africa, but Australia, he said, reminded him of a man who bought an inordinate amount of real estate and tried to prevent others from owning any adjoining land. Hughes' strategic arguments were irrelevant because in the new world order of collective security there would be no need for states to seek protection by annexing territory. Instead, the League of Nations would 'rally the whole world against an outlaw' aggressor in the future.[30]

Undeterred, Hughes launched into a broadside attack on mandates—at least as they might apply to New Guinea. Direct government, he argued, had always proved more effective than indirect. Australia, with its past experience in governing Papua, was worthy of German New Guinea: as a democracy it would not tolerate the ill-treatment of native peoples and, contrary to what Wilson said, the world did not dread annexation. Annexation was repugnant only when it was motivated by 'imperialistic purposes'.

For Wilson, however, the credibility of the League of Nations was at stake. The open diplomacy that the United States had championed would also be compromised if the peace conference parcelled out the German colonies in a traditionally realist manner. The issue of the German colonies therefore should not be resolved until the League had been established.[31] This, at least, was his public position. Privately, Wilson and his advisers were inclined to oppose the annexation of German colonies for reasons of *realpolitik* rather than liberal internationalism. If Australian and New Zealand claims to New Guinea and Samoa were granted, so too would be Japan's claim to the Caroline and Marshall islands. This would leave Japan positioned strategically in the mid-Pacific—a development that the US administration, with its eye on the changing regional power balance, did not welcome. The British, too, were growing uneasy about French claims in relation to Togoland and the Cameroons, which French officials supported with reference to Australia's arguments for New Guinea.[32]

Attempting to find a solution, the British delegation came up with a compromise: there should be a three-tier system of mandates, in which Class C should allow the mandated territories to be part of the legal and economic systems of the mandated power. As a draft by Latham, who was serving as assistant secretary to the British Empire delegation, put it with impeccable legal precision:

> There are territories such as South-West Africa and the Pacific Islands, which, owing to the sparseness of their population, or their small size, or their remoteness from the centres of civilisation, or their geographical contiguity to the mandatory State, and other circumstances, can be best administered under the laws of the mandatory State as integral portions thereof, subject to the safeguards above-mentioned in the interests of the indigenous population.[33]

It was an ingenious solution, giving everyone the essence of what they wanted. The custodial role of the League would be preserved and the territories would effectively be demilitarised, since the mandatory power could not fortify them. Moreover, Australia and other mandatory powers could control the trade and immigration of the territories they administered. Excluding Japanese commercial interests from New Guinea and preserving White Australia were at the forefront of Hughes' mind: as he said, if the principle of 'open door' were applied to New Guinea, it would 'become a Japanese or Japanese and German country' within ten years.[34]

Yet it would take several more torrid meetings before Hughes accepted the compromise. Oddly slow to appreciate the strategic implications of Japan's annexing the islands north of the equator, Hughes continued to campaign against the mandate system. There was, he claimed, no guarantee that Australia would be granted the mandate by the League—nor that the mandate, if granted, would extend beyond German New Guinea to include the Bismarck archipelago and the German Solomons. When Lloyd George, his patience fraying, told Hughes that he 'would not quarrel with the United States for the Solomon Islands' and that if Hughes persisted in his claim he could not expect the British Navy to help him enforce it, Hughes threatened to appeal to the English people. To quote Malcolm Booker, as an old trade unionist Hughes 'always used the threat of confrontation as a negotiating lever'. But Lloyd George said privately that he would not be bullied by 'a damned little Welshman'.[35]

Despite his irritation, Lloyd George managed to secure Wilson's in-principle agreement to the compromise mandate scheme, but by then Hughes, unable to help himself, had gone to press. On the very morning that Lloyd George was taking the British proposal for mandates to the Council of Ten, a Paris edition of the British *Daily Mail* carried an article that implied that Wilson was 'either a hypocrite or an egotistical fool' in insisting on a mandate system. Using obviously leaked information, it also stated that the existence of the British Empire was being threatened by the Dominions' concerns about mandates. Infuriated, Wilson dug in when he met the Dominion leaders, insisting that while the compromise proposal went a long way towards resolving the issue, the detail of mandates could not be resolved until the League was established. To Lloyd George's dismay, the compromise deal began to unravel. Hughes rose to his feet and, as Borden recalled, practically repudiated 'the whole arrangement as far as Australia was concerned'.[36]

What followed in the next meeting has become part of Hughes folklore. The details vary according to witnesses, but it seems that Wilson lost his temper after Massey spoke in support of the Class C mandate. Were Australia and New Zealand, the president asked, presenting an ultimatum to the conference? Hughes, fiddling with his hearing aid—either because he needed to or because it suited him to stall—asked for the question to be repeated. When it was, he replied: 'That's about the size of it, Mr President. That puts it very well.' When Wilson continued, asking Hughes whether he expected the five million Australians he represented to be set against the 1200 million represented by the conference, Hughes responded, 'I represent sixty thousand dead.' (The United States in fact had lost more—possibly 77,500 killed in combat—but no one thought that, given the size of its population, this was anything like the 'blood price' paid by Australia and other participants.) Finally, when Lloyd George tried to mediate by asking Hughes if Australia would grant free access for missionaries in any New Guinea mandate, Hughes replied, 'I understand that these poor people are very short of food, and for some time past they have not had enough missionaries.' Wilson did not see the joke.[37]

As the story of this confrontation spread around Paris, Hughes became something of folk hero, 'the little David facing the American Goliath, or the larrikin giving cheek to the dignified professor according to one's point of view', as Fitzhardinge has put it. But Eggleston (admittedly not the most objective of sources) questioned the value of Hughes' tactics:

> It is open to doubt . . . whether the brilliant eclecticism of Mr. Hughes was not somewhat out of place . . . At Paris, in fact, Australia was a 'Digger' among the nations and Mr. Hughes a typical leader of 'Diggers'. But the atmosphere of a Peace Conference is far different from and far less noble than that of the field where the 'Digger' is seen at his glorious best. There is a base, calculating Peace Conference spirit which takes no account of courage or sacrifice, but coldly weighs forces and mercilessly visits upon each party the results.

Certainly Hughes' maverick style did nothing to improve his standing with Wilson—or, for that matter, with Lloyd George or his Dominion counterparts. Borden, for example, apologised to Colonel House for Hughes.[38]

With bigger matters on the agenda, the storm finally blew over and the system of Class C mandates was accepted. In June, the Council of Three (Italy being absent) allocated to Japan the mandate for the islands north of the equator, to New Zealand the mandate for Samoa, and to Australia the mandate for the islands south of the equator. Nauru was not included. Its mandate went to the British Empire. A later agreement established joint control by Britain, Australia and New Zealand. Britain and Australia were each allocated 42 per cent of Nauru's valuable phosphate production and 16 per cent went to New Zealand.[39]

The racial equality clause

This was a victory of sorts for Hughes. So too—at least in his terms—was his battle to stop the inclusion in the Covenant of the League of a clause enshrining the principle of racial equality. This was proposed early in the conference by Japan's representatives at Paris, Makino and Sutemi Chindu. Having gained admission to the inner circles of the Allies by virtue of its role in the war, Japan was intent on eradicating any humiliating distinctions by gaining a formal statement that 'all alien nationals' of League members would be accorded 'equal and just treatment in every respect, [without] distinction, either in law or in fact, on account of their race and nationality'. Colonel House, whom the Japanese approached for advice as to how to proceed, seemed willing at first to consider the proposal. But Borden, Smuts and Hughes all protested, with the backing of the British, who wanted to avoid another crisis in imperial relations. Hughes was particularly agitated. For him, the proposed racial equality clause was nothing more than an insidious way for the Japanese to breach the walls of White Australia and penetrate the Australian economy.[40]

Long weeks of negotiations in search of compromise followed, during which Hughes would become the public face of opposition to the Japanese, although he was not alone in his reservations. In an effort to find agreement, the Japanese offered concessions. The clause might state only the principle of racial equality, leaving the practical applications to be settled in bilateral diplomacy; or there might be a declaration without binding force in the preamble of the League rather than in the Covenant itself. But Hughes was uncompromising.

To Smuts he said privately, 'Nothing shall go in, no matter how mild and in-offensive.' Publicly, he insisted that if there were to be a racial equality clause of any kind, it must explicitly exclude immigration and naturalisation.[41]

Once more he turned to the press, this time with the aim of inflaming opposition to the proposed clause in California, a community as deeply committed to racially discriminatory immigration as was Australia. For a man who jealously guarded his own nation's right to exclusive domestic juris-diction, this was a remarkable tactic—but it worked. Wilson and House soon became nervous that the racial equality clause might raise a storm of protest in the western United States. Opposition to the League itself was already growing in the US because of its potential erosion of national autonomy. Hence it became politically convenient for the US administration to shelter behind Hughes and his British backers.

When the Japanese presented their watered-down proposal for a statement in the League preamble to the final meeting of the League Commission on 11 April, it failed—even though it got majority support. Wilson insisted on a unanimous vote. Makino, who had made a dignified appeal for the redressing of the 'wrongs of racial discrimination', which caused 'deep resentment on the part of a large portion of the human race', was left to refer the matter to the final plenary session of the conference. Here, although Smuts and Borden were now willing to accommodate the Japanese, Hughes still held out for the exclusion of immigration and naturalisation—and the Japanese backed down.[42]

Hughes may have felt vindicated, but his intransigence on this issue damaged Australia's reputation in Japan. Makino told Keith Murdoch that public opinion in Japan would hold Australia accountable if no racial equality clause eventuated and that Australian–Japanese relations would be 'seriously compromised'. Other Japanese delegates in Paris spoke of their 'utmost mortification' at Hughes' refusal to meet with them. The Japanese press also attacked Hughes, demanding that Japan turn its back on the League and 'create her own Monroe doctrine in the Orient'.[43]

The egregious offence that Hughes had caused also troubled some of his colleagues in Australia. Watt was receiving advice from experts on

Japan—Professor James Murdoch, a scholar of Japanese, and Edmund Piesse, the head from May 1919 of the newly created Pacific Branch in the Prime Minister's Department—to the effect that Hughes' behaviour might fuel ultra-nationalism in Japan. He might be eroding rather than enhancing Australia's security by strengthening the hands of those who wanted to keep Japan out of the League. Concessions on the racial equality clause might have been enabled, and the integrity of Australia's immigration policy preserved, by a negotiated 'gentleman's agreement' with Japan, such as the one that existed with Canada. This could limit the intake of Japanese while removing the more gratuitously offensive aspects of the White Australia Policy. Hence Watt tried to soften Hughes' stance by cabling on 15 April that:

> Recent comments in Japanese papers, which I have been closely following for months, are couched in a tone which bodes no good to Australia. All information which I have indicates growing irritation in Japan against Australia's reaffirmation of its principles. This is obviously being fanned by Japanese Military Party whose power has been rapidly declining. Nothing so calculated, however, to revive it as this atmosphere of irritation.

Hughes, however, refused advice, blamed the Americans for all the trouble and assured Watt that his own interview with the Japanese press in Paris had 'greatly pleased' them. The Japanese preferred, he claimed, 'a straight-out opponent to those who promised support or led them to believe they would support'. Watt was left to try to convey a more conciliatory message at home. Speaking on Empire Day, he said that Japan had 'stood by our side as the lonely sentinel in the Pacific, guarding our boys while they were going across the oceans . . . and even guarding Australia itself'. Even though the Japanese had been regarded earlier as 'an utterly inferior race', Australians 'should cherish the friendship of Japan'.[44]

The episode was one in which, judged by today's values, Hughes brought little credit on Australia. Yet perhaps he read the Australian electorate better than Watt. White Australia was a core value of Australians on both the right and the left, and would remain so for decades to come. As the Melbourne

Argus wrote on 19 April 1919, Australians' fear of non-white immigration was 'deeper and more instinctive' than simple fear of economic competition in labour and the erosion of living standards:

> The East and the West [its leader writer proclaimed] are too far apart in tradition, in ethos or ethical tone and way of feeling, in religion and social instinct, in all the elements which really go to make up what is called civilisation . . . The intimacy and the meeting, the mixing and the mingling of two differing civilisations means demoralisation; means social, ethical and religious decadence.[45]

Reparations and indemnities

However ambiguous Hughes' 'success' on the racial equality clause may have been, he failed completely in his final battle at Paris, over indemnities from Germany. His position on this issue was again non-negotiable: Germany should be made to pay all the costs of the war. Reparations that simply 'restored' the physical damage Germany had inflicted on occupied territories were not enough. Indemnities must be paid so that Australia could discharge its accumulated war debt, which might otherwise impose a crushing burden of taxation on future generations. It would be invidious if nations that had fought the war for more than four years were to be left financially crippled while those that had held back (that is, Japan and the United States) emerged from the war with a competitive advantage.[46]

Hughes' views on the subject were so well known that in late 1918 Lloyd George had appointed him to chair an Imperial War Cabinet committee responsible for formulating the British position on reparations. The report of this committee, produced in a matter of weeks during the British election campaign that immortalised the phrase 'squeezing Germany like a lemon till the pips squeak', was 'farcical'. Hughes dominated proceedings, talking incessantly and being 'dogmatic, hectoring, impatient of evidence and scornful of logic'. Contrary to its instructions, the Committee ignored the question of Germany's capacity to pay and the effect reparations might have on the countries receiving them. It took little notice of awkward evidence presented by Treasury officials such as John Maynard Keynes and discounted the dissenting views of the Canadian Minister of Finance. In the end, it plucked from the air a figure of £24,000 million that Germany should pay. This was enough to enable Lloyd George to say, on the eve of the December election: 'First we have the absolute right to demand the whole cost of the war; second, we propose to demand the whole cost of the war; and third a Committee appointed by the direction of the Government believe it can be done.' The Imperial War Cabinet, meeting on 24 December, agreed—despite the reservations of some members—to instruct the British delegates to the proposed Inter-Allied Commission on reparations to 'endeavour to secure from Germany the greatest possible indemnity she can pay consistently with the economic well-being of the British Empire and the peace of the world, and without involving an army of occupation'.[47]

Hence Hughes seemed well positioned in Paris to win what he wanted for Australia, particularly as he was appointed as one of three representatives for Britain on the Reparations Commission. He was also vice-chairman of this commission and chair of the sub-committee that was assigned the task of considering how Germany would be compelled to meet the obligations imposed on it. However, it became clear almost immediately that there were profound divisions among the Allies on the issue of reparations. Wilson was on record as saying that indemnities symbolised all that was wrong with the politics of the Old World. Now the US representatives, led by the able 30-year-old John Foster Dulles (Secretary of State from 1953 to 1959), mounted a skilful, if legalistic, case against Germany's paying the full costs of the war. Arguing that Germany should be liable only for damages arising from its violations of international law, Dulles sought to limit reparations to all of Belgium's war costs, the restoration of the occupied areas of France, and compensation for all damage to property and persons caused directly by German military operations. It was not enough that Germany's actions were immoral or unjust, Dulles said. They had to be technically illegal for liability to be incurred.

For Hughes, this was of course unacceptable. The American position was too restrictive in its understanding of the damage to civilian populations and property. If Belgium was entitled to have its costs covered, why not also those countries that had come to her aid and incurred debt as a result of Germany's illegal actions? Justice—a concept that Wilson himself was prone to invoke—demanded that Germany as the aggressor should pay for the costs of the war.

The impasse seemed irreconcilable. Hughes, as ever, lobbied the press—in Britain, France and the United States—and looked to Australia for support. He asked Watt, whose support he wanted on this question at least, to get resolutions passed in Australia in favour of indemnities. But Wilson would not budge. Although his advisers conceded that the British position had some popular support, the Allies, as he saw it, were bound by the exchange of notes at the time of the armistice in which Allied demands were said to have been limited. Not that this placated Hughes. He had always had deep reservations about the terms of the armistice, which he now saw as 'a millstone round our necks'.[48]

Unable to get traction in the Reparations Commission, Hughes drew in Lloyd George. Australia's cause was also the British Empire's, since if the US view prevailed, France and Belgium would get the lion's share of reparations, leaving little for other Allies. Like Australia, Britain had significant war debts. It had suffered £800 million worth of damage, owed £100 million to the United States and had forfeited $900 million in securities and bullion to fund war purchases. It was also owed significant amounts by other countries. Although there was the option of all debts being cancelled and less being asked of Germany, the United States would not consider this. Hence Lloyd George, sceptical about any schedule of reparations that went for more than ten years and keen to avoid having to administer Germany to extract payment, concluded that the best option might be to calculate, in the first instance, what Germany could afford to pay. Then the different national claims could be prioritised and reparations shared out in agreed proportions. The concept of 'damages', Lloyd George also argued, should be extended to include the capitalised cost of pensions for the incapacitated and their dependants within the British Empire.

When he learned of this, Hughes was again aghast. As Neville Meaney puts it, 'Another betrayal was at hand. Another cause was lost.' But Hughes was isolated. Although the Reparations Commission continued to meet and produce reports, the crucial decisions about reparations were made by Wilson, Lloyd George, Clemenceau and, when he was available, Orlando. For advice, Lloyd George looked not to Hughes but to Smuts and British officials such as Keynes, who would later resign his position as adviser and publish a profoundly influential attack on what he saw as the 'Carthaginian Peace' of Versailles, *The Economic Consequences of the Peace*.[49]

By early April, Hughes' battle to get Germany to pay the full costs of the war was lost. Lloyd George had agreed to settle for a total bill of £11,000 million and persuaded Wilson to accept German liability for pensions, thus increasing the British Empire's proportion of the payout. When this compromise was presented to the British Empire Delegation on 11 April, Hughes alone of all the British and Dominion leaders refused to agree. He rehearsed all his well-worn arguments, lamenting that the British had 'truckled to the United States for too long'. But it had no effect. Borden told him to agree with Lloyd George or risk getting nothing at all. Massey found this compelling, and South Africa's P.W. Botha admitted he had not expected to get as much as Lloyd George had secured. After an agonising delay, Hughes capitulated. He did not accept the outcome on reparations and continued to hope for better terms, but he agreed in the interests of imperial unity that he would follow the lead of the British Empire and sign the peace treaty.

The Australian Cabinet, seeing the issue through Hughes' eyes, was also bitterly disappointed. The settlement that now seemed probable would be 'inequitable' between European allies; and it would confront two generations of Australians with taxation 'which will blight Australia's prosperity' and 'reflect itself on the sentiments of Empire which through all the great war had animated the Commonwealth and its people'. But for all their distress, the members of the Cabinet, like Hughes, could not countenance publicly breaking with Britain on this or any other question. 'Virtual secession from Empire partnership' was not an option. It was, after all, the survival of the empire that had been from the start a core Australian war aim.[50]

This is not the place to tell the tortured story of German reparations in the 1920s. Suffice to say that by 1931, when reparations payments finally ended,

Australia had received only £5.571 million against a total claim of £464 million, £364 million being for actual war expenditure and £100 million for the capitalised value of pensions, repatriation and loss to civilian property. Moreover, what it had received was largely made up of ships seized in Australian ports and the value of expropriated property in New Guinea.[51]

The gains and losses

Hughes described the Treaty of Versailles as 'not a good peace' for Australia, but a good one for the United States. As he had feared, Wilson's agenda had shaped the peace process—though not to the degree the president had hoped—and the compromises and pragmatism of international politics had denied Australia what Hughes thought were its entitlements. Though he drew some satisfaction from blocking the racial equality clause and was reconciled to the compromise on mandates, he thought the failure to extract full war costs from Germany was little short of catastrophic. Not only did it leave Australian burdened with its war costs but, as Hughes saw it, it would allow Germany to rise again to challenge British imperial dominance. The German delegation that came to Paris on 7 May to receive the Allied peace terms seemed only to confirm this. To Hughes, they seemed unbowed by their defeat, 'the very incarnation of all against which the world had been fighting for over 4½ years'. Yes, the League of Nations—which Hughes had grudgingly come to tolerate—might provide some international security against a resurgent Germany, but realist that he was, Hughes had his doubts (with good cause, as it happened).[52]

Beyond this, Hughes lamented that the war seemed to have left the United States triumphant and the British Empire, whose contribution to victory had been so much greater, diminished. He wrote to Munro Ferguson in May that it was:

a good peace for America. *She* who did not come into the war to make anything has made thousands of millions out it. *She* gets the best ships. *She* has a good chance of beating us for world mercantile supremacy. *She* prevented us getting the cost of the war.

Later in September 1919, when moving the ratification of the Treaty of Versailles by the Australian parliament, Hughes again said that 'this peace [is] not a harsh Peace to Germany, and it is not a just peace to us'. It was an odd judgement, given that the Treaty of Versailles remains notorious as a peace settlement so punitive that it sowed the seeds for another great European conflict two decades later.[53]

Yet in some ways, Hughes' disappointment was understandable. The quantifiable 'spoils of war' for Australia were few, and scarcely commensurate with the scale of the losses the country had suffered. No one would claim that a mandate to control German New Guinea was worth over 60,000 dead. But Hughes' expectations of the peace settlement were unrealistic. As the difficulties of extracting reparations from Germany in the 1920s would show, repayment of all war costs was impossible. Even if German aggression had caused the war—a question debated even today—this was an economic reality that no amount of diplomacy could change. Likewise, the rise of the United States and the relative decline of the British Empire that Hughes so lamented were trends that no peace treaty could reverse. The growth of American industrial might, which would make it a superpower in the twentieth century, was already in train before 1914. It was simply accelerated by the war. For all his realism, Hughes struggled to understand that this was not a matter of 'injustice'. It is in the nature of long general wars that they exhaust those who fight them and leave the international balance of power fundamentally transformed. Not only did World War I leave Britain and its empire exhausted and in debt, it also destroyed three of the dynastic monarchies that had dominated Europe for centuries. The world order that the Great Powers of Europe had gone to war to preserve in 1914 was shattered.

This, however, was more evident in retrospect than at the time. In 1919, many Australians took comfort in the fact that the Allies had at least won the war. The British Empire had survived and German power, it seemed, had been crushed—if not so conclusively in Europe, at least in the Asia-Pacific, the region most critical to Australia's security. Australia had not become a German colony, as might have been its fate if Britain had lost the war.

Its democratic systems were secure. Japan, to be sure, was a troubling presence to the north, but in 1919 there seemed little reason to doubt that British naval power would be able to contain it.

If these 'gains' do not seem today to be substantial, it is partly because we know they were illusory. World War I was not 'the war to end war'. Within a generation, Germany would launch another even more destructive conflict, and Japan would seek to create by force a Greater East Asia Co-Prosperity Sphere. The dominance of Europe that Britain and France secured by their 1918 victory would prove, as Michael Howard has said, to be a 'false hegemony', lasting only as long as Germany did not mobilise to challenge it. When it did, neither Britain nor France could maintain supremacy in Europe, or provide the strategic protection that Australia relied upon in the Asia-Pacific. When the long-feared Japanese advance south occurred in 1941–42, it was also of little value to Australia that it administered German New Guinea, which under the terms of its mandate it had not been able to fortify.[54]

We also struggle to see as 'gains' the protection of empire and racism. These values are anachronistic—even mortifying. How did they sustain a nation through four years of war? As Stéphane Audoin-Rouzeau and Annette Becker have written more generally:

> The system of representations which characterized First World War contemporaries—soldiers and civilians, men, women and children—is now almost impossible to accept. The sense of obligation, of unquestioned sacrifice, which held most people in its tenacious, cruel clutches for so long and so profoundly, and without which the war could never have lasted as long as it did, is no longer acceptable. The foundation on which the immense collective consensus of 1914–18 was based . . . has vanished into thin air.[55]

Most significantly, the cost of defending the values of 1914 seems, by almost any respective calculation, to be disproportionate. Almost 20 per cent of Australians who served overseas were killed, and many thousands more would die prematurely over the next two decades. These deaths (and those caused by the influenza pandemic) changed the demographics of the Australian population. The 1933 national census revealed 21,500 fewer men aged 35–39 years—who had been 16–20 in 1914–19—than in the 30–34-year-old cohort. The gender balance of Australian society changed too. Whereas in 1911 there were 109 men for every 100 women between 25 and 44 years of age, in 1933 there were 98 men for every 100 women between 35 and 39. The demographic 'gap' would have been even more pronounced had there not been unusually high levels of migration in the 1920s (an average of 121,000 per year between 1921 and 1928, as opposed to 57,000 per year between 1901 and 1908).[56]

This might not literally be 'a lost generation', but it must have seemed like it. So many young men who would have made a productive contribution to post-war Australia, providing labour and leadership and becoming husbands and fathers, had gone. Since another 160,000 men had been wounded, the damage to Australian social life was incalculable. Not for nothing did Manning Clark call the 1920s in Australia 'the age of the survivors'.[57]

Added to this was the less quantifiable embittering of public life. No community can wage battles as polarising as the conscription debates of 1916 and 1917 without carrying scars. Post-war Australia remained divided for years into the camps the war had spawned: a broken nation in which the volunteer was pitted against the 'shirker'; the conscriptionist against the anti-conscriptionist; and, though sectarianism was not created by the war, the Catholic against the Protestant. The insults, calumny and accusations traded in the hysteria of the war years were not forgotten—they echoed down the years. Even in April 1939, the incoming Prime Minister Robert Menzies had to defend himself against attacks from his political opponent, Earle Page, for his failure to enlist in World War I. As his mother—who flew, for the first time, to Canberra to defend him—explained, Menzies' family had urged him to stay at home after two brothers had enlisted.[58]

The war had also given free rein to a xenophobia and insularity that continued beyond the peace. The hapless 'enemy aliens' who had been interned during the war were not reintegrated into Australian society at the war's end, but rather hounded out of the country. Among those who bayed for their deportation were returned soldiers who thought German-Australians had 'got in first [with land claims] whilst our men were fighting'. They were joined by professional associations, such as the Australian branch of the British Medical Association, which wrote to the prime minister claiming that it was not in the public interest for doctors of alien birth and qualifications to continue to practise in Australia. Since the federal government itself was keen to eliminate German competition within the British Empire, and the Treaty of Versailles stated that all prisoners of war and interned civilians should be repatriated 'with the greatest rapidity', mass deportation was introduced with the same 'arbitrary and ruthless determination' that characterised internment during the war years. By September 1919, some 6150 people had been deported, 5414 of whom had previously been interned. Others were family members or enemy aliens who could not face staying in the country that had turned so viciously against them.[59]

The paranoia about left-wing radicalism that Hughes and other loyalists had exploited during the war years also persisted into the post-war years. The IWW may have been crushed, but there was now a new enemy in communism—almost literally, since the Australian government decided to send Australian troops to Russia as part of the Allied military intervention against the Bolsheviks. The internal security apparatus that the Australian state had created—purportedly for the duration of the war only—therefore was not completely dismantled. The offices of the censor and other agencies were closed, but their vast records on the Australian population were transferred to the Investigation Branch set up after the war as part of the Attorney-General's Department. Meanwhile, although the *War Precautions Act* was repealed in 1920, some regulations continued, and in 1926 an amendment to the *Crimes Act* resurrected many of the provisions of the *Unlawful Associations Act*. Under surveillance now were communists, non-British migrants, Irish nationalists, left-wing radicals and trade unionists.[60]

The loyalist elements of Australian society also remained mobilised against the 'threat' from the left. Initially, they conducted vigilante-style attacks against meetings of radicals and Russian-Australians in 1918 and 1919. The streets of Brisbane, for example, erupted in the so-called Red Flag Riots in the later months of 1919. Then, in later years, citizen forces were raised as they had been in 1917, to counter strike action, for example, by Victorian police in 1923. And when the Great Depression brought financial ruin and unemployment to many returned soldiers, their disillusion found an outlet in 'secret' armies—notably the Old and New Guard in New South Wales and the White Army in Victoria. The threat posed by these groups to the authority of Australian governments was never especially serious (even though they had high-level support, including from senior businessmen, conservative politicians and military leaders). They were certainly not comparable to the paramilitary organisations of the right and left that destroyed democracy in Weimar Germany. But even if more Dad's Armies than Sturmabteilungen, they reflected the degree to which the war had left a potential for violence within the Australian political culture.[61]

In many ways, then, post-war Australia was polarised and dominated by the forces of conservatism and reaction. Some historians have lamented that the shattering of the ALP federally meant that the 'party of progress' was overtaken by the 'parties of reaction or resistance'. The reforming energies of the pre-1914 period were dissipated and Australia lost the capacity for political and social experimentation which had placed it in a vanguard internationally in the years before 1914. This conclusion needs some qualification. Dominant though the non-Labor parties were at the federal level from 1917 to 1941, they were not monolithic and, under Prime Minister Stanley Bruce (1924–29) and the cautious reforming liberalism of Joseph Lyons (1931–39), they initiated their own agendas of national and infrastructure development. At the state level, too, power alternated between Labor and non-Labor, with Queensland having a long period of Labor government (and abolishing the bête noire of the left, the Legislative Council, in 1922). Yet despite this, the image of Australia as an inward-looking society, focused on grief and the rancour of the war years, is impossible to dispel.[62]

The Anzac legend

For all its negative legacy, World War I provided a foundational narrative of Australian nationalism in the form of the Anzac 'legend' or 'myth' which, if its resilience over subsequent decades is any indication, many Australians have seen as positive. Originating in the landing at Gallipoli and rapidly gaining a hold on the Australian cultural imagination thereafter, this heroic narrative would soon be embedded in the commemorative rituals, literature and public discourse of the inter-war period. There were many agents shaping its formation and perpetuation, but none was more important than Charles Bean. The monumental official history that he edited and wrote from 1919 to 1946 articulated a powerful representation of the Australian soldier as the product of a distinctive society and value system—a society in which the bush shaped the cultural imagination and social mores; in which men learned to be independent in spirit and thus natural and resourceful fighters; in which the relative lack of class made men willing to challenge rank and authority; and in which the quality of mateship was valued above all. Little of this was empirically verifiable, but this did not matter. 'Anzac' was a version of the past that many—though not all—Australians wanted to hear and which, like other myths, would soon serve as a charter for the present, justifying contemporary institutions and values, keeping them in existence.[63]

By World War II, the Anzac myth had become hegemonic in the sense that it seemed natural even to those who were not part of the elites that created it. The army of 1939–45 took the title of the Second Australian Imperial Force, its battalions were numbered after the battalions of 1914–18, and the dead of this conflict were more often than not commemorated on the same memorials as those of World War I. Figuratively as well as physically, the men who fought World War II were the heirs to the first Anzacs. Even prisoners of the Japanese, whose surrender in 1941–42 did not fit easily into a narrative of military heroism, were able to integrate their experiences into the Anzac narrative when they came to write their memoirs in the post-war years. Forced into humiliating captivity they may have been, but they were still able to display the 'Anzac' qualities of mateship, humour and resourcefulness in situations of duress.[64]

Within two decades, however—in the 1960s and 1970s—it seemed that the dominance of the Anzac 'legend' was being eroded. A generation radicalised by feminism, student activism and the use of selective conscription during the Vietnam War attacked the values of Anzac and its custodian, the Returned and Services League, as militaristic, misogynist and anachronistic. As Ken Inglis later said, it seemed that 'the ceremonies of Anzac would wither away and its monuments become ever more archaic'. However, to its critics' surprise, Anzac Day would rebound in the 1980s as part of a remarkable 'memory boom' that swept across Australia and the world. What caused this phenomenon is beyond the scope of this book, and remains a matter for ongoing debate. Suffice to say that with this 'turning to the past' came not only new commemorative activities—new war memorials at home and abroad, and an explosion of battlefield tours and pilgrimages, official and private—but a new affirmation of the narrative and values of Anzac in Australian public life.[65]

The form the Anzac legend now takes, it must be said, is somewhat different from that of earlier decades. Reflecting the values of a multicultural Australia, the language of Anzac has become more inclusive of gender and cultural diversity. It does not invoke military skills or killing, but rather courage, endurance, sacrifice and mateship—the words inscribed on the memorial unveiled at Isurava, on the Kokoda Trail, in 2002. These are not only qualities that resonate with the kinds of military operations that today's defence personnel often conduct—what might be called 'post-heroic' warfare in the form of peacekeeping and humanitarian interventions. They are also, like the qualities Bean saw in the AIF, civilian values. They affirm the behaviour that a materialistic and individualistic society still requires for the purposes of social cohesion and national security. Hence the mantle of 'the Anzac spirit' can now be claimed by any citizens who subordinate their individual desires to needs of the collective or team—be they police, firefighters, victims of terrorism or even football players. The coach of the defeated team in the 2009 Anzac Day AFL match in Melbourne, for example, claimed that his players 'let down the Anzacs', whereas the winning team 'showed the true Anzac spirit'.[66]

The memory of World War I has therefore been demilitarised—some might say sanitised and sentimentalised—by the passage of time. Yet some things remain unchanged. The landing at Gallipoli continues to be invoked, as it was in 1915–18, as the day on which Australian nationhood was born. The men and women who volunteer to risk their lives in the service of the nation continue to be honoured as superior Australians. Beyond this, the language of Anzac continues, as it did during the conscription crises of 1916 and 1917, to be used to mobilise public support for war. In the prelude to the 2003 Iraq War, for instance, there was considerable opposition to Australia's involvement, particularly without United Nations approval; but once the war began, this mood shifted. Thereafter, Iraq was positioned by the government and media within a lineage of wars from World War I on. The defence personnel serving in that theatre were thereby constructed as new Anzacs, entitled to honour and respect and beyond criticism. As John Howard said to personnel who had served Iraq in 2003:

> You went abroad as part of a great Australian military tradition, a tradition that has never sought to oppress people, a tradition that has never sought to impose the will of this country or the collective will of a group of countries of which Australia is part, on other people and other nations, but rather a tradition that seeks to defend what is good in the world, that seeks to uphold the values for which this nation stands and seeks to deliver freedom from tyranny, from terror and oppression.[67]

In some ways, this statement articulates values that are not so radically different from those of Australians of 1914. Perhaps, then, the challenge of understanding the generation that fought World War I is not so daunting as it may seem. One hundred years on, the tolerance for casualties on the scale of 1914–18 has evaporated. So too have the passion for the British Empire, and the willingness to consider conscription as a policy option. However, the appeal of nationalism and the readiness on the part of the Australian population to risk the lives of those who *choose* to fight in the defence of core national values continue to be uncontested. So too does the belief that these values may at times have to be defended far from Australian shores, and that war—for all its human cost—is a legitimate way of doing this.

APPENDIX 1
Organisation of the 1st AIF, 1918

1st Inf. Division	1st Inf. Brigade	1st, 2nd, 3rd, 4th Battalions
	2nd Inf. Brigade	5th, 6th, 7th, 8th Battalions
	3rd Inf. Brigade	9th, 10th, 11th, 12th Battalions
	1st Field Artillery	1st, 2nd, 3rd, 101st Batteries
	2nd Field Artillery Bde	4th, 5th, 6th, 102nd Batteries
2nd Inf. Division	5th Inf. Brigade	17th, 18th, 19th, 20th Battalions
	6th Inf. Brigade	21st, 22nd, 23rd, 24th Battalions
	7th Inf. Brigade	25th, 26th, 27th, 28th Battalions
	4th Field Artillery Bde	10th, 11th, 12th, 104th Batteries
	5th Field Artillery Bde	13th, 14th, 15th, 105th Batteries
3rd Inf. Division	9th Inf. Brigade	33rd, 34th, 35th, 36th Battalions
	10th Inf. Brigade	37th, 38th, 39th, 40th Battalions
	11th Inf. Brigade	41st, 42nd, 43rd, 44th Battalions
	7th Field Artillery Bde	25th, 26th, 27th, 107th Batteries
	8th Field Artillery Bde	29th, 30th, 31st, 108th Batteries
4th Inf. Division	4th Inf. Brigade	13th, 14th, 15th, 16th Battalions
	12th Inf. Brigade	45th, 46th, 47th, 48th Battalions
	13th Inf. Brigade	49th, 50th, 51st, 52nd Battalions
	10th Field Artillery Bde	37th, 38th, 39th, 110th Batteries
	11th Field Artillery Bde	41st, 42nd, 43rd, 111th Batteries

5th Inf. Division	8th Inf. Brigade	29th, 30th, 31st, 32nd Battalions
	14th Inf. Brigade	53rd, 54th, 55th, 56th Battalions
	15th Inf. Brigade	57th, 58th, 59th, 60th Battalions
	13th Field Artillery Bde	49th, 50th, 51st, 113th Batteries
	14th Field Artillery Bde	53rd, 54th, 55th, 114th Batteries
Australian and New Zealand Mounted Division	1st Light Horse Bde	1st, 2nd, 3rd LH Regiments
	2nd Light Horse Bde	5th, 6th, 7th LH Regiments
Australian Mounted Division	3rd Light Horse Bde	8th, 9th, 10th LH Regiments
	4th Light Horse Bde	4th, 11th, 12th LH Regiments
	5th Light Horse Bde	14th, 15th LH Regiments
	New Zealand Mounted Rifles Brigade*	Auckland, Canterbury and Wellington Regiments
Corps troops	13th Light Horse Regiment	
	3rd Army Artillery Bde	7th, 8th, 9th, 103rd Batteries
	6th Army Artillery Bde	16th, 17th, 18th, 106th Batteries
	12th Army Artillery Bde	45th, 46th, 47th, 112th Batteries
Miscellaneous units in France	36th Heavy Artillery Bde	1st, 2nd Siege Batteries
	1st, 2nd and 3rd General Hospitals	
	2nd, 3rd, 4th Australian Flying Corps	
HQ AIF depots in England	1st Training Bde	
	2nd Training Bde	
	3rd Training Bde	
	Australian Heavy Artillery Training Depot	
	Engineer Training Depot	

* Not part of the AIF.

Source: Albert Palazzo, The Australian Army: A History of its Organisation 1901–2001, Melbourne: Oxford University Press, 2001, p. 68.

APPENDIX 2
AIF enlistments by month, 1915–18

Month	Enlistments	Month	Enlistments
Jan. 1915	10,225	Jan. 1917	4575
Feb.	8370	Feb.	4924
Mar.	8913	Mar.	4989
Apr.	6250	Apr.	4646
May	10,526	May	4576
June	12,505	June	3679
July	36,575	July	4155
Aug.	25,714	Aug.	3274
Sept.	16,571	Sept.	2460
Oct.	9914	Oct.	2761
Nov.	11,230	Nov.	2815
Dec.	9119	Dec.	2247
Jan. 1916	22,101	Jan. 1918	2344
Feb.	18,508	Feb.	1918
Mar.	15,597	Mar.	1518
Apr.	9876	Apr.	2781
May	10,659	May	4888
June	6582	June	2540
July	6170	July	2741
Aug.	6345	Aug.	2959
Sept.	9325	Sept.	2451
Oct.	11,520	Oct.	3619
Nov.	5055	Nov.	1124
Dec.	2617		

Source: Ernest Scott, *The Official History of Australia in the War of 1914–1918*, vol. XI, pp. 871–2.

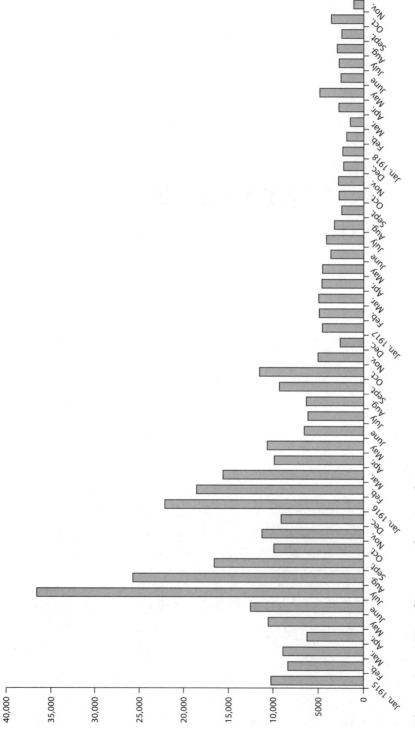

Figure A.1: AIF enlistments by month, 1915–18

Source: Ernest Scott, *The Official History of Australia in the War of 1914–1918*, vol. XI, pp. 871–2.

Note: The peaks in enlistments appear to be attributable to the following: May 1915: news of the landing at Gallipoli; July–September 1915: the first major recruitment campaign; September–October 1916: call-up prior to the conscription referendum and possibly news of the Somme; May 1918: the crisis on the Western Front and the governor-general's recruitment campaign.

NOTES

Preface

1 Quoted in Samuel H. Bowden (ed.), *The History of the Australian Comforts Fund*, n.p., 1922, p. 53.

2 F.G. Shedden, Secretary, Department of Defence, to Secretary, Prime Minister's Department, 15 March 1938, A461 H370/1/15 pt 3, National Archives of Australia (NAA).

3 Jay Winter, *Remembering War: The Great War Between Memory and History in the Twentieth Century*, New Haven, CT: Yale University Press, 2006, p. 4.

4 Stéphane Audoin-Rouzeau and Annette Becker, *14–18: Understanding the Great War*, New York: Hill and Wang, 2002, p. 2.

5 For the war memorial movement, see K.S. Inglis, *Sacred Places: War Memorials in the Australian Landscape*, Melbourne: Miegunyah Press, 1998, particularly pp. 199, 216–21; and 'War Memorials' in Peter Dennis et al., *The Oxford Companion to Australian Military History*, 2nd edn, Melbourne: Oxford University Press, 2008, pp. 580–3. By one calculation, there was one memorial for every 30 Australian dead. For France, in contrast, there was one memorial for every 45 dead.

6 A preliminary engagement with this vast topic may be found in Joan Beaumont, '"*Nation* oder *Commonwealth*?" Der gefallene Soldat und die Nationalidentität', in Manfred Hettling und Jörg Echternkamp (eds), *Der Tod des Soldaten und das politische Gemeinwesen. Gefallenengedenken im internationalen Vergleich* [*The death of the Soldier and the Polity: An International Comparison of Remembering Dead Soldiers*], Goettingen: Vandenhoeck & Rupprecht, 2012, pp. 43–68. The definition of myth is that of the anthropologist Bronislaw Malinowski (1922).

7   C.E.W. Bean, *The Official History of Australia in the War of 1914–1918*, vol. II, *The Story of Anzac: From 4 May, 1915, to the Evacuation of the Gallipoli Peninsula*, Sydney: Angus & Robertson, 1924, p. 910.

8   For Monash's celebration of the Australian soldier, see *The Australian Victories in France in 1918*, London: Hutchinson, 1920, pp. 263–7.

9   Ernest Scott, *The Official History of Australia in the War of 1914–1918*, vol. XI, *Australia During the War*, Sydney: Angus & Robertson, 1936, Appendix 3.

Prologue

1   C.E.W. Bean, *The Official History of Australia in the War of 1914–1918*, vol. IV, *The Australian Imperial Force in France 1917*, Sydney: Angus & Robertson, 1933.

2   Joanna Bourke, *Dismembering the Male: Men's Bodies, Britain and the Great War*, Chicago: University of Chicago Press, 1996, pp. 34, 11.

3   This is the estimate of the Influenza Specialist Group: <www.isg.org.au/index.php/about-influenza/pandemic-influenza/>, viewed July 2013.

Chapter 1

1   These and later statistics are those of the Australian War Memorial. They include deaths from 4 August 1914 to 31 March 1921.

2   Scott, *Official History*, vol. XI, p. 3.

3   Roger Chickering, *Imperial Germany and the Great War, 1914–1918*, Cambridge: Cambridge University Press, 1998, p. 1.

4   *Argus* (Melbourne), 28 July 1914.

5   *War Memoirs of David Lloyd George*, vol. 1, London: Nicholson & Watson, 1933, p. 32. British Prime Minister Herbert Asquith, quoted in Neville Meaney, *Australia and World Crisis*, Sydney: University of Sydney Press, 2009, p. 5. For Germany's 'grab for power', see the influential 1961 book of the German historian, Fritz Fischer, *Griff nach der Weltmacht*, Dusseldorf: Droste, published in English as *Germany's Aims in the First World War*, New York: W.W. Norton, 1967.

6   Peter McDermott, 'External Affairs and Treaties: The Founding Fathers' Perspective', *University of Queensland Law Journal*, vol. 16, 1990, pp. 138 ff. For the 1911 Imperial Conference see Neville Meaney, *A History of Australian Defence and Foreign Policy, 1901–23*, vol. I, *The Search for Security in the Pacific 1901–14*, Sydney, University of Sydney Press, 1976, pp. 213–23.

7   For a comprehensive history, see John Mordike, *An Army for a Nation: A History of Australian Military Developments 1880–1914*, Sydney: Allen & Unwin, 1992.

8   8 August 1914.

9   L.L. Robson, *The First A.I.F.: A Study of its Recruitment 1914–1918*, Melbourne: Melbourne University Press, 1982, p. 16.

10   Meaney, *Australia*, pp. 7, 8.

11   Scott, *Official History*, vol. XI, p. 11.

12   National Archives of Australia (NAA), Fact Sheet 67—Boer War Records.

13   *Argus*, 3 August 1914; Scott, *Official History*, vol. XI, p. 22; Bobbie Oliver, *War and Peace in Western Australia: The Social and Political Impact of the Great War 1914–1926*, Nedlands: University of Western Australia Press, 1995, p. 31.

14   Scott, *Official History*, vol. XI, pp. 24–5.

15   *West Australian*, quoted in Oliver, *War and Peace*, p. 28.

16   *Australian Baptist*, 3 November 1914; John McQuilton, *Rural Australia and the Great War: From Tarrawingee to Tangambalanga*, Melbourne: Melbourne University Press, 2001, p. 19; Oliver, *War and Peace*, p. 32.

17   *Labor Call*, 3, 6 August 1914; *Australian Worker*, 1 October, 6 August 1914.

18   Interview with *Herald*, quoted in *Woman Voter*, 11 August 1914.

19   Scott, *Official History*, vol. XI, p. 23; Robson, *The First A.I.F.*, p. 21.

20   Chickering, *Imperial Germany*, p. 14; Adrian Gregory, 'British "War Enthusiasm" in 1914: A Reassessment', in Gail Braybon, *Evidence, History and the Great War*, New York: Berghahn, 2003, pp. 78, 69.

21   Oliver, *War and Peace*, p. 27.

22   For recruitment, see Robson, *The First A.I.F.*, especially pp. 28–30. For Scotch College at war, see D.T. Merrett, '"The School at War", Scotch College and the Great War', in Stephen Murray-Smith (ed.), *Melbourne Studies in Education*, Melbourne: Melbourne University Press, 1983, pp. 209–30.

23   Enlistments per month from each state can be found in Scott, *Official History*, vol. XI, pp. 871–2.

24   Richard White, 'Motives for Joining Up: Self-sacrifice, Self-interest and Social Class, 1914–18', *Journal of the Australian War Memorial*, October 1986, p. 6.

25   ibid., p. 5.

26   Alistair Thomson, *Anzac Memories: Living with the Legend*, Melbourne: Melbourne University Press, 1994, pp. 218, 215.

27   White, 'Motives', pp. 4, 14. This summary also draws on a study of 216 veterans of World War I by J.N.I. Dawes and L.L. Robson, *Citizen to Soldier: Australia Before the Great War: Recollections of Members of the First A.I.F.*, Melbourne: Melbourne University Press, 1977.

28   White, 'Motives', p. 6.

29   Stuart Braga, *Anzac Doctor: The Life of Sir Neville Howse, VC*, Sydney: Hale & Iremonger, 2000, p. 94.

30   *Argus*, 31 August 1914; Australia, Parliament, House of Representatives, *Debates*, 14 October 1914.

31   White, 'Motives', p. 14.

32   Stirling, quoted in White, 'Motives', p. 7.

33   Audoin-Rouzeau and Becker, *14–18*, p. 100.

34   This account draws on David Stevenson, *Cataclysm: World War I as Political Tragedy*, New York: Basic Books, 2004, pp. 45–60.

35   For German strategy, see Annika Mombauer, *Helmuth von Moltke and the Origins of the First World War*, Cambridge: Cambridge University Press, 2001, Ch. 5.

36   Stevenson, *Cataclysm*, p. 58.

37   L.C. Reeves, quoted in Kevin Meade, *Heroes Before Gallipoli: Bita Paka and That One Day in September*, Brisbane: John Wiley & Sons, 2005, p. 13.

38   ibid., p. 36.

39   S.S. Mackenzie, *The Official History of Australia in the War of 1914–1918*, vol. X, *The Australians at Rabaul*, Sydney: Angus & Robertson, 1927, pp. 75–6.

40   Patsy Adam-Smith, *The Anzacs*, Melbourne: Nelson, 1978, p. 35.

41   Meade, *Heroes*, pp. 21, 35.

42   See Meaney, *Australia*, Ch. 3 for a full account.

43   C.E.W. Bean, *The Official History of Australia in the War of 1914–1918*, vol. I, *The Story of Anzac: From the Outbreak of War to the End of the First Phase of the Gallipoli Campaign, May 4, 1915*, Sydney: Angus & Robertson, 1921, p. 32.

44   Albert Palazzo, *The Australian Army: A History of its Organisation 1901–2001*, Melbourne: Oxford University Press, 2001, p. 62.

45   New South Wales and Victoria had large enough population bases to provide discrete battalions. Infantry from Queensland, South Australia, Tasmania and Western Australia, known then as the 'rural states', were amalgamated (though Queensland, with its huge cattle stations, provided a large proportion of light horse). Specialist arms such as the artillery, medical corps and engineers were drawn from across the country.

46   Bean, *Official History*, vol. I, p. 46. Of the men who had volunteered by the end of 1914, approximately 10,000 had served in the citizens' forces: Palazzo, *The Australian Army*, p. 65.

47   Jeffrey Grey, *A Military History of Australia*, Melbourne: Cambridge University Press, 1990, p. 94.

48   Quoted in David Stevens (ed.), *The Australian Centenary History of Defence*, vol. III, *The Royal Australian Navy*, Melbourne: Oxford University Press, 2001, p. 40.

49   Production was concentrated in textiles and clothing, food and drink, simple metal works, woodworking, vehicles (mostly horse-drawn and fittings) and processing pastoral and agricultural products. Marnie Haig-Muir, 'The economy at war' in Joan Beaumont (ed.), *Australia's War, 1914–18*, Sydney: Allen & Unwin, 1995, p. 95.

50   ibid., pp. 98–9.

51   Stuart Macintyre, *The Oxford History of Australia*, vol. 4, *1901–1942*, Melbourne: Oxford University Press, 1986, p. 145; Raymond Evans, *Loyalty and Disloyalty: Social Conflict on the Queensland Homefront 1914–18*, Sydney: Allen & Unwin, 1987, p. 23.

52   Scott, *Official History*, vol. XI, pp. 503, 515–16, 633.

53   Michael McKernan, *The Australian People and the Great War*, first published 1980, Sydney: Collins, 1984, p. 4.

54   Scott, *Official History*, vol. XI, pp. 636–9; T.R. Bavin and H.V. Evatt, 'Price-Fixing in Australia During the War', *Journal of Comparative Legislation and International Law*, 3rd series, vol. III, London: Society of Comparative Legislation, 1921, pp. 202–12.

55   The first Labor government came to power under John Watson in 1904 but lasted only four months.

56   Scott, *Official History*, vol. XI, p. 659.

57   See Ian Turner, *Industrial Labour and Politics: The Labour Movement in Eastern Australia 1900–1921*, Canberra: ANU Press, 1965, Ch. 2, for a full account of these tensions. Federal Labor conferences were made up of six delegates from each state party, among whom federal parliamentarians were invariably well represented.

58   Meaney, *Australia*, p. 14; for Hughes' proposal for an electoral truce, see pp. 26–7.

59   Sir Albert Gould, Australia, Parliament, Senate, *Debates*, 28 October 1914; Meaney, *Australia*, pp. 35, 8. The *War Precautions Act* was based on the UK *Defence of the Realm Act*.

60   Scott, *Official History*, vol. XI, p. 105. The term 'enemy within the gates' is Scott's.

61   Gerhard Fischer, *Enemy Aliens: Internment and the Homefront Experience in Australia 1914–1920*, Brisbane: University of Queensland Press, 1989, p. 75.

62   *Register*, 7 September 1914.

63   *Argus*, 20, 21, 23 October 1914.

64   Scott, *Official History*, vol. XI, pp. 106–7.

65   ibid., pp. 107–8.

66   Australia, Parliament, Senate, *Debates*, 14 October 1914.

67   The definitive work is John Horne and Alan Kramer, *German Atrocities, 1914: A History of Denial*, Newhaven and London: Yale University Press, 2001.

68   Judith Smart, '"Poor Little Belgium" and Australian Popular Support for War 1914–1915', *War & Society*, vol. 12, no. 1, 1994, p. 31.

69   Scott, *Official History*, vol. XI, p. 115.

70   Fischer, *Enemy Aliens*, p. 77.

71   Women's Peace Alliance, quoted in *Labor Call*, 24 December 1914; Ann-Mari Jordens, 'Anti-war Organisations in a Society at War, 1914–18', *Journal of Australian Studies*, no. 26, 1990, pp. 81, 87.

Chapter 2

1   Stevenson, *Cataclysm*, p. 81.

2   Norman Stone, *The Eastern Front 1914–1917*, London: Hodder & Stoughton, 1975, pp. 113–21.

3   ibid., p. 113.

4   For Turkey's entry into the war, see Stevenson, *Cataclysm*, pp. 89–90; and Hew Strachan, *The First World War*, vol. I, *To Arms*, Oxford: Oxford University Press, 2001, pp. 65–80.

5   R.G. Casey, Diary, 17 March 1915, MS6150, Series 4, Box 16, NLA.

6   Cutlack, quoted in K.S. Inglis, 'Anzac and the Australian Military Tradition', *Revue Internationale d'Histoire*, no. 72, 1990, p. 13; Bean, *Official History*, vol. I, p. 118.

7   Geoffrey Serle, *John Monash: A Biography*, Melbourne: Melbourne University Press, first published 1982, reprinted 1985, pp. 208–9; Bean, *Official History*, vol. I, p. 120. For an assessment of Birdwood as a military commander, see John Lee, 'William Birdwood', in Ian F.W. Beckett and Steven J. Corvi (eds), *Haig's Generals*, Barnsley: Pen & Sword Military, 2006, pp. 33–53.

8   Bean, *Official History*, vol. I, p. 125; Coe, quoted in Suzanne Brugger, *Australians and Egypt: 1914–1919*, Melbourne: Melbourne University Press, 1980, pp. 33–4.

9   Serle, *John Monash*, p. 211.

10 Brugger, *Australians and Egypt*, pp. 40, 42–3.

11 E.P.F. Lynch, *Somme Mud: The War Experiences of an Australian Infantryman in France 1916–1919*, Sydney: Random House, 2006, p. 5.

12 Bean, *Official History*, vol. I, p. 130; Bill Gammage, *The Broken Years: Australian Soldiers in the Great War*, first published 1974, Harmondsworth: Penguin, 1975, p. 36.

13 Bean press release, *Argus*, 21 January 1915; *Argus*, 25 January 1915. For Bean's private thoughts, see Kevin Fewster (ed.), *Gallipoli Correspondent: The Frontline Diary of C.E.W. Bean*, Sydney: George Allen & Unwin, 1983, p. 37.

14 Letters of L/Cpl F.C. Eric Mulvey, 2DRL/0233, AWM.

15 B.B. Leane papers, 23 April 1915, 1DRL/0412, AWM.

16 For planning of the campaign, see Robin Prior, *Gallipoli*, Sydney: UNSW Press, 2009, Chs 1–3; quote p. 239.

17 Prior, *Gallipoli*, p. 241.

18 Tim Travers, *Gallipoli: 1915*, first published 2001, Charleston, SC: Tempus, 2003, pp. 21, 35. For British planning for a coup in Turkey, see David French, 'The Origins of the Dardanelles Campaign Reconsidered', *History*, vol. 68, 1983, p. 217.

19 John Coates, *An Atlas of Australia's Wars*, Melbourne: Oxford University Press, 2001, p. 40.

20 Travers, *Gallipoli*, pp. 46, 67.

21 C.E.W. Bean, *Anzac to Amiens: A Shorter History of the Australian Fighting Services in the First World War*, Canberra: Australian War Memorial, 1946, p. 82; G.D. Mitchell, Diary, 25 April 1915, 2DRL/0928, AWM; J.M. Aitken, Diary (addressed to his mother), 29 April 1915, 1DRL/0013, AWM.

22 Tom Frame, *The Shores of Gallipoli: Naval Aspects of the Anzac Campaign*, Sydney: Hale & Iremonger, 2000, pp. 191–200; Travers, *Gallipoli*, p. 68; Peter D. Williams, *The Battle of Anzac Ridge: 25 April 1915*, Sydney: Australian Military History Publications, 2007, p. 65; Nigel Steel and Peter Hart, *Defeat at Gallipoli*, first published 1994, London:

Papermac, 1995, p. 60. The traditional view that there was machine-gun fire at Anzac has been challenged by Chris Roberts, *The Landing at Anzac, 1915*, Canberra: Army History Unit, 2013, pp. 169–72.

23 Cheney, Typescript for talk presented in London, p. 3, 1DRL/0199, AWM.

24 Guy Dawnay and Bennett, quoted in John Robertson, *Anzac and Empire: The Tragedy and Glory of Gallipoli*, Melbourne: Hamlyn, 1990, pp. 75–6.

25 Layh, quoted in Williams, *The Battle of Anzac Ridge*, p. 66.

26 Peter Pedersen, *The Anzacs: Gallipoli to the Western Front*, Melbourne: Viking, 2007, p. 49.

27 Roberts, *The Landing*, p. 92.

28 Cheney, Typescript for talk presented in London, p. 4, 1DRL/0199, AWM.

29 Bean, *Anzac to Amiens*, p. 108; Thomas Richards, Diary, 22 April 1915, 2DRL/0786, AWM; Harrison, quoted in Pedersen, *The Anzacs*, p. 54.

30 Travers, *Gallipoli*, p. 75. See also David Horner, *The Gunners: A History of Australian Artillery*, Sydney: Allen & Unwin, 1995, pp. 90ff.

31 Fewster, *Gallipoli Correspondent*, pp. 73–4; Bean, *Official History*, vol. I, p. 453; Travers, *Gallipoli*, p. 71.

32 Joanna Bourke, *Dismembering the Male: Men's Bodies, Britain and the Great War*, Chicago: Chicago University Press, 1996; Mitchell, Diary, 25 April 1915, 2DRL/0928; Ellis Silas, Diary, 27 April 1915, 1DRL/0566, AWM.

33 Braga, *Anzac Doctor*, p. 154; Cheney, Typescript for talk presented in London, p. 4, 1DRL/0199, AWM; Mitchell, Diary, 25 April 1915, 2DRL/0928, AWM.

34 Cheney, Typescript for talk presented in London, p. 5, 1DRL/0199, AWM.

35 E.W. King, quoted in Jan Bassett, *Guns and Brooches: Australian Army Nursing from the Boer War to the Gulf War*, Melbourne: Oxford University Press, 1992, p. 36.

36 Travers, *Gallipoli*, pp. 77–9.

37 For a full account, see Frame, *Shores of Gallipoli*, pp. 99–107.

38 For a detailed study, see Peter Stanley, *Quinn's Post, Anzac, Gallipoli*, Sydney: Allen & Unwin, 2005.

39 Captain Guy Geddes (1st Royal Munster Fusiliers), quoted in Travers, *Gallipoli*, p. 54.

40 Birdwood, Diary, 28 April 1915, quoted in Pedersen, *The Anzacs*, p. 64.

41 Silas, Diary, 2 May 1915, 1DRL/0566, AWM.

42 Pedersen, *The Anzacs*, p. 68.

43 An excellent account of the Australians' role at Krithia is to be found in Christopher Wray, *Sir James Whiteside McCay: A Turbulent Life*, Melbourne: Oxford University Press, 2002, Ch. 9, from which this account is drawn (Hamilton quote, p. 129).

44 Bean, *Anzac to Amiens*, p. 124; Wray, *Sir James Whiteside McCay*, p. 136.

45 Travers, *Gallipoli*, p. 103.

46 ibid., p. 104.

47 *SMH*, 8 May 1915.

48 *SMH*, 10, 15 May 1915; *Argus*, 10 May 1915; *Brisbane Courier*, 20 May 1915. See Fred and Elizabeth Brenchley, *Myth Maker: Ellis Ashmead-Bartlett: The Englishman Who Sparked Australia's Gallipoli Legend*, Brisbane: John Wiley & Sons, 2005, pp. 85–8 for full details; and Kevin Fewster, 'Ellis Ashmead-Bartlett and the Making of the Anzac Legend', *Journal of Australian Studies*, no. 10, 1982, pp. 17–30.

49 McKernan, *The Australian People*, p. 25; Brenchley and Brenchley, *Myth Maker*, p. 89.

50 A.G. Butler, *The Official History of the Australian Army Medical Services in the War of 1914–1918*, vol. I, *Gallipoli, Palestine and New Guinea*, Melbourne: Australian War Memorial, 2nd edn, 1938, p. 178; *Australian Baptist*, 11 May 1915; Tanja Luckins, *The Gates of Memory: Australian People's Experiences and Memories of Loss and the Great War*, Fremantle: Curtin University Books, 2004, pp. 57–61.

51 Noel Carthew, *Voices from the Trenches: Letters to Home*, Sydney: New Holland, 2002, pp. 40, 44, 75.

52 Butler, *Official History*, vol. I, p. 471; Kerry Neale, Reconstructed Lives: The Experiences of Facially Disfigured Australian Veterans of the Great War, Australian National University Honours thesis, 2007; for wounded returning to duty, Trevor Wilson, *The Myriad Faces of War: Britain and the Great War, 1914–1918*, Cambridge: Polity Press, 1986, p. 598. Butler's estimate for the AIF is lower: that 67.2 per cent of AIF casualties on the Western Front (excluding those who died of wounds or disease) re-joined their unit: A.G. Butler, *The Official History of the Australian Army Medical Services in the War of 1914–1918*, vol. III, *Special Problems and Services*, Australian War Memorial, 1943, p. 921.

53 E.M. Andrews, *The Anzac Illusion: Anglo-Australian Relations during World War I*, Melbourne: Cambridge University Press, 1993, p. 59; *Voices from the Trenches*, pp. 72–3, 71.

54 Jennifer Crew, 'Women's Wages in Britain and Australia During the First World War', *Labour History*, vol. 57, 1989, p. 31; Scott, *Official History*, vol. XI, pp. 703, 705–6. For Lady Helen Munro Ferguson, see Melanie Oppenheimer, '"The Best P.M. for the Empire in War"? Lady Helen Munro Ferguson and the Australian Red Cross Society 1914–1920', *Australian Historical Studies*, vol. 33, no. 119, 2002, pp. 108–34.

55 McKernan, *The Australian People*, p. 74. For accounts of the Comforts Fund, see Samuel H. Bowden, *The History of the Australian Comforts Fund*, n.p., 1922, and Melanie Oppenheimer, *Red Cross VADs: A History of the VAD Movement in New South Wales*, Sydney: Ohio Productions, 1999.

56 W.H. Frederick, 'Brookes, Sir Norman Everard (1877–1968)', *Australian Dictionary of Biography*, http://adb.anu.edu.au/biography/brookes-sir-norman-everard-5373; John Rickard, 'White, Vera Deakin (1891–1978)', ibid., http://adb.anu.edu.au/biography/white-vera-deakin-12014, viewed 2 July 2013.

57 Joy Damousi and Marilyn Lake (eds), *Gender and War: Australians at War in the Twentieth Century*, Melbourne: Cambridge University Press, 1995, p. 8; Cora V. Baldock, 'Public Policies and the Paid Work of Women', in Cora V. Baldock and Bettina Cass (eds), *Women, Social Welfare and the State*, Sydney: George Allen & Unwin, 1983,

p. 27. For a more detailed discussion of the marginalisation of patriotic women, see Joan Beaumont, 'Whatever Happened to Patriotic Women, 1914–1918?', *Australian Historical Studies*, vol. 31, no. 115, 2000, pp. 273–86.

58   Jan Bassett, '"Ready to Serve": Australian Women and the Great War', *Journal of the Australian War Memorial*, vol. 2, 1983, pp. 8–9.

59   Even though the Lord Mayor's Patriotic Fund in New South Wales was dealing primarily with women and children, it consistently excluded women from its executive committee: Melanie Oppenheimer, 'Alleviating Distress: The Lord Mayor's Patriotic Fund in New South Wales, 1914–1920', *Journal of the Royal Australian Historical Society*, vol. 81, pt 1, 1995, p. 92.

60   Peter Cochrane, *Simpson and the Donkey: The Making of a Legend*, Melbourne: Melbourne University Press, 1992, pp. 82–3.

61   John F. Hutchinson, *Champions of Charity: War and the Rise of the Red Cross*, Boulder, CO: Westview Press, 1996, pp. 256, 275.

62   Turner, *Industrial Labour*, p. 76.

63   Scott, *Official History*, vol. XI, pp. 485–95.

64   ibid., pp. 499–502. In addition to the seven war loans, there were two peace loans in 1919 and 1920 which raised over £51.6 million and a Diggers' Loan in 1921 that raised £10.08 million (ibid., p. 875).

65   Meaney, *Australia*, pp. 36–7. The account that follows draws on Robson, *The First A.I.F.*, Ch. 3.

66   *SMH*, 2 July 1915.

67   Holman to Senator Pearce, 27 July 1915, FPWC6, A13886, NAA; New South Wales Recruiting Campaign, The Call to Arms, AWM27 533/14, AWM; *Australian Worker*, 5 August 1915.

68   The records of the Federal Parliamentary War Committee are at A13886, NAA. The former Prime Minister, John Watson, was appointed to the FPWC in August 1915 with responsibility for coordinating state and Commonwealth cooperation regarding employment of returned servicemen (Memo, Duties of Honorary Organiser, FPWC1, A13886, NAA); *Worker*, 16 December 1916.

69   See Cochrane, *Simpson*, pp. 69, 75–81.

70   *Queanbeyan Age and Queanbeyan Observer*, 1 June 1915; G.J. Meyer, *A World Undone: The Story of the Great War 1914 to 1918*, New York: Batman Dell, 2006, pp. 251–2; *Horsham Times*, 14 May 1915.

71   Report of the Committee on Alleged German Outrages (Bryce Report, <www.firstworldwar.com/source/brycereport.htm#Conclusions>, viewed 2 February 2013).

72   Evans, *Loyalty*, pp. 51–2; Meaney, *Australia*, pp. 44–5.

73   Margaret Young and Bill Gammage (eds), *Hail and Farewell: Letters from Two Brothers Killed in France in 1916, Alec and Goldy Raws*, Sydney: Kangaroo Press, 1995, pp. 103–4.

74 Stanley, *Quinn's Post*, pp. 44–52.

75 ibid., pp. 59–61.

76 Bean, Diary, 19 May 1915, AWM 38, 3DRL/606/8/1, AWM; Robertson, *Anzac and Empire*, p. 94; Aitken, Diary, 19 May 1915, 1DRL/0013, AWM; Mitchell, Diary, 19 May, 2DRL/0928; AWM; Pedersen, *The Anzacs*, p. 75.

77 Richards, Diary, 21 May 1915, 2DRL/0786.

78 Stanley, *Quinn's Post*, pp. 84, 87, 99.

79 Orlo Williams, quoted in Robertson, *Anzac and Empire*, p. 99; C.D. Coulthard-Clark, *No Australian Need Apply: The Troubled Career of Lieutenant-General Gordon Legge*, Sydney: George Allen & Unwin, 1988, p. 104.

80 Sir Ronald East (ed.), *The Gallipoli Diary of Sergeant Lawrence of the Australian Engineers—1st A.I.F., 1915*, Melbourne: Melbourne University Press, 1981, p. 50.

81 Quoted in Robertson, *Anzac and Empire*, p. 80. For the problems of logistics at Gallipoli, and during the August 1915 offensive, see Rhys Crawley, 'Supplying the Offensive: The Role of Allied Logistics', in Ashley Ekins (ed.), *Gallipoli: A Ridge Too Far*, Wollombi: Exisle, 2013, pp. 252–71.

82 Butler, *Official History*, vol. I, pp. 240, 248.

83 ibid., p. 249.

84 East, *Gallipoli Diary*, p. 43; Silas, Diary, 1DRL/0566, AWM.

85 Young and Gammage, *Hail and Farewell*, pp. 36–7, 44.

86 East, *Gallipoli Diary*, pp. 27, 28.

87 Diary, 2, 3 May 1915, 1DRL/0566, AWM.

88 ibid., 5, 7, 16 May 1915.

89 S.T. Parkes, Diary, PR/01077, AWM; Durrant, '13th Australian Infantry Battalion', MSS143, folder 2, AWM 224, AWM; Richards, Diary, 2DRL/0786, AWM. For the impact of noise on the men's mental state see Eric Leed, *No Man's Land: Combat and Identity in World War I*, Cambridge: Cambridge University Press, 1979, p. 131.

90 Jackson, quoted in Cochrane, *Simpson*, p. 116; Richards, Diary, 2DRL/0786, AWM; East, *Gallipoli Diary*, pp. 27–8.

91 Barwick and Clune, quoted in Gammage, *The Broken Years*, pp. 101–2.

92 Bean, *Official History*, vol. I, pp. 6, 607.

93 Gammage, *The Broken Years*, p. 101.

94 For casualties of junior officers on the Western Front, see J.M. Winter, *The Great War and the British People*, Basingstoke: Macmillan, 1985, pp. 85–92.

95 C.D. Coulthard-Clark, *A Heritage of Spirit: A Biography of Major-General Sir William Throsby Bridges KC.B. C.M.G.*, Melbourne: Melbourne University Press, 1979, p. 175.

96 C.D. Coulthard-Clark, 'Legge', *Australian Dictionary of Biography*, <www.adb.online.anu.edu.au/biogs/A100059b.htm?hilite=legge>, viewed 2 February 2013; Coulthard-Clark, *No Australian Need Apply*, pp. 98–101.

97 Gary Sheffield, *The Chief: Douglas Haig and the British Army*, London: Arum Press, 2011, p. 115.

98 Prior, *Gallipoli*, pp. 161–3; Steel and Hart, *Defeat*, pp. 216–17.

99 Hamilton, quoted in Stanley, *Quinn's Post*, p. 132.

100 For a convincing critique, see Rhys Crawley, 'Our Second Great [Mis]adventure': A Critical Re-evaluation of the August Offensive, Gallipoli, 1915, PhD thesis, University College, University of New South Wales, Australian Defence Force Academy, 2010.

101 George Dewry, quoted in Robertson, *Anzac and Empire*, p. 119; East, *Gallipoli Diary*, pp. 60–1.

102 Bean, *Official History*, vol. II, p. 576.

103 Travers, *Gallipoli*, p. 125. Christopher Pugsley, *The Anzac Experience: New Zealand, Australia and Empire in the First World War*, Auckland: Reed, 2004, p. 102.

104 Travers, *Gallipoli*, p. 126.

105 Pedersen, *The Anzacs*, p. 99.

106 John McQuilton, 'Gallipoli and Contested Commemorative Space', in Jenny McLeod (ed.), *Gallipoli: Making History*, London: Frank Cass, 2004, p. 154.

107 Howe, quoted in Serle, *John Monash*, p. 238.

108 Tom Smith, quoted in Pedersen, *The Anzacs*, p. 99.

109 Travers, *Gallipoli*, p. 131.

110 Allanson, quoted in Serle, *John Monash*, p. 236; P.A. Pedersen, *Monash*, Melbourne: Melbourne University Press, 1985, p. 106; Bean, *Official History*, vol. II, pp. 663–4.

111 William Baylebridge, quoted in Jim Haynes (ed.), *Cobbers: Stories of Gallipoli 1915*, Sydney: ABC Books, 2005, p. 251. For details of Lone Pine, see Bean, *Official History* Vol. II, Chs XVIII and XIX.

112 East, *Gallipoli Diary*, p. 69.

113 Pedersen, *The Anzacs*, p. 92; Travers, *Gallipoli*, p. 117.

114 See <www.Anzacsite.gov.au/1landing/first-to-fall/cemeteries.html#8>, viewed 2 February 2013; Bart Ziino, *A Distant Grief: Australians, War Graves and the Great War*, Crawley: University of Western Australia Press, 2007, p. 173.

115 'The Lone Pine', <www.awm.gov.au/encyclopedia/lone.asp>, viewed 2 April 2013.

116 For watches not being synchronised as an explanation, see Les Carlyon, *Gallipoli*, Sydney: Pan Macmillan, 2001, p. 403. For a detailed discussion of the artillery issues, see Travers, *Gallipoli*, pp. 120–1.

117 Pedersen, *The Anzacs*, p. 96; Bean, *Official History*, vol. II, p. 615.

118 Pedersen, *The Anzacs*, p. 97; Carlyon, *Gallipoli*, p. 407.

119 Travers, *Gallipoli*, pp. 122–3.

120 Bean, *Official History*, vol. II, pp. 617–18.

121 Pedersen, *The Anzacs*, p. 98.

122 Interview with Weir on *Gallipoli* Special Features DVD, 20th Century Fox DVD.

123 White, quoted in Travers, *Gallipoli*, p. 118.

124 Birdwood, quoted in Serle, *John Monash*, p. 239; Godley, quoted in Pugsley, *The Anzac Experience*, p. 115.

125 Serle, *John Monash*, p. 236; Robin Prior, 'The Suvla Bay Tea-party: A Reassessment', *Journal of the Australian War Memorial*, no. 7, 1985, pp. 25–34.

126 *Advertiser* (Adelaide), 27 August 1915; *Register* (Adelaide), 27 August 1915; *Sunday Times* (Perth), 29 August 1915; *SMH*, 27 August 1915.

127 Bart Ziino, 'Mourning and Commemoration in Australia: The Case of Sir W.T. Bridges and the Unknown Australian Soldier', *History Australia*, vol. 4, no. 2, 2007, pp. 40.1–40.17.

128 *Worker*, 8 July 1915; Warren G. Osmond, *Frederic Eggleston: An Intellectual in Australian Politics*, Sydney: Allen & Unwin, 1985, p. 75.

129 Travers, *Gallipoli*, p. 202.

130 Prior, *Gallipoli*, pp. 211–12.

131 Carlyon, *Gallipoli*, p. 496; David Day, *Andrew Fisher: Prime Minister of Australia*, Sydney: Harper Collins, 2008, pp. 340–2.

132 Robertson, *Anzac and Empire*, p. 158.

133 Meaney, *Australia*, p. 115.

134 *Worker*, 21 January 1915, 24 April 1915, 3 June 1915, 17 June 1915, 24 June 1915, 1 July 1915, 27 July 1915.

135 *Worker*, 18 February 1915, 13 May 1915.

136 Meaney, *Australia*, p. 117; *Australian Worker*, 16 December 1915, 11 November 1915.

137 Scott, *Official History*, vol. XI, p. 643; Turner, *Industrial Labour*, pp. 80–1.

138 Hughes, quoted in *Worker*, 29 July 1915.

139 Evans, *Loyalty*, p. 85; *Worker*, 8 August 1915; Meaney, *Australia*, pp. 50–2; Robson, *The First A.I.F.*, p. 80.

140 Meaney, *Australia*, pp. 52–4; *Worker*, 16 December 1915.

141 Australian Imperial Force, FPWC7, A13886, NAA; Meaney, *Australia*, pp. 52–4.

142 Minutes of FPWC, 24 November 1915, FPWC2, NAA: Hughes, quoted in Robson, *The First A.I.F*, p. 64.

143 *Australian Worker*, 16 December 1915; Meaney, *Australia*, p. 121; *Worker*, 2 December 1915, 16 December 1915.

144 *Worker*, 16 December 1915.

145 John Bourne, 'Charles Monro', in Ian F.W. Beckett and Steven J. Corvi (eds), *Haig's Generals*, Barnsley: Pen & Sword Military, 2006, pp. 128–9.

146 Robertson, *Anzac and Empire*, pp. 178–9.

147 ibid., p. 185; Young and Gammage, *Hail and Farewell*, pp. 59–60.

148 Carlyon, *Gallipoli*, pp. 520–1.

149 Prior, *Gallipoli*, pp. 242–3.

150 B. Leane, 20 December 1915, 1DRL/0412, AWM.

151 *Daily Telegraph*, 22 December 1915; *Argus*, 22 December 1915.

152 *Daily Telegraph*, 22 December 1915.

153 The changing fortunes of Anzac Day since 1916 are currently the subject of a major study by Bruce Scates at Monash University, <artsonline.monash.edu.au/anzac-remembered>, viewed 2 July 2013.

154 Ashley Ekins, 'A "Precious Souvenir": The Making of *The Anzac Book*', in *The Anzac Book*, Sydney: UNSW Press, 2010, p. xxv; David Kent, '*The Anzac Book* and the Anzac Legend; CEW Bean as Editor and Image-maker', *Historical Studies*, vol. 21, no. 84, 1985, pp. 376–90.

155 Adrian Caesar, '"Kitsch" and Imperialism: *The Anzac Book* Re-Visited', *Westerly*, vol. 40, no. 4, 1995, pp. 76–85.

156 Cochrane, *Simpson*, pp. 96, 108–11. Graham Wilson's *Dust, Donkeys and Illusions: The Myth of Simpson and His Donkey Exposed*, Sydney: Big Sky Publishing, 2012, as its title suggests, provides an analysis of the gap between Simpson the man and Simpson the legend.

157 Cochrane, *Simpson*, p. 2.

158 See Cochrane, *Simpson*, pp. 201–10, for the debate about the Simpson at the Shrine of Remembrance.

Chapter 3

1 Mitchell, Diary, 2DRL/0928, AWM; Letter of 7 January 1916, Young and Gammage, *Hail and Farewell*, p. 61.

2 Serle, *John Monash*, p. 256.

3 Lee, 'Birdwood', p. 38. For the Light Horse details, see Jean Bou, *Light Horse: A History of Australia's Mounted Arm*, Melbourne: Cambridge University Press, 2010, pp. 149–50.

4 Major McConaghy, quoted in C.E.W. Bean, *The Official History of Australia in the War of 1914–1918*, vol. III, *The Australian Imperial Force in France, 1916*, Sydney: Angus & Robertson, 1929, pp. 48–9; Richards, Diary, 23 January 1916, 2DRL/786, AWM; Bean, *Anzac to Amiens*, p. 189.

5 Birdwood to Pearce, 24 March 1916, Birdwood Papers, Series 7, Folder 1, 3DRL/3376, AWM.

6 Serle, *John Monash*, pp. 258–60.

7 20 March 1916, Elliott papers, Series 3, Folder 4, 2DRL/0513, AWM.

8 Birdwood to Pearce, 24 March 1916, Series 3, Folder 2, 3DRL/2222, AWM.

9 Jean Bou, *Australia's Palestine Campaign*, Canberra: Army History Unit, 2010, pp. 11–12.

10 Murray, quoted in Bean, *Anzac to Amiens*, p. 273; C.E.W. Bean, 'Sidelights of the War on the Australian Character', *Journal of the Royal Australian Historical Society*, vol. XIII, pt 4, 1927, p. 222. Mounted rifles did all the tasks of cavalry but without swords or lances.

11 Young and Gammage, *Hail and Farewell*, p. 79.

12 ibid., p. 81.

13   Pedersen, *The Anzacs*, p. 120.

14   ibid., pp. 121–2.

15   The account that follows relies on Meaney, *Australia*, pp. 126–32.

16   L.F. Fitzhardinge, *William Morris Hughes: A Political Biography*, vol. II, *The Little Digger 1914–1953*, London: Angus & Robertson, 1979, p. 76. This remains the best account of Hughes' time in London and Paris. Hughes' quotes, unless otherwise stated, are drawn from this source.

17   Quoted in Peter Spartalis, *The Diplomatic Battles of Billy Hughes*, Sydney: Hale & Iremonger, 1983, p. 16.

18   Colonel A. Sutton, Diary, 31 May 1916, 2DRL/1227, AWM.

19   Meaney, *Australia*, p. 134; W.M. Hughes, *'The Day'—And After: War Speeches of the Rt. Hon. W.M. Hughes*, London: Cassell, 1916, p. vii.

20   For Kut, see Wilson, *The Myriad Faces*, p. 379.

21   Kosmas Tsokhas, *Markets, Money and Empire: The Political Economy of the Australian Wool Industry*, Melbourne: Melbourne University Press, 1990, pp. 18–29.

22   Scott, *Official History*, vol. XI, pp. 607, 610, 613.

23   For details of the London discussions, see Fitzhardinge, *William Morris Hughes*, vol. II, pp. 138–44.

24   Frank Brennan, *The Australian Commonwealth Shipping Line*, Canberra: Roebuck Books, 1978, pp. 5–6.

25   Meaney, *Australia*, pp. 145–6.

26   The account of the 1916 conference that follows is based on Spartalis, *The Diplomatic Battles*, pp. 24–8 and Fitzhardinge, *William Morris Hughes*, vol. II, pp. 121–36. Hughes' quotes are from Fitzhardinge.

27   Fitzhardinge, *William Morris Hughes*, vol. II, pp. 134, 136.

28   Makin, Letter to mother, 3 May 1916, 1DRL/0473, AWM. The best accounts, on which this description draws, are by E.M. Andrews, '25 April 1916: The First Anzac Day in Australia and Britain', *Journal of the Australian War Memorial*, no. 23, 1993, pp. 13–20, and Andrews, *Anzac Illusion*, pp. 84–91.

29   *Register* (Adelaide), 27 April 1916.

30   Day, *Fisher*, p. 366.

31   Evans, *Loyalty*, pp. 37–8; *Register* (Adelaide), 25 April 1916; R. Ely, 'The First Anzac Day: Invented or Discovered?', *Journal of Australian Studies*, no. 17, 1985, p. 57.

32   Andrews, *The Anzac Illusion*, p. 87; Andrews, '25 April 1916', p. 14.

33   Andrews, '25 April 1916', p. 15; Evans, *Loyalty*, p. 39.

34   Black, quoted, in Robertson, *Anzac and Empire*, p. 247; Evans, *Loyalty*, p. 37.

35   Inglis, *Sacred Places*, pp. 109–10.

36   Jay Winter, *Sites of Memory, Sites of Mourning: The Great War in European Cultural History*, Cambridge: Cambridge University Press, 1995, p. 5; *Australian Baptist*, 30 January 1917; Ely, 'The First Anzac Day', p. 58.

37 Stone, *The Eastern Front*, p. 228.

38 For blockade, see Gerd Hardach, *The First World War 1914–1918*, Ringwood: Penguin, 1987, Ch. 2.

39 Stevens, *The Australian Centenary History*, vol. III, p. 47.

40 Wilson, *The Myriad Faces*, pp. 93–4.

41 Robin Prior and Trevor Wilson, *Command on the Western Front: The Military Career of Sir Henry Rawlinson*, Oxford: Blackwell, 1992, pp. 139–41.

42 For details of defects in British artillery, see Robin Prior and Trevor Wilson, *The Somme*, New Haven, CT: Yale University Press, 2005, pp. 62–3.

43 ibid., pp. 112–18.

44 Sheffield, *The Chief*, p. 176; Haig, Diary, quoted in Peter Charlton, *Pozières: Australians on the Somme, 1916*, Sydney: Methuen, 1986, p. 49.

45 J.P. Harris, *Douglas Haig and the First World War*, Cambridge: Cambridge University Press, 2008, p. 239.

46 Sheffield, *The Chief*, p. 176.

47 For detailed accounts of Fromelles, see Ross McMullin, *Pompey Elliott*, first published 2002, Melbourne: Scribe, 2008, Ch. 9; Paul Cobb, *Fromelles 1916*, Stroud: Tempus, 2007; Charlton, *Pozières*, Chs 7 and 8; and Wray, *Sir James Whiteside McCay*, Ch. 12.

48 Bourne, 'Charles Munro', p. 133.

49 ibid., p. 134; McCay, quoted in McMullin, *Pompey Elliott*, p. 208.

50 For the artillery plan at Fromelles, see Roger Lee, *The Battle of Fromelles 1916*, Canberra: Army History Unit, 2010, pp. 104–12.

51 Folder 2, 3DRL/3623, AWM. McCrae provides the lead story in Ross McMullin's *Farewell Dear People: Biographies of Australia's Lost Generation*, Melbourne: Scribe, 2012.

52 26 July 1916, PR86/38/, AWM.

53 W.H. Downing, *To the Last Ridge*, Sydney: Duffy and Snellgrove, 1998, first published 1920, p. 8; Whiteside, quoted in Wray, *Sir James Whiteside McCay*, p. 190.

54 Bean, *Official History*, vol. III, p. 394.

55 H.R. Williams, quoted in Wray, *Sir James Whiteside McCay*, p. 197.

56 'Australians on the Western Front' <www.ww1westernfront.gov.au/fromelles/fromelles-casualties.html>, viewed 2 March 2013; McMullin, *Pompey Elliott*, pp. 222–3; R. Hugh Knyvett, *'Over There' with the Australians*, London: Hodder and Stoughton, 1918, pp. 155–6.

57 Bean, Diary, 20 July 1916, AWM38 3DRL/606/52/1, AWM; McMullin, *Pompey Elliott*, pp. 226, 229.

58 McMullin, *Pompey Elliott*, pp. 229–30.

59 *Canberra Times*, 18 July 1930.

60 Wray, *Sir James Whiteside McCay*, p. 202; Charlton, *Pozières*, pp. 113–14.

61   Charlton, *Pozières*, p. 116; Bean, quoted in *Tamworth Daily Observer*, 24 July 1916.

62   Wray, *Sir James Whiteside McCay*, pp. 199–204.

63   Bean, *Official History*, vol. III, p. 441; *Age*, 16 March 2008.

64   A full account of the search for the missing can be found in Patrick Lindsay, *Fromelles*, Melbourne: Hardie Grant Books, 2008.

65   *Australian*, 1 February 2010.

66   *Age*, 30 January 2010; *Australian*, 30 January 2010.

67   *Australian*, 1 February 2010; Winter, *Remembering War*, p. 40.

68   *Australian*, 1 February 2010; *Warrnambool Standard*, 30 January 2010; *Age*, 19 July 2009, 1 February 2010; *SMH*, 30 January 2010; Minister for Veterans' Affairs Alan Griffin, quoted in ABC News, 30 January 2010.

69   Harris, *Douglas Haig*, p. 242; Prior and Wilson, *Command*, pp. 185–95.

70   Pedersen, *The Anzacs*, pp. 148–9.

71   Champion, quoted in Charlton, *Pozières*, p. 134; letter by German, quoted in Bean, *Official History*, vol. III, p. 522.

72   Sergeant A.A. Barwick, 1st Battalion AIF 1914–1919, Diary, AWM, p. 58; Bean, *Official History*, vol. III, p. 514.

73   H. Preston, 'John Leak's V.C.', 'Sidelights on Pozières', *Reveille*, 1 August 1935; Barwick, Diary, AWM, p. 59.

74   Coates, *An Atlas*, p. 56; E.J. Rule, *Jacka's Mob*, Sydney: Angus & Robertson, 1933, p. 61.

75   Peter Gaffney, Diary, PR91/084, AWM.

76   Coates, *An Atlas*, Map 18a; Gaffney, Diary, PR91/084, AWM.

77   Leane, Diary, 3 August 1916, 1DRL/0412, AWM; Bean, Diary, 31 July, 4 August 1916, AWM 38, 3DRL/606/54/1, AWM.

78   Haig, quoted in Charlton, *Pozières*, p. 187; C.E.W. Bean, *Two Men I Knew: William Bridges and Brudenell White, Founders of the A.I.F.*, Sydney: Angus & Robertson, 1957, pp. 136–7.

79   Gaffney, Diary, PR91/084, AWM.

80   A.G. Butler, *The Official History of the Australian Army Medical Services in the War of 1914–1918*, vol. II, *The Western Front*, Canberra: Australian War Memorial, 1940, p. 61; Edmund Sullivan, Diary, 9 August 1916, PR00919, AWM.

81   Prior and Wilson, *The Somme*, p. 180.

82   *Jacka's Mob*, p. 102.

83   Butler, *Official History*, vol. II, p. 73.

84   Harris, *Douglas Haig*, pp. 255–6; Prior and Wilson, *The Somme*, pp. 186–90.

85   Harris, *Douglas Haig*, p. 266.

86   'Gallipoli', <www.awm.gov.au/encyclopedia/gallipoli/>, viewed 20 March 2013.

87   Butler, *Official History*, vol. II, pp. 495, 306, 310; Rule, *Jacka's Mob*, p. 108.

88 Leed, *No Man's Land*, p. 131; Rule, *Jacka's Mob*, p. 78.

89 Edwards, quoted in Butler, *Official History*, vol. III, pp. 114–15; Marina Larsson, *Shattered Anzacs: Living with the Scars of War*, Sydney: UNSW Press, 2009, pp. 159–60. For statistics, see Butler, *Official History*, vol. III, p. 102.

90 Scott Bennett, *Pozières: The Anzac Story*, Melbourne: Scribe, 2011, pp. 291–2.

91 Kevin Fewster, 'The Operation of State Apparatuses in Times of Crisis: Censorship and Conscription, 1916', *War & Society*, vol. 3, no, 1, 1985, p. 43; Young and Gammage, *Hail and Farewell*, p. 156.

92 Young and Gammage, *Hail and Farewell*, p. 159; *Australian Baptist*, 27 June 1916.

93 '1st Australian Division', AWM27 623/4, AWM.

94 Memo to Sir Fabian Ware, IWGC, 18 January 1930, A458 P337/6 pt 2, NAA; *SMH*, 4 August 1920; Bean, *Anzac to Amiens*, p. 264.

95 *Maffra Spectator* (Vic.), 14 August 1916; *Register* (Adelaide), 4 August 1917; Bou, *Light Horse*, pp. 157–8.

96 Fitzhardinge, *William Morris Hughes*, vol. II, p. 172; Scott, *Official History*, vol. XI, p. 334.

97 Turner, *Industrial Labour*, pp. 101–2; *Worker*, 13 April 1916.

98 Turner, *Industrial Labour*, p. 102. For developments in various states, see P.M. Gibson, 'The Conscription Issue in South Australia, 1916–1917', *University Studies in History*, vol. IV, no. 3, 1963–64, pp. 47–80; J.R. Robertson, 'The Conscription Issue and the National Movement in Western Australia, June 1916–December 1917', *University Studies in Western Australian History*, vol. II, no. 3, 1959, pp. 5–57; Peter Bastian, 'The 1916 Conscription Referendum in New South Wales', *Teaching History*, vol. 5, no. 1, 1971, pp. 30–1.

99 Fitzhardinge, *William Morris Hughes*, vol. II, pp. 175, 182–5.

100 Hughes, 18 September 1916, quoted in Leslie C. Jauncey, *The Story of Conscription in Australia*, London: George Allen & Unwin, 1935, p. 168; W.M. Higgs, 12 August 1916, quoted in Fitzhardinge, *William Morris Hughes*, vol. II, p. 178.

101 Fitzhardinge, *William Morris Hughes*, vol. II, p. 180.

102 Fewster, 'Operation', p. 40.

103 Australia, Parliament, House of Representatives, *Debates*, 30 August 1916.

104 Hughes, quoted in Jauncey, *The Story of Conscription*, p. 154.

105 Editorial, *Australian Baptist*, 17 October 1916.

106 Quoted in Jauncey, *The Story of Conscription*, pp. 169–70.

107 Manifesto of the NSW Methodist Conference, quoted in Bastian, '1916 Conscription Referendum', p. 28; *Australian Baptist*, 8 August 1916.

108 Australian Christian Commonwealth, 27 October 1916, quoted in Bastian, '1916 Conscription Referendum', p. 70; Fred Coleman in *The Question*, quoted in Jauncey, *The Story of Conscription*, p. 198; 'Conscription and Christianity', quoted in Jauncey, *The Story of Conscription*, p. 206.

109 MP Mathews (Melbourne Ports), Australia, Parliament, House of Representatives, *Debates*, 14 September 1916.

110 Forrest, Australia, Parliament, House of Representatives, *Debates*, 14 September 1916; 'An Appeal to the Women of New South Wales', MS5913, NLA.

111 Gibson, 'The Conscription Issue', p. 68; Manifesto to Australian people, quoted in Jauncey, *The Story of Conscription*, p. 171.

112 Richards, Diary, 1 June 1916, 2DRL/786, AWM.

113 Bastian, '1916 Conscription Referendum', p. 28; MPs Bamford (Herbert) and Pigott (Calare), Australia, Parliament, House of Representatives, *Debates*, 14, 15 September 1916.

114 'How Would the Kaiser Vote?' MS5913, NLA.

115 *Australian Worker*, 5 October 1916.

116 Anstey, quoted in Jauncey, *The Story of Conscription*, p. 155; *Australian Worker*, 12 October 1916.

117 Evans, *Loyalty*, p. 98; *Worker*, 5 October 1916.

118 Barry York, 'The Maltese, White Australia, and Conscription: "Il-tfal Ta Billy Hughes"', *Labour History*, no. 57, 1989, pp. 1–15.

119 Meaney, *Australia*, p. 176; *Australian Worker*, 7, 28 September 1916; *Worker*, 14 September 1916; *Alpine Observer* (Vic.), quoted in McQuilton, *Rural Australia*, p. 62.

120 *Australian Worker*, 24 September 1916; Frank Cotton, in *Australian Worker*, 5 October 1916.

121 *Australian Worker*, 7 September 1916; *Worker*, quoted in Jauncey, *The Story of Conscription*, p. 163.

122 Fewster, 'Operation', pp. 45–6.

123 Judith Smart, 'The Right to Speak and the Right to Be Heard: The Popular Disruption of Conscriptionist Meetings in Melbourne, 1916', *Australian Historical Studies*, vol. 23, no. 92, 1989, pp. 204–6.

124 *Direct Action*, 14 October 1914. For details of the IWW, including the trial of the 'Twelve', see Frank Cain, *The Wobblies at War: A History of the IWW and the Great War in Australia*, Melbourne: Spectrum, 1993, p. 172. For IWW ideology, see P.J. Rushton, 'Revolutionary Ideology of the I.W.W. in Australia', *Historical Studies*, vol. 15, no. 59, 1972, pp. 424–45.

125 Cain, *The Wobblies*, pp. 213–14; Hughes, quoted in Evans, *Loyalty*, p. 77.

126 Anstey, quoted in Jauncey, *The Story of Conscription*, p. 183.

127 Alan D. Gilbert, 'The Conscription Referenda, 1916–17: The Impact of the Irish Crisis', *Historical Studies*, vol. 14, no. 53, 1969, pp. 55–6; Patrick O'Farrell, *The Catholic Church and Community: An Australian History*, Sydney: UNSW Press, 1985, p. 324.

128 Gibson, 'The Conscription Issue', pp. 66–7; Michael McKernan, *Australian Churches at War: Attitudes and Activities of the Major Churches 1914–1918*, Sydney and Canberra:

Catholic Theological Faculty and Australian War Memorial, 1980, p. 113; Gilbert, 'The Conscription Referenda', p. 64; Evans, *Loyalty*, pp. 92–4.

129 *Australian Worker*, 15 November 1917.

130 *Australian Worker*, 24 September, 19 October 1916. See also 'Doomed! Married Men's Position', *Worker*, 26 September 1916.

131 Jauncey, *The Story of Conscription*, p. 247; Report by General Sellheim, 'Conscription 1st Referendum', 5 August 1919, AWM27/533, AWM; McQuilton, *Rural Australia*, p. 67.

132 For further details of the disruption of meetings, see Smart, 'The Right to Speak', pp. 208–11.

133 Butler, *Official History*, vol. II, p. 901; *Daily Standard*, quoted in Evans, *Loyalty*, p. 101.

134 To the Women of Australia: Manifesto from Mr. W.M. Hughes, MS5913, NLA. For women and propaganda, see Carmel Shute, '"Blood Votes" and the "Bestial Boche": A Case Study in Propaganda', *Hecate*, vol. II, no. 2, 1976, pp. 7–22; and Carmel Shute, 'Heroines and Heroes: Sexual Mythology in Australia, 1914–18', in Damousi and Lake, *Gender and War*, pp. 23–42.

135 'The Blood Vote' was written by E.J. Dempsey, an editor of a pro-conscriptionist paper, who asked William Winspear, editor of *The Radical*, to publish it under his name.

136 Reply to 'The Blood Vote', MS5913, NLA.

137 Judith Smart, 'Eva Hughes: Militant Conservative', in Marilyn Lake and Farley Kelly (eds), *Double Time: Women in Victoria—150 Years*, Ringwood: Penguin, 1985, pp. 184–7; Joy Damousi, 'Socialist Women and Gendered Space: Anti-conscription and Anti-war Campaigns 1915–18' in Damousi and Lake, *Gender and War*, pp. 258–9; Smart, 'The Right to Speak', p. 214.

138 Fitzhardinge, *William Morris Hughes*, vol. II, p. 213; *Australian Worker*, 28 September 1916.

139 Glen Withers, 'The 1916–1917 Conscription Referenda: A Cliometric Re-Appraisal', *Historical Studies*, vol. 20, no. 78, 1982, p. 43; A.R. Pearson, 'Western Australia and the Conscription Plebiscites of 1916 and 1917', *RMC Historical Journal*, vol. 3, 1974, p. 25.

140 Bastian, '1916 Conscription Referendum', p. 33; G.P. Shaw, 'Patriotism Versus Socialism: Queensland's Private War, 1916', *Australian Journal of Politics and History*, vol. XIX, 1973, p. 174; Ina Bertand, 'The Victorian Country Vote in the Conscription Referendums of 1916 and 1917: The Case of the Wannon Electorate', *Labour History*, vol. 26, 1974, p. 20; Withers, 'The 1916–1917 Conscription Referenda', pp. 43–4.

141 Fitzhardinge, *William Morris Hughes*, vol. II, pp. 207–9.

142 Short, Diary, 28 August 1916, 3DRL/3467, AWM; Davis, Diary, 2DRL/0547, AWM; Makin, Letter to mother, 1 February 1917, 1DRL/0473, AWM; Letter to Secretary of State for the Colonies, 3 November 1916, Munro Ferguson Papers, MS696, Series 7, Box 2, NLA; Bean, *Official History*, vol. III, pp. 891–2.

143 Fewster, 'Operation', p. 49.

144 Fitzhardinge, *William Morris Hughes*, vol. II, pp. 212–13.

145 ibid., pp. 212, 227, 230.

146 Marilyn Lake, 'Earle, John', *Australian Dictionary of Biography*, <www.adbonline.anu. edu.au>, viewed 20 March 2013.

147 Fitzhardinge, *William Morris Hughes*, vol. II, pp. 213–14.

148 ibid., p. 218.

149 L.F. Crisp, cited in Gilbert, 'Conscription Referenda', p. 68.

150 For a full account of the British debate, see Prior and Wilson, *The Somme*, Ch. 25. Haig, quoted p. 288.

151 Downing, *To the Last Ridge*, pp. 16–17.

152 For a detailed account these operations, see Bean, *Official History*, vol. III, pp. 902–15.

153 ibid., p. 919; A.W. Edwards Memoir, p. 31, PR89/050, AWM.

154 Bean, *Official History*, vol. III, p. 920; Major Parkinson, quoted in A.D. Ellis, *The Story of the Fifth Australian Division*, London: Hodder & Stoughton, 1920, p. 171.

155 Sutton, Diary, 2DRL/1227, AWM.

156 Gaffney, Diary, PR91/084, AWM; Pedersen, *The Anzacs*, p. 182.

157 George Mitchell, 'The Winter of 1916–17', *Reveille*, 1 December 1934, p. 15: Bean, *Official History*, vol. III, p. 957.

158 For an excellent discussion of sticks and carrots, see Niall Ferguson, *The Pity of War*, first published 1998, London: Penguin, 1999, Ch. 12; statistic, p. 345.

159 Gammage, *The Broken Years*, p. 236; John Connor, *Anzac and Empire: George Foster Pearce and the Foundations of Australian Defence*, Melbourne: Cambridge University Press, 2011, p. 106.

160 Ferguson, *The Pity*, pp. 350–1.

161 J.C. Fuller, *Troop Morale and Popular Culture in British and Dominion Armies 1914–1918*, Oxford: Clarendon Press, 1990, p. 52.

162 Gammage, *The Broken Years*, p. 101: M.J. Cotton, 'Operations at Pozières', 3DRL/3071, AWM; Edgar Thompson, Diary, 27 December 1916, PR84/331, AWM; G.D. Mitchell, *Backs to the Wall: A Larrikin on the Western Front*, first published 1937, Sydney: Allen & Unwin, 2007, p. 200.

163 Leed, *No Man's Land*, p. 131.

164 Bean, *Official History*, vol. III, p. 941; Ferguson, *The Pity*, pp. 369–70.

165 Butler, *Official History*, vol. III, p. 91; Joanna Bourke, '"Swinging the Lead": Malingering Australian Soldiers and the Great War', *Journal of the Australian War Memorial*, no. 26, 1995, pp. 10–18; Michael Tyquin, *Madness and the Military: Australia's Experience of the Great War*, Sydney: Australian Military History Publishing, 2006, pp. 33–7.

166 L. Mann, quoted in Gammage, *The Broken Years*, p. 251.

167 Prior and Wilson, *The Somme*, pp. 301–2; Harris, *Douglas Haig*, p. 271.

168 Wilson, *The Myriad Faces*, p. 351; Harris, *Douglas Haig*, p. 271.

169 Asquith, quoted in David Cannadine, 'War and Death, Grief and Mourning in Modern Britain', in Joachim Whaley, *Mirrors of Mortality: Studies in the Social History of Death*, London: Europa, 1981, p. 216.

170 Letter to Secretary of State for the Colonies, 28 November 1916, MS696, Series 7, Box 2, NLA; *Advertiser* (Adelaide), 3 November 1916; 'The Farmer and His Crops', handbill, MS5913, NLA; *West Australian*, 26 October 1916.

171 *Advertiser* (Adelaide), 1 December 1916; *SMH*, 13 November 1916.

172 'Recruiting Campaign, A Soldier's Letter', 27 December 1916, AWM27 533/19, AWM.

173 Australia, Parliament, House of Representatives, *Debates*, 18 December 1916; Turner, *Industrial Labour*, p. 130.

174 Thompson, Diary, 29 December 1916, PR84/331, AWM.

175 Stevenson, *Cataclysm*, p. 121; Chickering, *Imperial Germany*, p. 87.

176 Quoted in A.J. Hill, *Chauvel of the Light Horse*, Melbourne: Melbourne University Press, 1978, p. 87.

177 Bou, *Light Horse*, pp. 158–62; Hill, *Chauvel*, p. 89.

178 Hill, *Chauvel*, p. 89; *Mercury* (Hobart), 27, 28 December 1916.

179 *Brisbane Courier*, 4 January 1917; *SMH*, 5 January 1917.

Chapter 4

1 *Australian Baptist*, 19 December 1916.

2 Wilson, *The Myriad Faces*, pp. 428–9.

3 ibid., p. 432.

4 Lloyd George, quoted in Wilson, *The Myriad Faces*, p. 441.

5 Robert A. Doughty, *Pyrrhic Victory: French Strategy and Operations in the Great War*, Cambridge, MA: Belknap Press, 2005, p. 346.

6 For a detailed account, see David Woodward, *Lloyd George and the Generals*, Newark, DE: University of Delaware Press, 1983, Ch. 7.

7 See Fitzhardinge, *William Morris Hughes*, vol. II, pp. 237–48 for a detailed account of the negotiations.

8 Scott, *Official History*, vol. XI, p. 378.

9 For the Royal Commission into the Department of Defence, see Connor, *Anzac and Empire*, pp. 96–101.

10 R.J. Cassidy, *Worker*, 18 January 1917.

11 *Worker*, 18 January 1917.

12 See Meaney, *Australia*, pp. 185–6.

13 Fitzhardinge, *William Morris Hughes*, vol. II, p. 261.

14 Meaney, *Australia*, pp. 186, 188–9.

15 Guy Powles, *The New Zealanders in Sinai and Palestine*, Auckland: Whitcombe and Tombs, 1922, p. 90.

16 H.S. Gullett, *The Official History of Australia in the War of 1914–1918*, vol. VII, *The Australian Imperial Force in Sinai and Palestine, 1914–1918*, Sydney: Angus & Robertson, 1937.

17 Hill, *Chauvel*, p. 93; Bou, *Light Horse*, p. 158.

18 Coulthard-Clark, *No Australian Need Apply*, p. 153; Wray, *Sir James Whiteside McCay*, p. 211.

19 Miles, Diary, April 1917, 2DRL/0554, AWM; Bean, *Anzac to Amiens*, p. 318.

20 Albert Edwards, Memoir, pp. 45–6, PR89/050, AWM.

21 McMullin, *Pompey Elliott*, pp. 281, 268–71.

22 Hill, *Chauvel*, p. 102.

23 ibid., pp. 104–5; Bou, *Light Horse*, p. 160.

24 Bou, *Light Horse*, p. 162.

25 For British generals as 'donkeys' leading 'lions' (the soldiers), see Alan Clark, *The Donkeys*, London: Hutchinson, 1961.

26 See Paddy Griffith, *Battle Tactics of the Western Front: The British Army's Art of Attack, 1916–18*, New Haven, CT: Yale University Press, 1994, pp. 75–9.

27 John F. Williams, *Anzacs, The Media and the Great War*, Sydney: UNSW Press, 1999, p. 171.

28 Craig Deayton, *Battle Scarred: The 47th Battalion in World War I*, Sydney: Big Sky Publishing, 2011, Ch. 5, provides a useful summary of both Bullecourt battles. On Gough, see Gary Sheffield and Helen McCartney, 'Hubert Gough: Fifth Army, 1916–1918', in Ian W. Beckett and Steven J. Crovi (eds), *Haig's Generals*, Barnsley: Pen & Sword Military, 2006, pp. 75, 84.

29 Les Carlyon, *The Great War*, Sydney: Pan Macmillan, 2006, p. 327; Hubert Gough, *The Fifth Army*, London: Hodder & Stoughton, 1931, p. 181.

30 Paul Kendall, *Bullecourt 1917: Breaching the Hindenburg Line*, Stroud: Spellmount, 2010, p. 58; Eric Andrews, 'Bean and Bullecourt: Weaknesses and Strengths of the Official History of Australia in the First World War', *Revue Internationale d'Histoire Militaire*, 1972, p. 29.

31 48th Battalion history, quoted in Kendall, *Bullecourt*, p. 63; N.G. Imlay, 'Without Loss', *Reveille*, 1 June 1935, p. 26; Pedersen, *The Anzacs*, p. 200.

32 Gallwey, quoted in Bean, *Official History*, vol. IV, p. 289n.

33 David Coombes, *Crossing the Wire: The Untold Stories of Australian POWs in Battle and Captivity during WWI*, Sydney: Big Sky Publishing, 2011, p. 139.

34 Mitchell, Diary, 11 April 1917, 2DRL/0928, AWM; Pedersen, *The Anzacs*, p. 203; Gough, *The Fifth Army*, p. 184. A detailed account of the tanks can be found in Kendall, *Bullecourt*, Ch. 10.

35 Mitchell, Diary, 11 April 2017, 2DRL/0928; Denver Gallwey, quoted in Deayton, *Battle Scarred*, p. 95; Bert Knowles, 'Bullecourt Tragedy: Retrospect', *Reveille*, 30 April 1931, p. 15; Kendall, *Bullecourt*, p. 68.

36 Max McDowall, 'Bullecourt Tragedy', *Reveille*, 1 May 1935, p. 32.

37 Coates, *An Atlas*, p. 60; In Memoriam, (Hurstbridge) *Advertiser*, 29 April 1927.

38 Mitchell, *Backs to the Wall*, p. 128; Anthony Farrar-Hockley, *Goughie: The Life of General Sir Hubert Gough, CGB, GCMG, KCVO*, London: Hart-Davis, MacGibbon, 1975, p. 206; Pedersen, *The Anzacs*, p. 205.

39 Bean, *Official History*, vol. IV, p. 351; British official history, quoted in Coates, *An Atlas*, p. 60; Gough, *The Fifth Army*, p. 184.

40 Andrews, 'Bean and Bullecourt', p. 34.

41 Bean, *Official History*, vol. IV, p. 374.

42 Pedersen, *The Anzacs*, p. 208; Bean, *Official History*, vol. IV, p. 393.

43 This account relies on Doughty, *Pyrrhic Victory*, pp. 349–64.

44 Andrews, 'Bean and Bullecourt', p. 30. One of the more accessible accounts of Second Bullecourt is Peter S. Sadler, *The Paladin: A Life of Major-General Sir John Gellibrand*, Melbourne: Oxford University Press, 2000, Ch. 12.

45 Bean, *Anzac to Amiens*, p. 342.

46 Pedersen, *The Anzacs*, p. 216.

47 Downing, *To the Last Ridge*, pp. 59, 65.

48 Kinchington, quoted in Bean, *Official History*, vol. IV, p. 493.

49 ibid., pp. 496–7.

50 Pedersen, *The Anzacs*, p. 218.

51 Rupert Baldwin, Diary, 7 May 1917, PR00557, AWM.

52 Bean, *Official History*, vol. IV, p. 542; *Australian Worker*, 19 April 1917.

53 Letter, 25 April 1917, Papers of Allan Leane, 1DRL/0411, AWM; Letter from Brigadier J.C. Robertson, CO 12 Infantry Battalion to Mr Davis, 22 April 1917, papers of Henry Davis, 2DRL/0547, AWM.

54 Connor, *Anzac and Empire*, pp. 102–3; Munro Ferguson to Secretary of State for the Colonies, 26 June 1917, MS696, Series 8, Box 3, NLA.

55 Baldwin, Diary, 16 May 1917, PR00557, AWM; Maguire, Letter to mother, 14 May 1917, 2DRL/322, AWM.

56 Australian War Memorial, 'Prisoners of the Germans', <www.awm.gov.au/exhibitions/stolenyears/ww1/germany/>; 'Prisoners of Turkey', <www.awm.gov.au/exhibitions/stolenyears/ww1/turkey/>, viewed 20 March 2013.

57 Kendall, *Bullecourt*, p. 106.

58 Alan Stephens, *The Australian Centenary History of Defence*, vol. II, *The Royal Australian Air Force*, Melbourne: Oxford University Press, p. 8; Jennifer Lawless, 'Gallipoli POWs: Challenging the Myths', paper presented to conference, Prisoners of War: the Australian Experience of Captivity in the 20th Century, Australian National University, Canberra, June 2013.

59 John Lee, quoted in Kendall, *Bullecourt*, p. 107.

60 Coombes, *Crossing the Wire*, pp. 186–7.

61 *To the Last Ridge*, p. 62; Letter E. Sinclair-MacLagan to Lieut.-General Sir J. Talbot Hobbs, 28 March 1919, AWM 27/623/7, AWM.

62 '4th Australian Divisional Memorial', AWM 623/7, AWM; 'Bullecourt 1917', ; 'Slouch Hat Memorial at Bullecourt', <www.awm.gov. au/blog/tag/bullecourt>, viewed 20 March 2013.

63 'Cross Memorial, Bullecourt', <http://memorials.dva.gov.au/MemorialDetail.aspx? Id=123>; 'Bullecourt War Museum', <http://battlefields1418.50megs.com/bullecourt_ museum.html>; Bullecourt, The Bullecourt digger', <www.ww1westernfront.gov.au/ bullecourt/the-bullecourt-digger.html>, viewed 20 March 2013. For Percy Black painting, see ART3558, AWM.

64 *Canberra Times*, 27 August 2011; Embassy of France in Australia, 'Reopening of the 1917 Bullecourt Museum', <www.ambafrance-au.org/Reopening-of-the–1917-Bullecourt>, viewed 20 March 2013; Julia Gillard, Speech to the Australian Strategic Policy Institute and Boeing National Security Luncheon, Canberra, 17 April 2012, <www.pm.gov.au/ press-office>, viewed 20 April 2013.

65 Hughes' correspondence with religious leaders, Prime Minister's Office to Premier of Victoria, 18 April 1917, A2 1919/1622, pt 1, NAA.

66 Leonard Bryant, Diary, PR00142, AWM; *Sunday Times*, 29 April 1917.

67 *Advertiser*, 25 April 1917.

68 Munro Ferguson to Secretary of State for the Colonies, 22 March 1917, MS696, Series 8, Box 3, NLA; Scott, *Official History*, vol. XI, pp. 381–3; *Labor Call*, 8 March 1917.

69 Fitzhardinge, *William Morris Hughes*, vol. II, p. 259; Scott, *Official History*, vol. XI, cartoon, p. 387.

70 Fitzhardinge, *William Morris Hughes*, vol. II, p. 263.

71 Meaney, *Australia*, pp. 201–2.

72 ibid., p. 202; Hughes, quoted in *Australian Worker*, 19 April 1917.

73 *Labor Call*, 22 March 1917; *Worker*, 26 April 1917.

74 *Australian Worker*, 19, 26 April 1917; *Labor Call*, 22 March 1917.

75 Scott, *Official History*, vol. XI, p. 396; *Warrnambool Standard*, 12 April 1917.

76 Fitzhardinge, *William Morris Hughes*, vol. II, p. 263; Mannix, quoted in Meaney, *Australia*, p. 208.

77 For the growing anti-war sentiment within the industrial labour movement in 1917, see Turner, *Industrial Labour*, pp. 171–3.

78 Frank Cain, *Wobblies at War*, pp. 251–6.

79 Australia, Parliament, House of Representatives, *Debates*, 19 July 1917.

80 Frank Cain, 'The Industrial Workers of the World: Aspects of Its Suppression in Australia 1916–1919', *Labour History*, vol. 42, 1982, pp. 58–60; Turner, *Industrial Labour*, p. 135.

81 F.L. Carsten, *War Against War: British and German Radical Movements in World War I*, London: Batsford, 1982, p. 103; War Cabinet, quoted in Woodward, *Lloyd George*, p. 173.

82 Meyer, *A World Undone*, p. 486.

83 Stevens, *The Australian Centenary History*, vol. III, pp. 50–1.

84 Wilson, *The Myriad Faces*, pp. 433–7.

85 Peter Simkins, 'Herbert Plumer: Second Army, 1915–17, 1918', in Ian F.W. Beckett and Steven J. Corvi (eds), *Haig's Generals*, Barnsley: Pen & Sword Military, 2006, p. 140.

86 Serle, *John Monash*, pp. 287–9.

87 Coates, *An Atlas*, p. 64.

88 A good description of tunnelling at Hill 60 can be found in Bean, *Official History*, vol. IV, pp. 949–59.

89 Australian Memorials in France and Belgium, 19 December 1923, CP102/22, 23A, NAA.

90 'Beneath Hill 60', <www.beneathhill60.com.au/index.htm>, viewed 20 April 2013. The film was accompanied by a book by Will Davies, *Beneath Hill 60*, Sydney: Vintage Books, 2010.

91 Mitchell, Diary, 7 June 1917, 2DRL/0928, AWM; Hurley, Diary, 23 August 1917, MS883, NLA.

92 For details, see Pedersen, *Monash*, pp. 171–6.

93 *Barrier Miner (Broken Hill)*, 10 July 1917.

94 Serle, *John Monash*, p. 292; Robin Prior and Trevor Wilson, *Passchendaele: The Untold Story*, 2nd edn, New Haven, CT: Yale Nota Bene, 2002, p. 65; A.J.P. Taylor, *The First World War: An Illustrated History*, London: Hamish Hamilton, 1963, p. 175.

95 Prior and Wilson, *Command*, p. 269; Prior and Wilson, *Passchendaele*, pp. 50–1.

96 Bean gives a full account of this battle in *Official History*, vol. IV, pp. 960–4.

97 Hurley, Diary, 17 September 1917, MS883, NLA; Pedersen, *The Anzacs*, p. 246.

98 Wilson, *The Myriad Faces*, p. 467.

99 Serle, *John Monash*, p. 293.

100 This account relies on Turner, *Industrial Labour*, pp. 139–61; Robert Bollard, '"The Active Chorus": The Great Strike of 1917 in Victoria', *Labour History*, vol. 90, 2006, pp. 77–94; and Robert Bollard, 'How to Create a Tradition: The Seamen's Union and the Great Strike of 1917', *The History Cooperative Conference Proceedings*, <www.historycooperative.org/proceedings/asslh2/bollard.html>, viewed 20 April 2013.

101 Bollard, 'How to Create a Tradition', p. 8; Boote, quoted in Turner, *Industrial Labour*, p. 149.

102 Munro Ferguson, Letter to Sir Samuel Griffith, 27 September 1917, MS696, Series 12, Box 5, NLA; Robert Bollard, 'Victorian Workers in the 1917 Mass Strike', *Marxist Interventions*, <www/anu.edu.au/polsci/marx/interventions/1917strike.html>, viewed 20 April 2013, p. 16.

103 This account draws on Judith Smart, 'Feminists, Food and the Fair Price: The Cost-of-living Demonstrations in Melbourne: August–September 1917', in Damousi and Lake, *Gender and War*, pp. 274–301; quotes pp. 276, 281, 277.

104 Joy Damousi, *Women Come Rally: Socialism, Communism and Gender in Australia 1890–1955*, Melbourne: Oxford University Press, 1994, p. 85.

105 Hughes, quoted in Turner, *Industrial Labour*, p. 146; NSW Minister of Labour, quoted ibid., p. 154.

106 Hughes, quoted in Smart, 'Feminists, Food', p. 286.

107 Bollard, 'Victorian Workers', p. 9.

108 ibid., p. 10; Ross McMullin, *The Light on the Hill: The Australian Labor Party 1891–1991*, first published 1991, Melbourne: Oxford University Press, 1992, p. 113.

109 *Argus*, quoted in Smart, 'Feminists, Food', p. 287.

110 *Industrial Labour*, p. 159.

111 Bollard, 'How to Create a Tradition', p. 2; David T. Rowlands, 'Remembering the 1917 General Strike', *Green Left Weekly*, <www.greenleft.org.au/node/39343>, viewed 20 April 2013; Marilyn Lake and Henry Reynolds (eds), *What's Wrong with Anzac? The Militarisation of Australian History*, Sydney: UNSW Press, 2010, p. 10; Australian Bureau of Statistics data, quoted in *Australian*, 13 May 2012; David Lowenthal, *The Past is a Foreign Country*, Cambridge: Cambridge University Press, 1985.

112 Bean, *Official History*, vol. IV, p. 735.

113 ibid., p. 739.

114 ibid., p. 761.

115 Baldwin, Diary, 21 September 1917, PR00557, AWM; Lawrence, Letter, 20 September 1917, PR86/266, AWM; Prior and Wilson, *Passchendaele*, p. 118.

116 Douglas, Diary, 27 September 1917, 2DRL/0930, AWM; Lance-Corporal Horace Parton, quoted in Pedersen, *The Anzacs*, p. 251.

117 McMullin, *Pompey Elliott*, p. 305; Pedersen, *The Anzacs*, p. 253; Coates, *An Atlas*, Map 23a; Prior and Wilson, *Passchendaele*, p. 119.

118 Haig, 28 September 1917, quoted in Wilson, *The Myriad Faces*, p. 476.

119 For a detailed account, see McMullin, *Pompey Elliott*, pp. 310ff.; Downing, *To the Last Ridge*, p. 76.

120 Diary of Leonard Clyde Bryant, 2nd Field Ambulance, PR00142, AWM.

121 David Coombes, *The Lionheart: Lieutenant-General Sir Talbot Hobbs*, Sydney: Australian Military History Publications, 2007, p. 201.

122 Bean, *Official History*, vol. IV, p. 813; 3rd Division War Diary, quoted in Prior and Wilson, *Passchendaele*, p. 130.

123 '5th Australian Divisional Memorial', AWM 27 623/8, AWM.

124 McMullin, *Pompey Elliott*, p. 328.

125 ibid., p. 333.

126 Coates, *An Atlas*, map 23; Prior and Wilson, *Passchendaele*, p. 131.

127 Bryant, Diary, 21 September 1917, PR00142, AWM; Hurley, Diary, 20 September 1917, MS883, NLA.

128 Bryant, Diary, 26 September 1917, PR00142, AWM; Tilton, quoted in Peter Rees, *The Other Anzacs: Nurses at War, 1914–1918*, Sydney: Allen & Unwin, 2008, p. 234.

129 King, quoted in Rees, *The Other Anzacs*, pp. 219, 220.

130 ibid., p. 233; Tilton, quoted in ibid, p. 236.

131 Serle, *John Monash*, p. 297.

132 Bean, *Anzac to Amiens*, p. 369.

133 Miles, Diary, 4 October 1917, 2DRL/0554, AWM; Pedersen, *The Anzacs*, p. 258.

134 Miles, Diary, 4 October 1917, 2DRL/0554, AWM.

135 Prior and Wilson, *Passchendaele*, p. 137; Coates, *An Atlas*, map 23; Monash, quoted in Pedersen, *Monash*, p. 198.

136 Prior and Wilson, *Passchendaele*, p. 137; Bean, *Official History*, vol. IV, p. 856.

137 Prior and Wilson, *Passchendaele*, p. 155.

138 Miles, Diary, 5 October 1917, 2DRL/0554, AWM; Bean, *Official History*, vol. IV, p. 890.

139 Carthew, *Voices from the Trenches*, p. 214.

140 Pedersen, *The Anzacs*, p. 261; Bean, *Official History*, vol. IV, p. 900.

141 Sutton, Diary, nd, 2DRL/1227, AWM; Miles, Diary, 9 October 1917, 2DRL/0554, AWM.

142 Prior and Wilson, *Passchendaele*, p. 166.

143 Haig, quoted in Pedersen, *Monash*, p. 200; Hurley, Diary, 11 October 1917, MS883, NLA.

144 Hope Weatherhead, 2 Australian General Hospital, quoted in Kirsty Harris, *More than Bombs and Bandages: Australian Army Nurses at Work in World War I*, Sydney: Big Sky Publishing, 2011, pp. 160–1.

145 Bean, *Official History*, vol. IV, p. 911.

146 Serle, *John Monash*, p. 298; David Coombes, *Morshead: Hero of Tobruk and El Alamein*, Melbourne: Oxford University Press, 2001, p. 53; F.M. Cutlack, *The War Letters of General Monash*, Sydney: Angus & Robertson, 1934, p. 202.

147 Currie, quoted in Pugsley, *The Anzac Experience*, p. 194.

148 Stephens, *The Australian Centenary History*, vol. II, p. 18.

149 Sheffield, *The Chief*, pp. 247–8; Harris, *Douglas Haig*, p. 381.

150 Australian War Memorial, 'Third Battle of Ypres', <www.awm.gov.au/units/event_104.asp>, viewed 20 April 2013; Prior and Wilson, *Pascchendaele*, p. 195; Simon Robbins, *British Generalship on the Western Front 1914–18: Defeat into Victory*, Abingdon: Frank Cass, 2005, p. 128; Harris, *Douglas Haig*, p. 382.

151 *Argus*, 27 October 1917; *Age*, 21 October 1917; *Argus*, 7, 12 November 1917.

152 Bou, *Light Horse*, p. 164.

153 ibid., pp. 165–6.

154 Hill, *Chauvel*, p. 128.

155 Bou, *Australia's Palestine Campaign*, p. 52.

156 For press comment, see *SMH*, 3 November 1917; *Border Watch* (Mount Gambier), 2 November 1917; *West Gippsland Gazette*, 27 November 1917.

157 For Beersheba as 'forgotten': Paul Daley, *Beersheba: A Journey Through Australia's Forgotten War*, Melbourne: Melbourne University Press, 2009.

158 *SMH*, 1 November 2007; *Australian*, 29 April 2008.

159 Bou, *Light Horse*, p. 175.

160 Kempe, quoted in Ian Jones, *The Australian Light Horse*, Sydney: Time-Life Books, 1987, p. 115; Gullett, *Official History*, vol. VII, p. 417.

161 Bou, *Australia's Palestine Campaign*, p. 67.

162 A. Seager, 'The Conquest of Jerusalem', (Adelaide) *Register*, 15 December 1917.

163 Governor-General opening of Parliament speech, 11 July 1917, A29/19, AWM; Meaney, *Australia*, p. 212.

164 For details, see Robson, *The First A.I.F.*, Ch. 7.

165 ibid., p. 144.

166 Governor-General opening of Parliament speech, 11 July 1917, A29/19; Judith Smart, '"For the Good that We Can Do": Cecilia Downing and Feminist Christian Citizenship', *Australian Feminist Studies*, vol. 9, issue 19, 1994, p. 44; McKernan, *The Australian People*, pp. 111–12.

167 *Ballarat Accommodation and Tourism Directory*, 'The Ballarat Avenue of Honour', <www.ballarat.com/avenue.htm>, viewed 20 April 2013; Janine Haddow, 'Avenues of Honour: A Victorian Cultural Landscape', *Landscape Australia*, vol. 3, 1988, pp. 306–9.

168 Fitzhardinge, *William Morris Hughes*, vol. II, p. 280.

169 Mackinnon, 'Recruiting', 7 June 1917, 3DRL 6673/169 pt 1, AWM; Fitzhardinge, *William Morris Hughes*, vol. II, p. 281.

170 Fitzhardinge, *William Morris Hughes*, vol. II, p. 267; Meaney, *Australia*, pp. 216–17.

171 Connor, *Anzac and Empire*, p. 108.

172 Proclamation by Hughes, 17 November 1917, AWM 13 7041/8/20, AWM.

173 McQuilton, *Rural Australia*, p. 88.

174 Boote, Conscription special, *Australian Worker*, 19 November 1917; Hughes, quoted in Meaney, *Australia*, p. 218.

175 Meaney, *Australia*, pp. 219–20.

176 Alan D. Gilbert, 'The Conscription Referenda, 1916–17: The Impact of the Irish Crisis', *Historical Studies*, vol. 14, no. 53, 1969, p. 71; Fitzhardinge, *William Morris Hughes*, vol. II, p. 283; Meaney, *Australia*, pp. 215, 221.

177 O'Farrell, *The Catholic Church and Community*, p. 322; McKernan, *Australian Churches*, p. 123.

178 B.A. Santamaria, *Daniel Mannix*, Melbourne: Melbourne University Press, 1985, p. 83.

179 O'Farrell, *Catholic Church and Community*, pp. 336–7; Meaney, *Australia*, p. 224; T.E. Ruth, 'Dr Mannix as Political Commander-in-Chief of a "Sordid Trade War"', Patriotic Pamphlets 18, Melbourne, Critchley Parker, 1917, State Library of Victoria.

180 Sandra Thwaites, 'Rev T.E. Ruth: A City Preacher in a Time of War and After', *Our Yesterdays*, vol. 4, 1996, pp. 28–9.

181 D.J. Murphy, 'Queensland', in D.J. Murphy (ed.), *Labor in Politics: The State Labor Parties in Australia, 1880–1920*, Brisbane: University of Queensland Press, 1975, p. 201.

182 For the Ryan and *Hansard* incident, see Evans, *Loyalty*, pp. 106–7 and Fitzhardinge, *William Morris Hughes*, vol. II, pp. 289–91.

183 Evans, *Loyalty*, p. 107.

184 Fitzhardinge, *William Morris Hughes*, vol. II, p. 296; Meaney, *Australia*, p. 228.

185 McQuilton, *Rural Australia*, p. 91; Hilary Summy, 'Margaret Thorp and the Anti-Conscription Campaign in Brisbane 1915–1917', *Hecate*, vol. 32, no. 1, 2006, p. 70.

186 Raymond Evans, '"All the Passion of our Womanhood": Margaret Thorp and the Battle of the Brisbane School of Arts', in Damousi and Lake, *Gender and War*, pp. 247–8.

187 Fitzhardinge, *William Morris Hughes*, vol. II, pp. 291–5, is the best account of the Warwick incident.

188 Hughes, quoted in Fitzhardinge, *William Morris Hughes*, vol. II, p. 294; Robson, *The First A.I.F.*, p. 160.

189 RC00317, AWM, <http://cas.awm.gov.au/item/RC00317>, viewed 20 April 2013. Edith Cavell was a British nurse working in Brussels who assisted British soldiers to escape from Belgium to the Netherlands. She was shot by the Germans as a spy in 1915 and became a popular martyr. An Australian silent film about her was released in 1916. Michael Considine was the militant president of the Amalgamated Miners' Association, for a time a member of the Marist Australian Socialist Party and from 1917, a federal member of parliament. Maurice Blackburn was a Labor member of parliament in Victoria who lost his seat in 1917 because of his outspoken opposition to conscription and the war. Jack Brookfield was president of Labor's Volunteer Army. The haystack reference presumably was to one of the arson charges against the IWW.

190 Withers, 'The 1916–1917 Conscription Referenda', p. 40; Evans, *Loyalty*, p. 111; Scott, *Official History*, vol. XI, p. 27.

191 C.E.W. Bean, *The Official History of Australia in the War of 1914–1918*, vol. V, *The Australian Imperial Force in France during the Main German Offensive, 1918*, Sydney, Angus & Robertson, 1937, p. 22. Stephen Murray-Smith, 'On the Conscription Trail: The Second Referendum Seen from Beside W.M. Hughes', *Labour History*, no. 33, 1977, p. 102.

192 Letter, no author but from context almost certainly George Steward, to Hall (Admiral Sir William 'Blinker'), 30 January 1918, A8911/240, NAA.

193 Murray-Smith, 'On the Conscription Trail', p. 100.

194 Pearson, 'Western Australia and the Conscription Plebiscites', p. 24. Ina Bertrand suggests that Mannix's visits to country Victoria may have contributed to the higher 'no' vote in the Wannon electorate, although voting patterns were complex: 'The Victorian Country Vote', pp. 28–31.

195 Murdoch, 'Notes on the Australian Conscription Referendum', AWM 7041/8/20, AWM.

196 Fitzhardinge, *William Morris Hughes*, vol. II, p. 285.

197 'The Last Post Ceremony at Ypres', AWM27 623/17, AWM.

198 Letter Philip Cuthbertson to Secretary, Australian War Graves Commission, 9 May 1917, Principal Assistant Secretary, Imperial War Graves Commission to Official Secretary, Australia House, 20 June 1928, A2909, 6/1/48 pt 2, NAA.

199 'Will Longstaff's *Menin Gate at Midnight (Ghosts of Menin Gate)*', <www.awm.gov.au/encyclopedia/menin/notes.asp>, viewed 20 April 2013.

200 'Menin Gate lions', <www.awm.gov.au/encyclopedia/menin/lions.asp>, viewed 20 April 2013.

Chapter 5

1 Stevenson, *Cataclysm*, p. 305.

2 David R. Woodward, 'The Origins and Intent of David Lloyd George's January 5 War Aims Speech', *Historian*, vol. 34, no. 1, 1971, pp. 22–39.

3 Meaney, *Australia*, p. 241.

4 This account relies on Munro Ferguson to Secretary of State for the Colonies, 15 January 1918, MS696, Series 9, Box 4, NLA; Fitzhardinge, *William Morris Hughes*, vol. II, pp. 299–305; Scott, *Official History*, vol. XI, pp. 431–7.

5 Fitzhardinge, *William Morris Hughes*, vol. II, p. 30.

6 Munro Ferguson to Secretary of State for the Colonies, 19 January 1918, A11047, NAA.

7 Fitzhardinge, *William Morris Hughes*, vol. II, pp. 305–6.

8 The account that follows draws on Bou, *Australia's Palestine Campaign*, pp. 71–85, and Hill, *Chauvel*, pp. 143–4.

9 Stevenson, *Cataclysm*, pp. 332–3.

10 Harris, *Douglas Haig*, pp. 433–5.

11 Bean, *Official History*, vol. V, pp. 190, 188.

12 Pedersen, *The Anzacs*, p. 318.

13 Serle, *John Monash*, p. 312.

14 David Horner, *Australia's Military History for Dummies*, Milton: Wiley Publishing, 2010, pp. 139–40.

15 John Monash, *The Australian Victories in 1918*, London: Hutchinson, 1920, p. 28.

16 ibid., p. 29.

17 Hindenburg, quoted in Peter Edgar, *To Villers-Bretonneux with Brigadier-General William Glasgow, DSO and the 13th Australian Infantry Brigade*, Sydney: Australian Military History Publications, 2006, p. 224.

18 Pedersen, *The Anzacs*, pp. 322–3. For Morlancourt, see Bean, *Official History*, vol. V, pp. 230–5.

19 Pedersen, *The Anzacs* p. 323; Bean, *Official History*, vol. V, p. 304; Coombs, *Morshead*, p. 58.

20 McMullin, *Pompey Elliott*, p. 373.

21 Bean, *Official History*, vol. V, p. 318; McMullin, *Pompey Elliott*, p. 374.

22 Bean, *Official History*, vol. V, p. 344.

23 ibid., pp. 369, 390; Mitchell, *Backs to the Wall*, pp. 235–6. For Dernancourt on 5 April, see Deayton, *Battle Scarred*, Ch. 9; and Bean, *Official History*, vol. V, Ch. XII.

24 For a detailed account of the Battle of Lys, see Chris Baker, *The Battle for Flanders: German Defeat on the Lys 1918*, Barnsley, South Yorkshire: Pen & Sword Military, 2011.

25 Bean, *Official History*, vol. V, p. 437.

26 Quoted in Pedersen, *The Anzacs*, p. 332.

27 William Moore, quoted in Wilson, *The Myriad Faces*, p. 571.

28 Scott, *Official History*, vol. XI, p. 439.

29 Mackinnon's and Griffith's reports can be found in Scott, *Official History*, vol. XI, pp. 439–45; see also Robson, *The First A.I.F.*, pp. 182–3.

30 Meaney, *Australia*, p. 39. This account relies on Scott, *Official History*, vol. XI, pp. 445–58 and Memorandum on the Proceedings of the Conference, 20 April 1918, MS696, Series 8, Box 3, NLA.

31 Meaney, *Australia*, p. 237.

32 Robson, *The First A.I.F.*, p. 192.

33 Fitzhardinge, *William Morris Hughes*, vol. II, pp. 308–9.

34 Meaney, *Australia*, p. 225; *West Australian*, 22 March 1918; *Argus*, 25 March 1918.

35 Letter to Editor, *Argus*, by 'Catholic Englishman', 25 March 1918. For Mannix and the Vatican, see Meaney, *Australia*, pp. 226–7.

36 Scott, *Official History*, vol. XI, pp. 461–2.

37 *Western Mail* (Perth), 10 May 1918; *Argus*, 9 May 1918.

38 Scott, *Official History*, vol. XI, p. 459.

39 For 'The Gospel of Frightfulness', see ARTV00037, ARTVV01163, AWM.

40 Scott, *Official History*, vol. XI, pp. 460–1.

41 Quoted in the Australian press—for example, *Examiner* (Launceston) and *Register* (Adelaide), 25 April 1918.

42 Deayton, *Battle Scarred*, p. 266.

43 Evans, *Loyalty*, p. 142.

44 Bean, *Official History*, vol. V, p. 534.

45 See McMullin, *Pompey Elliott*, pp. 393–9.

46 Edgar, *To Villers-Bretonneux*, p. 230; Pedersen, *The Anzacs*, pp. 337–8; Bean, Diary and Notebooks, 25 April 1918, AWM38, 3DRL606/108/1, AWM.

47 Bean, *Official History*, vol. V, p. 603; McMullin, *Pompey Elliott*, p. 409.

48 Pedersen, *The Anzacs*, p. 342.

49 McMullin, *Pompey Elliott*, pp. 418–21; Coombs, *The Lionheart*, p. 241.

50 Pedersen, *The Anzacs*, p. 342; Peter Edgar, *Sir William Glasgow: Soldier, Senator and Diplomat*, Sydney: Big Sky Publishing, 2011, p. 212; McMullin, *Pompey Elliott*, p. 423.

51   Bean, *Official History*, vol. V, pp. 120, 177.

52   Ziino, *Distant Grief*, p. 91; 'Villers-Bretonneux, Australian National Memorial', <www.wwlwesternfront.gov.au/villers-bretonneux/town-of-villers-bretonneux.html>, viewed 20 April 2013; Foch, quoted in Inglis, *Sacred Places*, p. 265. The Villers-Bretonneux tablet was intended to tour each Australian state and then be included in a memorial to Australians at Villers-Bretonneux. However, at the request of the Australian War Memorial in 1928, the mayor of the town agreed to the tablet's remaining in Australia (Shepherd to Director, AWM, 6 May 1929, A461, H370/1/15, pt 1, NAA).

53   This account draws on Linda Wade, 'By diggers defended, by Victorians mended': searching for Villers Bretonneux, PhD thesis, School of History and Politics, University of Wollongong, 2008.

54   Hobbs to Secretary, Department of Defence, 26 January 1922, MP367/1 528/1/292, NAA.

55   Minutes of 7th meeting of Anglo-French mixed committee, 25 June 1926, A461 H370/1/15 pt 1, NAA.

56   *Canberra Times*, 23 July 1938.

57   Draft Speech, A461, H370/1/15 pt 3, NAA.

58   Inglis, *Sacred Places*, p. 455.

59   'Anzac Day, Australian National Memorial, Villers-Bretonneux, France, 2008', <www.dva.gov.au/commems_oawg/commemorations/commemorative_events/major_anniversaries/villers-bretonneux/Pages/index.aspx>; 'Australian Remembrance & Battlefield Tours', <www.battlefield-tours.com.au/html/dawn-service-villers-bretonneu.html>, both viewed 20 April 2013; *Australian*, 22 April 2008.

60   *Age*, 25 April 2008.

61   Bean, *Anzac to Amiens*, p. 445.

62   C.E.W. Bean, *The Official History of Australia in the War of 1914–1918*, vol. VI, *The Australian Imperial Force in France During the Allied Offensive, 1918*, Sydney: Angus & Robertson, 1942, pp. 104–5.

63   Bean, *Anzac to Amiens*, p. 459; Coates, *An Atlas*, p. 78.

64   Hill, *Chauvel*, p. 144.

65   Chetwode, quoted in Bou, *Light Horse*, p. 186. For the Es Salt raid see Hill, *Chauvel*, pp. 146–51.

66   Hill, *Chauvel*, p. 151; Coates, *An Atlas*, p. 104.

67   For Hughes in the United States and Britain, see Fitzhardinge, *William Morris Hughes*, vol. II, pp. 311–29; Meaney, *Australia*, pp. 256–79; Andrews, *The Anzac Illusion*, pp. 190–5.

68   Meaney, *Australia*, p. 258.

69   Fitzhardinge, *William Morris Hughes*, vol. II, p. 314; Meaney, *Australia*, p. 259.

70   Meaney, *Australia*, p. 260.

71 Fitzhardinge, *William Morris Hughes*, vol. II, pp. 315–16.

72 Meaney, *Australia*, p. 262.

73 Fitzhardinge, *William Morris Hughes*, vol. II, p. 320.

74 Bean, *Anzac to Amiens*, p. 447; Fitzhardinge, *William Morris Hughes*, vol. II, p. 319.

75 Stevenson, *Cataclysm*, p. 341.

76 Andrews, *The Anzac Illusion*, p. 192.

77 Meaney, *Australia*, p. 269; Andrews, *The Anzac Illusion*, p. 192.

78 On Haig, see Wilson, *The Myriad Faces*, pp. 547–9.

79 Fitzhardinge, *William Morris Hughes*, vol. II, p. 324; Meaney, *Australia*, p. 269.

80 Meaney, *Australia*, p. 271.

81 This account draws on Meaney, *Australia*, pp. 273–6, and Fitzhardinge, *William Morris Hughes*, vol. II, pp. 269–76.

82 Fitzhardinge, *William Morris Hughes*, vol. II, pp. 328–9.

83 Hughes, quoted in Meaney, *Australia*, p. 267.

84 Meaney, *Australia*, p. 277; Fitzhardinge, *William Morris Hughes*, vol. II, p. 332.

85 Andrews, *The Anzac Illusion*, p. 195; Fitzhardinge, *William Morris Hughes*, vol. II, pp. 331–3.

86 Andrews, *The Anzac Illusion*, p. 200.

87 Fitzhardinge, *William Morris Hughes*, vol. II, p. 325; Spartalis, *Diplomatic Battles*, p. 50.

88 Hughes, quoted in Meaney, *Australia*, p. 277. For visa, see Meaney, *Australia*, p. 279.

89 This account draws on Serle, *John Monash*, pp. 319–28, and Bean, *Official History*, vol. VI, Ch. VI.

90 Serle, *John Monash*, p. 320.

91 Bean, *Official History*, vol. VI, pp. 195–6; *Anzac to Amiens*, p. 458; Serle, *John Monash*, p. 322.

92 Serle, *John Monash*, p. 325.

93 Fitzhardinge, *William Morris Hughes*, vol. II, p. 321.

94 Serle, *John Monash*, p. 328.

95 Bean, *Official History*, vol. V, pp. 213–14: Andrews, *The Anzac Illusion*, pp. 141–2.

96 This account draws on McMullin, *Pompey Elliott*, Ch. 17.

97 Report on Parliamentary session of 24 April 1918 in *Queenslander* (Brisbane), 4 May 1918; Australian Labor Party (Vic.), Annual Conference, *Report of Proceedings*, 29 March to 1 April 1918, NLA.

98 *Report of the Seventh Commonwealth Commonwealth Conference of the Australian Labor Party, Opened at Perth, June 1917, 1918*, Melbourne: *Labor Call* print, 1918, pp. 11–14, NLA.

99 *Report of Seventh Commonwealth Conference*, pp. 23–8.

100 Scott, *Official History*, vol. XI, pp. 468–9.

101 Stevenson, *Cataclysm*, p. 342.

102 Pedersen, *The Anzacs*, p. 353.

103 Monash, *Australian Victories*, p. 56.

104 Coates, *An Atlas*, map 28.

105 Pedersen, *Monash*, p. 230.

106 Eric Andrews and B.G. Jordan, 'Hamel: Winning a Battle', *Journal of the Australian War Memorial*, no. 18, 1991, p. 6: Bean, *Anzac to Amiens*, p. 461.

107 Monash, *Australian Victories*, pp. 53–4.

108 Coates, *An Atlas*, p. 80; Andrews and Jordan, 'Hamel', pp. 7–8; Bean, *Official History*, vol. VI, p. 285; Private Shapcott, quoted in Pedersen, *The Anzacs*, p. 362.

109 Monash, *Australian Victories*, p. 56; Pedersen, *The Anzacs*, p. 365.

110 See McMullin, *Pompey Elliott*, pp. 457–60, for the Ville operation.

111 Serle, *John Monash*, p. 336.

112 Fuller and Essame, quoted in Serle, *John Monash*, p. 335.

113 Jonathan King, 'Disquiet on the Front', *Australian*, 8 August 1998; Madeleine Coorey, 'War Weary Faces Etched on Stonemason's Memory', *Australian*, 11 March 1998.

114 John Laffin to Gary Beck, Office of Australian War Graves, 24 May 1998, supplied under special access by DVA, file reference 981369.

115 DVA media release, 'Four WW1 Diggers to Go to France to Commemorate War's End', 17 June 1998; Address by Minister for Veterans' Affairs, supplied under special access by DVA, file reference 990975.

116 *Australian*, 11 March 1998, 9 July 2007.

117 DVA media release, 'Australian Corps Memorial Park, Le Hamel, France'.

118 Stevenson, *Cataclysm*, p. 345.

119 Serle, *John Monash*, pp. 337–40; Monash, *Australian Victories*, p. 64.

120 Coates, *An Atlas*, p. 82, map 29a; Pedersen, *The Anzacs*, p. 372.

121 Monash, quoted in Serle, *John Monash*, p. 343; David Wilson of 24th Battalion, quoted in Pedersen, *The Anzacs*, p. 374.

122 Downing, *To the Last Ridge*, p. 138; A.W. Bacon, quoted in Wilson, *The Myriad Faces*, p. 592.

123 Charles Montague, *Disenchantment*, London: Chatto & Windus, 1924, pp. 174–5.

124 Downing, *To the Last Ridge*, p. 143.

125 Coates, *An Atlas*, map 29.

126 Prior and Wilson, *Command*, p. 323.

127 Quoted in Pedersen, *The Anzacs*, p. 378.

128 German Official History, quoted in Richard Holmes, *The Western Front*, London: BBC Books, Random House, 1999, p. 231.

129 Wilson, *The Myriad Faces*, p. 593; Pedersen, *The Anzacs*, p. 378.

130 Bean, *Official History*, vol. VI, p. 684; Peter Pedersen, 'Maintaining the Advance: Monash, Battle Procedure and the Australian Corps in 1918', in Ashley Ekins (ed.), *1918 Year of Victory: The End of the Great War and the Shaping of History*, Titirangi, New Zealand: Exisle, 2010, pp. 130–45, provides an excellent account.

131 Pedersen, 'Maintaining the Advance', pp. 137–9; Prior and Wilson, *Command*, p. 330.

132 McMullin, *Pompey Elliott*, pp. 467–9.

133 Edgar, *Glasgow*, pp. 228–9.

134 For the patrol, see Dale Blair, *Dinkum Diggers: An Australian Battalion at War*, Melbourne: Melbourne University Press, 2001, pp. 52–5.

135 Bean, *Official History*, vol. VI, p. 693.

136 ibid., pp. 688–92.

137 Serle, *John Monash*, pp. 350–1.

138 Brisbane *Courier*, 17 August 1918.

139 Ballarat *Courier*, 23 August 1918; Brereton Greenhous, '"It was Chiefly a Canadian Battle": The Decision at Amiens, 8–11 August 1918', *Canadian Defence Quarterly*, 1988, pp. 73–80.

140 Elizabeth Greenhalgh, *Foch in Command: The Forging of a First World War General*, Cambridge: Cambridge University Press, 2011, pp. 423–5.

141 Serle, *John Monash*, p. 353; Greenhalgh, *Foch*, p. 426.

142 Doughty, *Pyrrhic Victory*, p. 480.

143 Rawlinson, quoted in Pedersen, *The Anzacs*, p. 385; Monash, quoted in Serle, *John Monash*, p. 353; Monash, *Australian Victories*, pp. 167–8.

144 Serle, *John Monash*, p. 354.

145 Peter Pedersen, 'The AIF on the Western Front: The Role of Training and Command', in M. McKernan and M. Browne (eds), *Australia: Two Centuries of War and Peace*, Canberra and Sydney: Australian War Memorial in association with Allen & Unwin, 1988, p. 190; Prior and Wilson, *Command*, pp. 344–5.

146 Peter Stanley, *Men of Mont St Quentin: Between Victory and Death*, Melbourne: Scribe, 2009, p. 81.

147 ibid., pp. 108, 120.

148 McMullin, *Pompey Elliott*, pp. 473–82; Coombes, *The Lionheart*, pp. 280–6.

149 Rawlinson, quoted in Monash, *Australian Victories*, p. 193; Stanley, *Men of Mont St Quentin*, pp. 141–5.

150 Bean, *Official History*, vol. VI, p. 873.

151 Stanley, *Men of Mont St Quentin*, pp. 252–3.

152 This account draws on Ashley Ekins, 'Fighting to Exhaustion: Morale, Discipline and Combat Effectiveness of the Armies of 1918', in Ekins, *1918 Year of Victory*, pp. 111–29.

153 ibid., pp. 114–15; Butler, *Official History*, vol. II, p. 708; Bean, *Official History*, vol. VI, p. 875.

154 McMullin, *Pompey Elliott*, p. 488; Pedersen, *Monash*, p. 278.

155 Bean, *Official History*, vol. VI, p. 875.

156 Pedersen, *The Anzacs*, p. 391.

157 Blair, *Dinkum Diggers*, pp. 157ff.

158 Pedersen, *The Anzacs*, p. 392. The battalions to be disbanded were the 19th, 21st, 25th, 29th, 37th, 42nd, 54th and 60th.

159 McMullin, *Pompey Elliott*, pp. 489–91.

160 Pedersen, *Monash*, p. 280.

161 Ekins, 'Fighting to Exhaustion', p. 199.

162 Estimate of six million: Wilson, *The Myriad Faces*, p. 600.

163 Pedersen, *Monash*, pp. 284–7.

164 Wilson, *The Myriad Faces*, p. 602. A useful account of this battle is to be found in Sadler, *The Paladin*, pp. 175–81.

165 Serle, *John Monash*, pp. 365–6. David Horner, *Blamey: The Commander-in-Chief*, Sydney: Allen & Unwin, 1998, p. 54.

166 Serle, *John Monash*, p. 366; Sadler, *The Paladin*, p. 181.

167 Bean, *Official History*, vol. VI, p. 1021; Coates, *An Atlas*, map 32b.

168 For details of AFC movements, see Coates, *An Atlas*, map 33.

169 The best accounts of Megiddo are Hill, *Chauvel*, pp. 153–73, and Bou, *Australia's Palestine Campaign*, pp. 103–28. For force numbers, see Coates, *An Atlas*, p. 106.

170 Bean, *Anzac to Amiens*, p. 503.

171 Bou, *Light Horse*, p. 194; Hill, *Chauvel*, p. 167.

172 Bean, *Anzac to Amiens*, p. 505.

173 ibid., p. 508.

174 'Before Damascus', *SMH*, 5 October 1918.

175 Hill, *Chauvel*, pp. 173, 171; Brisbane *Courier*, 5 October 1918.

176 Hill, *Chauvel*, p. 171; 'Before Damascus', *SMH*, 5 October 1918.

177 Lawrence, quoted in David Murphy, *The Arab Revolt, 1916–1918*, Oxford: Osprey, 2008, p. 77.

178 Hill's *Chauvel*, pp. 184–5, contains Chauvel's detailed notes of the meeting between Allenby and Feisal.

179 Wilson, *The Myriad Faces*, p. 604.

180 Meaney, *Australia*, pp. 287, 292.

181 Letter to Watt, 13 November 1918, quoted in Fitzhardinge, *William Morris Hughes*, vol. II, p. 357. For the Hughes–Lloyd George exchange, see Meaney, *Australia*, pp. 290ff.

182 Meaney, *Australia*, p. 291.

183 ibid., p. 292.

184 ibid.

185 Hughes, quoted in Fitzhardinge, *William Morris Hughes*, vol. II, p. 356.

186 *SMH*, 14 November 1918.

187 Fitzhardinge, *William Morris Hughes*, vol. II, p. 355; Leonie Foster, *High Hopes: The Men and Motives of the Australian Road Table*, Melbourne: Melbourne University Press, 1986, p. 84.

188 British papers, quoted in *West Australian*, 11 November 1918, *North Western Advocate and Emu Bay Times* (Tas.), 6 November 1918, and *SMH*, 9 November 1918.

189 *Sunday Times* (Perth), 17 November 1918; Fitzhardinge, *William Morris Hughes*, vol. II, p. 356.

190 *Queenslander*, 16 November 1918. For other criticisms, see *Mail* (Adelaide), 9 November 1918, *Courier* (Brisbane), 12 November 1918, *Examiner* (Launceston), 11 November 1918, *Register* (Adelaide), 14 November 1918, *Queenslander*, 16 November 1918, *Examiner* (Launceston), 11 November 1918.

191 *Barrier Miner*, 16 November 1918; *North Western Advocate and the Emu Bay Times*, 6 November 1918; Australia, Parliament, House of Representatives, *Debates*, 14 November 1918.

192 *North Western Advocate and the Emu Bay Times*, 6 November 1918.

193 Australia, Parliament, House of Representatives, *Debates*, 14 November 1918.

194 Fitzhardinge, *William Morris Hughes*, vol. II, pp. 358–9; Meaney, *Australia*, p. 297.

195 Finlayson and Fowler, members of House of Representatives, quoted in *Argus*, 16 November 1918, and *Courier* (Brisbane), 16 November 1918.

196 A.W. Jose, *The Official History of Australia in the War of 1914–1918*, vol. IX, *The Royal Australian Navy*, Angus & Robertson, 1928, pp. 330–1.

197 *West Australian*, 18 November 1918.

198 *SMH*, 13 November 1918; *Argus*, 14 November 1918; *Register*, 14 November 1918; *West Australian*, 13, 14 November 1918. For a full description of celebrations, see McKernan, *The Australian People*, pp. 201–7.

199 Evans, *Loyalty*, pp. 147–8.

200 Gammage, *The Broken Years*, p. 264–5; T.A. Miles, Diary, pp. 51–2, 2DRL/0054, AWM; R.N. Fry, Diary, 11 November 1918, 3DRL/0461, AWM; Peter Yule (ed.), *Sergeant Lawrence Goes to France*, Melbourne: Melbourne University Press, 1987, p. 182; Mitchell, *Backs to the Wall*, p. 318.

201 Bean, 'Sidelights of the War', p. 211; Allan R. Millett and Williamson Murray, *Military Effectiveness*, vol. I, *The First World War*, Sydney: Allen & Unwin, 1988, pp. 334–5.

202 For an example of such calculations, see Pedersen, 'The AIF on the Western Front', p. 192.

203 John Ellis and Michael Cox, *World War I Databook*, London: Arum Press, 2001, pp. 269–70.

Chapter 6

1 Peter Curson and Kevin McCracken, 'An Australian Perspective of the 1918–1919 Influenza Pandemic', *NSW Public Health Bulletin*, vol. 17, nos 7–8, n.d., pp. 103–4.

2 Scott, *Official History*, vol. XI, p. 825. There were some 15,000 men who returned home with a wife or fiancée (see Larsson, *Shattered Anzacs*, p. 86).

3 Fitzhardinge, *William Morris Hughes*, vol. II, pp. 351–2; Bourne, 'An Engineer at War', MSS1206, AWM; Scrivener, 29 November 1918, PR03563, AWM.

4 Serle, *John Monash*, p. 406; Connor, *Anzac and Empire*, p. 131.

5   Scott, *Official History*, vol. XI, pp. 825–8; Connor, *Anzac and Empire*, p. 132; Serle, *John Monash*, p. 411.

6   This account relies on Curson and McCrackern, 'An Australian Perspective', pp. 103–6.

7   Anthea Hyslop, 'Fever Hospital', in David Dunstan, *Victorian Icon: The Royal Exhibition Building, Melbourne*, Melbourne: Australian Scholarly Publishing, 1996, pp. 323–4.

8   Melanie Oppenheimer, '"Fated to a Life of Suffering": Graythwaite, the Australian Red Cross and Returned Soldiers, 1916–1919', in Martin Crotty and Marina Larsson (eds), *Anzac Legacies: Australians and the Aftermath of War*, Melbourne: Australian Scholarly Press, 2010, p. 21; Marilyn Lake, 'The Power of Anzac', in McKernan and Browne, *Australia*, pp. 197–202.

9   Clem Lloyd and Jacqui Rees, *The Last Shilling: A History of Repatriation in Australia*, Melbourne: Melbourne University Press, 1994, pp. 23–31; Lake, 'Power of Anzac', pp. 195–6; Scott, *Official History*, vol. XI, p. 838.

10   Lake, 'Power of Anzac', pp. 204–6; Martin Crotty, 'The Anzac Citizen: Towards a History of the RSL', *Australian Journal of Politics and History*, vol. 53, no. 2, 2007, p. 190, and Martin Crotty, 'The Returned Sailors' and Soldiers' Imperial League of Australia 1916–46', in Crotty and Larsson, *Anzac Legacies*, pp. 170–1.

11   Marina Larsson, '"The Part We Do Not See": Disabled Australian Soldiers and Family Caregiving After World War I', in Crotty and Larsson, *Anzac Legacies*, p. 40; Butler, *Official History*, vol. III, p. 963. See Lloyd and Rees, *Last Shilling*, pp. 19–41 for details of the evolution of the pensions scheme.

12   Lloyd and Rees, *Last Shilling*, pp. 141, 146, 151; George Johnston, *My Brother Jack*, first published 1964, Sydney: Angus & Robertson, 1990, p. 6.

13   For facial disfigurement see Neale, Reconstructed Lives.

14   See Michael Tyquin, *Madness and the Military: Australia's Experience of the Great War*, Sydney: Australian Military History Publications, 2006, Chs 5 and 6, for shellshock.

15   Larsson, '"The Part We Do Not See"', pp. 44, 41, 51–2; Larsson, *Shattered Anzacs*, pp. 79–80.

16   Johnston, *My Brother Jack*, pp. 6–7.

17   Larsson, '"The Part We Do Not See"', p. 41.

18   Lake, 'Power of Anzac', pp. 218–20.

19   Lloyd and Rees, *Last Shilling*, pp. 44–9; Lake, 'Power of Anzac', p. 200.

20   Lake, 'Power of Anzac', pp. 212–17. For a more detailed account of soldier settlement in Victoria, see Marilyn Lake, *The Limits of Hope: Soldier Settlement in Victoria 1915–38*, Melbourne: Oxford University Press, 1987. For New South Wales, see 'A Land Fit for Heroes: A History of Soldier Settlement in New South Wales, 1916–1939', <http://soldiersettlement.records.nsw.gov.au/index.php/about/>, viewed 20 April 2013.

21   Amery, quoted in Meaney, *Australia*, pp. 302–3.

22   See W.J. Hudson, *Billy Hughes in Paris: The Birth of Australian Diplomacy*, Melbourne: Nelson, 1978, pp. 8–9.

23 Meaney, *Australia*, p. 304.

24 Meaney, *Australia*, p. 400. See W.J. Hudson and M.P. Sharp, *Australian Independence: Colony to Reluctant Kingdom*, Melbourne: Melbourne University Press, 1988, for Australia's reluctance to embrace constitutional change.

25 Meaney, *Australia*, p. 340; Fitzhardinge, *William Morris Hughes*, vol. II, p. 370.

26 Osmond, *Frederic Eggleston*, p. 92.

27 Fitzhardinge, *William Morris Hughes*, vol. II, p. 370.

28 ibid., p. 373.

29 ibid., p. 388; Meaney, *Australia*, p. 348.

30 Fitzhardinge, *William Morris Hughes*, vol. II, pp. 388–9.

31 ibid.; Hudson, *Billy Hughes*, p. 21.

32 Fitzhardinge, *William Morris Hughes*, vol. II, p. 390.

33 Latham, quoted in Hudson, *Billy Hughes*, p. 24. For details of the three classes of mandates, see Meaney, *Australia*, pp. 350–1.

34 Fitzhardinge, *William Morris Hughes*, vol. II, p. 390.

35 Meaney, *Australia*, p. 351. Malcolm Booker, *The Great Professional: A Study of W.M. Hughes*, Sydney: McGraw Hill, 1980, p. 238; Fitzhardinge, *William Morris Hughes*, vol. II, pp. 391–2.

36 Meaney, *Australia*, p. 356.

37 Fitzhardinge, *William Morris Hughes*, vol. II, pp. 394–6.

38 ibid., p. 397; Osmond, *Frederic Eggleston*, p. 95.

39 For detail see Meaney, *Australia*, pp. 358–63; Hudson, *Billy Hughes*, pp. 30–1.

40 This accounts draws on Meaney, *Australia*, pp. 363–79, a definitive account of the issue, and Fitzhardinge, *William Morris Hughes*, vol. II, pp. 400–10; quote, p. 402.

41 Fitzhardinge, *William Morris Hughes*, vol. II, p. 405.

42 Makino, quoted in Meaney, *Australia*, p. 372.

43 ibid., p. 374.

44 ibid., pp. 375–7.

45 ibid., p. 379.

46 Unless otherwise stated this account draws on Meaney, *Australia*, pp. 379–91.

47 Fitzhardinge, *William Morris Hughes*, vol. II, pp. 380–2.

48 Meaney, *Australia*, p. 381.

49 ibid., p. 387.

50 ibid., p. 390.

51 Scott, *Official History*, vol. XI, p. 808; Fitzhardinge, *William Morris Hughes*, vol. II, p. 387.

52 Meaney, *Australia*, pp. 396–7.

53 Hughes, quoted ibid., pp. 397, 399.

54 Michael Howard, *The Causes of War*, Cambridge: Cambridge University Press, 1984, p. 19.

55 Audoin-Rouzeau and Becker, *14–18*, p. 10.

56   Australian Bureau of Statistics, *Reflecting a Nation: Stories from the 2011 Census*, 2012–
      2013, <www.abs.gov.au/ausstats/abs@.nsf/Lookup/2071.0main+features952012–2013>,
      viewed 20 April 2013.

57   Manning Clark, *A Short History of Australia*, first published 1963, Melbourne: Penguin,
      2006, p. 255.

58   See A.W. Martin, *Robert Menzies: A Life*, vol. 1, *1894–1943*, Melbourne: Melbourne
      University Press, 1993, pp. 274–8.

59   See Fischer, *Enemy Aliens*, Ch. 15.

60   ibid., pp. 306–7.

61   See Raymond Evans, '"Agitation, Ceaseless Agitation": Russian Radicals in Australia and
      the Red Flag Riots', in John McNair and Thomas Poole, *Russia and the Fifth Continent:
      Aspects of Russian–Australian Relations*, Brisbane: University of Queensland Press, 1992,
      pp. 126–71, and Raymond Evans, '"Some Furious Outbursts of Riots": Returned Soldiers
      and Queensland's "Red Flag" Disturbances, 1918–19', *War & Society*, vol. 3, no. 2, 1985,
      pp. 75–98. For the secret armies, see Andrew Moore, 'Guns Across the Yarra: Secret
      Armies and the 1923 Melbourne Police Strike', in Sydney Labour Group (ed.), *What
      Rough Beast? The State and Social Order in Australian History*, Sydney: George Allen &
      Unwin, 1982, pp. 220–33; Andrew Moore, *The Secret Army and the Premier: Conservative
      Paramilitary Organisations in New South Wales 1930–32*, UNSW Press, 1989; Michael
      Cathcart, *Defending the National Tuckshop: Australia's Secret Army Intrigue of 1931*,
      Melbourne: McPhee Gribble, 1988. For Australian intervention in Russia, see Jeffrey
      Grey, 'A Pathetic Sideshow: Australians and the Russian Intervention 1918–1919', *Journal
      of the Australian War Memorial*, no. 7, 1985, pp. 12–17; Peter Burness, 'The Australians in
      North Russia 1919', *Sabretache*, vol. XXII, no. 4, 1976, and Peter Burness, 'The Forgotten
      War in North Russia', *Defence Force Journal*, vol. 22, 1980, pp. 31–41.

62   See Rob Watts, *The Foundations of the National Welfare State*, Sydney: Allen & Unwin,
      1987, pp. 2–7, for further discussion of this issue.

63   For a discussion of the evolution of the Anzac legend, see Joan Beaumont, 'The Anzac
      Legend', in Joan Beaumont (ed.), *Australia's War 1914–18*, Sydney: Allen & Unwin,
      1995, pp. 149–80.

64   For further discussion, see Joan Beaumont, 'Prisoners of War in Australian National
      Memory', in Bob Moore and Barbara Hately-Broad, *Prisoners of War: Prisoners of Peace*,
      Oxford: Berg, 2005, pp. 185–94.

65   Inglis, *Sacred Places*, p. 9.

66   *Sunday Herald Sun*, 26 April 2009. This argument is developed more fully in Joan
      Beaumont, '*Nation* oder *Commonwealth?*', pp. 43–68.

67   For public opinion and Iraq, see Murray Goot, 'Public Opinion and the Democratic
      Deficit: Australia and the War Against Iraq', *Australian Humanities Review*, issue 29, May
      2003. For the positioning of Iraq and Afghanistan in the Anzac lineage, see 'For Freedom's
      Flame', by Rupert McCall, read at the 2009 Anzac Day ceremony at the Melbourne Shrine
      of Remembrance. For Howard, see Mark McKenna, 'Howard's Warriors', in Raimond
      Gaita (ed.), *Why the War was Wrong*, Melbourne: Text, 2003, p. 184.

BIBLIOGRAPHY

Primary sources

Research for this book has primarily drawn on archives of the Australian War Memorial, the National Library of Australia, the National Archives of Australia and the Noel Butlin Archives Centre at the Australian National University. Details of primary sources are cited in endnotes. The surviving footage of *The Heroes of the Dardanelles* was viewed at the National Film and Sound Archive, Canberra. Every reasonable effort has been made to secure permission for the use of private records.

Secondary sources

Adam-Smith, Patsy, *The Anzacs*, Melbourne: Nelson, 1978.

Andrews, E.M., '25 April 1916: The First Anzac Day in Australia and Britain', *Journal of the Australian War Memorial*, no. 23, 1993, pp. 13–20.

——'Bean and Bullecourt: Weaknesses and Strengths of the Official History of Australia in the First World War', *Revue Internationale d'Histoire Militaire*, 1972, pp. 25–47.

——*The Anzac Illusion: Anglo-Australian Relations During World War I*, Melbourne: Cambridge University Press, 1993.

Andrews, Eric and Jordan, B.J., 'Hamel: Winning a Battle', *Journal of the Australian War Memorial*, no. 18, 1991, pp. 5–12.

Audoin-Rouzeau, Stéphane and Becker, Annette, *14–18: Understanding the Great War*, New York: Hill and Wang, 2002.

Baker, Chris, *The Battle for Flanders: German Defeat on the Lys 1918*, Barnsley, South Yorkshire: Pen & Sword Military, 2011.

Baldock, Cora V., 'Public Policies and the Paid Work of Women', in Cora V. Baldock and Bettina Cass (eds), *Women, Social Welfare and the State*, Sydney: George Allen & Unwin, 1983.

Bassett, Jan, *Guns and Brooches: Australian Army Nursing from the Boer War to the Gulf War*, Melbourne: Oxford University Press, 1992.

——'"Ready to serve": Australian Women and the Great War', *Journal of the Australian War Memorial*, no. 2, 1983, pp. 8–16.

Bastian, Peter, 'The 1916 Conscription Referendum', *Teaching History*, June 1971, pp. 25–36.

Bavin, T.R. and Evatt, H.V., 'Price-Fixing in Australia During the War', *Journal of Comparative Legislation and International Law*, 3rd series, vol. III, London: Society of Comparative Legislation, 1921, pp. 202–12.

Bean, C.E.W., *Anzac to Amiens: A Shorter History of the Australian Fighting Services in the First World War*, Canberra: Australian War Memorial, 1946.

—— *The Official History of Australia in the War of 1914–1918*, vol. I, *The Story of Anzac: From the Outbreak of War to the End of the First Phase of the Gallipoli Campaign, May 4, 1915*, Sydney: Angus & Robertson, 1921.

—— *The Official History of Australia in the War of 1914–1918*, vol. II, *The Story of Anzac: From 4 May, 1915, to the Evacuation of the Gallipoli Peninsula*, Sydney: Angus & Robertson, 1924.

—— *The Official History of Australia in the War of 1914–1918*, vol. III, *The Australian Imperial Force in France, 1916*, Sydney: Angus & Robertson, 1929.

—— *The Official History of Australia in the War of 1914–1918*, vol. IV, *The Australian Imperial Force in France 1917*, Sydney: Angus & Robertson, 1933.

—— *The Official History of Australia in the War of 1914–1918*, vol. V, *The Australian Imperial Force in France during the Main German Offensive, 1918*, Sydney: Angus & Robertson, 1937.

—— *The Official History of Australia in the War of 1914–1918*, vol. VI, *The Australian Imperial Force in France During the Allied Offensive, 1918*, Sydney: Angus & Robertson, 1942.

—— 'Sidelights of the War on the Australian Character', *Journal of the Royal Australian Historical Society*, vol. XIII, pt 4, 1927, pp. 209–23.

—— *Two Men I Knew: William Bridges and Brudenell White, Founders of the A.I.F.*, Sydney: Angus & Robertson, 1957.

Beaumont, Joan (ed.), *Australia's War 1914–18*, Sydney: Allen & Unwin, 1995.

——'Rank, Privilege and Prisoners of War', *War & Society*, vol. 1, no. 1, 1983.

——'Whatever Happened to Patriotic Women, 1914–1918?', *Australian Historical Studies*, vol. 31, no. 115, 2000, pp. 273–86.

Bennett, Scott, *Pozières: The Anzac Story*, Melbourne: Scribe, 2011.

Bertrand, Ina, 'The Victorian Country Vote in the Conscription Referendums of 1916 and 1917: The Case of the Wannon Electorate', *Labour History*, no. 26, 1974, pp. 19–31.

BIBLIOGRAPHY

Blair, Dale, *Dinkum Diggers: An Australian Battalion at War*, Melbourne: Melbourne University Press, 2001.

Bollard, Robert, '"The Active Chorus": The Great Strike of 1917 in Victoria', *Labour History*, vol. 90, 2006, pp. 77–94.

——'How to Create a Tradition: The Seamen's Union and the Great Strike of 1917', *The History Cooperative Conference Proceedings*, <www.historycooperative.org/proceedings/asslh2/bollard.html>, viewed 20 March 2013.

——'Victorian Workers in the 1917 Mass Strike', *Marxist Interventions*, <www.anu.edu.au/polsci/marx/interventions/1917strike.htm>, viewed 20 March 2013.

Booker, Malcolm, *The Great Professional: A Study of W.M. Hughes*, Sydney: McGraw Hill, 1980.

Bou, Jean, *Australia's Palestine Campaign*, Canberra: Army History Unit, 2010.

——*Light Horse: A History of Australia's Mounted Arm*, Melbourne: Cambridge University Press, 2010.

Bourke, Joanna, *Dismembering the Male: Men's Bodies, Britain and the Great War*, Chicago: Chicago University Press, 1996.

——'"Swinging the Lead": Malingering Australian Soldiers and the Great War', *Journal of the Australian War Memorial*, no. 26, 1995, pp. 10–18.

Bourne, John, 'Charles Monro', in Ian F.W. Beckett and Steven J. Corvi (eds), *Haig's Generals*, Barnsley: Pen & Sword Military, 2006, pp. 122–40.

Bowden, Samuel H. (ed.), *The History of the Australian Comforts Fund*, n.p., 1922.

Braga, Stuart, *Anzac Doctor: The Life of Sir Neville Howse, VC*, Sydney: Hale & Iremonger, 2000.

Brenchley, Fred and Brenchley, Elizabeth, *Myth Maker: Ellis Ashmead-Bartlett: The Englishman Who Sparked Australia's Gallipoli Legend*, Brisbane: John Wiley & Sons, 2005.

Brennan, Frank, *The Australian Commonwealth Shipping Line*, Canberra: Roebuck Books, 1978.

Brugger, Suzanne, *Australians and Egypt: 1914–1919*, Melbourne: Melbourne University Press, 1980.

Burness, Peter, 'The Australians in North Russia', *Sabretache*, vol. XII, no. 4, 1976, pp. 266–79.

——'The Forgotten War in North Russia', *Defence Force Journal*, no. 22, 1980, pp. 31–41.

——*The Nek: A Gallipoli Tragedy*, Titirangi, New Zealand: Exisle, 2012.

Butler, A.G., *The Official History of the Australian Army Medical Services in the War of 1914–1918*, vol. I, *Gallipoli, Palestine and New Guinea*, Melbourne: Australian War Memorial, 2nd edn, 1938.

——*The Official History of the Australian Army Medical Services in the War of 1914–1918*, vol. II, *The Western Front*, Canberra: Australian War Memorial, 1940.

——*The Official History of the Australian Army Medical Services, 1914–1918*, vol. III, *Special Problems and Services*, Canberra: Australian War Memorial, 1943.

Caesar, Adrian, '"Kitsch" and Imperialism: *The Anzac Book* Re-Visited', *Westerly*, vol. 40, no. 4, 1995, pp. 76–85.

Cain, Frank, 'The Industrial Workers of the World: Aspects of its Suppression in Australia 1916–1919', *Labour History*, vol. 42, 1982, pp. 54–62.

——*The Wobblies at War: A History of the IWW and the Great War in Australia*, Melbourne: Spectrum, 1993.

Carlyon, Les, *Gallipoli*, Sydney: Pan Macmillan, 2001.

——*The Great War*, Sydney: Pan Macmillan, 2006.

Carsten, F.L. *War Against War: British and German Radical Movements in the First World War*, London: Batsford, 1982.

Carthew, Noel, *Voices from the Trenches: Letters to Home*, Sydney: New Holland, 2002.

Charlton, Peter, *Pozières: Australians on the Somme, 1916*, Sydney: Methuen, 1986.

Chickering, Roger, *Imperial Germany and the Great War, 1914–1918*, Cambridge: Cambridge University Press, 1998.

Clark, Alan, *The Donkeys*, London: Hutchison, 1961.

Clark, Manning, *A Short History of Australia*, first published 1963, Ringwood: Penguin, 2006.

Coates, John, *An Atlas of Australia's Wars*, Melbourne: Oxford University Press, 2001.

Cobb, Paul, *Fromelles 1916*, Stroud, Gloucestershire: Tempus, 2007.

Cochrane, Peter, *Simpson and the Donkey: The Making of a Legend*, Melbourne: Melbourne University Press, 1992.

Connor, John, *Anzac and Empire: George Foster Pearce and the Foundations of Australian Defence*, Melbourne: Cambridge University Press, 2011.

Coombes, David, *Crossing the Wire: The Untold Stories of Australian POWs in Battle and Captivity During WWI*, Sydney: Big Sky Publishing, 2011.

——*Morshead: Hero of Tobruk and El Alamein*, Melbourne: Oxford University Press, 2001.

——*The Lionheart: Lieutenant-General Sir Talbot Hobbs*, Sydney: Australian Military History Publications, 2007.

Coulthard-Clark, C.D., *A Heritage of Spirit: A Biography of Major-General Sir William Throsby Bridges K.C.B., C.M.G.*, Melbourne: Melbourne University Press, 1979.

——*No Australian Need Apply: The Troubled Career of Lieutenant-General Gordon Legge*, Sydney: George Allen & Unwin, 1988.

Crawley, Rhys, 'Our Second Great [Mis]adventure': A Critical Re-evaluation of the August Offensive, Gallipoli, 1915, PhD thesis, University of New South Wales, Australian Defence Force Academy, 2010.

——'Supplying the offensive: the role of Allied logistics', in Ashley Ekins (ed.), *Gallipoli: A Ridge Too Far*, Wollombi: Exisle, 2013, pp. 252–71.

Crew, Jennifer, 'Women's Wages in Britain and Australia During the First World War', *Labour History*, no. 57, 1989, pp. 27–43.

Crotty, Martin, 'The Anzac Citizen: Towards a History of the RSL', *Australian Journal of Politics and History*, vol. 53, no. 2, 2007, pp. 183–93.

——'The Returned Sailors' and Soldiers' Imperial League of Australia 1916–46', in Martin Crotty and Marina Larsson (eds), *Anzac Legacies*, Melbourne: Australian Scholarly Publishing, 2010, pp. 166–86.

Curson, Peter and McCracken, Kevin, 'An Australian Perspective of the 1918–1919 Influenza Pandemic', *NSW Public Health Bulletin*, vol. 17, nos 7–8, 2006, pp. 103–7.

Cutlack, F.M., *War Letters of General Monash*, Sydney: Angus & Robertson, 1934.

Daley, Paul, *Beersheba: A Journey through Australia's Forgotten War*, Melbourne: Melbourne University Press, 2009.

Damousi, Joy, 'Socialist Women and Gendered Space: Anti-conscription and Anti-war Campaigns 1915–18', in Joy Damousi and Marilyn Lake (eds), *Gender and War: Australians at War in the Twentieth Century*, Melbourne: Cambridge University Press, 1995, pp. 254–73.

——*Women Come Rally: Socialism, Communism and Gender in Australia 1890–1955*, Melbourne: Oxford University Press, 1994.

Damousi, Joy and Lake, Marilyn (eds), *Gender and War: Australians at War in the Twentieth Century*, Melbourne: Cambridge University Press, 1995.

Davies, Will, *Beneath Hill 60*, Sydney: Vintage Books, 2010.

Dawes, J.N.I. and Robson, L.L., *Citizen to Soldier: Australia Before the Great War: Recollections of Members of the First A.I.F.*, Melbourne: Melbourne University Press, 1977.

Day, David, A*ndrew Fisher: Prime Minister of Australia*, Sydney: Harper Collins, 2008.

Deayton, Craig, *Battle Scarred: The 47th Battalion in the First World War*, Sydney: Big Sky Publishing, 2011.

Doughty, Robert A., *Pyrrhic Victory: French Strategy and Operations in the Great War*, Cambridge, MA: Belknap Press, 2005.

Downing, W.H., *To the Last Ridge*, first published 1920, Sydney: Duffy and Snellgrove, 1998.

East, Sir Ronald (ed.), *The Gallipoli Diary of Sergeant Lawrence of the Australian Engineers— 1st A.I.F., 1915*, Melbourne: Melbourne University Press, 1981.

Edgar, Peter, *Sir William Glasgow: Soldier, Senator and Diplomat*, Sydney: Big Sky Publishing, 2011.

——*To Villers-Bretonneux with Brigadier-General William Glasgow, DSO and the 13th Australian Infantry Brigade*, Sydney: Australian Military History Publications, 2006.

Ekins, Ashley, (ed.), *Gallipoli: A Ridge Too Far*, Wollombi: Exisle, 2013.

——'A "Precious Souvenir": The Making of *The Anzac Book*', in *The Anzac Book*, Sydney: UNSW Press, 2010.

——'Fighting to Exhaustion: Morale, Discipline and Combat Effectiveness of the Armies of 1918', in Ashley Ekins (ed.), *1918 Year of Victory: The End of the Great War and the Shaping of History*, Titirangi, New Zealand: Exisle, 2010, pp. 111–29.

Ellis, A.D., *The Story of the Fifth Australian Division*, London: Hodder & Stoughton, 1920.

Ely, R., 'The First Anzac Day: Invented or Discovered?' *Journal of Australian Studies*, no. 17, 1985, pp. 41–58.

Evans, Raymond, '"Agitation, Ceaseless Agitation": Russian Radicals in Australia and the Red Flag Riots', in John McNair and Thomas Poole (eds), *Russia and the Fifth Continent: Aspects of Russian–Australian Relations*, Brisbane: Queensland University Press, 1992, pp. 126–71.

——'"All the Passion of Our Womanhood": Margaret Thorp and the Battle of the Brisbane School of Arts', in Joy Damousi and Marilyn Lake (eds), *Gender and War: Australians at War in the Twentieth Century*, Melbourne: Cambridge University Press, 1995, pp. 239–53.

——*Loyalty and Disloyalty: Social Conflict on the Queensland Homefront 1914–18*, Sydney: Allen & Unwin, 1987.

——'"Some Furious Outbursts of Riots": Returned Soldiers and Queensland's "Red Flag" Disturbances, 1918–19', *War & Society*, vol. 3, no. 2, 1985, pp. 75–98.

Facey, A.B., *A Fortunate Life*, first published 1981, Camberwell: Penguin, 1985.

Farrar-Hockley, Anthony, *Goughie: The Life of General Sir Hubert Gough, CGB, GCMG, KCVO*, London: Hart-Davis, MacGibbon, 1975.

Ferguson, Niall, *The Pity of War*, first published 1998, Harmondsworth: Penguin, 1999.

Fewster, Kevin, 'Ellis Ashmead-Bartlett and the Making of the Anzac Legend', *Journal of Australian Studies*, no. 10, 1982, pp. 17–30.

——(ed.), *Gallipoli Correspondent: The Frontline Diary of C.E.W. Bean*, Sydney: George Allen & Unwin, 1983.

——'The Operation of State Apparatuses in Times of Crisis: Censorship and Conscription, 1916', *War & Society*, vol. 3, no. 1, pp. 37–54.

Fischer, Gerhard, *Enemy Aliens: Internment and the Homefront Experience in Australia 1914–1920*, Brisbane: University of Queensland Press, 1989.

Fitzhardinge, L.F., *William Morris Hughes: A Political Biography*, vol. II, *The Little Digger 1914–1953*, London: Angus & Robertson, 1979.

Foster, Leonie, *High Hopes: The Men and Motives of the Australian Road Table*, Melbourne: Melbourne University Press, 1986.

Frame, Tom, *The Shores of Gallipoli: Naval Aspects of the Anzac Campaign*, Sydney: Hale & Iremonger, 2000.

French, David, 'The Origins of the Dardanelles Campaign Reconsidered', *History*, vol. 68, 1983, pp. 210–24.

Fuller, J.G., *Troop Morale and Popular Culture in British and Dominion Armies 1914–1918*, Oxford: Clarendon Press, 1990.

Fussell, Paul, *The Great War and Modern Memory*, London: Oxford University Press, 1975.

Gammage, Bill, *The Broken Years: Australian Soldiers in the Great War*, first published 1974, Harmondsworth: Penguin, 1975.

Gibson, P.M., 'The Conscription Issue in South Australia, 1916–1917', *University Studies in History*, vol. IV, no. 3, 1963–64, pp. 47–80.

Gilbert, Alan D., 'The Conscription Referenda, 1916–17: The Impact of the Irish Crisis', *Historical Studies*, vol. 14, no. 53, 1969, pp. 54–72.

Gough, Hubert, *The Fifth Army*, London: Hodder & Stoughton, 1931.

Greenhalgh, Elizabeth, *Foch in Command: The Forging of a First World War General*, Cambridge: Cambridge University Press, 2011.

Greenhous, Brereton, '"It was Chiefly a Canadian Battle": The Decision at Amiens, 8–11 August 1918', *Canadian Defence Force Quarterly*, 1988, pp. 73–80.

Gregory, Adrian, 'British "War Enthusiasm" in 1914: A Reassessment', in Gail Braybon (ed.), *Evidence, History and the Great War*, New York: Berghahn, 2003, pp. 67–85.

Grey, Jeffrey, *A Military History of Australia*, Cambridge: Cambridge University Press, 1990.

——'A "Pathetic Sideshow": Australians and the Russian Intervention 1918–19', *Journal of the Australian War Memorial*, no. 7, 1985, pp. 12–17.

Griffith, Paddy, *Battle Tactics of the Western Front: The British Army's Art of Attack 1916–18*, New Haven, CT: Yale University Press, 1994.

Gullett, H.S., *The Official History of Australia in the War of 1914–1918*, vol. VII, *The Australian Imperial Force in Sinai and Palestine, 1914–1918*, Sydney: Angus & Robertson, 1937.

Haddow, Janine, 'Avenues of Honour: A Victorian Cultural Landscape', *Landscape Australia*, vol. 3, 1988, pp. 306–9.

Haig-Muir, Marnie, 'The economy at war' in Joan Beaumont (ed.), *Australia's War, 1914–18*, Sydney: Allen & Unwin, 1995, pp. 93–124.

Harris, Kirsty, *More than Bombs and Bandages: Australian Army Nurses at Work in World War I*, Sydney: Big Sky Publishing, 2011.

Harris, J.P., *Douglas Haig and the First World War*, Cambridge: Cambridge University Press, 2008.

Haynes, Jim (ed.), *Cobbers: Stories of Gallipoli 1915*, Sydney: ABC Books, 2005.

Hill, A.J., *Chauvel of the Light Horse*, Melbourne: Melbourne University Press, 1978.

Holmes, Richard, *The Western Front*, London: BBC Books, 1999.

Horne, John and Kramer, Alan, *German Atrocities, 1914: A History of Denial*, New Haven, CT: Yale University Press, 2001.

Horner, David, *Australia's Military History for Dummies*, Milton: Wiley Publishing, 2010.

——*Blamey: The Commander-in-Chief*, Sydney: Allen & Unwin, 1998.

——*The Gunners: A History of Australian Artillery*, Sydney: Allen & Unwin, 1995.

Hudson, W.J., *Billy Hughes in Paris: The Birth of Australian Diplomacy*, Melbourne: Nelson, 1978.

Hudson W.J. and Sharp, M.P., *Australian Independence: Colony to Reluctant Kingdom*, Melbourne: Melbourne University Press, 1988.

Hughes, W.M., *'The Day'—And After: War Speeches of the Rt. Hon. W.M. Hughes*, London: Cassell, 1916.

Hurst, James, *Game to the Last: The 11th Australian Infantry Battalion at Gallipoli*, 2nd edn, Newport: Big Sky Publishing, 2011.

Hutchinson, John F., *Champions of Charity: War and the Rise of the Red Cross*, Boulder, CO: Westview Press, 1996.

Hyslop, Anthea, 'Fever Hospital', in David Dunstan, *Victorian Icon: The Royal Exhibition Building, Melbourne*, Melbourne: Australian Scholarly Publishing, 1996, pp. 302–7.

Imlay, N.G., 'Without Loss', *Reveille*, 1 June 1935, pp. 6–7.

Inglis, K.S., 'Anzac and the Australian Military Tradition', *Revue Internationale d'Histoire*, no. 72, 1990, pp. 1–24.

——*Sacred Places: War Memorials in the Australian Landscape*, Melbourne: Miegunyah Press, 1998.

Jauncey, Leslie C., *The Story of Conscription in Australia*, London: George Allen & Unwin, 1935.

Johnston, George, *My Brother Jack*, first published 1964, Sydney: Angus & Robertson, 1990.

Jones, Ian, *The Australian Light Horse*, Sydney: Time-Life Books, 1987.

Jordens, Ann-Mari, 'Anti-war Organisations in a Society at War, 1914–18', *Journal of Australian Studies*, no. 26, 1990, pp. 80–93.

Jose, A.W., *The Official History of Australia in the War of 1914–1918*, vol. IX, *The Royal Australian Navy*, Sydney: Angus & Robertson, 1928.

Kendall, Paul, *Bullecourt 1917: Breaching the Hindenburg Line*, Stroud: Spellmount, 2010.

Kent, David, '*The Anzac Book* and the Anzac Legend: C.E.W. Bean as editor and image-maker', *Historical Studies*, vol. 21, no. 84, 1985, pp. 376–90.

Knowles, Bert, 'Bullecourt Tragedy: Retrospect', *Reveille*, 30 April 1931, pp. 15–16.

Knyvett, R. Hugh, *'Over There' with the Australians*, London: Hodder and Stoughton, 1918.

Lake, Marilyn, *The Limits of Hope: Soldier Settlement in Victoria 1915–38*, Melbourne: Oxford University Press, 1987.

——'The power of Anzac', in M. McKernan and M. Browne (eds), *Australia: Two Centuries of War and Peace*, Canberra and Sydney: Australian War Memorial and Allen & Unwin, 1988, pp. 194–222.

Lake, Marilyn and Reynolds, Henry (eds), *What's Wrong with Anzac? The Militarisation of Australian History*, Sydney: UNSW Press, 2010.

Larsson, Marina, *Shattered Anzacs: Living with the Scars of War*, Sydney: UNSW Press, 2009.

——'"The Part We Do Not See": Disabled Australian Soldiers and Family Caregiving After World War I', in Martin Crotty and Marina Larsson (eds), *Anzac Legacies: Australians and the Aftermath of War*, Melbourne: Australian Scholarly Publishing, 2010, pp. 39–60.

Lee, John, 'William Birdwood', in Ian F.W. Beckett and Steven J. Corvi, *Haig's Generals*, Barnsley: Pen & Sword Military, 2006, pp. 33–53.

Lee, Roger, *The Battle of Fromelles, 1916*, Canberra: Army History Unit, 2010.

Leed, Eric, *No Man's Land: Combat and Identity in World War I*, Cambridge: Cambridge University Press, 1979.

BIBLIOGRAPHY

Lindsay, Patrick, *Fromelles*, Melbourne: Hardie Grant Books, 2008.

Lloyd, Clem and Rees, Jacqui, *The Last Shilling: A History of Repatriation in Australia*, Melbourne: Melbourne University Press, 1994.

Lloyd George, David, *War Memoirs of David Lloyd George*, vol. 1, London: Nicholson & Watson, 1933.

Longworth, Philip, *The Unending Vigil: The History of the Commonwealth War Graves Commission*, first published 1967, 2nd edn, 1985.

Lowenthal, David, *The Past is a Foreign Country*, Cambridge: Cambridge University Press, 1985.

Luckins, Tanja, *The Gates of Memory: Australian People's Experiences and Memories of Loss and the Great War*, Fremantle: Curtin University Books, 2004.

Lynch, E.P.F., *Somme Mud: The War Experiences of an Australian Infantryman in France 1916–1919*, Sydney: Random House, 2006.

McDowall, Max, 'Bullecourt Tragedy', *Reveille*, 1 May 1935, p. 32.

Macintyre, Stuart, *The Oxford History of Australia*, vol. 4, *1901–1942,* Melbourne: Oxford University Press, 1986.

Mackenzie, S.S., *The Official History of Australia in the War of 1914–1918*, vol. X, *The Australians at Rabaul*, Sydney: Angus & Robertson, 1927.

McKernan, Michael, *Australian Churches at War: Attitudes and Activities of the Major Churches 1914–1918*, Sydney and Canberra: Catholic Theological Faculty and Australian War Memorial, 1980.

——*The Australian People and the Great War*, first published 1980, Sydney: Collins, 1984.

McMullin, Ross, *Farewell Dear People: Biographies of Australia's Lost Generation*, Melbourne: Scribe, 2012.

——*Pompey Elliott*, first published 2002, 2nd edn, Melbourne: Scribe, 2008.

——*The Light on the Hill: The Australian Labor Party 1891–1991*, first published 1991, 2nd edn, Melbourne: Oxford University Press, 1992.

McQuilton, John, 'Gallipoli and Contested Commemorative Space', in Jenny McLeod (ed.), *Gallipoli: Making History*, London: Frank Cass, 2004.

——*Rural Australia and the Great War: From Tarrawingee to Tangambalanga*, Melbourne: Melbourne University Press, 2001.

Martin, A.W., *Robert Menzies: A Life,* vol. 1, *1894–1943*, Melbourne: Melbourne University Press, 1993.

Meade, Kevin, *Heroes Before Gallipoli: Bita Paka and That One Day in September*, Brisbane: John Wiley & Sons, 2005.

Meaney, Neville, *Australia and World Crisis, 1914–1923*, Sydney: Sydney University Press, 2009.

——*A History of Australian Defence and Foreign Policy, 1901–23*, vol. I, *The Search for Security in the Pacific 1901–14*, Sydney: Sydney University Press, 1976.

Merrett, D.T., '"The School at War", Scotch College and the Great War', in Stephen Murray-Smith (ed.), *Melbourne Studies in Education*, Melbourne: Melbourne University Press, 1983, pp. 209–30.

Meyer, G.J., *A World Undone: The Story of the Great War 1914 to 1918*, New York: Batman Dell, 2006.

Millett, Allan R. and Murray, Williamson, *Military Effectiveness*, vol. I, *The First World War*, Boston: Allen & Unwin, 1988.

Mitchell, G.D., *Backs to the Wall: A Larrikin on the Western Front*, first published 1937, Sydney: Allen & Unwin, 2007.

——'The Winter of 1916–17', *Reveille*, 1 December 1934, pp. 15, 62, back cover; 1 January 1935, pp. 13, 30–1; 1 February 1935, pp. 12–13; 1 March 1935, pp. 13, 30; 1 May 1935, pp. 12–13; 1 June 1935, pp. 12–13, 19.

Mombauer, Annika, *Helmuth von Moltke and the Origins of the First World War*, Cambridge: Cambridge University Press, 2001.

Monash, John, *The Australian Victories in France in 1918*, London: Hutchinson, 1920.

Montague, Charles, *Disenchantment*, London: Chatto & Windus, 1924.

Moore, Andrew, 'Guns Across the Yarra: Secret Armies and the 1923 Melbourne Police Strike', in Sydney Labour Group, *What Rough Beast: The State and Social Order in Australian History*, Sydney: George Allen & Unwin, 1982, pp. 220–33.

——*The Secret Army and the Premier: Conservative Paramilitary Organisations in New South Wales 1930–32*, Sydney: UNSW Press, 1989.

Mordike, John, *An Army for a Nation: A History of Australian Military Developments 1880–1914*, Sydney: Allen & Unwin, 1992.

Murphy, D.J., 'Queensland', in D.J. Murphy (ed.), *Labor in Politics: The State Labor Parties in Australia, 1880–1920*, Brisbane: University of Queensland Press, 1975.

Murphy, David, *The Arab Revolt, 1916–1918*, Oxford: Osprey, 2008.

Murray-Smith, Stephen, 'On the Conscription Trail: The Second Referendum Seen from Beside W.M. Hughes', *Labour History*, no. 33, 1977, pp. 98–104.

Neale, Kerry, Reconstructed Lives: The Experiences of Facially Disfigured Australian Veterans of the Great War, Honours thesis, Australian National University, 2007.

O'Farrell, Patrick, *The Catholic Church and Community: An Australian History*, Sydney: UNSW Press, 1985.

Oliver, Bobbie, *War and Peace in Western Australia: The Social and Political Impact of the Great War 1914–1926*, Nedlands: University of Western Australia Press, 1995.

Oppenheimer, Melanie, 'Alleviating Distress: The Lord Mayor's Patriotic Fund in New South Wales, 1914–1920', *Journal of the Royal Australian Historical Society*, vol. 81, pt. 1, 1995, pp. 85–98.

——'"Fated to a Life of Suffering": Graythwaite, the Australian Red Cross and Returned Soldiers, 1916–1919', in Martin Crotty and Marina Larsson (eds), *Anzac Legacies: Australians and the Aftermath of War*, Melbourne: Australian Scholarly Publishing, 2010, pp. 18–38.

BIBLIOGRAPHY

——*Red Cross VADs: A History of the VAD Movement in New South Wales*, Sydney: Ohio Productions, 1999.

——'"The Best P.M. for the Empire in War?": Lady Helen Munro Ferguson and the Australian Red Cross Society, 1914–1920', *Australian Historical Studies*, vol. 33, no. 119, 2002, pp. 108–24.

Osmond, Warren G., *Frederic Eggleston: An Intellectual in Australian Politics*, Sydney: Allen & Unwin, 1985.

Palazzo, Albert, *The Australian Army: A History of its Organisation 1901–2001*, Melbourne: Oxford University Press, 2001.

Pearson, A.R., 'Western Australia and the Conscription Plebiscites of 1916 and 1917', *RMC Historical Journal*, vol. 3, 1974, pp. 21–6.

Pedersen, Peter, 'Maintaining the Advance: Monash, Battle Procedure and the Australian Corps in 1918', in Ashley Ekins (ed.), *1918 Year of Victory: The End of the Great War and the Shaping of History*, Titirangi, New Zealand: Exisle, 2010, pp. 130–45.

——*Monash as Military Commander*, Melbourne: Melbourne University Press, 1985.

——'The AIF on the Western Front: The Role of Training and Command', in M. McKernan and M. Browne (eds), *Australia: Two Centuries of War and Peace*, Canberra and Sydney: Australian War Memorial and Allen & Unwin, 1988, pp. 167–93.

——*The Anzacs: Gallipoli to the Western Front*, Camberwell, Vic.: Viking, 2007.

Phillips, Walter, 'Six O'Clock Swill: The Introduction of Early Closing of Hotel Bars in Australia', *Historical Studies*, vol. 19, no. 75, 1980, pp. 250–66.

Powley, Guy, *The New Zealanders in Sinai and Palestine*, Auckland: Whitcombe and Tombs, 1922.

Prior, Robin, *Gallipoli: The End of the Myth*, Sydney: UNSW Press, 2009.

——'The Suvla Bay Tea-party: A Reassessment', *Journal of the Australian War Memorial*, no. 7, 1985, pp. 25–34.

Prior, Robin and Wilson, Trevor, *Command on the Western Front: The Military Career of Sir Henry Rawlinson*, Oxford: Blackwell, 1992.

——*Passchendaele: The Untold Story*, 2nd edn, New Haven, CT: Yale Nota Bene, 2002.

——*The Somme*, New Haven, CT: Yale University Press, 2005.

Pugsley, Christopher, *The Anzac Experience: New Zealand, Australia and Empire in the First World War*, Auckland: Reed, 2004.

Rees, Peter, *The Other Anzacs: Nurses at War, 1914–1918*, Sydney: Allen & Unwin, 2008.

Robbins, Simon, *British Generalship on the Western Front 1914–18: Defeat into Victory*, Abingdon: Frank Cass, 2005.

Roberts, Chris, *The Landing at Anzac, 1915*, Canberra: Army History Unit, 2013.

Robertson, J.R., 'The Conscription Issue and the National Movement in Western Australia, June 1916–December 1917', *University Studies in Western Australian History*, vol. 2, no. 3, 1959, pp. 5–57.

Robertson, John, *Anzac and Empire: The Tragedy and Glory of Gallipoli*, Melbourne: Hamlyn, 1990.

Robson, L.L. *The First A.I.F.: A Study of its Recruitment 1914–1918*, Melbourne: Melbourne University Press, 1982.

——'The Origin and Character of the First A.I.F., 1914–18: Some Statistical Evidence', *Historical Studies*, vol. 15, no. 61, 1973, pp. 737–49.

Rule, E.J., *Jacka's Mob*, Sydney: Angus & Robertson, 1933.

Rushton, P.J., 'Revolutionary Ideology of the I.W.W. in Australia', *Historical Studies*, vol. 15, no. 59, 1972, pp. 424–45.

Sadler, Peter S., *The Paladin: A Life of Major-General Sir John Gellibrand*, Melbourne: Oxford University Press, 2000.

Santamaria, B.A., *Daniel Mannix*, Melbourne: Melbourne University Press, 1985.

Scates, Bruce, *Return to Gallipoli: Walking the Battlefields of the Great War*, Cambridge: Cambridge University Press, 2006.

Scott, Ernest, *The Official History of Australia in the War of 1914–1918*, vol. XI, *Australia During the War*, Sydney: Angus & Robertson, 1936.

Serle, Geoffrey, *John Monash: A Biography*, first published 1982, Melbourne: Melbourne University Press, 1985.

Shaw, G.P. 'Patriotism Versus Socialism: Queensland's Private War, 1916', *Australian Journal of Politics and History*, vol. XIX, 1973, pp. 167–93.

Sheffield, Gary, *The Chief: Douglas Haig and the British Army*, London: Arum Press, 2011.

Sheffield, Gary and McCartney, Helen, 'Hubert Gough: Fifth Army, 1916–18', in Ian F.W. Beckett and Steven J. Corvi (eds), *Haig's Generals*, Barnsley: Pen & Sword Military, 2006, pp. 75–96.

Shute, Carmel, '"Blood Votes" and the "Bestial Boche": A Case Study in Propaganda', *Hecate*, vol. 2, no. 2, 1976, pp. 7–22.

——'Heroines and Heroes: Sexual Mythology in Australia, 1914–18', in Joy Damousi and Marilyn Lake (eds), *Gender and War: Australians at War in the Twentieth Century*, Melbourne: Cambridge University Press, 1995, pp. 23–42.

Simkins, Peter, 'Herbert Plumer: Second Army, 1915–17, 1918', in Ian F.W. Beckett and Steven J. Corvi (eds), *Haig's Generals*, Barnsley: Pen & Sword Military, 2006, pp. 141–63.

Smart, Judith, 'Eva Hughes: Militant Conservative', in Marilyn Lake and Farley Kelly (eds), *Double Time: Women in Victoria—150 Years*, Ringwood: Penguin, 1985.

——'Feminists, Food and the Fair Price: The Cost-of-living Demonstrations in Melbourne: August–September 1917', in Joy Damousi and Marilyn Lake (eds), *Gender and War: Australians at War in the Twentieth Century*, Melbourne: Cambridge University Press, 1995, pp. 274–301.

——'"For the Good that We Can Do": Cecilia Downing and Feminist Christian Citizenship', *Australian Feminist Studies*, vol. 9, no. 19, 1994, pp. 39–60.

——'The Panacea of Prohibition: The Reaction of the Woman's Christian Temperance Union of Victoria to the Great War', in Sabine Willis (ed.), *Women, Faith and Fetes*, Melbourne: Dove Communication, 1977, pp. 162–92.

——'"Poor Little Belgium" and Australian Popular Support for War 1914–1915', *War & Society*, vol. 12, no. 1, 1994, pp. 27–46.

——'The Right to Speak and the Right to Be Heard: The Popular Disruption of Conscriptionist Meetings in Melbourne, 1916', *Australian Historical Studies*, vol. 23, no. 92, 1989, pp. 201–19.

Spartalis, Peter, *The Diplomatic Battles of Billy Hughes*, Sydney: Hale & Iremonger, 1983.

Stanley, Peter, *Men of Mont St Quentin Between Victory and Death*, Melbourne: Scribe, 2009.

——*Quinn's Post, Anzac, Gallipoli*, Sydney: Allen & Unwin, 2005.

Steel, Nigel and Hart, Peter, *Defeat at Gallipoli*, first published 1994, London: Papermac, 1995.

Stephens, Alan, *The Australian Centenary History of Defence*, vol. II, *The Royal Australian Air Force*, Melbourne: Oxford University Press, 2001.

Stevens, David (ed.), *The Australian Centenary History of Defence*, vol. III, *The Royal Australian Navy*, Melbourne: Oxford University Press, 2001.

Stevenson, David, *Cataclysm: The First World War as Political Tragedy*, New York: Basic Books, 2004.

Stone, Norman, *The Eastern Front 1914–1917*, London: Hodder & Stoughton, 1975.

Strachan, Hew, *The First World War*, vol. I, *To Arms*, Oxford: Oxford University Press, 2001.

Summy, Hilary, 'Margaret Thorp and the Anti-Conscription Campaign in Brisbane 1915–1917', *Hecate*, vol. 32, no. 1, 2006, pp. 59–76.

Tanner, Thomas W., *Compulsory Citizen Soldiers*, Sydney: Alternative Publishing Co-Operative, 1980.

Taylor, A.J.P., *The First World War: An Illustrated History*, London: Hamish Hamilton, 1963.

Thomson, Alistair, *Anzac Memories: Living with the Legend*, Melbourne: Melbourne University Press, 1994.

Thwaites, Sandra, 'Rev T.E. Ruth, a City Preacher in a Time of War and After', *Our Yesterdays*, vol. 4, 1996, pp. 19–41.

Travers, Tim, *Gallipoli: 1915*, first published 2001, Charleston, SC: Tempus, 2003.

Tsokhas, Kosmas, *Markets, Money and Empire: The Political Economy of the Australian Wool Industry*, Melbourne: Melbourne University Press, 1990.

Turner, Ian, *Industrial Labour and Politics: The Labour Movement in Eastern Australia 1900–1921*, Canberra: ANU Press, 1965.

Tyquin, Michael, *Madness and the Military: Australia's Experience of the Great War*, Sydney: Australian Military History Publications, 2006.

Wade, Linda, 'By Diggers Defended, by Victorians Mended': Searching for Villers-Bretonneux, PhD thesis, School of History and Politics, University of Wollongong, 2008.

Watts, Rob, *The Foundations of the National Welfare State*, Sydney: Allen & Unwin, 1987.

White, Richard, 'Motives for Joining Up: Self-sacrifice, Self-interest and Social Class, 1914–18', *Journal of the Australian War Memorial*, October 1986, pp. 3–16.

Williams, John F., *Anzacs, The Media and the Great War*, Sydney: UNSW Press, 1999.

Williams, Peter D., *The Battle of Anzac Ridge: 25 April 1915*, Sydney: Australian Military History Publications, 2007.

Wilson, Graham, *Dust, Donkeys and Illusions: The Myth of Simpson and His Donkey Exposed*, Sydney: Big Sky Publishing, 2012.

Wilson, Trevor, *The Myriad Faces of War: Britain and the Great War, 1914–1918*, Cambridge: Polity Press, 1986.

Winter, Denis, *Making the Legend: The War Writings of C.E.W. Bean*, Brisbane: University of Queensland Press, 1992.

Winter, Jay, *Remembering War: The Great War Between Memory and History in the Twentieth Century*, New Haven, CT: Yale University Press, 2006.

——*Sites of Memory, Sites of Mourning: The Great War in European Cultural History*, Cambridge: Cambridge University Press, 1995.

Winter, J.M., *The Great War and the British People*, Basingstoke: Macmillan, 1985.

Withers, Glen, 'The 1916–1917 Conscription Referenda: A Cliometric Re-Appraisal', *Historical Studies*, vol. 20, no. 78, 1982, pp. 38–46.

Woodward, David, *Lloyd George and the Generals*, Newark, DE: University of Delaware Press, 1983.

——'The Origins and Intent of David Lloyd George's January 5 War Aims Speech', *Historian*, vol. 34, no. 1, 1971, pp. 22–39.

Wray, Christopher, *Sir James Whiteside McCay: A Turbulent Life*, Melbourne: Oxford University Press, 2002.

York, Barry, 'The Maltese, White Australia, and Conscription: "Il-tfal Ta Billy Hughes"', *Labour History*, no. 57, 1989, pp. 1–15.

Young, Margaret and Gammage, Bill (eds), *Hail and Farewell: Letters from Two Brothers Killed in France in 1916, Alec and Goldy Raws*, Sydney: Kangaroo Press, 1995.

Yule, Peter (ed.), *Sergeant Lawrence Goes to France*, Melbourne: Melbourne University Press, 1987.

Ziino, Bart, *A Distant Grief: Australians, War Graves and the Great War*, Perth: University of Western Australia Press, 2007.

——'Mourning and Commemoration in Australia: The Case of Sir W.T. Bridges and the Unknown Australian Soldier', *History Australia*, vol. 4, no. 2, 2007, pp. 40.1–40.17.

INDEX

In this index, page numbers in **_bold italic_** indicate illustrations.

INDEX